W9-CUT-303

Perception Checking (page 42)

Skill
Making a verbal statement that reflects your understanding of another person's behavior.

Use
To enable you to test the accuracy of your perceptions.

Procedure
1. Describe the behaviors of the other person that have led to your perception.
2. Add your interpretation of the behavior to your statement.

Example
After taking a phone call, Shimika comes into the room with a completely blank expression and neither speaks to Donnell nor acknowledges that he is in the room. Donnell says, "Shimika, from your blank look, I get the feeling that you're in a state of shock. Has something happened?"

Communication Skills

PULL OUT SECTION☞

Communicate!

Kathleen S. Verderber
Northern Kentucky University

Rudolph F. Verderber
Distinguished Teaching Professor of Communication,
University of Cincinnati

Deanna D. Sellnow
University of Kentucky

WADSWORTH
CENGAGE Learning

Australia • Brazil • Japan • Korea • Mexico • Singapore • Spain • United Kingdom • United States

***Communicate!* Thirteenth Edition**
Kathleen S. Verderber, Rudolph
F. Verderber, and Deanna D. Sellnow

Senior Publisher: Lyn Uhl

Executive Editor: Monica Eckman

Senior Development Editor: Greer Lleuad

Assistant Editor: Rebekah Matthews

Editorial Assistant: Colin Solan

Media Editor: Jessica Badiner

Marketing Manager: Bryant Chrzan

Marketing Coordinator: Darlene Macanan

Marketing Communications Manager:
Christine Dobberpuhl

Senior Content Project Manager: Rosemary
Winfield

Senior Art Director: Linda Helcher

Senior Print Buyer: Justin Palmeiro

Permissions Account Manager, Text:
Margaret Chamberlain-Gaston

Production Service: Elm Street Publishing
Services

Text Designer: Rokusek Design

Senior Permissions Account Manager,
Images: Dean Dauphinais

Cover Designer: Linda Kuhn

Cover Image: © enjoynz, © Talex,
© rangepuppies, © illustrious

Compositor: Integra Software Services Pvt.
Ltd.

For product information and technology assistance, contact us at
Cengage Learning Customer & Sales Support, 1-800-354-9706.

For permission to use material from this text or product,
submit all requests online at **www.cengage.com/permissions.**
Further permissions questions can be emailed to
permissionrequest@cengage.com.

Library of Congress Control Number: 2009940613

ISBN-13: 978-1-4390-3640-2

ISBN-10: 1-4390-3640-3

Wadsworth
20 Channel Center Street
Boston, MA 02210
USA

Cengage Learning is a leading provider of customized learning solutions
with office locations around the globe, including Singapore, the United
Kingdom, Australia, Mexico, Brazil, and Japan. Locate your local office at
international.cengage.com/region.

Cengage Learning products are represented in Canada by
Nelson Education, Ltd.

For your course and learning solutions, visit **www.cengage.com.**

Purchase any of our products at your local college store or at our
preferred online store **www.ichapters.com.**

Printed in the United States of America
1 2 3 4 5 6 7 13 12 11 10 09

Brief Contents

Contents iv
Preface xiii

PART **I** FOUNDATIONS OF COMMUNICATION

Chapter 1 Communication Perspectives 1
Chapter 2 Perception of Self and Others 23
Chapter 3 Communicating Verbally 47
Chapter 4 Communicating Nonverbally 66
Chapter 5 Listening and Responding 87

PART **II** INTERPERSONAL COMMUNICATION

Chapter 6 Communicating Across Cultures 111
Chapter 7 Understanding Interpersonal Relationships 133
Chapter 8 Communication Skills in Interpersonal Relationships: Providing Emotional Support, Managing Privacy, and Negotiating Conflict 157

Appendix Interviewing 185

PART **III** GROUP COMMUNICATION

Chapter 9 Communicating in Groups 207
Chapter 10 Problem Solving in Groups 224

PART **IV** PUBLIC SPEAKING

Chapter 11 Developing and Researching a Speech Topic 250
Chapter 12 Organizing Your Speech 275
Chapter 13 Adapting Verbally and Visually 304
Chapter 14 Overcoming Speech Apprehension by Practicing Delivery 332
Chapter 15 Informative Speaking 363
Chapter 16 Persuasive Speaking 388

References 419
Index 430

Contents

Brief Contents   iii
Preface   xiii

PART I   FOUNDATIONS OF COMMUNICATION

Chapter 1   Communication Perspectives   1

The Communication Process   3
  Participants   3
  Messages   3
  Context   4
  Channels   5
  Interference (Noise)   5
  Feedback   7
  A Model of the Basic Communication Process   8
  Communication Settings   8

Communication Principles   10
  Communication Has Purpose   10
  Communication Is Continuous   11
  Communication Messages Vary in Conscious Thought   11
  Communication Is Relational   11
  Communication Is Guided by Culture   12
  Communication Has Ethical Implications   14
  Communication Is Learned   15

Increasing Our Communication Competence   15
  Develop Communication Skills Improvement Goals   18

Chapter 2   Perception of Self and Others   23

The Perception Process   24
  Attention and Selection   24
  Organization of Stimuli   25
  Interpretation of Stimuli   26

Perceptions of Self: Self-Concept and Self-Esteem   26
  Forming and Maintaining a Self-Concept   26

Developing and Maintaining Self-Esteem   28
  The Influence of Gender and Culture on Self-Perceptions   30
  Changing Self-Perceptions   31
  Accuracy and Distortion of Self-Perceptions   31
  The Effects of Self-Perceptions on Communication   34

Presenting Self to Others   35
    Self-Monitoring   36
    Social Construction of Self   36
Perception of Others   37
    Observing Others   38
    Using Stereotypes   38
    Emotional State   39
    Perceiving Others' Messages   40
    Improving the Accuracy of Social Perceptions   41

Chapter ——— 3   Communicating Verbally   47
The Nature and Purposes of Language   48
    Purposes of Language   49
    The Relationship Between Language and Meaning   49
    Cultural and Gender Influences on Language Use   51
Improving Language Skills   52
    Use Clear Language   52
    Use Language That Makes Your Messages Memorable   55
    Use Linguistic Sensitivity   58

Chapter ——— 4   Communicating Nonverbally   66
Characteristics of Nonverbal Communication   68
Types of Nonverbal Communication   69
    Use of Body: Kinesics   69
    Use of Voice: Vocalics   71
    Use of Space: Proxemics   73
    Use of Time: Chronemics   75
    Self-Presentation Cues   76
Guidelines for Improving Nonverbal Communication   79
    Sending Nonverbal Messages   79
    Interpreting Nonverbal Messages   82

Chapter ——— 5   Listening and Responding   87
What Is Listening?   88
Types of Listening   88
    Appreciative Listening   89
    Discriminative Listening   89
    Comprehensive Listening   90
    Empathic Listening   90
    Critical Listening   90

Steps in the Listening Process   91
    Attending   91
    Understanding   93
    Remembering   97
    Evaluating   98
    Responding   100
Conversation and Analysis   102

PART II — INTERPERSONAL COMMUNICATION

Chapter 6 — Communicating Across Cultures — 111

Culture and Communication   112
    Intercultural Communication   112
    Dominant Cultures and Co-Cultures   113
    Cultural Identity   116
Identifying Cultural Norms and Values   117
    Individualism–Collectivism   117
    Uncertainty Avoidance   121
    Power Distance   121
    Masculinity–Femininity   122
Barriers to Effective Intercultural Communication   123
    Anxiety   123
    Assuming Similarity or Difference   123
    Ethnocentrism   124
    Stereotypes and Prejudice   125
    Incompatible Communication Codes   126
    Incompatible Norms and Values   127
Intercultural Communication Competence   127
    Adopt Correct Attitudes   127
    Acquire Knowledge About Other Cultures   128
    Develop Culture-Specific Skills   129

Chapter 7 — Understanding Interpersonal Relationships — 133

Types of Relationships   134
    Acquaintances   134
    Friends   136
    Close Friends or Intimates   137
Disclosure and Feedback in Relationship Life Cycles   141
    The Open Pane   141
    The Secret Pane   142
    The Blind Pane   142
    The Unknown Pane   142
Communication in the Stages of Relationships   143
    Beginning Relationships   143
    Developing Relationships   144

Maintaining Relationships   145
Deteriorating and Dissolving Relationships   148

Dialectics in Interpersonal Relationships   149

Relational Dialectics   149
Managing Dialectical Tensions   151

Conversation and Analysis   152

Chapter   8   Communication Skills in Interpersonal Relationships: Providing
Emotional Support, Managing Privacy, and Negotiating Conflict   157

Comforting Messages   158

Skills for Comforting   158
Gender and Cultural Considerations in Comforting   160

Managing Privacy and Disclosure in Relationships   161

Effects on Intimacy   164
Expectations of Reciprocity   164
Information Co-Ownership   165
Guidelines and Communication Strategies for Disclosure   165
Communication Strategies for Managing Privacy   171

Negotiating Different Needs, Wants, and Preferences in Relationships   172

Communicating Personal Needs, Wants, and Preferences: Passive,
    Aggressive, and Assertive Behavior   173
Cultural Variations in Passive, Aggressive, and Assertive Behavior   174

Managing Conflict in Relationships   176

Styles of Conflict   176
Guidelines for Collaboration   178

Conversation and Analysis   179

Appendix   Interviewing   185

Structuring Interviews   186

The Interview Protocol   186
Effective Questions   187
Order and Time Constraints in Interview Protocols   188

Guidelines for Conducting Information Interviews   189

Doing Research About Interviewees   189
Conducting an Information Interview   190

Conducting Employment Interviews   191

Preparing for the Interview   191
Conducting the Interview   191

Interviewing Strategies for Job Seekers   192

Applying for the Job   192
Electronic Cover Letters and Résumés   194
Preparing to Be Interviewed   196
Guidelines for Job Interviewees   197

Conversation and Analysis	198
Following Up After the Interview	200
Strategies for Interviews with the Media	200
Before the Interview	201
During the Interview	201

PART III   GROUP COMMUNICATION

Chapter 9   Communicating in Groups   207

Characteristics of Healthy Groups	208
Healthy Groups Have Ethical Goals	208
Healthy Groups Are Interdependent	210
Healthy Groups Are Cohesive	210
Healthy Groups Develop and Abide by Productive Norms	210
Healthy Groups Are Accountable	212
Healthy Groups Are Synergetic	213
Stages of Group Development	213
Forming	213
Storming	214
Norming	214
Performing	214
Adjourning	214
Types of Groups	215
Families	215
Social Friendship Groups	216
Support Groups	216
Interest Groups	217
Service Groups	217
Work Groups	217
Evaluating Group Dynamics	219

Chapter 10   Problem Solving in Groups   224

The Problem-Solving Process	225
Step One: Identify and Define the Problem	226
Step Two: Analyze the Problem	226
Step Three: Determine Criteria for Judging Solutions	227
Step Four: Identify Alternative Solutions	228
Step Five: Evaluate Solutions and Decide	229
Step Six: Implement the Agreed-Upon Solution	230
Shared Leadership	230
Task Roles	230
Maintenance Roles	231
Procedural Roles	232

Making Meetings Effective 235
    Guidelines for Meeting Leaders 235
    Guidelines for Meeting Participants 238
Conversation and Analysis 239
Communicating Group Solutions 242
    Written Formats 242
    Oral Formats 243
    Virtual Reports 243

PART IV PUBLIC SPEAKING

Chapter 11 Developing and Researching a Speech Topic 250

Identify Topics 252
    List Subjects 252
    Brainstorm and Concept Map for Topic Ideas 253
Analyze the Audience 254
    Identify Audience Analysis Information Needs 254
    Gather Audience Data 255
Analyze the Setting 257
Select a Topic 258
Write a Speech Goal 259
    Identify Your General Goal 259
    Phrase a Specific Goal Statement 259
Locate and Evaluate Information Sources 261
    Personal Knowledge, Experience, and Observation 262
    Secondary Research 262
    Primary Research 264
Evaluate Sources 265
Identify and Select Relevant Information 267
    Factual Statements 267
    Expert Opinions 268
    Elaborations 268
Draw Information from Multiple Cultural Perspectives 269
Record Information 269
    Prepare Research Cards 269
Cite Sources in Speeches 270

Chapter 12 Organizing Your Speech 275

Developing the Body of the Speech 276
    Determining Main Points 276
    Writing a Thesis Statement 279

Outlining the Body of the Speech — 280
Selecting and Outlining Supporting Material — 284
Preparing Section Transitions and Signposts — 286

Creating the Introduction — 287
Gaining Attention — 287
Establishing Listener Relevance — 289
Stating the Thesis — 290
Establishing Your Credibility — 290
Setting a Tone — 290
Creating a Bond of Goodwill — 291

Crafting the Conclusion — 291
Summary — 292
Clincher — 292

Listing Sources — 294

Reviewing the Outline — 296

Chapter 13   Adapting Verbally and Visually — 304

Adapting to Your Audience Verbally — 305
Relevance — 305
Common Ground — 306
Speaker Credibility — 307
Information Comprehension and Retention — 309
Adapting to Cultural Differences — 312

Adapting to Audiences Visually — 315
Types of Presentational Aids — 316
Criteria for Choosing Presentational Aids — 323
Designing Effective Presentational Aids — 323

Methods for Displaying Presentational Aids — 326
Posters — 326
Whiteboards or Chalkboards — 326
Flip Charts — 327
Handouts — 327
Document Cameras — 328
CD/VCR/DVD Players and LCD Projectors — 328
Computer-Mediated Slide Show — 328

Chapter 14   Overcoming Speech Apprehension by Practicing Delivery — 332

Public Speaking Apprehension — 333
Symptoms and Causes — 333
Managing Your Apprehension — 334

Characteristics of an Effective Delivery Style — 336
Use a Conversational Style — 336
Be Animated — 336

Effective Use of Your Voice — 337
Speak Intelligibly — 337
Use Vocal Expressiveness — 338

Effective Use of Your Body   341
     Facial Expressions   341
     Gestures   342
     Movement   342
     Eye Contact   343
     Posture   343
     Poise   343
     Appearance   344

Delivery Methods   345
     Impromptu Speeches   346
     Scripted Speeches   346
     Extemporaneous Speeches   346

Rehearsal   346
     Preparing Speaking Notes   347
     Handling Presentational Aids   347
     Recording, Analyzing, and Refining Speech Delivery   349

Criteria for Evaluating Speeches   351

Sample Informative Speech   353

Chapter 15   Informative Speaking   363

Characteristics of Effective Informative Speaking   364
     Intellectually Stimulating   364
     Relevant   365
     Creative   365
     Memorable   366
     Address Diverse Learning Styles   367

Methods of Informing   368
     Description   368
     Definition   369
     Comparison and Contrast   369
     Narration   370
     Demonstration   370

Common Informative Speech Frameworks   371
     Process Speech Frameworks   371
     Expository Speech Frameworks   372

Sample Informative Speech   379

Chapter 16   Persuasive Speaking   388

How We Process Persuasive Messages:
The Elaboration Likelihood Model (ELM)   389

Writing Persuasive Speech Goals as Propositions   390
     Types of Persuasive Goals   390
     Tailoring Your Proposition to Your Audience   391

Developing Arguments (Logos) That Support Your Proposition   393
    Finding Reasons to Use as Main Points   393
    Selecting Evidence to Support Reasons   394
    Types and Tests of Arguments   395
    Avoiding Fallacies in Your Reasons and Argument   397

Increasing Audience Involvement Through Emotional Appeals (Pathos)   398

Cueing Your Audience Through Credibility (Ethos): Demonstrating Goodwill   400

Motivating Your Audience to Act Through Incentives   401
    Using Incentives to Satisfy Unmet Needs   401
    Creating Incentives That Outweigh Costs   403

Organizational Patterns for Persuasive Speeches   403
    Statement of Reasons   404
    Comparative Advantages   404
    Criteria Satisfaction   404
    Refutative   405
    Problem-Solution   405
    Problem-Cause-Solution   406
    Motivated Sequence   406

Sample Persuasive Speech   409

REFERENCES   419

INDEX   431

BONUS CHAPTER   PREPARING AND PRESENTING PUBLIC SPEECHES

We are delighted to welcome Deanna D. Sellnow, Ph.D., to the author team for *Communicate!* A proven textbook author, Dr. Sellnow is the Gifford Blyton Endowed Professor and Director of Undergraduate Studies in Communication at the University of Kentucky. Her scholarly interests include instructional communication, educational assessment, popular culture, and gender communication. A past president of the Central States Communication Association, she has taught a wide variety of communication courses and enjoys directing basic communication courses. Dr. Sellnow's voice blends well with ours, as her writing has an appealing conversational quality that keeps the reader's interest. While the contributions she has made to this book will not be evident to those of you who are reading the book for the first time, those of you familiar with Dr Sellnow's work will recognize and appreciate her influence. We look forward to a long and successful collaboration.

To Students

Congratulations! You are beginning to study communication, a subject that is important and useful to you in all parts of your life. When you want to establish or improve a relationship, when you need to work with others on a group project for class or for a cause you support, or when you are required to make a presentation at work, your success will depend on how effective you are at communicating in those settings.

Most of you have probably never studied communication formally. Rather, you've learned the communication skills and strategies you use every day informally, in your home and from your friends. By taking this communication course and learning tested communication skills, you'll strengthen your existing abilities and improve your relationships. You can improve the likelihood that your group project is successful by understanding the predictable patterns of group process and communication. And you can more effectively overcome stage fright and give better presentations when you have studied public speaking and know how to plan and deliver a formal speech. So again, we say, congratulations! You'll find that this course will be instantly relevant to your day-to-day living. We are confident that by the end of this term you will be glad you spent your time and money on it.

The textbook you're reading, *Communicate!*, was one of the first college texts about human communication. A lot has changed since Rudy wrote that first edition. Over the years we have worked to make sure that students, like you, have a book that is easy and enjoyable to read and learn from. We have also worked hard to make sure that the information, theories, and skills discussed and relevant to the real relationships and communication situations you face. So every three years we examine the book in light of how the world has changed. Just ten years ago, cell phones were not in wide use, *texting* wasn't a verb, many social networking sites and YouTube didn't exist, and "to twitter" simply meant to speak excitedly about something. Despite these huge changes in the way we communicate, this textbook is as up-to-date and useful as the first edition was because we work hard to make sure that the information we present reflects what it takes to be an effective communicator *today*.

Communicate! is written with six specific goals in mind:

1. **To explain important communication concepts, frameworks, and theories** that have been consistently supported by careful research so that you can understand the conceptual foundations of human communication.
2. **To teach specific communication skills** that research has shown facilitate effective relationships.
3. **To describe and encourage you to adopt the ethical frameworks** that can guide competent communication.
4. **To increase awareness of how culture affects communication practices.**
5. **To stimulate critical and creative thinking** about the concepts and skills you learn.
6. **To provide tools for practice and assessment** that enable you to monitor how well you are learning communication concepts and skills.

So we hope you will read and enjoy this textbook and that it will be a resource you will want to maintain in your personal library. We appreciate it when students who are using our text take time to share their reactions to the book with us. So we encourage you to email us with questions, comments, and suggestions. Our email address is Communicate.Authors@cengage.com.

To Instructors

Thank you for considering and using *Communicate!* We are grateful for the colleagues who have used previous editions of this text and to those of you who are considering using this edition. We believe that the revisions we have made will surprise and delight those of you who have used *Communicate!* in the past. We also believe that those of you who are looking for a different textbook will find *Communicate!* is precisely the learning tool that will encourage your students to read and think about the important role of communication in their lives.

As we prepared this edition, we were acutely aware of how our students' lives are changing and how these changes are influencing their learning process and the nature of communication in their lives. So we have revised the text with these new realities in mind while at the same time retaining the hallmarks that have made this textbook useful to students and instructors in the past. And, as with every new edition, we have incorporated the suggestions of colleagues who use the text, and we've reviewed the latest scholarship so that this new edition reflects what users want and what recent scholarship has discovered about human communication. In the sections that follow, we detail what's new and highlight the continuing features that have made *Communicate!* a perennial favorite with both students and faculty.

New to This Edition

- **Pop Comm! articles,** found in each chapter, highlight how the communication concepts addressed in this book play out in popular culture. Each article demonstrates the universal and omnipresent role of communication in our culture and how communication practices change and evolve. Many articles spotlight how the uses of new technologies are changing basic communication processes. Topics include online mourning, the ghostwriting of online dating profiles, managing privacy on social networking sites, the dark side of online social groups, and the persuasive messages of infomercials.
- Relevant *Communicate!* pedagogy has been revamped to facilitate **active learning and assessment**. Chapter-opening questions prompt students to consider what

they already know and to engage with the main ideas of each chapter as they read (pre-assessment). Review questions in the margins throughout the chapters and activities at the ends of chapters encourage students to think critically about what they're learning (formative assessment). And end-of-part and online quizzes help students determine how well they've absorbed chapter content (summative assessment).

- **New and updated examples** throughout the text highlight student-friendly topics, such as pop culture and new technologies.
- If your course doesn't emphasize public speaking but, rather, is a general survey of the discipline, a **single chapter on public speaking** is available through Cengage Learning's Flex-Text customization program. This new bonus chapter, written by the *Communicate!* authors, presents a concise overview of public speaking and the speech-making process. It replaces Chapters 11–16 of *Communicate!* (For more information about the Flex-Text program, see the Instructor Resources section later in this preface.)
- **Chapter 1, "Communication Perspectives,"** now includes a section on communication settings that distinguishes among intrapersonal, interpersonal, small group, and public communication.
- **Chapter 2, "Perception of Self and Others,"** introduces the important role media images play in distorting one's self-perception, the relationship between self-perceptions and communication apprehension, and how perception is shaped via images constructed on social networking sites such as Facebook and MySpace.
- Reflecting the fact that today we rely heavily on computer-mediated communication, **Chapter 4, "Communicating Nonverbally,"** includes a discussion of how nonverbal messages that clarify meaning and convey emotions can be communicated in online environments.
- Because listening and responding is a foundational element of communication in any setting, we moved the discussion of this topic forward to **Chapter 5, "Listening and Responding,"** in Part I of the book. This chapter now includes a section on the types of listening, which distinguishes among appreciative, discriminative, comprehensive, empathic, and critical listening purposes. In addition, we added a section on responding effectively to public speakers in the form of speech critiques.
- **Chapter 6, "Communicating Across Cultures,"** has been updated to reflect what we know today about dominant cultures and co-cultures, including the distinction among sex, gender, and sexual orientation.
- For this edition, we have reworked the two interpersonal chapters, which now focus, first, on understanding relationships and, second, on specific skills. **Chapter 7, "Understanding Interpersonal Relationships,"** walks readers through the types of interpersonal relationships, the role of disclosure and feedback in relationship life cycles, communication in the various relationship stages, and the dialectical tensions inherent in interpersonal relationships. In **Chapter 8, "Communication Skills in Interpersonal Relationships,"** we describe communication skills for comforting, managing the competing urges between self-disclosure and privacy management, and conflict management styles.
- Many instructors have indicated that they simply don't have time to teach the chapter on interviewing in their courses. Still, because we believe effective interviewing skills are so important, we have retained the content in the form of an **internal appendix, "Interviewing."** So, even if teachers cannot include the content in their courses, students can still benefit from learning about it on their own. The content of this appendix has been refined so that it first focuses on developing

good questions and then proposes some guidelines for conducting both information and employment interviews. Tips for presenting oneself in employment and media interviews are also discussed.

- The unit on group communication has been extensively revised. For this edition, **Chapter 9, "Communicating in Groups,"** focuses on understanding the characteristics of groups, stages of development, different types of groups, and guidelines for communicating effectively in groups. In **Chapter 10, "Problem Solving in Groups,"** we focus specifically on the nature of effective problem solving, including leadership, member responsibilities, and formats for sharing results with others.

- As in the previous edition, the unit on public speaking continues to describe the process for preparing and presenting public speeches using the Speech Plan Action Steps. The chapters in this part include many important revisions. **Chapter 11, "Developing and Researching a Speech Topic,"** now includes a discussion of concept mapping as a means by which students can generate topic ideas. In **Chapter 12, "Organizing Your Speech,"** we added narrative order as a method for arranging main points. **Chapter 13, "Adapting Verbally and Visually,"** includes a section about addressing diverse learning styles when adapting to an audience. In addition, we expanded the discussion of visual aids to include guidelines for using audio and audiovisual presentational aids. And **Chapter 14, "Overcoming Speech Apprehension by Practicing Delivery,"** offers an expanded discussion of public speaking apprehension and ways to overcome it.

- New to **Chapter 15, "Informative Speaking,"** are a discussion of learning styles as they relate to effective informative speaking, revised informative speech critique forms, and a new sample student speech, "Understanding Hurricanes."

- Finally, in **Chapter 16, "Persuasive Speaking,"** we have expanded our discussion of reasoning fallacies to include the either-or and straw person fallacies, we have expanded the discussion of organizational patterns to include both the refutative and problem-cause-solution patterns as options, and we offer a new sample student speech, "Sexual Assault Policy a Must," which uses the motivated sequence pattern.

Hallmark Features

- **Communication Skill boxes** provide a step-by-step guide for each of the communication skills presented in the text. Each of these boxes includes the definition of the skill, a brief description of its use, the steps for enacting the skill, and an example that illustrates the skill. A convenient tear-out chart at the beginning of the book provides a summary of all the Communication Skill boxes. The **Skill Building activities**, adjacent to each Communication Skill box, reinforce and provide an immediate opportunity for students to practice the skills. Students can complete these activities online and then compare their answers with models provided by the authors.

- **Conversation and Analysis communication scenarios** offer print and video exemplars of important concepts. Transcripts of these conversations appear in the text and online—students can download the transcripts to use for note taking as they view the videos. Once they have analyzed the conversation by answering a series of critical-thinking questions, they can compare their assessments with the authors'.

- The principles of effective speech making are organized into five **Speech Plan Action Steps**, presented in Chapters 11–14. The activities that accompany each of these action steps guide students through an orderly process that results in better speeches. *Communicate!*'s online resources provide students with the opportunity to view examples of each activity prepared by other students and to complete many of the action steps with Speech Builder Express. (See the section Student Resources for more about these online resources.)

- **Sample student speeches** appear in the text, each accompanied by an audience adaptation plan, an outline, and a transcript and analysis. Two of the three sample speeches in this edition are new. Students can use their online resources to view videos of these speeches, see the transcript and two different kinds of outlines and sample note cards, prepare their own critiques, and compare their critiques to the authors'.

- In Parts I and II, **Communicate On Your Feet speech assignments** encourage students to begin building their public-speaking skills immediately while also addressing the needs of instructors who assign prepared speeches throughout the course. In Part IV, these assignments correspond to the speech types discussed in Chapters 15–16. In this edition, we have added a number of new assignments so that each chapter now includes at least one.

- Exercises that were called "Observe and Analyze" and "Test Your Competence" in previous editions are now called **Skill Learning Activities** and are grouped at the ends of chapters. Some of these exercises challenge students to observe events related to concepts they are learning, use the theories and concepts from the chapter to analyze what happened, and, in some cases, improve what occurred by applying the communication skills they've learned. Other activities provide opportunities for students to self-evaluate or practice specific skills. Students can use their online resources to complete these activities and download worksheets and data collection forms.

- **Self-Reviews** appear at the end of each part to encourage students to commit to improving their skills in interpersonal, group, and public communication. In accord with the findings of learning motivation research, students have the opportunity to inventory their current skill levels and set specific goals for skill improvement. The Self-Reviews can be completed online and, if requested, emailed to the instructor.

- **Diverse Voices articles** give voice to the communication experiences of people from a wide range of social and cultural backgrounds. Each article, which presents the personal thoughts and experiences of the writer on topics related to chapter concepts, helps students understand and appreciate the relationship between culture and communication. Six of these articles are new to this edition.

- **What Would You Do? A Question of Ethics boxes** are short case studies that appear near the end of chapters. These cases, several of which are new to this edition, present ethical challenges and require students to think critically, sorting through a variety of ethical dilemmas faced by communicators. Conceptual material presented in Chapter 1 lays groundwork for the criteria on which students may base their assessments, but each case focuses on issues raised in a specific chapter.

Teaching and Learning Resources

Communicate! is accompanied by a full suite of integrated materials that will make teaching and learning more efficient and effective. **Note to faculty:** If you want your students to have access to the online resources for this book, please be sure to order them for your course. The content in these resources can be bundled with every new copy of the text or ordered separately. If you do not order them, your students will not have access to the online resources. *Contact your local Wadsworth Cengage Learning sales representative for more details.*

Student Resources

- The **Premium Website for** *Communicate!* provides students with one-stop access to all the integrated technology resources that accompany the book. These resources include an enhanced eBook, Audio Study Tools chapter downloads, Speech Builder Express™ 3.0, InfoTrac College Edition, interactive versions of the Skill Learning activities, interactive video activities, Web Resources links, and self-assessments. All resources are mapped to show both key discipline learning concepts as well as specific chapter learn lists.

- The *Communicate!* **interactive video activities** feature the Conversation and Analysis communication scenario clips presented in the text so students can see and hear how the skills they are studying can be used to create effective conversations in various circumstances. Students can answer the critical-thinking questions that accompany each video and then compare their answers to the authors'. This online resource also features videos of the sample informative and persuasive student speeches included in the book. Each speech is accompanied by a transcript, a preparation outline and a speaking outline, note cards, a speech critique checklist, and critical-thinking questions.

- Many of the Speech Plan Action Steps can be completed with the **Speech Builder Express 3.0 organization and outlining program.** This interactive Web-based tool coaches students through the speech organization and outlining process. By completing interactive sessions, students can prepare and save their outlines—including a plan for visual aids and a works cited section—formatted according to the principles presented in the text. Text models reinforce students' interactive practice.

- **InfoTrac College Edition with InfoMarks.** This virtual library features more than 18 million reliable, full-length articles from 5,000 academic and popular periodicals that can be retrieved almost instantly. They also have access to InfoMarks—stable URLs that can be linked to articles, journals, and searches to save valuable time when doing research—and to the InfoWrite online resource center, where students can access grammar help, critical-thinking guidelines, guides to writing research papers, and much more.

- The **Audio Study Tools for** *Communicate!* provide mobile content that offers students a fun and easy way to review chapter content whenever and wherever. For each chapter of the text, students will have access to a brief conversation or speech example and a five- to seven-minute review consisting of a brief summary of the main points in the text and review questions. Students can access the Audio Study Tools for *Communicate!* on the Premium Website or can purchase them through iChapters (see below) and download files to their computers, iPods, or other MP3 players.

- The **Cengage Learning Enhanced eBook** is a Web-based, multimedia version of *Communicate!* that offers ease of use and maximum flexibility for students who want to create their own learning experience. The enhanced eBook includes advanced book tools such as a hypertext index, bookmarking, easy highlighting, and faster searching, easy navigation, and a vibrant Web-based format. Students get access to the enhanced eBook with the printed text, or they can just purchase access to the stand-alone enhanced eBook.

- **Speech Studio™ Online Video Upload and Grading Program** improves the learning comprehension of public speaking students. This unique resource empowers instructors with a new assessment capability that is applicable for traditional, online, and hybrid courses. With Speech Studio, students can upload video files of practice speeches or final performances, comment on their peers' speeches, and review their grades and instructor feedback. Instructors create courses and assignments, comment on and grade student speeches with a library of comments and grading rubrics, and allow peer review. Grades flow into a gradebook that allows instructors to easily manage their course from within Speech Studio.

- The **iChapters.com** online store provides students with exactly what they've been asking for: choice, convenience, and savings. A 2005 research study by the National Association of College Stores indicates that as many as 60 percent of students do not purchase all required course material; however, those who do are more likely to succeed. This research also tells us that students want the ability to purchase "à la carte" course material in the format that suits them best. Accordingly, iChapters. com is the only online store that offers eBooks at up to 50 percent off, eChapters for as low as $1.99 each, and new textbooks at up to 25 percent off, plus up to 25 percent off print and digital supplements that can help improve student performance.
- *A Guide to the Basic Course for ESL Students* can be bundled and is designed to assist the nonnative speaker. The *Guide* features FAQs, helpful URLs, and strategies for accent management and speech apprehension.
- *Service Learning in Communication Studies: A Handbook* is an invaluable resource for students in the basic course that integrates, or will soon integrate, a service-learning component. This handbook provides guidelines for connecting service-learning work with classroom concepts and advice for working effectively with agencies and organizations. It also provides model forms and reports and a directory of online resources.

Instructor Resources

- The **Instructor's Resource Manual with Test Bank** by Katrina Bodey, University of North Carolina, Chapel Hill, changes from the twelfth edition to the thirteenth edition, sample syllabi, chapter-by-chapter outlines, summaries, vocabulary lists, suggested lecture and discussion topics, classroom exercises, assignments, and a comprehensive test bank with answer key and rejoinders. In addition, this manual includes the **Spotlight on Scholars boxes** that were in the textbook in past editions. These boxes feature the work of eight eminent communication scholars, putting a face on scholarship by telling each scholar's "story." These boxes can be used as discussion starters, as enrichment for students who are interested in communication scholarship, or in any other way instructors would like to integrate them into the course.
- **Special-Topic Instructor's Manuals.** Written by Deanna Sellnow, University of Kentucky, these three brief manuals provide instructor resources for teaching public speaking online, with a service-learning approach, and with a problem-based learning approach that focuses on critical thinking and teamwork skills. Each manual includes course syllabi; icebreakers; information about learning cycles and learning styles; and public speaking basics such as coping with anxiety, outlining, and speaking ethically.
- *The Teaching Assistant's Guide to the Basic Course,* based on leading communication teacher training programs, covers general teaching and course management topics as well as specific strategies for communication instruction—for example, providing effective feedback on performance, managing sensitive class discussions, and conducting mock interviews.
- The **PowerLecture** CD-ROM contains an electronic version of the Instructor's Resource Manual, ExamView® Computerized Testing, predesigned Microsoft

PowerPoint presentations, and JoinIn® classroom quizzing. The PowerPoint presentations contain text, images, and cued videos of student speeches and can be used as they are or customized to suit your course needs.

- **Communication Scenarios for Critique and Analysis on Video and DVD** include the communication scenarios included in the *Communicate!* interactive videos as well as additional scenarios covering interpersonal communication, interviewing, and group communication.

- Launch your lectures with **ABC News DVDs: Human Communication, Interpersonal Communication, and Public Speaking.** Footage from *Nightline, World News Tonight,* and *Good Morning America* provides context and real-life examples of communication theories and practices. Footage includes discussion of dozens of communication topics—including family "virtual visitation," cell phone spam, and professional nonverbal communication—as well as significant speeches by public figures.

- The **BBC News and CBS News DVDs: Human Communication, Interpersonal Communication, and Public Speaking,** provide footage of news stories that relate to current topics in human and interpersonal communication, and footage of famous historical and contemporary public speeches, as well as clips that relate to current topics in speech communication. Available Spring 2010.

- The **Student Speeches for Critique and Analysis on Video and DVD** offer a variety of sample student speeches, including those featured in the *Communicate!* interactive videos, that your students can watch, critique, and analyze on their own or in class. All of the speech types are included, as well as speeches featuring nonnative English speakers and the use of visual aids.

- **ABC News DVD: Speeches by Barack Obama.** This DVD includes nine famous speeches by President Barack Obama, from 2004 to the present day, including his speech at the 2004 Democratic National Convention; his 2008 speech on race, "A More Perfect Union"; and his 2009 inaugural address. Speeches are divided into short video segments for easy, time-efficient viewing. This instructor supplement also features critical-thinking questions and answers for each speech, designed to spark class discussion.

- The *Media Guide for Interpersonal Communication* provides faculty with media resource listings focused on general interpersonal communication topics. Each listing provides compelling examples of how interpersonal communication concepts are illustrated in particular films, books, plays, Web sites, or journal articles. Discussion questions are provided.

- **TeamUP technology training and support.** Get trained, get connected, and get the support you need for seamless integration of technology resources into your course with Cengage Learning's TeamUP Program. This unparalleled service and training program provides robust online resources, peer-to-peer instruction, personalized training, and a customizable program you can count on. Visit http://academic.cengage.com/tlc to sign up for online seminars, first days of class services, technical support, or personalized face-to-face training. Our online or onsite training sessions are frequently led by one of our lead teachers, faculty members who are experts in using Wadsworth Cengage Learning technology and can provide the best practices and teaching tips.

- **Flex-Text customization program.** Create a text as unique as your course: quickly, simply, and affordably. As part of our Flex-Text program, you can add your personal touch to *Communicate!* with a course-specific cover and up to 32 pages of your own content, at no additional cost. Bonus chapters available now include a single chapter on public communication.

Acknowledgments

This thirteenth edition of *Communicate!* has benefitted from the work of many people we would like to recognize.

First, we thank our colleagues who reviewed the book and offered their insights and suggestions including Karen Anderson, University of North Texas; Thomas Bovino, Suffolk County Community College; Jon Croghan, Northwestern State University; Sheryl Davis, Kaiser University; James Floss, Humboldt State University; Thomas Gaines, Johnson & Wales University; King Godwin, Grambling State University; Daria Heinemann, Kaiser University; Tracey Holley, Tarleton State University; Keri Keckley, Crowder College; Nancy Levin, Palm Beach Community College; and Charlotte Toguchi, Kapiolani Community College.

We also want to thank Zach Leitch, Debbie Sellnow, and Rick Sellnow, who read the previous edition of this text and suggested where examples needed to be updated so that today's 21st-century students would find illustrations they could relate to.

We are fortunate to have the best editorial team in Communication Studies today. We are grateful for the support of Lyn Uhl, our senior publisher; Monica Eckman, executive editor; Colin Solan, editorial assistant; Jessica Badiner, media editor; Bryant Chrzan, marketing manager; Christine Dobberpuhl, marketing communications manager; Rosemary Winfield, senior content product manager; Linda Helcher, art director; Kristin Jobe, project manager at Elm Street Publishing Services; Barbara Armentrout, copy editor; Rokusek Design, designer; Dean Dauphinais, permissions acquisitions manager for images; Raquel Sousa, photo researcher; and Margaret Chamberlain-Gaston, permissions acquisitions manager for text. We give special thanks to Rebekah Matthews, assistant editor, who in addition to her usual duties helped us write the new Pop Comm! feature. As always, we are indebted to Greer Lleuad, senior development editor, who is simply the best in the business. We trust and respect her opinions and advice unconditionally. We simply could not have done this book without her.

We also thank our families for their continued patience, understanding, and support.

Finally, we thank God for the many ways that our lives have been blessed. We hope this book helps readers glimpse what Martin Buber called the "I-Thou" respect and love that we believe God planned us to have in our human relationships.

Kathleen S. Verderber
and
Deanna D. Sellnow

Martin Barraud/Getty Images

Communication Perspectives

Questions you'll be able to answer after reading this chapter:

- How does the communication process work?
- What characterizes each of the communication settings you will study in this course?
- What are the basic principles of communication?
- What major ethical issues face communicators?
- What is *communication competence* and what can you do to achieve it?
- What is *communication apprehension* and how does it relate to communication competence?

Mimi and Marcus finished talking with the fifth car salesperson.

"From what I could understand, most of the basic features we need are about the same," said Mimi. "So, for me, it comes down to who we feel most comfortable with."

"Yeah, that's pretty much the way I see it. And from that standpoint, I'd pick Carrie," Marcus responded.

"She really seemed nice, didn't she?" asked Mimi. "She seemed friendly and—unlike Paul—she talked to both of us, not just you."

Marcus replied, "She talked about features, price, and financing options that were tailored to our specific needs—unlike Dempsey, who spent most of his time talking about luxury features that cost more than we can afford."

Mimi added, "Yeah, and Gloria was so disorganized . . ."

"And she was so focused on getting through her presentation that she didn't even notice when you tried to ask a question!" Marcus interjected.

"I sort of liked Steve," Mimi continued, "but when we suggested that the price range he was quoting was out of our budget, he wasn't much help. Once he got off his 'script,' he seemed lost."

"Well," Marcus replied, "not only did Carrie offer a car with features we can use and a financing plan we can afford, she also led me to believe that we could call her with questions later about when and where to service our vehicle."

"OK," Mimi said as she nodded. "So we agree; we're buying our car from Carrie!"

Why was Carrie successful? Was it the car she was promoting or her specialized expertise in the automobile business? Not necessarily. From this conversation, it appears that Carrie's success was due to her ability to communicate with Mimi and Marcus. Carrie's success is not unusual. Time and time again, studies have concluded that, for almost any job, employers seek oral communication skills, teamwork skills, and interpersonal abilities (College learning for the new global century, 2008; Hansen & Hansen, 2007; Young, 2003). For example, an article on the role of communication in the workplace reported that in engineering, a highly technical field, speaking skills were very important for 72 percent of the employers surveyed (Darling & Dannels, 2003, p. 12). A survey by the National Association of Colleges and Employers (Koncz, 2008) reported the top 10 personal qualities and skills that employers seek from college graduates. The number one skill was communication, including face-to-face speaking, presentational speaking, and writing. Other skills ranked in the top 10 that you will learn about and practice in this course include teamwork skills (number three), analytical skills (number five), interpersonal skills (number eight), and problem-solving skills (number nine). The employers also said these very skills are, unfortunately, the ones many new graduates lack. So this course can significantly increase your ability to get a job and be successful in your chosen career.

How effectively you communicate with others is important not only to your career, but also to your personal relationships. Your ability to make and keep friends, to be a good family member, to have satisfying intimate relationships, to participate in or lead groups, and to prepare and present speeches depends on your communication skills. During this course, you will learn about the communication process and have an opportunity to practice basic communication skills that will help you improve your relationships.

In this chapter, we begin by explaining the process of communication. Next, we describe several communication settings and how we'll address improving communication skills for them in this book. From there, we describe several fundamental principles of communication. Finally, we discuss communication competence, the role managing communication apprehension plays in achieving it, and a strategy for improving your communication skills.

The Communication Process

Communication is the process of creating or sharing meaning in informal conversation, group interaction, or public speaking. To understand how this process works, we begin by describing its essential elements: participants (who), messages (what), context (where), channels (how), interference (distractions), and feedback (reaction).

How does the communication process work?

Participants

The **participants** are the individuals who assume the roles of senders and receivers during an interaction. As senders, participants form and transmit messages using verbal symbols, visual images, and nonverbal behavior. As receivers, they interpret the messages that have been transmitted to them.

Messages

Messages are the verbal utterances, visual images, and nonverbal behaviors to which meaning is attributed during communication. To understand how messages are created and received, we need to understand meanings, symbols, encoding and decoding, and form (organization).

Meanings

Meanings include the thoughts in your mind as well as the interpretations you make of another's message. Meanings are the ways participants make sense of messages. It is important to realize that meanings are not transferred from one person to another, but are created together in an exchange. Some communication settings enable participants to verify that they have shared meanings; in other settings this is more difficult. For instance, if Sarah says to Tiffany that many female celebrities are unhealthily underweight, through the exchange of verbal messages, they can together come to some degree of understanding of what that means. But if Sarah is giving a speech on the subject to an audience of 200 people, Tiffany's ability to question Sarah and negotiate a mutual meaning is limited. If Sarah shows a slideshow of before-and-after photographs of some of the celebrities she is referring to, she can make the meaning clear even for a large audience.

Symbols

To express yourself, you form messages made of verbal symbols (words), nonverbal cues (behaviors), and visual images. **Symbols** are words, sounds, and actions that represent specific ideas and feelings. As you speak, you choose word symbols to express your meaning. At the same time, you also use facial expressions, eye contact, gestures, and tone of voice—all symbolic, nonverbal cues—in an attempt to express your meaning. Your listeners make interpretations or attribute meaning to the messages they receive. When you offer your messages through a variety of symbols, the meaning you are trying to convey becomes clearer.

Encoding and decoding

Encoding is the process of putting your thoughts and feelings into words, nonverbal cues, and images. **Decoding** is the process of interpreting another's message. Ordinarily you do not consciously think about either the encoding or the decoding process. Only when there is a difficulty, such as speaking in a second language or having to use an easier vocabulary with children, do you become aware of encoding. You may not think about decoding until someone seems to speak in circles or uses unfamiliar technical words and you have difficulty interpreting or understanding what is being said. Have you ever taken a course where the instructor used lots of unfamiliar technical words? If so, how did that affect the decoding process for you?

communication
the process of creating or sharing meaning in informal conversation, group interaction, or public speaking.

participants
individuals who assume the roles of senders and receivers during an interaction.

messages
verbal utterances, visual images, and nonverbal behaviors to which meaning is attributed during communication.

meanings
thoughts in our minds and interpretations of others' messages.

symbols
words, sounds, and actions that are generally understood to represent ideas and feelings.

encoding
the process of putting our thoughts and feelings into words and nonverbal cues.

decoding
the process of interpreting another's message.

Form (Organization)

When the meaning we wish to share is complex, we may need to organize it in sections or in a certain order. Message form is especially important when one person talks without interruption for a relatively long time, such as in a public speech or when reporting an event to a colleague at work. Visual images also need to be organized and in good form if they are to aid understanding.

Context

The **context** is composed of the (1) physical, (2) social, (3) historical, (4) psychological, and (5) cultural situations in which a communication encounter occurs, including what precedes and follows what is said. According to noted German philosopher Jürgen Habermas, the ideal speech situation is impossible to achieve, but considering its contexts as we communicate with others can move us closer to that goal (Littlejohn & Foss, 2007 p. 335). The context affects the expectations of the participants, the meaning these participants derive, and their subsequent behavior.

Physical context

The **physical context** includes the location, the environmental conditions (temperature, lighting, and noise level), the distance between communicators, and the time of day. Each of these factors can affect the communication. For instance, the meaning shared in a conversation may be affected by whether it is held in a crowded company cafeteria, an elegant candlelit restaurant, over the telephone, or on the Internet.

Today, more and more of our communication exchanges occur in technologically mediated spaces. When you call someone on your cell phone, for instance, you are in different physical places and your conversation will be influenced by the physical contexts each of you occupy as well as by the quality of your phone connection. Moreover, the messages and meaning are affected by whether the technology used is synchronous or asynchronous. Synchronous technologies allow us to exchange messages in real time, while asynchronous technologies allow delays between sending, receiving, and responding to messages. Telephone calls are synchronous, and voice mail messages and e-mail are typically asynchronous. Instant messages (IMs) and text messages may be either synchronous or asynchronous.

Social context

The **social context** is the nature of the relationship between the participants. Whether communication takes place among family members, friends, acquaintances, work associates, or strangers influences what and how messages are formed, shared, and interpreted. For instance, most people change how they interact when talking with their parents or siblings as compared to how they interact when talking with their friends.

Historical context

The **historical context** is the background provided by previous communication episodes between the participants. It influences understandings in the current encounter. For instance, suppose one morning Chad tells Shelby that he will pick up the rough draft of a paper they had given to their professor for feedback to help prepare the final manuscript. When Shelby joins Chad for lunch in the cafeteria, she says, "Did you get it?" Another person listening to the conversation would have no idea what the *it* is. Yet Chad quickly replies, "It's on my desk." Shelby and Chad would understand each other because the content of their previous conversation provides the context for understanding what "it" is in this exchange.

context
the setting in which communication occurs, including what precedes and follows what is said.

physical context
a communication encounter's location, environmental conditions (temperature, lighting, noise level), distance between communicators, seating arrangements, and time of day.

social context
the nature of the relationship that exists between the participants.

historical context
the background provided by previous communication episodes between the participants that influence understandings in the current encounter.

Psychological context

The **psychological context** includes the moods and feelings each person brings to the interpersonal encounter. For instance, suppose Corinne is under a lot of stress. While she is studying for an exam, a friend stops by and pleads with her to take a break and go to the gym with her. Corinne, who is normally good-natured, may explode with an angry tirade. Why? Because her stress level provides the psychological context within which she hears this message and it affects how she responds.

Cultural context

The **cultural context** includes the values, beliefs, orientations, underlying assumptions, and rituals prevalent among people in a society (Samovar, Porter, & McDaniel, 2007). Culture penetrates into every aspect of our lives, affecting how we think, talk, and behave. Each of us belongs to many cultural groups, though we may differ in how much we identify with each group. Mina, for example, was born in Taiwan but was raised in Boston, where she attended Chinese elementary school. She is also a college student and a Democrat. Each of these groups helps characterize her cultural setting. When two people from different cultures interact, misunderstandings may occur because of the cultural variations between them. For example, the role of a "good student" in many Asian cultures typically means being quiet, respectful, and never challenging others' views, but the good-student role in U.S. classrooms often includes being talkative, assertive, and debating the views expressed by others. The Pop Comm article in this chapter describes how the cultural ritual of mourning is changing in the U.S.A.

Channels

Channels are both the route traveled by the message and the means of transportation. Messages are transmitted through sensory channels. Face-to-face communication has three basic channels: verbal symbols, nonverbal cues, and visual images. Technologically mediated communication uses these same channels, though nonverbal cues such as movements, touch, and gestures are represented by visual symbols like **emoticons** (textual images that symbolize the sender's mood, emotion, or facial expressions) and **acronyms** (abbreviations that stand in for common phrases). For example, in a face-to-face inter-action, Barry might express his frustration about a poor grade on an assignment by ver-bally noting why he thought the grade was unfair, by visually showing the assignment along with the grading criteria for it, and by nonverbally raising his voice and shaking his fist. In an online interaction, he might insert a frowning-face emoticon (☹) or the acronym "POed" to represent those nonverbal behaviors.

Interference (Noise)

Interference (noise) is any stimulus that hinders the process of sharing meaning. Interference can be physical or psychological.

Physical interference includes the sights, sounds, and other stimuli in the environment that draw people's attention away from intended meaning. For instance, while a

psychological context
the mood and feelings each person brings to a conversation.

cultural context
the values, attitudes, beliefs, orientations, and underlying assumptions prevalent among people in a society.

channel
both the route traveled by the message and the means of transportation.

interference (noise)
any stimulus that interferes with the process of sharing meaning.

physical interference
sights, sounds, and other stimuli in the environment that draw people's attention away from intended meaning.

Did you know that 2.5 billion text messages are sent each day in the United States?

Leland Bobbe/Photonica/Getty images

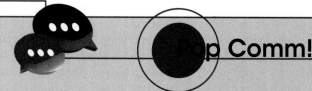

Mourning in the United States, 21st-Century Style

CHIP EAST/Reuters/Landov

Mourning is a universal human communication activity. It is the process of celebrating the life of someone while grieving his or her death. Mourning rituals and traditions vary by culture and religion and change over time. So it is not surprising that mourning in the United States

in the 21st century is adapting past practices to modern life.

Mourning rituals include norms for how the body of the deceased is dealt with, burial and commemorative rituals, symbols of mourning, and comforting practices. In the past, personally washing, dressing, and preparing the body for burial enabled mourners to present the deceased as they would like the person to be remembered. Burial and commemorative rituals gave family, friends, and the larger community an opportunity to gather, exchange memories of the deceased, comfort those closest to the deceased, and receive comfort in return. Graves were places where those close to the deceased could go to "talk" to the departed and recall memories. Family members would often withdraw into their homes for a period of time to grieve. Friends and community members would visit with the family in their home during this intense period of mourning. Those closest to the person who had died chose or were expected to wear symbols of their status as mourners. Mourning clothes and tokens served as signals to others in the community that the person so dressed was in mourning and should be accorded extra gentleness.

Today, in the U.S.A. most families do not personally prepare the body of their loved one for burial

---

friend is giving you instructions on how to work the new MP3 player, your attention may be drawn away by the external noise of your favorite TV show, which is on in the next room. External noise does not have to be a sound, however. Perhaps, while your friend is giving instructions, your attention is drawn momentarily to an attractive man or woman. Such visual distractions are also physical interference.

Psychological interference includes internal distractions based on thoughts or feelings and can fall into two categories: internal noise and semantic noise. **Internal noise** refers to the thoughts and feelings that compete for attention and interfere with the communication process. If you have ever tuned out the lecture your professor is giving and tuned into a daydream or a past conversation, then you have experienced internal noise. **Semantic noise** refers to the distractions aroused by certain symbols that take our attention away from the main message. If a friend describes a 40-year-old secretary as "the girl in the office," and you think *girl* is an odd and condescending term for a 40-year-old

psychological interference
internal distractions based on thoughts, feelings, or emotional reactions to symbols.

internal noise
thoughts and feelings that compete for attention and interfere with the communication process.

or wear special mourning clothes. Increasingly, one or more members of the family may honor their loved one by preparing a commemorative Web page that memorializes the life of the departed. Web sites such as Legacy.com, MyDeathSpace.com, and Memory-Of.com have been around for over a decade to facilitate the creation of interactive online memorials. An article in *The Boston Globe* recounted the story of Shawn Kelley who created a "moving tribute" to his brother Michael, a National Guardsman killed in Afghanistan. The 60-second video features a slide show of Michael growing up, from a toddler to a clean-cut teen, while quiet classical music plays softly and a voice-over recounts Michael's attributes and interests. Shawn reported that it made him feel good to be able to "talk" about his brother, and over a year later he was still visiting the site to watch the video and to view the messages left by family members and friends (Plumb, 2006). Today the rituals traditionally associated with funerals and memorial services such as eulogies, visitations, and expressions of condolence now often take place online.

Interactive memorial Web sites also have become a "place" where mourners can "visit" with their departed loved one and connect with other mourners, activities that traditionally occurred at a funeral or memorial service. Most Web sites that host memorial Web pages allow visitors to leave messages of condolence, share stories about the deceased, and leave messages directed to the deceased. Denise McGrath, a mother who created "R.I.P. Tony," a memorial Web page for her teenage son on MySpace explained that it was "just a place for his friends to go" (Plumb, 2006). Today Legacy.com hosts over 50,000 permanent memorials and reports being visited by over 10 million users each month (Plumb, 2009).

The somber mourning clothes of past generations have given way to newer ways of marking oneself as in mourning. Today family members and friends may wear T-shirts imprinted with pictures of the deceased. This practice is most common when the departed is young and died a violent death. According to Montana Miller, professor of popular culture at Bowling Green State University, the tradition of wearing commemorative t-shirts originated with West Coast gangs in the early 1990s (Moser, 2005).

Not only are people using T-shirts to signal mourning, but they are also designing decals to place on cars and bikes to memorialize those who have died. In a highly mobile society, decals are visual markers that can not only memorialize a loved one who has died but can also connect mourners to others who have suffered a similar loss. When one 17-year-old was shot and killed, hundreds of people in his town put memorial decals in their car windows. Four years later the young man's mother reported that seeing those decals continued to help her with her grieving process (Moser, 2005).

Although we may no longer personally prepare the dead for burial or wear somber formal mourning clothes, we still need to connect and communicate with others as we grieve, and we continue to evolve new methods for doing so.

woman, you might not even hear the rest of what your friend has to say. Whenever we react emotionally to a word or a behavior, we are experiencing semantic noise.

Feedback

Feedback is the reactions and responses to a message that indicate to the sender whether and how that message was heard, seen, and interpreted. In face-to-face communication, we can express feedback verbally through words or nonverbally through body language. In online interactions, we can express feedback verbally through words or nonverbally through emoticons and acronyms. We continuously give feedback when we are listening to another, if only by paying attention, giving a confused look, or showing signs of boredom. Or we may give direct verbal feedback by saying, "I don't understand the point you are making" or "That's a great comment you just made." In online interactions, we might use an acronym like CC (I understand) or WDYM (What do you mean?).

semantic noise
distractions aroused by certain symbols that take our attention away from the main message.

feedback
reactions and responses to messages.

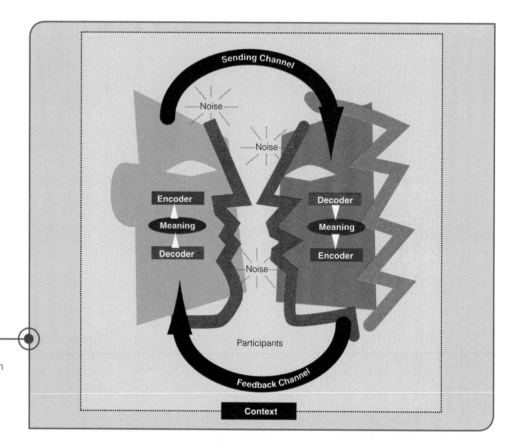

Figure 1.1
A model of communication between two individuals

Skill Learning Activity 1.1

What characterizes each of the communication settings discussed in this book?

communication setting
the different communication environments within which people interact, characterized by the number of participants and the extent to which the interaction is formal or informal; also called communication contexts.

intrapersonal communication
the interactions that occur in a person's mind when he or she is talking with himself or herself.

A Model of the Basic Communication Process

Figure 1.1 illustrates the communication process between two people. In the minds of these people are meanings, thoughts, and feelings that they intend to share. These thoughts and feelings are created and shaped by the people's values, culture, environment, experiences, occupation, sex, interests, knowledge, and attitudes. To communicate a message, the sender encodes thoughts and feelings into messages that are sent using one or more channels.

The receiver decodes or interprets the symbols in an attempt to understand the speaker's meaning. This decoding process is affected by the receiver's total field of experience—that is, by all the same factors that shape the encoding process. Feedback completes the process so that the sender and receiver can arrive at a similar understanding of the message.

The model depicts the context as the area around the participants. This may include the physical, social, historical, psychological, and cultural contexts that permeate all parts of the process. Similarly, the model shows that during conversation physical and psychological interference (noise), including internal and semantic distractions, may interfere at various points and therefore affect the people's ability to arrive at similar meanings. As you might imagine, the process becomes more complex when more than two people are conversing or when someone is speaking to a large and diverse audience.

Communication Settings

The basic communication process describes how meanings are shared and in this course you will learn skills that will help you communicate effectively regardless of the type of interaction you are experiencing. But there are also important skills to learn that are specific to a particular communication setting. **Communication settings** differentiate interactions based on the number of participants and the extent to which the interaction is characterized by formal or informal exchanges. Also called *communication contexts* by some scholars these classifications describe the different communication environments within which we interact. (Littlejohn & Foss, 2008, pp. 52–53). In this book, you will learn skills that will help you in intrapersonal settings, interpersonal settings, small group settings, and public communication settings.

Intrapersonal communication refers to the interactions that occur in your mind when you are talking with yourself. While we may occasionally think out loud, we usually don't verbalize our internal dialog. When you sit in class and think about what you'll do later that day, you are communicating intrapersonally. Similarly, when you send yourself a reminder note as an e-mail or text message, you are communicating intrapersonally. A lot of our intrapersonal communication occurs subconsciously (Kellerman, 1992). When we drive into the driveway "without thinking," we are communicating intrapersonally on a subconscious level. The study of intrapersonal communication often focuses on its role in shaping self-perceptions and in managing communication apprehension, that is, the fear associated with communicating with others (McCroskey, 1977). Our study of intrapersonal communication will focus on self-talk as a means to improve your self-concept and self-esteem and, ultimately, your communication competence in a variety of situations.

Interpersonal communication is characterized by informal interaction between two people who have an identifiable relationship with each other (Knapp & Daly, 2002). Talking to a friend between classes, visiting on the phone with your mother, texting or chatting online with your brother, and comforting someone who has suffered a loss are all examples of interpersonal communication. In Part II, our study of interpersonal communication includes the exploration of how we develop, maintain, improve, or end our relationships with others. We will also focus on listening and responding to others with empathy and on sharing personal information.

Small group communication typically involves three to 20 people who come together to communicate with one another (Beebe & Masterson, 2006; Hirokawa, Cathcart, Samovar, & Henman, 2003). There are many kinds of small groups; examples include a family, a group of friends, a group of classmates working on a project, and a management team in the workplace. Small group communication can occur in face-to-face settings, as well as online through electronic mailing lists, discussion boards, and blogs. In Part III, our study of small groups focuses on the characteristics of effective groups, ethical and effective communication in groups, leadership, problem-solving, conflict, and group presentations.

Public communication is communication delivered to audiences of more than 20 people. Public communication includes public speeches and other types of mass communication that you may experience live, in person, or on a delayed or mediated basis. For example, when President Barack Obama delivered his inaugural address some people were there, others watched on TV or the

interpersonal communication
informal interaction between two people who have an identifiable relationship with each other.

small group communication
two to 20 people who participants come together for the specific purpose of solving a problem or arriving at a decision.

public communication
one participant, the speaker, delivers a prepared message to a group or audience who has assembled to hear the speaker.

Karen Kapoor/Getty Images

How might the conversation of these people differ if they were in the library working on a class project?

Internet at the time he spoke, and still others have experienced his speech after Inaugural Day by viewing it in the form of televised snippets or via a Web site such as YouTube. The Internet is also becoming the medium of choice for posting job ads and résumés, for advertising and buying products, and for political activism. In Part IV, our study of public communication will focus on preparing, practicing, and delivering effective oral presentations in both face-to-face and virtual environments.

Skill Learning Activity 1.2

Communication Principles

Principles are general truths. Understanding the principles of communication is important as you begin your study because they will provide a foundation for practicing and improving your communication skills. In this section, we discuss seven generally agreed-upon principles: communication has purpose, communication is continuous, communication messages vary in conscious thought, communication is relational, communication is guided by culture, communication has ethical implications, and communication is learned.

Communication Has Purpose

What are the fundamental principles of communication?

When people communicate with each other, they have a purpose for doing so. The purpose may be serious or trivial, and they may or may not be aware of it at the time. Here we list five basic purposes for communicating that we'll be addressing throughout the book.

1. **We communicate to develop and maintain our sense of self.** Through our interactions, we learn who we are, what we are good at, and how people react to how we behave.

2. **We communicate to meet our social needs.** Just as we need food, water, and shelter, so too do we, as social animals, need contact with other people. Two people may converse happily for hours, chatting about inconsequential matters that neither remembers afterward. Still, their communication has functioned to meet the important need simply to talk with another human being.

3. **We communicate to develop and maintain relationships.** Not only do we get to know others through our communication with them but, more importantly, we develop relationships with them—relationships that grow and deepen or stagnate and wither away. For example, when Beth calls Leah to ask whether she'd like to join her for lunch to discuss a project they are working on, her purpose actually may be to resolve a misunderstanding they've had because she wants to maintain a positive relationship with Leah.

4. **We communicate to exchange information.** Some information we get through observation, some through reading, some through media, and a great deal through direct communication with others, whether face-to-face, via text messaging, or online through e-mail and social networking sites such as Facebook and MySpace. Whether we are trying to decide how warmly to dress or whom to vote for in the next election, all of us have countless exchanges that involve sending and receiving information.

5. **We communicate to influence others.** It is doubtful that a day goes by in which you don't engage in behavior such as trying to convince your friends to go to a particular restaurant or to see a certain movie, to persuade your supervisor to alter your schedule, or to convince an instructor to change a grade.

Skill Learning Activity 1.3

Communication Is Continuous

Because communication is nonverbal and visual as well as verbal, we are always sending behavioral messages from which others draw inferences or meaning. Even silence communicates if another person infers meaning from it. Why? Because your nonverbal behavior represents reactions to your environment and to the people around you. If you are cold, you shiver; if you are hot or nervous, you perspire; if you are bored, happy, or confused, your face or body language probably will show it. Not only that, we are continuously sending and receiving multiple messages when we communicate with others. For example, as you talk with your friend about where to go on spring break, both of you are simultaneously sending and receiving multiple verbal and nonverbal messages to each other. As skilled communicators, we need to be aware of the explicit and implicit messages we are constantly sending to others.

Communication Messages Vary in Conscious Thought

Recall that sharing meaning with another person involves encoding and decoding verbal messages, nonverbal cues, and even visual images. Our messages may (1) occur spontaneously, (2) be based on a "script" we have learned or rehearsed, or (3) be carefully constructed based on our understanding of the unique situation in which we find ourselves.

Many of our messages are **spontaneous expressions,** spoken without much conscious thought. For example, when you burn your finger, you may blurt out, "Ouch!" When something goes right, you may break into a broad smile.

At other times, our messages are **scripted,** phrasings that we have learned from our past encounters and judge to be appropriate to the present situation. Many of these scripts are learned in childhood. For example, when you want the sugar bowl but cannot reach it, you may say, "Please pass the sugar," followed by "Thank you" when someone complies. This conversational sequence comes from your "table manners script," which may have been drilled into you at home. Scripts enable us to use messages that are appropriate to the situation and are likely to increase the effectiveness of our communication. One goal of this text is to acquaint you with general scripts (or skills) that can be adapted for use in your communication encounters across a variety of relationships, situations, and cultures.

Finally, our messages may be carefully constructed to meet the unique requirements of a particular situation. **Constructed messages** are those that we put together with careful thought when we recognize that our known scripts are inadequate for the situation.

Communication Is Relational

In any communication setting, in addition to sharing content meaning, our messages also reflect two important aspects of our relationships: immediacy and control.

Immediacy is the degree of liking or attractiveness in a relationship. For instance, when José passes Josh on campus he may say, "Josh, good to see you" (a verbal expression of friendliness); the nonverbal behavior that accompanies the words may show Josh whether José is genuinely happy to see him or is only expressing recognition. For instance, if José smiles, has a sincere sound to his voice, looks Josh in the eye, and perhaps pats him on the back or shakes hands firmly, then Josh will recognize these signs of friendliness. If, however, José speaks quickly with no vocal inflection and with a deadpan facial expression, Josh will probably perceive the comment as impersonal communication offered merely to meet some social expectation.

Control is the degree to which one participant is perceived to be more dominant or powerful. Thus, when Tom says to Sue, "I know you're concerned about

spontaneous expressions
messages spoken without much conscious thought.

scripted messages
phrasings learned from past encounters that we judge to be appropriate to the present situation.

constructed messages
messages put together with careful thought when we recognize that our known scripts are inadequate for the situation.

immediacy
the degree of liking or attractiveness in a relationship.

control
the degree to which one participant is perceived to be more dominant or powerful.

© Michael Keller/CORBIS

What message about immediacy and control do wedding couples send as they feed each other cake? Power in relationships is influenced by both verbal and nonverbal messages.

the budget, but I'll see to it that we have money to cover everything," his words and the sound of his voice may be saying that he is "in charge" of finances—that he is in control. How Sue responds to Tom determines whether, on this issue, she submits to his perception of control. If Sue says, "Thanks, I know you have a better handle on finances than I do," then she accepts that on this issue, she is willing to submit to Tom at this time. A few days later, if Tom says to Sue, "I think we need to cut back on credit card expenses for a couple of months," and Sue responds, "No way! I need a new suit for work, the car needs new tires, and you promised we could replace the couch," then the nature of the relationship will require further discussion.

Communication Is Guided by Culture

Culture may be defined as systems of knowledge shared by a relatively large group of people. It includes a system of shared beliefs, values, symbols, and behaviors. How messages are formed and interpreted depends on the cultural background of the participants. We need to look carefully at ourselves and our communication behavior; as we interact with others whose cultural backgrounds differ from our own, so we don't unintentionally communicate in ways that are culturally inappropriate or insensitive and thereby undermine our relationships. In addition to national and ethnic culture we also need to be sensitive to the sex, age, class, and sexual orientation of our listeners. Failure to take those differences into account when we interact can also lead us to behave insensitively.

Throughout the history of the United States, we've experienced huge migrations of people from different parts of the world. According to the *New York Times Almanac* (Wright, 2002), at the turn of the 21st century, people of Latin and Asian descent constituted 12.5 percent and 3.8 percent, respectively, of the total U.S. population. About 2.4 percent of the population regards itself as multiracial. Combined with the approximately 13 percent of our population that is of African descent, these four groups account for nearly 32 percent of the total population. According to the U.S. Census Bureau, this figure is predicted to rise to nearly 50 percent by 2050.

According to Samovar, Porter, and McDaniel (2007) "a number of cultural components are particularly relevant to the student of intercultural communication. These include (1) perception, (2) patterns of cognition, (3) verbal behaviors, (4) nonverbal behaviors, and the influence of context" (p. 13). Because cultural concerns permeate all of communication, in each chapter of this book we will point out when the concepts and skills you are learning are viewed differently by cultural groups other than the dominant American one. In the Diverse Voices feature found in many chapters, authors explain how they or their culture views a concept presented in the text. In this chapter, Harlan Cleveland describes how the diverse peoples in the United States have learned to live together.

Web Resource 1.1

culture
systems of knowledge shared by a relatively large group of people.

Lessons from American Experience

by Harland Cleveland

 **Diverse Voices**

The late Harland Cleveland was president of the University of Hawaii and the World Academy of Art and Science. In this selection, Cleveland explains how Hawaii, the most diverse of our 50 states, achieves ethnic and racial peace. He argues that the Hawaiian experience is no different from the experience of immigrants to the mainland; the ability to tolerate diversity is not unique in the world.

We Americans have learned, in our short but intensive 200-plus years of history as a nation, a first lesson about diversity: that it cannot be governed by drowning it in "integration."

I came face-to-face with this truth when, just a quarter of a century ago, I became president of the University of Hawaii. Everyone who lives in Hawaii, or even visits there, is impressed by its residents' comparative tolerance toward each other. On closer inspection, paradise seems based on paradox: Everybody's a minority. The tolerance is not despite the diversity but because of it.

It is not through the disappearance of ethnic distinctions that the people of Hawaii achieved a level of racial peace that has few parallels around our discriminatory globe. Quite the contrary. The glory is that Hawaii's main ethnic groups managed to establish the right to be separate. The group separateness, in turn, helped establish the rights of individuals in each group to equality with individuals of different racial aspect, ethnic origin, and cultural heritage.

Hawaii's experience is not so foreign to the transatlantic migrations of the various more-or-less white Caucasians. On arrival in New York (passing that inscription on the Statue of Liberty, "Send these, the homeless, tempest-tossed, to me"), the European immigrants did not melt into the open arms of the white Anglo Saxon Protestants who preceded them. The reverse was true. The new arrivals stayed close to their own kind; shared religion, language, humor, and discriminatory treatment with their soul brothers and sisters; and gravitated at first into occupations that did not too seriously threaten the earlier arrivals.

The waves of new Americans learned to tolerate each other—first as groups, only thereafter as individuals. Rubbing up against each other in an urbanizing America, they discovered not just the old Christian lesson that all men are brothers, but the hard, new, multicultural lesson that all brothers are different. Equality is not the product of similarity; it is the cheerful acknowledgement of difference.

What's so special about our experience is the assumption that people of many kinds and colors can together govern themselves without deciding in advance which kinds of people (male or female, black, brown, yellow, red, white, or any mix of these) may hold any particular public office in the pantheon of political power.

For the twenty-first century, this "cheerful acknowledgement of differences is the alternative to a global spread of ethnic cleansing and religious rivalry. The challenge is great, for ethnic cleansing and religious rivalry are traditions as contemporary as Bosnia and Rwanda in the 1990s and as ancient as the Assyrians.

In too many countries, there is still a basic (if often unspoken) assumption that one kind of people is anointed to be in general charge. Try to imagine a Turkish chancellor of Germany, an Algerian president of France, a Pakistani prime minister of Britain, a Christian president of Egypt, an Arab prime minister of Israel, a Jewish president of Syria, a Tibetan ruler of Beijing, anyone but a Japanese in power in Tokyo. Yet in the United States during the twentieth century, we have already elected an Irish Catholic as president, chosen several Jewish Supreme Court justices, and racially integrated the armed forces right up to the chairman of the Joint Chiefs of Staff . . . .

I wouldn't dream of arguing that we Americans have found the Holy Grail of cultural diversity when, in fact, we're still searching for it. We have to think hard about our growing pluralism. It's useful, I believe, to dissect in the open our thinking about it, to see whether the lessons we are trying to learn might stimulate some useful thinking elsewhere. We still do not quite know how to create "wholeness incorporating diversity," but we owe it to the world, as well as to ourselves, to keep trying.

Reflective Questions

1. To what degree to you think America has moved forward since Harland Cleveland offered these statements?
2. Name some specific examples to support your opinion.

Excerpted from Harland Cleveland, "The Limits to Cultural Diversity," in Intercultural Communication: A Reader *(12th ed.), eds. Larry A. Samovar, Richard E. Porter, and Erwin R. McDaniel (Belmont, CA: Wadsworth, 2009), pp. 431–434. Reprinted by permission of the World Future Society.*

Communication Has Ethical Implications

What ethical issues face communicators?

In any encounter, we choose whether or not to communicate ethically. **Ethics** is a set of moral principles that may be held by a society, a group, or an individual. Although what is considered ethical is a matter of personal judgment, various groups still expect members to uphold certain standards. These standards influence the personal decisions we make. When we choose to violate the standards that are expected, we are viewed to be unethical. Here are five ethical standards that influence our communication and guide our behavior.

1. Truthfulness and honesty mean refraining from lying, cheating, stealing, or deception. "An honest person is widely regarded as a moral person, and honesty is a central concept to ethics as the foundation for a moral life" (Terkel & Duval, 1999, p. 122). Although most people accept truthfulness and honesty as a standard, they still confess to lying on occasion. We are most likely to lie when we are caught in an **ethical dilemma,** a choice involving an unsatisfactory alternative. An example of an ethical dilemma would be a boss asking us if our coworker arrived to work late today and knowing that telling the truth would get the coworker fired.

2. Integrity means maintaining a consistency of belief and action (keeping promises). Terkel and Duval (1999) say, "A person who has integrity is someone who has strong moral principles and will successfully resist the temptation to compromise those principles" (p. 135). Integrity, then, is the opposite of hypocrisy. A person who had promised to help a friend study for the upcoming exam would live up to this promise even when another friend offered a free ticket to a sold-out concert for the same night.

3. Fairness means achieving the right balance of interests without regard to one's own feelings and without showing favor to any side in a conflict. Fairness implies impartiality or lack of bias. To be fair to someone is to listen with an open mind, to gather all the relevant facts, consider only circumstances relevant to the decision at hand, and not let prejudice or irrelevancies affect how you treat others. For example, if two of her children are fighting, a mom is exercising fairness if she listens openly as the children explain "their side" before she decides what to do.

4. Respect means showing regard or consideration for others and their ideas, even if we don't agree with them. Respect is not based on someone's affluence, job status, or ethnic background. In a classroom, students show respect for others by attentively listening to another student's speech even when the main point violates their political or religious position.

ethics
a set of moral principles that may be held by a society, a group, or an individual.

ethical dilemma
a choice involving two unsatisfactory alternatives.

5. **Responsibility** means being accountable for one's actions and what one says. Responsible communicators recognize the power of words. Messages can hurt and messages can soothe. Information is accurate or it may be faulty. A responsible communicator would not spread a false rumor about another friend.

Web Resource 1.2

In our daily lives, we often face ethical dilemmas and must sort out what is more or less right or wrong. In making these decisions, we usually reveal our ethical standards. At the end of each chapter of this book, the feature What Would You Do? A Question of Ethics will ask you to think about and resolve an ethical dilemma that relates to that chapter's content. Your instructor may use these as a vehicle for class discussions, or you may be asked to prepare a written report.

© George Simian/CORBIS

Just as children learn how to behave from their parents, so too do they learn to communicate. What specific communication behaviors can you identify that you learned at home?

Communication Is Learned

Just as you learned to walk, so too you learned to communicate. But talking is a complex undertaking. You may not yet have learned all of the skills you will need to develop healthy relationships. Because communication is learned, you can improve your ability. Throughout this text, we identify communication skills that can help you become a more competent communicator.

Increasing Our Communication Competence

Communication competence is the impression that communicative behavior is both appropriate and effective in a given situation (Spitzberg, 2000, p. 375). Communication is *effective* when it achieves its goals; it is *appropriate* when it conforms to what is expected in a situation. We create the perception that we are competent communicators through the verbal messages we send, and the nonverbal behaviors and visual images that accompany them. Competence is an impression or judgment that people make about others. Because communication is at the heart of how we relate to each other, one of your goals in this course will be to learn strategies to increase the likelihood that others will view you as competent.

What is communication competence, and what can you do to achieve it?

communication competence
the impression that communicative behavior is both appropriate and effective in a given situation.

Perceptions of competence depend, in part, on personal motivation, knowledge, and skills (Spitzberg, 2000, p. 377). Motivation is important because we will only be able to improve our communication if we are *motivated*—that is, if we want to. People are likely to be more motivated if they are confident and if they see potential rewards. Knowledge is important because we must know what is involved in increasing competence. The more knowledge people have about how to behave in a given situation, the more likely they are to be able to develop competence. Skill is important because we must know how to act in ways that are consistent with our communication knowledge. *Skills* are goal-oriented actions or action sequences that we can master and repeat in appropriate situations. The more skills you have, the more likely you are to be able to structure your messages effectively and appropriately.

In addition to motivation, knowledge, and skills, credibility and social ease are important components of communication competence. **Credibility** is a perception of a speaker's knowledge, trustworthiness, and warmth. Listeners are more likely to be attentive to and influenced by speakers they see as credible. **Social ease** means managing communication apprehension so you do not appear nervous or anxious. To be seen as a competent communicator, it is important that you can speak in a style that conveys confidence and poise. Communicators that appear apprehensive are not likely to be regarded as competent, despite their motivation or knowledge.

Although most people think of public speaking anxiety when they hear the term *communication apprehension* (CA), there are actually four different forms of CA. Generally speaking, **communication apprehension** is "the fear or anxiety associated with real or anticipated communication with others" (McCroskey, 1977, p. 78). The four specific types are traitlike CA, audience-based CA, situational CA, and context-based CA. If you experience *traitlike communication apprehension*, you feel anxious in most speaking situations. About 20 percent of all people experience traitlike CA (Richmond and McCroskey, 2000). If you experience *audience-based communication apprehension*, you feel anxious about speaking only with a certain person or group of people. *Situational communication apprehension* is a short-lived feeling of anxiety that occurs during a specific encounter, for example, during a job interview. Finally, *context-based communication apprehension* is anxiety only in a particular situation, for example, when speaking to a large group of people. All these forms of communication anxiety can be managed effectively in ways that help you convey social ease when communicating with others. Throughout this book, we will offer strategies for managing communication apprehension in various settings.

The combination of our motivation, knowledge, skills, credibility, and social ease leads us to perform effectively in our encounters with others. The rest of this book is aimed at helping you increase the likelihood that you will be perceived as competent. In the pages that follow, you will learn about theories of interpersonal, group, and public speaking that can increase your knowledge and your motivation. You will also learn how to perform specific skills, and you will be provided with opportunities to practice them. Through this practice, you can increase the likelihood that you will be able to perform these skills when needed.

> **What is communication apprehension and what can you do to manage it effectively?**

credibility
a perception of a speaker's knowledge, trustworthiness, and warmth.

social ease
communicating without appearing to be anxious or nervous.

communication apprehension
fear or anxiety associated with real or anticipated communication with others.

Peanuts: © United Feature Syndicate, Inc.

Speech Assignment: Communicate on Your Feet

Introduce a Classmate

The Assignment

Following your instructor's directions, partner with someone in the class. Spend some time talking with this person, getting to know him or her, so that next class period you can give a short 2-minute speech introducing your partner to the rest of the class.

Questions to Ask

1. What is your background? (Where were you born and raised? What is the makeup of your family? What else do you want to share about your personal background?)
2. What are you majoring in and why?
3. What are some of your personal and professional goals after college?
4. What are two personal goals you have for this class and why?
5. What is something unique about you that most people probably don't know?

Speeches of Introduction

A speech of introduction is given to acquaint a group with someone they have not met. We make short "speeches" of introduction all the time. When a friend from high school comes to visit for a weekend, you introduce her to your friends. Not only will you tell them her name, but you will probably mention other things about her that will make it easy for your friends to talk with her. Likewise, a store manager may call the sales associates together in order to introduce a new hire. The manager might mention the new team member's previous experience, interests, and other items of information that will make it easy for the team to respect, help, and become acquainted with the new employee.

Speeches of introduction also often precede formal addresses. The goal of the introducer is to establish the credibility of the main speaker by letting the audience know the education, background, and expertise of the speaker related to the topic of the speech and to build audience interest. The introducer usually concludes by identifying the topic or title of the address.

Speech to Introduce a Classmate

Because your classmate will not be giving a formal address after you introduce him or her, we suggest you organize your speech as follows:

1. **The introduction:** Start with an attention catcher—a statement, story, or question tied to something about the speaker that will pique audience curiosity. Then offer a thesis and a preview of main points, which can be as simple as "I'm here today to introduce [name of person] to you by sharing something about his personal background, personal and professional goals, and something unique about him."

2. **The body:** Group the information you plan to share under two to four main points. For example, your first main point might be "personal background," your second main point "personal and professional goals," and your third main point "something unique." Then offer two or three examples or stories to illustrate what you learned regarding each main point. Create a transition statement to lead from the first main point to the second main point, as well as from the second main point to the third main point. These statements should remind listeners of the main point you are concluding and introduce the upcoming main point. For example, "Now that you know a little bit about [name of person]'s personal background, let's talk about his personal and professional goals."

3. **The conclusion:** Ideally, in your conclusion, you'll remind listeners of the name of the classmate you introduced and the two to four main points you discussed about him or her. Then, end with a clincher—a short sentence that wraps the speech up by referring to something you said in the speech (usually in the introduction) that will encourage listeners to want to know him or her better.

Develop Communication Skills Improvement Goals

To get the most from this course, we suggest that you write personal goals to improve specific skills in your own interpersonal, group, and public communication repertoire.

Before you can write a goal statement, you must first analyze your current communication skills repertoire. After you read each chapter and practice the skills described, select one or two skills to work on. Then write down your goal statement in four parts.

1. State the problem. Start by stating a communication problem that you have. For example: "*Problem*: Even though some of my group members in a team-based class project have not produced the work they promised, I haven't spoken up because I'm not very good at describing my feelings."

2. State the specific goal. A goal is specific if it is measurable and you know when you have achieved it. For example, to deal with the problem stated above, you might write: "*Goal*: To describe my disappointment to other group members about their failure to meet deadlines."

3. Outline a specific procedure for reaching the goal. To develop a plan for reaching your goal, first consult the chapter that covers the skill you wish to hone. Then translate the general steps recommended in the chapter to your specific situation. For example: "*Procedure*: I will practice the steps of describing feelings. (1) I will identify the specific feeling I am experiencing. (2) I will encode the emotion I am feeling accurately. (3) I will include what has triggered the feeling. (4) I will own the feeling as mine. (5) I will then put that procedure into operation when I am talking with my group members."

4. Devise a method of determining when the goal has been reached. A good goal is measurable, and the fourth part of your goal-setting effort is to determine your minimum requirements for knowing when you have achieved a given goal. For example: "*Test for Achieving Goal*: I will have achieved this goal when I have described my disappointment to my group members about missed deadlines."

At the end of each section, you will be challenged to develop a goal statement related to the material presented. Figure 1.2 provides another example of a communication improvement plan, this one relating to a public speaking problem.

Problem: When I speak in class or in the student senate, I often find myself burying my head in my notes or looking at the ceiling or walls.

Goal: To look at people more directly when I'm giving a speech.

Procedure: I will take the time to practice oral presentations aloud in my room. (1) I will stand up just as I do in class. (2) I will pretend various objects in the room are people, and I will consciously attempt to look at those objects as I am talking. (3) When giving a speech, I will try to be aware of when I am looking at my audience and when I am not.

Test for Achieving Goal: I will have achieved this goal when I am maintaining eye contact with my audience most of the time.

Figure 1.2
Communication improvement plan

A Question of Ethics

Molly has just been accepted at Stanford University and calls her friend Terri to tell her the good news.

MOLLY: Hi Terri! Guess what? I just got accepted to Stanford Law School!

TERRI [*Surprised and disappointed*]: Oh, cool.

MOLLY: Thanks—you sound so enthusiastic!

TERRI: Oh, I am. Listen, I have to go—I'm late for class.

MOLLY: Oh, OK. See you.

The women hang up, and Terri immediately calls her friend Monica.

TERRI: Monica, it's Terri.

MONICA: Hey, Terri. What's up?

TERRI: I just got some terrible news—Molly got into Stanford!

MONICA: So, what's wrong with that? I think it's great. Aren't you happy for her?

TERRI: No, not at all. I didn't get in, and I have better grades and a higher LSAT score.

MONICA: Maybe Molly had a better application.

TERRI: Or maybe it was what was on her application.

MONICA: What do you mean?

TERRI: You know what I mean. Molly's black.

MONICA: Yes, and . . . ?

What Would You Do?

TERRI: Don't you see? It's called affirmative action.

MONICA: Terri, give it a rest!

TERRI: Oh, please. You know it, and I know it. She only got in because of her race and because she's poor. Her GPA is really low and so is her LSAT.

MONICA: Did you ever stop to think that maybe she wrote an outstanding essay? Or that they thought the time she spent volunteering in that free legal clinic in her neighborhood was good background?

TERRI: Yes, but we've both read some of her papers, and we know she can't write. Listen, Monica, if you're black, Asian, American Indian, Latino, or any other minority and poor, you've got it made. You can be as stupid as Forrest Gump and get into any law school you want. It's just not fair at all.

MONICA [*Angrily*]: No, you know what isn't fair? I'm sitting here listening to my so-called friend insult my intelligence and my ethnic background. How dare you tell me that the only reason I'll ever get into a good medical school is because I'm Latino. Listen, honey, I'll get into medical school just the same way that Molly got into law school—because of my brains, my accomplishments, and my ethical standards. And based on this conversation, it's clear that Molly and I are way ahead of you.

Describe how well each of these women followed the ethical standards for communication discussed in this chapter.

Adapted from "Racism," a case study posted on the Web site of the Ethics Connection, Markkula Center for Applied Ethics, Santa Clara University. Retrieved from http://www.scu.edu/ethics/practicing/focusareas/education/racism.html. Used with permission.

Summary

We have defined communication as the process of creating or sharing meaning, whether the setting is informal conversation, group interaction, or public speaking. The elements of the communication process are participants, messages, context, channels, interference (noise), and feedback.

Our communication is guided by at least seven principles. First, communication is purposeful. Second, communication is continuous. Third, communication messages vary in degree of conscious encoding. Messages may be spontaneous, scripted, or constructed. Fourth, communication is relational, defining the power and affection between people. Fifth, communication is guided by culture. Sixth, communication has ethical implications. Ethical standards that influence our communication include truthfulness, integrity, fairness, respect, and responsibility. And seventh, interpersonal communication is learned.

A primary issue in this course is competence—we all strive to become better communicators. Competence is the perception by others that our communication behavior is appropriate and effective. It involves a desire to improve our communication, increasing our knowledge of communication, identifying and attaining goals, being able to use various skills, and presenting ourselves as credible and confident communicators. Skills can be learned, developed, and improved, and you can enhance your learning this term by writing goal statements to systematically improve your own skill repertoire.

Communicate! Active Online Learning

Now that you have read Chapter 1, use your Premium Web site for *Communicate!* for quick access to the electronic resources that accompany this text. These resources include

- **Study tools** that will help you assess your learning and prepare for exams (*digital glossary, key term flash cards, review quizzes*).
- **Activities and assignments** that will help you hone your knowledge, analyze communication

situations (*Skill Learning Activities*), and build your public speaking skills throughout the course (*Communication on Your Feet speech assignments, Action Step activities*). Many of these activities allow you to compare your answers to those provided by the authors, and, if requested, submit your answers to your instructor.

- **Media resources** that will help you explore communication concepts online (*Web Resources*), develop your speech outlines (*Speech Builder Express 3.0*), watch and critique videos of communication situations and sample speeches (*Interactive Video Activities*), upload your speech videos for peer reviewing and critique other students' speeches (*Speech Studio online speech review tool*), and download chapter review so you can study when and where you'd like (*Audio Study Tools*).

This chapter's Key Terms, Skill Learning Activities, and Web Resources are also featured on the following pages, and you can find this chapter's *Communicate on Your Feet* assignment in the body of the chapter.

Key Terms

channel (5)
communication (3)
communication apprehension (16)
communication competence (15)
communication setting (8)
constructed messages (11)
context (4)
control (11)
credibility (16)
cultural context (5)
culture (12)
decoding (3)

encoding (3)
ethical dilemma (14)
ethics (14)
feedback (7)
historical context (4)
immediacy (11)
interference (noise) (5)
internal noise (6)
interpersonal communication (9)
intrapersonal communication (8)
meanings (3)
messages (3)
participants (3)

physical context (4)
physical interference (5)
psychological context (5)
psychological interference (6)
public communication (9)
scripted messages (11)
semantic noise (7)
social context (4)
social ease (16)
small group communication (9)
spontaneous expressions (11)
symbols (3)

Skill Learning Activities

1.1: Identifying Elements of the Communication Process (8)

For the following interaction, identify the contexts, participants, channels, message, interference (noise), and feedback:

Maria and Damien are meandering through the park, talking and drinking bottled water. Damien finishes his bottle, replaces the lid, and tosses the bottle into the bushes at the side of the path. Maria, who has been listening to Damien talk, comes to a stop, puts her hands on her hips, stares at Damien, and says angrily, "I can't believe what you just did!" Damien blushes, averts his gaze, and mumbles, "Sorry, I'll get it—I just wasn't thinking." As the tension drains from Maria's face, she gives her head a playful toss, smiles, and says, "Well, just see that it doesn't happen again."

1. Contexts
   a. Physical_____
   b. Social_____
   c. Historical_____
   d. Psychological_____

2. Participants_____
3. Channels_____
4. Message_____
5. Interference (Noise)_____
6. Feedback_____

When you're done with this activity, compare your answers to the authors' at the Premium Web site for *Communicate!* Look for them in the Skill Learning activities for Chapter 1.

1.2: Communication over the Internet (10)

The Internet has thoroughly revolutionized communication over the last 20 years. Consider the advantages and disadvantages of communicating via the following Internet-based mediums: e-mail, newsgroups, Internet chat, social networking sites, social messaging services (e.g., Twitter), and blogs. Spend some time evaluating these mediums if you are not already familiar with them. Enter your thoughts into a two-column table, with advantages in the first column and disadvantages in the second. Did your analysis produce any discoveries that surprised you?

To help you complete this activity, you can use the table provided in your Premium Web site for *Communicate!* Look for it in the Skill Learning activities for Chapter 1.

1.3: Communication Functions (10)

Keep a log of the various communications you have today. Tonight, categorize each episode by one of the five functions it served. Each episode may serve more than one function. Were you surprised by the variety of your communication in such a relatively short period?

To help you complete this activity, you can use the log sheet provided in your Premium Web site for *Communicate!* Look for it in the Skill Learning activities for Chapter 1.

Web Resources

1.1: Profile of Foreign-Born Population (12)

Read more about the U.S. foreign-born population at the U.S. Census Bureau Web site. This site provides reports, data tables, and other information about people living in the United States who were not U.S. citizens at birth.

1.2: Ethics Connection (15)

Learn more about ethics at the Markkula Center for Applied Ethics at Santa Clara University, a forum for research and discussion on ethical issues in American life. The Center's site features information about ethics in business, health care and biotechnology, education, government and public policy, and technology.

Hristo Shindov(RM)/Jupiter Images

Perception of Self and Others

Questions you'll be able to answer after reading this chapter:

- How does the perception process work?
- What is a self-concept, and how is it formed and maintained?
- What is self-esteem, and how is it developed and maintained?
- How might culture or gender influence our perceptions of self?
- How can our perceptions of self change?
- How can our perceptions of self become distorted?
- How do perceptions of self affect our communication with others?
- What influences our perceptions of others?
- What can we do to improve the accuracy of our perceptions of others?

As Dwayne and Miguel leave their Spanish literature class on the first day of the semester, Dwayne comments: "I give up! This course is going to be impossible—I don't want to take it."

"Really?" replies Miguel. "I thought the course sounded interesting. The professor was funny, and I really liked how we could choose our own paper topic."

"But did you see what we're reading?" asks Dwayne. "We've got four books to read—with a test over each book, and then we're supposed to write a paper!"

"But the books look pretty interesting," replies Miguel. "They're novels and some even have movies based on them. And because the professor seems to know what he's talking about—I mean he was born and educated in Spain—he'll probably be able to tell us a lot about Spain."

"Right," says Dwayne, "but I'm taking four other courses that look pretty tough. I like Spanish, but four books and a paper!"

Have you had this kind of disagreement with a friend after a first day of class? How do we come to have different takes on the same event? As we analyze this conversation, we can see that Dwayne focuses on the time requirements and workload in the class whereas Miguel focuses on what he can learn. They attended the same class but carried away different perceptions. Because much of the meaning we share with others is based on our perceptions, this chapter begins with a discussion of the perception process before moving into perceptions of self, perceptions of others, and how these perceptions influence and are influenced by our communication with others. We end by offering suggestions for improving the accuracy of your perceptions.

The Perception Process

Perception is the process of selectively attending to information and assigning meaning to it (Gibson, 1966). At times, our perceptions of the world, other people, and ourselves agree with the perceptions of others. At other times, our perceptions are significantly different from the perceptions of other people. For each person, perception becomes reality. What one person sees, hears, and interprets is real and considered true to that person. Another person who may see, hear, and interpret something entirely different from the same situation will regard that different perception as real and true. When your perceptions are different from those with whom you interact, sharing meaning becomes more challenging. So how does perception work? Essentially, your brain selects some of the information it receives from your senses (sensory stimuli), organizes the information, and then interprets it.

> How does the perception process work?

Attention and Selection

Although we are subject to a constant barrage of sensory stimuli, we focus attention on relatively little of it. To help clarify, consider how many television channels you watch regularly compared to the number of channels offered. Why? Your choices of sensory stimuli depend in part on your needs, interests, and expectations.

Needs

We are likely to pay attention to information that meets our biological and psychological needs. When you go to class, how well you focus on what is being discussed is likely to depend on whether you believe the information is relevant to you. Your brain communicates intrapersonally by asking such questions as, "Will what I learn here help me in school, in the work world, in my personal life?"

Interests

We are likely to pay attention to information that pertains to our interests. For instance, you may not even recognize that music is playing in the background until you suddenly find yourself listening to some old favorite. Similarly, when you are

perception
the process of selectively attending to information and assigning meaning to it.

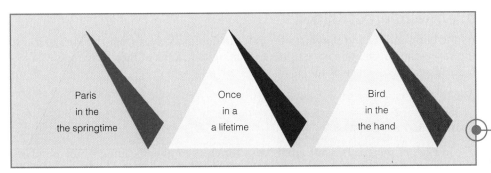

Figure 2.1
A sensory test of expectation

really attracted to a person, you are more likely to pay attention to what that person is saying. Likewise, when you get an e-mail from someone you don't like, don't recognize, or that appears to be spam, you might simply delete it.

Expectations

Finally, we are likely to see what we expect to see and to miss information that violates our expectations. Take a quick look at the phrases in the triangles in Figure 2.1. If you have never seen these triangles, you probably read "Paris in the springtime," "Once in a lifetime," and "Bird in the hand." But if you re-examine the words, you will see that what you perceived was not exactly what is written. Do you now see the repeated words? It is easy to miss the repeated word because we don't *expect* to see the word repeated.

Organization of Stimuli

Even though our attention and selection process does reduce the number of stimuli our brain must process, the number of stimuli we attend to at any one moment is still substantial. Our brains arrange these stimuli so that they make sense according to organizing principles such as simplicity and pattern.

Simplicity

If the stimuli we attend to are very complex, the brain simplifies the stimuli into some commonly recognized form. Based on a quick look at what someone is wearing, how she is standing, and the expression on her face, we may perceive her as a business executive, a doctor, or a soccer mom. Similarly, we simplify the verbal messages we receive. For example, after an hour-long performance review in which his boss described four of Tony's strengths and two areas for improvement, Tony might say to Jerry, his coworker, "Well, I'd better shape up or I'm going to get fired!"

Pattern

A **pattern** is a set of characteristics used to differentiate some things from others. For example, when you see a crowd of people, instead of perceiving each individual, you may focus on a characteristic of sex and "see" men and women, or you may focus on age and "see" children, teens, adults, and seniors. In our interactions with others, we try to find patterns that help us organize and respond to their behavior. For example, each time Jason and Bill encounter Sara, she hurries over to them and begins an animated conversation. Yet when Jason is alone and runs into Sara, she barely says "Hi." After a while, Jason may detect a pattern to Sara's behavior. She is warm and friendly when Bill is around and not so friendly when Bill is absent. Based on this pattern, Jason may construe Sara's friendly behavior as flirting with Bill.

pattern
a set of characteristics used to differentiate some things from others.

Interpretation of Stimuli

As the brain selects and organizes the information it receives from the senses, it also **interprets** the information by assigning meaning to it. Look at these three sets of numbers. What do you make of them?

A. 631 7348
B. 285 37 5632
C. 4632 7364 2596 2174

In each of these sets, your mind looks for clues to give meaning to the numbers. Because you use similar patterns of numbers every day, you probably interpret A as a telephone number. How about B? A likely interpretation is a Social Security number. And C? People who use credit cards may interpret this set as a credit card number.

Our interpretation of others' behavior in conversation affects how we interact with them. If Jason believes that Sara is only interested in Bill, he may not participate in conversations that she initiates.

In the remainder of this chapter, we apply this basic information about perception to the study of perceptions of self and others as they influence and are influenced by communication.

Perceptions of Self: Self-Concept and Self-Esteem

Self-concept and self-esteem are the two perceptions of self that have the greatest impact on how we communicate. **Self-concept** is your self-identity (Baron, Byrne, & Brascombe, 2006). It is the mental image that you have about your skills, your abilities, your knowledge, your competencies, and your personality. **Self-esteem** is your overall evaluation of your competence and personal worthiness (based on Mruk, 1999, p. 26). In this section, we describe how you come to understand who you are (self-concept) and how you evaluate yourself (self-esteem). Then we examine what determines how well these self-perceptions match others' perceptions of you. Finally, we discuss the role self-perceptions play when you communicate with others.

Forming and Maintaining a Self-Concept

> What is a self-concept and how is it formed and maintained?

Our self-concept is essentially our identity, that is, who we think we really are. We develop our self-concept based on our experiences and others' reactions and responses to us.

Personal experiences

One way we form our self-concept is through our interpretation of our personal experiences regarding our skills, abilities, knowledge, competencies, and personality. Positive experiences shape our self-concept in positive ways. For example, if you perceive that it is easy for you to talk in front of a group of people because you don't feel anxious when doing so, you may conclude that you are a "natural" public speaker.

We place a great deal of emphasis on our first experience with a particular phenomenon, particularly if it is a negative one. For instance, if you get anxious and draw a blank while giving a speech for the first time, you may conclude you are a poor public speaker. If additional experiences produce similar results, this first perception will be strengthened. Even if the first experience is not immediately repeated, you will probably need more than one contradictory experience to change the original negative perception.

interpret
assigning meaning to information.

self-concept
your self-identity.

self-esteem
your overall evaluation of your competence and personal worthiness.

Reactions and responses of others

Our self-concept is also formed and maintained by how others react and respond to us (Rayner, 2001, p. 43). Other people's comments serve to validate, reinforce, or alter our perception of who and what we are. For example, if during a trip to Cancun, your best friend tells you, "You're really an excellent planner," you may decide this comment fits your image of who you are. Such comments are especially powerful in affecting our self-concept if we respect the person making the comment. And the power of such comments is increased when the praise is immediate rather than delayed (Hattie, 1992, p. 251).

Our self-concept begins to form early in life, and information we receive from our families shapes our self-concept (Demo, 1987). One of the major responsibilities that family members have is to talk and act in ways that will help develop accurate and positive self-concepts in other family members. For example, the mom who says, "Roberto, your room looks very neat. You are very organized," or the brother who comments, "Kisha, the $20 you lent to Tomika really helped her out. You are very generous," is helping Roberto or Kisha to recognize important parts of their personalities.

Unfortunately, in some families, members do not fulfill these responsibilities. Sometimes family members do real damage to each other's self-concepts. Communicating blame, name-calling, and repeatedly pointing out another's shortcomings are particularly damaging. What are some characteristics of your self-concept and in what specific ways did your family members help shape it?

As we interact with others and with the media, we not only develop an understanding of who we are, but we also form an **ideal self-concept,** which is what we would like to be. For example, although Jim may know that he is really not naturally athletic, in his ideal self-concept he is a jock. So he plays intramural basketball on his dorm team, hangs out at the gym, and tries to befriend the university scholarship athletes. The Pop Comm! article in this chapter describes how products are marketed in order to appeal to our ideal self-concepts.

Skill Learning Activity 2.1

ideal self-concept
what you would like to be

David Young-Wolff/PhotoEdit

Our family members shape our self-concept. Can you recall a time when someone in your family praised you for something you had done? Is that something you still consider yourself to be good at?

Marketing Self-Concept Individuality

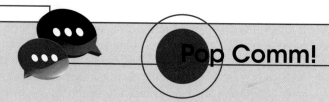

In 2005 it was "I am what I am." In 2007 it was "There are two people in everyone." And in 2008 it was "Your move." Recognize the campaigns? Each was part of Reebok's global effort to position itself as the brand that "celebrates individuality, and supports those who choose to do things their way"[1] All three campaigns used celebrity endorsers—from sports figures to hip hop artists—to convince young consumers that the number two sneaker maker should be their brand.

Using celebrities to endorse a product is nothing new. For years advertisers have used celebrities because they know that doing so is effective at persuading us to buy a product. Research has found that when we see the celebrity as being "like us" or like how we would like to believe we are, we listen and are persuaded. In other words, when the celebrity's image fits our self-concept or our ideal self-concept, then we will choose the same product that the celebrity is using.[2] So world-class sports figures, musicians, and other pop culture icons appear in commercials in order to sell the product to those of us who identify with the celebrity.

Recently, marketers have expanded this approach by paying celebrities to be seen in public wearing or using their products. If we think we are savvy and not susceptible to overt advertisements, we may be persuaded by seeing a celebrity with whom we identify using particular product

in a situation that appears more real. Tiger Woods usually wears clothes with Nike's logo. But he doesn't buy those clothes; they are given to him and he has to wear them as part of his multi-million-dollar endorsement contract with Nike. Nevertheless, today countless young men and women sport attire adorned with the distinctive "swoosh" label of Nike.

What makes the Reebok campaigns different, however, is that the ads suggest that people wear a Reebok product not because they identify with the celebrity but because they are asserting their individuality. In a telephone interview with *USA Today*, tennis star Andy Roddick, who appeared in Reebok's 2005 "I am what I am" commercials, explained, "Every other sporting goods commercial is about buying the shoe to become something you're not. This is about being yourself."[3] In the same article, rap artist 50 Cent, another celebrity featured in this campaign, said, "The experiences I have been through in my life have shaped my character. The Reebok ads are just another opportunity for me to express myself. Love it or hate it, I am what I am."[4]

The "I am what I am" campaign depicted celebrities' comfort with their self-images and called on consumers to be comfortable with who they are. In contrast, the "There are two people in everyone" campaign was designed to convince people to embrace their individuality in all of its diversity.

Developing and Maintaining Self-Esteem

You'll recall that our self-esteem is our positive or negative evaluation of our self-concept. Our self-esteem is rooted in our values and develops over time as a result of our experiences. Self-esteem is not just how well or poorly we do things (self-concept) but also the importance or value we place on what we do well or poorly (Mruk, 1999, p. 27). For instance, Chad believes he is good with kids (self-concept). But if he doesn't believe that nurturing children is a valuable attribute for a man to have, then this characteristic is unlikely to help him have positive self-esteem and may even hurt his

Print, video, and Web-based ads showcased two distinctively different sides of the celebrity endorser's personality. Basketball superstar Yao Ming is also an avid conservationist, and NBA star Allen Iverson is a working dad. Not only did the campaign use the typical advertising media, but it also included a Web site (www.2ineveryone.com) where visitors could view the videos of the celebrities and interact by identifying the two people inside of them: "Each one of us is made up of different ideas, passions, and interests. We believe it's time to stop glorifying extremes. We don't need to be defined by one thing. We're free to embrace the 2 people inside of us. So tell us, what 2 are you?" This campaign's message is "Wear Reebok products and embrace your duality."

Reebok's 2008 campaign, "Your move," shows celebrities doing what they do best and challenges people to live in ways that are true to themselves. In the words of one ad:

So what will it be? All play or have to work for it? Fame? Fortune? The love of the game or maybe a little slice of both? It's time to exercise your free will. Do you break records or make them? Play to win or for the hell of it? Whisper? Scream your face off? Or let actions speak louder than words?...The only thing you need to fit into is your own skin....The ball, as they say, is in your court.... So what will it be? "Just doing it" because someone else said so or living life according to your own rulebook? Your move.[5]

Again, the ads used celebrities showing what they do best and then inviting consumers to make "Your move."

Although the success of most celebrity endorsements depends on consumers identifying with some aspect of the celebrity's image,

Reebok is positioning its celebrity marketing on "celebrating the distinct qualities that make people who they are—their unique points of view, their individual style, and their remarkable talents and accomplishments."[6] So when you wear Reebok products, you're not saying that you think you're like Allen Iverson or Yao Ming. Instead, you're saying that, like Allen or Yao, "I am what I am." An interesting way to sell shoes, don't you think?

[1]*Reebok (n.d.). Reebok Marketing. Retrieved from http:// corporate.reebok.com/en/about_reebok/faq_section /marketing/default.asp*

[2]*See, for example, Onkvisit, S., & Shaw, J. (1987). Self-concept and image congruence: Some research and managerial implications. Journal of Consumer Marketing, 4(1), 13–23; Solomon, M., Bamossy, G., & Askegaard, S. (2002). Consumer Behaviour: A European Perspective (2nd ed.). Upper Saddle River, NJ: Prentice Hall Financial Times.*

[3]*McCarthy. M. (2005) New theme for Reebok. USATODAY.com. Retrieved from http://usatoday.com /money/advertising/2005-02-09-reebok-usat_x.htm*

[4]*Ibid.*

[5]*Reebok (n.d.). Reebok Your Move campaign. YouTube. Retrieved from http://www.youtube.com /watch?v=IK_5TwmvuWo*

[6]*Reebok. (n.d.). Reebok's positioning. About Reebok. Retrieved from http://corporate.reebok.com/en/about _reebok/default.asp*

self-esteem. High self-esteem requires both the perception of having a characteristic and a belief that the characteristic is valuable. Our self-esteem can affect the types of relationships that we form and who we form them with. For example, research has shown that a person who has high self-esteem is more likely to be committed to a partner who perceives him or her very favorably, whereas a person with low self-esteem is more likely to be committed to a partner who perceives him or her less favorably (Leary, 2002, p. 130). In both cases, the individual finds a partner who reinforces their own self-perceptions, but the low self-esteem person ends up reinforcing a negative self-image.

Why is self-esteem important to communication?

The Influence of Gender and Culture on Self-Perceptions

A person's culture has a strong influence on the self-perception process (Samovar, Porter, & McDaniel, 2009). In individualistic cultures, such as the United States, people stress the self and personal achievement. In individualistic cultures, people care about self-concept, self-esteem, and self-image. In fact, all the information thus far in this chapter reflects an individualistic perspective of perception, self-concept, and self-esteem. In an individualistic culture, you tend to think first of what is best for yourself when making a decision, such as taking a new job. You might move far away from family for the job. At work, we want to be paid, judged, and promoted based on our own work rather than how the group is performing. In collectivist cultures, such as China, groups and social norms tend to be more important than individuals. People are expected to be interdependent and to see themselves in terms of the group. Notions of self-concept and self-esteem have little meaning in collectivist cultures. In a collectivist culture, your decision about taking a new job would likely be made collectively by your family. Your salary, performance evaluations, and promotions would naturally be based on how well the entire group, team, or department was functioning. We should note, however, that these generalizations are not absolutes. As more people raised in individualistic cultures and in collectivist cultures live and work together, a blending of values is beginning to emerge.

> How might culture or gender influence our perception of self?

Web Resource 2.1

Similarly, generally speaking, men and women may be socialized to view themselves differently and to value who they are based on whether their characteristics or behaviors correspond to or challenge the characteristics or behaviors expected of their sex in their culture. There are norms of what it means to be "feminine" and what it means to be "masculine" in any culture. The cultural expectations for your gender inevitably influence your self-perceptions. In the past, boys in the United States were taught to base their self-esteem on their achievements, status, and income, and girls learned that their culture valued their appearance and their relationship skills, so boys and girls formed their self-perceptions based on how well they met these criteria (Wood, 2007).

Today in the United States these definitions of "appropriate" characteristics and behaviors for males and females are becoming less rigid, but they do still exist and are promoted incessantly in popular culture. Consider television sitcoms like *Two and a Half Men*, *Everybody Loves Raymond*, and *According to Jim*, for example. Such programs continue to portray women as the "natural" caregivers for the family, and when men attempt a caregiver behavior, they make a mess of the situation. Think about your family experiences growing up. How do they compare? Similarly, in terms of appearance, you only need to flip through the pages of any fashion magazine to see the narrowly defined perception of "beauty" for women. If you read Christy Haubegger's story, "I'm

CBS /Landov

Can you think of a television program that depicts men rather than women as the caregivers?

Not Fat, I'm Latina," in the Diverse Voices feature, you'll learn about her reaction to cultural perceptions about appearance.

Changing Self-Perceptions

Self-concept and self-esteem are enduring characteristics, but they can be changed. At times, comments that contradict your current self-perception lead you to slowly change it. Certain situations seem to expedite this process, for example, when you experience a profound change in your social environment. When children begin school or go to sleep-away camp; when teens start part-time jobs; when young adults go to college; or when people begin or end jobs or relationships, become parents, or grieve the loss of someone they love, they are more likely to absorb messages that are at odds with their current self-perceptions.

> How can our perceptions of self change?

Therapy and self-help techniques can assist us when we want to alter our self-concept and improve our self-esteem. In his analysis of numerous research studies, Christopher Mruk (1999) found that self-esteem is increased through "hard work and practice, practice, practice—there is simply no escaping this basic existential fact" (p. 112).

So why is this important to communication? Because our self-esteem affects with whom we choose to form relationships, how we interact with them, how we participate when we are in small groups, and how comfortable we feel when we are called on to present a speech. Essentially, improving your perception of self will improve how you interact with others and improving how you interact with others will improve your self-perception.

Web Resource 2.2

Accuracy and Distortion of Self-Perceptions

The accuracy of our self-concept and self-esteem depends on the accuracy of our own perceptions and how we process others' perceptions of us. All of us experience success and failure, and all of us hear praise and criticism. If we are overly attentive to successful experiences and positive responses, our self-concept and self-esteem may become inflated. If you've seen the Disney classic *Beauty and the Beast*, Gaston is a prime example of one with an inflated perception of self. We tend to describe such individuals as "arrogant," "pompous," "haughty," or "snobbish." Who have you known that you might describe in this way? Do you enjoy interacting with them? Conversely, if we perceive and dwell on failures and give little value to our successes, or if we only remember the criticism we receive, our self-concept and our self-esteem may be deflated. Winnie the Pooh's friend Eeyore, the donkey, who is always "having a bad day," is an example of one with a deflated sense of self. We tend to describe such individuals as "depressed," "despondent," "sullen," or "gloomy." Who have you known that you might describe in this way? Do you enjoy interacting with them? In neither case does their self-concept or self-esteem accurately reflect who they are.

> How can our perceptions of self become distorted?

Incongruence, the gap between our inaccurate self-perceptions and reality, is a problem because our perceptions of self are more likely than our true abilities to affect our behavior (Weiten, 1998, p. 491). For example, Raul may actually possess all the skills, abilities, knowledge, competencies, and personality characteristics for effective leadership, but if he doesn't perceive that he has these characteristics, he won't step forward when leadership is needed. Unfortunately, individuals tend to reinforce their self-perceptions by behaving in ways that conform to their perceived self-perceptions. The inaccuracy of a distorted picture of oneself is magnified through self-fulfilling prophecies, filtering messages, and reliance on media images.

incongruence
the gap between our inaccurate self-perceptions and reality.

Self-fulfilling prophecies

self-fulfilling prophecy
a false perception of a situation or characteristic or skill that leads to behaviors that perpetuate that false perception as true.

A **self-fulfilling** prophecy is a *false* perception of a situation or characteristic or skill that leads to behaviors that perpetuate that false perception as *true* (Merton, 1968). Self-fulfilling prophesies may be self-created or other-imposed.

Self-created prophecies are predictions you make about yourself. We often talk ourselves into success or failure. For example, researchers have found that when people expect rejection, they are more likely to behave in ways that lead others to reject them (Downey, Freitas, Michaelis, & Khouri, 2004, p. 437). So Aaron, who sees himself as unskilled in establishing new relationships, says to himself, "I doubt I'll know anyone at the party—I'm going to have a miserable time." Because he fears encountering strangers, he feels awkward about introducing himself and, just as he predicted, spends much of his time standing around alone thinking about when he can leave. In contrast, Stefan sees himself as quite social and able to get to know people easily. As a result, he looks forward to the party and, just as he predicted, makes several new acquaintances and enjoys himself.

I'm Not Fat, I'm Latina

by Christy Haubegger

Diverse Voices

"Beauty is in the eye of the beholder." But when you are a "large" person, whether your size enhances or detracts from your own or others' perceptions of your beauty may depend on your cultural group.

I recently read a newspaper article that reported that nearly 40 percent of Hispanic and African American women are overweight. At least I'm in good company. Because according to even the most generous height and weight charts at the doctor's office, I'm a good 25 pounds overweight. And I'm still looking for the panty-hose chart that has me on it (according to Hanes, I don't exist). But I'm happy to report that in the Latino community, my community, I fit right in.

Latinas in this country live in two worlds. People who don't know us may think we're fat. At home, we're called *bien cuidadas* (well cared for). I love to go dancing at Cesar's Latin Palace here in the Mission District of San Francisco. At this hot all-night salsa club, it's the curvier bodies like mine that turn heads. I'm the one on the dance floor all night while some of my thinner friends spend more time waiting along the walls.

Come to think of it, I wouldn't trade my body for any of theirs.

But I didn't always feel this way. I remember being in high school and noticing that none of the magazines showed models in bathing suits with bodies like mine. Handsome movie heroes were never hoping to find a chubby damsel in distress. The fact that I had plenty of attention from Latino boys wasn't enough. Real self-esteem cannot come from male attention alone.

My turning point came a few years later. When I was in college, I made a trip to Mexico, and I brought back much more than sterling-silver bargains and colorful blankets.

I remember hiking through the awesome ruins of the Mayan and Aztec civilizations, which created pyramids as large as the ones in Egypt. I loved walking through the temple doorways, whose clearance was only 2 inches above my head, and I realized that I must be a direct descendant of those ancient priestesses for whom those doorways had originally been built.

For the first time in my life, I was in a place where people like me were the beautiful ones.

Self-esteem has an important effect on our self-perception and, thus, on the prophecies we make. For instance, people with low self-esteem attribute their successes to luck, and so they prophesy that they will not repeat them whereas people with positive self-esteem see their successes as self-created, so they prophesy that they will repeat them (Hattie, 1992, p. 253).

The prophecies others make about us also affect our perception of self and behavior. For example, when teachers act as if their students are bright, students buy into this expectation and learn more as a result. Likewise, when teachers act as if students are not bright, students may "live down" to these imposed prophecies and fail to achieve. A good example takes place in the popular book *Harry Potter and the Order of the Phoenix*. A prophesy was made that suggested Harry Potter would vanquish the Dark Lord (Voldemort). So the Dark Lord sets out to kill Harry Potter. Dumbledore explains to Harry that the prophecy is only true because the Dark Lord believes it. Still, because the Dark Lord will not rest until he kills Harry, it becomes inevitable that Harry will, in fact, have to kill Voldemort (or vice versa). Have you ever experienced a self-fulfilling prophecy based on what others have said? How did that influence your self-concept and self-esteem?

And I began to accept, and even like, the body that I have.

I know that medical experts say that Latinas are twice as likely as the rest of the population to be overweight. And yes, I know about the health problems that often accompany severe weight problems. But most of us are not in the danger zone; we're just *bien cuidadas*. Even the researchers who found that nearly 40 percent of us are overweight noted that there is a greater "cultural acceptance" of being overweight within Hispanic communities. But the article also commented on the cultural-acceptance factor as if it were something unfortunate, because it keeps Hispanic women from becoming healthier. I'm not so convinced that we're the ones with the problem.

If the medical experts were to try to get to the root of this so-called problem, they would probably find that it's part genetics, part enchiladas. Whether we're Cuban American, Mexican American, Puerto Rican, or Dominican, food is a central part of Hispanic culture. While our food varies from fried plantains to tamales, what doesn't change is its role in our lives.

You feed people you care for, and so if you're well cared for, *bien cuidada*, you have been fed well. I remember when I used to be envious of a Latina friend of mine who had always been on the skinny side. When I confided this to her a while ago, she laughed. It turns out that when she was growing up, she had always wanted to look more like me. She had trouble getting dates with Latinos in high school, the same boys I dated. When she was little, the other kids in the neighborhood had even given her a cruel nickname: *la seca*, "the dry one." I'm glad I never had any of those problems.

Our community has always been accepting of us well-cared-for women. So why don't we feel beautiful? You only have to flip through a magazine or watch a movie to realize that beautiful for most of this country still means tall, blond, and underfed. But now we know it's the magazines that are wrong. I, for one, am going to do what I can to make sure that *mis hijas*, my daughters, won't feel the way I did.

Reflective questions

1. To what degree do you think these perceptions of weight for women continue to exist in the dominant American culture?
2. What are some reasons it continues to be the norm?
3. What can we do to embrace a variety of body types as beautiful for women?

Reprinted from Christy Haubegger, "I'm Not Fat, I'm Latina," in Readings for Diversity and Social Justice: An Anthology on Racism, Anti-Semitism, Sexism, Heterosexism, Ableism, and Classism, *eds. M. Adams, W. J. Blumenfeld, R. Castañeda, H. W. Hackman, M. L. Peters, & X. Zúñiga (New York: Routledge, 2000), pp. 242–243.*

How do media portrayals of "ideal" male and female figures distort self-perception?

Filtering messages

A second way that our self-perceptions can become distorted is through the way we filter what others say to us. We are prone to pay attention to messages that reinforce our current self-image, whereas messages that contradict this image may not "register" or may be downplayed. For example, suppose you prepare an agenda for your study group. Someone comments that you're a good organizer. If you spent your childhood hearing how disorganized you were, you may not really hear this comment, or you may downplay it. If, however, you think you are good at organizing, you will pay attention to the compliment and may even reinforce it by responding, "Thanks, I'm a pretty organized person. I learned it from my mom."

Media images

A third way our perceptions of self can become distorted is through verbal and visual images we see in the media such as on television, in the movies, and in popular magazines. Social learning theory suggests that we strive to copy the characteristics and behaviors of the characters portrayed as perfect examples or "ideal types" (Bandura, 1977). Persistent media messages of violence, promiscuity, use of profanity, bulked-up males, and pencil-thin females have all been linked to distorted perceptions of self among viewers. One particularly disturbing study found that before TV was widely introduced on the Pacific Island of Fiji, only 3 percent of girls reported vomiting to lose weight or being unhappy with their body image. Three years after the introduction of TV, that percentage had risen to 15 percent, and an alarming 74 percent reported being too big or too fat (Becker, 2004). Unfortunately, distorted body image perceptions lead to low self-esteem and, sometimes, to self-destructive behaviors such as anorexia and bulimia.

The Effects of Self-Perceptions on Communication

How do perceptions of self affect our communication with others?

Just as our self-concept and self-esteem affect how accurately we perceive ourselves, so too do they influence our communication by moderating competing internal messages in our self-talk, influencing how we communicate about ourselves with others, and affecting communication apprehension.

Self-perceptions moderate how we talk to ourselves.

Self-talk (intrapersonal communication) is the internal conversations we have with ourselves. A lot of these conversations are also about ourselves. People who have high self-esteem are more likely to engage in positive self-talk, such as "I know I can do it" or "I did really well on that test." People with low self-esteem are more likely to overemphasize negative self-talk or, ironically, they may overinflate their sense of self-worth to compensate and tell themselves they are good at everything they do.

self-talk
the internal conversations we have with ourselves.

Self-perceptions influence how we talk about ourselves with others.
If we feel good about ourselves, we are likely to communicate positively. For instance, people with a strong self-concept and higher self-esteem usually take credit for their successes. Likewise, people with healthy self-perceptions are inclined to defend their views even in the face of opposing arguments. If we feel bad about ourselves, we are likely to communicate negatively by downplaying our accomplishments.

Why do some people put themselves down regardless of what they have done? People who have low self-esteem are likely to be unsure of the value of their contributions and expect others to view them negatively. As a result, people with a poor self-concept or low self-esteem may find it less painful to put themselves down than to hear the criticism of others. Thus, to preempt the likelihood that others will comment on their unworthiness, they do it first.

Self-perceptions affect communication apprehension.
Perhaps one the most unfortunate consequences of a poor self-concept and low self-esteem is a heightened level of communication apprehension. People who harbor fear about speaking with others (whether in one-on-one situations, with certain individuals or groups, or in public speaking situations) tend to engage in negative self-talk that leads to a self-fulfilling prophesy (Richmond & McCroskey, 1995). Even as a young child, Tina was told by friends, family members, and teachers that she was shy. By the time she reached adolescence, she feared going to social events because she "knew nobody would talk to her" and she feared giving speeches because she "would certainly fail." The negative self-talk that leads to communication apprehension can be reversed by replacing negative self-talk with positive self-talk.

For more detailed information about how to manage communication apprehension, go to your Premium Web site for Communicate!, click on "Chapter Learn Lists" in the left-hand menu, select the Chapter 2 resources, and click on "Managing Communication Apprehension."

Speech Assignment: Communicate on Your Feet

Presenting Your Self-Concept

The Assignment

On a piece of paper, write down ten terms that describe your self-concept. Then create a short poem, rap, cheer, or song using those terms to present *who you see yourself as.* Perform it for the class. The presentation should take less than 2 minutes to perform.

Presenting Self to Others

Your self-concept and self-esteem are the "true" perceptions of what you think of yourself. But when we interact with others, most of us mask some of who we really think we are so that we can meet or violate others expectations. As a result we create different "selves" to present in different situations and with different people. How differently you present yourself across different social situations and relationships depends on how actively you self-monitor.

Self-Monitoring

When people are in social situations or relationships, they can feel vulnerable. So they analyze and make predications about the situation or relationship and decide how to behave. **Self-monitoring** is an internal process of being aware of yourself and how you are coming across to others. It involves being sensitive to other people's expressions and reactions (feedback) and using this information in deciding how to act and what roles to play. In other words, it is a process of observing, analyzing, and regulating your own behavior in relation to the response of others (Gangestad & Snyder, 2000). Self-monitoring is an internal thought process, so others probably don't know that you are monitoring and making choices about how to act. Think of the times when you consciously monitored how you were coming across in a situation. If you have ever been in an unfamiliar situation and made a flip remark that was met with stares or glares, you may have said to yourself, "Wow, that was a stupid thing to say! Let, me see if I can fix it." Then, based on this self-monitoring, you are able to make a repair.

People differ in when and how carefully they self-monitor. Some people are very cautious and are always vigilant in monitoring situations and relationships. Other people are careful to self-monitor when they perceive themselves to be in a risky or new situation, but are less attentive in situations or relationships that they perceive as safer. A few people seem unable to self-monitor. As a result, they tend to say and do the wrong things because they are not paying attention to how they are coming across. You may know someone who seems to always say the wrong thing or act inappropriately. The saying "Think before you speak" is really a call to self-monitor.

We are most likely to self-monitor when we are in a new relationship or an unfamiliar situation. Because we are not sure of how to act in an unfamiliar situation, there is more uncertainty and more analysis about how to present ourselves. When we are communicating in an unfamiliar situation, we may be saying to ourselves things like "Why did I make that silly remark? It sounded lame" or "Well, that seemed to go over well." Even in familiar and comfortable situations, skilled communicators do some self-monitoring by remaining attentive to the feedback they are receiving from others.

Skill Learning Activity 2.2

self-monitoring
the internal process of observing, analyzing, and regulating your own behavior based on your analysis of the situation and others' responses to you.

role
a pattern of learned behaviors that people use to meet the perceived demands of a particular context.

Skill Learning Activity 2.3
Web Resource 2.3

Social Construction of Self

While our self-concept and self-esteem are "true" perceptions that we have of ourselves, our self-monitoring enables us to decide what role we want to play and what persona we want to assume in a certain situation or relationship. As a result, we present different personas in response to different situations and relationships, and we change ourselves in the process. We socially construct ourselves through the roles we enact. A **role** is a pattern of learned behaviors that we use to meet the perceived demands of a particular context. For instance, think of your behavior when enacting the role of "sibling" while talking with your sister or brother or the role of "employee" at your job. How is what you say and do different in these contexts than when you are interacting with your classmates or your professor?

Do you have a MySpace or Facebook page? Think of the time and effort you spent creating that "self." Does it accurately reflect all of who you are? Or did you pick and choose what you would present to those who would view your page? The Internet allows you to experiment with a wide variety of roles. Some users experiment with gender and age switching or pretend to have a different job. The ethics of intentionally misrepresenting oneself in cyberspace is problematic because the people with whom you interact have no way to verify the accuracy of your persona. Nonetheless, many people engage in intentional deception, and child predators are a particular problem. In real life, as in cyberspace, we choose what parts of ourselves we allow others to see not only by what we talk about but also by how we behave, and we alter who we are to fit the situation and the relationship.

Let's look at the different personas or selves that Ashley enacts over a few days. As a restaurant server, Ashley is very polite, helpful, agreeable, and attentive to others. She does not talk about herself much or use profanity. She is confident, moves quickly, and cares about being efficient and productive. When Ashley goes out with her friends after work, she is more casual and less concerned about time. She is louder and more boisterous, talks about herself more, occasionally swears, and gets into heated debates of issues and ideas. When Ashley visits her grandmother, she behaves in a more childlike way: She never uses pro-

Chris Jackson/Getty Images

fanity, is careful to observe social politeness, is careful not to mention topics that may offend her grandmother, and listens more than she talks. Online, Ashley may present a party-girl image through a personal profile, photos, and listings of favorite activities, or she may assume totally different identities through avatars in multiplayer games. Ashley will enact other selves when she is at school, when she babysits her five-year-old niece, when she is on a date, and with her rock-climbing partners. Which is Ashley's real self? They all are because our when she is "self" is created in the interactions we have with others. We begin this process at birth and continue it throughout our lives.

If you have a Facebook or MySpace account, how does your profile picture and status information influence how others might perceive you?

Perception of Others

As we encounter new people, or as we experience new situations in our ongoing relationships, most of us feel somewhat to profoundly anxious. Questions such as: Do we have anything in common? Will others accept and value us? Will we be able to get along? How will our partner react to this new situation? etc. can raise our anxiety levels and so it is natural that we search for ways to alleviate it. This process of monitoring the social environment to learn more about self and others is called **uncertainty reduction** (Littlejohn & Foss, 2007). As people interact, they gain information and form impressions of others. For example, when Nicole and Justin meet for the first time at a party, they probably pay much attention to how each other looks, because that's the only source of information they have about each other at first. Then they ask each other questions about their majors, jobs, hobbies, interests, and people they both may know. This small talk helps them gain information in order to find things they have in common. The more they learn about each other and find commonalities, the less uncertain they are about each other. These perceptions will be reinforced, intensified, or changed as their relationship develops. The factors likely to influence perceptions of others include our observations of their physical characteristics and social behaviors, our interpretation of their messages, our use of stereotyping, and our emotional state.

What influences our perceptions of others?

uncertainty reduction
the process of monitoring the social environment to learn more about self and others.

Observing Others

Can you recall being shown a photo of someone you had not met? What impressions did you form on the basis of that photo alone? Recall meeting someone for the first time and forming an impression based on how he or she acted in that situation. Did your impression change once you got to know that person better? Our initial social perceptions or first impressions of others are usually made from our observations of how they look and act. We often judge people to be friendly, intelligent, or "cool" based on how physically attractive we find them (Aronson, 1999, p. 380). And these impressions can influence how we act toward them. For this reason, women in business are advised to wear a suit with pumps or flats as a way of increasing the likelihood that they will be perceived as credible and move ahead in their field ("How to Dress," 2008).

Likewise, first impressions are also made on the basis of how someone acts. If, on the first day of class, a fellow student strikes up conversations with the strangers sitting near him, makes humorous remarks in class, and gives the best self-introduction in a class activity, you are likely to form the impression that he is confident, extroverted, and friendly. Similarly, if you try to strike up a conversation with someone at a party, and the person gives short yes-or-no answers to your questions, you may perceive the person to be unfriendly and dull.

We make similar judgments about people we meet online. We use the profile and other pictures that people post, as well as the nicknames they use for themselves, the personal information they disclose, and the timeliness of their responses to perceive what they are like. Today, potential employers can make judgments about job applicants based on impressions gleaned from the applicants' home pages, profiles, and even the e-mail address they provide. For example, an employer may make different inferences about the character of an applicant whose e-mail address is realhottie@ hotmail.com than one whose e-mail address is more generic.

Sometimes we make judgments of other people based on **implicit personality theories** (Asch, 1946), which are assumptions about which physical characteristics and personality traits or behaviors are associated with one other (Michener & DeLamater, 1999, p. 106). Because your own implicit personality theory connects certain traits, you might assume that a person has a whole set of characteristics, traits, and behaviors when you have actually observed only one. When you do this, your perception is based on the **halo effect** (Thorndike, 1920). For instance, Heather sees Martina personally greeting and welcoming every person who arrives at the meeting. According to Heather's implicit personality theory, this behavior is a sign of the characteristic of warmth. She further associates warmth with goodness, and goodness with honesty. As a result, she perceives that Martina is good and honest, as well as warm.

In reality, Martina may be a con artist who uses her warmth to lure people into a false sense of trust. This example demonstrates a "positive halo" (Heather assigned Martina positive characteristics), but we also use implicit personality theory to inaccurately impute negative characteristics. Given limited amounts of information, we fill in details and come up with a "negative halo." The tendency to do so leads to another factor that influences our perception of others, stereotyping.

Using Stereotypes

One perceptual shortcut that we use in forming our initial perceptions of others is stereotyping. A **stereotype** is "a generalization, usually exaggerated or oversimplified and often offensive, used to describe or distinguish a group" ("Stereotype," 2005). Because

implicit personality theories
assumptions about which physical characteristics and personality traits or behaviors are associated with one another.

halo effect
to generalize and perceive that a person has a whole set of characteristics when you have actually observed only one characteristic, trait, or behavior.

stereotypes
generalizations, usually exaggerated or oversimplified and often offensive, use to describe or distinguish a group.

it is human nature to name, label, and organize in order to make sense of the stimuli we encounter, we develop generalized perceptions about groups we come in contact with personally or learn about through media portrayals. Subsequently, any number of perceptual cues—skin color, style of dress, a religious medal, gray hair, a loud voice, an expensive car, and so on—can lead us to apply the characteristics associated with a stereotype. A professor may see a student's purple spiked hair and numerous tattoos and assume the student is a rebel who will defy authority, slack off on classroom assignments, and seek attention. In reality, this person may be a polite, quiet, serious honor student who aspires to graduate school. According to B. J. Hall (2002), we don't form most of the stereotypes we use from our personal experience. Instead we learn them from family, friends, coworkers, and media. So we adopt stereotypes before we have any personal proof. And because stereotypes guide what we perceive, they can lead us to attend to information that confirms them and to overlook information that contradicts them.

Unfortunately, stereotyping can lead to prejudice and discrimination. According to Hall (2002), **prejudice** is "a rigid attitude that is based on group membership and predisposes an individual to feel, think, or act in a negative way toward another person or group" (p. 208). Notice the distinction between a stereotype and a prejudice. Whereas a stereotype is a set of beliefs or expectations, a prejudice is a positive or negative attitude about them; both relate to group membership. Stereotypes and prejudice are cognitive—that is, things we think.

prejudice
a rigid attitude that is based on group membership and predisposes an individual to feel, think, or act in a negative way toward another person or group.

discrimination
a negative action toward a social group or its members on account of group membership.

Skill Learning Activity 2.4
Web Resource 2.4

Discrimination goes a step further in that it involves a negative action toward a social group or its members based on a stereotype and prejudice (Jones, 2002, p. 8). For instance, when Ben discovers that he has been paired with Bobby Jo, a cheerleader, for a class project, he might stereotype her as a ditz who is not too concerned about grades. If he acts on his prejudice, he may discriminate against her by refusing to partner with her. So, without having gotten to know Bobby Jo, Ben uses her stereotype to prejudge her and discriminate. Bobby Jo may never get the chance to be known for who she really is, and Ben may have lost an opportunity to get to work with the best student in class. The movie *Legally Blonde* enacts this form of prejudice and discrimination.

G. Baden/zefa Value/Corbis

What is the relationship between these colleagues? How did stereotyping influence your perception?

Emotional State

A final factor that affects how accurately we perceive others is our emotional state at the time of the interaction (Forgas, 1991). For example, if you meet Carol for the first time after you have just received the good news that you got the internship you applied for, your good mood is likely to spill over so that you perceive her more positively than you might under different circumstances. If, however, you just learned that your car needs $1,500 in repairs, your perception of her might be influenced by your negative mood and anxiety about paying the bill.

Our emotions also cause us to engage in selective perceptions, so that we "see" data that supports our previous knowledge and we ignore inconsistent information. For instance, if Nick is physically attracted to Jessica, he is likely to focus on the positive aspects of Jessica's personality and may overlook or ignore the negative ones that are apparent to others.

Our emotional state also affects our attributions (Forgas, 2000). **Attributions** are reasons we give for others' behavior (Heider, 1958). According to attribution theory, what we determine—rightly or wrongly—to be the causes of others' behavior has a direct impact on our perceptions of them. For instance, suppose a coworker with whom you had made a noon lunch date has not arrived by 12:20 p.m. If you like and respect your coworker, you may attribute his lateness to something out of his control: an important phone call at the last minute, the need to finish a job before lunch, or some accident that may have occurred. If you are not particularly fond of your coworker, you are more likely to attribute his lateness to something in his control: forgetfulness, inconsiderateness, or malicious intent. In either case, your attribution will affect your perception of him and probably how you treat him.

Like prejudices, the attributions we make can be so strong that we ignore contrary evidence. If you are not particularly close to your coworker, when he finally arrives and explains that he had an emergency long-distance phone call, you may believe he is lying.

Perceiving Others' Messages

Our observations of others and our emotional state certainly affect how we perceive others. Not only that, they also tend to influence how we perceive the messages others send to us. Two additional factors that influence how we perceive others' messages are context and shared language.

First, we interpret the content and intent of the speaker based on the context. For example, at a family dinner Jeorge's dad, who dislikes conflict, sought to distract family members from a quarrel between two aunts by looking up at the crystal chandelier hanging above the table and asking, "How do you suppose they clean that chandelier?" Because the aunts were aware that Jeorge's dad hated conflict, they immediately understood "the message" and stopped arguing. Thereafter, regardless of the situation, when anyone in the family wanted to avoid a brewing conflict, they would simply say, "How about that chandelier?" and the potential conflict would usually be diffused. Obviously, people who had not been present at the initial dinner would not have understood the historical context of this message and would likely be confused by it.

The better we know someone, the more likely we are to share an understanding of the context in which our messages are sent and received. When we don't know someone well or when we are speaking with several people or a large audience, there are expanded opportunities for messages to be perceived differently.

Second, even when both participants speak the same language, they might not enjoy a "shared language" in terms of how each one perceives specific words, visual images, and nonverbal cues. To clarify, the sender might use a word with which the receiver is unfamiliar, ambiguously use a word that has multiple meanings, misuse a symbol, or use a personal and idiosyncratic definition of a word. When Justin tells his wife that he's "going out with the guys for an hour or so," she may expect him home in 60–90 minutes. When he shows up five hours later, she might be upset. Justin may

attributions
reasons we give for others' behavior.

have figured that "or so" would cover any additional time he was away, but his wife may have viewed it as something less than two hours. Although the message was sent in a language that both "understood," they did not share meaning because they perceived the message to mean different lengths of time.

Understanding how observations and emotional states, as well as context and shared language affect our perceptions of others and the messages they send is a first step in improving your perceptual accuracy. Now we'll describe four guidelines and a communication skill you can use to improve the accuracy of your perceptions of others and the messages they send.

Improving the Accuracy of Social Perceptions

Because distortions in our perception of others and their messages are common and because they influence how we communicate, improving perceptual accuracy is an important first step in becoming a competent communicator. The following guidelines can aid you in constructing accurate impressions of others and in assessing your perceptions of others' messages.

> What can we do to improve the accuracy of our perceptions of others?

1. **Question the accuracy of your perceptions.** Questioning accuracy begins by saying, "I know what I think I saw, heard, tasted, smelled, or felt, but I could be wrong. What other information should I be aware of?" By accepting the possibility that you have overlooked something, you will become interested in increasing your accuracy.

2. **Seek more information to verify perceptions.** If your perception is based on only one or two pieces of information, try to collect additional information so that your perceptions are better grounded. Note that your perception is tentative—that is, subject to change.

   The best way to get additional information about people is to talk with them. It's OK to be unsure about how to treat someone from another group. But rather than letting your uncertainty cause you to make mistakes, talk with the person and ask for the information you need to become more comfortable.

3. **Realize that your perceptions of a person will change over time.** People often base their behavior on perceptions that are old or based on incomplete information. So when you encounter someone you haven't seen for a while, you will want to become reacquainted and let the person's current behavior rather than their past actions or reputation inform your perceptions. A former classmate who was wild in high school may well have changed and become a mature, responsible adult.

4. **Use the skill of perception checking.** One way to assess the accuracy of a perception is to verbalize it and see whether others agree with what you see, hear, and interpret. A **perception check** is a message that reflects your understanding of the meaning of another person's nonverbal behavior. It is a process of describing what you have seen and heard and then asking for feedback from the other person. Perception checking calls for you to (1) watch the behavior of the other person, (2) ask yourself "What does that behavior mean to me?" and (3) describe the behavior and put your interpretation into words to verify your perception.

perception check
a message that reflects your understanding of the meaning of another person's nonverbal behavior.

The following examples illustrate the use of perception checking. In each of the examples, the final sentence is a perception check. Notice that the perception-checking statements do not express approval or disapproval of what is being received—they are purely descriptive statements of the perceptions.

Valerie walks into the room with a completely blank expression. She does not speak to Ann or even acknowledge that Ann is in the room. Valerie sits down on the edge of the bed and stares into space. Ann says, "Valerie, did something happen? You look like you're in a state of shock. Am I right? Is there something I can do?"

While Marsha is telling Jenny about the difficulty of her midterm exam in chemistry class, she notices Jenny smiling. She says to Jenny, "You're smiling. I'm not sure how to interpret it. What's up?" Jenny may respond that she's smiling because the story reminded her of something funny or because she had the same chemistry teacher last year and he purposely gave an extremely difficult midterm to motivate students, but then he graded them on a favorable curve.

Cesar, the shift foreman, speaking in short, precise sentences with a sharp tone of voice, gives Bill his day's work assignment. Bill says, "From the sound of your voice, Cesar, I get the impression that you're upset with me. Are you?"

So when we use the skill of perception checking, we encode the meaning that we have perceived from someone's behavior and feed it back so that it can be verified or corrected. For instance, when Bill says, "I can't help but get the impression that you're upset with me. Are you?" Cesar may say: (1) "No, whatever gave you that impression?" in which case Bill can further describe the cues that he received; (2) "Yes, I am," in which case Bill can get Cesar to specify what has caused the feelings; or (3) "No, it's not you, it's just that three of my team members didn't show up for this shift." If Cesar is not upset with him, Bill can examine what caused him to misinterpret Cesar's feelings; if Cesar is upset with him, Bill has the opportunity to change the behavior that caused Cesar to be upset.

Skill Learning Activity 2.5

Perception Checking

Communication Skill

Skill	Use	Procedure	Example
Making a verbal statement that reflects your understanding of another person's behavior.	To enable you to test the accuracy of your perceptions.	1. Describe the behaviors of the other person that have led to your perception. 2. Add your interpretation of the behavior to your statement.	After taking a phone call, Shimika comes into the room with a completely blank expression and neither speaks to Donnell nor acknowledges that he is in the room. Donnell says, "Shimika, from your blank look, I get the feeling that you're in a state of shock. Has something happened?"

Perception Checking

Skill Building

For each of the following situations, write a well-phrased perception check.

1. When Franco comes home from the doctor's office, you notice that he looks pale and his shoulders are slumped. Glancing at you with a sad look, he shrugs his shoulders.
   You say:

2. As you return the basketball you borrowed from Liam, you smile and say, "Thanks, here's your ball." You notice Liam stiffen, grab the ball, and, turning abruptly, walk away.
   You say:

3. Natalie, who has been waiting to hear about a scholarship, dances into the room with a huge grin on her face.
   You say:

4. You see your adviser in the hall and ask her if she can meet with you on Wednesday afternoon to discuss your schedule of classes for next term. You notice that she pauses, frowns, sighs, turns slowly, and says, "I guess so."
   You say:

Compare your written responses to the guidelines for effective perception checking discussed earlier. Edit your responses where necessary to improve them. Now say them aloud. Do they sound "natural"? If not, revise them until they do.

Skill Learning Activity 2.6

A Question of Ethics

UniConCo, a multinational construction company, successfully bid to build a new minor league stadium in a Midwestern city that had very little diversity. Miguel Hernandez was assigned to be the assistant project manager, and he moved his family of seven to town. He quickly joined the local chamber of commerce, affiliated with the local Rotary group, and was feeling the first signs of acceptance. One day Mr. Hernandez was working at his desk when he accidentally overheard a group of local Anglo construction workers who were on the project talking about their Mexican American coworkers. Hernandez was discouraged to hear the negative stereotypes that were being used. The degree of hatred expressed was clearly beyond what he was used to, and he was further upset when he recognized several of the voices as belonging to men he had fought to hire.

What Would You Do?

A bit shaken, Hernandez returned to his office. He had a problem. He recognized his workers' prejudices, but he wasn't sure how to change them. Moreover, he wanted to establish good work relationships with his Anglo workers for the sake of the company, but he also wanted to create a good working atmosphere for the other Latino workers who would soon be moving to town to work on the project. What could Mr. Hernandez do?

Devise a plan for Mr. Hernandez. How could he use his social perceptions to address the problem in a way that is within ethical interpersonal communication guidelines?

Summary

Perception is the process of selectively attending to information and assigning meaning to it. Our perceptions are a result of our selection, organization, and interpretation of sensory information. Self-concept is our self-identity, the idea or mental image that we have about our skills, abilities, knowledge, competencies, and personality. Self-esteem is our overall evaluation of our competence and personal worthiness. Self-concepts come from interpretations of self based on our own experience and on the reactions and responses of others. The inaccuracy of a distorted picture of oneself becomes magnified through self-fulfilling prophecies, filtering messages, and media images. Our self-concept and self-esteem moderate competing internal messages in our self-talk, influence our perception of others, and influence our personal communication style. Our self-concept is socially constructed by us and by others, and the different roles we play in various situations create our multiple selves.

Perception plays an important role in forming impressions of others. We form these impressions based on others' physical characteristics and social behaviors, our stereotyping, and our emotional state. These factors, along with context and shared language, influence how we perceive others and the messages they send. You can improve the accuracy of your perceptions of others and the messages they send by questioning the accuracy of your perceptions, seeking more information about your perceptions, realizing that your perceptions will change over time, and practicing perception checking.

Communicate! Active Online Learning

Now that you have read Chapter 2, use your Premium Web site for *Communicate!* for quick access to the electronic resources that accompany this text. These resources include

- **Study tools** that will help you assess your learning and prepare for exams (*digital glossary, key term flash cards, review quizzes*).
- **Activities and assignments** that will help you hone your knowledge, analyze communication situations (*Skill Learning Activities*), and build your public speaking skills throughout the course (*Communication on Your Feet speech assignments, Action Step activities*). Many of these activities allow you to compare your answers to those provided by the authors, and, if requested, submit your answers to your instructor.

- **Media resources** that will help you explore communication concepts online (*Web Resources*), develop your speech outlines (*Speech Builder Express 3.0*), watch and critique videos of communication situations and sample speeches (*Interactive Video Activities*), upload your speech videos for peer reviewing and critique other students' speeches (*Speech Studio online speech review tool*), and download chapter review so you can study when and where you'd like (*Audio Study Tools*).

This chapter's Key Terms, Skill Learning Activities, and Web Resources are also featured on the following pages, and you can find this chapter's Skill Building activity in the body of the chapter.

Key Terms

attributions (40)
discrimination (39)
halo effect (38)
ideal self-concept (27)
implicit personality theories (38)

incongruence (31)
interpret (26)
pattern (25)
perception (24)
perception check (41)
prejudice (39)
role (36)

self-concept (26)
self-esteem (26)
self-fulfilling prophecy (32)
self-monitoring (36)
self-talk (34)
stereotypes (38)
uncertainty reduction (37)

Skill Learning Activities

2.1: Who Am I? (27)

Complete this journal activity to help you assess how your self-concept aligns with how others see you.

First ask, *How do I see myself?* List the skills, abilities, knowledge, competencies, and personality characteristics that describe how you see yourself. To generate this list, try completing these sentences: "I am skilled at..., I have the ability to...," "I know things about..., I am competent at doing...," and "One part of my personality is that I am...." List as many characteristics in each category as you can think of. What you have developed is an inventory of your self-concept.

Second ask, *How do others see me?* List the skills, abilities, and so on that describe how you think others see you by completing these sentences: "Other people believe I am skilled at...," "Other people believe I have the ability to...," "Other people believe I know things about...," "Other people believe I am competent at doing...," and "One part of my personality is that other people believe I am...."

Compare your two lists. How are they similar? Where are they different? Do you understand why they differ? After you have thought about each, write a paragraph titled "Who I Am, and How I Know This."

2.2: The Speech of Introduction About You (36)

Listen to the speech of introduction that a classmate gives about you. How do you feel about what was said? Did anything the speaker said embarrass you? On a scale of 1 to 10, rate how pleased you were to be introduced as you were. What did you

like about what the speaker said about you? What did you dislike? Do you think that the other members of the class have an accurate perception of who you are based on what the speaker said about you? Why or why not? Is there anything the speaker did not know about you that, if he or she had included it in the speech, would have helped the speaker to do a better job? If you could go back and have your get-acquainted conversation with the speaker again, what would you do or say differently to help the speaker do a better job of presenting you as you would like others to know you? How does all of this relate to the concept of self-monitoring?

2.3: Monitor Your Enacted Roles (36)

For three days, record your roles in various situations such as "lunch with a best friend" or "meeting professor about a class project." Describe the roles you chose to enact in each setting such as student, friend, or customer.

At the conclusion of this three-day observation period, analyze what you observed. To what extent does your role behavior change across situations? What factors seem to trigger you to enact a particular role? Are there certain roles that you take on more than others? Are there roles you need to modify? Are there roles you are reluctant to enact that would help you be a more effective communicator? How satisfied are you with the roles you took? With which are you most and least pleased?

Write a paragraph explaining what you have learned.

You can find a data collection sheet for this activity at your Premium Web site for *Communicate!* Look for the Skill Learning activities for Chapter 2.

2.4: Stereotypes and Media (39)

For a few days, catalog the stereotypes in mass media. Enter your research into a log broken out by the following categories: (1) medium of communication (TV, radio, magazines, newspapers, the Internet, signage/posters); (2) source (general content or advertising); (3) target (race, ethnicity/culture, religion, gender, sexual orientation, age, income, profession, hobby, appearance); and (4) connotation (positive or negative).

After you have completed your research, analyze the results. What target was most frequently stereotyped in your findings? Did some mediums of communication indulge in more stereotyping the others? Did regular programming or advertising employ more stereotyping than the other? Were the majority of the stereotypes positive or negative in connotation? Did anything in your research surprise you? Write a paragraph explaining what you learned in this activity.

You can find a data collection sheet for this activity at your Premium Web site for *Communicate!* Look for the Skill Learning activities for Chapter 2.

2.5: Culture and Perception (42)

1. Describe a recent encounter you had with someone of a different race or ethnic group.

   _____

   _____

2. How comfortable did you feel talking with this person?

   _____

   _____

3. In what ways did this person's race or ethnic group influence how you acted or reacted?

   _____

   _____

4. Did it affect the topics you discussed or the care with which you phrased your messages?

   _____

   _____

Web Resources

2.1: Real Self-Esteem? (30)

Read this provocative article about self-esteem by Dr. Richard O'Connor, "Self-Esteem: In a Culture Where Winning Is Everything and Losing Is Shameful." What points does O'Connor make? How does his conclusion coincide with what you have observed?

2.2: Self-Esteem Model (31)

The Web site Coping.org is the home of manuals for coping with a variety of life's stressors, including the Model of Self-Esteem. This site provides information about self-esteem and offers suggestions for improving one's self-esteem.

2.3: Identity in Cyberspace (36)

With the advent of the Internet and anonymity it affords, we now create roles that are quite different from our offline roles. Read about five interlocking factors that are useful in understanding how people manage identities in cyberspace.

2.4: Fighting Words with Words (39)

Learn how to identify the sweeping generalizations behind stereotypes and how to use balancing statements to counteract them with this Coverdell World Wise Schools activity. Coverdell World Wise Schools seeks to foster student inquiry about the world and others and began as a correspondence "match" program between Peace Corps volunteers and U.S. school students.

David Young-Wolff/PhotoEdit

Communicating Verbally

Questions you'll be able to answer after reading this chapter:

- What are the purposes of language?
- What is the relationship between language and meaning?
- How do culture and gender affect language use?
- How can you make your language more clear?
- How can you make your messages more memorable?
- What can you do to ensure your listener will understand the words you choose?
- How can you phrase messages to demonstrate linguistic sensitivity?

Donna approached her friend Mary and said, "Ed and I are having a really tough time."

"I'm sorry to hear that," replied Mary. "What's happening?"

"Well, you know, it's just the way he acts."

"Is he being abusive?"

"Uh, no—it's not that. I just can't seem to figure him out."

"Well, is it what he says?"

"No, it's more what he doesn't say."

"What do you mean 'what he doesn't say'?"

"You know, he comes home and I ask him where he's been."

"And . . . ?"

"He says he was working overtime."

"And you don't believe him?"

"No, I believe him. It's just that he's working so much, I'm starting to feel lonely."

"Have you talked with him about this?"

"No, I don't know how to say it, and I don't think he'd understand me."

Given what Donna has said and the way she has said it, would you understand? Sometimes, for a variety of reasons, the way we form our messages makes it difficult for others to understand. Sometimes the problem is what we say; other times it's how we say it.

As Thomas Holtgraves (2002), a leading scholar in language use, reminds us, "Language is one of those things that we often take for granted" (p. 8). Yet we could all improve our use of language. In this chapter, we discuss the nature of and purposes for language and improving our verbal language skills.

The Nature and Purposes of Language

Language is both a body of symbols (most commonly words) and the systems for their use in messages that are common to the people of the same speech community.

A **speech community**, also called a language community, is a group of people who speak the same language. There are between 3,000 and 4,000 speech communities in the world. Around 60 percent of the world's speech communities have fewer than 10,000 speakers. The five largest speech communities, in order, are Mandarin Chinese, Spanish, English, Arabic, and Hindi (World Almanac, 2007).

Words are symbols used by a speech community to represent objects, ideas, and feelings. Although the word used to represent a particular object or idea varies from language to language, for a word to be a symbol all the members of the speech community must recognize it as standing for the same object, idea, or feeling. Different speech communities use different word symbols for the same phenomenon. For example, the season for planting is called *spring* in English-speaking communities but *printemps* in French-speaking communities.

Speech communities also vary in how they put words together to form messages. The structure a message takes depends on the rules of grammar and syntax that have evolved in a particular speech community. For example, in English a sentence must have at least a subject (a noun or pronoun) and a predicate (a verb). To make a statement in English, the subject is placed before the predicate. In Mandarin Chinese, however, an idea is usually expressed with a verb and a complement (which is rarely a noun and usually another verb or an adjective).

Language affects how people think and what they pay attention to. This concept is called the **Sapir–Whorf hypothesis**, named after two theorists, Edward Sapir and Benjamin Lee Whorf (Littlejohn & Foss, 2008). Language allows us to perceive certain aspects of the world by naming them and allows us to ignore other parts of the world by not naming them. For instance, if you work in a job such as fashion or interior design that deals with many different words for color distinctions, you will be able to perceive finer differences in color. Knowing various words for shades of white, such as *ecru, eggshell, cream, ivory, pearl, bone china white*, and *antique white*, actually helps you see differences in shades of white. Similarly, there are concepts that people do not fully perceive until a word is coined to describe them. Think of words added to American English vocabulary in the last few years such as *google,*

language
a body of symbols (most commonly words) and the systems for their use in messages that are common to the people of the same speech community.

speech community
a group of people who speak the same language (also called a language community).

words
symbols used by a speech community to represent objects, ideas, and feelings.

Sapir–Whorf hypothesis
a theory claiming that language influences perception.

texting, couch potato, or *mouse potato.* The behaviors to which those words refer certainly existed before the terms were coined. But as a society, we did not collectively perceive these behaviors until language allowed us to name them.

Purposes of Language

Although language communities vary in the words they use and in their grammar and syntax systems, all languages serve the same purposes.

Today we know what a *couch potato* is, but that was not the case 30 years ago.

1. **We use language to designate, label, define, and limit.** So, when we identify music as "punk," we are differentiating it from other music labeled rap, rock, pop, indie, country, or R&B.

2. **We use language to evaluate.** Through language we convey positive or negative attitudes toward our subject. For instance, if you see Hal taking more time than others to make a decision, you could describe Hal positively as "thoughtful" or negatively as "dawdling." Or you might describe a comedy like the movie *Superbad* positively as "hilarious" or negatively as "vulgar." Kenneth Burke (1968), a prominent language theorist, describes this as the power of language to emphasize hierarchy and control. Because language allows us to compare things, we tend to judge them as better or worse, which leads to social hierarchy or a pecking order. Certainly, programs like *What Not to Wear* and *Flip This House* use language to suggest how to judge certain looks as better or worse.

3. **We use language to discuss things outside our immediate experience.** Language lets us talk about ourselves, learn from others' experiences, share a common heritage, talk about past and future events, and communicate about people and things that are not present. Through language, we can discuss where we hope to be in five years, where we plan to go for spring break, or learn about the history that shapes the world we live in. If you ever watch television programs on the discovery channel, you are learning from things outside your own experiences.

4. **We use language to talk about language.** We also use language to communicate about how we are communicating. For instance, if your friend said she would see you "this afternoon," but she didn't arrive until 5 o'clock, and you ask her where she's been, the two of you are likely to discuss your communication and the different interpretations you each bring to the phrase "this afternoon." You might also relate to this if you've ever had a professor tell you an assignment is due "next week," and then asks for it first thing Monday morning with a comment that she "will not accept late papers."

What are the purposes of language?

The Relationship Between Language and Meaning

On the surface, the relationship between language and meaning seems perfectly clear: We select the correct words, structure them using the rules of syntax and grammar agreed upon by our speech community, and people will interpret our meanings correctly. In fact, the relationship between language and meaning is not nearly so simple for five reasons.

Ulrich Niehoff/imagebroker/Alamy

> What is the relationship between language and meaning?

First, the meaning of words is in people, not in the words themselves. If Juan says to Julia that the restaurant is expensive, each of them probably has a different meaning of the word *expensive.* Maybe Juan thinks one meal will cost $40, whereas for Julia, *expensive* might mean a $20 meal. All words, especially abstract ones, have multiple meanings depending on who is using them and who is hearing them. What does *expensive* mean to you?

Second, words have two levels of meaning: denotation and connotation. **Denotation** is the direct, explicit meaning a speech community formally gives a word—it is the meaning found in a dictionary. Different dictionaries may define words in slightly different ways. For instance, the *Encarta World English Dictionary* defines *bawdy* as "ribald in a frank, humorous, often crude way," and the *Cambridge American English Dictionary* defines *bawdy* as "containing humorous remarks about sex." Similar? Yes, but not the same. Not only that, but many words have multiple definitions. For instance, the *Random House Dictionary of the English Language* lists 23 definitions for the word *great.* **Connotation**, the feelings or evaluations we associate with a word, may be even more important to our understanding of meaning than denotation. C. K. Ogden and I. A. Richards (1923) were among the first scholars to consider the misunderstandings resulting from the failure of communicators to realize that their subjective reactions to words are based on their life experiences. For instance, when Tina says, "We bought an SUV; I think it's the biggest one Chevy makes," Kim might think "Why in the world would anyone want one of those gas guzzlers that take up so much space to park?" and Lexia might say, "Oh, I envy you. I'd love to own a vehicle that has so much power and sits so high on the road." Word denotation and connotation are important because the only message that counts is the message that is understood, regardless of whether it is the one you intended.

Third, meaning may vary depending on its **syntactic context** (the position of a word in a sentence and the other words around it). For instance, in the same sentence a person might say, "I love to vacation in the mountains, where it's really cool in mornings and you're likely to see some really cool animals." Most listeners would understand that "mornings are really cool" refers to temperature and "see some really cool animals" refers to animals that are uncommon or special.

Fourth, the language of any speech community will change over time. Language changes in many ways, including the creation of new words, the abandonment of old words, changes in word meanings in segments of society, and the influx of words from the mixing of cultures. For instance, the latest edition of *Merriam-Webster's Collegiate Dictionary* contains 10,000 new words and usages. New words are created to express new ideas. For example, younger generations, businesspeople, and scientists, among others, will invent new words or assign different meanings to words to better express the changing realities of their world. For example, *bling* is used to describe flashy jewelry, *marathoning* is the practice of watching an entire season of a TV series in one sitting, a *desktop* is the visual surface we see on our computer screen, and *greenwashing* is the practice of making a misleading claim about the environmental benefits of a product, service, technology, or company practice. In the past 20 years, entire vocabularies have been invented to allow us to communicate about new technologies. So we *google* to get information, use the *wi-fi* on our *laptop*, and listen to a *podcast* while writing a *blog.* Words used by older generations may fade as they no longer describe current realities or are replaced by new words. We once used a *mimeograph*, but now we use a *copy machine.* In addition, some members of the speech community will invent new meanings for old words to differentiate themselves from other subgroups of the language community. For instance, in some parts of the country, young people use the word *bad* to mean "intense," as in "That movie was really bad," or *sick* to mean

denotation
the direct, explicit meaning a speech community formally gives a word.

connotation
the feelings or evaluations we associate with a word.

syntactic context
the position of a word in a sentence and the other words around it.

"cool" as in "That bike is really sick," or the word *kickin'* to mean "really great" as in "That concert was really kickin'."

Fifth, as a society absorbs immigrants who speak different languages and becomes more multicultural, the language of the dominant group gradually absorbs some words from the languages of the immigrants. In English we use and understand what were once foreign words, such as *petite, siesta, kindergarten,* and *ciao.* Similarly, the slang used by a subgroup may also eventually be appropriated by the larger speech community. For example, the African American slang terms for "girlfriend," *shorty* or *boo,* are now used and understood by a more diverse group of American speakers.

Cultural and Gender Influences on Language Use

Culture and gender both influence how words are used and interpreted. Cultures vary in how much meaning is embedded in the language itself and how much meaning is interpreted from the context in which the communication occurs. In **low-context cultures**, like the United States and most northern European countries, messages are typically quite direct and language is very specific. Speakers say exactly what they mean, and the verbal messages are very explicit, with lots of details provided. In low-context cultures, what the speaker intends the message to mean is not heavily influenced by the setting or context; rather, it is embedded in the verbal message. In **high-context cultures**, like Latin American, Asian, and American Indian, what a speaker intends for you to understand from the verbal message depends heavily on the setting or context in which it is sent. So verbal messages in high-context cultures may be indirect, using more general and ambiguous language. Receivers in high-context cultures, then, rely on contextual cues to help them understand the speaker's meaning (Samovar, Porter, & McDaniel, 2009).

Elena Rooraid/PhotoEdit

People in high-context cultures rely on contextual cues to understand a speaker's meaning.

When people from low-context cultures interact with others from high-context cultures, misunderstandings often occur. Imagine that Isaac from a German company and Zhao from a Chinese company are trying to conduct business.

ISAAC: "Let's get right down to it. We're hoping that you can provide 100,000 parts per month according to our six manufacturing specifications spelled out in the engineering contract I sent you. If quality control finds more than a 2-percent error, we will have to terminate the contract. Can you agree to these terms?"

ZHAO: "We are very pleased to be doing business with you. We produce the highest quality products and will be honored to meet your needs."

ISAAC: "But can you supply that exact quantity? Can you meet all of our engineering specifications? Will you consistently have less than a 2-percent error?"

ZHAO: "We are an excellent, trustworthy company that will send you the highest quality parts."

> How do culture and gender influence language use?

low-context cultures
cultures in which messages are direct, specific, and detailed.

high-context cultures
cultures in which messages are indirect, general, and ambiguous.

Isaac is probably frustrated with what he perceives as general, evasive language used by Zhao, and Zhao may be offended by the direct questions, specific language, and perceived threat in Isaac's message. Global migration, business, and travel are increasing the interactions that occur between people accustomed to high- or low-context expectations. As this happens, the likelihood of misunderstanding increases. To be a competent communicator, you will need to be aware of, compensate for, or adapt to the cultural expectations of your conversational partner.

Societal expectations for masculinity and femininity also influence language use. According to Wood (2007), **feminine styles of language** typically use words of empathy and support, emphasize concrete and personal language, and show politeness and tentativeness in speaking. **Masculine styles of language** often use words of status and problem solving, emphasize abstract and general language, and show assertiveness and control in speaking.

Feminine language often includes empathic phrases like "I can understand how you feel" or "I've had a similar experience, so I can sense what you are going through." Likewise, feminine language often includes language of support such as "I'm so sorry that you are having difficulty" or "Please let me know if I can help you in any way." Feminine language often goes into detail by giving specific examples and personal disclosures. To appear feminine is to speak politely by focusing on others and by not being too forceful with language. Words and phrases like "I may be wrong but . . .";
"It's just my opinion"; "maybe"; ."perhaps"; and "I don't want to step on anyone's toes here" are associated with feminine styles of speaking.

By contrast, masculine styles of speaking often emphasize status through phrases like "I know that . . ." and "My experience tells me" and communicates problem solving or advice giving through such language as "I would . . ."; "You should . . ."; and "The way you should handle this is . . ." Masculine styles of communication may favor theoretical or general discussions and avoid giving personal information about oneself. To appear masculine, one's language must be forceful, direct, and in control through such phrases as "definitely," "I have no doubt," "It is clear to me," and "I am sure that . . . "

Women and men can use both masculine and feminine language, although, generally, dominant American society expects women to use feminine language and men to use masculine language. One style is not inherently better than another, but each may be better suited to certain communication situations.

Improving Language Skills

Regardless of whether we are conversing with a friend, working on a task force, or giving a speech, we should strive to use language in our messages that accurately conveys our meanings. We can improve our messages by choosing words that make our meaning clear, choosing language that makes our messages memorable, and choosing language that demonstrates linguistic sensitivity.

Use Clear Language

We ought to choose words that help listeners assign meaning that is similar to what we intended. Compare these two descriptions of a near miss in a car: *"Some nut almost got me a while ago"* versus *"An hour ago, an older man in a banged-up Honda Civic ran the light at Calhoun and Clifton and almost hit me broadside while I was in the intersection waiting to turn left at the cross street."* In the second message,

feminine styles of language
use words of empathy and support, emphasize concrete and personal language, and show politeness and tentativeness in speaking.

masculine styles of language
use words of status and problem solving, emphasize abstract and general language, and show assertiveness and control in speaking.

Frank and Ernest

the language is much more specific, so both parties would be likely to have a more similar perception of the situation than would be possible with the first message.

Often as we try to express our thoughts, the first words that come to mind are general in nature. **Specific words** clear up confusion caused by general words by narrowing what is understood from a general category to a particular group within that category. Specific words are more concrete and precise than general words. What can we do to speak more specifically?

For one, we can select a word that most accurately captures the sense of what we are saying. At first I might say, "Waylon was angry during our work session today." Then I might think, "Was he really showing anger?" So I say, "To be more accurate, he wasn't really angry. Perhaps he was more frustrated or impatient with what he sees as a lack of progress by our group." What is the difference between the two statements in terms of words? By carefully choosing words, you can show shades of meaning. Others may respond quite differently to your description of a group member showing anger, frustration, or impatience. The interpretation others get of Waylon's behavior depends on the word or words you select. Specific language is achieved when words are concrete or precise or when details or examples are used.

Concrete words are words that appeal to our senses. Consider the word *speak*. This is an abstract word—that is, we can speak in many different ways. So instead of saying that Jill *speaks in a peculiar way*, we might be more specific by saying that Jill *mumbles, whispers, blusters*, or *drones*. Each of these words creates a clearer sense of the sound of her voice.

We speak more specifically when we use **precise words**, narrowing a larger category to a smaller group within that category. For instance, if Nevah says that Ruben is a "blue-collar worker," she has named a general category; you might picture an unlimited number of occupations that fall within this broad category. If, instead, she is more precise and says he's a "construction worker," the number of possible images you can picture is reduced; now you can only select your image from the specific subcategory of construction worker. So your meaning is likely to be closer to the one she intended. To be even more precise, she may identify Ruben as a "bulldozer operator"; this further limits your choice of images and is likely to align with the one she intended you to have.

Clarity also can be achieved by adding detail or examples. For instance, Linda says, "Rashad is very loyal." The meaning of *loyal* ("faithful to an idea, person, company, and so on") is abstract, so to avoid ambiguity and confusion, Linda might add, "He defended Gerry when Sara was gossiping about her." By following up her use of the abstract concept of loyalty with a concrete example, Linda makes it easier for her

How can you make your language more clear?

specific words
words that clarify meaning by narrowing what is understood from a general category to a particular item or group within that category.

concrete words
words that appeal to the senses and help us see, hear, smell, taste, or touch.

precise words
words that narrow a larger category to a smaller group within that category.

Web Resource 3.1
Skill Learning Activity 3.1

Skill Learning Activity 3.2

dating information
specifying the time or time period that a fact was true or known to be true.

indexing generalizations
the mental and verbal practice of acknowledging the presence of individual differences when voicing generalizations.

listeners to ground their idea of this personal quality in a concrete or real experience. We can also clarify our messages by providing details. The statement "He lives in a really big house" can be clarified by adding details: "He lives in a 14-room Tudor mansion on a six-acre estate."

We can also increase clarity by dating information. **Dating information** are details that specify the time or period that a fact was true or known to be true. Because nearly everything changes with time, not dating our statements can lead some people to conclude that what we are saying is current when it is not. For instance, Parker says, "I'm going to be transferred to Henderson City." Laura replies, "Good luck—they've had some real trouble with their schools." On the basis of Laura's statement, Parker may worry about the effect his move will have on his children. What he doesn't know is that Laura's information about this problem in Henderson City is over five years old. Henderson City still may have problems, or the situation may have changed. Had Laura replied, "Five years ago, I know they had some real trouble with their schools. I'm not sure what the situation is now, but you may want to check," Parker would look at the information differently.

Here are two additional examples:

Undated: Professor Powell is really enthusiastic when she lectures.
Dated: Professor Powell is really enthusiastic when she lectures—at least she was *last semester* in communication theory.

Undated: You think Mary's depressed? I'm surprised. She seemed her regular, high-spirited self when I talked with her.
Dated: You think Mary's depressed? I'm surprised. She seemed her regular, high-spirited self when I talked with her *last month.*

To date information, before you make a statement (1) consider when the information was true and (2) verbally acknowledge the date or period when the information was true. When you date your statements, you increase the clarity of your messages and enhance your credibility.

Finally, we can increase clarity through indexing generalizations. **Indexing generalizations** is the mental and verbal practice of acknowledging individual differences when voicing generalizations. Although we might assume that someone who buys a Mercedes is rich, that may not be true for all Mercedes buyers. Thus, just because Brent has bought a top-of-the-line, very expensive Mercedes, Brent is not necessarily rich. If we said, "Brent bought a Mercedes; he must be rich," we should add, "Of course not all people who buy Mercedes are rich."

Let's consider another example:

Generalization: Your Toyota should go 50,000 miles before you need a brake job; Jerry's did.
Indexed Statement: Your Toyota may well go 50,000 miles before you need a brake job; Jerry's did, *but of course, all Toyotas aren't the same.*

To index, consider whether what you are about to say applies a generalization to a specific person, place, or thing. If so, qualify it appropriately so that your assertion does not go beyond the evidence that supports it.

To ensure that our listeners decode our messages as we intend them, we can use words that are specific, concrete, and precise. We can also provide details and examples, as well as date our information and index our generalizations. Ultimately, our goal is to be understood. Practicing these strategies will help us achieve that goal.

Use Language That Makes Your Messages Memorable

Because your listeners cannot simply re-read what you have said, effective verbal messages use vivid wording and appropriate emphasis to help listeners understand and remember the message.

Vivid wording is full of life, vigorous, bright, and intense. For example, a novice football announcer might say, "Jackson made a great catch," but a more experienced commentator's vivid account would be "Jackson leaped into the air with double-coverage, made a spectacular one-handed catch, and landed somehow with both feet planted firmly in the end zone." The words *spectacular, leaped, one-handed catch*, and *planted firmly* paint an intense verbal picture of the action. Vivid messages begin with vivid thoughts. You are much more likely to *express* yourself vividly when you have physically or psychologically *sensed* the meanings you are trying to convey.

Vividness can be achieved quickly through using similes and metaphors. A **simile** is a direct comparison of dissimilar things and is usually expressed with the words *like* or *as*. Clichés such as "She walks like a duck" and "She sings like a nightingale" are both similes. A **metaphor** is a comparison that establishes a figurative identity between objects being compared. Instead of saying that one thing is like another, a metaphor says that one thing *is* another. Thus, a problem car is a "lemon" and an aggressive driver is a "road hog." As you think about and try to develop similes and metaphors, stay away from trite clichés. Although we use similes and metaphors frequently in conversations, they are an especially powerful way to develop vividness when we are giving a speech. Try developing and practicing one or two different original metaphors or similes when you rehearse a speech to see which works best.

Finally, although your goal is to be vivid, be sure to use words that are understood by all your listeners. Novice speakers can mistakenly believe they will be more impressive if they use a large vocabulary, but using big words can be off-putting to the audience and make the speaker seem pompous, affected, or stilted. When you have a choice between a common vivid word or image and one that is more obscure, choose the more common.

> How can you make your messages more memorable?

Skill Learning Activity 3.3

vivid wording
wording that is full of life, vigorous, bright, and intense.

simile
a direct comparison of dissimilar things.

metaphor
a comparison that establishes a figurative identity between objects being compared.

Using Specific Language

Communication Skill

Skill	Use	Procedure	Example
Clarify meaning by narrowing what is understood from a general category to a particular group within that category, by appealing to the senses, by choosing words that symbolize exact thoughts and feelings, or by using concrete details or examples.	To help the listener picture thoughts analogous to the speaker's.	1. Assess whether the word or phrase to be used is less specific (or concrete or precise) than it could be. 2. Pause to consider alternatives. 3. Select a more specific (or concrete or precise) word, or give an example or add details.	Instead of saying, "Bring the stuff for the audit," say, "Bring the records and receipts from the last year for the audit." Or instead of saying, "Make sure you improve your grades," say, "This term, we want to see a B in Spanish and at least a C in algebra."

Clarifying General Statements

Rewrite each of these statements to make it more specific by making general and abstract words more concrete and precise. Add details and examples.

1. My neighbor has a lot of animals that she keeps in her yard.
2. When I was a little girl, we lived in a big house in the Midwest.
3. My husband works for a large newspaper.
4. She got up late and had to rush to get to school. But she was late anyway.
5. Where'd you find that thing?
6. I really liked going to that concert. The music was great.
7. I really respect her.
8. My boyfriend looks like a hippie.
9. She was wearing a very trendy outfit.
10. We need to have more freedom to choose our courses.

Skill Learning Activity 3.4

emphasis
the importance given to certain words or ideas.

Emphasis is the importance you give to certain words or ideas. Emphasis tells listeners what they should seriously pay attention to. Ideas are emphasized through proportion of time, repetition, and transitions. Ideas to which you devote more time are perceived by listeners to be more important, whereas ideas that are quickly mentioned are perceived to be less important. Emphasizing by repeating means saying important words or ideas more than once. You can either repeat the exact words, "A ring-shaped coral island almost or completely surrounding a lagoon is called *an*

The Language of the Frontier

by Gloría Anzaldúa

Diverse Voices

The late Gloría Anzaldúa was a writer, poet, activist, and instructor of Chicano studies, women's studies, and creative writing at the University of California at Santa Cruz. The selection below is from her book Borderlands/La Frontera. In this excerpt, Anzaldúa embraces the use of multiple English and Spanish dialects to express the many cultural and social influences in her life.

"*Pocho*, cultural traitor, you're speaking the oppressor's language by speaking English,

you're ruining the Spanish language." I have been accused by various Latinos and Latinas. Chicano Spanish is considered by the purist and by most Latinos deficient, a mutilation of Spanish.

But Chicano Spanish is a border tongue which developed naturally. Change, *evolución, enriquecimiento de palabras nuevas por invención* or *adopción* have created variants of Chicano Spanish, *un nuevo lenguaje. Un lenguaje que corresponde a un modo de vivir.* Chicano Spanish is not incorrect, it is a living language.

For people who are neither Spanish nor live in a country in which Spanish is the first language; for a people who live in a country in which English is the reigning tongue but who are not Anglo; for a people who cannot entirely identify with either standard (formal, Castilian) Spanish nor standard English, what recourse is left to them but to create their own language? A language which they can connect their identity to, one capable of communicating the realities and values true to themselves—a language with the terms that are neither *español ni ingles*, but both. We speak a patois, a forked tongue, a variation of two languages.

Chicano Spanish sprang out of the Chicanos' need to identify ourselves as a distinct people. We needed a language with which we could communicate with ourselves, a secret language. For some of us, language is a homeland closer than the Southwest—for many Chicanos today live in the Midwest and the East. And because we are a complex, heterogeneous people, we speak many languages. Some of the languages we speak are

1. Standard English
2. Working-class and slang English
3. Standard Spanish
4. Standard Mexican Spanish
5. North Mexican Spanish dialect
6. Chicano Spanish (Texas, New Mexico, Arizona, and California have regional variations)
7. Tex-Mex
8. *Pachuco* (called *caló*)

My "home" tongues are the languages I speak with my sister and brothers, with my friends. They are the last five listed, with 6 and 7 being the closest to my heart. From school, the media, and job situations, I've picked up standard and working class English. From Mamagrande Locha and from reading Spanish and Mexican literature, I've picked up Standard Spanish and Standard Mexican Spanish. From *los recién llegados*, Mexican immigrants, and *braceros*, I have learned the North Mexican dialect. From my parents and Chicanos living in the Valley, I picked up Chicano Texas Spanish, and I speak it with my

mom, younger brother (who married a Mexican and who rarely mixes Spanish with English), aunts, and older relatives.

With Chicanas from *Nuevo Mérico* or Arizona I will speak Chicano Spanish a little, but often they don't understand what I'm saying. With most California Chicanas I speak entirely in English (unless I forget). When I first moved to San Francisco, I'd rattle off something in Spanish, unintentionally embarrassing them. Often it is only with another Chicana *tejano* that I can talk freely.

Words distorted by English are known as anglicisms or *pochismos*. The *pocho* is an anglicized Mexican or American of Mexican origin who speaks Spanish with an accent characteristic of North Americans and who distorts and reconstructs the language according to the influence of English. Tex-Mex, or Spanglish, comes most naturally to me. I may switch back and forth from English to Spanish in the same sentence or in the same word. With my sister and my brother Nune and with Chicano *tejano* contemporaries I speak in Tex-Mex.

From kids and people my own age I picked up *Pachuco*. *Pachuco* (the language of the zoot suiters) is a language of rebellion, both against Standard Spanish and Standard English. It is a secret language. Adults of the culture and outsiders cannot understand it. It is made up of slang words from both English and Spanish. *Ruca* means girl or woman, *vato* means guy or dude, *chale* means no, *simón* means yes, *churro* is sure, talk is *periquiar, pigionear* means petting, *que gacho* means how nerdy, *ponte águila* means watch out, death is called *la pelona*. Through lack of practice and not having others who can speak it, I've lost most of the *Pachuco* tongue.

Reflective Questions

1. Can you identify ways you adjust your language choices based on who you are speaking with?
2. How are these language choices different and similar to what Gloría Anzaldúa describes?

Excerpted from Gloría Anzaldúa, Borderlands/La Frontera: The New Mestiza. (San Francisco, CA: Aunt Lute Books, 1987, 1999). Reprinted by permission of Aunt Lute Books.

atoll—an atoll," or you can restate the idea using different words, "The test will contain about four essay questions; that is, all the questions on the test will be the kind that require you to discuss material in some detail." Emphasizing through transitions means using words that show the relationship between your ideas. For example, some transitions summarize *(therefore, and so, so, finally, all in all, on the whole, in short, thus, as a result)*, some clarify *(in fact, for example, that is to say, more specifically)*, some forecast *(also, and, likewise, again, in addition, moreover, similarly, further)*, and some indicate changes in direction or provide contrasts *(but, however, on the other hand, still, although, while, no doubt)*.

Use Linguistic Sensitivity

Linguistic sensitivity means choosing language and symbols that demonstrate respect for your listener(s). Through appropriate language, we communicate our respect for those who are different from us. To do so, we need to avoid language our listeners might not understand, as well as language that might offend them. Linguistic sensitivity can be achieved by using vocabulary our listeners understand, using jargon sparingly, using slang that is appropriate to our listeners and the situation, using inclusive language and using language that is not offensive.

> How can you phrase your messages to demonstrate linguistic sensitivity?

1. **Adapt your vocabulary to the level of your listener.** If you have made a conscious effort to expand your vocabulary, are an avid reader, or have spent time conversing with others who use a large and varied selection of words, then you probably have a large vocabulary. As a speaker, the larger your vocabulary, the more choices you have from which to select the words you want. Having a larger vocabulary, however, can present challenges when communicating with people whose vocabulary is more limited. One strategy for assessing another's vocabulary level is to listen to the types and complexity of words the other person uses and to take your signal from your communication partner. When you have determined that your vocabulary exceeds that of your partner, you can use simpler synonyms for your words or use word phrases composed of more familiar terms. Adjusting your vocabulary to others does not mean talking down to them. Rather, it demonstrates respect and effective communication to select words that others understand.

2. **Use jargon sparingly. Jargon** refers to technical terms whose meanings are understood only by a select group of people based on their shared activity or interests. We may form a special speech community, which develops a common language (jargon) based on a hobby or occupation. Medical practitioners speak a language of their own, which people in the medical field understand and those outside of the medical field do not. The same is true of lawyers, engineers, educators, and virtually all occupations. For instance, lawyers may speak of briefs and cases, but the general public might associate such terms with underwear (briefs) and packages of beer or soda (cases). If you are an avid computer user, you may know many terms that non-computer users do not. Likewise, there are special terms associated with sports, theatre, wine tasting, science fiction, and so on. The key to effective use of jargon is to use it only with people who you know will understand it or to explain the terms the first time you use them. Without explanation, jargon is basically a type of foreign language. Have you ever tried to listen to a professor who uses jargon of his or her field without defining it? If so, how did it affect your learning of the material?

3. **Use slang appropriate to the listeners and to the situation. Slang** is informal vocabulary developed and used by particular groups in society. Slang performs

jargon
technical terms whose meanings are understood only by select groups.

linguistic sensitivity
language choices that demonstrate respect for listener(s).

an important social function. Slang bonds those in an inner circle who use the same words to emphasize a shared experience. But slang simultaneously excludes others who don't share the terminology. The simultaneous inclusion of some and exclusion of others is what makes slang popular with youth and marginalized people in all cultures. Slang may emerge from teenagers, urban life, college life, gangs, or other contexts. A young adult, for instance, might say, "My bad" for "I made a mistake." *Sweet* could be translated as "That's great, fine, or excellent." Using slang appropriately means using it in situations where people understand the slang and avoiding it with people who do not share the slang terminology.

There is a new type of slang developing with digital and Internet technology. Experts in computer-mediated communication (Thurlow, Lengel, & Tomic, 2004) explain that with texting, for example, many of the rules of grammar, style, and spelling are broken. Many people adopt a phonetic type of spelling, which increasingly is understandable to this speech community but may not be understandable to others. Texters know, for example, that *lol* is short for "laugh out loud," *brb* stands for "be right back," and *jk* means "just kidding." Some communication experts who emphasize traditional styles of communication regard this new language of texters as incorrect, deficient, or inferior. Although this shorthand is convenient in cyberspace, using it in other settings could be problematic.

4. **Use inclusive language. Generic language** uses words that apply only to one sex, race, or other group as though they represent everyone. This usage is a problem because it excludes a portion of the population it ostensibly includes. For example, English grammar traditionally used the masculine pronoun *he* to stand for all humans regardless of gender. According to this rule, we would say, "When a person shops, he should have a clear idea of what he wants to buy."

Web Resource 3.2

slang
informal vocabulary used by particular groups in society.

generic language
using words that may apply only to one sex, race, or other group as though they represent everyone.

Why do you suppose someone felt compelled to add *woman* to this sign?

Jeffrey Blankfort/Jeroboam

Don Imus and Three Extreme Curse Words

Pop Comm!

UPI Photo/Monika Graff/Landov

On April 4, 2007, shock jock and member of the National Broadcasters Hall of Fame, Don Imus ignited a firestorm of criticism that eventually led to his firing and to a national discussion of offensive language in music and broadcasting. During his morning program on MSNBC he called the 2006–2007 Rutgers women's basketball team a bunch of "nappy-headed hos."[1] Lewd and misogynistic language has been a hallmark of both shock radio personalities and hip-hop artists for years. But Imus crossed a line when, as a white man, he used words common to hip-hop music to describe a group of highly accomplished young women, eight of whom were black. The Rutgers women's basketball team had overcome considerable odds as individuals and as a team and had made it to the finals of the NCAA tournament.[2] Yet in discussing them on his program, Imus's misogynistic comments demeaned both the women and their accomplishments.

Coach C. Vivian Stringer and the Rutgers's administration refused to let this hate speech go unchallenged. Coach Stringer's coaching philosophy is based on teaching her players to first respect themselves and once they have accomplished this to never let anyone else disrespect them.[3] So it was not surprising that Rutgers quickly called a press conference during which Coach Stringer, called Mr. Imus on his "racist and

sexist remarks that are deplorable, despicable and unconscionable." Several of the players also spoke of the personal pain that Imus's comments had caused. "This week and last, we should have been celebrating our accomplishments the past season," said Heather Zurich, a sophomore forward from Montvale, New Jersey. "We fought, we persevered, and most of all, we believed in ourselves. But all of our accomplishments were lost; our moment was taken away. We were stripped of this moment by the degrading comments made by Mr. Imus. My team did nothing to deserve Mr. Imus's... deplorable comments."[4]

Coach Stringer's reaction was mirrored by many influential media watchers and in the days and months that followed the country debated not only the Imus incident but also the causes, consequences, and use of crude, demeaning, obscene, racist, and misogynistic speech found in hip-hop lyrics and on shock talk radio. Within days, Al Sharpton, the NAACP, the National Association of Black Journalists, the National Organization for Women, and the Hip-Hop Summit Action Network all weighed in on the controversy.

The Hip-Hop Summit Action Network, a nonprofit nonpartisan national coalition of hip-hop artists, entertainment industry leaders, education advocates, civil rights proponents, and youth leaders was particularly active in the debate.[5] On April 13 Russell Simmons, chairman of the Hip-Hop Summit Action Network, and Benjamin Chavis, president, issued a joint statement in which they tried to differentiate between the use of derogatory and misogynistic speech within the artistic and cultural realm of hip-hop music and the use of the same language in other contexts: "Don Imus is not a hip-hop artist or a poet. Hip-hop artists rap about what they see, hear and feel around them, their experience of the world.... Language can be a powerful tool. That is why one's intention, when using the power of language, should be made clear. Comparing Don Imus's language with hip-hop artists' poetic expression is misguided and inaccurate and feeds into a mindset that can be a catalyst for unwarranted, rampant censorship."[6]

But the following week after hosting a private closed door meeting with executives of the recording industry, Mr. Simons and Dr. Hooks appear to have had a change of heart and they issued three recommendations to the recording and broadcasting industries. In their communiqué the men were careful to acknowledge that the recommendations were not attempts at censorship but rather recommendations for "corporate social responsibility of the industry to voluntarily show respect to African Americans and other people of color, African American women and to all women in lyrics and images." The first of the three recommendations was "that the recording and broadcast industries voluntarily remove/bleep/delete the misogynistic words *bitch* and *ho* and the racially offensive word *nigger*. Going forward, these three words should be considered with the same objections to obscenity as 'extreme curse words.' The words *bitch* and *ho* are utterly derogatory and disrespectful of the

painful, hurtful, misogyny that, in particular, African American women have experienced in the United States as part of the history of oppression, inequality, and suffering of women. The word *nigger* is a racially derogatory term that disrespects the pain, suffering, history of racial oppression, and multiple forms of racism against African Americans and other people of color."[7]

By September when the U.S. House of Representatives Energy and Commerce Subcommittee held its hearing titled "From Imus to Industry: The business of stereotypes and degrading images" the public had moved on to other issues.[8]

On Monday December 3, 2007 Don Imus returned to the air with a new early morning talk show on WABC-AM. And in August 2008 hip-hop artist Ludacris released a song titled "Politics as Usual" in which he supported Barack Obama's bid for president while referring to Senator Hillary Clinton as a "bitch." Although there was extensive mainstream media coverage of Imus's return and his subsequent questionable comments about Adam (PacMan) Jones, coverage of Ludacris's misogynistic comment about Senato Clinton seemed to only be covered by the conservative press like FOX News.

[1]Carr, David. (2007, April 7). Network condemns remarks by Imus." *New York Times.* Retrieved from http://www.nytimes.com/2007/04/07/arts/television/07imus.html

[2]Newman, Maria. (2007, April 10). Rutgers women to meet with Imus over remark." *New York Times.* Retrieved from http://www.nytimes.com/2007/04/10/business/media/10cnd-imus.html?hp

[3]C. Vivian Stringer took the Imus firestorm in stride. (2008, March 1). *New York Daily News.* Retrieved from http://www.nydailynews.com/entertainment/arts/2008/03/02/2008-03-02_c_vivian_stringer_took_the_imus_firestor.html

[4]Newman, op. cit.

[5]Hip-Hop Summit Action Network. (2007April 13) Differentiating between Don Imus and hip hop: A statement from Russell Simmons, Chairman, and Dr. Benjamin Chavis, President of the Hip-Hop Summit Action Network." Retrieved from http://hsan.org/Content/Main. aspx?PageId=242

[6]Hip-Hop Summit Action Network. Mission statement. Retrieved from http://www.hsan.org/content/main.aspx?pageid=7

[7]Hip-Hop Summit Action Network. (2007, April 23). Recommendation to the recording and broadcast industries: A statement by Russell Simmons and Dr. Benjamin Chavis on behalf of the Hip-Hop Summit Action Network. Retrieved from http://hsan.org/Content/Main. aspx?PageId=246]]

[8]Abrams, J. (2007, Sept. 25). House panel debates hip-hop lyrics. *USA Today.com.* Retrieved from http://www.usatoday.com/news/washington/2007-09-25-3649050705_x.htm

Despite traditional usage, it is hard to picture people of both sexes when we hear the masculine pronoun *he*.

The following techniques can help you be more inclusive: First, use plurals. For instance, instead of saying, "Because a doctor has high status, his views may be believed regardless of the topic," you could say, "Because doctors have high status, their views may be believed regardless of the topic." Second, use both male and female pronouns: "Because a doctor has high status, his or her views may be believed regardless of the topic." Stewart, Cooper, Stewart, and Friedley (1998) cite research showing that when speakers refer to people using "he and she," and to a lesser extent "they," listeners often visualize *both* women and men (p. 68). Thus, when speakers avoid generic language, it's more likely that listeners will perceive a message that is more gender balanced. Third, avoid using words that are gender specific. For most sex-biased expressions, you can use or create suitable alternatives. For instance, use *police officer* instead of *policeman* and substitute *synthetic* for *man-made*. Instead of saying *mankind*, change the wording—for example, change "All of mankind benefits" to "Everyone benefits."

5. Use nonoffensive language. Finally, you can demonstrate linguistic sensitivity by choosing words that do not offend your listeners. Do you swear when you are with your friends but clean up your act when you are with your grandparents? If so, you are self-monitoring your language so that you don't offend your grandma. Just as you modify your speech when you are with your grandmother, so too you should avoid language that is offensive to those you are talking with. The Pop Comm! feature on pages 63–64 describes how shock jocks and hip-hop artists have come under attack for their use of offensive language.

Speech Assignment: Communicate on Your Feet

What Does It Mean?

The Assignment

Following your instructor's instructions, work alone, partner with someone in the class, or form a small group. Make up a nonsensical word and then develop a short speech clarifying its meaning using the tools you have learned in this chapter. If you work with a partner or in a small group, identify a representative to present the speech to the class. After each speech has been presented, ask a volunteer from the audience to paraphrase the meaning of the word.

Guidelines

1. Be sure to include an attention catcher, listener relevance link, speaker credibility, and thesis with preview in your introduction. Be sure to include transitions between each main point. And be sure to restate the thesis with summary of main points and clincher in your conclusion.
2. Be sure to incorporate the concepts for clarifying meaning in ways that are vivid and linguistically sensitive in your speech.

A Question of Ethics

What Would You Do?

One day Heather, Terry, Paul, and Martha stopped at the Student Union Grill before their next class. After they had talked about their class for a few minutes, the conversation shifted to students who were taking the class.

"By the way," Paul said, "do any of you know Fatty?"

"Who?" the group responded in unison.

"The really fat guy who was sitting a couple of seats from me. We've been in a couple of classes together—he's a pretty nice guy."

"What's his name?" Heather asked.

"Carl—but he'll always be Fatty to me."

"Do you call him that to his face?" Terry asked.

"Aw, I'd never say anything like that to him—I wouldn't want to hurt his feelings."

"Well," Martha chimed in, "I'd sure hate to think that you'd call me 'skinny' or 'the bitch' when I wasn't around."

"Come on—what's with you guys?" Paul retorted. "You trying to tell me that you never talk about another person that way when they aren't around?"

"Well," said Terry, "maybe a couple of times—but I've never talked like that about someone I really like."

"Someone you like?" queried Heather. "Why does that make a difference? Do you mean it's OK to trash-talk someone so long as you don't like the person?"

1. Sort out the ethical issues in this case. How ethical is it to call a person you supposedly like by an unflattering name that you would never use if that person were in your presence?

2. From an ethical standpoint, is whether you like a person what determines when such name-calling is OK?

Summary

Language is a body of symbols and the systems for their use in messages that are common to the people of the same language community. Language allows us to perceive the world around us. Through language we designate, label, and define; we evaluate; discuss things outside our immediate experience; and talk about language.

The relationship between language and meaning is complex because the meaning of words varies with people, people interpret words differently based on both denotative and connotative meanings, the context in which words are used affects meaning, and word meanings change over time.

Culture and gender influence how words are used and how we interpret others' words. In low-context cultures, messages are direct and language is specific. In high-context cultures, messages are indirect, general, and ambiguous. Societal expectations of masculinity and femininity influence language.

We can increase language skills by using specific, concrete, and precise language; by providing details and examples, dating information, and indexing generalizations; and by developing verbal vividness and emphasis. We can speak more appropriately by choosing vocabulary the listener understands, using jargon sparingly, using slang situationally, and demonstrating linguistic sensitivity.

Communicate! Active Online Learning

Now that you have read Chapter 3, use your Premium Website for *Communicate!* for quick access to the electronic resources that accompany this text. These resources include

- **Study tools** that will help you assess your learning and prepare for exams (*digital glossary, key term flash cards, review quizzes*).
- **Activities and assignments** that will help you hone your knowledge, analyze communication situations (*Skill Learning Activities*), and build your public speaking skills throughout the course (*Communication on Your Feet speech assignments, Action Step activities*). Many of these activities allow you to compare your answers to those provided by the authors, and, if requested, submit your answers to your instructor.

- **Media resources** that will help you explore communication concepts online (*Web Resources*), develop your speech outlines (*Speech Builder Express 3.0*), watch and critique videos of communication situations and sample speeches (*Interactive Video Activities*), upload your speech videos for peer reviewing and critique other students' speeches (*Speech Studio online speech review tool*), and download chapter review so you can study when and where you'd like (*Audio Study Tools*).

This chapter's Key Terms, Skill Learning Activities, and Web Resources are also featured on the following pages, and you can find this chapter's Communicate on Your Feet assignment and Skill Building activity in the body of the chapter.

Key Terms

concrete words (53)
connotation (50)
dating information (54)
denotation (50)
emphasis (56)
feminine styles of language (52)
generic language (59)
high-context cultures (51)

indexing generalizations (54)
jargon (58)
language (48)
linguistic sensitivity (58)
low-context cultures (51)
masculine styles of language (52)
metaphor (55)
precise words (53)
Sapir–Whorf hypothesis (48)

simile (55)
slang (59)
specific words (53)
speech community (48)
syntactic context (50)
vivid wording (55)
words (48)

Skill Learning Activities

3.1: Identifying Specific Language (54)

Pick an article or essay from your favorite magazine (either the print or online version). Read through the piece, highlighting instances in which the writer uses concrete words and precise words. Also identify places in which the writer employs abstractions or generalizations that could be made more specific if they were expressed with either concrete or precise words.

3.2: Dating and Indexing Messages (54)

Read the examples below and practice adjusting messages so that they are dated or indexed. After

writing your first draft, check to make sure that your revision is more concrete, precise, and provides examples and details. Now read your response aloud. Does it sound natural? If not, revise it until it does.

When you're done with this activity, compare your answers to the authors' at the Premium Website for *Communicate!* Look for them in the Skill Learning activities for Chapter 3.

1. Oh, Jamie's an accounting major, so I'm sure she keeps her checkbook balanced.
2. Forget taking statistics; it's an impossible course.
3. Never trying talking to Jim in the morning; he's always grouchy.

4. Don't bother to buy that book for class. You'll never use it.

5. I can't believe you bought a dog. I mean, all they do is shed.

3.3: Similes and Metaphors (56)

Over the next three days, as you read books, newspapers, and magazine articles and listen to people around you talk, make notes of both the trite and original similes and metaphors you hear. Choose three that you thought were particularly vivid. Write a paragraph in which you briefly describe how and why they impressed you.

3.4: Clarifying General Statements (57)

See page 57 in this chapter. When you're done with this activity, compare your answers to the authors' at the Premium Website for *Communicate!* Look for them in the Skill Learning activities for Chapter 3.

Web Resources

3.1: Merriam-Webster Online (54)

Merriam-Webster's online dictionary and thesaurus is an excellent resource that can help you not only at school but also in the workplace.

3.2: Slang Dictionary (59)

The Online Slang Dictionary is a collaborative project that features slang contributed by people from all around the world.

Archives du 7eme Art/Photos 12/Alamy

Communicating Nonverbally

Questions you will be able to answer after reading this chapter:

- What are the characteristics of nonverbal communication?
- In what ways do we communicate nonverbally with our bodies?
- In what ways do we communicate nonverbally with our voices?
- In what ways do we communicate nonverbally with our use of space?
- In what ways do we communicate nonverbally with our use of time?
- In what ways do we communicate nonverbally with our appearance?
- What can you do to improve your nonverbal communication skills?

"You don't want me to buy that denim jacket we looked at this morning, do you?" Clay asked.

"What do you mean 'I don't want you to'?" Maya replied.

"You've got that look on your face."

"What look?"

"You know the look—the one you always get on your face when you don't want me to do something I want to do. But I'm going to get that jacket anyway."

"I don't know what you're talking about, Clay."

"Sure you do. You know how I can tell? Because now you're embarrassed that I know and so you're acting weird."

"I'm not acting weird."

"Oh yes you are."

"Clay, you're making me angry."

"You're just saying that because I know you too well and it bothers you."

"Know me too well? I really don't care whether you get that jacket or not."

"Of course you do. You don't have to tell me in words."

"Clay, it's your decision. If you want to get the jacket, get it."

"Well, I don't think I want to—but don't think you changed my mind."

We've all heard—and said—"actions speak louder than words." In fact, actions are so important to our communication that researchers have estimated that in face-to-face communication as much as 60 percent of the social meaning is a result of nonverbal behavior (Burgoon & Bacue, 2003, p. 179). In other words, the meaning we assign to any communication is based on both the content of the verbal message and our interpretation of the nonverbal behavior that accompanies and surrounds the verbal message. And, as Clay found out, interpreting nonverbal behaviors is not always the easiest thing to do.

We begin this chapter by briefly identifying the characteristics of nonverbal communication. Next, we describe the types of nonverbal information we use to communicate with others: use of body (kinesics), use of voice (paralanguage), use of space (proxemics), use of time (chronemics), and self-presentation cues (appearance, including clothing and grooming). Finally, we offer suggestions to help you improve your clarity in sending nonverbal messages and your accuracy in interpreting the nonverbal messages you receive from others.

In the broadest sense, the term *nonverbal communication* describes all human communication messages that transcend spoken or written words (Knapp & Hall, 2006). Specifically, **nonverbal communication behaviors** are those signals that typically accompany our verbal message; our eyes and face, our gestures, our use of voice, and even our appearance. These behaviors are usually interpreted as intentional and may have agreed-upon interpretations in a particular culture or speech community (Burgoon & Hoobler, 2002, p. 244).

The widespread use of computer-mediated communication (CMC—e-mail, Facebook, blogs, texting, and so forth) has highlighted nonverbal communication's role in clarifying meaning and conveying emotion. It has become obvious that when CMC is limited to only words, chances for misunderstanding skyrocket (Olaniran, 2002 & 2003). Recognition of this fact led CMC users to improvise and create **emoticons**: symbolic pictures made with keyboard characters that represent the emotional tone that nonverbal behaviors add to face-to-face verbal messages.

nonverbal communication behaviors
bodily actions and vocal qualities that typically accompany a verbal message.

emoticons
typed symbols that convey emotional aspects of an online message.

Ei Katsumata-CMC/Alamy

Nonverbal communication is so important that we've developed emoticons to represent it in our computer-mediated messages.

Characteristics of Nonverbal Communication

When used effectively, nonverbal communication helps clarify what we are trying to convey verbally. Nonverbal communication has four important characteristics: it is inevitable, it is the primary conveyer of emotions, it is multichanneled, and it is ambiguous.

First, nonverbal communication is *inevitable*. In their germinal book *Pragmatics of Human Communication*, Watzlawick, Bavelas, and Jackson (1967) coined the phrase "We cannot NOT communicate." Though grammatically awkward, this phrase captures the essence of what we mean when we say that nonverbal communication is inevitable. If you are in the presence of someone else, your nonverbal behaviors (whether intentional or not) are sending messages. Moreover, although we can choose what we say in our verbal message, we often don't control our nonverbal behavior and how it is interpreted. When Austin yawns and stares off into the distance during class, his classmates will notice this behavior and assign meaning to it. One classmate may interpret it as a sign of boredom, another might see it as a sign of fatigue, and yet another may view it as a message of disrespect. Meanwhile, Austin may be oblivious to all of the messages his behavior is sending. Have you ever noticed a classmate checking e-mail or Facebook during class? How did you interpret what you saw? Have you ever done this during a class? If so, what possible messages might your behavior be sending to your instructor and classmates?

Second, nonverbal communication is the *primary conveyor of our emotions*. When we listen to others, we base our interpretation of their feelings and emotions almost totally on their nonverbal behavior. In fact, about 93 percent of the emotional meaning of messages is conveyed nonverbally (Mehrabian, 1972). So, when Janelle says, "I'm fine, but thanks for asking," her sister Renee will understand the real message based on the nonverbal behaviors that accompany it. For example, if Janelle uses a sarcastic tone, Renee may decide that Janelle is angry about something. If Janelle sighs, averts her eyes, tears up, and almost whispers her message, Renee may decide that Janelle is sad and emotionally upset.

Third, nonverbal communication is *multichanneled*. We perceive meaning from a variety of nonverbal behaviors including posture, gestures, body movements, appearance, and vocal mannerisms. When we interpret nonverbal behavior, we usually base our perception on a combination of these behaviors. So, when Anna observes Mimi's failure to sustain eye contact, her bowed head, and her repetitive toe-stubbing in the dirt, she may decide that her daughter is lying about not hitting her brother. The fact that nonverbal communication is multichanneled is one reason people are more likely to believe nonverbal communication when nonverbal behaviors contradict the verbal message (Burgoon, Blair, & Strom, 2008).

Finally, nonverbal communication is *ambiguous*. Very few nonverbal behaviors mean the same thing to everyone. The meaning of one nonverbal behavior can vary, for example, based on culture, sex, gender, and even context or situation. For example, in mainstream American culture, direct eye contact tends to be understood as a sign of respect. That's why parents often tell their children, "Look at me when I'm talking to you." In many Native American, Latin American, Caribbean, and African cultures, however, a direct gaze can be interpreted as disrespectful if the speaker is a superior. In this case, averting one's eyes signals respect. Not only can the meaning of a nonverbal behavior vary in different cultures, but the meaning of the same nonverbal behavior also can differ based on the situation. For example, a furrowed brow might convey Byron's confusion when he did not understand his professor's explanation of the assignment, or Monica's anger when she discovered she did not get the internship she had worked so hard for, or Max's disgust when he was dissecting a frog during biology lab.

What are the characteristics of nonverbal communication?

kinesics
the interpretation of how body motions communicate.

gestures
movements of our hands, arms, and fingers that we use to describe or to emphasize.

illustrators
gestures that augment a verbal message.

emblems
gestures can substitute for words.

Web Resource 4.1

Types of Nonverbal Communication

There are a variety of types of nonverbal messages that we interpret from others and display ourselves. These include the use of the body (kinesics), the voice (vocalics/paralanguage), space (proxemics), and time (chronemics), as well as self-presentation cues.

In what ways do we communicate nonverbally with our bodies?

Use of Body: Kinesics

Of all the research on nonverbal behavior, you are probably most familiar with **kinesics**, the technical name for the interpretation of what and how body motions communicate (Birdwhistell, 1970). Body motions are movements of the body or body parts that others interpret and assign meaning to. These include gestures, eye contact, facial expression, posture, and touch.

Gestures

Gestures are the movements of our hands, arms, and fingers to describe or emphasize a point. People vary, however, in the amount of gesturing that accompanies their spoken messages; for example, some people "talk with their hands" far more than others. Unfortunately, using our hands too much can defeat our purpose and distract listeners from the message we are trying to convey. Some gestures, called **illustrators**, augment the verbal message. When you say "about this high" or "nearly this round," your listeners expect to see a gesture accompanying your verbal description. Other gestures, called **emblems**, can stand alone and substitute completely for words. When you raise your finger and place it vertically across your lips, it signifies "Quiet." An emblem has an automatic agreed-upon meaning in a particular culture, but the meaning assigned to a specific gesture can vary across cultures. For example, the American hand sign for "OK" has an obscene sexual meaning in some European countries and stands for "I'll kill you" in Tunisia. **Adaptors** are gestures that occur unconsciously as a response to a physical need. For example, you may scratch an itch, adjust your glasses, or rub your hands together when they are cold. You do not mean to communicate a message with these gestures, but others do notice

adaptors *gestures that respond to a physical need.*

eye contact or gaze *how and how much we look at people with whom we are communicating.*

oculesics *how and how much we look at others when communicating.*

The same nonverbal cue can mean very different things in different cultures.

and attach meaning to them. Some research suggests differences between how much women and men use adaptors. For example, women tend to play more often with their hair or clothing and tap their fingers more often than men (Pearson, Turner, & West, 1995). Do you know anyone who tends to use a lot of gestures when they talk to you? Does it help or hurt message clarity? Why?

Eye contact

The technical term for **eye contact**, or **gaze**, is **oculesics**. It has to do with how and how much we look at others when we are communicating. Although the amount of eye contact differs from person to person and from situation to situation, studies show that talkers hold eye contact about 40 percent of the time, and listeners nearly 70 percent of the time (Knapp & Hall, 2006).

Christian Steinhausen/Taxi/Getty Images

Our facial expressions are especially important in conveying emotions. What is the message on this face?

Through eye contact, we both express our emotions and monitor what is occurring in the interaction. How we look at a person can convey a range of emotions such as anger, fear, or affection. The saying "The eyes are the windows to the soul" acknowledges how powerfully we express emotions through eye contact. With eye contact, you can tell whether a person or an audience is paying attention to and interested in what you are saying, as well the person's or the audience's reaction to your comments.

A majority of people in the United States and other Western cultures expect those with whom they are communicating to look them in the eye. Samovar, Porter, and McDaniel (2009) explain, however, that direct eye contact is not a custom throughout the world. For instance, in Japan, prolonged eye contact is considered rude, disrespectful, and threatening. For people from many Latin American, Caribbean, and African cultures, avoiding eye contact is a sign of respect.

In the United States, women tend to have more frequent eye contact during conversations than men do (Cegala & Sillars, 1989). Moreover, women tend to hold eye contact longer than men, regardless of the sex of the person they are interacting with (Wood, 2007). It is important to note that these differences, which we have described according to biological sex, are also related to notions of gender and standpoint in society. In other words, people (male or female) will give more eye contact when they are displaying feminine-type behaviors than when they are displaying masculine-type behaviors. Both women and men using a feminine style of communication tend to smile frequently.

Facial expression

Facial expression is the arrangement of facial muscles to communicate emotional states or reactions to messages. Our facial expressions are especially important in conveying the six basic human emotions of happiness, sadness, surprise, fear, anger, and disgust. Studies show that there are many similarities in nonverbal communication across cultures with regard to facial expressions. For instance, a slight raising of the eyebrow communicates recognition, whereas the wrinkling of one's nose communicates repulsion (Martin & Nakayama, 2000, pp. 183–184). The comedic actor Jim Carrey is notorious for his use of exaggerated facial expressions to reveal emotions in his films (for example, *The Mask, Dumb and Dumber, Liar Liar, The Truman Show*, and *Bruce Almighty)*. If you've ever watched the sitcom *Seinfeld*, you may also recall that Kramer (played by Michael Richards) is a master at using facial expressions to make his messages more poignant.

Facial expressions are so important to communicating the emotional part of a message that people often use representative smiley face ☺, sad face ☹, and other emoticons to represent facial expressions when texting, sending e-mail, or posting comments on social networking sites like Facebook (Walther & Parks, 2002).

Posture

Posture is how we position (body orientation) and move our body (body movement). From our posture, others interpret how attentive, respectful, and dominant we are. **Body orientation** refers to posture in relation to other people. Facing another person squarely is called *direct body orientation*. When two people's bodies are at angles to each other, this is called *indirect body orientation*. In many situations, direct body orientation signals attentiveness and respect, and indirect body orientation shows inattentiveness and disrespect. In a job interview, you are likely to sit up straight and face the interviewer directly because you want to communicate your interest and

facial expression
the arrangement of facial muscles to communicate emotional states or reactions to messages.

posture
the position and movement of the body.

body orientation
posture in relation to another person.

respect. Interviewers tend to interpret a slouched posture and indirect body orientation as inattentiveness and disrespect. Yet in other situations, such as talking with friends, a slouched posture and indirect body orientation may be appropriate and may not carry messages about attention or respect. When you are making a speech, an upright stance and squared shoulders will help your audience perceive you as poised and self-confident. So when you are giving a speech, be sure to distribute your weight equally on both feet to appear confident. **Body movement** can be motivated (movement that helps clarify meaning) or unmotivated (movement that distracts listeners from the point being made). Pacing, for example, is unmotivated movement.

Haptics

Haptics is the technical term for what and how touch communicates. Touching behavior is a fundamental aspect of nonverbal communication. We use our hands, our arms, and other body parts to pat, hug, slap, kiss, pinch, stroke, hold, embrace, and tickle others. People differ in their use of touching behavior and their reactions to unsolicited touch from others. Some people like to touch others and be touched; other people do not. How we interpret appropriate and inappropriate touch varies not only among individuals but also varies with culture, sex, and gender.

Although American culture uses relatively little contact, we are likely to shake hands to be sociable and polite, pat a person on the back for encouragement, and hug a person to show love. Still, the kinds and amounts of touching behavior within our society vary widely. Touching behavior that seems appropriate to one person may be perceived as overly intimate or threatening by another. Moreover, the perceived appropriateness of touch differs with the context. Touch that is considered appropriate in private may embarrass a person when done in public or in a large group of people. For example, a couple holding hands while strolling in the park or at a shopping mall might seem appropriate, but kissing and fondling each other might not.

Lots of contact and touching is considered normal behavior in some cultures but not encouraged in others (Samovar, Porter, & McDaniel, 2009). Some cultures in South and Central America, as well as many in southern Europea, encourage contact and engage in frequent touching (Neuliep, 2006). In many Arabic countries, for instance, two grown men walking down the street holding hands is a sign of friendship. In the United States, however, it might be interpreted as a sign of an intimate relationship. Many northern European cultures tend to be medium to low in contact, and many Asian cultures are mainly low-contact cultures. The United States, which is a country of immigrants, is generally perceived to be medium in contact, though there are wide differences between individual Americans due to variations in family heritage.

Some research also suggests that women tend to touch others less than men do, but value touching more than men do. Women view touch as an expressive behavior that demonstrates warmth and affection, whereas men view touch as instrumental behavior, so that touching females is considered as leading to sexual activity (Pearson, West, & Turner, 1995, p. 142). Of course, these are generalizations based on gender and standpoints. They do not apply to every woman and man.

Use of Voice: Vocalics

The interpretation of a verbal message based on the paralinguistic features is called **vocalics. Paralanguage** is the voiced but not verbal part of a spoken message. Paralanguage comprises six vocal characteristics: pitch, volume, rate, quality, intonation, and vocalized pauses.

Skill Learning Activity 4.1

body movement
movement that helps clarify meaning (motivated) or movement that distracts listeners from the point being made (unmotivated).

haptics
what and how touch communicates.

vocalics
the interpretation of the message based on the paralinguistic features.

paralanguage
the voiced but not verbal part of a spoken message.

In what ways do we communicate nonverbally with our voices?

Pitch

Pitch is the highness or lowness of vocal tone. People raise and lower vocal pitch to emphasize ideas and emotions and to indicate question,. People sometimes raise their pitch when they are nervous or afraid. They may lower the pitch to convey peacefulness or sadness (as in a speech given at a funeral), or when they are trying to be forceful. When parents reprimand a child for misbehaving, for example, they typically lower their pitch.

Volume

Volume is the loudness or softness of tone. Whereas some people have booming voices that carry long distances, others are normally soft-spoken. People who speak too loudly run the risk of appearing obnoxious or pushy, whereas people who speak too softly might appear timid and unsure of themselves. Regardless of their normal volume level, however, people also tend to vary their volume depending on the situation, the topic of discussion, and emotional intent. For example, people talk loudly when they wish to be heard in noisy settings. They may speak louder when they are angry and softer when they are being romantic or loving. We should point out here that there are a few cultural and gender variations in the meanings we attach to volume. Samovar, Porter, and McDaniel (2009) suggest, for example, that Arabs tend to speak with a great deal of volume to convey strength and sincerity, whereas soft voices are preferred in Britain, Japan, and Thailand.

Rate

Rate is the speed at which a person speaks. Most people naturally speak between 100 and 200 words per minute. People tend to talk more rapidly when they are happy, frightened, nervous, or excited and more slowly when they are problem solving out loud or are trying to emphasize a point. People who speak too slowly run the risk of boring listeners, and those who speak too quickly may not be intelligible.

Quality (Timbre)

Quality is the sound of a person's voice that distinguishes it from others. Voice quality may be breathy (Marilyn Monroe or Kathleen Turner), strident (Joan Rivers or Marge Simpson), throaty (Nick Nolte or Jack Nicholson), or nasal (Fran Drescher in *The Nanny*). Although each person's voice has a distinct quality, too much breathiness can make people sound frail, too much stridence can make them seem hypertense, too much throatiness can make them seem cold and unsympathetic, and too much nasality can make them sound immature or unintelligent.

Intonation

Intonation is the variety, melody, or inflection in one's voice. Voices with little intonation are described as monotone and tend to bore listeners. If you have ever seen the movie *Ferris Bueller's Day Off*, you may recall the teacher (played by Ben Stein) who is portrayed as boring via a monotone pitch as he questions the class: "Anyone? Anyone? Bueller? Bueller?" Other voices have too much intonation and may be perceived as sing-songy and childlike. Too much intonation is often interpreted as ditzy or even dim-witted. People prefer to listen to voices with a moderate amount of intonation.

In the United States, there are stereotypes about masculine and feminine voices. Masculine voices are expected to be low-pitched and loud, with moderate to low intonation; feminine voices are expected to be higher-pitched, softer in volume, and more expressive. Although both sexes have the option to portray a range of masculine and feminine paralanguage, most people usually conform to the expectations for their sex (Wood, 2007).

pitch
the highness or lowness of vocal tone.

volume
the loudness or softness of tone.

rate
the speed at which a person speaks.

quality
the sound of a person's voice that distinguishes it from others.

intonation
the variety, melody, or inflection in one's voice.

Vocalized pauses

Vocalized pauses are extraneous sounds or words that interrupt fluent speech. The most common vocalized pauses that creep into our speech include "uh," "um," "er," "well," "OK," and those nearly universal interrupters of American conversations, "you know" and "like." At times we may use vocal pauses to hold our turn when we momentarily search for the right word or idea. Because they are not part of the intended message, occasional vocalized pauses are generally ignored by those who are interpreting the message. However, when we begin to use them to excess, listeners are likely to perceive us as nervous or unsure of what we are saying. As the use of vocalized pauses increases, people are less able to understand what we are saying, and they may perceive us as confused and our ideas as not well thought out. For some people, vocalized pauses are so pervasive that listeners are unable to concentrate on the meaning of the message.

We can interpret the paralinguistic part of a message as complementing, supplementing, or contradicting the meaning conveyed by verbal message. So when Joan says, "Well, isn't that an interesting story," how we interpret her meaning will depend on her paralanguage. If she alters her normal voice so that "Well" is varied both in pitch and tone and the rest of her words are spoken in a staccato monotone, we might interpret the vocalics as contradicting the words and perceive her message as sarcasm. But if her voice pitch rises with each word, we might perceive the vocalics as supplementing the message and understand that she is asking a question.

Skill Learning Activity 4.2

Use of Space: Proxemics

Have you ever been in the midst of a conversation with someone who you felt was standoffish or pushy? If you had analyzed your feeling, you might have discovered that your impression stemmed from how far the person chose to stand from you. If the person seemed to be farther away than you are accustomed to, you might have interpreted the distance as aloofness. If the distance was less than you would have expected, you might have felt uncomfortable and perceived the person as being overly familiar or pushy. **Proxemics** is the formal term for how space and distance communicate (Hall, 1968). People will interpret how you use the personal space around you, the physical spaces that you control and occupy, and the things you choose to decorate your space.

Personal space

Personal space is the distance we try to maintain when we interact with other people. Our need for and use of personal space stems from our biological territorial nature, for which space is a protective mechanism. How much space we perceive as appropriate depends on our individual preference, the nature of our relationship to the other person or people, and our culture. Although the absolute amount of space varies from person to person, message to message, and culture to culture, in general the amount of personal space we view as appropriate decreases as the intimacy of our relationship increases. For example, in the dominant U.S. culture, four distinct distances are generally perceived as appropriate and comfortable, depending on the nature of the conversation. *Intimate distance* is defined as up to 18 inches and is appropriate for private conversations between close friends. *Personal distance*, from 18 inches to 4 feet, is the space in which casual conversation occurs. *Social distance*, from 4 to 12 feet, is where impersonal business such as a job interview is conducted. *Public distance* is anything more than 12 feet (Hall, 1966).

> In what ways do we communicate nonverbally with our use of space?

vocalized pauses
extraneous sounds or words that interrupt fluent speech.

proxemics
the interpretation of a person's use of space and distance.

personal space
the distance you try to maintain when you interact with other people.

Robert Azzi - Woodfin Camp

Of greatest concern to us is the intimate distance—that which we regard as appropriate for intimate conversation with close friends, parents, and younger children. People usually become uncomfortable when "outsiders" violate this intimate distance. For instance, in a movie theater that is less than one-quarter full, people will tend to leave one or more seats empty between themselves and others whom they do not know. If a stranger sits right next to us in such a setting, we are likely to feel uncomfortable or threatened and may even move away. Intrusions into our intimate space are acceptable only in certain settings and then only when all involved follow the unwritten rules. For instance, people will tolerate being packed into a crowded elevator or subway and even touching others they do not know, provided that the others follow the "rules." The rules may include standing rigidly, looking at the floor or the indicator above the door, but not making eye contact with others. The rules also include ignoring or pretending that they are not touching.

People have differing concepts of personal space. Although you might find it rude for someone who was not an intimate friend to get this close to you in conversation, these men would find it rude if you backed away.

Skill Learning Activity 4.3

Physical space

Physical space is the part of the physical environment over which we exert control. Our territorial natures not only lead us to maintain personal distance but also to assert ownership claims to parts of the physical space that we occupy. Sometimes we do not realize the ways we claim space as our own; in other instances, we go to great lengths to visibly "mark" our territory. For example, Ramon arrives early for the first day of class, finds an empty desk, and puts his backpack next to it on the floor and his coat on the seat. He then makes a quick trip to the restroom. If someone comes along while Ramon is gone, moves Ramon's backpack and coat, and sits down at the desk, that person is violating what Ramon has marked as his territory. If you regularly take the same seat in a class, that habit becomes a type of marker, signaling to others that a particular seat location is yours. Other students will often leave that seat empty because they have perceived it as yours. Not only can we interpret someone's ownership of space by their markers, but we also can understand a person's status in a group by noting where the person sits and the amount of space over which ownership is claimed. In a well-established group, people with differing opinions will often choose to sit on opposite sides of the table, while allies will sit in adjacent spots. So if you are observant, you can tell where people stand on an issue by noticing where they choose to sit. Many other meanings can be discerned from how people use physical space. Have you ever attended a middle-school dance and noticed how the boys typically sit on one side of the room and the girls on the other? If so, what might that be communicating?

physical space
the physical environment over which you exert control.

artifacts
objects and possessions we use to decorate the physical space we control.

Artifacts

Artifacts are the objects and possessions we use to decorate the physical space we control. When others enter our homes, our offices, or our dorm rooms, they look around and notice what objects we have chosen to place in the space and how we have arranged them. Then they assign meaning to what they see. For example, when Katie visited her boyfriend, Peter, at school, the first thing she noticed was a picture on his bulletin board of him hugging a cute woman she did not recognize. The second thing she noticed was that the framed picture she had given him of her before he left for school was nowhere to be found. From this, she concluded that Peter wasn't honoring his promise not to see anyone at school.

The way we arrange the artifacts in our space also can nonverbally communicate to others. Professors and businesspeople have learned that by choosing and arranging the artifacts in their space, they can influence interactions. We once knew a professor who was very softhearted. So when he had to handle the students who were petitioning to enter closed classes, he turned his desk, which normally faced the window, so that it was directly in front of the door. That way, the students couldn't get into his office, sit down, and break his resolve with their sad stories. Instead, they had to plead their case standing in the very public hall. In this case, his desk served as a barrier and protected him from his softhearted self.

People choose artifacts not just for their function but also for the message that the objects convey about them. When Lee, the baby of his family, got his first job, the first items he purchased for his new apartment were a large flat-screen TV and a stuffed leather couch and chair. He chose these primarily to impress his older and already successful brother. Whether the artifacts you choose are conscious attempts to impress or simply reflect your taste, when others enter your space, they will notice the artifacts and draw conclusions. Have you ever gone to visit someone and been turned off by how messy or dirty their home was? Why? What did their artifacts communicate to you?

As is the case with most forms of nonverbal communication, one's use of space and territory is associated with culture (Samovar, Porter, & McDaniel, 2009). Western cultures like the United States generally demand more space than do collectivist cultures such as India, China, and Japan and will defend space more strongly. Seating and furniture placement may also vary by cultural expectations. For example, Americans in groups tend to talk to those seated opposite them, but Chinese prefer to talk to those seated next to them. Furniture arrangement in the United States and Germany often emphasizes privacy. In France and Japan, furniture is typically arranged for group conversation or participation.

Use of Time: Chronemics

Chronemics is how we interpret use of time and is based largely on cultural context (Hall, 1959). People from Western cultures tend to be very time conscious. We carry daily planners and wear digital watches so we can arrive at precisely the "right time." People from many other cultures are far less time conscious. In some cultures, for example Mexican, it's rare to specify an exact time for guests to arrive for dinner. In another example, American executives tend to get right down to business and finish quickly, whereas Japanese executives expect to devote time to social interaction first (Samovar, Porter, & McDaniel, 2009).

Moreover, people can have either a monochronic or a polychronic orientation to time. Those of us with a **monochronic time orientation** tend to concentrate our efforts on one task, and only when it is finished or when the time we have allotted to it is over, do we move on to another task. If we are monochronic, we see time as "real" and think about "spending time," "losing time," and so on. As a result, monochronic people subordinate interpersonal relationships to their schedule (Dahl, 2004, p. 11). When Margarite's sister comes into the room and interrupts her study time to share some good news, Margarite, who is monochronic, screams, "Get out!

> In what ways do we nonverbally communicate with our use of time?

chronemics
the interpretation of a person's use of time.

monochronic time orientation
a time orientation that emphasizes doing one thing at a time.

polychronic time orientation
a time orientation that emphasizes doing multiple things at once.

Can't you see I'm studying!" Others of us with a **polychronic time orientation** tend to tackle multiple tasks at once. For example, while writing a paper, we might periodically check our e-mail and Facebook messages and cook dinner too. Polychronic people see time as flexible and fluid and view appointment times and schedules as variable and subordinate to interpersonal relationships; they easily alter or adapt their schedule to meet the needs of their relationships (Dahl, 2004, p. 11). For example, George, who is polychronic, shows up for a noon lunch with Raoul at 12:47 p.m. because as he was leaving his office, his coworker stopped him to ask for help on a problem.

How Margarite's sister or Raoul interpreted the time behavior they experienced depends on their time orientation. If Margarite's sister is also monochronic, she probably apologized, perceiving her own behavior to have been at fault. If Raoul is polychronic, he will not be offended by George's late arrival because he will view George's delay as understandable. We tend to view others' use of time through the lens of the culture from which we come. So if we are monochronic in our orientation to time, we will view the polychronic time behavior of someone else as being "rude" and vice versa.

As you probably recognize, the dominant U.S. culture has a monochronic time orientation; Swiss and German cultures tend to be even more monochronic. On the other hand, many Latin American and Arab cultures have a polychronic orientation. Immigration has led to an influx of Arab workers into northern Europe and of Latin American workers into the United States. As a result, you are quite likely to encounter people whose use of time is different from your own. Dr. Charles Okigbo, talks about moving to and from what he calls "African time" to "American time" in the Diverse Voices feature entitled "Chronemics."

Self-Presentation Cues

People learn a lot about us based on how we look. This includes our physical appearance as well as our clothing and grooming.

Physical Appearance

People make judgments about others based on how they look. We can control our physique to some extent through exercise, diet, cosmetic surgery, and so on. But we also inherit much of our physical appearance, including our body type and physical features such as hair and eyes. Our body is one of the first things that others notice about us, and there are culture-based stereotypes associated with each of the three general body shapes. **Endomorphs,** who are shaped round and heavy, are stereotyped as kind, gentle, and jovial. **Mesomorphs,** who are muscular and strong, are believed to be energetic, outgoing, and confident. **Ectomorphs,** whose bodies are lean and have little muscle development, are stereotyped as brainy, anxious, and cautious. Although not everyone fits perfectly into one of these categories, each person tends toward one body type. Even though these stereotypes are far from accurate, there is ample anecdotal evidence to suggest that many of us form our first impressions based on body type stereotypes.

Clothing and Grooming

Our clothing and personal grooming communicate a message about us. Today, more than ever, people use clothing choices, body art, and other personal grooming to communicate who they are and what they stand for. Likewise, when we meet someone, we are likely to form our impression of them from how they are dressed and groomed. Because clothing and grooming can be altered to suit the

---

In what ways do we communicate non verbally with our appearance?

endomorph
round and heavy body type.

mesomorph
muscular and athletic body type.

ectomorph
lean and little muscle development.

Chronemics

by Charles Okigbo

Professor of Communication, North Dakota State University and Head, Policy Engagement & Communication African Population and Health Research Center Nairobi, Kenya

It is ironical that time is universal in the sense that every society understands the passage of time, which is also connected to growth, aging, and transitions from one life stage to another. And yet, the concept of time is so varied from one society to another. I have experienced the sameness and variation in understanding or appreciating time in my life history, starting from growing up in Nigeria, coming to the United States for higher education, and traveling between the United States and different African countries. In much of Africa, there are two time modes—cultural time, which is imprecise, and Western or, as we call it in Nigeria, "English" time. In Nigeria, we call this precise clock-based accounting for time "English time" because the British colonized us. Other African countries that had different colonists might call it by a different name.

Time in much of traditional Africa is seen as an inexhaustible resource that flows endlessly and is hardly in short supply. Growing up in my Igbo village in southeastern Nigeria, the setting for Chinua Achebe's novel, *Things Fall Apart*, I saw my people mark time with the rising and setting of the sun. Longer periods were marked by the rainy and dry seasons, which could come late or early, and people's ages were gauged by historic events such as the world wars, the invasion of locusts, or the British colonialists' confiscation of all guns. Such loose characterization meant that precision was not possible. I vividly remember my people saying with utmost imprecision that a morning meeting would start "after sunrise" or "at the first cockcrow" or "after the morning

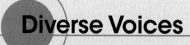

market." Whereas this would appear confusing and imprecise to Western time observers, to us, it presented no problems at all.

My first experience with Western time was when I went to kindergarten and later elementary school. We were taught to be punctual, and tardiness exacted strict sanctions, usually severe flogging. The severity of the punishment depended on how late one came to school.

When I came to the United States in 1978 for the first time for graduate studies at Ohio University, I was already comfortable with Western time and never had any problem with punctuality. In fact, many Africans in the United States who come from backgrounds of cultural time are often hypersensitive about punctuality issues and tend to be too punctual. This may be a case of overcompensating to avoid relapsing to cultural time. The adjustment to Western time can present some challenges, especially in situations when we have exclusive African events in the United States. For example, I remember from my personal experiences as an African student and teacher in the United States that many meetings organized by Nigerian or other African students hardly ever started "on time" by Western standards because we often relapsed to our cultural time for exclusively African events.

We also tend to operate by cultural time when hosting exclusively African events in U.S. communities. For example, the Igbo Cultural Association in Minneapolis (Umunne) holds an annual masquerade festival in the fall. Even when the published program states that the celebration will start at 4:00 p.m., the organizers and their African guests know that the event will probably begin about 8:00 p.m. or so, because it is largely an exclusive African event.

So, we seem capable of successfully weaving in and out of cultural time depending on

(Continued)

our expectation of whether the occasion is for Africans only or for Africans and "others." When the "others" are people with Western time orientation, we make every effort to be punctual. But when they are people who seem to share our sense of time, we respond accordingly. This represents a chronemics co-orientation, by which I mean that unconsciously we size up the other to know where to position them on the continuum of "cultural" and "Western" time. If they are closer to the former, we expect them to have a more relaxed approach to time, but if they are closer to the latter, we try to be punctual and seriously time conscious in dealing with them.

The tendency is for people to adjust their sense of time depending on the situation or the expectation of the audience. Professional meetings, conferences, even appointments with doctors or lawyers are loosely treated depending on one's expectations of how the other side sees time.

I must say that we Africans are not the only ones who could benefit from engaging in chronemics co-orientation. People who are usually Western in their approach to keeping appointments may decide not to be so punctual if they expect that the other party will keep them waiting. For example, in the 1960s my village, Ojoto, was so small that we had no resident priest for the local church. Every Sunday, an Irish priest came from the cathedral in Onitsha to conduct mass. Whereas many priests observed Western time and were usually punctual and expected us to be as well, Revered Father Nicholson, went so native in his sense of time that the joke then became that if Fr. Nicholson was the celebrant for the Sunday mass, you could go to the market and do five other chores before coming to his Sunday morning mass, and you would not be late! So, we could say that whereas sometimes Africans may need to adjust to the precision of Western time, at other times and in other situations, other people, including Europeans and Americans who are dealing with exclusive

African groups, should consider adjusting to cultural time.

I have noticed that many African Americans in the United States are similar to Africans from the continent with respect to time consciousness, and many Native Americans in North Dakota and Minnesota share a similar cultural time orientation. So when African Americans host a party where most of the guests are also African American, the invitation may state that the party starts at 7:00 p.m., but the host may not expect most guests to arrive until after 9:30 p.m.

While both cultural time and Western time continue to guide human behavior, increasing globalization and the information technological revolution are dictating a global approach to time that runs by the precision of the clock rather than by the natural rhythms of the rising or setting of the sun or the beginning or ending of seasons. Whether this move is ultimately in the best interest of humankind remains to be seen.

There appears to be no rule of thumb about how Africans take time. In fact, we have obviously overgeneralized in talking about "African time," knowing that it is impossible to have all 53 African countries or 750 million African peoples adopt a uniform outlook on how to use time. The expectation is that educated Africans adopt Western time more than their uneducated compatriots, but this is also an overgeneralization since there are many educated Africans who have a very poor sense of punctuality, whereas there are uneducated ones to whom punctuality is second nature. There are many exceptions to any generalization. My personal experience, which has many limitations, is that being tardy is more readily tolerated in Africa, although there are many Africans who value punctuality and cannot stand tardy time keeping. Every culture has people who are punctual and others who are tardy. We have them both in Africa as well.

occasion, we rely heavily on these nonverbal cues to understand who other people are and how to treat them. As a result, you can change how people perceive you by altering your clothing and grooming. For example, a successful sales representative may wear an oversize white T-shirt, baggy shorts, and a backward ball cap when hanging out with his friends; put on khakis and a golf shirt to go to the office; and dress in a formal blue suit to make a major presentation to a potential client group. In each case, he uses what he is wearing to communicate who he is and how others should treat him. Body art (piercings and tattoos) have become quite popular in the United States today. Although body art can be an important means of self-expression, the Pop Comm! feature points out some serious considerations regarding body art and the impression it might make on an employer. Clothing choices vary based on gender, as well. In the United States, feminine clothing is more decorative, and masculine clothing is more functional (Wood, 2007). In professional settings today, masculine clothing (a two-piece suit) is considered most appropriate for both women and men, but women will often wear feminine clothing on a date.

From Wall Street Journal. Permission, Cartoon Features Syndicate. Reprinted by permission.

"Tell me about yourself, Kugelman—your hopes, dreams, career path, and what that damn earring means."

Skill Learning Activity 4.4

Guidelines for Improving Nonverbal Communication

Because nonverbal messages are inevitable, multichanneled, ambiguous, and sometimes unintentional, decoding them accurately can be tricky. Add to this the fact that the meaning for any nonverbal behavior can vary by situation, culture, and gender, and you begin to understand why we so often misread the behavior of others. The following guidelines can help you improve the likelihood that the messages you send will be perceived accurately and that you will accurately interpret the nonverbal messages you receive.

> What can you do to improve your nonverbal communication skills?

Sending Nonverbal Messages

1. **Be conscious of the nonverbal behaviors you are displaying.** Remember that you are always communicating nonverbally. Some nonverbal cues will always be out of your level of consciousness, but you should work to bring more of your nonverbal behavior into your conscious awareness. Pay attention to what you are doing with your body, voice, space, and self-presentation cues. If you initially have difficulty doing this, ask a friend to point out the nonverbal behaviors you are displaying.

Body Art Then and Now: Its Messages and Meanings

Cora Reed, 2009/Used under license from Shutterstock.com

Since ancient times, people have been painting, piercing, scarring, tattooing, and shaping their bodies. In fact, there is no culture that didn't or doesn't use body art to signal people's place in society, mark a special occasion, or just make a fashion statement (American Museum of Natural History, 1999). The body art you see today is simply an extension of ancient human practice that has been adapted to our 21st-century definitions of status, ritual, and beauty.

Body painting is a temporary means of creating a different identity or celebrating a particular occasion. For centuries Eastern cultures have used henna to dye hands and other body parts to celebrate rites of passage such as marriages. Traditionally in India, married women wore a *bindi*, a red spot, between their eyebrows. Native Americans used a variety of natural dyes to paint their bodies in preparation for war. Today, women use cosmetics, sports fans decorate their faces and bodies before big games, and children have their faces painted at community festivals.

Roman soldiers and Masai warriors voluntarily underwent body piercings as a sign of strength. Some tribal cultures had a rite of passage in which the person hangs from large piercings in the limbs or body trunk. Some societies used piercings as a sign of slavery, and others viewed them as signs of beauty or royalty (Schurman, n.d.). Today piercing is voluntary, and common parts of the body to be pierced are the ears and nose. Some people choose to pierce other body parts including eyebrows, tongues, navels, and genitals. Often, piercings are a rite of passage signaling some personal milestone. At a certain age girls may have their ears pierced. Less traditional piercings or multiple piercings may be undertaken as a sign of rebellion or to express membership in a particular subculture.

Scarification is the deliberate cutting or burning of the skin in such a way as to control the scarring and create a pattern or picture. Sometimes the freshly made cuts are purposely irritated so that they form raised or keloid scars. Scarification was widely practiced in Africa, where facial scars could identify a person's ethnic group or family, or just be an individual statement of beauty. The Jewish rite of circumcision practiced since the time of Abraham is a form of scarification. Today, scarification may be part of a fraternity or gang initiation rite. Some individuals use cutting to escape from feeling trapped in an intolerable psychological and emotional situation (Jacobs, 2005). The scars that result from this type of cutting are seen as badges of survival.

2. Be purposeful in your use of nonverbal communication. Sometimes, it is important to control what you are communicating nonverbally. For instance, if you want to be persuasive, you should use nonverbal cues that demonstrate confidence and credibility. These may include direct eye contact, a serious facial expression, a relaxed posture, a loud and low-pitched voice with no vocal interferences, and a professional style of clothing and grooming. Although there are no absolute prescriptions for communicating nonverbally, we can make strategic choices to convey the message we desire.

Tattooing is the oldest form of body art; tattooed mummies have been found in various parts of the world. Tattoos are permanent alterations to the body using inks or dyes, and they are symbolic in nature. Like other body art, tattoos can be either a statement of group solidarity or an expression of individuality. They can be sources of shame or pride. They can be public statements of outsider status or privately enjoyed personal symbols.

Like piercings, tattoos have also been used to mark people who were considered property or inferior in some other way. African American slaves were often tattooed. During World War II, the Nazis tattooed a five-digit number on the inner forearm of Jews and other "undesirables" in concentration camps to strip them of their individual identities. Unlike self-initiated tattoos, which are a source of pride for the wearer, these tattoos were a source of shame. For years after their ordeal, many Holocaust survivors covered their forearms and refused to talk about their experiences. The number on their arm was a grim reminder that they had survived while others had perished.

Today tattoos are losing their outsider status. Celebrities, soccer moms, corporate executives, sports stars, and high school students sport tattoos as statements of individuality and personal aesthetic. Teenagers may "rebel" by having a small butterfly tattooed on their shoulder blade or a Native American–patterned band tattooed on their bicep. Some people have tattoos strategically placed so that they can choose to display them or hide them from view depending on the self they want to portray.

Shaping, another type of body art, is altering the silhouette or shape of the body based on a culturally validated aesthetic (Australian Museum, 2009). Cranial shaping, neck stretching, corsetry, and foot binding have been practiced in various cultures at various times. Native American and African tribes practiced head shaping. In Africa, Burma, and Thailand rings or beaded necklaces are used to give the appearance of an elongated neck ("African Neck Stretching," 2008–2009). Corsetry began in ancient times as a means of protecting the wearer from hernias and other body damage that occurs during strenuous activity. By the time of the Romans, wearing a corset became a sign of lower status. Slaves, who did manual labor, wore corsets while their owners wore flowing garments. In the 16th century, fashionable French women cinched their corsets to achieve a 13-inch waist (Wilson, 2002). For over two thousand years, Chinese girls' feet were bound so that they would have the ideal tiny feet and would be able to marry well (Lim, 2007).

When Madonna donned a merry widow corset, she was just following a practice that is several centuries old. And the Spanx undergarments that many women wear today have their origins in body shaping. But today, we body shape in a variety of additional ways including weight lifting and other workouts that go beyond keeping us healthy. We also body shape through cosmetic surgeries, allowing us to rid ourselves of our familial nose, take years off of our face, or suck off unwanted weight. Some people become addicted to cosmetic surgery, and others develop eating disorders in order to conform their natural bodies to the current definitions of beauty.

When it comes to body art, everything old is new again.

3. Make sure that your nonverbal cues do not distract from your message. When you are not aware of what nonverbal cues you are displaying or when you are anxious, certain nonverbal behaviors may hinder your communication. Fidgeting, tapping your fingers on a table, pacing, mumbling, and using vocal interferences and adaptors can hinder other people's interpretation of your message. Try to use nonverbal behaviors that enhance rather than distract from your message.

4. **Make your nonverbal communication match your verbal communication.** When nonverbal messages contradict verbal messages, people are more likely to believe the nonverbal messages, so it is important to have your verbal and nonverbal messages match. In addition, the various kinds of nonverbal communication behavior should match each other. If you are feeling sad, your voice should be softer and less expressive, and you should avoid smiling, which would contradict your voice. People get confused and frustrated by inconsistent messages.

5. **Adapt your nonverbal behavior to the situation.** Situations vary in their formality, familiarity among the people, and purpose. Just like you would select different language for different situations, you should adapt your nonverbal messages to the situation. Assess what the situation calls for in terms of body motions, paralanguage, proxemics and territory, artifacts, chronemics, and physical appearance. Of course, you already do some situational adapting with nonverbal communication. You would not dress the same way for a wedding as you do to walk the dog. You do not treat your brother's space and territory the same way you treat your doctor's space and territory. The more you can consciously adapt your nonverbal behavior to what seems appropriate to the situation, the more effective you will be as a communicator.

Interpreting Nonverbal Messages

1. **Do not automatically assume that a particular behavior means the same thing to everyone.** There is much room for error when people draw quick conclusions about an aspect of nonverbal behavior. Instead, assume multiple possibilities based on culture, gender, and even individual differences. You may have learned over time that your friend grinds her teeth when she is excited. You may never encounter another person who uses this behavior in this way.

2. **Consider nonverbal behaviors as they relate to the context of the message.** Because the same nonverbal cue can mean different things in different contexts, take the time to consider how it is intended in a given situation. Realize, too, that you might not understand all the details of the situation. One behavior that often offends teachers is a student answering a cell phone during class. Before assuming the worst, however, it might be best if the teacher tried to discover why the student did so. The student might be in the midst of a serious family situation that demanded instant access.

3. **Pay attention to the multiple nonverbal cues being sent and their relationship to the verbal message.** In any one interaction, you are likely to get simultaneous messages from a person's eyes, face, gestures, posture, voice, and use of space and touch. Even in electronic communication, where most nonverbal communication is impossible, facial expression and touch can be communicated through emoticons, paralanguage through capitalization of words, and chronemics through the timing and length of the electronic message. By taking into consideration all nonverbal cues, you will be more effective in interpreting others' messages.

4. **Use perception checking.** The skill of perception checking lets you see if your interpretation of another person's message is accurate. By describing the nonverbal behavior you have noticed and tentatively sharing your interpretation of it, you can get confirmation or correction of your interpretation.

Speech Assignment: Communicate on Your Feet

Communicating Emotions Nonverbally: Encoding and Decoding Skill and Practice

The Assignment

Your instructor will write a simple sentence on the board that you will recite to your classmates while attempting to convey a particular emotion nonverbally. First, you will use only your voice; then you will use your voice and face; and finally you will use your voice, face, and body. The sentence could be as simple as "I had bacon and eggs for breakfast this morning."

1. To find out the emotion you will convey, draw a card from a stack offered by your instructor. Without letting your classmates see, turn the card over to read what emotion is written on the front. Some possible emotions include *anger, excitement, fear, joy, worry*, and *sadness*. Consider how you will use vocalics and kinesics to convey that emotion.
2. When your instructor calls on you, go to the front of the classroom and face the wall (so your classmates cannot see your face). Try to convey that emotion with only your voice while saying the sentence with your back to the class.
3. The class might make some guesses about the emotion you are conveying and give some reasons for their guesses. You should not tell them whether they are correct at this point.
4. Turn around to face your classmates and say the sentence again, this time trying to reinforce the emotion with your face and eyes.
5. The class might again make some guesses and why.
6. Repeat the sentence once more, this time using your voice, face, and body to convey the emotion.
7. The class might again make some guesses and why.
8. Tell them the emotion that was on the card and what you did with your voice, face, and body to convey it.
9. Your instructor may lead a discussion about what worked and didn't, as well as how you could have made the emotional message more clear.

A Question of Ethics

What Would You Do?

After the intramural mixed-doubles tennis matches on Tuesday evening, most of the players adjourned to the campus grill for a drink and a chat. Marquez and Lisa sat down with Barry and Elana, the couple they had lost a match to that night largely because of Elana's improved play. Although Marquez and Lisa were only tennis friends, Barry and Elana had been going out together for much of the season.

After some general conversation about the tournament, Marquez said, "Elana, your serve today was the best I've seen it this year."

"Yeah, I was really impressed. And as you saw, I had trouble handling it," Lisa added.

"And you're getting to the net a lot better too," Marquez added.

"Thanks, guys," Elana said in a tone of gratitude, "I've really been working on it."

"Well, aren't we getting the compliments today," sneered Barry in a sarcastic tone. Then after a pause, he said, "Oh, Elana, would you get my sweater—I left it on that chair by the other table."

"Come on, Barry; you're closer than I am," Elana replied.

Barry got a cold look on his face, moved slightly closer to Elana, and said emphatically, "Get my sweater for me, Elana. Now."

Elana quickly backed away from Barry as she said, "OK, Barry—it's cool," and she then quickly got the sweater for him.

"Gee, isn't she sweet," Barry said to Marquez and Lisa as he grabbed the sweater from Elana.

Lisa and Marquez both looked down at the floor. Then Lisa glanced at Marquez and said, "Well, I'm out of here. I've got a lot to do this evening."

"Let me walk you to your car," Marquez said as he stood up.

"See you next week," they both said in unison as they hurried out the door, leaving Barry and Elana alone at the table.

1. Analyze Barry's nonverbal behavior. What was he attempting to achieve?
2. How do you interpret Lisa's and Marquez's nonverbal reactions to Barry?
3. Was Barry's behavior ethically acceptable? Explain.

Summary

Nonverbal communication refers to the interpretations of bodily actions, vocal qualities, use of space and time, and self-presentation cues. Nonverbal communication is inevitable, multichanneled, intentional or unintentional, possibly ambiguous, and the primary means by which we convey our emotions. The sources of nonverbal messages include use of body motions (kinesics: gestures, eye contact, facial expression, posture, and touch), use of voice (vocalics: pitch, volume, rate, quality and intonation, and vocalized pauses), use of space (proxemics: personal space, physical space, and use of artifacts), use of time (chronemics), and self-presentation cues (physical appearance as well as clothing and grooming).

Although the meanings we attach to nonverbal behaviors are influenced by culture and gender, we can become more adept at sending and interpreting nonverbal messages. In terms of sending nonverbal messages, we can improve by being conscious of the nonverbal behavior we are displaying, by being purposeful in its use, by making sure that our nonverbal cues do not distract from our message, by making our nonverbal communication match our verbal messages, and by adapting our nonverbal behavior to the situation. In terms of receiving nonverbal messages, we can improve by not jumping to conclusions, by acknowledging context, by paying attention to multiple nonverbal cues and their relationship to the verbal message, and by perception checking.

Communicate! Active Online Learning

Now that you have read Chapter 4, use your Premium Website for *Communicate!* for quick access to the electronic resources that accompany this text. These resources include

- **Study tools** that will help you assess your learning and prepare for exams (*digital glossary, key term flash cards, review quizzes*).
- **Activities and assignments** that will help you hone your knowledge, analyze communication situations (*Skill Learning Activities*), and build your public speaking skills throughout the course (*Communication on Your Feet speech assignments, Action Step activities*). Many of these activities allow you to compare your answers to those provided by the authors, and, if requested, submit your answers to your instructor.
- **Media resources** that will help you explore communication concepts online (*Web Resources*), develop your speech outlines (*Speech Builder Express 3.0*), watch and critique videos of communication situations and sample speeches (*Interactive Video Activities*), upload your speech videos for peer reviewing and critique other students' speeches (*Speech Studio online speech review tool*), and download chapter review so you can study when and where you'd like (*Audio Study Tools*).

This chapter's Key Terms, Skill Learning Activities, and Web Resources are also featured on the following pages, and you can find this chapter's Communicate on Your Feet assignment in the body of the chapter.

Key Terms

adaptors (69)
artifacts (74)
body movement (71)
body orientation (70)
chronemics (75)
ectomorph (76)
emblems (68)
emoticons (67)
endomorph (76)
eye contact or gaze (69)
facial expression (70)

gestures (68)
haptics (71)
illustrators (68)
intonation (72)
kinesics (68)
mesomorph (76)
monochronic time orientation (75)
nonverbal communication
    behaviors (67)
oculesics (69)
paralanguage (71)
personal space (73)

physical space (74)
pitch (72)
polychronic time orientation (75)
posture (70)
proxemics (73)
quality (72)
rate (72)
vocalics (71)
vocalized pauses (73)
volume (72)

Skill Learning Activities

4.1: Body Motions (71)

Go to a public place (for example, a restaurant) where you can observe two people having a conversation. You should be close enough so that you can observe their eye contact, facial expression, and gestures, but not close enough to hear what they are saying.

Carefully observe the interaction, with the goal of answering the following questions: What is their relationship? What seems to be the nature of the conversation (social chitchat, plan making, problem solving, argument, intimate discussion)? How does each person feel about the conversation? Do feelings change over the course of the conversation? Is one person more dominant? Take note of the specific nonverbal behaviors that led you to each conclusion, and write a paragraph describing this experience and what you have learned.

To help you complete this activity, you can use the observation sheet provided in your Premium Website for *Communicate!* Look for it in the Skill Learning activities for Chapter 4.

4.2: Vocal Characteristics (73)

Spend a few hours listening to public or talk radio. If possible, listen to a station that broadcasts in a language with which you are unfamiliar. Attempt to block out your awareness of the speakers' words, and instead focus on the meaning communicated by the pitch, volume, rate, and quality of their speech. Be sure to listen to a number of different speakers and record your results in a log. Can you detect any variations in the vocal characteristics of the different speakers? If so, what do you make of these variations and what they say about each speaker's message?

To help you complete this activity, you can use the log sheet provided in your Premium Website for *Communicate!* Look for it in the Skill Learning activities for Chapter 4.

4.3: Violating Intimate Space Norms (74)

Enter a crowded elevator. Get on it and face the back. Make direct eye contact with the person you are standing in front of. When you disembark, record the person's reactions. On the return trip, introduce yourself to the person who is standing next to you and engage in an animated conversation. Record the reaction of the person and others around you. Then get on an empty elevator and stand in the exact center. Do not move when others board. Record their reactions. Be prepared to share what you have observed with your classmates.

4.4: Self-Presentation Audit (79)

The Self-Presentation Audit allows you to analyze the image you project, using the dimensions you have studied in Chapter 4. These include body type, clothing and personal grooming, poise, touch, and use of time. Once you have completed the audit, review how you have described yourself with respect to each of the self-presentation dimensions. Then write a short essay in which you describe how you present yourself, evaluate how satisfied you are with this image, and list what, if any, adjustments to your self-presentation you would like to make so that your self-presentation matches the image you are trying to project.

To complete this activity, you'll need the audit provided in your Premium Website for *Communicate!* Look for it in the Skill Learning activities for Chapter 4.

Web Resources

4.1: Maria Brazil (69)

Maria-Brazil.org is a U.S.-based Web site dedicated to Brazilian culture. The link at your Premium Website will take you to a page on the site that depicts how Brazilians use body language to communicate. How does Brazilian body language compare to body language used in the United States?

Mark Richards/PhotoEdit

Listening and Responding

Questions you will be able to answer after reading this chapter:

- What is listening and why is it important?
- What are the five different types of listening?
- How can you improve your listening skills by focusing your attention?
- How can you improve your listening skills to increase understanding?
- What are three tactics that can help you remember what you hear?
- How can you improve your listening skill of evaluating what you've heard?
- How can you improve your listening skills so that you respond appropriately to what you've heard?

Beth, do you have my opener to the garage? I can't find it and I have to take the car or I'll be late for class."

"No, but it doesn't matter because . . ."

"I can't believe it. I was sure I left it here on the counter last night."

"Bart, it's okay . . ."

"It just figures. Just because I'm in a hurry, I can't find it."

"Bart, I've been trying to tell you, the . . ."

"I swear I put it here on the counter. Did you stuff it in a drawer or move it when you were cleaning the kitchen or something?"

"Bart, chill out. The door's . . ."

"Chill out?! If I'm late, I won't be able to do my presentation and it's worth 50 percent of the course grade! I won't pass the class and I need at least a B to get accepted into the major. Beth, this is a very big deal."

"Bart, I've been trying to tell you . . ."

"Oh sure—I just go in to the professor's office and say, 'By the way, the reason I wasn't in class was that I couldn't find the garage door opener. Can I please do my presentation tomorrow?' I'll sound like a slacker who wasn't ready. There's no way he'll buy that argument even though it's true."

"Bart, listen!!! I've been trying to tell you—I don't know where your opener is, but I went out this morning and knew you would be leaving soon so I left the door open for you."

"Geez, Beth, why didn't you tell me?"

Are you a good listener when you are under pressure? Or, like Bart, do you occasionally find that your mind wanders when others are talking to you? We must not underestimate the importance of listening, because it can provide clarification, connect us to others, build trust and empathy, help us learn and remember material, and improve our ability to evaluate information (Donoghue & Siegel, 2005). We begin this chapter with a discussion of what listening is and the different types of listening. Then, we focus on specific ways you can improve your listening skills during each phase of the listening process.

What Is Listening?

People sometimes make the mistake of thinking listening and hearing are the same thing, but they're not. Hearing is a physiological process, whereas listening is a cognitive process. In other words, listening occurs only when we choose to attach meaning to what we hear. Members of the International Listening Association define **listening** as "the process of receiving, constructing meaning from, and responding to spoken and/or nonverbal messages" (Brownell, 2002, p. 48).

Listening is important for effective communication because 50 percent or more of the time we spend communicating is spent listening (Janusik & Wolvin, 2006). Although most of us have spent a great deal of time learning to read and write, fewer than 2 percent of us have had any formal listening training (Listening Factoid, 2003). According to research by the International Listening Association, even when we try to listen carefully, most of us remember only about 50 percent of what we hear shortly after hearing it and only about 20 percent two days later. One survey of top-level North American executives revealed that 80 percent believe listening is one of the most important skills needed in the corporate environment (Salopek, 1999). It simply makes sense to improve our listening skills.

Types of Listening

Although we spend most of the time we are communicating listening to what others are saying, the type of listening that is required of us depends on the situation. So in order to be an effective listener in different situations, you must first consider your purpose for listening. Scholars have identified five types of listening based on five different purposes. These types are appreciative, discriminative, comprehensive, empathic, and critical listening (Wolvin & Coakley, 1996). Each type of listening requires a different

What is listening and why is it important?

listening
the process of receiving, constructing meaning from, and responding to spoken and/or nonverbal messages.

Monkey Business Images, 2009/Used under license from Shutterstock.Com

Do you ever choose to listen to a particular song just because it makes you feel good? If so, you are engaging in appreciative listening.

degree of psychological processing. By considering your purpose, you can engage in the most appropriate type of listening in a given situation and devote the degree of psychological processing necessary.

What are the five different types of listening?

Appreciative Listening

In an **appreciative listening** situation, your goal is to simply enjoy the thoughts and experiences of others by listening to what they are saying. (Wolvin & Coakley, 1996). With appreciative listening, you do not have to focus as closely or as carefully on specifics as you do in other listening situations. You might use appreciative listening during a casual social conversation while watching a ball game with friends or when listening to your daughter describe the fish she caught on an outing with her grandpa. Most people listen to music in this way. Do you ever turn on the TV or radio just for background sound?

Discriminative Listening

In a **discriminative listening** situation, your goal is to accurately understand the speaker's meaning. At times this involves listening "between the lines" for meaning conveyed in other ways than the words themselves. Discriminative listening requires us to pays attention not only to the words but also to nonverbal cues such as rate, pitch, inflection, volume, voice quality, inflection, and gestures. So when a doctor is explaining the results of a test, a patient not only listens carefully to what the doctor is saying but also pays attention to the nonverbal cues that indicate whether these results are troubling or routine. Likewise, we often choose to support political candidates based on whether, when we listen, we believe that we can trust that they will fulfill their campaign promises. If you've ever questioned the truthfulness of a friend's claim, what nonverbal cues helped convince you they were not telling the whole truth?

appreciative listening
listening for enjoyment.

discriminative listening
listening to understand the meaning of a message.

AP Photo/Rob Carr

What are some nonverbal cues that hot line volunteers can use to show their empathy?

Comprehensive Listening

In a **comprehensive listening** situation, your goal is not only to understand the speaker's message but also to learn, remember, and be able to recall what has been said. We listen comprehensively to professors lecturing about key concepts, speakers at training seminars, and broadcast news reports that provide timely information about traffic conditions.

Empathic Listening

When the situation calls for us to try to understand how someone else is feeling about what they have experienced or are talking about, we use **empathic listening**. Therapists, counselors, psychologists, and psychiatrists engage in empathic listening with their clients as do those who answer telephone hotlines. When your goal is to be a sounding board or help a friend sort through feelings, you will want to begin with empathic listening.

Critical Listening

comprehensive listening
listening to learn or remember.

empathic listening
listening to understand the speakers feelings about the message.

critical listening
listening to evaluate the truthfulness or honesty of a message.

In **critical listening** situations, your ultimate goal is to evaluate the worth of a message. Because you need to hear, understand, evaluate, and assign worth to the message, it requires more psychological processing than the other types. Critical listening is the most demanding of the types of listening because it requires that you understand and remember both the verbal and nonverbal message, assess the speaker's credibility, and effectively analyze the truthfulness of the message. Fortunately, we don't need to engage in critical listening all the time. But when we are talking with salespeople or listening to political candidates, when we are receiving an apology from someone who has violated our trust or when we are being solicited for a donation, we need to engage in critical listening.

Steps in the Listening Process

Listening is a complex process made up of five steps. These steps are (a) attending, (b) understanding, (c) remembering, (d) evaluating, and (e) responding to the message.

Attending

Attending is the process of focusing on what a speaker is saying regardless of the potential distractions of other competing stimuli. Poor listeners have difficulty exercising control over what they attend to, often letting their minds drift to thoughts unrelated to the topic. One reason is that people typically speak at a rate of about 120–150 words per minute, but our brains can process between 400 and 800 words per minute (Wolvin & Coakley, 1996). This means we usually assume we know what a speaker is going to say before he or she finishes saying it, so our mind has lots of time to wander from the message. Moreover, research suggests that the average attention span for adults is 20 minutes or less (Stephens, 1999). Some reports even claim that, thanks to the Internet, our attention span is considerably shorter.

To be a good listener then, you must train yourself to focus on or attend to what people are saying regardless of potential distractions. Let's consider five techniques that can help you improve your attending.

> How can you improve your listening skills by focusing your attention?

1. **Get physically ready to listen.** Good listeners create a physical environment that will aid listening, and they adopt a listening posture. They eliminate distractions from the physical environment. If the music is playing so loudly that it competes with your roommate who is trying to talk with you, turn it down. If you are checking e-mail or Facebook, stop. Shut down the site so you won't be tempted to check it while you are supposed to be listening. Similarly, turn off or silence your cell phone.

    A listening posture is one that moves the listener toward the speaker, allows direct eye contact, and stimulates the senses. For instance, when the professor tells the class that the next bit of information will be on the test, effective listeners are likely to sit upright in their chairs, lean forward slightly, cease any unnecessary physical movement, and look directly at the professor.

2. **Resist mental distractions while you listen.** Block out wandering thoughts when they creep into your head while you listen. These thoughts may stem from a visual distraction associated with something you see (such as a classmate who enters the room while the professor is lecturing), an auditory distraction associated with something you hear (such as classmates chatting beside you during class), or a physical distraction associated with body aches, pains, or discomfort (such as wondering what you'll eat for lunch because your stomach is growling) Obviously, the more you can do to eliminate the potential for mental distractions, the less likely you'll be to experience wandering thoughts while you listen.

3. **Resist interrupting others.** In conversation, we switch from speaker to listener so frequently that we may find it difficult at times to make these shifts completely. Instead of listening, it is easy to rehearse what we are going to say as soon as we have a chance. It is especially important to when trying to be a good listener that you let the other person finish before you take your turn to speak. Good listeners resist interrupting others. Especially when you are in a heated conversation or excited about what you just heard, you will consciously need to stop yourself from preparing a response or interrupting the speaker. The Pop Comm! feature for this chapter focuses on the lost art of listening on cable news programs, where interrupting and talking over one another seems to have become the norm.

attending
the process of focusing on what a speaker is saying regardless of the potential distractions of other competing stimuli.

4. **Hear a person out before you react.** Far too often, we stop listening before the person has finished speaking because we think we know what the person is going to say. Yet often we are wrong. In addition, we often stop listening to people because their mannerisms or words turn us off. Think of the times you may have stopped listening to a professor's lecture and missed important information because of the teacher's accent or gestures. Most of us need to learn the value of patience and silence in allowing others to express themselves and in helping us to listen closely and carefully.

5. **Observe nonverbal cues.** Listeners interpret messages more accurately when they observe the nonverbal behaviors accompanying the words. For instance, when your friend says, "Don't worry about me. I'm fine, really," we must interpret cues

Pundit "Debates": The Lost Art of Listening and the Future of Civil Democratic Discourse in America

Pop Comm!

AP Photo/Jeff Christensen

During their August 2009 recess, members of the U.S. Congress returned to their home states amidst partisan wrangling over health care reform. Many of them held town hall meetings, allowing citizens to debate the government's proposed changes to the health care system. They were shocked to encounter citizens shouting at one another and at their elected representatives, refusing to listen to explanations and differing points of view. But could this situation have been predicted, given the steady diet of what now passes for "debate" on televised news and opinion programs?

Today, the uncivil discourse spouted by television's self-proclaimed pundits is so widespread

that comedian Stephen Colbert created a TV show, *The Colbert Report*, devoted entirely to satirizing them. Mimicking real cable TV hosts, Colbert frequently interrupts his guests, manipulates data, and has the unshakeable faith that his opinions are always right.

One of the first and most popular of these pundits is Bill O'Reilly, host of Fox's *The O'Reilly Factor* (Colapinto, 2006; Johnson, 2006). O'Reilly's aggressive pundit style has been widely copied by others such as Lou Dobbs on CNN, Nancy Grace on Headline News, Chris Matthews on NBC, and Keith Olbermann on MSNBC. Taken as a group, these TV talk show hosts are influencing a generation of Americans, whose only exposure to the concept of democratic debate is informed by these programs.

But news programming that features in-depth interviews and discussion about policy issues is not new. In 1945, *Meet the Press* debuted as a radio show, providing discussion and debate among public officials and other policy experts about the issues of the day. The program migrated to the NBC television network in 1947 and has been broadcast continuously ever since.

In its original format, *Meet the Press* was considered part of the NBC's public information programming, featuring a government official or a prominent expert who was quizzed by a

such as tone of voice, body actions, and facial expression to tell whether she is really fine or whether she is upset but reluctant to tell you about it.

Understanding

Understanding is decoding a message accurately to reflect the meaning intended by the speaker. Sometimes we do not understand because the message is encoded in words that are not in our vocabulary; other times the meaning that we find in the message may not be the meaning intended by the speaker; and at still other times our misunderstanding may stem from our missing the emotional, nonverbal meaning of a message. We can improve our understanding by asking questions, paraphrasing the message, and empathizing with the speaker.

> How can you improve your listening skills to increase understanding?

understanding
decoding a message accurately to reflect the meaning intended by the speaker.

panel of well-known journalists. These discussions were moderated by the host of the show, also a respected journalist. This format changed in the early 1990s, when journalist and lawyer Tim Russert began hosting the show. Under the new format, Russert interviewed the guests alone, and a panel of people with opposing viewpoints discussed the interview. Russert was known for ambushing his guests on air, confronting them with statements they'd made in the past that differed from their current views and asking them to reconcile the differing positions. In addition, the show's panels were often populated by the same combative pundits who appear on other TV news and opinion talk shows.

There are two reasons why public information programs meant to educate us about important issues have become "gotcha" scream-fests. First, such shows are profitable for TV networks because the costs to produce them are relatively low—they don't require writers or elaborate sets, and guests receive no compensation for sharing their opinions (Farhi, 2009).

Second, viewers like edginess. Professor Dale Harrison of Auburn University explains, "Rants add passion to news events and inspire people to take sides on issues" (Johnson, 2006). This is certainly not a new phenomenon. As journalist James Maguire (2007) points out, as far back as 80 B.C., Roman philosopher Cicero speculated that people are more convinced by pathos (emotion) than by logos (logic). Professor Harrison acknowledges the effectiveness of pathos, saying, "That's not all bad, as long as

viewers are skeptical about the facts presented on TV rants and balance their media diet with more reliable sources of facts and information" (Johnson, 2006, p. 71). But with newspaper circulation dropping precipitously (Hau, 2008), more Americans are getting their news from TV sources, often choosing those whose ideological bent mirrors their own. As a result, they are less likely to be exposed to valid arguments made by people with opposing views.

Furthermore, as explored in a presentation by Diana Mutz, Byron Reeves, and Kevin Wise (2003) at an annual meeting of the International Communication Association, experiments show that although viewers are more likely to remember the main emphasis of the arguments in less civil debates, they are also less likely to remember the actual arguments underlying the positions. Compared to more civil debate, viewers are also less likely to remember the arguments that are opposed to their own opinion.

Despite what viewers say they want, how well does the pundit debate style serve our democracy? What would Thomas Jefferson—who said, "Information is the currency of democracy"—think of Bill O'Reilly? How would John F. Kennedy—who said, "The ignorance of the voter in a democracy impairs the security of all"—grade Keith Olbermann? And what must Jesse Jackson—who said, "A full and fair discussion is essential to democracy"—make of the talk-show round tables he participates in, where guests interrupt, fail to listen, and insult other guests? Fair and balanced? You decide.

1. **Ask questions to gain additional information.** A **question** is a statement designed to get further information or to clarify information already received. Effective questioning begins by identifying the kind of information you need to increase your understanding. Suppose Maria says to you, "I am totally frustrated. Would you stop at the store on the way home and buy me some more paper?" You may be a bit confused by her request and need more information to understand. Yet if you simply respond "What do you mean?" Maria, who is already frustrated, may become defensive. Instead, you might think about what type of information you need and form a question to meet that need. To increase your understanding, you can ask one of these three types of questions:

   - *To get details*: "What kind of paper would you like me to get, and how much will you need?"
   - *To clarify word meanings*: "Could you tell me what you mean by *frustrated*?"
   - *To clarify feelings*: "What's frustrating you?"

2. **Paraphrase the message to check your understanding.** **Paraphrasing** is putting into words the ideas or feelings you have perceived from the message. For example, during an argument with your sister, after she has stated her concern about your behavior, you might paraphrase what she has said as follows: "You say that you are tired of my talking about work and that you feel that I try to act better than you when I talk about my successes at work." Paraphrases may focus on content, on feelings underlying the content, or on both. A **content paraphrase** focuses on the denotative meaning of the message. The first part of the example above ("You say that you are tired of my talking about work") is a content paraphrase. A **feelings paraphrase** is a response that captures the emotions attached to the content of the message. The second part of the example ("you feel that I try to act better than you") is a feelings paraphrase.

   By paraphrasing, you give the speaker a chance to verify your understanding. The longer and more complex the message, the more important it is to paraphrase. When the speaker appears to be emotional or when English is not the speaker's native language, paraphrasing is also important.

   To paraphrase effectively, (1) listen carefully to the message, (2) notice what images and feelings you have experienced from the message, (3) determine what the message means to you, and (4) create a message that conveys these images or feelings.

3. **Empathize with the speaker. Empathy** is intellectually identifying with or vicariously experiencing the feelings or attitudes of another. To empathize, we generally try to put aside our own feelings or attitudes about another. Three approaches people use when empathizing are empathic responsiveness, perspective taking, and sympathetic responsiveness (Weaver & Kirtley, 1995, p. 131).

   - **Empathic responsiveness** occurs when you experience an emotional response parallel to, and as a result of observing, another person's actual or anticipated display of emotion (Omdahl, 1995, p. 4; Stiff, Dillard, Somera, Kim, & Sleight, 1988, p. 199). For instance, when Jackson tells Janis that he is in real trouble financially, and Janis senses the stress and anxiety that Jackson is feeling, we would say that Janis has experienced empathic responsiveness.
   - **Perspective taking,** imagining yourself in the place of another, is the most common form of empathizing. Although perspective taking is difficult for many of

question
a statement designed to get further information or to clarify information already received.

paraphrasing
putting into words the ideas or feelings you have perceived from the message.

content paraphrase
one that focuses on the denotative meaning of the message.

feelings paraphrase
a response that captures the emotions attached to the content of the message.

empathy
intellectually identifying with or vicariously experiencing the feelings or attitudes of another.

empathic responsiveness
experiencing an emotional response parallel to, and as a result observing, another person's actual or anticipated display of emotion.

perspective taking
imagining yourself in the place of another; the most common form of empathizing.

Paraphrasing
Communication Skill

Skill
A response that conveys your understanding of another person's message.

Use
To increase listening efficiency; to avoid message confusion; to discover the speaker's motivation.

Procedure
1. Listen carefully to the message.
2. Notice what images and feelings you have experienced from this message.
3. Determine what the message means to you.
4. Create a message that conveys these images or feelings.

Example
Grace says, "At two minutes to five, the boss gave me three letters that had to be in the mail that evening!" Bonita replies, "If I understand, you were really resentful that your boss dumped important work on you right before quitting time when she knows you have to pick up the baby at day care."

Questions and Paraphrases
Skill Building

Provide an appropriate question and paraphrase for each of these statements. To get you started, look at this model:

Example: "It's Dionne's birthday, and I've planned a big evening. Sometimes I think Dionne believes I take her for granted—well, after tonight she'll know I think she's something special!"

Question: "What specific things do you have planned?"

Paraphrase: "If I'm understanding you, you're really proud that you've planned a night that's going to be a lot more elaborate than what Dionne expects on her birthday."

1. Luis: "It was just another mind-numbing class. I keep thinking one of these days Professor Romero will get excited about something. He is a real bore!"
2. Angie: "Everyone seems to be raving about the new reality show on Channel 5 last night, but I didn't see it. You know, I don't watch the boob tube."
3. Kaelin: "I don't know if it's me or Mom, but lately she and I just aren't getting along."
4. Aileen: "I've got a report due at work and a paper due in management class. On top of that, it's my sister's birthday, and so far I haven't even had time to get her anything. Tomorrow's going to be a disaster."

Skill Learning Activity 5.1

Skill Learning Activity 5.2

us (Holtgraves, 2002), with conscious effort we can learn to imagine ourselves in the place of another. For example, if Janis personalizes the message by picturing herself in serious financial debt, anticipates the emotions she might experience, and then assumes that Jackson might be feeling the same way, then Janis is empathizing by perspective taking.

- **Sympathetic responsiveness** is feeling concern, compassion, or sorrow for another because of the other's situation or plight. Having sympathy differs from the other two approaches. Rather than attempting to experience the feelings of the other, when you sympathize, you translate your intellectual understanding of what the speaker has experienced into your own feelings of concern, compassion, and sorrow for that person. In our previous example, Janis has sympathy for Jackson when she understands that Jackson is embarrassed and worried, but instead of trying to feel those same emotions, she feels concern and compassion for her friend. Because of this difference in perspective, many scholars differentiate sympathy from empathy.

How well you empathize also depends on how observant you are of others' behavior and how clearly you read the nonverbal messages they are sending. To improve your observational skills when another person begins a conversation with you, develop the habit of silently posing two questions to yourself: (1) What emotions do I believe the person is experiencing right now? and (2) On what cues from the person am I basing this conclusion? Consciously asking these questions helps you focus on the nonverbal aspects of messages, which convey most of the information on the person's emotional state.

sympathetic responsiveness
feeling concern, compassion, or sorrow for another because of the other's situation or plight.

To further increase the accuracy of reading emotions, you can use the skill of perception checking. This is especially helpful when the other person's culture is different from yours. Let's consider an example. Atsuko, who was raised in rural Japan (a collectivist culture) and is now studying at a university in Rhode Island may feel embarrassed when her professor publically compliments her for her part of a group

"Cheer up, Nicole! What does Princeton know? Say, you got any plans for that last bit of cobbler?"

project. Her friend Meredith might notice Atsuko's reddened cheeks and downcast eyes and comment, "Atsuko, you look like I do when I'm embarrassed. Are you uncomfortable that Professor Shank singled you out for praise?"

Remembering

Remembering is being able to retain information and recall it when needed. Too often, people forget almost immediately what they have heard. For instance, you can probably think of many times when you were unable to recall the name of a person to whom you had just been introduced.

Think of how much the education system depends on listening and recalling information. Given the common use of lectures, class discussions, and other listening-based learning experiences, it is not surprising that research shows a link between effective listening and school success (Bommelje, Houston, & Smither, 2003). Three techniques that can help you improve your ability to remember information are repeating, constructing mnemonics, and taking notes.

> What are the three tactics that can help you to remember what you hear?

1. **Repeat the information.** Repetition—saying something aloud or mentally rehearsing it two, three, or four times immediately after hearing it—helps listeners store information in long-term memory by providing necessary reinforcement (Estes, 1989). If information is not reinforced, it will be held in short-term memory for as little as 20 seconds and then forgotten. When you are introduced to a stranger, increase the chances that you will remember the person's name by immediately using it: "It's nice to meet you, Jack…McNeil right?" If you also mentally say "Jack McNeil, Jack McNeil, Jack McNeil, Jack McNeil" to yourself, you'll further increase your chances of remembering his name. Likewise, when you receive the directions "Go two blocks east, turn left, turn right at the next light, and it's in the next block," immediately repeat to yourself "two blocks east, turn left, turn right at light, next block—that's two blocks east, turn left, turn right at light, next block."

2. **Construct mnemonics.** Constructing mnemonics helps listeners put information in forms that are more easily recalled. A **mnemonic device** is any artificial technique used as a memory aid. One of the most common mnemonic techniques is to form a word with the first letters of a list of items you are trying to remember. For example, a popular mnemonic for the five Great Lakes is HOMES (*H*uron, *O*ntario, *M*ichigan, *E*rie, *S*uperior).

    When you want to remember items in a sequence, you can form a sentence with the words themselves or use words starting with the same first letters. For example, most beginning music students learn the mnemonic "*every good boy does fine*" for the notes on the lines of the treble clef (E, G, B, D, F). (And the word *face* is a common mnemonic for the notes on the treble clef spaces, F, A, C, E.)

3. **Take notes.** Although note taking would be inappropriate in casual interpersonal encounters, it is a powerful tool for increasing your recall when important information is being shared. Note taking is an important strategy for learners when they attempt to listen to and absorb information from lecture-type speech (Dunkel & Pialorsi, 2005). Note taking does more than provide a written record that you can go back to; it also allows you to take an active role in the listening process (Wolvin & Coakley, 1996, p. 239).

Useful notes may consist of a brief list of main points or key ideas, plus a few of the most significant details. Or they may be a short summary of the entire concept (a type of paraphrase) after the message is completed. For lengthy and

Skill Learning Activity 5.3
Skill Learning Activity 5.4
Web Resource 5.1

remembering
being able to retain information and recall it when needed.

mnemonic device
any artificial technique used as a memory aid.

Dana White/PhotoEdit

Effective managers understand the value of making notes about problems that employees point out. How can you use note taking at work to improve your performance?

detailed information, however, good notes likely will consist of a brief outline of what the speaker has said, including the overall idea, the main points of the message, and key developmental material. Good notes are not necessarily long. In fact, many classroom lectures can be summarized in a simple outline. Figure 5.1 is an example of notes based on the material in this chapter.

Evaluating

How can you improve your listening skills of evaluating what you've heard?

The fourth listening process is to evaluate or critically analyze what has been said. **Evaluation** is critically analyzing what you have heard to determine its truthfulness. Critical listening is especially important when you are asked to believe, act on, or support what is being said. For instance, if a person is trying to convince you to vote for a particular candidate, support efforts to legalize gay marriage, or buy an expensive gadget, you will want to listen critically in order to evaluate the information and arguments presented. If you don't critically analyze what you hear, you risk going along with ideas or plans that violate your values, are counterproductive to your interests, or mislead others (including the speaker) who value your judgment.

To evaluate a message, you must learn to separate statements of fact from statements based on inferences. **Factual statements** are those whose accuracy can be verified as true. **Inferences** are conjectures which may be based on facts or observations. If we comment, "You are reading this sentence," we have stated a fact. If we say, "You are understanding and enjoying what you are reading," we have made an inference. Once you've determined what in the message is being offered as fact and what is being offered as inference, you need to (1) analyze the "facts" to determine if they are true and (2) test the inferences to determine whether they are valid.

evaluation
critically analyzing what you have heard to determine its truthfulness.

factual statements
statements whose accuracy can be verified or proven.

inferences
statements made by the speaker that are based on facts or observations.

1. **Analyze "facts" to determine if they are true.** If a statement is offered as a fact, you need to determine if it is true and not simply rely on the speaker's statement. Doing so often requires asking questions that probe the evidence. For example, if Raoul states, "It's going to rain tomorrow." You might ask, "Oh did you see hear the weather report this morning?"

I.   What is listening?
A.   Attaching meaning to what we hear
B.   50% of communication time is listening

II.   Types of listening (appreciative, discriminative, comprehensive, empathic, critical)

III.   Steps in listening process

A.   Attending—focusing
1.   Get ready (physically & mentally)
2.   Resist mental distractions
3.   Don't interrupt (Make complete shift, don't rehearse)
4.   Hear person out (don't check out)
5.   Watch nonverbal cues (do they match words?)

B.   Understanding—decoding message
1.   Ask questions (get details & clarify words & feelings)
2.   Paraphrase (content & feelings)
3.   Empathize (empathy, perspective taking, sympathy)
4.   Check perceptions

C.   Remembering
1.   Repeat info
2.   Construct mnemonics (e.g., Great Lakes = HOMES)
3.   Take notes

D.   Evaluating
1.   Analyze facts
2.   Test inferences

E.   Responding

1.   Supportive messages (state aim to help, acceptance of other, concern, availability to listen, being ally; acknowledge & validate feelings; encourage elaboration)
2.   Disagree respectfully ("I" language, specific examples, points of agreements)

Figure 5.1
Notes based on a lecture on listening

2.   **Test inferences to determine whether they are valid.** If a statement offered is an inference, you need to determine whether it is valid. You can ask yourself (or the speaker) three questions: (1) What are the facts that support this inference? (2) Is this information really central to the inference? (3) Are there other facts or information that would contradict this inference? For example, if someone says, "Better watch it—Katie's in one bad mood today. Did you catch the look on her face? That's one unhappy girl," you should stop and think, is Katie really in a bad mood? The support for this inference is her facial expression. Is this inference accurate? Is Katie's expression one of unhappiness, or is it anger? Is the look on her face enough to conclude that she's in a bad mood? Or are there other cues that those of us who know her would expect to see? Is there anything else about Katie's behavior today that could lead us to believe that she's not in a bad mood?

You are listening critically when you separate facts from inferences and then evaluate them as true or valid.

Skill Learning Activity 5.5
Skill Learning Activity 5.6

Speech Assignment: **Communicate on Your Feet**

Critical Listening

Find and attend a formal public presentation that is being given on campus or in your community. Your goal is to listen so that you remember and can critically evaluate what you have heard. Be sure to take notes and record the main ideas the speaker presents. After you have heard the speech, analyze what you have heard. You can use the following questions to guide your initial thinking:

- What was the purpose of the speech? What was the speaker trying to explain to you or convince you about?
- Was it easy or difficult to identify the speaker's main ideas? What did you notice about how the speaker developed each point she or he made?
- Did the speaker use examples or tell stories to develop a point? If so, were these typical examples, or did the speaker choose examples that were unusual but seemed to prove the point?
- Did the speaker use statistics to back up what was said? If so, did the speaker tell you where the statistics came from? Did the statistics surprise you? If so, what would you have needed to hear that would have helped you to accept them as accurate?
- Do you think that the speaker did a good job? If so, why? If not, what should the speaker have done to be more effective?

When you have finished your analysis, follow your instructor's directions. You may be asked to write a short essay about the speech or to present what you have learned to the class.

Responding

How can you improve your listening skills so that you respond appropriately to what you've heard?

At times, to be truthful and ethical, we will need to disagree with someone or provide negative feedback or a negative critique. When we respond to a friend or family member who appears emotionally upset, respond to a work-group colleague's ideas, or respond to a public speech by critiquing it, we need to respond supportively. Supportive responses confirm the speaker's feelings, and when we are disagreeing or critiquing, they demonstrate respect for the speaker. Let's take a look at several guidelines.

1. **Guidelines for responses that offer emotional support.** At times the appropriate response is one that is related to the emotional content of the message we have heard. So the goal of our response will be to reassure, encourage, soothe, console, or cheer up. **Supportive messages** are helpful when they create a conversational environment that encourages the other person to talk about and make sense of the situation that is causing distress. Supporting does not mean making false statements or telling someone only what he or she wants to hear. Effective supporting responses are based on the facts but focus on how those facts can provide emotional support for the speaker.

supportive messages
comforting statements that have a goal to reassure, bolster, encourage, soothe, console, or cheer up.

Research suggests several key characteristics of **supportive messages** in interpersonal settings (Burleson, 2003, pp. 565–568). The following guidelines are based on this research:

- *Clearly state that your aim is to help.*
  Example: "I'd like to help you, what can I do?"
- *Express acceptance or affection; do not condemn or criticize.*
  Example: "I understand that you just can't seem to accept this."
- *Demonstrate care, concern, and interest in the other's situation; do not give a lengthy recount of a similar situation.*
  Example: "What are you planning to do now?" Or "Gosh, tell me more; what happened then?"
- *Indicate that you are available to listen and support the other without intruding.*
  Example: "I know we've not been that close, but sometimes it helps to have someone to listen, and I'd like to do that for you."
- *State that you are an ally.*
  Example: "I'm with you on this." Or "Well, I'm on your side; this isn't right."
- *Acknowledge the other's feelings and situation as well as expressing your sincere sympathy; do not condemn or criticize the other's behavior or feelings.*
  Example: "I'm so sorry to see you feeling so bad; I can see that you're devastated by what has happened."
- *Assure the other that what he or she is feeling is legitimate; do not tell the other how to feel or to ignore his or her feelings.*
  Example: "With what has happened to you, you have a right to be angry."
- *Use prompting comments to encourage the other to elaborate on his or her story.*
  Example: "Uh-huh," "yeah," or "I see. How did you feel about that?" Or "What happened before that? Can you elaborate?"

Effective supportive messages are in touch with the facts and provide emotional support for the speaker.

2. **Guidelines for responses that demonstrate respect when disagreeing or critiquing others.** When you cannot agree with what a speaker has said, or when you are in a position where it is appropriate for you to critique what someone else has said or done, the following guidelines can help you demonstrate that you respect the person and that your goal is to provide the person with your point of view.

- *Use "I" language so that you clearly own the comments you are making and do not ascribe them to others.*
  Example: "Carla, I really like the way you cited the reference for your opening quotation."
- *Use specific language and specific examples to point out areas of disagreement and areas for improvement.*
  Example: "I apologize, but I can't agree to that deadline or to another meeting about this project until I have had a chance to see the entire presentation. I'd suggest that by Monday at 10:00 a.m. each of us e-mails other team members a copy of the report section we are drafting. Then let's have a short meeting right after class to see if we need to meet again and, if so, to set a time."
- *Find a point to agree with or something positive to say before expressing your disagreement or offering a negative critique.*
  Example: "I really appreciate what you had to say on this topic. But it was hard for me to follow your argument, and I

David R. Frazier/Photoresearchers/First Light

think that if you had used transitional statements, they could have helped me understand your points better."

In this course, you may be asked to respond to a speech given by one of your classmates. If so, you will want to remember that your goal is to be supportive, honest, and helpful. A good critique will address three topics: the content of the speech, the structure of the speech, and the delivery of the speech.

- When critiquing the content, you can comment on the appropriateness of the speech for that particular audience and the use of facts and inferences; you can also analyze the logic of the arguments and the evidence used to support ideas.
- When critiquing structure, you can focus on the introduction, the use of transitions, the choice of organizational pattern, and the concluding remarks.
- When critiquing delivery, you can comment on how the speaker used voice and gesture, whether the tone was appropriately conversational or formal, and how effectively the speaker used visual aids such as PowerPoint slides.

When you critique a classmate's speech, it is especially important to offer specific suggestions for improvement. Figure 5.2 provides examples of ineffective and effective speech critique statements.

Figure 5.3 on pages 104 and 105 summarizes the five processes involved in listening and describes how good and poor listeners approach each process.

Conversation and Analysis

Use your Premium Website for *Communicate!* to access the **Skill Learning Activity 5.7**, which is a video clip of Damien and Chris's conversation. As you watch the interaction, analyze how well Damien uses the skills of active listening and how well his responses

	Ineffective critique	Effective critique
Content	"The sources you cited are old and no longer represent current thinking on the topic."	"I noticed you relied heavily on Johnson's 1969 essay about global warming. For me, your argument would be more compelling if you were to cite research that has been published in the last five years."
Structure	"You were really hard to follow."	"I really appreciate what you had to say on this topic. I would have been able to follow your main points better if I had heard clear transitions between each one. Transitions would have helped me notice the switch from one topic to the next."
Delivery	"You talk too fast!"	"I was fascinated by the evidence you offered to support the first main point. It would have been even more compelling for me if you were to slow down while explaining that information. That would give me time to understand the material more fully before we moved on to the next main point."

Figure 5.2

Examples of effective and ineffective speech critiques

demonstrate effective support and comforting. You can respond to this and other analysis questions by clicking on "Critique" in the menu bar at the top of the screen. When you've answered all the questions, click "Done" to compare your answers to those provided by the authors.

Damien and Chris work in a small shop selling shirts and gifts. Usually they get along well, but lately Chris has seemed standoffish. Damien decides to talk with Chris to see if anything is wrong. Damien approaches Chris in the break room.

Skill Learning Activity 5.7

Conversation

DAMIEN: Chris, you've been kind of quiet lately, man. What's been going on?

DAMIEN: Come on, man, what's going on?

CHRIS: Just life. *(He shrugs.)* I'm just kind of down right now.

DAMIEN: Well, what am I here for? I thought we were friends.

CHRIS: *(He thinks briefly and decides to talk about it.)* Well, Carl's been on my case the last few weeks.

DAMIEN: Why? Did you do something?

CHRIS: Oh, he says that I'm sloppy when I restock and that I'm not always "polite" to our customers. You know, just 'cuz I don't smile all the time. I mean, what does he want—Little Mary Sunshine?

DAMIEN: So you're angry with the boss.

Jason Harris/Thomson Higher Education/ Wadsworth Publishing Group

CHRIS: Yeah, I guess. . . . No, no, not so angry. I'm just frustrated. I come in to work every day, and I try to do my job, and I don't complain. You know, I'm sick and tired of getting stuck back there in the stock room reorganizing everything. It's not like they're paying us big bucks here. And Carl shouldn't expect us to be charming with everybody who walks through that door. I mean, half of the people who walk through that door are, well, they're totally rude and act like jerks.

DAMIEN: Yeah, I feel like you on that. Some of those people shouldn't be allowed out in public. What is Carl saying about how you're dealing with the customers?

CHRIS: Oh, he just says that I've changed and that I'm not being "nice." I mean, he used to call me his top guy.

DAMIEN: I mean, you know how Carl is. He's a fanatic about customer service. You know how, when we first started, he drilled us about being polite and smiling and being courteous at all times. So maybe when he says "you're not being nice," he just means that you're not doing it the way you used to. I mean, I've noticed a change. I mean, you're just not yourself lately. Is anything going on outside of work?

Jason Harris/Thomson Higher Education/ Wadsworth Publishing Group

CHRIS: You could say that. Sarah and I just bought a house, so money's been a bit tight. Now, she wants to quit her job and start a family, and I'm not sure we can afford it. On top of it all, my kid sister shows up a few weeks ago on our doorstep, pregnant, and so she's living with us. So yeah, it is a bit overwhelming. And I'm a bit worried that Carl's going to fire me.

DAMIEN: Wow, that is a lot of stuff! I can understand why you're down, but did Carl really threaten to fire you?

Figure 5.3
A summary of the five aspects of listening

	ATTENDING	UNDERSTANDING	REMEMBERING
	The process of focusing on what a speaker is saying regardless of competing stimuli that are potential distractions.	The process of decoding a message accurately to reflect the meaning intended by the speaker.	The process of being able to retain information and recall it when needed.
Good listeners	Good listeners attend to important information. They • ready themselves physically and mentally • listen objectively regardless of emotional involvement • listen differently depending on situations	Good listeners assign appropriate meaning to what is said. They • seek out apparent purpose, main points, and supporting information • ask mental questions to anticipate information • silently paraphrase to solidify understanding • seek out subtle meanings based on nonverbal cues	Good listeners mentally work to retain what has been said. They • repeat key information • mentally create mnemonics for lists of words and ideas • take notes
Poor listeners	Poor listeners may not hear what a person is saying because of daydreaming or distractions. They • fidget in their chairs, look out the window, and let their minds wander • visibly react to emotional language • listen the same way regardless of the type of material	Poor listeners hear what is said but are either unable to understand or assign different meaning to the words. They • ignore the way information is organized • fail to anticipate coming information • seldom or never mentally review information • ignore nonverbal cues	Poor listeners rely on a single hearing to retain what has been said. They • assume they will remember • seldom single out any information as especially important • rely on memory alone

EVALUATING

The process of critically analyzing what you have heard to determine its truthfulness.

Good listeners assess the accuracy, truthfulness, and extent to which they agree with the speaker's ideas. They
- assess facts to determine if they are true.
- test the logic underlying speaker inferences to see if they are valid.

Poor listeners hear and understand but don't take time to consider the accuracy, truthfulness, and extent to which they agree. They
- accept information at face value.
- don't analyze the logic behind inferences.

RESPONDING SUPPORTIVELY

The process of confirming the speaker's feelings and, when disagreeing or critiquing, demonstrating respect for the speaker

Good listeners provide emotional comfort or demonstrate respect for the speaker while disagreeing or critiquing. They
- offer statements that acknowledge the legitimacy of the speaker's emotional state.
- use "I" centered statements that begin by agreeing or acknowledging positives before offering specific disagreements or commenting on problems.

Poor listeners ignore the speaker's emotional message or disagree or critique in a manner that demeans. They
- respond without acknowledging the explicit emotional pain or joy of the speaker.
- couch statements in other-centered language, fail to acknowledge positives or areas of agreement, and make comments that are overly general, not specific, or negative.

Jason Harris/Thomson Higher Education/
Wadsworth Publishing Group

CHRIS: No, no, but I'm not perfect, and he could use my "attitude" as an excuse to fire me.

DAMIEN: Well, did you think about telling him what's been going on? And maybe, you know, he'll understand and cut you some slack.

CHRIS: Or he could see that I really have changed and he'd can me.

DAMIEN: OK, well, just tell me this. Do you like working here?

CHRIS: Yeah, of course I do.

DAMIEN: OK, well, then, you've just got to tough it out. I mean, you've just got to use the game face on these people. You used to be the best at doing that. So you're just gonna have to get back to being a salesman, and leave everything else behind.

CHRIS: I guess I never realized how much my problems were affecting my work. I thought Carl was just out to get me, but now you're noticing something too, then maybe I have changed. Thanks, thanks for talking this out.

?? A Question of Ethics

Janeen always disliked talking on the telephone—she thought it was an impersonal form of communication. Thus, college was a wonderful respite. When friends called her, instead of staying on the phone she could quickly run over to their dorm or meet them at a coffeehouse.

One day during reading period before exams, Janeen received a phone call from Barbara, an out-of-town friend. Before she was able to dismiss the call with her stock excuses, she found herself bombarded with information about old high school friends and their whereabouts. Not wanting to disappoint Barbara, who seemed eager to talk, Janeen tucked her phone under her chin and began straightening her room, answering Barbara with the occasional "uh-huh," "hmm," or "wow, that's cool!" As the "conversation" progressed, Janeen began reading through her mail and then her notes from class. After a few minutes, she realized there was silence on the other end of the line. Suddenly very ashamed, she said, "I'm sorry, what did you say? The phone...uh, there was just a lot of static."

Barbara replied with obvious hurt in her voice, "I'm sorry I bothered you. You must be terribly busy."

What Would You Do?

Embarrassed, Janeen muttered, "I'm just really stressed, you know, with exams coming up and everything. I guess I wasn't listening very well; you didn't seem to be saying anything really important. I'm sorry. What were you saying?"

"Nothing 'important,'" Barbara answered. "I was just trying to figure out a way to tell you. I know that you are friends with my brother Billy, and you see, we just found out yesterday that he's terminal with a rare form of luekemia. But you're right; it obviously isn't really important." With that, she hung up.

1. How ethical was Janeen's means of dealing with her dilemma of not wanting to talk on the phone but not wanting to hurt Barbara's feelings?

2. Identify ways in which both Janeen and Barbara could have used better and perhaps more ethical interpersonal communication skills. Rewrite the scenario incorporating these changes.

Summary

Listening is a complex activity made up of five simple processes: attending, understanding, remembering, evaluating, and responding. Listening skill is important to both effective personal and professional relationships. Because we spend so much time listening, we adjust our listening depending on its purpose in a particular situation. The five types of listening we might use are appreciative, discriminative, comprehensive, empathic, and critical. To be an effective listener, you must master each of the five processes of listening.

Attending is the process of selecting and focusing on specific stimuli from among the countless ones that we receive. We can be more effective in attending if we (1) get ready physically, (2) resist mental distractions, (3) resist interrupting (don't rehearse), (4) hear a person out before responding, and (5) observe nonverbal clues.

Understanding is the process of decoding a message so that the meaning accurately reflects that intended by the speaker. Empathizing, which is identifying with or vicariously experiencing the feelings of another, can increase understanding. We can also increase understanding by asking questions to clarify and get details and by paraphrasing the speaker's content and feelings.

Remembering is the process of retaining information so that it can be recalled when it is needed. By repeating information, using mnemonics, and taking notes, we can increase the likelihood that we will remember what we hear.

Critical analysis is the process of evaluating what has been said to determine its truthfulness. Critical analysis is especially important when a speaker is asking you to believe, act on, or support what is being said. One important skill of critical analysis is to separate statements of fact from inferences. Statements of fact should be analyzed to see if they are true. Inferences should be tested to see if they are valid. Three questions can help us to test inferences: (1) What facts support this inference? (2) Is the information really central to the inference? (3) Do other facts contradict the inference?

Responding supportively helps people feel better about themselves and their behavior. Whenever you respond to others, you want to confirm their feelings and demonstrate respect. You can offer emotional support by bolstering, reassuring, encouraging, or consoling the speaker. You can show respect when disagreeing or critiquing others by using "I" language, being specific, and offering something positive first.

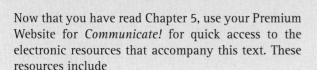
Communicate! Active Online Learning
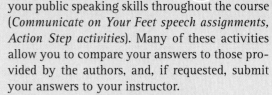

Now that you have read Chapter 5, use your Premium Website for *Communicate!* for quick access to the electronic resources that accompany this text. These resources include

- **Study tools** that will help you assess your learning and prepare for exams (*digital glossary, key term flash cards, review quizzes*).
- **Activities and assignments** that will help you hone your knowledge, analyze communication situations (*Skill Learning Activities*), and build

your public speaking skills throughout the course (*Communicate on Your Feet speech assignments, Action Step activities*). Many of these activities allow you to compare your answers to those provided by the authors, and, if requested, submit your answers to your instructor.
- **Media resources** that will help you explore communication concepts online (*Web Resources*), develop your speech outlines (*Speech Builder Express 3.0*), watch and critique videos of communication

situations and sample speeches (*Interactive Video Activities*), upload your speech videos for peer reviewing and critique other students' speeches (*Speech Studio online speech review tool*), and download chapter review so you can study when and where you'd like (*Audio Study tools*).

This chapter's Key Terms, Skill Learning Activities, and Web Resources are also featured on the following pages, and you can find this chapter's Communicate on Your Feet assignment and Skill Building activity in the body of the chapter.

Key Terms

appreciative listening (89)
attending (91)
comprehensive listening (90)
content paraphrase (94)
critical listening (90)
discriminative listening (89)
empathic listening (90)

empathic responsiveness (94)
empathy (94)
evaluation (98)
factual statements (98)
feelings paraphrase (94)
inferences (98)
listening (88)
mnemonic device (97)

paraphrasing (94)
perspective taking (94)
question (94)
remembering (97)
supportive messages (100)
sympathetic responsiveness (96)
understanding (93)

Skill Learning Activities

5.1: Questions and Paraphrases (96)

Finish the in text activity.

5.2: Empathizing Effectively (97)

Write a paragraph describing a time when you effectively empathized with another person. What was the person's emotional state? How did you recognize it? What were the nonverbal cues? Verbal cues? What type of relationship did you have with this person? How similar were the two of you? What type of empathizing did you use? Why?

5.3: Creating Mnemonics (98)

Mnemonics are useful memory aids. Construct a mnemonic for the five phases of the listening process: attending, understanding, remembering, evaluating, and responding. Record your mnemonic.

Tomorrow, while you are getting dressed, see whether you can recall the mnemonic you created. Then see whether you can recall the phases of the listening process from the cues in your mnemonic. Write a brief paragraph describing your experience.

5.4: Listening to Remember (98)

Take an online listening test to evaluate how well you remember what you hear, with and without notes. Access this test at your Premium Website

for *Communicate!* Look for it in the Skill Learning activities for Chapter 5.

5.5: Evaluating Inferences (100)

For each of the following statements, identify the fact(s) and the inference(s). Then, write three specific questions that "test" the validity of the inference. Here's an example:

The campus walk-in health clinic is understaffed. I stopped by the other day and had to wait two hours to be seen.

Fact: I had to wait two hours to be seen at the walk-in clinic.

Inference: The clinic is understaffed.

Questions:

1. Is one person's experience alone enough to support the inference?
2. Are there times when there is not a backup?
3. Are there other things besides staffing levels that could account for the wait?

When you're done with this activity, compare your answers to the authors' at the Premium Website for *Communicate!* Look for them in the Skill Learning activities for Chapter 5.

1. Christy got a 96 percent on the first test. She must have crammed all weekend.
2. Kali's pregnant. Just look at how tight her jeans are; she can barely keep them buttoned.

3. You can't get a good job unless you know some-one. Mike searched everywhere for six months before he finally talked to his next-door neigh-bor, who hired him for his construction company.

4. If you want to go to dental school when you graduate, forget it. In the past three years, none of the students from this program who applied got in.

5. Kids today are growing up too fast. I mean, they carry cell phones and everything.

5.6: Critically Analyzing the Use of Facts and Inferences in the Media (100)

Watch a political talk show and an infomercial on television. If possible, record the two programs so you can watch them more than once. While you are watching each program, note as many individual factual statements and inferences as you can. Next, write a paragraph in which you answer these ques-tions: What was the ratio of factual statements to inferences in each program (for example, 1 to 1, 1 to 2, or 1 to 3)? Did these results surprise you? If so, how? Were the ratios different for the two programs? If so, how did the results conform to or differ from your expectations? How did evaluating the inferences used in the two programs change your perception of their messages?

To help you complete this activity, you can use the log provided in your Premium Website for *Communicate!* Look for it in the Skill Learning activi-ties for Chapter 5.

5.7: Damien and Chris (105)

After you've watched the video of Damien and Chris and have read the transcript of their conversa-tion, answer the following questions.

1. What does Damien do that shows he's attending?
2. What does Damien do that demonstrates his understanding?
3. Does Damien use critical listening to separate facts from inferences?
4. How does Damien show empathy?

When you're done with this activity, compare your answers to the authors' at the Premium Website for *Communicate!* Look for them in the Skill Learning activities for Chapter 5.

Web Resources

5.1: Mnemonics (98)

Mindtools.com is a great site that describes and provides links to a variety of mnemonic techniques.

Self Review

Foundations of Communication

Establishing a Communication Foundation from Chapters 2 through 5

What kind of a communicator are you? This review looks at several specifics that are basic to effective communicators. On the line provided for each statement, indicate the response that best captures your behavior: 1, almost always; 2, often; 3, sometimes; 4, rarely; 5, never.

_____ When I speak, I tend to present a positive image of myself. (Chapter 2)

_____ In my behavior toward others, I look for more information to confirm or negate my first impressions. (Chapter 2)

_____ Before I act on perceptions drawn from people's nonverbal cues, I seek verbal verification of their accuracy. (Chapter 2)

_____ I use specific language when I speak, avoiding generalizations that could be misinterpreted. (Chapter 3)

_____ I speak clearly, using words that people readily understand. (Chapter 3)

_____ When I am speaking with people of different cultures or of the opposite sex, I am careful to monitor my word choices. (Chapter 3)

_____ I tend to look at people when I talk with them. (Chapter 4)

_____ Most of my sentences are free from such expressions as "uh," "well," "like," and "you know." (Chapter 4)

_____ I consider the effect of my dress on others. (Chapter 4)

_____ I try to make sure that my nonverbal messages match my verbal messages. (Chapter 4)

_____ I listen attentively, regardless of my interest in the person or the ideas. (Chapter 5)

_____ When I'm not sure whether I understand, I seek clarification. (Chapter 5)

_____ When a person describes an unfortunate experience, I am able to provide appropriate comfort. (Chapter 5)

Based on your responses, select the communication behavior you would most like to change. Write a communication-improvement goal statement similar to the sample improvement plan in Chapter 1 (page 18). If you would like verification of your self-analysis before you write a goal, have a friend or co-worker complete this same analysis for you.

You can complete this Self-Review online and, if requested, e-mail it to your instructor. Go to your Premium Website for Communicate! to access Part I Self-Review.

Wally McNamee/Wally McNamee/Corbis

Communicating Across Cultures

◉

6

Questions you will be able to answer after reading this chapter:

- What is intercultural communication?
- What is the relationship between a dominant culture and a co-culture?
- How does the communication of people from individualistic cultures differ from that of people in collectivist cultures?
- How does the communication of people from high uncertainty-avoidance cultures differ from that of people from low uncertainty-avoidance cultures?
- How does the communication of people from high power-distance cultures differ from that of the people from low power-distance cultures?
- How does the communication of people from masculine cultures differ from that of people from feminine cultures?
- What barriers do we face when communicating interculturally?
- How can you improve your intercultural communication?

"Jack, I don't think we should take this flight," Alicia said. "Why don't we wait and take the next one?"

"What are you talking about?" Jack replied. "Our reservations are confirmed, our bags are probably on board by now, and why would we want to sit around here for hours?"

"But Jack, over there," Alicia muttered behind her hand while nodding to her far right. Jack turned his head. There on the end of the long bench sat a large bearded man in a turban.

"Jack, I'm afraid," Alicia whispered urgently. "He could be a terrorist."

"Relax, Alicia," Jack said. "There is nothing to worry about. Anyway, what makes you think that all Muslims are terrorists? For that matter, anyone on our flight could be a terrorist."

How could we evaluate Alicia's assumptions in this situation? Are the inferences underlying Jack's responses more accurate? In both cases, their judgments are based on their perceptions of people who are culturally different from themselves.

Because culture has a profound impact on not only our perceptions but also our communication behavior, in this chapter we examine how culture affects our communication behavior and how it influences our perception of the communication we receive from others. We begin by taking a look at some basic concepts of culture, identifying important values and norms that set cultures apart. Then we discuss the barriers that arise from cultural difference and offer strategies for improving intercultural communication competence.

Culture and Communication

How often have we heard people observe that the world is getting smaller and the people in it increasingly similar? Today, through the globalization of trade and the Internet, our lives are affected by the decisions and actions of people in other parts of the world, and we can make instant personal contact with people around the globe through the click of a mouse. Some people celebrate this trend as a step toward world unity, but others mourn the loss of local cultures, traditions, and control and feel overwhelmed by the pervasiveness of communication.

Culture includes the values, attitudes, beliefs, orientations, and underlying assumptions prevalent among people in a society (Samovar, Porter, & McDaniel, 2009). Yet, we do not have to journey to other countries to meet people of different cultures. As a nation of immigrants, the United States is a multicultural society. Our population includes not only recent immigrants from Asia, Latin America, Eastern Europe, and other countries, but also the descendents of earlier voluntary immigrants and of African slaves brought here against their will, as well as native peoples. So understanding how cultural groups vary in their approach to communication can help us as we interact with the people we meet each day.

Intercultural Communication

culture
the values, attitudes, beliefs, orientations, and underlying assumptions prevalent among people in a society.

culture shock
the psychological discomfort you may feel when you attempt to adjust to a new cultural situation

We are so familiar with our own language, gestures, facial expressions, conversational customs, and norms that we may experience anxiety when these familiar aspects of communication are disrupted. This occurs frequently when we interact with people from different cultures. **Culture shock** is the psychological discomfort you may feel when you attempt to adjust to a new cultural situation (Klyukanov, 2005, p. 33). Because culture shock is caused by an absence of shared meaning, you are likely to feel it most profoundly when you are thrust into another culture through travel, business, or studying abroad. In the film *Lost in Translation*, for example, Bill Murray's character struggles with culture shock when filming a commercial in Japan.

Culture shock can also occur when you have contact with people from another culture within your home country. For example, Brittney, who is from a small town in Minnesota, experienced culture shock when she visited Miami for the first time. She was overwhelmed by the distinct Hispanic flavor of the city, hearing Spanish spoken on the street and seeing signs and billboards written in Spanish, the prevalence of Latin beat music, and the ways people looked and dressed. Brittney was disoriented not only because of the prominence of Spanish but also because the values, attitudes, beliefs, and behaviors of the people she encountered seemed quite foreign to her. Likewise, if Maria, who lives in Miami, were to visit the small Minnesota

Image Source/Getty Images

If you plan to study abroad, how might you prepare yourself to manage initial feelings of culture shock?

town where Brittney grew up, she would also be likely to experience culture shock as Brittney's hometown is like the rural Minnesota towns whose values and customs are humorously highlighted on Garrison Keillor's public radio program *A Prairie Home Companion*.

Intercultural communication refers to interactions between people whose cultural assumptions are so different that the communication between them is altered (Samovar, Porter, & McDaniel, 2009). In other words, when we interact with people whose attitudes, values, beliefs, customs, and behaviors are culturally different from ours, we are communicating across cultural boundaries, which can lead to misunderstandings that would not commonly occur between people who are culturally similar. It is important to recognize that not every exchange between people of different cultures exemplifies intercultural communication. For example, when Brittney is on the beach in Miami and joins a group of Hispanics in a friendly game of beach volleyball, the cultural differences between them are unlikely to affect their game-related exchanges. However, should Brittney decide to join the group for a night of club hopping, she is more likely to experience conversations in which cultural differences lead to difficulty in understanding or interpreting what is said.

What is intercultural communication?

intercultural communication *interactions that occur between people whose cultural assumptions are so different that the communication between them is altered.*

dominant culture *the attitudes, values, beliefs, and customs that the majority of people in a society hold in common.*

Dominant Cultures and Co-Cultures

Although the United States is a multicultural society, there are many attitudes, values, beliefs, and customs that a majority of people hold in common. This shared system of meaning constitutes our **dominant culture**, and like the dominant culture of any country, ours has evolved over time. The dominant culture of the United States once reflected the values of white, Western European, English-speaking, Protestant, heterosexual men. But as we have recognized our diversity, the dominate culture has evolved and incorporated aspects of other cultural groups. The result is a dominant culture that better reflects the diversity of the people in the United States.

What is the relationship between a dominant culture and a co-culture?

Still, there are cultural groups whose values, attitudes, beliefs, and customs differ from the dominant culture. These groups, called **co-cultures**, exhibit communication that is sufficiently different to distinguish them from the dominant culture. The following are some of the major contributors to co-cultures in United States society today:

Race

Traditionally, the term *race* was used to classify people in terms of biological characteristics, such skin and eye color, hair texture, and body shape. However, scientific justifications for such divisions have proven elusive, and the classification system itself has changed drastically over time (Hotz, 1995). Despite the difficulty of scientifically defining race, people have experienced the social effects of perceived race and have formed communities and cultures based on racialized experiences. So race is an important cultural signifier for many people, and racial identity can influence communication in a number of ways. For example, African Americans "code switch" at times using the linguistic and non verbal patterns of the dominant culture and at other times using the communication style that is unique to their race (Jackson, 2004). Which code is used may depend on their attitude, the topic, or who is listening (Bonvillain, 2003). Likewise, members of co-cultures based on gender, ethnicity, or social class may also change their communication style from time to time, to be more similar to or distant from that of the dominant culture.

Ethnicity

Like race, ethnicity is an inexact distinction. **Ethnicity** refers to a classification of people based on combinations of shared characteristics such as nationality, geographic origin, language, religion, ancestral customs, and tradition. So, people may identify themselves as Italian Americans, Irish Americans, Mexican Americans, and so on. People vary greatly in the importance they attach to their ethnic heritage and the degree to which it affects their attitudes, values, and behavior. You may descend from Italians and this heritage may affect your closeness to family, your religion, the foods you prefer, and many other aspects of your identity. Your roommate may also have Italian ancestors but may not identify herself as Italian and may not follow any family traditions based on this ethnicity.

Language or mother tongue is an obvious influence of ethnicity on communication. Immigrants bring with them the language of their original country, and they may or may not speak English when they arrive. Even after they learn English, many immigrants choose to speak their mother tongue at home, intentionally live close to other people from their home country, and interact with these people in their primary language. English is the first language of most people in the United States. But Spanish is quickly becoming a de facto second language. The U.S. Census Bureau data indicates that 15 percent of the U.S. population is Hispanic and that figure is projected to grow to 30 percent by 2050. Furthermore, in Hispanic homes 78 percent report that Spanish is the primary language used in the home (U.S. Census Bureau, 2007). So today most toll-free 800 and 888 numbers offer the option of conversing in English or Spanish; most cable companies have several Spanish-language channels as part of their basic package; and Spanish-language radio stations can be heard across the country.

Sex and gender

"Frogs and snails and puppy dog tails, that's what little boys are made of." "Sugar and spice and everything nice, that's what little girls are made of." "He's a real man's man." "She's such a girlie girl." These traditional childhood rhymes and sex-specific generalizations capture the traditional thinking about men's and women's co-cultures. Women and men tend to belong to different co-cultures within each larger cultural

Skill Learning Activity 6.1

co-cultures

groups of people living within a dominant culture but exhibiting communication that is sufficiently different to distinguish them from the dominant culture.

ethnicity

a classification of people based on combinations of shared characteristics such as nationality, geographic origin, language, religion, ancestral customs, and tradition.

group. Part of what men and women learn from their co-culture is expectations of how they are to behave and communicate. Because women's co-culture values the nurturing role, women who identify with the feminine co-culture may tend to speak more about their personal relationships, more easily describe their feelings, and be more likely to include others in conversation and actively respond to others. On the other hand, men who identify with masculine co-cultural norms may focus more on tasks or outcomes when they communicate. They may tend to talk more about content and problem solving, emphasize control and status, and be less responsive to others (Wood, 2007). Obviously, people differ in the extent to which they identify with these gendered co-cultures, and those who do not strongly identify with the co-culture may not behave in line with co-cultural expectations. In addition, over time the values and norms of each co-culture can change. For example, in Western societies many of the value differences between men's and women's co-cultures have decreased, but in many Middle Eastern societies such differences still exist.

Julie Toy/Taxi/Getty Images

Women and men tend to communicate differently because of their cultural differences. Some research suggests that women focus on feelings, whereas men focus on outcomes. What about you? Do you communicate as women tend to do, as men tend to do, or do you communicate in different ways?

Religion

A **religion** is a system of beliefs that is shared by a group and that supplies the group with an entity (or entities) for devotion, rituals for worshipping that entity, and a code of ethics. Although the dominant culture of the United States values religious freedom and diversity, historically it has reflected Judeo-Christian values and practices. All observant practitioners of a religion participate in a co-culture. Those who strongly identify with a religious group that is outside the Judeo-Christian tradition have different orientations that shape their relationships and their communication behavior. For example, Buddhism advises individuals to embrace rather than to resist personal conflict. Adversity, emotional upheaval, and conflict are seen as natural parts of life (Chuang, 2004). So a Buddhist is apt to communicate openly and calmly during an interpersonal conflict and embrace the positive aspects of conflict in strengthening interpersonal ties. Throughout history, we can point to religious differences as the source of many culture wars. Many of the conflicts in the Middle East today are essentially culture wars based on religious differences.

Sexual orientation

In most places in the world today, the dominant culture values heterosexuality. Although the dominant cultures of many Western countries have changed their laws reflecting a change in attitudes toward homosexuality, people who are not heterosexual still face discrimination in Western societies and legal and physical threats in many parts of the world. As a result, gay, lesbian, bisexual, and transgender people may participate in and identify with "underground" co-cultural communities. These communities have attitudes, values, customs, rites, and rituals that are supportive of homosexual behavior. So people may frequent gay, lesbian, or bi- bars, join gay churches, sing in local gay men's or women's choruses, and participate in commitment ceremonies where the dominant society has laws against homosexual marriage.

Social class

Social class is a level in the power hierarchy of a society. Membership in each social class is determined by income, education, occupation, and social habits. The dominant culture of the United States is the middle class culture. Because social class often determines where people live, people of the same social class often establish communities where they reinforce co-cultures with distinct values, rituals, and communication practices. For

religion
a system of beliefs shared by a group and that supplies the group with an entity(ies) for devotion, rituals for worship, and a code of ethics.

social class
an indicator of a person's position in a social hierarchy, as determined by income, education, occupation, and social habits.

Focus Features/The Kobal Collection/Picture Desk

In the 1970's, Harvey Milk, who became the first openly gay politician in California, urged other gay people to come out of the closet and stand up for their human rights. Assassinated at the height of his popularity, he became the face of the nascent gay pride movement. Do you have friends or family members who are gay? How are their lives different from yours?

example, lower-class parents tend to emphasize obedience, acceptance of what others think, and hesitancy in expressing desires to authority figures, whereas middle-class parents more often emphasize self-control, self-direction, and intellectual curiosity. Such differences in values based on social class may lead those from middle-class backgrounds to speak more directly and assertively than do people from working-class backgrounds (Gilbert & Kahl, 1982).

Age

The period in which we are born and raised can have a strong formative influence on us. People of the same generation form a cultural cohort whose personal values, beliefs, and behaviors have been influenced by the common life experiences and events they encountered as they aged. People who grew up during the Great Depression tend to be frugal; those alive during World War II value sacrifice of self for cause and country; the baby boom generation, who came of age during the counterculture sixties, are likely to question authority; Generation Xers, who were born in the 1960s and 1970s and experienced latchkey childhoods and other consequences of widespread divorce, value self-sufficiency; and those called Generation Next, who came of age after 9/11 and grew up with personal computers, cell phones, and the Internet, tend to value fortune, fame, and tolerance (Pew Research Center, 2007).

Whether in family relationships or in the workplace, when people from different generations interact, their co-cultural orientations can create communication difficulties. Miscommunication, misunderstandings, and conflict are likely to occur when people work with others of different generations. For example, people from earlier generations are unlikely to question authority figures such as parents, teachers, religious leaders, or bosses. They demonstrate respect by using formal terms of address, such as Mr., Ms., Dr., and sir. People who came of age in the 1960s or later, on the other hand, tend to be skeptical of authority and less formal in dealing with authority figures. They are more likely to question their managers and to openly disagree with decisions made by those in authority (Zempke, Raines, & Filipczak, 2000).

Cultural Identity

Recall that your self-concept is the mental image that you have of yourself, and that image is negotiated and reinforced through your communication with others. Membership in the co-cultural groups described above contributes to your cultural identity, but how much your identity is affected by each co-culture depends on the extent to which you identify with it (Ting-Toomey et al., 2000). For example, 20-year-old Kelly is a devout Catholic who attends Mass every morning and is a leader at the Newman Center on campus. She volunteers at the local pregnancy crisis center, where she tutors pregnant teens, and she dates only men who are Catholic. By contrast, Kelly's roommate, Nicole, is also Catholic, but rarely goes to Mass, is not involved at the Newman Center, is pro-choice, and is engaged to a classmate who is Jewish. As you would expect, being a Catholic is central to how Kelly views herself, and it is one of the first things she shares about herself when she meets someone. By contrast, the values of Catholicism don't seem to be central to Nicole's self-image, what she believes, or how she behaves.

Identifying Cultural Norms and Values

Some aspects that identify members of a culture may be easy to spot. We may be able to figure out people's cultural background by the language they speak, their dress, or artifacts such as religious markers they wear as jewelry or place in their home. For example, when people meet Shimon, from his sidecurls, his yarmulke, and his black clothes, they can quickly discern that he is a Hassidic Jew. But beyond style of dress, what does it mean to be a Hassidic Jew? How do Hassidic Jews differ from the dominant culture and from other cultural groups? What are other cultural groups to which they are similar?

The work of Geert Hofstede gives us a way to understand how cultures are similar to and different from one another and to understand how that variation affects communication. Hofstede (1980) identifies four major dimensions of culture that affect communication: individualism–collectivism, uncertainty avoidance, power distance, and masculinity–femininity. Table 6.1 shows where the United States falls on each of these dimensions.

Karl Walter/Getty Images Entertainment /Getty Images

Matisyahu displays an interesting blend of cultural identities. His clothing represents how important his Jewish faith is to him. Yet he performs reggae music. Does this blending of cultural identities seem odd to you? Why or why not?

Web Resource 6.1

Individualism–Collectivism

In **individualistic cultures** (for example, the United States, Australia, Great Britain, Canada, as well as northern and eastern European countries), people place primary value on the self and personal achievement. In an individualistic society, people tend to consider the interests of others primarily in relationship to how they affect the interest of the self. If you come from an individualistic culture, you may consider your family and close friends when you act, but mainly because your interests and theirs align. People in individualistic cultures view competition between people as desirable and useful. Because of this, individualistic cultures emphasize personal rights and responsibilities, privacy, voicing one's opinion, freedom, innovation, and self-expression (Andersen, Hecht, Hoobler, & Smallwood, 2003).

In contrast, **collectivist cultures** (for example, countries in South and Central

How does the communication of people from individualistic cultures differ from that of people in collectivist cultures?

individualistic culture *emphasizes personal rights and responsibilities, privacy, voicing one's opinion, freedom, innovation, and self-expression.*

Table 6.1 U.S. Ranking Among 53 Countries/Regions

Individualism	High uncertainty-avoidance	High power-distance	Masculinity
✓ (1st)			
			✓ (15th)
		✓ (38th)	
	✓ (43rd)		
Collectivism	Low uncertainty-avoidance	Low power-distance	Femininity

America, east and Southeast Asia, and Africa) place primary value on the interests of the group and group harmony. In a collectivist society, an individual's decision is shaped by what is best for the group whether it serves the individual's interests or not. Collectivist societies are highly integrated, and maintaining harmony and cooperation are valued over competitiveness and personal achievement. As a result, members of collectivist societies will probably have stronger bonds within the groups to which they belong (family, workplace, and community). Collectivist cultures emphasize community, collaboration, shared interest, harmony, the public good, and avoiding embarrassment (Andersen, Hecht, Hoobler, & Smallwood, 2003).

Notions of individualism and collectivism influence many aspects of communication, including most notably our self-concept formation, conflict management style, and group communication behavior (Samovar, Porter, & McDaniel, 2009). In individualistic cultures, people stress the self and personal achievement, and the individual is treated as the most important element in a social setting. In a collectivist culture, what affects self-concept and self-esteem is not individual achievement; rather, it is whether the group thrives and how people's actions have contributed to their group's success. So if Marie has been raised in an individualist culture and she is the highest scoring player on her basketball team, she will feel good about herself and identify herself as a "winner" even if her team has a losing season. But if Marie is from a collectivist culture, being the highest scoring player will have little effect on her self-esteem, but the fact that her team had a losing season will likely cause her to feel less personal esteem.

People from each of these cultural perspectives also view conflict differently. In individualistic cultures, the emphasis on the individual leads its members to value and practice assertiveness and confrontational argument, whereas members of collectivist cultures value accord and harmony and so practice tentativeness and collaboration or avoidance of arguments. In the United States, we teach assertiveness and argumentation as useful skills and expect them in interpersonal and work relationships, politics, consumerism, and other aspects of civic life. By contrast, to maintain harmony and avoid interpersonal clashes, Japanese business has evolved an elaborate process called *nemawashi*, a term that literally means digging around the roots of a tree before transplanting it. In Japan, any subject that might cause conflict at a meeting should be discussed in advance, so that the interaction at the meeting will not seem rude or impolite (Samovar & Porter, 2001). In collectivist societies, a style of communication that respects the relationship is more important than the information exchanged (Jandt, 2001). In collectivist societies, group harmony, sparing others embarrassment, and a modest presentation of oneself are important ways to show respect. A person does not speak directly if it might hurt others in the group.

How people work in groups also depends on the type of culture they come from. Because members of collectivist cultures see group harmony and the welfare of the group to be of primary importance, they strive for consensus on group goals and may, at times, sacrifice optimal outcomes for the sake of group accord. Your cultural assumptions affect how you work to establish group goals, how you interact with other group members, and how willing you are to sacrifice for the sake of the group. Groups with members from both individualistic and collectivist cultures may experience difficulties due to their varying cultural assumptions. In the Diverse Voices feature in this chapter, a Chinese-born communication professor, Min Liu, talks about how she dealt with the transition from China (a collectivist culture) to the United States (an individualistic culture) as a graduate student and how she has learned to manage both perspectives today.

collectivist culture
emphasizes community, collaboration, shared interest, harmony, the public good, and avoiding embarrassment.

Web Resource 6.2

Individualism and Collectivism

by Min Liu

Assistant Professor of Communication
Southern Illinois University at Edwardsville

I was born and raised in China, which is a collectivist country. I arrived in the United States for the first time in August of 2002 when I entered the Ph.D. program as a graduate student at North Dakota State University (NDSU) in Fargo, North Dakota. I chose NDSU for a number of reasons, but one that stands out in my mind as important is the fact that Fargo was listed as one of the safest cities in the United States at the time. You see, my family was concerned about sending their daughter to study in the United States, which is the most individualistic country in the world. They felt a bit more at ease knowing I would be studying in one of the safest cities in that country. Even my decision to come to NDSU was influenced by my family and our collectivist ideals. Little did I know, however, how much culture shock I would experience beginning with the first day I set foot on the NDSU campus.

I officially became an international student studying Communication at North Dakota State University in August of 2002. I felt prepared to study in the United States because I had learned English and was trained to become a college English instructor back in China. I had also aced the English proficiency test (TOEFL) required of international students. I remember feeling pretty confident about communicating with my American colleagues. As I walked across campus for my first day of orientation, I thought to myself, "Worst-case scenario, I'll forget how to say something in English and that's what my digital Chinese-English dictionary is for."

I would soon learn, however, that the issue of translating vocabulary was not the worst-case scenario. For most of my communication struggles, I could not find an answer in the dictionary. For example, in one of the first graduate classes I took, the professor asked everyone to call her by her first name (Deanna). Without hesitation, all my American classmates began doing so. Calling a professor by her first name was unheard of for Chinese students like me! As a sign of respect, we always call our teachers by their titles—Dr. Sellnow, Professor Sellnow, or Teacher Sellnow. Wherever you are on a college campus in China, it's clear who is the teacher and who are the students. I thought, "How am I to call a professor of mine by her first name?"

For a long time, I felt torn as to what to do—continuing to call her Dr. Sellnow may seem too distant and she might correct me. I want to honor her request out of respect for her authority. But everything in my collectivist values suggested that calling her Deanna was simply too disrespectful. So I simply avoided calling her anything. This solution worked fairly well in face-to-face communication situations—I would walk up to her, smile, and then start the conversation. This approach was working fairly well for me until the day came when I needed to e-mail her. I remember sitting in front of my computer for almost an hour trying to fine-tune a one-paragraph e-mail. Soon I realized the e-mail message was fine. The reason I couldn't bring myself to press "Send" was with the beginning of the e-mail, which read "Hello Deanna." I finally changed it to "Dr. Sellnow," followed by an apologetic explanation asking her to understand my dilemma and why I addressed her in this way. To my surprise, she responded by saying there was nothing wrong in addressing her as "Dr. Sellnow" and that I should continue to do so if that is what feels most appropriate to me.

In another class, I studied intercultural communication concepts. What I learned there proved helpful to me in reconciling my collectivist-individualistic predicament and better understand the cultural shock I was experiencing. As a Chinese, I grew up in a high power-distance culture. Professors and teachers are seen as having more power than students because, in my culture, people hold more or less power depending on where they are situated in certain formal, hierarchical positions. Students are to respect and honor their teachers by acknowledging their higher position of authority and status. The United States, however, is a low power-distance culture. People demonstrate respect for one another by addressing each other more as equals regardless of the formal positions they may hold. So, as uncomfortable as I felt, I tried to call my professors by their first names when they suggested it was appropriate to do so. I reminded myself that in the United States doing so was culturally appropriate and not a sign of disrespect.

Another culture shock experience I had to reconcile as a result of the differences between my collectivist values and the individualistic values of the United States had to do with disagreeing with my professor. In the United States, students learn to form opinions and defend their viewpoints and are rewarded for doing so in classroom presentations and debates. Professors perceive students who challenge their viewpoints with evidence and reasoning as intelligent and motivated. Students who do so are perceived very differently in the Chinese culture, where public disagreement with an authority figure is not only rare, but also inappropriate. Because of this value clash, I found it difficult to express and defend my opinions in class, especially if they differed from something the professor said. Doing so, it seemed to me, would be extremely disrespectful. Yet I observed classmates doing so and being lauded for their comments. Many times, I chose not to say anything during a face-to-face meeting with a professor, but found the courage to write an e-mail later. In the online environment, I found I could be honest and explain my disagreement with respect. Fortunately, many of my professors soon realized my cultural-values dilemma and adapted their communication styles toward me. Still today, though, I prefer to present my viewpoints concerning controversial

issues in a paper, a letter, an e-mail message, or an online post rather than in a meeting or other face-to-face discussion. I have found a way to honor my collectivist values in a way that also allows me to express myself in an individualistic cultural setting.

Finally, I recall struggling with how to behave in group settings as a result of the cultural differences along the individualism versus collectivism continuum. When I first arrived in the United States, I was very conflict avoidant, probably because in collectivistic cultures maintaining the harmony of the collective is an important priority. The approaches I had learned to value and enact in small group settings were actually perceived negatively by my peers and professors in the United States. My conflict avoidant style—which I engaged in as a sign of respect—would actually frustrate some of my group members. They perceived it as a sign that I did not care about the group's success and was a "slacker." I felt frustrated, too, as I tried to help the group become more cohesive and successful by avoiding conflict! I eventually learned that, to be successful, we all had to begin by being upfront about where we come from and our values. Once we all understood the differences, we could create a workable plan for success.

I have been in the United States for seven years now, am married, and have a son. I have also earned my Ph.D. and am working as an assistant professor of communication at the University of Southern Illinois at Edwardsville. Even now, I continue to learn new things about how to communicate best in this individualistic culture as compared to my collectivist home in China. Based on my experiences, I would have to say the most important thing for successful communication when interacting with people who come from a different place on the collectivism-individualism continuum is for all of us to always be mindful.

Used with permission.

Uncertainty Avoidance

Cultures differ in how their members feel about and deal with unpredictable people, relationships, or events. **Low uncertainty-avoidance cultures** (such as the United States, Sweden, and Denmark) are more tolerant of uncertainty in how people behave in relationships and in events, and so put little cultural emphasis on reducing unpredictability. People from cultures with low uncertainty avoidance more easily accept the unpredictability and ambiguity in life. They tend to be tolerant of the unusual, prize initiative, take risks, and think that there should be as few rules as possible. People who come from **high uncertainty-avoidance cultures** have a lower tolerance for unpredictable people, relationships, and events. These cultures create systems of formal rules and believe in absolute truth as the way to provide more security and reduce the risk. They also tend to be less tolerant of people or groups with deviant ideas or behavior. Because their culture emphasizes the importance of avoiding uncertainty, they often view life as hazardous and experience anxiety and stress when confronted with unpredictable people, relationships, or situations. Nations whose cultures are marked by high uncertainty-avoidance include Japan, Portugal, Greece, Peru, and Belgium (Samovar, Porter, & McDaniel, 2009).

How our culture has taught us to view uncertainty affects our communication with others. It shapes how we use language, develop relationships, and negotiate with others. People from high uncertainty-avoidance cultures use and value precise language because they believe that careful word choice makes the meaning of a message easier to understand. Imagine a teacher declaring to a class that "the paper must be well researched, with evidence cited, and professional in format and appearance." Students from high uncertainty-avoidance cultures would find the teacher's remarks to be too general and vague. They would most likely experience anxiety and ask a lot of questions about what kind of research is appropriate, how to cite evidence, how much evidence is needed, what writing style to use, and the length of the paper in order to reduce their uncertainty. These students would welcome a specific checklist or rubric that enumerated the exact criteria by which the paper would be graded. By contrast, students from low uncertainty-avoidance cultures would be annoyed by an overly specific list of rules and guidelines, viewing it as a barrier to creativity and initiative. As you can imagine, a teacher with students from both these backgrounds faces a difficult challenge when trying to explain an assignment.

How people approach new relationships and how they communicate in developing relationships is also affected by their culture's view of uncertainty. As you would expect, people from high uncertainty-avoidance cultures are wary of strangers and may not seek out new relationships or relationships with others they perceive as different (unpredictable). They generally prefer meeting people through friends and family and refrain from being alone with strangers. When developing relationships, people from high uncertainty-avoidance cultures tend to guard their privacy, refrain from self-disclosure early in a relationship, and proceed more slowly through relationship development. Members of low uncertainty-avoidance cultures, on the other hand, are likely to initiate relationships with people who differ from them, and enjoy the excitement of disclosing personal information in earlier stages of relationship development.

Power Distance

Cultures differ in how accepting they are of wide differences in power held by different groups of people and how people of unequal power expect to be treated. In cultures characterized as having **high power-distance**, inequalities in power, status, and rank are viewed as natural and these differences are acknowledged by all members of the

How does the communication of people from high uncertainty-avoidance cultures differ from that of people from low uncertainty-avoidance cultures?

low uncertainty-avoidance cultures
cultures characterized by greater acceptance of, and less need to control, unpredictable people, relationships, or events.

high uncertainty-avoidance cultures
cultures characterized by a low tolerance for, and a high need to control, unpredictable people, relationships, or events.

high power-distance
the cultural belief that inequalities in power, status, and rank are "natural" and that these differences should be acknowledged and accentuated.

How does the communication of people from high power-distance cultures differ from that of the people from low power-distance cultures?

Spencer Grant/PhotoEdit

In the United States, a low power-distance culture, employers and employees often interact informally in many work settings. How have you interacted with your bosses or employees? Has it varied from workplace to workplace?

low-power distance
the cultural belief that inequalities in power, status, and rank should be underplayed and muted.

masculine culture
a culture in which people are expected to adhere to traditional sex roles.

feminine culture
a culture in which people, regardless of sex, are expected to assume a variety of roles based on the circumstances and their own choices.

How does the communication of people from masculine cultures differ from that of people from feminine cultures?

culture. These cultures believe that everyone in the culture has a rightful place and that members who have higher power, status, and rank should be deferred to by those with less power, status, and rank. High power-distance cultures include most Arab countries of the Middle East as well as India, Malaysia, Guatemala, Venezuela, and Singapore.

In cultures characterized as having **low power-distance**, inequalities in power, status, and rank are muted. People know that some individuals have more clout, authority, and influence, but lower-ranking people are not in awe of, are not more respectful toward, and do not fear people with more power. Even though power differences exist, these cultures value democracy and egalitarian behavior. Austria, Finland, Denmark, Norway, the United States, New Zealand, and Israel are examples of countries whose dominant cultures are characterized by low power-distance.

Our cultural beliefs about power distance affect how we interact with others, including how we communicate with authority figures, our language use, and our nonverbal behavior. If you were a student, unskilled worker, or average citizen in a high power-distance culture, you would not challenge a person in authority, because you would expect to be punished for doing so. You would expect the more powerful person to control the interaction and would listen to what that person said and do what was ordered without question. When talking with more powerful people, you would address them formally by using their title as a sign of respect. Formal terms of address like Mr. or Mrs., proper and polite forms of language, as well as nonverbal signals of your status differences would be evident in the exchange. If you come from a low power-distance culture, you would be more comfortable challenging those in authority because differences in status are muted. When interacting with a more powerful people, you would feel comfortable directing the course of the conversation and would question or confront them if you needed to. You would not feel compelled to use a formal title when addressing a more powerful person.

Masculinity-Femininity

Cultures differ in how strongly they value traditional sex role distinctions. Cultures that Hofstede (2000) called **masculine cultures** expect people to maintain traditional sex roles and maintain different standards of behavior for men and women. Hofstede called these cultures "masculine" because, for the most part, groups that maintain distinct sex-based roles also value masculine roles more highly than feminine ones. If you come from a masculine culture like the ones that are dominant in Mexico, Italy, and Japan, you are likely to value men when they are assertive and dominant and to value women when they are nurturing, caring, and service oriented. When you encounter people who don't meet these expectations, you are likely to be uncomfortable. Overall, however, if you come from a masculine culture regardless of your sex, you will see masculine behaviors as more worthwhile, so you are likely to value the masculine characteristics of performance, ambition, assertiveness, competitiveness, and material success more than you value traditionally feminine traits such as service, nurturing, investment in relationships, and helping behaviors. **Feminine cultures** expect that people, regardless of sex, will assume a variety of roles depending on the circumstances and their own choices; they do not have any sex-role expectations. If you are from a feminine culture, like the national cultures of Sweden, Norway, and Denmark, not only will you feel free to act in ways that are not traditionally assigned to people of your sex, but you will also value traits that have traditionally been associated with feminine roles.

Whether you come from a masculine or a feminine culture has a significant effect on how much behavioral flexibility you demonstrate. People from masculine cultures have strict definitions of appropriate behavior for people of each sex. As a result, they learn and are reinforced for only those behaviors that are seen to be appropriate for their sex. So men in these cultures are unprepared to engage in nurturing and caring behaviors, such as empathizing and comforting, and women are unprepared to be assertive and argue persuasively. This is one of the reasons why those of us raised in masculine cultures find movies portraying men as bumbling caregivers humorous. Both men and women in feminine cultures learn to and are reinforced for demonstrating both traditionally masculine and feminine behaviors. As a result, people from feminine cultures are more flexible in their communication behavior. Both men and women learn to nurture, empathize, assert, and argue, although any single individual may lack skill in one or more behaviors. In fact, some situation comedies created in the United States that have been translated for audiences in feminine cultures have flopped because the humorous anecdotes about men who fail as caregivers don't translate.

Barriers to Effective Intercultural Communication

What barriers do we face when communicating interculturally?

Now that you have developed an understanding of culture and the variations that can exist among cultures and co-cultures, you are in a better position to appreciate the specific barriers caused by cultural differences, including anxiety, assumptions of similarity or difference, ethnocentrism, stereotypes and prejudice, incompatible communication codes, and incompatible norms and values.

Anxiety

It is normal to feel some discomfort or apprehension when we recognize that we are different from most everyone else or when we enter a cultural milieu that has unfamiliar customs. Most people experience fear, dislike, and distrust when first interacting with someone from a different culture (Luckmann, 1999). So when Marissa, who is from a barrio in Los Angeles, decided to attend a small, liberal arts college in New England, she was nervous and wondered if her decision to attend school in the northeast had been a good one. The other students had been friendly enough during orientation week, but it had become clear that she didn't really have much in common with them. While the others easily shared stories of spring-break trips with their families and joked about the cars they had wrecked, Marissa found she had little to add—her family always went to see her grandmother in Mexico when her parents took time off from their jobs. She didn't even have a driver's license. When she hesitantly mentioned her quinceañera party, everyone turned and stared at her and one guy said, "What in the world is a 'keensy snare yah' party?" And all of the guys laughed. At first, the other women listened politely, but by that time Marissa was so nervous that she stumbled over her words and really didn't do a good job of explaining this coming-of-age tradition that was so important to her community. Most of us are like Marissa when we are anxious—we don't do a good job of sharing our ideas and feelings. So, our anxiety becomes a barrier to our communication.

Assuming Similarity or Difference

When people cross into an unfamiliar cultural environment, they often assume that the norms, values, and traditions that applied in their familiar situation match those that apply in the new one. When traveling internationally from the United States, for example, many people expect to eat their familiar hamburgers and fries, provided with rapid and efficient service. Likewise, they may be annoyed when shops and restaurants closing during midday in countries that observe the custom of siesta.

It can be just as great a mistake to assume that everything about an unfamiliar culture will be different. With time, Marissa is likely to find that the other students really aren't as different from her friends at home, and that school is still school even when there is snow on the ground. As she makes friends, she learns that although Rachel, who is Jewish, didn't have a quinceañera party, she did have a bat mitzvah celebration, and Kate, who is Irish Catholic, had a big party to celebrate her confirmation. Because our assumptions guide our communication behavior, incorrectly assuming similarities or differences can lead to miscommunication. The wisest way to overcome this barrier is not to assume anything, but to be aware of the feedback you receive, which provides cues to the real similarities and differences that exist between your cultural expectations and those of your interaction partners.

Skill Learning Activity 6.2

Ethnocentrism

ethnocentrism
the belief that one's own culture is superior to others.

Ethnocentrism is the belief that one's own culture is superior to others. The stereotype of the immigrant in the host country, loudly complaining of how much better everything is back home, is the classic example of ethnocentrism. In varying degrees, ethnocentrism is found in every culture (Haviland, 1993) and can occur in co-cultures as well.

Professor Gates, Sergeant Crowley, and the Rose Garden Beer Summit

Pop Comm!

Chip Somodevilla/ Getty Images News/Getty Images

In July 2009, Henry Louis Gates, Jr., a distinguished Harvard professor who is black, was arrested at his home in Cambridge, Massachusetts, for "disorderly conduct." The arresting officer was Sergeant James Crowley, a white police officer who teaches police academy courses on how to avoid racial profiling. What might have been a national story for one day became a cause

célèbre for over a week when President Obama weighed in with his opinion. The event culminated in what became known as the Rose Garden Beer Summit, where Gates and Crowley met with President Obama and Vice President Biden over a beer in the White House's Rose Garden and agreed to disagree about the events of that night and to continue a dialogue (Williams, 2009).

It appears that during this incident both Professor Gates and Sergeant Crowley were influenced by deeply ingrained co-cultural messages about race and police authority. Professor Gates, returning home after what must have been an exhausting trip to China, was confronted with a front door that was stuck, so he had to force his way into his own home. A short time later, when confronted by a white officer at his door who claimed to be investigating a break-in, Gates's normal civility was probably overridden by his exhaustion and his co-cultural experience of racial profiling. According to the

An ethnocentric view of the world leads to attitudes of superiority and messages that are directly and subtly condescending in content and tone. As you would expect, these messages are offensive to receivers from other cultures or co-cultures.

Stereotypes and Prejudice

Stereotypes are the attributions that cover up individual differences and ascribe certain characteristics to a group of people. Basing our interactions on stereotypes can lead to misunderstandings and can strain relationships. For example, when Laura anticipates meeting Joey, who she has heard is gay, she may expect him to be effeminate in his mannerisms and interested in fashion. So she embarrasses him and herself when, early in their conversation, she attempts to find common ground and asks him for advice on what type of cologne to buy her boyfriend—to which he replies, "What is your problem? I may be gay, but I'm not that Clinton Kelly dude from *What Not to Wear!* Just because I'm gay doesn't make me a fashion consultant."

Prejudice is defined as a rigid attitude based on group membership that predisposes us to think, feel, or act in a negative way toward another person or group. Thinking that Xue, a Chinese student in your class, will get the best grade in the course because, supposedly, all Chinese students excel intellectually or assuming that Alberto, who is Mexican, is working in the United States illegally would be examples

stereotypes
attributions that cover up individual differences and ascribe certain characteristics to a group of people.

prejudice
a rigid attitude based on group membership.

---

police report filed by Sergeant Crowley, Gates's response to Crowley's request to step out to the porch was to demand, "Why, because I'm a black man in America?" (Associated Press, 2009).

On the other hand, Sergeant Crowley was responding to a 911 call about a possible home invasion and asked Gates to step outside and provide identification to support Gates's statement that he was the homeowner. This procedure is designed to ensure that if a home invader answers the door and has hostages, the person is drawn out of the residence. Crowley indicated in his police report that he was "surprised and confused" by Gates's continued accusations that he was a racist police officer ("Henry Louis Gates, Jr., Police Report," 2009). We can speculate that Crowley, who prided himself on his race-neutral approach to his work, may have been offended and angered by what he probably perceived as an unfair attack.

So, when confronted with a stressful and personally humiliating situation, two otherwise good men who make it their professional mission to overcome racism allowed their egos and their co-cultural stereotypes to escalate a routine police call into a national incident.

That two men who seem especially understanding and aware about the issue of racial profiling still clashed so intensely with one another is an example of how deep co-cultural conflict runs in the United States. This event also illustrates how the approaches we advocate in this chapter—listening, empathy, and flexibility—are often times easier said than done, especially when sensitive buttons are pushed. Rosie Sizer, chief of police in Portland, Oregon, says, "I think there's been…very little attention [paid] to how communications can sometimes break down in the heat of discussions of race" (Goodwin, 2009). To help avoid these kinds of communication breakdowns, Reverend Jim Wallis, author of *God's Politics: Why the Right Gets It Wrong and the Left Doesn't Get It*, encourages respect even when it might seem undeserved: "The best way to defuse, diminish, and ultimately dismantle the power of [prejudice] is to show even excessive respect in potential situations of conflict" (Jonsson, 2009). We can only hope that as Professor Gates and Sergeant Crowley continue their dialogue, they will inspire all of us as we seek to overcome our own co-culturally ingrained stereotypes.

Doug Pensinger/Getty Images News/Getty Images

Prejudice and stereotypes can negatively affect our relationships not only with people we know personally but also with our larger communities. How do you suppose this protester's sign will affect the young girls in the photo?

of prejudice. Colin is prejudiced and believes that all white people try to take advantage of people of color. So when his coworker John, who is white, offers to refer a client to Colin, Colin replies, "Forget it—you're not going to pawn off a deadbeat on me." When we interact based on stereotypes and prejudice, we risk creating messages that are inaccurate and damage our relationships. When we listen with our stereotypes and prejudices in mind, we may misperceive the intent of the person with whom we are talking. In the Pop Comm! article in this chapter you can read about how prejudice and stereotyping created a conflict that resulted in what is now know as the Rose Garden Beer Summit.

Incompatible Communication Codes

At times, we misunderstand one another because the language or other communication behavior of our culture or co-culture differs from that of another cultural group. For example, Zeke could not understand why those Chinese guys who were continually fighting—screaming at each other and waving their arms—always sat together in the dining hall. Zeke had no idea what they were saying but he from his standpoint they looked pretty angry.

Because he didn't understand Mandarin, Zeke was judging the conversation of the Chinese students based on their paralanguage and body movement, which he interpreted as hostile and angry. Zeke did not know that Mandarin is a tonal language. How the words are voiced affects their meaning. The large changes in pitch and volume that he heard were not expression of strong emotion, but only the voicing of different words.

When our conversational partners, people in our group, or audience members speak a different language, it is easy to see that we have incompatible communication codes. But even when people speak the same language, cultural variations can result from their belonging to different co-cultures. For example, people from Great Britain take a *lift* to reach a higher floor, while Americans ride an elevator. Even within a national group, co-cultural use of the language can lead to incompatible communication codes. In fact, less powerful co-cultural groups will often purposefully develop in-group codes that are easily understood by co-culture members but unintelligible to those from the outside. Just try to have a conversation about your computer problem with your friend Sam who is a "techno geek." As an insider, Sam's vocabulary is likely to be as foreign to you as if he were speaking Icelandic.

People who speak different languages quickly comprehend their inability to communicate verbally and invariably turn to some type of nonverbal signing in an effort to overcome the language barrier. As we have seen, however, there are also significant differences in the use and meaning of nonverbal behaviors. Not only do incompatible verbal communication codes create barriers to intercultural communication, so do our differences in how we use and interpret nonverbal behavior. For example, in some cultures, belching after eating signifies that the meal did not agree with the diner, whereas in other cultures, it is a compliment to the cook. Such cultural differences in nonverbal behavior often account for misunderstandings or embarrassment when people from different cultures attempt to communicate with each other.

Incompatible Norms and Values

All cultures base their communication behaviors on cultural norms and rules and on personal values based on those cultural norms and rules. Sometimes the norms and values of two people of different cultures create barriers that make it difficult for them to understand each other. For example, Jeff and Abdul have been best friends since elementary school. They have shared everything: school work, summer vacations, sports, and camping trips. Now that they are in high school, their interests seem to be changing. One day Jeff tells Abdul that he has a six-pack of beer and offers to share it with Abdul. Abdul simply says, "No," and offers no explanation. Jeff is confused by Abdul's behavior. To Jeff, a fourth-generation American whose family is not religious and is individualistic in their cultural orientation, drinking a couple of beers is no big deal. He figures, "Even if we get caught, neither of us has ever been in trouble before, so all we'd get is a slap on the wrist." He doesn't consider how his arrest might affect his family and chides Abdul, saying, "Come on, don't wimp out on me now." What Jeff does not understand is that Abdul, coming from a first-generation Saudi American Muslim family, has religious norms and the collectivist values of his parents. Being caught with alcohol would not only violate his religious beliefs but it would also bring great disgrace upon his whole family. To Abdul, honoring Allah as well as maintaining his family honor is much more important than having fun with a friend. But because they are life long friends, Abdul and Jeff don't recognize that their cultural backgrounds have led them to have different expectations that they don't really know how to discuss, so this incident puts a strain on their relationship

> How can you improve your intercultural communication?

Intercultural Communication Competence

Competent intercultural communicators overcome cultural barriers by adopting the correct attitudes toward other cultures, acquiring accurate information about other cultures' values and practices, and developing specific skills needed to be effective across cultures.

Adopt Correct Attitudes

The right attitudes for intercultural communication involve one's motivations and flexibility in interacting with others from different cultures (Neuliep, 2006). In other words, we must be willing to try and must have a desire to succeed when communicating interculturally. We must be willing to try new behaviors rather than expecting the other person to adjust to our style of communicating. Tolerating ambiguity, being open-minded, and acting altruistically enable us to effectively communicate across cultural differences.

1. **Tolerate ambiguity.** Communicating with strangers creates uncertainty, and when the stranger also comes from a different culture, we can become anxious about what he or she will expect of us. People beginning intercultural relationships must be prepared to tolerate a high degree of uncertainty about the other person and to tolerate it for a long time. If you enter an intercultural interaction believing that it is OK to be unsure about how to proceed, you are likely to pay closer attention to

One way to develop intercultural communication competence is to tolerate ambiguity. How well do you tolerate ambiguity when meeting someone from a different culture or co-culture?

altruism
a display of genuine and unselfish concern for the welfare of others.

egocentricity
a selfish interest in one's own needs, to the exclusion of everything else.

Skill Learning Activity 6.3

the feedback you receive from the other person, and you can then work to adjust your behavior and messages so that together the two of you can achieve understanding. Accepting the ambiguity in the interaction can help you work hard to make the conversation successful; you will be much less apt to become frustrated or discouraged by the inevitable false starts and minor misunderstandings.

When Jerome read the Partner Assignment List posted on the bulletin board outside the lab, he discovered that his lab partner had an Indian-sounding name, but he resolved to work hard to make the relationship a success. So when he met Meena in class and found that she was an exchange student from Mumbai, he worked hard to attune his ear to her accent and was pleased to discover that although her accent was at first difficult to understand, her command of English was as good as his. Over the semester, Jerome worked hard to understand Meena's English. He was rewarded, because she really had a much better grasp of chemistry than he did and was willing to tutor him as they worked on assignments.

2. **Be open-minded.** An open-minded person is willing to dispassionately receive the ideas and opinions of others. Open-minded people are aware of their own cultural values and recognize that other people's values are different. They resist the impulse to judge the values of other cultures in terms of those of their own culture. In other words, they resist ethnocentrism.

3. **Be altruistic.** **Altruism** is a display of genuine and unselfish concern for the welfare of others. The opposite of altruism is **egocentricity**, a selfish interest in one's own needs to the exclusion of everything else. Egocentric people are self-centered, whereas altruistic people are other-centered. Altruistic communicators do not neglect their own needs, but they recognize that for a conversation to be successful, both parties must be able to contribute what they want and take what they need from the exchange.

Acquire Knowledge About Other Cultures

The more we know about other cultures, the more likely we are to be competent intercultural communicators (Neuliep, 2006). There are several ways to learn about other cultures.

1. **Observe.** You can simply watch as members of another culture interact with each other. As you watch, you can notice how their values, rituals, and communication styles are similar to and different from your own and other cultures with which you are familiar. The technique of watching the communication behaviors used by members of a particular culture is called "passive observation."

2. **Formally study.** You can learn about other cultures by reading accounts by their members and ethnographic research studies, by taking courses, and by interviewing members of the culture about their values, rituals, and so on.

3. **Immerse yourself in the culture.** You can learn a great deal about another culture by actively participating in it. When you live or work with people whose cultural assumptions are different from yours, you not only acquire obvious cultural information, but you also learn nuances that escape passive observers and are generally not accessible through formal study alone. One reason that study-abroad programs often include home stays is to ensure that students become immersed in the culture of the host country. We hope that you will consider participating in a study-abroad experience. The international or global studies office at your college or university can point you to a variety of study-abroad opportunities and may even guide you to scholarships or grants to help pay your expenses.

Speech Assignment: **Communicate on Your Feet**

Acquiring Cultural Knowledge

The Assignment

Choose a culture you're not familiar with but are curious about. Prepare a 3- to 5-minute speech to deliver in class by gathering materials from (a) reviewing an encyclopedia entry (b) researching two or three academic sources about the culture, and (c) interviewing someone from that country either face-to-face or online. Use what you learn from the encyclopedia and the academic sources to shape the questions you ask in the interview. In your speech discuss what you learned from each source, answering the following questions:

1. What did you know about the culture before you began your research?
2. What did you learn from the encyclopedia article that changed or deepened your knowledge?
3. How was your understanding enriched from the additional academic sources you read?
4. What did you learn from your interviewee, and how did the interview compare to your other sources?

Using Diverse Resources

When we are researching any topic, we can be tempted to limit our quest to only one type of information source. But as you will learn in this assignment, what you know about a subject is often the result of where you look. That is why it is important to consult a variety of information sources. Whether online or in print, encyclopedias are good jumping-off points to acquire information and can provide a wonderful overview of the subject. Specialized sources like books and articles by experts provide additional details and can confirm or disconfirm information in the encyclopedia. Finally, personal interviews with experts add another dimension or level of specificity. For example, in this assignment when you interview the person from the other culture, you can ask for specific examples of his or her experiences and whether what you have read is accurate. Good speeches depend on accurate information, so learning to use diverse sources is important to your success.

Develop Culture-Specific Skills

To be effective in intercultural situations, you may need to adapt the basic communication skills that you learn in this course to the demands of a particular culture. To this end, the three most useful skills that you will study are listening, empathy, and flexibility.

1. **Practice listening.** By carefully listening and demonstrating you're listening, you can improve your communication with people from other cultures. Because language and nonverbal communication vary across cultures, it is vitally important that you focus closely on the other and listen attentively. There are cultural differences in how people engage in listening and the value that cultures place on listening. In the United States, we listen closely for concrete facts and information and often ask

questions while listening. In other cultures, such as Japan, Finland, and Sweden, listeners are more reserved and do not ask as many questions (Samovar, Porter, & McDaniel, 2009). For many cultures in the Far East, listening is much more valued than speaking. Regardless of your cultural background, however, becoming a more skillful listener will help you in your intercultural encounters.

2. **Practice intercultural empathy.** **Intercultural empathy** means imaginatively placing yourself in the other person's cultural world to attempt to experience what he or she is experiencing (Ting-Toomey, 1999). The saying "Don't judge a person until you have walked a mile in his shoes" captures this idea. By paying close attention to the other person and focusing on the emotions displayed, we can improve our empathic skills.

3. **Develop flexibility.** We discussed the concept of flexibility as part of an appropriate attitude toward intercultural encounters, but we can also provide concrete strategies for becoming more flexible in communication. **Flexibility** is the ability to adjust your communication to fit the other person and the situation. With flexibility, you can use a wide variety of communication skills during an interaction and modify your behavior within and across situations. Being flexible means analyzing a situation, making good decisions about how to communicate in that situation, and then modifying your communication when things are not going well.

intercultural empathy
imaginatively placing yourself in the dissimilar other person's cultural world to attempt to experience what he or she is experiencing.

flexibility
the ability to adjust your communication to fit the other person and the situation.

A Question of Ethics

Tyler, Jeannie, Margeaux, and Madhukar were sitting around Margeaux's dining-room table working on a group marketing project. It was 2:00 a.m. They had been working since 6:00 p.m. and still had several hours' work remaining.

"Oh, the misery," groaned Tyler, pretending to slit his own throat with an Exacto knife. "If I never see another photo of a veggie burger, it will be too soon. Why didn't we choose a more interesting product?"

"I think it had something to do with *someone* wanting to promote a healthy alternative to greasy hamburgers," Jeannie replied sarcastically.

"Right," said Tyler, "I don't know what I could have been thinking. Speaking of greasy hamburgers, is anyone else starving? Anybody want to order pizza or something?"

"No one will deliver up here this late," Margeaux replied, "but I have a quiche that I could heat up."

"Fancy," Tyler quipped.

"You wish," Margeaux said. "It came out of a box."

"Sure, that sounds great, thanks," Jeannie said. "I'm hungry too."

What Would You Do?

"It doesn't have any meat in it, does it?" asked Madhukar. "I don't eat meat."

"Nope, it's a cheese and spinach quiche," Margeaux said.

Tyler and Margeaux went off to the kitchen to prepare the food. Tyler took the quiche, still in its box, from the fridge. "Uh-oh," he said. "My roommate is a vegetarian, and he won't buy this brand because it has lard in the crust. Better warn Madhukar. He's a Hindu, so I imagine it's pretty important to him."

"Shhh!" said Margeaux, "I don't have anything else to offer him, and he'll never know the difference anyway. Just pretend you didn't notice that."

"Okay," Tyler said. "It's your kitchen."

1. What exactly are Margeaux's ethical obligations to Madhukar in this situation? Why?
2. Does the fact that Tyler is not the host relieve him of all ethical responsibility in this case?

Summary

Culture encompasses the values, attitudes, beliefs, orientations, and underlying assumptions prevalent among people in a society. Culture shock is the psychological discomfort people have when they attempt to adjust to a new cultural situation. Intercultural communication takes place when people's distinct cultural assumptions alter the communication event. A shared system of meaning exists within the dominant culture, but meanings can vary within co-cultures based on race, ethnicity, sex and gender, religion, sexual orientation, social class, and age. Cultural norms and values vary in systematic ways, and we can understand how similar or different one culture is from others by understanding where the culture is on the dimensions of individualism–collectivism, uncertainty avoidance, power distance, and masculinity–femininity.

Barriers to intercultural communication include anxiety, assumptions about differences and similarities, ethnocentrism, stereotypes and prejudice, incompatible communication codes, and incompatible norms and values. To develop intercultural communication competence, we should learn to tolerate ambiguity, be open-minded, and be altruistic. We can acquire knowledge of other cultures through observing, formal study, and cultural immersion. Useful skills for intercultural communication competence are listening, intercultural empathy, and flexibility.

Communicate! Active Online Learning

Now that you have read Chapter 6, use your Premium Website for *Communicate!* for quick access to the electronic resources that accompany this text. These resources include

- **Study tools** that will help you assess your learning and prepare for exams (*digital glossary, key term flash cards, review quizzes*).
- **Activities and assignments** that will help you hone your knowledge, analyze communication situations (*Skill Learning Activities)*, and build your public speaking skills throughout the course (*Communication on Your Feet speech assignments, Action Step activities*). Many of these activities allow you to compare your answers to those provided by the authors, and, if requested, submit your answers to your instructor.

- **Media resources** that will help you explore communication concepts online (*Web Resources*), develop your speech outlines (*Speech Builder Express 3.0*), watch and critique videos of communication situations and sample speeches (*Interactive Video Activities*), upload your speech videos for peer reviewing and critique other students' speeches (*Speech Studio online speech review tool*), and download chapter review so you can study when and where you'd like (*Audio Study Tools*).

This chapter's Key Terms, Skill Learning Activities, and Web Resources are also featured on the following pages, and you can find this chapter's Communicate on Your Feet assignment in the body of the chapter.

Key Terms

altruism (128)
co-culture (114)
collectivist culture (118)
culture (112)
culture shock (112)
dominant culture (113)
egocentricity (128)

ethnicity (114)
ethnocentrism (124)
feminine culture (122)
flexibility (130)
high power-distance (121)
high uncertainty-avoidance
   cultures (121)
individualistic culture (117)
intercultural communication (113)

intercultural empathy (130)
low power-distance (122)
low uncertainty-avoidance cultures
   (121)
masculine culture (122)
prejudice(125)
religion (115)
social class (115)
stereotypes (125)

Skill Learning Activities

6.1: Race and Ethnicity (114)

What is the difference between race and ethnicity? Can you think of examples of people who are ethnically different but racially the same? racially different but ethnically the same? Can you think of anyone for whom both designations might be identical? For whom the two designations might be contradictory? What does this analysis suggest about the accuracy and legitimacy of such classification systems?

6.2: Similarities and Differences (124)

Recall a time when you visited a place that was different from your usual social milieu: a different country, a different city, a different kind of club or market. Did you assume any similarities or differences? Were your assumptions correct? How did they affect your perception of the place? How did they affect your appreciation for, or enjoyment of, the place?

6.3: Acquiring Accurate Cultural Knowledge (128)

For the next week, conduct research into a distinct culture with which you have little or no familiarity. This can be a co-culture based on gender, race, religion, ethnicity, social class, sexual orientation, age, or some combination of these factors, but whatever culture you choose to study, be sure you can access it locally. First, arrange to observe members of the culture engaged in a typical activity and note as many of their individual communication behaviors as you can. Take your notes respectfully, being careful not to offend those you observe. Next, spend some time formally researching the culture and its communication behaviors at a library or over the Internet, consulting only reputable sources for your information. Finally, observe members of the culture once more and then write a paragraph in which you answer these questions: What were your impressions of the culture's communication behaviors the first time you observed its members? How were these first impressions altered, if at all, by your formal research into the culture? How did your formal research affect your second observation of the culture?

To help you complete this activity, you can use the log provided in your Premium Website for *Communicate!* Look for it in the Skill Learning activities for Chapter 6.

Web Resources

6.1: Hofstede's Cultural Dimensions (117)

Geert Hofstede's Web site lists national scores in five cultural dimensions: power-distance index, individualism, masculinity, uncertainty-avoidance index, and long-term orientation.

6.2: Individualism and Collectivism (118)

This page from WestEnd.com, an agency that does research in education, offers resources about the differences between individualism and collectivism and their implications for teaching. One of its publications, a knowledge brief called *Bridging Cultures in Our Schools: New Approaches That Work,* discusses sources of cross-culture conflicts and describes strategies for resolving them. To read the brief online, click on the link "View online/PDF."

Gabe Palmer/Alamy

Understanding Interpersonal Relationships

Questions you will be able to answer after reading this chapter:

- What is competent communication in acquaintance, friendship, and intimate relationships?
- How do disclosure and feedback affect relationship life cycles?
- What role does communication play in beginning, developing, maintaining, and deteriorating relationships?
- How do dialectal tensions operate in interpersonal relationships?

It was Monday, between classes, and Jennifer had an hour before her next class. She decided to walk over to the bookstore. On the way, she spotted Maria, a woman in her accounting class, and asked, "Hey, how you doing?"

"OK," Maria replied. "What did you think of that test we had yesterday?"

"Not sure I want to think about it now," Jennifer replied with a little laugh.

"I know what you mean," Maria said. "I hope we get them back soon. See you in class tomorrow."

"Right," Jennifer replied as Maria made her way across the street.

A minute later, Jennifer was startled as she heard, "Hey beautiful, what are you doing here?"

"Greg!" Jennifer said with a big smile on her face. "You scared me. I thought you were working today!"

"Well," Greg replied, "as it turned out, my plans to work with Ken kind of fell through. Have you got time to get lunch?"

"You know I've always got time to spend with you."

"Like to decide what we're going to do this weekend?"

"Sounds good to me!"

relationship

sets of expectations two people have for their behavior based on the pattern of interaction between them.

good relationship

ones in which the interactions are satisfying to and healthy for those involved.

Interpersonal communication skills help you start, build, and maintain healthy **relationships,** sets of expectations two people have for their behavior based on the pattern of interaction between them (Littlejohn & Foss, 2008). We form relationships to satisfy our innate human need for connection with others. That is, we want to feel a sense of belonging and that someone else is here for us . Relationships run the gamut from impersonal acquaintances (like Maria and Jennifer) to intimate friends (like Greg and Jennifer). Regardless of the level of intimacy, we seek **good relationships,** ones in which the interactions are satisfying to and healthy for those involved. How we communicate is central to achieving that goal (Littlejohn & Foss, 2008).

In this chapter, we describe three types of interpersonal relationships and provide guidelines for healthy communication in each of them. Next, we talk about the role of self-disclosure and feedback in relationship life cycles. Finally, we talk about the dialectical tensions in relationships and ways to manage them.

Types of Relationships

We behave differently depending on whether our relationships are personal or impersonal. Moving on a continuum from impersonal to personal (Dindia & Timmerman, 2003), we can classify our relationships as acquaintances, friendships, and close friends or intimates. Specific communication competencies help establish and maintain each type of relationship.

> What is competent communication in acquaintance relationships?

Acquaintances

Acquaintances are people we know by name and talk with when the opportunity arises, but with whom our interactions are limited. Many acquaintance relationships grow out of a particular context. We become acquainted with those who live in our apartment building or dorm or in the house next door, who sit next to us in class, who go to our church, or belong to our club. Thus Whitney and Paige, who meet in calculus class, may talk with each other about class-related issues but make no effort to share personal ideas or to see each other outside of class. Most conversations with acquaintances can be defined as **impersonal communication,** which is essentially interchangeable chit-chat (Buber, 1970). In other words, I may talk about the same thing—for instance, the weather—with the grocery clerk, the sales associate, the bank teller, or the server at dinner. If you have an online social networking profile on Facebook, Twitter, or MySpace, many of your online "friends" would probably be most accurately defined as acquaintances if your online conversations are surface-level ones.

Our goals when communicating with acquaintances are usually to reduce uncertainty and maintain face. We engage in impersonal conversations to gain information that may help us connect with other people by discovering that their

acquaintances

people we know by name and talk with when the opportunity arises, but with whom our interactions are largely impersonal.

impersonal communication

interchangeable polite chit-chat involving no or very little personal disclosure.

beliefs, attitudes, and values are similar to our own (Berger, 1987). In doing so, however, either of us may say or do something that produces unintended consequences. That is, we could offend the other person or say something that is taken the wrong way. So, our second goal is to monitor verbal and nonverbal feedback and provide opportunities to help the other person save face. **Saving face** is the process of attempting to maintain a positive self-image in a relational situation (Ting-Toomey, 2004).

David J. Green-lifestyle themes/Alamy

Acquaintanceship guidelines

To meet other people and develop acquaintance relationships, it helps to be good at starting and developing conversations. The following guidelines can help you become more competent in conversing with others:

- **Initiate conversations** by introducing yourself, referring to the physical context, referring to your thoughts or feelings, referring to another person, or making a joke. For example, "Hi, I'm Whitney. Do you think it's hot in here, or is it just me?"
- **Develop an other-centered focus** by asking questions, listening carefully, and following up on what has been said. Here is an example:

WHITNEY: "Have you ever taken a class from this professor?"

PAIGE: "Yeah, I took algebra from her."

WHITNEY: "What was she like?"

PAIGE: "She was pretty good. Her tests were hard, but they were fair. I learned a lot."

WHITNEY: "Did she offer study guides?"

PAIGE: "Yes, and we reviewed as a class by playing what she called 'algebra jeopardy.' That worked well for me."

WHITNEY: "Sounds like I'm going to like this class and this instructor!"

- **Engage in appropriate turn-taking.** Effective conversationalists balance talking with listening and do not interrupt the other. Not only do we need to avoid dominating the conversation, but we also need to uphold our part by talking enough.
- **Make your comments relevant** to what has previously been said before you change subjects.
- **Be polite.** Consider how your conversational partner will feel about what you say and work to phrase your comments in a way that allows your partner to save face. Here is an example:

WHITNEY: "I wish I wouldn't have signed up for this section that meets right at noon. I'm famished. Here, do you want some M&Ms?"

PAIGE: "No thanks."

WHITNEY: "Are you sure? I don't mind sharing. A little sugar never hurt anyone."

PAIGE: "I'm diabetic."

WHITNEY: "Oh, I'm so sorry. I'll save these for later."

Which of your online "friends" would you describe as acquaintances and why?

saving face
the process of attempting to maintain a positive self-image in a relational situation.

Web Resource 7.1

Friends

Over time, some acquaintances become our friends. **Friends** are people with whom we have voluntarily negotiated more personal relationships (Patterson, Bettini, & Nussbaum, 1993, p. 145). As friendships develop, people move toward interactions that are less role bound and more interpersonally satisfying. For example, Whitney and Paige, who are acquaintances in calculus class and have only talked about class-related subjects, may decide to get together after class to work out at the gym. If they find that they enjoy each other's company, they may continue to meet outside of class and eventually become friends.

What is competent communication in friendships?

Some of our friendships are context bound. Thus, people often refer to their tennis friends, office friends, or neighborhood friends. These context friendships may fade if the context changes. For instance, your friendship with a person at the office may fade if you or your friend takes a job with a different company. Did you move a great distance from your hometown to attend college? If so, how many of your high school friends do you still consider friends?

Friendship guidelines

For friendships to develop and continue, some key behaviors must occur. These behaviors help friendships continue whether you are face to face or separated by distance. Computer-mediated communication (CMC) and cell phones have proven helpful in maintaining long distance relationships (Walther & Parks, 2002). The following five competencies can help you develop and maintain your friendships (Samter, 2003):

- **Initiation.** Be proactive in setting up times to spend together. One person must get in touch with the other, and the interaction must be smooth, relaxed, and enjoyable. A friendship is not likely to form between people who rarely interact or who have unsatisfying interactions.
- **Responsiveness.** Each person must listen. Listen to others and respond to what they say. It is difficult to form friendships with people who focus only on themselves or their issues, and it is equally difficult to maintain relationships with people who are uncommunicative.
- **Self-disclosure.** Friends share feelings with each other. Although acquaintances can be maintained by conversations that discuss surface issues or abstract ideas, a friendship is based on the exchange of more personal and specific information including personal history, opinions, and feelings. For example, after Paige and Whitney start to spend more time together outside of class, they might have this conversation:

PAIGE: "Can I tell you something and trust you to keep it between us?"

WHITNEY: "Of course."

PAIGE: "Well, you know I've been seeing David for a while now."

WHITNEY: "Yeah, he seems like a nice guy."

PAIGE: "Well, the other night we got into a little fight and he pushed me onto the couch. I actually have a bruise here on my arm from it."

- **Emotional support.** Provide comfort and support when needed. When we are emotionally or psychologically vulnerable, we expect to be helped by those we consider to be friends. When your friends are hurting, they need you to support them by confirming their feelings and helping them make sense of what has happened.

friends
people with whom we have negotiated more personal relationships that are voluntary.

WHITNEY: "Oh no."

PAIGE: "He said he was sorry and I believe him, but I just don't feel comfortable around him now."

WHITNEY: "I understand. I'm not sure I would feel comfortable either. Is there anything I can do?"

PAIGE: "No, not really. I guess I just wanted someone to confirm that I'm not overreacting."

WHITNEY: "Well, I don't think you're overreacting at all. Please let me know what I can do to help, OK?"

PAIGE: "OK. I'm so lucky to have you for a friend."

- **Conflict management.** Manage conflicts so that both parties' needs are met. It is inevitable that friends will disagree about ideas or behaviors. Friendship depends on successfully handling these disagreements through conversation. In fact, by competently managing conflict, people can strengthen their friendship.

WHITNEY: "Maybe you should talk to a campus counselor about this."

PAIGE: "No, I don't want to make a big deal out of it."

WHITNEY: "Paige, you got a bruise. That seems like a big deal to me."

PAIGE: "Actually, I bruise really easily. I don't want to see a counselor."

WHITNEY: "Well, if anything like this happens again, will you please talk to someone?"

PAIGE: "OK, if something happens again, I promise I will."

close friends or intimates
people with whom we share a high degree of commitment, trust, interdependence, disclosure, and enjoyment.

platonic relationship
an intimate relationship in which the partners are not sexually attracted to each other or do not act on an attraction they feel.

romantic relationship
an intimate relationship in which the partners act on their sexual attraction.

Close Friends or Intimates

Close friends or **intimates** are those few people with whom we share close, caring, and trusting relationships characterized by a high degree of commitment, trust, interdependence, disclosure, and enjoyment. We may have countless acquaintances and many friends, but we are likely to have only a few truly intimate relationships. Intimacy is not synonymous with "love" or exclusivity, and both platonic and romantic relationships may become intimate. A **platonic relationship** is one in which the partners are not sexually attracted to each other or do not act on an attraction they feel. If you're familiar with the television series, *Will and Grace*, their relationship is platonic. Although Will and Grace live together and are intimate friends, Will is homosexual and Grace is heterosexual. Conversely, a **romantic relationship** is one in which the partners act on their sexual attraction. Today, many people use social networking and matchmaking sites to find romantic relationship partners. Sometimes people use ghostwriters to help create the online profile they would like to project. The Pop Comm! feature talks about the role of ghostwriters and the ethical decisions to consider when using matchmaking sites to find romantic partners.

Original Artist/CSL CartoonStock Ltd

"Jerkins and I worked it out. He can have the office with the window."

trust

placing confidence in another in a way that almost always involves some risk.

What is competent communication in intimate relationships?

Regardless of whether the relationship is platonic or romantic, for it to remain intimate, both partners must continue to trust the other. **Trust** is placing confidence in another in a way that almost always involves some risk. We show trust by having positive expectations of the other person and believing that he or she will behave fairly and honestly. With our close friends, our lives are interdependent or intertwined. We are more likely to share personal, private information about ourselves with close friends. In close relationships, there is some fusion of the self and the other. The partner is perceived as part of yourself. In other words, you come to define who you are, in part, through your close relationships (Aron, Aron, Tudor, & Nelson, 2004). As we disclose personal information, we monitor how well our partner keeps our confidence. Once we perceive our partner to be untrustworthy, we are likely to withdraw and not continue to disclose. As a result, over time the intimacy in the relationship will decrease. When there is a severe breach of trust, we may even abruptly end the relationship.

Research shows that women and men tend to differ on the factors that lead to intimacy in relationships. This may be because society teaches women and men to behave differently, according to the norms of femininity and masculinity. Women tend to develop close relationships with others based on talking, opening up with the other, and sharing personal feelings. By gaining knowledge of the innermost being of their partner, women develop a sense of "we-ness" with others. Men tend to develop

Why Don't You Speak for Yourself, John?: Using Ghostwritten Online Dating Profiles

Pop Comm!

AP Photo/Jeff Christensen

Throughout history—in life, literature, and the media—people hoping to find love have solicited others to help them with self-expression. In Henry Wadsworth Longfellow's poem "The Courtship of Miles Standish," the shy Miles asks his friend John

Alden to plead his case with the beautiful Priscilla Mullins. John complies, but in a classic love triangle scenario, Priscilla asks John, "Why don't you speak for yourself, John?" More recently, in an episode of *Seinfeld*, Kramer asks his friend Newman to write a poem for Kramer to recite to a woman he is wooing. But Newman's poetry leaves something to be desired: "He imbibed her glistening spell / Just before the other shoe fell." And most of us remember at least one occasion in junior high when we asked our best friend to find out if that cute classmate was interested in us.

Today we've expanded our search for love to online dating services, but advanced technologies don't eliminate the need some of us have to seek outside help in expressing ourselves. A quick Amazon search shows several titles promising online dating success: *I Can't Believe I'm Buying This Book: A Commonsense Guide to Successful Internet Dating* by Evan Marc Katz; *Online Dating for Dummies* by Judy Silverstein and Michael Lasky; *Fine, I'll Go Online!: The Hollywood Publicist's Guide to Successful Internet Dating* by Leslie Oren; and

close friendships through joint activities, doing favors for each other, and being able to depend on one another. Men are less likely to define a close friend as someone with whom you can share feelings. For men, close friends are the people you can depend on to help you out of a jam and the people you regularly choose for pursuing enjoyable activities together (Wood & Inman, 1993). It is important to note that these differences are more pronounced in same-sex friendships. When men and women develop close friendships or intimate relationships with each other, these distinctions may not apply.

Intimacy guidelines

Maintaining intimacy depends on developing and maintaining trust in your partner and commitment to your relationship. The following guidelines can help you establish and maintain trust (Boon, 1994, pp. 97–101):

- **Be dependable** so your partner learns he or she can rely on you at all times and under all circumstances. Of course, nobody is perfect. But striving to be dependable will provide a foundation for understanding when something does come up.

Romancing The Web: A Therapist's Guide To The Finer Points Of Online Dating by Diane M. Berry.

Personal coaching for online dating is also on the rise. Online services such as Dating-Profile.com, ProfileHelper.com, and E-Cyrano.com help online daters write their profiles for a fee ranging from $29 to $2,000 (Alsever, 2007). On the ProfileHelper.com home page, the founder, Eric Resnic, says:

Everyone has something unique that makes them special. Together we will figure out that special thing that attracts people to you and exactly what qualities you are looking in a partner. Then, I will create or enhance your profile so that it is one of a kind, charming, entertaining and impossible to resist.

Opinions vary on what it means to "speak for yourself" on dating profile sites. Jenny Cargile, a Match.com user, says hiring someone to help write her profile would obscure who she truly is. "I'm not a person who is put together or always knows the right thing to say," she says. "I would feel like if I went out on a date with someone, I would have to be what they read instead of myself" (Alsever, 2007).

However, online dater Jim West sings the praises of ProfileHelper.com, where he learned to be more specific and inquisitive when communicating on online dating sites (Alsever, 2007). In his case,

a profile-writing coach stressed basic communication principles that helped West more accurately convey the kind of person he was, the types of things he enjoyed, and what he was looking for in a potential partner. Steve Zologa, founder of a similar company in Washington, D.C., looks at it as a simple matter of marketing: "My hypothesis is that there are many great men and women in the D.C. area who can't market themselves. You have about seven seconds to make a good impression, then you're done" (McCarthy, 2008).

However you feel about profile-writing coaches, most would agree that communication on online dating sites is tricky. An article in *Skeptic* explores the pros and cons of self-disclosing when dating online (King, Austin-Oden, & Lohr, 2009): On one hand, information presented online is easy to manipulate and control, so people can present themselves in any way they like—even if what they present isn't 100 percent accurate. On the other hand, the relative anonymity of online communication "accelerates intimacy through increased openness about aspects of the self." When what we disclose about ourselves is true, self-disclosure is an important step in making a successful relationship.

What do you think—is true self-disclosure encouraged or obscured by online dating?

- **Be responsive** in meeting your partner's needs. At times, this will require you to put their needs before your own.
- **Be collaborative in managing conflict.** Doing so includes saying you're sorry for something you've done or said, agreeing to disagree, and letting go of the need to be "right."
- **Be faithful** by maintaining your partner's confidential information and by abiding by sexual or other exclusivity agreements between you and your partner. If your partner tells you something in confidence, honor that request.
- **Be transparent** by honestly sharing your real ideas and feelings with your partner.
- **Be willing to put your relationship first.** This may mean giving up some activities or relationships to spend time with your partner. This is not to say you should give up all other activities and relationships. Rather, healthy intimate relationships are characterized by a balance between doing things together and doing things apart (Baxter & Montgomery, 1996).

Skill Learning Activity 7.1

Speech Assignment: **Communicate on Your Feet**

Friendship Speech

The Assignment

Prepare a 3- to 5-minute speech about your friends. Identify one person you have known for some time that you would consider an acquaintance, one that you would consider a friend, and one that you would consider a best friend. Describe each person and your relationship, as well as why you placed them in the category you did. Talk about the kinds of topics you typically discuss with them and the kinds you would not be likely to talk about with them. Be sure to follow the Speech Organization Guidelines here as you prepare. At your instructor's request, deliver your speech for your classmates.

Speech Organization Guidelines

Introduction
1. Catch attention
2. Provide listener relevance and speaker credibility
3. State thesis with preview of main points

Body
1. Acquaintance
2. Friend
3. Best friend

Conclusion
1. Restate thesis with summary of main points
2. Clincher

Throughout our lives, we interact in relationships with lots of people. But as you will learn in this assignment, most of our interpersonal relationships fall into the categories of acquaintances or friends. If we are honest with ourselves, most of us can probably name only a few best friends. As you prepare the speech, you will begin to see how the topics and feelings you share are deeper and more personal with best friends than with acquaintances or even friends.

Disclosure and Feedback in Relationship Life Cycles

Relationships are not something we *have*, but rather are something we *make* as we communicate with others. Over time, in the give and take of our conversations, we create, recreate, and sometimes even destroy our relationships (Parks, 2006). Even though no two relationships develop in exactly the same manner, all relationships tend to move through identifiable stages that include beginning, developing, maintaining, and perhaps deteriorating (Baxter; 1982, Duck, 1987; Knapp & Vangelisti, 2005; Taylor & Altman, 1987). Relationships don't move through these stages in a linear fashion: rather, we seem to cycle back and forth through the stages, so we say that these stages occur within the life cycle of a relationship (Honeycutt, 1993; Duck, 2007). How a relationship moves through these stages depends on the interpersonal communication between the partners. In fact, talking is basic to all relationship stages—whether they are beginning, deepening, getting worse, or maintaining at a status quo. (Duck, 2007). What enables a relationship to move between stages is the disclosure and feedback that occurs between partners. So let's take a look at how disclosure and feedback work together in relationship development.

A healthy interpersonal relationship is marked by an appropriate balance of **self-disclosure** (sharing biographical data, personal ideas, and feelings that are unknown to the other person) and **feedback** (the verbal and physical responses to people and/or their messages) within the relationship. The **Johari window**, named after its two originators, Joe Luft and Harry Ingham, is a tool for examining the relationship between disclosure and feedback in a relationship (Luft, 1970). The window represents all of the information about you that can be known. You and your partner each may know some (but not all) of this information. The window has four "panes" or quadrants, as shown in Figure 7.1.

The Open Pane

The first quadrant is called the "open" pane of the window because it represents the information about you that both you and your partner know. It includes information

> How do disclosure and feedback affect relationship life cycles?

self-disclosure
sharing biographical data, personal ideas, and feelings that are unknown to the other person.

feedback
verbal and physical responses to people (and/ or their messages) within the relationship.

Johari window
a tool for examining the relationship between disclosure and feedback in the relationship.

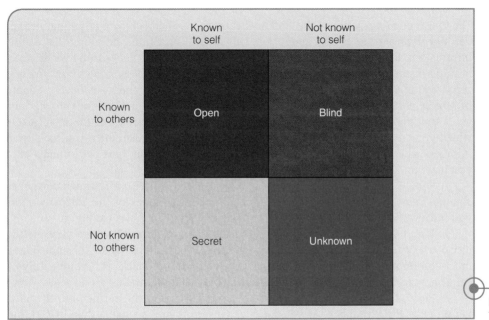

Figure 7.1
The Johari window

that you have disclosed and the observations about you that your partner has shared with you. It might include mundane information that you share with most people, such as your college major, but it also may include information that you disclose to relatively few people. Similarly, it could include simple observations that your partner has made, such as how you doodle when you're bored, or more serious feedback such as how you behave when you're angry.

The Secret Pane

The second quadrant is called the "secret" pane. It contains all those things that you know about yourself but that your partner does not yet know about you. Secret information is made known through the process of self-disclosure. The information moves into the open pane of the window once you share it with your partner. For example, suppose that you had been engaged to be married, but on the day of the wedding your fiancé(e) had backed out. You may not want to share this part of your history with casual acquaintances, so it will be in the secret pane of your window in many of your relationships. But when you disclose this fact to a friend, it moves into the open part of your Johari window with this person. As you disclose information, the secret pane of the window becomes smaller and the open pane is enlarged.

The Blind Pane

The third quadrant is called the "blind" pane. This is the place for information that the other person knows about you, but about which you are unaware. Most people have blind spots—parts of their behavior or the effects of their behavior of which they are unaware. Information moves from the blind area of the window to the open area through feedback from others. When someone gives you an insight about yourself and you accept the feedback, then the information moves into the open pane . Thus, like disclosure, feedback enlarges the open pane of the Johari window, but in this case, it is the blind pane that becomes smaller.

The Unknown Pane

The fourth quadrant is called the "unknown" pane. It contains information that neither you nor your partner knows about you. Obviously, you cannot develop a list of this information. So how do we know that it exists? Well, because periodically we discover it. If, for instance, you have never tried hang gliding, then nobody knows how you will react. You might chicken out or follow through, do it well or crash, love every minute of it or be paralyzed with fear. But until you try it, this information is unknown. Once you try it, you gain information about yourself that becomes part of the secret pane, which you can move to the open pane through disclosure. Also, once you have tried it, others who observe your flight will have information about your performance that you may not know unless they give you feedback.

As you disclose and receive feedback, the sizes of the various windowpanes change. These changes reflect the relationships. So the panes of the Johari window you have with different people will vary in size. Figure 7.2 shows examples.

In Figure 7.2a we see an example of a person in a relationship where there is little disclosure or feedback. The open pane is very small because this person has not shared much information with the other and has received little feedback. This pattern is typical of new relationships and ones between casual acquaintances.

Figure 7.2b shows the panes when a person discloses to the partner, but the partner provides little feedback. As you can see, the secret pane is smaller than in 7.2a, but

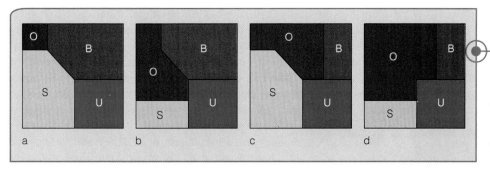

Figure 7.2
Sample Johari windows: (a) low disclosure, low feedback; (b) high disclosure, low feedback; (c) low disclosure, high feedback; (d) high disclosure, high feedback.

the hidden pane is unchanged. Because feedback from others is one of the ways we learn about who we are, relationships in which one partner does not provide feedback can become very unsatisfying to the other individual.

Figure 7.2c shows the panes when a partner is good at providing feedback, but the individual does not disclose. Because most of us disclose only when we trust our partner, this pattern may indicate that the individual does not have confidence in the partner.

Figure 7.2d shows the panes when the individual discloses information and receives feedback. The open pane of the window has enlarged as a result of both processes. Windows that look like this indicate sufficient trust and interest in the relationship that both partners are willing to risk disclosing and giving feedback.

Obviously, to get a complete "picture" of a relationship, each partner's Johari window would need to be examined. A balance of appropriate disclosure and feedback for both partners is a sign of a healthy relationship.

Skill Learning Activity 7.2
Web Resource 7.2

Communication in the Stages of Relationships

Regardless of whether your relationship is with an acquaintance, a friend, or an intimate partner, every relationship develops and changes with time. Even though no two relationships develop in exactly the same manner, they tend to follow a life cycle that has four identifiable stages: beginning, developing, maintaining, and deteriorating (Baxter, 1982; Duck, 1987; Knapp & Vangelisti, 2000; Taylor & Altman, 1987). Your relationship moves among the stages based on the conversations you have with your partner. Your relationship develops based not only on the information you share with each other, but "by the interpretation of such things by the partners" (Duck, 2007, p. 80). In other words, your relationship develops as you and your partner realize the similar ways in which the two of you see the world. Not only that, relationships can alternate almost imperceptibly between stages, so it may be difficult at any point in time to accurately label a stage of the relationship. At times, relationship stages may merge, and at other times, they may be quite distinct. But if you are observant, you can detect which way the relationship is moving over time.

Beginning Relationships

Communication during the beginning stage of a relationship focuses on reducing uncertainty by increasing your knowledge of the other person Your goal is to understand how he or she sees the world (Berger, 1987). Noted interpersonal communication scholar Steve Duck (1999) conceived the Relationship Filtering Model to explain the

What role does communication play in beginning relationships?

process that relationships go through in the beginning stage. When you first meet someone, the model suggests you assume they are similar to you until what they say or do tells you otherwise. You begin by communicating very generally about noncontroversial topics and ask questions about surface information such as where they grew up and if they have any hobbies. Based on what you learn, you make inferences about their general attitudes, values, and ways of thinking. If you decide you have enough common interests and attitudes, you will choose to develop the relationship by disclosing more about yourself.

One exciting thing about the college experience is the opportunity to meet new people and form new friendships. What new relationships have you begun since arriving on campus?

Let's look again at Whitney and Paige, who have decided to become college roommates. At first, they are nervous, wondering if they will be compatible as roommates. To reduce this uncertainty, they get to know each other better through disclosure and feedback They may talk about what they did in high school, what major each is pursuing, what hobbies they like, and their favorite foods, movies, and music. As they learn more about each other, they find that although Whitney is majoring in fine arts and Paige is in pre-med, they both are passionate environmentalists and vegetarians. As they learn more, they begin to relax and find that although they have many differences, they like and respect each other. Over the semester, they each socialize with different friends, but they continue to have evening meals in the dining hall together. Life in the room they share begins to take on a predictable pattern. When Whitney is working on a class project, materials are strewn all over the room, so Paige accommodates her by studying in the library. When Paige is freaking out over her mid-term exam in chemistry, Whitney gets her a Red Bull from the Quick Mart and then goes to the lounge to watch TV while Paige studies.

Relationships can begin in face-to-face or online environments. Increasingly, the beginning stage may occur online (Ward & Tracy, 2004). Online communication may present a potentially less difficult way to meet others than traditional face-to-face interactions. The initial interaction can occur in the comfort of your own home and at your own pace. You need not be concerned about physical aspects of the self or the other, and you can more precisely select what you are going to say (Ward & Tracy, 2004).

Developing Relationships

What role does communication play in developing relationships?

As the relationship develops, you disclose more to one another and begin to engage in more physical contact and feel a deepening psychological closeness (Duck, 1999). As healthy relationships develop, partners will identify and capitalize on their similarities and tolerate or negotiate their differences.

As the relationship develops, partners also tend to share greater physical contact. Physical contact may involve sitting closer together, leaning toward each other, more eye contact, and more touch. Such physical behaviors may or may not involve romantic feelings. Even platonic friends increase physical contact with each other as the relationship develops, though females and males may differ in how they show physical contact in same- and opposite-sex friendships. Females may hold hands or hug other female friends, whereas males may high-five each other or punch each other's shoulder. Let's say the relationship between Whitney and Paige is working out well. They spend time together, get to know each other well, and consider themselves to be close friends. By second semester, they hug each other when they return from spring break, share clothes, and do each other's hair, makeup, and nail polish.

Of course, cultural norms also affect how people engage in physical contact in relationships. In some cultures, for instance, male friends who are not romantic partners may hold hands in public or kiss to greet one another. In contrast, for orthodox Jews and observant Muslim women, touching men is abhorred. Take a moment to read the Diverse Voices article by Saba Ali in which she recounts how holding hands with a man she considered marriage material short-circuited the relationship.

As a relationship develops, partners will feel psychologically closer as well (Duck, 1999). Partners who do not feel relaxed and comfortable will remain casual acquaintances and may even decide to avoid having any relationship with one another. If you share no common interests, attitudes, or ways of interpreting the world, you are not likely to choose to develop a deeper relationship. Consider, for example, the people you met during your first weeks on campus. Which ones did not become your friends and why? Most likely, during your initial encounters you gathered information that reduced uncertainty about them, but what you learned was that they did not share enough common interests or attitudes to warrant developing a relationship.

Relationships can develop via face-to-face or online interactions. Some people even report that they achieve more closeness in online relationships than in equivalent face-to-face relationships (Walther, 1996). Indeed, rapid and exaggerated intimacy can be part of the fun of online relationships (Rabby & Walther, 2003).

Web Resource 7.3

Maintaining Relationships

Maintaining a relationship means that both people participate in ways that keep the relationship at a particular level of closeness. Researchers have catalogued many strategies, such as spending time together, merging friendship networks, sacrifice, and forgiveness that people use to maintain relationships (Rusbult, Olsen, Davis, & Hannon, 2004). You probably unconsciously use many of these techniques to maintain your relationships. Whitney and Paige used these strategies to maintain their relationship. Second term, they decided to take a few classes together, join some of the same clubs, and get to know each other's friends. They even visited each other's hometowns and met each other's families and high school friends.

You can maintain your relationship by choosing to spend time together face to face or online. In fact online communication can be the main vehicle for maintaining long distance relationships (Shedletsky & Aitken, 2004).

Another relationship maintenance strategy involves a willingness to sacrifice. Sacrifice means putting your own needs or desires on hold. For example, when Whitney was ill, Paige sacrificed a date in order to stay home and take care of her sick roommate. Because all relationships involve give-and-take, being willing at times to do what is best for the other person or for the relationship itself can help maintain the relationship.

Another strategy people sometimes practice is "positive illusion." This means emphasizing others' virtues and downplaying their faults.

Relationships can also be maintained by forgiveness. Because conflict is inevitable in close relationships, we may do or say things that hurt our partner. If not handled

What communication strategies help maintain relationships?

Close Enough to Touch Was Too Far Apart

by Saba Ali

Diverse Voices

Saba Ali lives in upstate New York.

Who knew that holding hands, the very act that signals the start of so many relationships, would be the end of mine? It seems the mullahs were onto something when they wagged their fingers against premarital relations, of any kind.

Born in Kenya, I came to the United States at age 6, settling with my family in upstate New York. Growing up Muslim, I missed out on the "Dawson's Creek" method of courtship.

For scarf-wearing Muslims like me, premarital interaction between the sexes (touching, talking, even looking) is strictly controlled. Men and women pray, eat, and congregate separately. At private dinner parties, women exit the dining room so the men can serve themselves. Boys sit on one side of the hall, girls on the other, and married couples in the middle.

When out in public, interactions with non-Muslim boys tend to be less constrained but still formal. A playful push from a boy would bring an awkward explanation of how touching is against my religion.

So my friends and I had high expectations for marriage, which was supposed to quickly follow graduation from college. That's when our parents told us it was time to find the one man we would be waking up with for the rest of our lives, God willing. They just didn't tell us how.

There were no tips from our mothers or anyone else on how to meet the right man or to talk to him. It's simply expected that our lives will consist of two phases: unmarried and in the company of women, and then married and in the company of a man.

It's all supposed to start with a conversation, but not a private one. My friends and I call them "meetings." The woman comes with her chaperone, a family member, and the man comes with his. Talking points include such questions as "What do you expect from your husband?" and

"Would you mind if my parents were to move in with us after the reception?"

Yet now, at 29, despite all of my "meetings," I remain unmarried. And in the last five years I've exhausted the patience of my matchmaking aunties and friends who have offered up their husbands' childhood playmates.

All I wanted was to feel secure, to look forward to spending my days and nights with my match. Which is why my interest was piqued last year when a friend from college told me about a radiologist in his early 30s who was also frustrated by the challenges of the contemporary Muslim hookup. Our first get-together was for brunch at a little French café near Central Park. I listened as he talked about his past relationships. Not the most appropriate topic for a first date, perhaps, but more comfortable for me than the typical pressurized questions: "Do you cook?" and "How many children do you want?" As he talked about the girls who either broke his heart, or whose hearts he had broken, I watched his hands, wondering what they would feel like to touch.

After brunch, we walked through the park. I spoke with ease about my own confusions, ambitions, faith, and fear of making the wrong decision about marriage. I told him I wanted someone who liked eating out, prayed five times a day and didn't drink alcohol, and who made eye contact when talking with girls. He said he wanted a wife who wasn't conservative and could fit in with his non-Muslim friends. He had most of the items on my mental checklist.

We kept getting to know each other by phone, often talking for hours at a time. If I was driving when he called, I would roam around aimlessly just so our exchange wouldn't end when I reached my destination. I hadn't yet told my parents about him, not wanting to get my mother's hopes up.

Our lingering problem, however, was the difference in how religious we each were; he hadn't planned on marrying someone who wore the traditional head scarf. His ideal woman was less strict, more secular. But I reveled in the recognition. Covering was a choice I had made in high school, partly out of a need for identity, and partly out of fear. The fear came from what I had heard at Muslim summer camp, which scared me enough to start covering and praying. Instead of ghost stories, we had "judgment day" stories about the terrible things that would happen if you strayed from God, which scared me enough to start covering and praying.

In the years since, that fear has evolved into understanding. Most girls will say the scarf is for modesty. I see it as a protection. It keeps me from making stupid decisions. To me, the scarf is more than a piece of fabric—it's a way of life. On my wedding night, going topless would mean unpinning my scarf and letting it fall down.

In order to get him over his hesitation, I planned our dates to take place in very public places. We played miniature golf, ate out at restaurants, and went blueberry picking. I looked at his objection as a challenge, a project. I wanted to convince him that even though I did stand out with my hijab, it didn't matter because no one really took notice of the scarf after the first glance.

And I had my own doubts, although I was afraid to admit them: Namely, why should I push forward with this when we weren't aligned in terms of our faith? How could we be a good match if he didn't approve of my hijab? Would I have to change? Should I?

One evening he called to tell me he had gone to a lounge with a few of his buddies. "I visualized what it would feel like to have you sitting next to me," he told me.

"And how did I feel?" I asked.

"Pretty good," he said. "Manageable."

After, I finally called my mother and told her about him.

Before him, I had never gone past the second date. But by now he and I were approaching our fourth date—plenty of time, in my mind, to decide whether a man is right for you.

And then came the night of the movie, his idea. I'm a movie fanatic and remember the details of almost every movie I've ever seen. I can't remember the title of the one we saw that night. I looked over at him and smiled, convincing myself that the weightiness I felt was because I was in uncharted territory. We were moving forward, talking about meeting each other's families. So when he leaned over and asked, "Can I hold your hand?" I didn't feel I could say no. I liked him for taking the risk.

Nearly 30 years old, I had thought about holding hands with a boy since I was a teenager. But it was always in the context of my wedding day. Walking into our reception as husband and wife, holding hands, basking in that moment of knowing this was forever.

Non-Muslim girls may wonder about their first kiss or, later, about losing their virginity. I thought I was running the same risk, though for me it would be the first time actually touching the hand of a potential husband. How would it feel? Would it convince me that he was the one?

A lifetime's worth of expectations culminated in this single gesture in a dark theater over a sticky armrest. I'm not sure it's possible to hold hands wrong, but we were not doing it right. It felt awkward with my hand under his, so we changed positions: my arm on top, his hand cradling mine. It was still uncomfortable, and soon my hand fell asleep, which was not the tingling sensation I was hoping for. Finally, I took it away.

But the damage had been done. We had broken the no-contact rule, and in doing so, I realized I wasn't willing to be the kind of girl he wanted. I believe in my religion, the rules, the reasons, and even the restrictions. At the same time, I've always wanted to be married, and the thought of never knowing that side of myself, as a wife and a mother, scares me. Being with him made me compromise my faith, and my fear of being alone pushed me to ignore my doubts about the relationship.

When we took it too far, I shut down. It wasn't supposed to happen that way. So after the date, I split us up. And I never saw him again.

Excerpted from the New York Times, October 7, 2007.

properly, such transgressions can harm the relationship and move it to a level of less intimacy. By forgiving minor transgressions, we can keep a relationship at the desired level of closeness. For example, Whitney and Paige each have little habits that annoy the other, but they choose not to let these annoyances get in the way of a good friendship.

Other ways that people maintain their relationships include continuing mutually acceptable levels of affection, self-disclosure, favors, and support.

Deteriorating and Dissolving Relationships

> **What role does communication play in deteriorating and dissolving relationships?**

The less highly developed a relationship is, the more likely it is to dissolve (Parks, 2007). Relationships between acquaintances, casual friends, coworkers, and neighbors will probably end at some point. Over time, a developed relationship may become less satisfying to one or both partners so that a partner will invest less time in the relationship. But this doesn't mean that the relationship will end. Instead it may revert to a different, less intimate level. The communication in deteriorating relationships is marked by three stages: recognition of dissatisfaction, disengaging, and at times, ending.

The first sign that a relationship is deteriorating is a subtle indication of dissatisfaction. The partners may feel less connected to each other, begin to share fewer activities, and communicate less frequently. They may begin to emphasize each other's faults and downplay virtues. Subjects that once involved deep, private, and frequent communication may become off-limits or sources of conflict. As the relationship begins to be characterized by an increase in touchy subjects and more unresolved conflicts, partners become more defensive and less willing to foster a positive communication climate.

If the relationship continues to be dissatisfying, people begin to drift apart. They become less willing to sacrifice for each other, and they show less forgiveness. Their communication changes from sharing ideas and feelings, to making small talk and other "safe" communication, and then, to having no significant communication at all. It may seem strange that people who once had so much to share can find themselves with nothing to talk about. They depend less on each other and more upon other people for favors and support. Hostility need not be present; rather, this stage is likely to be marked by indifference. Even though Whitney and Paige were very close during their first year at college, they may drift apart over time. Maybe one of them betrayed the trust of the other and the tension led to their becoming more annoyed with each other's faults. Once this happens, they will probably spend less time together, share fewer activities, talk about less important topics, and generally interact less frequently with each other.

When a relationship can't be maintained at a less developed level, it will end. A relationship has ended when the people no longer interact with each other. As Cupach and Metts (1986) show, people give many reasons for terminating relationships, including poor communication, lack of fulfillment, differing lifestyles and interests, rejection, outside interference, absence of rewards, and boredom.

Unfortunately, when people decide to end a relationship, they sometimes look for reasons to blame each other rather than trying to find equitable ways of bringing the relationship to an acceptable conclusion. To clarify, people sometimes use strategies of manipulation, withdrawal, and avoidance (Baxter, 1982). Though misguided and inappropriate, manipulation involves being indirect and failing to take any responsibility for ending the relationship. Manipulators may purposely sabotage the relationship in hopes that the other person will break it off. Withdrawal and avoidance, also less than competent ways of communicating desires to terminate a relationship, are passive approaches, which lead to the slow and often painful death of the relationship.

The most competent way to end a relationship is to be direct, open, and honest. It is important to clearly state your wish to end the relationship while being respectful of the other person and sensitive to the resulting emotions. If two people have had a satisfying and close relationship, they owe it to themselves and to each other to be forthright and fair about communicating during the final stage of the relationship.

Perhaps Whitney and Paige decide, separately, that they want to room with someone else next year. As effective communicators, they would discuss the sensitive topic without blame or manipulation, acknowledge that their relationship is less close than it once was, and move in with new roommates for the second year of college.

Michael Newman/PhotoEdit

How relationships end depends on the interpersonal competence of both people. Do you know people who have amicable divorces? How do they differ from people who have hostile divorces?

Even when the participants agree that their relationship is over, they may continue to interact and influence each other through a different type of relationship. This is called **relationship transformation**. Romantic relationships may transform into friendships, best friends may become casual friends, and even marriages may continue on friendly terms or as a type of business relationship where child-rearing practices and expenses are coordinated. (Parks, 2006). After Whitney and Paige graduate, they may try to keep in touch, but as the years pass and they form other attachments, their friendship may wane until they are simply acquaintances who enjoy seeing each other at reunions.

Dialectics in Interpersonal Relationships

Have you ever felt ambivalent about a relationship? On the one hand, you really wanted to become close to someone but at the same time you wanted your "space." Or have you met someone who seemed a bit too nosy but you really wanted to get to know the person? Or have you ever felt that a relationship you were in was in a rut and wished that there could be some excitement like when you first met? If so, you were experiencing what scholars call a relationship dialectic. A **dialectic** is a tension between conflicting forces. **Relational dialectics** are the competing psychological tensions that exist in any relationship. At any one time, one or both people may be aware of these tensions. Let's take a look at the specific dialectics and then discuss how you can use interpersonal communication skills to manage these inevitable tensions in your relationships.

> How do dialectal tensions operate in interpersonal relationships?

relationship transformation
the process of changing a relationship from one level of intimacy to another.

dialectic
a tension between conflicting forces.

relational dialectics
the competing psychological tensions in a relationship.

Relational Dialectics

Three dialectics that are common to most relationships are the tugs between autonomy and connection, openness and closedness, and novelty and predictability (Baxter & Montgomery, 1996; Baxter & West, 2003). How these tensions are dealt with can alter the stage and life cycle of a relationship. We'll describe each dialectic and then discuss how you can effectively manage them in your relationships.

Autonomy-Connection

Autonomy is the desire to do things independent of your partner. **Connection** is the desire to link your actions and decisions with your partner. Joel and Shelly have been dating for about a year. At this point in their relationship, Shelly wants to spend most of her free time with Joel and enjoys talking with Joel before acting or making decisions, but Joel has begun to feel hemmed in. For example, he wants to be able to play basketball with the guys without having to clear it first with Shelly. At the same time, however, he doesn't want to hurt Shelly's feelings or ruin the closeness of their relationship. Shelly is at peace and may not recognize any tension between autonomy and connection. On the other hand, Joel is feeling the tension between wanting to be more autonomous without jeopardizing his connection to Shelly. If Joel begins to act autonomously, he may relieve his own tension but at the same time create tension in the relationship.

Openness-Closedness

Openness is the desire to share intimate ideas and feelings with your partner. **Closedness** is the desire to maintain privacy. Let's say that Shelly discloses quite a bit to Joel. She believes it is important to divulge her feelings to Joel, and she expects him to do the same. In other words, the open quadrant of Shelly's Johari window in her relationship with Joel is quite large. Joel, however, is a more private person. He does disclose to Shelly, but not as much as she would like. The secret pane of his Johari window is larger than Shelly would like it to be. The fact that Shelly and Joel differ in their preferred levels of self-disclosure is one source of tension in their relationship. But Shelly does not want complete openness all the time. She realizes that it is appropriate to be closed, or to refrain from self-disclosure with Joel, at times. So she seeks both openness and closedness in this relationship. Likewise Joel, although wanting more closedness than Shelly does, still wants some openness. So, like Shelly, he wants both forces to occur simultaneously in this relationship.

Novelty-Predictability

Novelty is the desire for originality, freshness, and uniqueness in your own or your partner's behavior or in the relationship. **Predictability** is the desire for consistency, reliability, and dependability. People experience tension between their desires for novelty and predictability. Because Shelly and Joel have been dating for a year, much of the uncertainty is gone from their relationship. But they do not want to eliminate uncertainty altogether. With no uncertainty at all, a relationship becomes so predictable and so routine that it is boring. Although Shelly and Joel know each other well, can predict much about each other, and have quite a few routines in their relationship, they also want to be surprised and have new experiences with each other. Shelly and Joel may differ in their needs for novelty and predictability. Shelly may yearn for Joel to surprise her with a mystery date, or she may shock Joel by spontaneously breaking into their favorite song in the middle of the mall. At this point in their relationship, Joel may be comfortable operating by the routines they have established and may be embarrassed and shocked by Shelly's song. Here is another tension between the two that must be managed in their relationship. But they must also cope with the fact that they each need some amount of both novelty and predictability in the relationship.

Although our example of Shelly and Joel is an intimate relationship, it is important to remember that dialectical tensions exist in all relationships—not just romantic ones—and they are always in flux. Sometimes these dialectical tensions are active

---

autonomy
the desire to do things independent of one's partner.

connection
the desire to do things and make decisions with one's partner.

openness
the desire to share intimate ideas and feelings with one's partner.

closedness
the desire to maintain one's privacy in a relationship.

novelty
originality, freshness, and uniqueness in the partner's behaviors or in the relationship.

predictability
consistency, reliability, and dependability in a relationship.

and in the foreground; at other times they are in the background. Nevertheless, when these tension are experienced, they change what is happening in the relationship (Wood, 2000).

Managing Dialectical Tensions

You may be wondering how you can cope with dialectical tensions in relationships. How do people satisfy opposite needs at the same time in relationships? Several researchers (Baxter & Montgomery, 1996; Wood, 2000) have studied how people manage dialectical tensions in relationships. Four strategies have been reported: temporal selection, topical segmentation, neutralization, and reframing.

Temporal selection is the strategy of choosing one desire and ignoring the other for the time being. Perhaps you and a friend realize that you have spent too much time apart lately (autonomy), so you make a conscious decision to pursue connection. That is, you agree that over the next few months, you will make a point of spending more time together. You schedule lots of activities together so you can be more connected. Over time, however, you may feel that you are spending too much time together, and so you may find yourself cancelling dates. Seesawing back and forth like this is one way to temporarily manage a relational dialectic.

Topical segmentation is the strategy of choosing certain topics with which to satisfy one desire and other topics for the opposite desire. You and your mom may practice openness by sharing your opinions and feeling about certain topics such as school, work, or politics but maintain your privacy concerning your sex lives. This segmentation satisfies both your needs for balance in the openness-closedness dialectic.

Neutralization is the strategy of compromising between the desires of one person and the desires of the other. Neutralization partially meets the needs of both people but does not fully meet the needs of either. A couple might pursue a moderate level of novelty and spontaneity in their lives, which satisfies both of them. The amount of novelty in the relationship may be less than what one person would ideally want and more than what the other would normally desire, but they have reached a middle point comfortable to both.

Reframing is the strategy of changing your perception about the level of tension. Reframing involves putting less emphasis on the dialectical contradiction. It means looking at your desires differently so they no longer seem quite so contradictory. Maybe you are tense because you perceive that you are more open and your partner is more closed. So, you think about how much you disclose to him and how little he discloses to you. You might even discuss this issue with your partner. Perhaps during the conversation, you begin to realize the times that you have held back (closedness), as well as the instances when he was open. After the conversation, you no longer see as strong a contradiction. You see yourselves as more similar than different on this dialectic. You have reframed your perception of the tension.

In most cases when you are developing, maintaining, or trying to repair a deteriorating relationship, it is helpful if you can openly talk with your partner about the tensions that you are feeling and come to an agreement about how you will manage the dialectic going forward. Through self-disclosure and feedback, you and your partner may be able to negotiate a new balance that both of you find satisfying. At times, however, partners will be unable to resolve the tensions. When this happens, it is likely that one or both of you will experience dissatisfaction with the relationship and the relationship may deteriorate or end.

temporal selection
the strategy of choosing one dialectical tension and ignoring its opposite for a while.

topical segmentation
the strategy of choosing certain topics with which to satisfy one dialectical tension and other topics for its opposite.

neutralization
the strategy of compromising between the desires of the two partners.

reframing
the strategy of changing one's perspective about the level of tension.

Skill Learning Activity 7.3

A Question of Ethics

Jeff and Magda, seniors at a small rural college, had been dating each other since they were freshmen. Jeff loved Magda, and he planned to propose to her after they graduated in spring. At the same time, though, he reluctantly recognized that their relationship had fallen into a bit of a rut over the last six months, and he missed the excitement and romance of their first year together. Although he was troubled by these conflicting feelings, Jeff was unsure what to do about them.

One day while he was surfing MySpace.com, Jeff decided, on a whim, to create a fake user profile for the person he wanted to be in his fantasies. He spent quite a bit of time researching and designing the profile of his imaginary persona, a rap singer/flamenco guitarist/snowboarder/kung fu expert who went by the user name "MoonDog13." Jeff inserted photos of an obscure young Romanian actor he found online into MoonDog13's user profile. He posted lyrics to rap songs he wrote on MoonDog13's page and joined online user groups for those interested in flamenco guitar, snowboarding, and kung fu. In very little time, MoonDog13 had made a number of online friends, many of whom were admiring

What Would You Do?

young women. MoonDog13 loved to flirt with these girls.

Jeff told Magda nothing about MoonDog13, even when the time he spent online managing the fictitious life of his alter ego began to interfere in his relationship with her. He justified this decision with the belief that MoonDog13 was an imaginary figure who existed only in cyberspace. As long as fantasy didn't cross into reality, there was no reason Jeff had to feel guilty about anything MoonDog13 said online.

1. How is Jeff acting ethically or unethically in this situation?
2. Like Jeff, most people act differently in cyberspace than they do in the real world. Are the ethics of cyberspace any different from those of the real world? What about fantasy—are the ethics of our private desires different from the real world? Are we ethically obliged to disclose our fantasies to our loved ones?

Conversation and Analysis

Use your Premium Website for *Communicate!* to access the **Skill Learning Activity 7.4**, which is a video clip of Trevor and Meg's conversation. As you watch Trevor and Meg discuss the future of their relationship, focus on how effectively they are communicating. How do Trevor and Meg engage in disclosure and feedback? What stage of their relationship life cycle do they seem to be in and why? What dialectical tensions are they dealing with and what strategies are they, or should they be, using to manage them? What really is Meg's fear? You can respond to these and other analysis questions by clicking on "Critique" in the menu bar at the top of the screen. When you've answered all the questions, click "Done" to compare your answers to those provided by the authors.

Trevor and Meg have been going together for the last several months of their senior year at college. Now that graduation is approaching, they are trying to figure out what to do about their relationship. They sit and talk.

Skill Learning Activity 7.4

Conversation

TREVOR: Meg, I think it's time we talk about making plans for the future. After all, we'll be graduating next month.

MEG: Trevor, you know how uncomfortable I feel about making any long-range plans at this time. We still need to know a lot more about each other before we even think about getting engaged.

TREVOR: Why? We've both said we love each other, haven't we? (*Meg nods.*) So why's this too soon? What else do we need to know?

MEG: For starters, I'll be going to law school this fall, and this year is going to be difficult. And, you haven't gotten a job yet.

TREVOR: Come on, Meg. You're going to law school in the city, so I'll have a degree in business, so I can probably get a job most anywhere.

MEG: But Trevor, that's just my point. I know I'll be starting law school; I've always wanted to be a lawyer. And you don't really have any idea what you want to do. And that bothers me. I can't be worrying about you and your career when I'm going to need to focus on my classes.

TREVOR: But I told you, I can get a job anywhere.

MEG: Yes, Trevor, but you need more than a job. You need to figure out what kind of job really turns you on, or else you risk waking up one day and regretting your life. And, I don't want to be there when that happens. I watched my dad go through a midlife crisis, and he ended up walking out on us.

TREVOR: I'm not your dad, Meg. I won't leave you. And don't worry about me; I'll find a job.

MEG: Really? You knew I was going to law school in the city for over a month, but you still haven't even begun a job search. Trevor, right now is the time when people are hiring, and you haven't even done your résumé. The longer you wait, the more difficult your search is going to be.

TREVOR: Come on, Meg. You've already said I'm irresistible. What company wouldn't want me?

MEG: I'm serious, Trevor. Look, I've got a scholarship to law school, but it's only going to pay half of my expenses. I'll be taking a loan to get enough money to pay the rest and to have money to live on. I won't have the money or the time to be very supportive of you if you haven't found work. I need the security of knowing that you've got a job and that you are saving money.

TREVOR: Well, they say that "two can live as cheaply as one." I was thinking that once you got settled, I'd move in and that will save us a lot of money.

MEG: Whoa, Trevor. You know how I feel about that. I do love you, and I hope that we have a future together. But living together this year is not an option. I think we need at least a year of living on our own to get ourselves settled and make sure that we really are compatible. After all, we come from totally different backgrounds. I practically raised myself, and I've paid my own bills since I was 18, while you've been lucky enough to have parents who footed your bills. There have been several times when we've talked about important issues and the differences between us have been obvious, and they worry me.

TREVOR: You mean when I was joking around about our different taste in cars?

MEG: No, Trevor, not cars; that's minor. But we also have greatly different feelings about money and family. You've told me that once you get married you want to start a family immediately. As I see it, I've got a three-year commitment to law school, then seven to 10 years of hard work to make partner at a good firm. So I'm not sure when I want to start a family. But I know it won't be for at least six years.

TREVOR: So, what are you saying, Meg? Is it over? "Thanks for the good time, Trevor, but you're not in my plans?"

MEG: Please don't be sarcastic. I'm not trying to hurt you. It makes me happy to think that we'll spend the rest of our lives together. But I'm worried about several things, so I'm just not ready to commit to that now. Let's just take a year, get settled, and see what happens. I'll love it if you do get a job near where I'm in school. That way we can have time to sort through some of the issues between us.

TREVOR: You mean if you can fit me into your schedule? Meg, if we love each other now, aren't we still going to love each other next year? If we wait until we have everything settled, we might never get married; there'll always be something. After all, we are two different people. We're never going to agree on everything!

MEG: Are you saying that as unsettled as our lives are right now, we can shoulder the additional stress of planning for a marriage?

TREVOR: No, what I'm saying is that we live together this year, see how it goes, then if it isn't working, we don't have to get married.

Summary

Interpersonal communication helps develop and maintain relationships. A good relationship is any mutually satisfying interaction with another person. We have three types of relationships. Acquaintances are people we know by name and talk with, but with whom our interactions are limited in quality and quantity. Friendships are marked by degrees of warmth and affection, trust, self-disclosure, commitment, and expectation that the relationships will endure. Close or intimate friends are those with whom we share a high degree of commitment, trust, interdependence, disclosure, and enjoyment.

A healthy relationship is marked by a balance of self-disclosure and feedback. The Johari window is a tool for analyzing this balance helping us to identify the information in our relationships that are open, hidden, secret, or unknown.

Relationships go through a life cycle that includes beginning, developing, maintaining, and perhaps deteriorating or dissolving. In the first stage of beginning a relationship, we try to get to know each other to reduce uncertainty. If we decide to develop the relationship, we engage in more disclosure and experience feelings of relaxation and confirmation. There are various ways to maintain a relationship including spending time together, merging social networks, making sacrifices, and forgiving. When relationships deteriorate, we tend to recognize feelings of dissatisfaction, notice each other's faults, experience more conflict, discuss only safe topics, and spend less time together.

In any relationship, we negotiate dialectics, the tensions that tug at us as individuals and the relationship. These tensions focus on autonomy-connectedness, openness-closedness, and novelty-predictability. We can manage these tensions through temporal selection, topical segmentation, neutralization, and reframing. Effective communicators talk openly with their partners rather than manipulating or withdrawing.

Communicate! Active Online Learning

Now that you have read Chapter 7, use your Premium Website for *Communicate!* for quick access to the electronic resources that accompany this text. These resources include

- **Study tools** that will help you assess your learning and prepare for exams (*digital glossary, key term flash cards, review quizzes*).
- **Activities and assignments** that will help you hone your knowledge, analyze communication situations (*Skill Learning Activities)*, and build your public speaking skills throughout the course (*Communication on Your Feet speech assignments, Action Step activities*). Many of these activities allow you to compare your answers to those provided by the authors, and, if requested, submit your answers to your instructor.

- **Media resources** that will help you explore communication concepts online (*Web Resources*), develop your speech outlines (*Speech Builder Express 3.0*), watch and critique videos of communication situations and sample speeches (*Interactive Video Activities*), upload your speech videos for peer reviewing and critique other students' speeches (*Speech Studio online speech review tool*), and download chapter review so you can study when and where you'd like (*Audio Study Tools*).

This chapter's Key Terms, Skill Learning Activities, and Web Resources are also featured on the following pages, and you can find this chapter's Communicate on Your Feet assignment in the body of the chapter.

Key Terms

acquaintances (134)
autonomy (150)
close friends or intimates (137)
closedness (150)
connection (150)
dialectic (149)
feedback (141)
friends (136)

good relationship (134)
impersonal communication (134)
Johari window (141)
neutralization (151)
novelty (150)
openness (150)
platonic relationship (137)
predictability (150)
reframing (151)

relational dialectics (149)
relationship (134)
relationship transformation (149)
romantic relationship (137)
saving face (135)
self-disclosure (141)
temporal selection (151)
topical segmentation (151)
trust (138)

Skill Learning Activities

7.1: Distinguishing between Types of Relationships (140)

1. List five people you have known for some time whom you consider to be acquaintances. Why do you consider these people to be acquaintances rather than friends? What do you talk about with each of these people? What subjects do you avoid? Do any of these relationships

have the potential to become friendships? If so, what would you have to do to make that transition?

2. List five people you have known for some time whom you consider to be friends. Why do you consider each of these people to be a friend? How does your relationship with each differ from your relationships with your acquaintances? What do you talk about with each of these people? What subjects do you avoid? Do any of these relationships have the potential to become best

friendships or intimate relationships? If so, what would you have to do to make the transition?

3. List one to three people you have known for some time whom you consider to be your best friends or your intimates. Why do you consider each of these people to be best friends or intimates? What do you talk about with each of these people? What subjects do you avoid? How does each of these relationships differ from those you have with your friends?

Write an essay in which you describe what you have learned about your relationships.

7.2: Johari Window (143)

Access **Web Resource 7.2: Interactive Johari Window.** Select five or six adjectives from the grid provided that you feel accurately describe yourself. Enter your name (or an alias if you'd prefer) and save your grid. Then ask a few of your friends, relatives, or colleagues to access your grid and pick out five or six adjectives from that grid that they feel describe you.

When you have finished, write a paragraph discussing what you have learned. Did the adjectives other people picked to describe you match the adjectives you picked for yourself? How does this information explain your experiences in developing and sustaining relationships? Does this suggest any changes you need to make to improve your relationships?

7.3: Dialectics in Your Relationships (151)

Choose one of your current close friendship or intimate relationships. It can be with a friend or family member. Briefly explain this assignment and ask your relationship partner if she or he is willing to help you with this assignment and to have what you discuss become part of a short paper you are doing for this class. Only if your partner consents should you proceed. Otherwise, find another friend or intimate.

1. Briefly explain the concept of relationship dialectics to your partner. You may want to have them read the section of this chapter that explains these.
2. Once your partner understands the concepts, have a conversation about how each of you has experienced each of these tensions over the course of your relationship. Can you each think of specific instances when you were "out of sync"? How did this play out in the relationship? Be specific and be sure to talk about each of the three dialectical tensions.

3. Based on your conversation, write a short paper/journal entry in which you describe what you learned. How has hearing your partner talk about how he or she experienced these changed your understanding?
4. Given what you have learned in this conversation, how can you use this to improve this relationship going forward.

7.4: Trevor and Meg (152)

After you've watched the video of Trevor and Meg and have read the transcript of their conversation, answer the following questions.

1. How do Trevor and Meg disclose their feelings and offer feedback?
2. What stage of their relationship life cycle do they seem to be in and why?
3. What dialectical tensions are they dealing with and what strategies are they, or should they be, using to manage them?
4. What is Meg's real fear?

When you're done with this activity, compare your answers to the authors' at the Premium Website for *Communicate!* Look for them in the Skill Learning activities for Chapter 7.

Web Resources

7.1: Holding Effective Conversations (135)

This bonus chapter discusses how to hold effective conversations.

7.2: Interactive Johari Window (143)

This interactive site allows you to gauge your personality awareness. Describe yourself from the adjectives provided, then ask your friends and colleagues to describe you from the same adjectives. This site will build a window of overlap and difference for you—a type of Johari window.

7.3: In-Person versus Cyberspace Relationships (145)

Go to this page at the Psychology of Cyberspace Website to read a thorough comparison of the differences between relationships in person and electronically mediated relationships.

Communication Skills in Interpersonal Relationships:

Providing Emotional Support, Managing Privacy, and Negotiating Conflict

Questions you will be able to answer after reading this chapter:

- What are the characteristics of comforting messages?
- How can you manage disclosure and privacy in your relationships?
- How do people negotiate different needs, wants, and preferences?
- How do we deal with conflict in our relationships?
- What is a collaborative approach to conflict?

"Chuck, when that interviewer at the movie theatre asked you whether you'd rather see a comedy or a thriller, you said 'thriller!' We've been dating for four years, and I'm just now learning that you'd rather see a thriller? We've *never* gone to a thriller in all the time we've been dating." Susan said, her voice becoming shrill.

"Gosh, I'm sorry, Susan," Chuck said sheepishly. "But truthfully, I didn't want to upset you. I know you don't like thrillers and so I've never suggested seeing one with you. If I do want to see one, I just go with my friend Larry."

"Chuck, it's not that I don't like them. In fact, I wanted to see *Twilight*." Susan asks, "Are there other things that you like or don't like that you haven't told me about?"

"Well, um, probably."

"Probably? Probably? Why haven't you been leveling with me?"

"Well, I don't know. I guess I just didn't think they were all that important."

"Not important? Chuck, I thought we trusted each other enough to be honest. Now I find out you keep things from me. I just don't know what to think!"

"Sue, why didn't you ever tell me that you wanted to see *Twilight*?"

"Well I, uh, uh . . ."

Poor Chuck—poor Susan! Although this opening story might seem silly, every day in your relationships you make decisions about three fundamental issues: (1) how you will respond to the emotional distress of your partner, (2) the information you will share or keep private, and (3) how you will negotiate the differences between your own and your partner's needs, wants, and preferences. The decisions you make and how you choose to behave will affect the degree of intimacy and satisfaction you experience in your relationships. We begin this chapter by discussing emotional support and the communication skills for effective comforting. Next, we discuss how to manage the competing urges between wanting to share information and keeping it to yourself. We conclude the chapter by describing various conflict management styles that can damage your relationships and then present the skills associated with collaboration, a conflict management style that can lead to a win-win situation for both you and your partner.

Comforting Messages

Can you recall a time when you were emotionally distraught? Perhaps someone close to you died unexpectedly, or the person you believed you would spend the rest of your life with dumped you, or someone you trusted betrayed you, or you were unjustly harmed by someone with power over you. If you have experienced any of these or other emotionally devastating events, you probably appreciated the emotional support you received from some of your friends and family members and might have been perplexed, annoyed, or angered by inappropriate statements made by others. In most long-term relationships, we will encounter incidents when we are expected to respond to the emotional distress of a partner. **Comforting** is helping people feel better about themselves, their behavior, or their situation by creating a safe conversational space where they can express their feelings and work out a plan for the future. Effective comforting aids the person who is comforted, helping him or her cope with the future and improving his or her relationship with the comforter. Skilled comforting also benefits the comforter, improving his or her self-esteem and relationship with the person being comforted (Burleson, 2002). Comforting rarely happens in a single statement. Instead, it usually occurs over several turns in a conversation or over several conversations that may span weeks, months, or even years.

comforting
helping people feel better about themselves, their behavior, or their situation by creating a safe conversational space where they can express their feelings and work out a plan for the future.

buffering messages
comforting messages that are phrased very politely in ways that address another person's face needs.

positive face needs
the desires to be appreciated and approved, liked, and honored.

Skills for Comforting

The following skills can help you succeed when providing emotional comfort:

1. **Clarify supportive intentions.** When people are experiencing emotional turmoil, they may have trouble trusting the motives of those who want to help. You can

clarify your supportive intentions by openly stating that your goal in the conversation is to help your partner. Notice how David does this:

DAVID: (*noticing Paul sitting in his cubicle with his head in his lap and his hands over his head*): Paul, is everything OK?

PAUL: (*sitting up with a miserable but defiant look on his face*): Like you should care. Yeah, everything is fine.

DAVID: Paul, I do care. You've been working for me for five years. You're one of our best technicians. So if something is going on, I'd like to help, even if all I can do is listen. Now, what's up?

2. **Buffer face threats with politeness. Buffering messages** cushion the effect of what is said by using both positive and negative politeness skills. The very act of providing comfort can threaten the positive and negative face needs of your partner. **Positive face needs** are the desires to be appreciated and approved, liked, and honored. **Negative face needs** are the desires to be free from imposition and intrusion. On the one hand, your partner might worry that you will respect, like, or value him less because of his situation. On the other hand, the very act of comforting suggests that he cannot independently handle the situation. So comforting messages are phrased very politely in ways that address the other person's face needs. Notice how David says to Paul, "You're one of our best technicians," which reaffirms his admiration for Paul's work. David also attends to Paul's need for independence by stating that maybe all he "can do is listen," which implies that Paul will be able to do the rest.

R. Eko Bintoro/istockphoto.com

3. **Encourage understanding through other-centered messages.** To reduce emotional distress, people need to make sense out of what has happened (Burleson & Goldsmith, 1998). People feel better if they can re-evaluate specific parts of the situation or change their opinion about what happened. An important way people do this is by repeatedly telling and elaborating on the story (what happened to them). We can help this process by using **other-centered messages**, those that encourage our partner to talk about and elaborate on what happened and how she feels about it. Many of us find this difficult to do because we have been taught it is rude to pry or we are uncomfortable hearing someone's problems, so our initial reaction may be to change the subject or to talk about similar experiences we have had.

Other-centered messages can be questions that allow the other to elaborate, or they can simply be vocalized encouragement (um, uh-huh, wow, I see). They encourage the person to explore her feelings, and they demonstrate understanding and empathy.

Can you recall a time when you were upset and someone comforted you? Did you feel closer to this person as a result?

negative face needs
the desires to be free from imposition and intrusion.

other-centered messages
comforting messages that encourage relational partners to talk about and elaborate on what happened and how they feel about it.

4. **Reframe the situation.** When people are in the midst of strong emotions, they are likely to perceive events in a limited way. In these cases, it may be helpful for you to **reframe the situation** by offering ideas, observations, information, or alternative explanations that might help your partner understand the situation in a different light. For example, imagine that Travis returns from class and tells his roommate, Abe, "Well, I'm flunking calculus. It doesn't matter how much I study or how many of the online practice problems I do, I just can't get it. I might as well just drop out of school before I flunk out completely. I can ask for a full-time schedule at work and not torture myself with school anymore." To reframe the situation, Abe might remind Travis that he has been putting in many hours at work and ask Travis if he thinks that the heavy work schedule might be cutting into his study time. Or he might tell Travis that he heard calculus instructors curve grades at the end of the term because the material is so difficult. In each case, Abe is offering new observations and providing alternative explanations that can help Travis reframe the situation from an impossible one to a manageable one.

5. **Give advice.** At times, we can comfort people by **giving advice**—presenting relevant suggestions and proposals that a person can use to resolve a situation. You should not give advice, however, until your supportive intentions have been understood, you have attended to your partner's face needs, and you have sustained other-centered conversation for some time. Only when your partner has had time to make his or her own sense out of what has happened should you move the conversation to addressing next steps. Then you might begin by asking your partner what he or she thinks could help. After listening carefully to the response, you can ask your partner if some feedback and advice would be welcome. Always ask permission and acknowledge that your advice is only one suggestion of many that might work. Present the potential risks or costs associated with your advice, and let your partner know that it's OK if he or she chooses to ignore it.

Gender and Cultural Considerations in Comforting

reframing the situation *offering ideas, observations, information, or alternative explanations that might help a relational partner understand a situation in a different light.*

giving advice *presenting relevant suggestions and proposals that a person can use to resolve a situation.*

Many people believe that women expect, need, and provide more emotional support than men. However, a growing body of research suggests that both men and women place a high value on emotional support from their partners in a variety of relationships: siblings, same-sex friendships, opposite-sex friendships, and romantic relationships (Burleson, 2003). Studies also find that both men and women report that other-centered messages encouraging them to explore and elaborate on their feelings provide the most comfort. However, men are less likely to use other-centered messages when comforting.

Researchers have also examined cultural differences in comforting. Again, members of all social groups find solace strategies, especially other-centered messages, the most sensitive and comforting way to provide emotional support (Burleson, 2003, p. 574). Research does suggest, however, several differences related to race and ethnicity:

1. European Americans, more than other American ethnic groups, believe that openly discussing feelings will help a person feel better.
2. Americans are more sensitive to other-centered messages than are Chinese.
3. Both Chinese and Americans view avoidance strategies as less appropriate than approach strategies, but Chinese see avoidance as more appropriate than Americans do.
4. Married Chinese and married Americans both view the emotional support provided by their spouse to be the most important type of social support they receive.

5. African Americans place lower value on their partner's emotional support skills than do European or Asian Americans. This is especially true for African American women.

Although some differences exist, it appears that people are more alike than different in the desire for emotional support from close friends and intimate partners.

Managing Privacy and Disclosure in Relationships

In any relationship, both people will at times experience opposite pulls or dialectical tensions. One of these dialectics is the tension between openness and closedness. When we want openness, we use the skills of disclosure to share information and feelings with others. When we are feeling the pull of closedness, we manage our privacy to control what others know about us.

Disclosure is revealing confidential or secret information. Although it includes self-disclosure—which is sharing your own biographical data, personal ideas, and feelings that were unknown to others—disclosure is a larger concept because it includes confidential information about others as well as yourself (Petronio, 2002). Suppose Jim tells Mark that he wet the bed until he was 12 years old, but had never told anyone about it before because he was afraid of being teased. Jim has self-disclosed something confidential to Mark. If Mark later tells someone else that Jim was once a bed wetter, Mark is also disclosing, but he is disclosing Jim's private information, not his own.

Privacy management is the exercise of control over confidential or secret information in order to enhance autonomy or minimize vulnerability (Margulis, 1977, p. 10). The concept of **privacy** rests on the assumption that people *own* their personal information and have the right to control it by determining whether that information is to be communicated (Petronio, 2002). Like Jim, you can choose to reveal or conceal personal information from your partner. As your relationship develops, you and your partner will share sensitive information with each other. Then, either one of you could choose to reveal that sensitive information to others outside of the relationship or maintain it within the privacy of your relationship.

If your partner has your permission to share some item of your personal information, then disclosing it to others is unlikely to affect your relationship. However, if you have not given your partner permission to disclose that information and you expect that information to be held privately within your relationship, then its disclosure is likely to damage your trust in your partner and your relationship. So when Jim hears that Mark has "outed" him as a former bed wetter, he may be embarrassed, hurt, and feel violated because Mark breached his confidentiality, or he may be unaffected if he doesn't care that others know. How Jim reacts to Mark's disclosure of this private information can vary with age. If Jim and Mark are 16 when Jim discloses his bed wetting, Jim may see this as a very risky disclosure and be much more sensitive than he would if they are 35 when Mark discloses the information. The communication or the withholding of personal information is a very complex matter.

People use culture, gender, motivation, context, and risk-benefit analysis as criteria in creating rules for revealing and concealing of information (Petronio, 2002):

- Individualistic cultures value privacy more than collectivist cultures do. Members of individualistic cultures are less likely to disclose personal information to anyone but close intimates.

How can you manage privacy and disclosure in your relationships?

disclosure
revealing confidential or secret information about others as well as yourself.

privacy
the right of an individual to keep biographical data, personal ideas, and feelings secret.

privacy management
exercising personal control over confidential information in order to enhance autonomy or minimize vulnerability.

- Men or women who strongly identify themselves as masculine or feminine are likely to use rules for disclosure and privacy that correspond to sex-role stereotypes (Snell, Belk, & Hawkins, 1986). In cultures where the male stereotype includes "strong and silent" and competitive, men are likely to keep their feelings to themselves and to avoid disclosing private information that might be used against them.
- We are more likely to disclose when we have a specific motive. For example, we are more likely to disclose to avoid loneliness or to attract someone we are interested in knowing.
- Privacy and disclosure rules, like other communication rules, are influenced by the situation. We may disclose private information to a therapist or counselor in order to cope with a problem. In times of crisis, we may open up to people with whom we do not normally disclose.

Long Overdue

by Naomi Shihab Nye

Diverse Voices

Poets like Naomi Shihab Nye devote their lives to using words to communicate their feelings and ideas, yet when Shihab Nye, whose father was Palestinian, encountered anti-Arab prejudice, she was unable to disclose her Arab roots and to respond. In the excerpt that follows, Shihab Nye explores her silence.

The words we didn't say. How many times? Stones stuck in the throat. Endlessly revised silence. What was wrong with me? How could I, a person whose entire vocation has been dedicated one way or another to the use of words, lose words completely when I needed them? Where does vocal paralysis come from? Why does regret have such a long life span? My favorite poet, William Stafford, used to say, "Think of something you said. Now write what you *wish you* had said."

But I am always thinking of the times I said nothing.

In England, attending a play by myself, I was happy when the elderly woman next to me began speaking at intermission. Our arms had been touching lightly on the armrest between our seats.

"Smashingly talented," she said of Ben Kingsley, whose brilliant monologue we'd been watching. "I don't know how he does it—transporting us so effortlessly; he's a genius. Not many in the world like him." I agreed. But then she sighed and made an odd turn. "You know what's wrong with the world today? It's Arabs. I blame it all on the Arabs. Most world problems can really be traced to them."

My blood froze. Why was she saying this? The play wasn't about Arabs. Ben Kingsley was hardly your blue-blooded Englishman, either, so what brought it up? Nothing terrible about Arabs had happened lately in the news. I wasn't wearing a keffiyeh [traditional Arab headdress] around my neck.

But my mouth would not open.

"Why *did* so many of them come to England?" she continued, muttering as if she were sharing a confidence. "A ruination, that's what it is."

It struck me that she might be a landlady having trouble with tenants. I tried and tried to part my lips. Where is the end of the tangled thread? How will we roll it into a ball if we can't find an end?

She chatted on about something less consequential, never seeming to mind our utterly one-sided conversation, till the lights went down. Of course, I couldn't concentrate on the rest of the play. My precious ticket felt wasted. I twisted my icy hands together while my cheeks burned.

Even worse, she and I rode the same train afterwards. I had plenty of time to respond, to find a vocabulary for prejudice and fear. The dark night buildings flew by. I could have said, "Madam, I am half Arab. I pray your heart grows larger someday." I could have sent her off, stunned and embarrassed, into the dark.

My father would say, "People like that can't be embarrassed."

But what would he say back to her?

Oh I was ashamed for my silence and I have carried that shame across oceans, through the summer when it never rained, in my secret pocket, till now. I will never feel better about it. Like my reckless angry last words to the one who took his own life.

Years later, my son and I were sitting on an American island with a dear friend, the only African American living among 80 or so residents. A brilliant artist and poet in his seventies, he has made a beautiful lifetime of painting picture books, celebrating expression, encouraging the human spirit, reciting poems of other African American heroes, delighting children and adults alike.

We had spent a peaceful day riding bicycles, visiting the few students at the schoolhouse, picking up rounded stones on the beach, digging peat moss in the woods. We had sung hymns together in our resonant little church. Our friend had purchased a live lobster down at the dock for supper. My son and I were sad when it seemed to be knocking on the lid of the pot of boiling water. "Let me out." We vowed quietly to one another never to eat a lobster again.

After dinner, a friend of our friend dropped in, returned to the island from her traveling life as an anthropologist. We asked if she had heard anything about the elections in Israel—that was the day Shimon Peres and Benjamin Netanyahu vied for prime minister and we had been unable to pick up a final tally on the radio.

She thought Netanyahu had won. The election was very close. But then she said, "Good thing! He'll put those Arabs in their places. Arabs want more than they deserve."

My face froze. Was it possible I had heard correctly? An anthropologist speaking. Not a teenager, not a blithering idiot. I didn't speak another word during her visit. I wanted to. I should have, but I couldn't. My plate littered with red shells.

After she left, my friend put his gentle hand on my shoulder. He said simply, "Now you know a little more what it feels like to be black."

So what happens to my words when the going gets rough? In a world where certain equalities for human beings seem long, long, long, overdue, where is the magic sentence to act as a tool? Where is the hoe, the tiller, the rake?

Pontificating, proving, proselytizing leave me cold. So do endless political debates over coffee after dinner. I can't listen to talk radio, drowning in jabber.

The poetic impulse—to suggest, hint, shape a little picture, to find a story, metaphor, scene—abides as a kind of music inside. Nor can I forget the journalist in Dubai who called me donkey for talking about vegetables when there was injustice in the world.

I can talk about sumac, too. When a friend asks what's that purple spice in the little shake-up jar at the Persian restaurant, tears cloud my eyes.

Is it good for you?

Are vegetables, in some indelible way, smarter than we are? Are animals?

But then the headlines take the power. The fanatical behavior.

"Problem is, we can't hear the voices of the moderates," said the Israeli man, who assured me his house was built on a spot where Arabs had never lived. "Where are *they*? Why don't they speak *louder*?"

(They don't like to raise their voices.)

(Maybe they can't hear you either.)

Excerpt from Naomi Shihab Nye, "Long Overdue," Post Gibran: An Anthology of New Arab American Writing (Syracuse University Press, 2000), p. 127.

- One of the most important criteria we use to decide whether to disclose information or keep it private is the risk-benefit analysis. That is, we weigh the advantages we might gain by disclosing or maintaining private information against the disadvantages of disclosing or maintaining private information. Common benefits of disclosing include building the relationship, coping with stress, and emotional or psychological catharsis. Benefits of maintaining privacy include control and independence. The risks of disclosing include loss of control, vulnerability, and embarrassment. The risks of maintaining privacy include social isolation and having others misunderstand you.

In the Diverse Voices feature "Long Overdue," Naomi Shihab Nye describes her experiences with anti-Arab prejudice. As you read this excerpt from an interview with Shihab Nye, try to empathize with her frustration about Arab stereotypes, and consider her courage in disclosing information about herself and her feelings.

Although privacy and disclosure decisions affect relationships in many ways, the three most important are related to levels of intimacy, expectations for reciprocity, and information co-ownership—how jointly held private information is shared with others outside the relationship.

Effects on Intimacy

The effects of privacy and disclosure on intimacy in a relationship are not straightforward. You might think that as relationships develop, people move in a clear-cut way toward deeper disclosure. But research shows that over time, due to the dialectical tensions in relationships, people move back and forth between greater disclosure and moves to reestablish privacy (Altman, 1993).

Sometimes disclosure deepens intimacy. In your relationships you will probably find yourself and your partner cycling between times when you actively disclose and times when you back off and re-establish privacy boundaries. This can create problems when one partner craves greater intimacy at the same time her partner needs to re-establish privacy.

Other times, disclosure can decrease intimacy. People may disclose something to relieve their guilt or stress, as a type of confession. Some disclosures can do irreparable damage to a relationship, such as when one partner in a romantic relationship discloses an infidelity. So, sometimes opting for privacy may preserve the intimacy in a relationship (Hendrick, 1981) and avoid conflict (Roloff & Ifert, 2000). We may choose privacy over disclosure for many legitimate reasons, including protecting the other person's feelings, avoiding unnecessary conflict, sensitivity to the other's face needs, and protecting the relationship. Similarly, people whose religious, social, political, or sexual orientations conflict with the value systems of their partners may choose to keep their orientations private (Petronio, 2002). For example, some gays and lesbians choose not to "come out" to their parents because doing so may lead to estrangement.

Expectations of Reciprocity

Whether your disclosure is matched by similar disclosure from your partner also can affect your relationship. Although you may expect reciprocity, recent research (Dindia, 2000b) suggests there can be a long time lag after one person discloses before the other reciprocates. In between, their conversations may center on non-personal topics. One person may not be ready to disclose his or her feelings, even though the conversational partner had revealed private information. After a fourth date, Tom blurts out, "Nancy,

I love you and I know that I'm going to marry you." Nancy, who thinks she loves Tom but wants to make sure she is not just taken with the idea of being in love, may not voice her feelings for many more months. Nevertheless, the two of them continue to see each other, building common history, and sharing other personal information even though Nancy did not reciprocate at the moment when Tom first declared his love for her.

Information Co-Ownership

A third way that decisions about disclosure and privacy affect relationships has to do with how partners treat the private information that each has shared with the other. When you disclose a secret to your partner, you expect your partner to respect your privacy and not disclose your private information with others. Similarly, you and your partner may share experiences and make decisions that you consider private, and you expect your partner to protect these as well. Whether we hold revealed information in confidence or share it with others outside the relationship may affect the relationship.

As people use technology to develop and maintain their relationships, their decisions about what to disclose and what to keep private as well as the rules that guide those decisions are changing. Both mobile communication technology and the Internet are affecting the disclosure-privacy dialectic by blurring the distinction between what is public and what is private communication (Kleinman, 2007). Cell phones and other wireless technology allow people to carry on private conversations in public spaces. You may IM your friend, and that friend may pass your message around to others you would prefer did not have access to that thought. Social networking sites also blur the edges. Once we post information, it is there for others to take and share with anyone. Whereas paper diaries are considered private thoughts in written form to be guarded from others, online diaries in the form of blogs or tweets are purposely made accessible to friends, acquaintances, and often to hundreds of millions of strangers on the Web.

Skill Learning Activity 8.1

In the Pop Comm! feature "Our Right to Privacy in a Mediated Society," we talk about managing privacy in our mediated society. Do you think it is okay for gossip magazines to disclose information about celebrities without their permission? Why or why not?

Guidelines and Communication Strategies for Disclosure

The following communication guidelines can help you make wise decisions regarding disclosure when sharing personal information, sharing feelings, and providing feedback.

Sharing personal information

The following strategies can help you make good decisions about disclosing personal information.

1. Self-disclose the kind of information you want others to disclose to you. One way to determine what information is appropriate to disclose is to ask yourself whether you would feel comfortable if the other person were to disclose that kind of information to you.

2. Self-disclose more intimate information only when the disclosure represents an acceptable risk. There is always some risk that self-disclosure will distress your partner and damage your relationship, but the better you know your partner, the more likely a difficult self-disclosure will be well received.

The Right to Privacy in a Mediated Society

  p Comm!

ROBYN BECK/AFP/Getty Images

For over a century, celebrities have complained that the media invades their privacy, but it was the death of Princess Diana in 1997 that focused worldwide attention on the extent to which celebrities are denied any right to privacy. From the paparazzi who literally hounded Princess Diana to her death, to the newspapers who publicized the college antics of the Bush twins, it appears that anyone the media takes an interest in can no longer expect even a basic right to privacy. Certainly, public figures expect to be scrutinized regarding their professional lives, but the current cult of celebrity has created a situation in which the media thinks little about also prying into their private lives. Not only that, but anyone connected to these public figures, including their families, is also subject to invasive media coverage.

For example, during the 2008 presidential campaign, the media covered the pregnancy of vice-presidential candidate Sarah Palin's 17-year-old unmarried daughter, Bristol, extensively. In addition, the father of Bristol's child and his parents were subjected to intense media scrutiny. Although Bristol's pregnancy didn't seem relevant to Palin's campaign, Reverend Debra Haffner (2008) argued in a *Huffington Post* column that when "family matters relate directly to policy matters"—such as Palin's positions on sexuality education and teenage pregnancy—they are fair game. She maintained that calls for personal privacy could sometimes shroud political issues. But then-presidential candidate Barack Obama urged media to "back off these kinds of stories," saying, "People's families are off-limits, and people's children are especially off-limits. This shouldn't be a part of our politics. It has no relevance to

3. **Continue self-disclosure only if it is reciprocated.** Although a self-disclosure may not immediately be reciprocated, when it is apparent that it is not being returned, you should consider limiting the amount of self-disclosure you make. The choice not to reciprocate indicates that the person does not yet feel comfortable with the level of intimacy.

4. **Gradually move to deeper levels of self-disclosure.** Because receiving self-disclosure can be as threatening as giving it, most people become uncomfortable when the level of disclosure exceeds their expectations. The depth of self-disclosure should gradually increase as the relationship develops. So we should disclose surface information early in a relationship and more personal information in a more developed relationship (Dindia, Fitzpatrick, & Kenny, 1997, p. 408).

5. **Reserve very personal self-disclosure for ongoing relationships.** Disclosures about intimate matters are appropriate in close, well-established relationships. Making intimate self-disclosures before a bond of trust is established risks alienating the other person. Moreover, people are often embarrassed by and hostile toward others who try to saddle them with intimate information in an effort to establish a personal relationship where none exists.

Governor Palin's performance as a governor or her potential performance as a vice-president" (Seelye, 2008).

The debate over invasive media coverage was not clouded by politics in February 2009 when the celebrity Web site *TMZ.com* posted a photo of pop star Rihanna after she was physically assaulted by her then-boyfriend, R&B artist Chris Brown. The photo had been leaked by someone at the Los Angeles Police Department and, embarrassed, the department opened an internal investigation about the publication of the photo, saying it "takes seriously its duty to maintain the confidentiality of victims of domestic violence" (Itzkoff, 2009). However, *TMZ.com*'s executive producer, Harvey Levin, defended the publication of the photo, saying it helped put a face to the victims of domestic abuse ("TMZ Responds," 2009). Even people who fight for the rights of victims of domestic abuse hesitantly supported the decision to publish the photo. Chicago author and advocate for battered women Susan Murphy-Milano speculated, "Maybe it is a good idea, if it's her, if young girls see this." She added that she hoped it would make young women think "Is the next picture going to be of her in a morgue?" (McCartney, 2009).

But what about Rihanna's right to privacy? *PR Week* points out that typical standards of journalism prevent reporters and editors from publishing names of victims. However, in the case of Rihanna, David Hauslaib, editorial director of *Jossip.com*, says, "We have this appetite for celebrity culture and it brings down any sort of safeguards we, as a media industry, have implemented to protect people" (Maul, 2009). *The Gawker.com* further explored this debate about media ethics: "Critics say running the picture humiliates Rihanna at a time when she's already in emotional agony, that it pierces a zone of emotional and physical privacy already grossly violated in the apparent attack on her" (Tate, 2009). Nonetheless, profit-seeking publishers know that publishing such a shocking image will increase their traffic hits, and thus they simply choose to run the risk of exploitation accusations.

In both these cases, proponents of breaking privacy boundaries argued that they did so for a greater good. In Palin's case, they maintained that the media coverage highlighted important political issues; in Rihanna's case, publishing her photo furthered awareness of the seriousness of domestic violence. What do you think? Is the media justified in exposing the private moments of celebrities' lives, no matter how personal or painful, if doing so raises public awareness? Or is this sort of coverage just exploitive?

Sharing feelings

At the heart of intimate self-disclosure is sharing personal feelings. When we do so, we demonstrate that we trust our partner not to use the information to do us harm. Once we decide to share our feelings, we have to know how to do so appropriately.

The best way to share feelings is by describing them. **Describing feelings** is the skill of naming the emotions you are feeling without judging them. When we describe our feelings, we teach others how to treat us by explaining how what has happened affects us. For example, if you tell Paul that you enjoy it when he visits you, your description of how you feel should encourage him to visit you again. Likewise, when you tell Gloria that it bothers you when she borrows your iPod without asking, she may be more likely to ask the next time. Describing feelings allows you to exercise a measure of control over others' behavior simply by making them aware of the effects their actions have on you.

To practice describing your feelings, try following these four steps:

1. **Identify the behavior that triggered the feeling.** What specifically has someone said or done to or about you?

describing feelings
the skill of naming the emotions you are feeling without judging them.

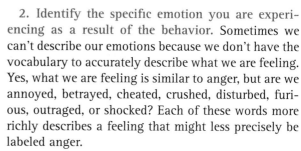

Describing feelings is difficult for many people because it makes them vulnerable. Can you recall a situation in which you masked your feelings because you didn't trust the other person? Was your fear justified?

2. Identify the specific emotion you are experiencing as a result of the behavior. Sometimes we can't describe our emotions because we don't have the vocabulary to accurately describe what we are feeling. Yes, what we are feeling is similar to anger, but are we annoyed, betrayed, cheated, crushed, disturbed, furious, outraged, or shocked? Each of these words more richly describes a feeling that might less precisely be labeled anger.

3. Frame your response as an "I" statement. For example, "I feel *happy/sad/irritated/excited/vibrant.*" "I" statements help neutralize the impact of an emotional description because they do not blame the other or evaluate the other's behavior. Instead, a first-person message accurately conveys what you are expressing and why. Be careful, however, not to couch a blaming statement as an "I" statement. For example, "I feel like you don't respect me" is a criticism of the other person. It doesn't let the other person know how you feel about what happened. You might have felt hurt, betrayed, or angry. But you haven't disclosed this.

4. Verbalize the specific feeling. Here are two examples of describing feelings effectively. The first one begins with the trigger, and the second one begins with the feeling—either order is acceptable:

"Thank you for your compliment [trigger]; I [the person having the feeling] feel gratified [the specific feeling] that you noticed the effort I made."

"I [the person having the feeling] feel very resentful [the specific feeling] when you criticize my cooking after I've worked as many hours as you have [trigger]."

To begin with, you may find it easier to describe positive feelings: "I felt so much happier after you took me to the movie" or "When you offered to help me with the yard work, I really felt relieved." As you become comfortable describing positive feelings, you can move to describing negative feelings caused by environmental factors: "It's cold and cloudy; I feel gloomy" or "When there's a thunderstorm, I get jumpy." Finally, you can risk describing the difficult emotions you feel resulting from what people have said or done: "When you use a sarcastic tone while you are saying that what I did pleased you, I really feel confused."

Skill Learning Activity 8.2

Providing personal feedback

Sometimes it is appropriate to go beyond sharing feelings to also disclose our thoughts about another's message or behavior. When personal feedback is shared with sensitivity, it can help the other person to develop a more accurate self-concept, and it can increase the openness in the relationship. Three skills can guide us when giving personal feedback: describing behavior, praising positive behavior, and criticizing negative behavior constructively.

1. Describing behavior. As is the case when sharing feelings, both effective praising and critiquing are based on being descriptive rather than evaluative, as well as being specific rather than vague. Unfortunately, people are quick to share ambiguous conclusions and evaluations. "You're so mean," "She's a tease," "You're a real friend," and countless statements like these are attempts to provide feedback, but they are evaluative and vague.

Describing Feelings

Communication Skill

Skill
Naming the emotions you are feeling without judging them.

Use
For self-disclosure; to teach people how to treat you.

Procedure
1. Identify the behavior that has triggered the feeling.
2. Identify the specific emotion you are experiencing as a result of the behavior. Anger? Joy? Be specific.
3. Frame your response as an "I" statement. "I feel _____."
4. Verbalize the specific feeling.

Example
"I just heard I didn't get the job, and I feel cheated and bitter" or "Because of the way you defended me when I was being belittled by Leah, I feel both grateful and humbled."

Identifying Descriptions of Feelings

Skill Building

For each of these statements, determine if the message is a description of feelings. If it is, place a "D" next to it. If you determine that the message is not a description of feelings, supply a message that provides a description of feelings.

_____ 1. That was a great movie!
_____ 2. I was really cheered by the flowers.
_____ 3. I feel that you are not respecting my rights.
_____ 4. Yuck!

_____ 5. Damn—I screwed that up again. I feel like an idiot.
_____ 6. I feel certain I got the job because I was the most qualified person.
_____ 7. Congratulations, I feel happy for you.
_____ 8. When Pam's around, I feel like a third wheel.
_____ 9. I'm ecstatic about winning the award.
_____10. I'm sick and tired of you.

Skill Learning Activity 8.3

Describing behavior is accurately recounting the specific behaviors of another without commenting on their appropriateness. To describe behavior, we move backward to identify the specific behaviors that led to our perception. What led you to conclude someone was "mean"? Was it something the person said or did? If so, what? Once you have identified the specific behaviors, actions, or messages that led to your conclusion, you can share that information as feedback. For

describing behavior
accurately recounting the specific behaviors of another without commenting on their appropriateness.

example, "Giorgio, you called me a liar in front of the team, and you know I have no way to prove that I told the truth." "Shana, you came to my graduation even though it was on your twenty-first birthday." "You stayed and comforted me when Tyrone left, and you even volunteered to stay with my son so I could job hunt. You're a real friend."

2. **Praising positive behavior.** **Praise** is describing a specific positive behavior or accomplishment of another person and the effect that behavior has on others. Praise is not the same as flattery. When we flatter someone, we use insincere compliments to ingratiate ourselves to that person. When we praise, our compliments are sincere. Too often we fail to acknowledge the positive and helpful things people say and do. Yet our view of who we are—our identity as well as our behavior—is shaped by how others respond to us. Praise can be used to reinforce positive behavior and to help another develop a positive self-concept.

   For praise to be effective, we need to focus on the specific behavior we want to reinforce. If your sister, who tends to be forgetful, remembers your birthday, you might want to praise that behavior. To say "You're so wonderful; you're on top of everything" does not reinforce the behavior because it does not identify the behavior. Instead, saying something like "Thanks for the birthday card; I really appreciate it" would be appropriate. The response acknowledges the accomplishment by describing the specific behavior you want to reinforce.

   Praise, when appropriate, doesn't cost much, and it is usually appreciated. Not only does praise provide feedback and build esteem, it can also deepen our relationship with that person. To praise behavior effectively, always begin by identifying the specific behavior or accomplishment that you want to reinforce. Then, describe the specific behavior or accomplishment and any positive feelings you or others experienced as a result of the behavior or accomplishment. Finally, phrase your comment so that the level of praise appropriately reflects the significance of the behavior or accomplishment.

3. **Giving constructive criticism.** **Constructive criticism** is describing specific behaviors of another that hurt the person or that person's relationships with others. Although the word *criticize* can mean judgment, constructive criticism does not condemn or judge but is based on empathy and a sincere desire to help someone understand the impact of his or her behavior. Use the following guidelines when providing constructive criticism.

   - *Ask the person's permission before giving criticism.* A person who has agreed to hear constructive criticism is likely to be more receptive to it than is someone who was not accorded the respect of being asked beforehand.
   - *Describe the behavior and its consequences by accurately recounting precisely what was said or done and the reaction of those affected by it.* Your objective description allows the other to maintain face while receiving accurate feedback about the damaging behavior. For example, DeShawn asks, "What did you think of the visuals I used when I delivered my report?" If you reply, "They weren't very effective," you would be too general and evaluative to be helpful. In contrast, to give descriptive feedback, you might say, "Well, the type on the first two was too small, and I had trouble reading them." Notice this constructive criticism does not attack DeShawn's competence. Instead, it points out a problem and in so doing enables DeShawn to see how to improve.
   - *Preface constructive criticism with an affirming statement.* Remember, even constructive criticism threatens the innate human need to be liked and admired. So, prefacing constructive criticism with statements that validate your respect

praise
describing the specific positive behaviors or accomplishments of another and the effect that behavior has on others.

constructive criticism
describing specific behaviors of another that hurt the person or that person's relationships with others.

for the other person is important. One way to do this is to offer praise before criticism. You could begin your feedback to DeShawn by saying, "First, the chart showing how much energy we waste helped me see just how much we could improve. The bold colors you chose also really helped me see the problems. But the type size on the first two slides was too small for me to see from the back of the room. It would have helped me read them if they had been larger."

- *When appropriate, suggest how the person can change the behavior.* Because the goal of constructive criticism is to help, it is appropriate to provide suggestions that might lead to positive change. In responding to DeShawn's request for feedback, you might also add, "In my Communication class, I learned that most people in an audience will be able to read 18-point font or larger. You might want to give that a try." By including a positive suggestion, you not only help the person by providing useful information, you also show that your intentions are positive.

Skill Learning Activity 8.4

Communication Strategies for Managing Privacy

Maintaining privacy during interpersonal interactions can be awkward especially if you want to maintain or further develop your relationship. Because reciprocal disclosures are part of relationship development, your partner may expect you to respond to their disclosure with a similar one of your own. Or you may encounter someone who asks you personal questions that you do not want to answer. In both cases, you will want to respond in a way that maintains your privacy without damaging the relationship. We offer three indirect and one direct communication strategy you can use when you are being pressed to disclose something that you are not comfortable sharing.

Jason Harris/Thomson Higher Education/Wadsworth Publishing Group

Learning to give constructive criticism can help you avoid a defensive reaction when you describe a person's negative behavior.

Indirect strategies for maintaining privacy

Sometimes you may choose to maintain your privacy by deflecting attention or by simply deceiving the other person. These strategies can be effective in the short term, but don't make them a habit because over the long term, they may damage the relationship.

1. **Change the subject.** Partners who are sensitive will recognize a change of subject as a signal that you don't want to disclose. For example, when Pat and Eric are leaving economics class, Pat says to Eric, "I got an 83 on the test, how about you?" If Eric doesn't want to share his grade, he might redirect the conversation by saying, "Hey, that's a B. Good going. Did you finish the homework for calculus?"

2. **Mask feelings.** When you have decided that sharing your feelings is too risky, you may choose to mask your emotions. A good poker player who develops a poker face, a neutral look that is impossible to decipher and stays the same whether the

player's cards are good or bad, has learned to mask emotions. Likewise, if Alita laughs along with the others as Manny makes fun of her, this display may mask her feelings of betrayal and embarrassment. On occasion masking your feelings can be an effective strategy. However, if we rely too much on this strategy, we might experience health problems because we are turning our feelings inward and not expressing them. We also run the risk of stunting the growth of our relationships because our partners won't really know or understand us.

3. **Tell a white lie.** A white lie is a false or misleading statement that might be acceptable if telling the truth would embarrass you or your partner and if the untruth will not cause serious harm to either person or to the relationship. So when Pat asks Eric about his grade on the test, Eric might respond, "I'm not sure. I got a few tests back this week."

Direct strategy for maintaining privacy: Establish a boundary

Changing the subject, masking feelings, and telling white lies are indirect ways to maintain your privacy and generally work in one-time situations. But these strategies will eventually damage your relationships if used repeatedly. When you wish to keep information private over a longer period of time, you will want to use a more direct approach. The skill of **establishing a boundary** allows you to effectively respond to people who expect you to disclose information you prefer to keep private. In essence, it is a polite way to let your partner know that questions requiring you to disclose about a specific topic are unacceptable.

1. **Recognize why you are choosing not to share the information.** For example, when Pat asks Eric about the grade he received on a history term paper, Eric may hesitate to share this recognizing that he feels uncomfortable doing so.

2. **Identify your rule that guided this decision.** Eric relates his discomfort in sharing the test score to his inability to predict how Pat will react when he finds out that Eric has received an "A+" while Pat got only a "B". Eric, who in the past has been teased for his good grades has developed a rule that he does not disclose the grades he receives unless he knows that the person he is talking to respects academic achievement.

3. **Form an "I"-centered message that briefly establishes a boundary.** For example, when Pat asks Eric about his test grade, Eric might reply, "I know that everyone's different, and I don't mean to be rude, but it's my policy not to ask other people about their grades and not to discuss my own. I know you may think this is weird, but please don't be offended." This lets Pat know that Eric's decision is based on a personal rule rather than an indication of his trust in Pat. Similarly, we sometimes need to establish a boundary regarding private information that another person has entrusted to us. So when Julie asks Ilaria why Emma isn't going on the alternative spring break trip this year, Emma may say, "You know, I'd like to share that with you, but Emma told me her reasons in confidence, and I pride myself on honoring commitments I've made to guard others' privacy. I know you can appreciate that."

Negotiating Different Needs, Wants, and Preferences in Relationships

Even two people who are in a mutually satisfying, intimate relationship have different needs, wants, and preferences. The dialectical tension between our need for autonomy and need for connection can affect whether we choose to push to have a preference honored by our partner or whether we are willing to subordinate our

establishing a boundary
effectively respond to people who expect you to disclose information you prefer to keep private.

Speech Assignment: **Communicate on Your Feet**

Personal Narrative

Prepare a 3- to 5-minute speech that is a story about something that happened to you and is not generally known by others. Your story might be humorous, serious, or somewhere in between. It might be about something that happened recently or about an event from your past.

Begin by making a list of stories you might tell. As you think about the stories on your list, use the privacy and disclosure guidelines in this chapter to determine whether the story is appropriate for a class-room setting. Remember to consider not only your own privacy, but also the privacy of others who are part of the story.

As you prepare your speech, think about how to tell the story so that your audience can easily follow what you are saying. We tell most stories in chronological order, introducing people in the story as they make their appearance in the events. You can help your audience follow your story if you chunk it into two, three, or four sequential parts, similar to the chapters of a book. For example, if you are going to tell a story about a cake-baking disaster, you could divide your story into three parts: problems with ingredients, problems with mixing, and problems with baking.

Briefly introduce your story in a way that piques the interest of your audience members. End your story by summarizing what you learned from the experience.

---

wishes to maintain connectedness with our partner. For example, Anna may enjoy watching college football all day every Saturday. But she has begun to date Jack, who hates all sports. So Anna may forego her Saturday habit in order to spend time with Jack. Or Jack may initially indulge Anna by watching with her, getting pleasure from just spending time with her. As they get to know each other better, the person who has made the personal sacrifice may choose to express his or her real preference. How Anna and Jack communicate their preferences and how the other one responds will affect the quality of their relationship. We negotiate our differences in relationships by communicating our personal needs and preferences and by managing the conflict that occurs when our needs, wants, and preferences do not match those of our partner.

> How do people negotiate different needs, wants, and preferences in relationships?

Communicating Personal Needs, Wants, and Preferences: Passive, Aggressive, and Assertive Behavior

We can communicate our needs, wants, and preferences in one of three ways. We can be passive, aggressive, or assertive.

Passive behavior

Passive behavior is expressing our personal preferences or defending our rights because we value our connection with the other person more than we value our independence and we fear that we will lose our connection if we stand

> **passive behavior**
> *not expressing personal preferences or defending our rights because we fear the cost and are insecure in the relationships, have very low self-esteem, or value the other person above ourself.*

up for ourselves. We behave passively when we submit to other people's demands even when doing so is inconvenient, against our best interests, or when it violates our rights. For example, Aaron and Katie routinely go to the gym at 10 a.m. Saturday mornings, but Aaron's Friday work schedule has changed and he doesn't get home until 3 a.m. on Saturday morning. Aaron behaves passively if he doesn't say anything to Katie but drags himself out of bed even though he'd much rather sleep.

Aggressive behavior

Aggressive behavior is forcefully making claims for our preferences, feelings, needs, or rights with little or no regard for the situation or for the feelings or rights of our partner. People behave aggressively when they perceive themselves to be powerful, do not value the other person, lack emotional control, or feel defensive. Although aggressive behavior may stem from the need to establish more independence in a relationship, it also weakens feelings of connection and damages relationships. Research shows that people who receive aggressive messages from their partner are likely to feel hurt by them regardless of their relationship (Martin, Anderson, & Horvath, 1996). Suppose that, without letting her know of his schedule change, Aaron continues to meet Katie at the gym. If Katie suggests they meet next week at 8 a.m. instead of 10 a.m., Aaron may explode and aggressively reply, "No way! In fact, I don't care if I ever work out on Saturday again!" Katie, who has no context for understanding this aggressive outburst, may be startled, hurt, and confused.

Assertive behavior

Assertive behavior is expressing our personal preferences and defending our personal rights while respecting the preferences and rights of others. Assertiveness is an effective way to establish our independence while continuing to nurture the relationship because our assertive messages teach our partners how to treat us. When we assert our needs and preferences effectively, we provide our partners with the honest and truthful information they need to understand and meet our needs. When Aaron's schedule changed, he could have behaved assertively and called Katie, explained his situation, and negotiated a more convenient time for working out together.

Assertive messages balance our rights and needs with the rights and needs of others. For a review of the characteristics of assertive behavior, see Figure 8.1.

Here are some useful guidelines for practicing assertive behavior: (1) identify what you are thinking or feeling; (2) analyze the cause of these feelings; (3) identify what your real preferences and rights are; and (4) use describing feelings and describing behavior skills to make "I" statements that explain your position politely.

Skill Learning Activity 8.5
Web Resource 8.1

Cultural Variations in Passive, Aggressive, and Assertive Behavior

Assertiveness is typically valued in individualistic cultures. Whereas North American culture is known for its assertive communication style, Asian and South American cultures, which are collectivist, tend to value accord and harmony (Samovar, Porter, & McDaniel, 2007). In collectivist cultures, passive behavior is more prevalent, and personal needs, wants, and preferences are subordinate to the needs of the group. In some cultures, such as Latino or Hispanic societies, men exercise a form of self-expression that goes far beyond the guidelines presented here for assertive behavior. In these societies, the concept of "machismo" guides male behavior (Arboleda-Florez & Weisstub, 2000). Although what is labeled appropriate behavior varies across cultures,

aggressive behavior
belligerently or violently confronting another with your preferences, feelings, needs, or rights with little regard for the situation or for the feelings or rights of others.

assertive behavior
expressing your personal preferences and defending your personal rights while respecting the preferences and rights of others.

Own your feelings	Assertive individuals acknowledge that the thoughts and feelings expressed are theirs.
Avoid confrontational language	Assertive individuals do not use threats, evaluations, or dogmatic language.
Use specific statements directed to the behaviors at hand	Instead of focusing on extraneous issues, assertive individuals use descriptive statements that focus on the issue that is most relevant.
Maintain eye contact and firm body position	Assertive individuals look people in the eye rather than shifting gaze, looking at the floor, swaying back and forth, hunching over, or using other signs that may be perceived as indecisive or lacking conviction.
Maintain a firm but pleasant tone of voice	Assertive individuals speak firmly but at a normal pitch, volume, and rate.
Avoid hemming and hawing	Assertive individuals avoid vocalized pauses and other signs of indecisiveness.

Figure 8.1
Characteristics of assertive behavior

the results of passive and aggressive behaviors seem universal. Passive behavior can cause resentment and aggressive behavior leads to fear and misunderstanding. When talking with people whose culture, background, or lifestyle differs from your own, you may need to observe their behavior and their responses to your statements before you can be sure about the kinds of behavior that are likely to effectively communicate your needs, wants, and preferences.

Assertiveness

Communication Skill

Skill	Use	Procedure	Example
Standing up for yourself and doing so in interpersonally effective ways that describe your feelings honestly and exercise your personal rights while respecting the rights of others.	To show clearly what you need, want, or prefer.	1. Identify what you are thinking or feeling. 2. Analyze the cause of these feelings. 3. Identify what your real preferences and rights are. 4. Use describing feelings and describing behavior skills to make "I" statements that politely explain your position.	When Gavin believes he is being charged too much, he says, "I have never been charged for a refill on iced tea before—has there been a change in policy?"

Assertive Messages

Skill Building

For each of the following situations, write an assertive response.

1. You come back to your dorm, apartment, or house to finish a paper that is due tomorrow, only to find that someone else is using your computer.
   Assertive response:

2. You work part time at a clothing store. Just as your shift is ending, your manager says to you, "I'd like you to work overtime, if you would. Martin's supposed to replace you, but he just called and can't get here for at least an hour." You have tickets to a concert that starts in an hour.
   Assertive response:

3. During a phone call with your elderly grandmother, she announces, "Your great-aunt Margie called, and I told her you'd be happy to take us grocery shopping and out to lunch on Sunday." You were planning

to spend Sunday working on your résumé for an interview on Monday.
   Assertive response:

4. You and your friend made a date to go dancing, an activity you really enjoy. When you meet, your friend says, "I don't feel like dancing tonight. Let's go to Joey's party instead."
   Assertive response:

5. You're riding in a car with a group of friends on the way to a party when the driver begins to clown around by swerving the car back and forth, speeding up to tailgate the car in front, and honking his horn. You believe this driving is dangerous, and you're becoming scared.
   Assertive response:

 Skill Learning Activity 8.6

Managing Conflict in Relationships

How do we deal with conflict in our relationships?

When two people have an honest relationship, there will be times when one person's attempt to satisfy his or her own needs will conflict with the other person's desires. When this happens, the partners experience conflict. **Interpersonal conflict** exists when the needs or ideas of one person are at odds with the needs or ideas of another. In these conflict situations, participants have choices about how they act and how they communicate with each other.

Many people view conflict as a sign of a bad relationship, but in reality conflict occurs in all relationships. Although cultures differ in how they view conflict (for example, Asian cultures see it as dysfunctional), whether conflict hurts or strengthens a relationship depends on how you deal with it. In this section, we discuss five styles people use to manage conflict and how you can skillfully initiate and respond to conflict in your relationships.

Styles of Conflict

interpersonal conflict
when the needs or ideas of one person are at odds with the needs or ideas of another.

Think about the last time you experienced a conflict. How did you react? Did you avoid it? Give in? Force the other person to accept your will? Did you compromise? Or did the two of you use a problem-solving approach? When faced with a conflict, you can withdraw, accommodate, force, compromise, or collaborate (Lulofs & Cahn, 2000).

One of the most common ways to deal with conflict is withdrawing. **Withdrawing** involves physically or psychologically removing yourself from the conflict. You withdraw physically by leaving the site. For instance, imagine Eduardo and Justina get into an argument about their financial situation. Eduardo may withdraw physically by saying, "I don't want to talk about this" and walking out the door. Or he may psychologically withdraw by simply ignoring Justina. When you withdraw repeatedly, you risk damaging your relationship. First, in terms of dialectical tension, withdrawing signals closedness rather than openness and autonomy rather than connection. Further, withdrawing doesn't eliminate the source of the conflict and it often increases the tension. In many cases, not confronting the problem when it occurs only makes it more difficult to deal with in the long run. Nevertheless, as a temporary strategy, withdrawing may allow tempers to cool and may be appropriate when the issue or the relationship isn't important.

A second style of managing conflict is **accommodating**, which means satisfying others' needs or accepting others' ideas while neglecting your own. People who adopt the accommodating style use passive behavior. For instance, during a discussion of their upcoming vacation, Mariana and Juan disagree about whether to invite friends to join them. Juan, who would really prefer to be alone with Mariana, uses accommodation when Mariana says, "I think it would be fun to go with another couple, don't you?" and he replies, "OK, whatever you want."

Accommodating can result in ineffective conflict resolution because important facts, arguments, and positions are not voiced. There are situations, of course, when accommodating is appropriate. When the issue is not important to you, but the relationship is, accommodating is the preferred style. Hal and Yvonne are trying to decide where to go for dinner. Hal says, "I really have a craving for some Thai food tonight." Yvonne, who prefers pizza, says, "OK, that will be fine." Yvonne's interest in pizza was not very strong, and because Hal really seemed excited by Thai food, Yvonne accommodated.

A third style of dealing with conflict is forcing. **Forcing** means satisfying your own needs or with no concern for the needs of the other and no concern for the harm done to the relationship. Forcing may use aggressive behavior such as physical threats, verbal attacks, coercion, or manipulation. If you use forcing in a conflict and your partner avoids or accommodates, the conflict seems to subside. If, however, your partner answers your forcing style with a forcing style, the conflict escalates.

Although forcing may result in a person getting her or his own way, it usually hurts a relationship, at least in the short term. There are times, however, when forcing is an effective means to resolve conflict. In emergencies, when quick and decisive action must be taken to ensure safety or minimize harm or when an issue is critical to your own or the other's welfare, or if you are interacting with someone who will take advantage of you if you do not force the issue, this style is appropriate. For example, David knows that, statistically speaking, the likelihood of death or serious injury increases dramatically if one does not wear a helmet when riding a motorcycle. So he insists that his sister wear one when she rides with him, even though she complains bitterly.

withdrawing
managing conflict by physically or psychologically removing yourself.

accommodating
managing conflict by satisfying others' needs or accepting others' ideas while neglecting our own.

forcing
managing conflict by satisfying your own needs or advancing your own ideas, with no concern for the needs or ideas of the other and no concern for the harm done to the relationship.

©1995 Baby Blues Partnership. Reprinted by permission of King Features Syndicate, Inc.

compromising
managing conflict by giving up part of what you want, to provide at least some satisfaction for both parties.

A fourth way to manage conflict is **compromising,** which occurs when partners each give up part of what they want to provide at least some satisfaction for both parties. For example, if Heather and Paul are working together on a class project and need to meet outside of class but both have busy schedules, they may compromise on a time to meet that isn't particularly ideal for either one.

Although compromising is a popular and effective style, there are drawbacks associated with it. One drawback is that the quality of a decision is affected if one of the parties "trades away" a better solution to find a compromise. Compromising is appropriate when the issue is moderately important, when there are time constraints, and when attempts at collaborating have not been successful.

A fifth style for dealing with conflict is collaborating. When you **collaborate,** you view the disagreement as a problem to be solved, discuss the issues, describe your feelings, and identify the characteristics of an effective solution. With collaboration, both people's needs are met and both sides feel that they have been heard. For example, if Juan and Mariana decide to collaborate on their conflict about asking friends to join them on vacation, Mariana may explain how she thinks that vacationing with friends lower the cost of the trip. Juan may describe his desire to have "alone time" with Mariana. As they explore what each wants from the vacation, they can arrive at a plan that meets both of their needs. So, they may end up vacationing alone, but spending several nights camping to lower their expenses. Or they may share a condo with friends but agree to schedule alone time each day.

Skill Learning Activity 8.7
Web Resource 8.2

Guidelines for Collaboration

You may be the person to initiate a conflict or you may have to respond to a conflict initiated by your partner. In either case, several guidelines can help you guide the conversation. You can initiate a collaborative conflict by following these guidelines:

> What is a collaborative approach to conflict?

- Identify the problem and own it as your own: "Hi, I'm trying to study and I need your help."
- Describe the problem in terms of behavior, consequences, and feelings: "When I hear your music, I listen to it instead of studying, and then I get frustrated and behind schedule."
- Don't evaluate the other person's motives. Refrain from blaming or accusing: "That person isn't trying to ruin your study; she's just enjoying her music."
- Find common ground: "I would guess that you have had times when you became distracted from something you needed to do, so I'm hoping that you can help me out by lowering the volume a bit."
- Mentally rehearse so that you can state your request briefly.

It is more difficult to create a collaborative climate when you have to respond to a conflict that someone initiates in a confrontational manner. But you can shape the conversation toward collaboration by following these guidelines:

collaborating
managing conflict by fully addressing the needs and issues of each party and arriving at a solution that is mutually satisfying.

- Disengage. Mentally "put up your shield" and avoid a defensive response by emotionally disengaging." Remember your partner has a problem and you want to help.
- Respond empathically and with genuine interest and concern. Sometimes you need to allow your partner to vent before the partner will be ready to problem solve: "I can see that you're angry. Tell me about it."

- Paraphrase your understanding of the problem and ask questions to clarify issues: "Is it the volume of my music or the type of music that is making it difficult for you to study?"
- Seek common ground by finding some aspect of the complaint that you can honestly agree with: "I can understand that you would be upset about losing precious study time."
- Ask the other person to suggest alternative solutions: "Can you give me a couple of ideas about how we could resolve this so your study is more effective?"

Web Resource 8.3

Conversation and Analysis

Use your Premium Website for *Communicate!* to access the **Skill Learning Activity 8.8**, which is a video clip of Jan and Ken's conversation. As you watch Jan and Ken talk, focus on how the nature of their relationship influences their interaction. What does each person do to help maintain the relationship? How does each person handle this conflict? How well does each person listen to the other? Are Jan and Ken appropriately assertive? Notice how well each provides feedback and describes feelings. You can respond to these and other analysis questions by clicking on "Critique" in the menu bar at the top of the screen. When you've answered all the questions, click "Done" to compare your answers to those provided by the authors.

Skill Learning Activity 8.8

Jan and Ken are in their early to middle twenties. They meet at Jan's apartment. Jan and Ken have been good friends for most of their lives. But because of what she said last week, Ken believes Jan has betrayed their friendship.

Conversation

KEN: Jan, we need to talk. Why'd you tell Shannon about what happened between Katie and me? Now Shannon doesn't want to talk to me.

JAN: (*Silent for a moment as she realizes that he knows*): Ken, I'm sorry, I didn't mean to tell her. It just kind of slipped out when we were talking.

KEN: Sorry? Sorry is not enough. I told you that in private, and you promised that you'd keep it just between you and me.

JAN: Ken, I told her that long before the two of you started dating. You know, Shannon and I, we've been friends for a long time. We were just talking about guys and cheating and stuff. It wasn't about you specifically.

KEN: It wasn't about me? It was totally about me. You had no right to tell anyone that, under any circumstances. Now Shannon doesn't trust me. She thinks I'm a lowlife that sleeps around.

JAN: Well, I'm sorry, but the two of you weren't even dating yet.

KEN: Oh, that's irrelevant. You know, it would be irrelevant even if Shannon and I weren't dating. But, you know, the point is I thought I could trust you and tell you anything and that it would go no further.

JAN: Yeah, like the time I told you I was thinking about dropping out of school for a semester and you just happened to tell my dad?

Jason Harris/Thomson Higher Education/Wadsworth Publishing Group

KEN: Ah, that's not the same thing.

JAN: You know what? It's *exactly* the same. I trusted you and you squealed. My dad lit into me big-time. He should have never known I was thinking about that. I trusted you, and you betrayed me.

KEN: Well look, I was just trying to look out for you. I knew you were making a big mistake, and I was just trying to stop you. And besides, you know I was right! (*Gets discouraged.*) Don't change the subject here. Are you saying that your telling Shannon is some sort of payback for me telling your dad?

JAN: No, I'm just trying to point out that you've got no right to throw stones!

KEN: You know what? Then maybe neither of us can trust the other. Maybe we just shouldn't tell each other anything that we don't want broadcast to the world, huh?

JAN: Don't be such a jerk. I'm sorry, OK?

KEN: Well, that's not good enough. You ruined any chance I had with her.

JAN: Are you saying that something I said about what you did a long time ago is ruining your chances?

KEN: Yeah, it might.

JAN: Ken, if she truly valued your friendship, something that you did a long time ago shouldn't matter.

KEN: Well, maybe you're right.

JAN: Look, I said I'm sorry, and I meant it. I'm also sorry about, you know, throwing in what you told my dad. I know that wasn't fair, but you know, you really hurt my feelings when you blew up at me like that.

KEN: Listen, listen, I shouldn't have, and I shouldn't have told your dad. I should have probably encouraged you to talk to him. We still friends?

A Question of Ethics

Ronaldo sat in the study hall cramming for a final examination when two of his classmates, Chauncey and Doug, walked up to his table.

"Studying hard, huh?" Chauncey asked.
"Yeah. I'm stressing hard over this final," said Ronaldo. "What about you guys?"
"Hardly studying," said Chauncey.
Doug laughed.

What Would You Do?

Ronaldo looked at the two and saw that they both seemed relaxed and confident. "Something's not right with this picture," he said. "You're not going to tell me you guys are ready for this thing, are you?"
"Yep," said Chauncey.

Doug nodded.

"I don't get it," said Ronaldo. "You mean you've already gone back and studied everything we've covered this semester?"

"Hey, bright boy, you only need to study what's actually on the test," said Chauncey.

"And how would you know that when McAllister didn't even give us a study sheet to help us know what would be on the test?" asked Ronaldo. He was beginning to put the puzzle together.

Doug placed his hand on Chauncey's arm. "Don't tell him anything else, man," he said.

"No, it's all right. Ronaldo's cool," said Chauncey. "He knows how to keep a secret. Don't you?"

"I guess," Ronaldo said uneasily.

"It's like this," said Chauncey. "Doug's little brother is a super geek with computers. He hacked into McAllister's system and downloaded a copy of the final exam. You interested in getting a head start?"

1. Assuming that Ronaldo declines Chauncey's offer to cheat, what are the remaining ethical issues he faces? Which would be more ethically compromising: letting Chauncey and Doug get away with cheating, or betraying their trust by notifying the professor about their actions?

2. When, if ever, is it ethically acceptable to divulge information that you have sworn not to share with others?

Summary

We develop and maintain our interpersonal relationships through communication with our partner. How satisfied we are with our relationships depends on how well we accomplish basic relationship communication tasks including: (1) providing emotional support and comfort, (2) managing our competing needs for privacy and disclosure, and (3) negotiating our differences.

We can provide emotional comfort for our partner by clarifying our supportive intentions, buffering face threats, using other-centered messages, reframing the situation, and giving advice.

The openness vs. closedness dialectical tension gives rise to our needs to disclose or maintain privacy within our relationships. When we disclose, we will be most effective when we own our feelings and describe feelings. We can also effectively disclose feedback by describing behavior, offering praise, and giving constructive feedback. When we want to maintain privacy, we can use three indirect methods: change the subject, mask feelings, or tell "white lies." Alternatively, we can directly express our desire for privacy by establishing a boundary.

Finally, our relationship satisfaction depends on our ability to negotiate differences with our partner. We can communicate our needs, wants, and preferences through passive, aggressive, or assertive behavior and messages. The skill of assertiveness is most useful in individualistic cultures. When our needs, wants, and preferences conflict with those of our partner, we can adopt one of five conflict styles: withdrawal, accommodation, forcing, compromising, or collaborating. While each style may be appropriate under certain circumstances, when we want to maintain a good relationship and our differences are serious, collaborative methods are most appropriate. Whether you initiate or respond to the conflict initiation of your partner, several guidelines can help you collaboratively resolve the conflict.

Communicate! Active Online Learning

Now that you have read Chapter 8, use your Premium Website for *Communicate!* for quick access to the electronic resources that accompany this text. These resources include

- **Study tools** that will help you assess your learning and prepare for exams (*digital glossary, key term flash cards, review quizzes*).
- **Activities and assignments** that will help you hone your knowledge, analyze communication situations (*Skill Learning Activities*), and build your public speaking skills throughout the course (*Communication on Your Feet speech assignments, Action Step activities*). Many of these activities allow you to compare your answers to those provided by the authors, and, if requested, submit your answers to your instructor.

- **Media resources** that will help you explore communication concepts online (*Web Resources*), develop your speech outlines (*Speech Builder Express 3.0*), watch and critique videos of communication situations and sample speeches (*Interactive Video Activities*), upload your speech videos for peer reviewing and critique other students' speeches (*Speech Studio online speech review tool*), and download chapter review so you can study when and where you'd like (*Audio Study Tools*).

This chapter's Key Terms, Skill Learning Activities, and Web Resources are also featured on the following pages, and you can find this chapter's Communicate on Your Feet assignment and Skill Building activities in the body of the chapter.

Key Terms

accommodating (177)
aggressive behavior (174)
assertive behavior (174)
buffering messages (159)
collaborating (178)
comforting (158)
compromising (178)
constructive criticism (170)

describing behavior (169)
describing feelings (167)
disclosure (161)
establishing a boundary (172)
forcing (177)
giving advice (160)
interpersonal conflict (176)
negative face needs (159)
other-centered messages (159)

passive behavior (173)
positive face needs (159)
praise (170)
privacy (161)
privacy management (161)
reframing the situation (160)
self-disclosure (161)
withdrawing (177)

Skill Learning Activities

8.1: Self-Disclosure and Popular Media (165)

Popular American culture has a reputation for promoting self-disclosure that probably exceeds that of any other culture in the world. Yet clearly, as the phrase "too much information" indicates, inappropriate self-disclosure still happens in popular American culture. Of course, what may be inappropriate for one person can be appropriate for another. Find three instances of self-disclosure in popular media (film, television, radio, magazines, newspapers, or the Internet) and write a paragraph on each, explaining why you think the particular instance of self-disclosure is appropriate or inappropriate.

To help you complete this activity, you can use the log provided in your Premium Website for

Communicate! Look for it in the Skill Learning activities for Chapter 8.

8.2: Building Your Vocabulary of Emotions (168)

Go to your Premium Website for *Communicate!* and look for Skill Learning Activity 8.2. There you'll find a list of words related to emotions such as *angry* and *happy*. For each of the following statements, select three words from the list that might fit the statement but would represent three different emotional reactions. As you select the words, try to visualize the feeling that each of the words arouses.

1. I feel _____ when you call me late at night.
2. I was _____ that she told everyone about that.
3. He was _____ when he discovered what she had done.

4. Witnessing that accident really made me feel _____.
5. When my father died, I felt _____.
6. I'm _____ about graduating.
7. I'm _____ about losing my job.
8. I was _____ when the doctor told me I needed surgery.
9. I suppose I should understand that it was a mistake, but I feel _____.
10. When you look at me like that, I feel _____.

When you're done with this activity, compare your answers to the authors'.

8.3: Identifying Descriptions of Feelings (169)

Finish the in text activity. When you're done with this activity, compare your answers to the authors' at the Premium Website for *Communicate!* Look for them in the Skill Learning activities for Chapter 8.

8.4: Praising and Criticizing (171)

Think of someone you need to praise and someone to whom you would like to give constructive criticism. Prepare feedback for each person. Use the following steps:

1. Begin by writing a sentence that identifies your general impression of each person.
2. For each person, recall and write down the specific behaviors, actions, and messages that led to your impression.
3. Identify all the consequences that have resulted from the way this person has acted or spoken.
4. If you have any advice that seems appropriate to give to this person, record it.
5. Write a short feedback message for each person that follows the guidelines for effective praise or criticism.

In the next day or two, have a feedback conversation with at least one of these people and use your preparation to help you deliver the feedback. Then write a paragraph describing what happened and how well the feedback was received. Analyze why you believe the feedback was received as it was.

To help you complete this activity, you can use the worksheet provided in your Premium Website for *Communicate!* Look for it in the Skill Learning activities for Chapter 8.

8.5: Passive and Aggressive Behavior (174)

Describe two incidents in the past where you behaved passively or aggressively. Now analyze each situation. What type of situation was it? Did someone make a request? Did you need to express a preference or right? Was someone imposing on you? What type of relationship did you have with the person (stranger, acquaintance, friendship, business, intimate, romantic)? How did you feel about how you behaved? If you had used assertive messages, what might you have said?

8.6: Assertive Messages (176)

Finish the in text activity. When you're done with this activity, compare your answers to the authors' at the Premium Website for *Communicate!* Look for them in the Skill Learning activities for Chapter 8.

8.7: Your Conflict Profile (178)

Access and print out **Web Resource 8.2: Your Conflict Profile**, which is an article called "How Do You Manage Conflict?" by Dawn M. Baskerville. Fill out and score the self-assessment questionnaire and graph your results. Read the description of each pattern. Study these results. Do they seem to capture your perception of your conflict profile accurately? Which are your dominant styles? Are your scores close together, or are there one or two styles that seem to dominate and other styles you prefer not to use? How does this pattern equip you to handle the conflicts you have experienced? Based on the information from this self-assessment, what do you need to do to become better able to handle conflict in your relationships? Write a paragraph in which you describe what you have learned about your conflict profile.

8.8: Jan and Ken (179)

After you've watched the video of Jan and Ken and have read the transcript of their conversation, answer the following questions.

1. How does each person handle this conflict?
2. How well does each person listen to the other?
3. Are Jan and Ken appropriately assertive?
4. Comment on how well each provides feedback and describes feelings?

When you're done with this activity, compare your answers to the authors' at the Premium Website for *Communicate!* Look for them in the Skill Learning activities for Chapter 8.

Web Resources

8.1: How to Say No (174)

The University of Florida's counseling Web site and the Hampden-Sydney College Counseling Center's Web site provide good advice about how to refuse requests, including unfair and unreasonable requests.

8.2: Your Conflict Profile (178)

Learn about conflict management and determine your conflict management style by reading the article "How Do You Manage Conflict?" by Dawn M. Baskerville.

8.3: Skills for Collaborative Conflict (179)

This article, "Resolving Conflicts through Collaboration," describes how to initiate conflict and how to respond to conflicts initiated by others.

Jeff Cadge

Appendix: Interviewing

Questions you will be able to answer after reading this appendix:

- What types of questions are used in interviews?
- How do you prepare for and conduct an information gathering interview?
- How do you conduct an employment interview?
- How do you present yourself successfully in a job interview?
- How do you participate in a media interview?

Terrence, the manager at Qwik In and Out, a convenience store and gas station, needed a new night cashier and was interviewing applicants. His first candidate arrived on time, and after taking a tour around the store, they retired to Terrence's office for the interview.

Terrence began, "Take a seat. What did you say your name was again?"

"Bobby. And, um, . . . I'm not sure where you want me to sit."

"Oh, well, just sit on that box over there. Sorry for the mess, but, you know, I've had a lot to do. So, Bobby, you want to work here at Qwik In and Out?"

"Yeah."

"Well, you understand that you will be working alone at night, right?"

"Yeah."

"So, it says on your application that you went to Highlands High School. Is that right?"

"Uh-huh."

"And now you're a student at CSCTU?"

"Yeah."

"Will school interfere with your work schedule?"

"Nope."

"Is there anything else I should know?"

"No."

"Well, I've got several other people to talk to, and I'll let you know by Monday what I decide."

"Okay."

After Bobby left the store, Terrence turned to Mary, the day cashier, and said, "Boy, that guy was sure a loser. He just wasn't at all prepared for the interview. I sure hope the next one's better."

What do you think about Terrence's assessment of Bobby? What do you think about Terrence's conducting of the interview? Interviewing is a powerful method of collecting or presenting firsthand information that may be unavailable elsewhere. So, it is an important communication skill to master. An **interview** is a highly structured conversation in which one person asks questions and another person answers them. Effective interview participants prepare in advance for the interview conversation, unlike most interpersonal communication. By *highly structured*, we mean that the purpose of the conversation and the questions to be asked are determined ahead of time. Because interviews are highly structured, they can be used to make comparisons. For example, an interviewer may ask two potential employees the same set of questions, compare the answers, and hire the person whose answers fit best with the needs of the organization. Although we all are experienced in informal conversation, few people know how to conduct an effective interview, and few of us have practice in effectively presenting ourselves and our ideas in an interview.

Because the heart of effective interviewing is developing a structured series of good questions, we begin by describing how to do so. Then we propose some guidelines for conducting both information and employment interviews. Finally, we offer tips about how to present yourself in an employment interview and in a media interview.

Structuring Interviews

The questions you develop for any interview depend on the specific purpose of the interview. Defining the purpose will give you insight into the major topic areas you will need to cover during the interview conversation. With these topics in mind, you can then structure the interview by forming and ordering a series of questions to use during the meeting.

The Interview Protocol

The **interview protocol** is the list of questions you prepare to elicit the information you want to know from the interviewee. To prepare the interview protocol, begin by listing the topic areas to be covered in the interview. Then prioritize them. Figure A.1 presents a list of topics for an interview with a music producer when the goal is to learn about how producers find and sign new talent.

interview
a planned, structured conversation in which one person asks questions and another person answers them.

interview protocol
the list of questions prepared to elicit relevant information from the interviewee.

- Finding artists
- Decision process
- Criteria
- Stories of success and failure

Figure A.1
Topics for interview with the
music producer

Effective Questions

Just as the topics in a well-developed speech are structured in an outline with main points, subpoints, and supporting material, an effective interview protocol is structured into primary and secondary questions. The questions should be a mix of open-ended and closed questions, as well as neutral and leading questions. Let's briefly examine each type.

> What types of
> questions are used
> in interviews?

Primary and secondary questions

Primary questions are the lead-in questions about one of the major topics of the interview. They are like the main points of an essay or speech. The interview with the music producer may have four primary questions corresponding to the topics in Figure A.1: (1) How do you find artists to consider for contract? (2) Once an artist has been brought to your attention, what course of action do you follow? (3) What criteria do you use when deciding to offer a contract? (4) Can you tell me the story of how you came to sign one of your most successful artists and then one about an unsuccessful artist?

   Secondary questions are follow-up questions designed to probe the answers given to primary questions. You can anticipate some of the follow-up questions you may want to ask. For example, if in his response to your primary question about the criteria used in selecting artists, the music producer doesn't mention music genre or demographic considerations, you might probe with a follow-up question. Some follow-up questions are not as directive and simply encourage the interviewee to continue ("And then?" or "Is there more?"); some probe into what the person has said ("What does 'regionally popular' mean?" or "What were you thinking at the time?"); and some probe the feelings of the person ("How did it feel when her first record went platinum?" or "Did you expect them to become so popular?"). The major purpose of follow-up questions is to encourage the interviewee to expand on an answer they've given. Sometimes the interviewee may not understand how much detail you are looking for, and occasionally he or she may be purposely evasive.

primary questions
lead-in questions that introduce one of the major topics of the interview conversation.

secondary questions
follow-up questions designed to probe the answers given to primary questions.

Open and closed questions

Open questions are broad-based probes that allow the interviewee to provide perspectives, ideas, information, feelings, or opinions as he or she wishes. For example, in a job interview you might be asked, "What one accomplishment has best prepared you for this job?" In a customer service interview, a representative might ask, "What seems to be the problem?" or "Can you tell me the steps you took when you first set up this product?" Open questions encourage the interviewee to talk and allow the interviewer an opportunity to listen and observe. Open questions take time to answer and give respondents more control, which means that interviewers can lose sight of their original purpose if they are not careful (Tengler & Jablin, 1983).

   By contrast, **closed questions** are narrowly focused and control what the interviewee can say. They require very brief (one- or two-word) answers. Closed questions range from those that can be answered yes or no, such as "Have you had a course in marketing?" to those that require only a short answer, such as "Which of the artists

open questions
broad-based probes that call on the interviewee to provide perspective, ideas, information, feelings, or opinions as he or she answers the question.

closed questions
narrowly focused questions that require the respondent to give very brief (one- or two-word) answers

Skill Learning Activity A.1

that you have signed have won Grammys?" By asking closed questions, interviewers can control the interview and obtain specific information quickly. But the answers to closed questions cannot reveal the nuances behind responses, nor are they likely to capture the complexity of the story.

Effective interview conversations contain a combination of open and closed questions. With this in mind, look again at the opening interview. What kinds of questions did Terrence ask Bobby? How did this affect what happened?

Neutral and leading questions

Open and closed questions may be either neutral or leading. **Neutral questions** do not direct a person's answer. "What can you tell me about your work with Habitat for Humanity?" or "What criteria do you use in deciding whether to offer an artist a contract?" are both neutral questions. The neutral question gives the respondent free rein to answer the question without any knowledge of what the interviewer thinks or believes.

By contrast, **leading questions** guide respondents toward providing certain types of information and imply that the interviewer prefers one answer over another. "What do you like about working for Habitat for Humanity?" steers respondents to describe only the positive aspects of their volunteer work. "Having a 'commercial sound' is an important criteria, isn't it?" directs the answer by providing the standard for comparison. In most types of interviews, neutral questions are preferable because they are less likely to create defensiveness in the interviewee. In the opening interview, which of Terrence's questions were neutral and which were leading?

Order and Time Constraints in Interview Protocols

The final step in creating the interview protocol is to develop a sequence for the questions. Here are a few tips about sequencing an interview:

- As in an interpersonal conversation, your initial questions should be short and designed to get the interviewee involved in the conversation. In general, it is better to leave more complex or controversial questions until later, after you have established rapport.
- Be sure to place topics of great importance earlier in the interview, so you will have plenty of time for follow-up questions.
- Answering fact questions can be boring for the interviewee, so you might consider spreading these throughout the interview.
- Finally, it is usually easier for people to talk about things in the present than it is for them to remember things from the past or to hypothesize about the future, so begin by asking about current practices or events, then work backward or forward.

Once you have generated a complete question list, you will need to estimate how long it will take to ask and answer all the questions. Typically, allow four minutes for an open question and one minute for a closed question. If your estimate for the length of time needed to answer all the questions exceeds the time allotted for the interview, mark the less-important questions with an asterisk (*)so you can skip them if necessary. You never want an interview to take longer than what you told the interviewee when you scheduled it. Figure A.2 shows what an interview protocol for a music producer might look like.

When you have finalized your interview protocol, make a version to use during the interview with enough space between questions for you to take complete notes of the answers.

neutral questions
questions that do not direct a person's answer.

leading questions
questions that guide respondents toward providing certain types of information and imply that the interviewer prefers one answer over another.

1. How do you find artists to consider for contract?
   a. Is this different than the methods used by other producers?
   b. Do artists ever come to you in other ways?
2. Once an artist has been brought to your attention what course of action follows?
   a. Do you ever just see an artist and immediately sign them?
   *b. What's the longest period of time you have ever "auditioned" an artist before signing them?
3. What criteria do you use in deciding to offer a contract?
   a. How important are the artists' age, sex, or ethnicity?
4. Can you tell me the story of how you came to sign one of your most successful artists and then one about an unsuccessful artist?
   *a. What do you think made this artist so successful?
   b. What single factor led to this artist's failure?
   c. In retrospect was it a mistake to sign this artist?
   *d. What could you have done differently with this artist so that they would have been successful?

Figure A.2
Protocol for interview with music producer

Guidelines for Conducting Information Interviews

Interviewing is a valuable method for obtaining information on nearly any topic. Lawyers and police interview witnesses to establish facts; health care providers interview patients to obtain medical histories before making diagnoses; reporters interview sources for their stories; social workers and sales representatives interview clients; managers interview employees to receive updates on projects; and students interview experts to obtain information for research papers. Assuming you have prepared a good interview protocol, the quality of the information you receive will depend on choosing the right person to interview and effectively conducting the interview conversation.

Doing Research About Interviewees

Sometimes it is obvious who you should interview. Other times, you may have to do research to identify the right person or people to interview. Suppose your purpose is to learn about how to get a recording contract. You might begin by asking a professor in the music department for the name of a music production agency in your community or nearby. Or you could find the name of an agency by searching online. Once you find a Web site, you can usually find an "About Us" or "Contact Us" link on it, which will offer names, titles, e-mail addresses, and phone numbers. You should be able to identify someone appropriate to your purpose from this list. Once you have identified the person or people to be interviewed, you should contact them to make an appointment. Today, it is generally best to do so by both e-mail and telephone if possible. When you contact them, be sure to clearly state the purpose of the interview, how the interview information will be used, and how long you expect the interview to take. When setting a date and time, suggest several dates and time ranges and ask which would be best for them.

You don't want to bother your interviewee with information you can get elsewhere. So to prepare appropriate questions, do some research on the topic in advance. If, for instance, you are going to interview a music producer, you will want to find out what a music producer is and does. If your purpose is to understand what criteria producers use to sign an artist or group, you will want to find out first if general "best practices" exist. Then, you can ask the interviewee if he or she has additional criteria, different criteria, or even to expand on how the criteria is used in making judgments. Interviewees will be more likely to enjoy talking with you if you're well informed. And being familiar with your subject will enable you to ask better questions.

Conducting an Information Interview

By applying the communication skills we have been discussing in this book, you'll find that you can turn your careful planning into an excellent interview. To guide you in the process, we offer this list of best practices:

1. **Be prompt.** Your interviewee deserves your respect, which you can show by showing up prepared to begin at the time you have agreed to. Remember to allow enough time for potential traffic and parking problems.

2. **Be courteous.** Begin by thanking the person for taking the time to talk to you. Remember, although interviewees may enjoy talking about the subject, may be flattered, and may wish to share knowledge, they have nothing to gain from the interview. So, you should let them know are grateful to them for taking the time to talk with you. Most of all, respect what the interviewee says regardless of what you may think of the answers.

3. **If you want to tape record the interview, ask permission.** If the interviewee says no, respect his or her wishes and take careful notes.

4. **Listen carefully.** For key information in the interview, paraphrase what the interviewee has said to be sure that you really understand.

5. **Keep the interview moving.** You do not want to rush the person, but you do want to get your questions answered during the allotted time.

6. **Make sure that your nonverbal reactions—your facial expressions and your gestures—are in keeping with the tone you want to communicate.** Maintain good eye contact with the person. Nod to show understanding, and smile occasionally to maintain the friendliness of the interview. How you look and act is likely to determine whether the person will warm up to you and give you an informative interview.

7. **Get permission to quote the interviewee.** If you are going to publish the substance of the interview, be sure to get written permission for exact quotes. As a courtesy, offer to let the person see a copy of the article (or at least tell the person exactly when and where it will be published). Under some circumstances, you may want to show the interviewee a draft before it goes into print, if only to allow him or her to double-check the accuracy of direct quotations. If so, provide the draft well before the deadline, to give the person the opportunity to read it and to give you time to deal with any suggestions.

8. **Always close the interview by thanking the interviewee for his or her time.** This closure leads to positive rapport should you need to follow up later and demonstrates that you realize the person gave up valuable time to visit with you.

Skill Learning Activity A.2
Web Resource A.1

Conducting Employment Interviews

Almost all organizations use interviewing as part of their hiring process. Employment interviews help organizations assess which applicants have the knowledge, experience, and skills to do a job and which applicants will fit into the organization's culture best. Interviews allow organizations to evaluate personal characteristics (such as ambition, energy, and enthusiasm) and interpersonal skills (such as conversing and listening) that cannot be judged from a résumé.

Did you know that in the past 50 years, the average number of years a person continues to work with the same organization has gone from 23 ½ years to 3 ½ years (Taylor & Hardy, 2004)? What this means is that we spend more time doing employment interviews both as job seekers and employers than ever before.

Historically, human resource professionals or managers did most of the employment interviewing, but today organizations are relying more and more on coworkers as interviewers. You may have already helped conduct employment interviews, or you may be asked to do so in the near future.

> How do you conduct an employment interview?

Skill Learning Activity A.3

Preparing for the Interview

As with information interviews, your preparation begins by doing research. In the case of employment interviewing, this means becoming familiar with the knowledge, skills, and aptitudes someone must have to be successful in the job. It also means studying the résumés, references, and, if available, the test scores for each person you will interview.

In most employment interviewing situations, you will see several candidates. You will want to make sure that all applicants are asked the same (or very similar) questions and that the questions selected allow applicants to disclose information you will need to know to make an informed hiring decision. To accomplish this, you will want to use a moderately to highly structured interview. This means that you will prepare a general interview protocol to use with all interviewees. Your protocol should have questions designed to probe the interviewees' knowledge, skills, and experiences that are relevant to the job.

It is also important to avoid questions that violate fair employment practice legislation. The Equal Opportunity Commission has detailed guidelines that spell out what questions are unlawful.

Web Resource A.2
Web Resource A.3

Conducting the Interview

As with the information interview, a well-planned employment interview begins with an introduction designed to establish rapport and help the interviewee relax. What follows are some best-practice tips to follow when conducting employment interviews.

1. **Greet the applicant.** Warmly greet the applicant by name, shake hands, and introduce yourself. If you will be taking notes or recording the interview, you should explain that as well. If the applicant is extremely nervous, you may want to ask a couple of "warm-up" questions designed to put the applicant at ease. Once the applicant seems comfortable, you can proceed.
2. **Ask the series of prepared questions.** Here is where you ask your well-planned questions to determine whether the applicant's knowledge, skills, experiences, personal characteristics, and interpersonal style fit the demands of the job and the organizational culture. It is important to keep the interview moving. You want to give the applicant sufficient time to answer your questions, but don't waste time by allowing the applicant to over-answer questions.

3. Consider your verbal and nonverbal cues. As you ask questions, strive to sound spontaneous and to speak in a voice that is easily heard. Be sensitive to the nonverbal messages you are sending. Be careful that you are not leading applicants to answer in certain ways through your nonverbal cues.

4. Use follow-up questions. You should probe the applicant to expand on answers that are vague or too brief. Remember, your goal is to understand the applicant, which includes his or her strengths, weaknesses, and potential fit with the position and your organization.

5. Conclude with a clarification of next steps. As the interview comes to an end, tell the applicant what will happen next. Explain how and approximately when the hiring decision will be made, as well a how the applicant will be notified. Unless you are the person with hiring authority, remain neutral about the applicant. You don't want to mislead the applicant with false hope or discouragement.

Skill Learning Activity A.4

Interviewing Strategies for Job Seekers

The steps involved in getting a job include preparing a résumé and cover letter, preparing for and participating in the interview, and then following up afterward.

A **job seeker** is anyone who is looking for a job or considering a job change. Some job seekers are unemployed and dedicating 100 percent of their time to finding a job. A job seeker also could be a happily employed person who is recruited to apply for another position. Or a job seeker could be an employed person seeking a more rewarding position. All job seekers must master certain skills to be competitive. As many employment experts will tell you, "As a rule, the best jobs do *not* go to the best-qualified individuals—they go to the best job seekers" (Graber, 2000, p. 29). Successful job seekers begin with a winning résumé and cover letter that helps them get an interview.

Applying for the Job

Because interviewing is time consuming, most organizations do not interview all the people who apply for a job. Rather, they use a variety of screening devices to eliminate people who don't meet their qualifications. Chief among these are evaluating the qualifications presented on the résumé and in the cover letter. The goal of your résumé with cover letter "is to communicate your qualifications in writing and sell yourself to prospective employers" (Kaplan, 2002, p. 6).

It all begins with research

To write an effective cover letter and résumé that highlight your qualifications for a particular job, you need to know something about the company and about the job requirements. The career center advisers at your college or university can assist you with your research. And you can go online to review the company's Web site.

Write an effective cover letter

A **cover letter** is a short, well-written letter expressing your interest in a particular job. In a cover letter, it is important to focus on the employer's needs—not on your needs. The letter should capture the reader's attention, demonstrate your qualifications, and request an interview. To write your cover letter, follow these simple steps:

1. Identify the job for which you are applying.
2. Provide a brief summary of your qualifications. If you have special qualifications that you cannot emphasize adequately in your résumé, you can mention

job seeker
anyone who is looking for a job or considering a job change

cover letter
a short, well-written letter expressing your interest in a particular job

them in your cover letter. Also, be sure to direct the potential employer to the most relevant and impressive parts of your résumé related to the position for which you are applying. Keep in mind, however, that most employers are unlikely to read a cover letter that is longer than two or three paragraphs.

3. Indicate that you hope to be contacted for an interview and how you can be reached.
4. Close by saying that you look forward to hearing from them soon.
   Figure A.3. provides a sample of a cover letter that follows these steps.

Web Resource A.4

2326 Tower Place
Cincinnati, OH 45220
April 8, 2009

Mr. Kyle Jones
Acme Marketing Research Associates
P.O. Box 482
Cincinnati, OH 45201

Dear Mr. Jones:

I am applying for the position of first-year associate at Acme Marketing Research Associates, which I learned about through the Office of Career Counseling at the University of Cincinnati. I am a senior mathematics major at the University of Cincinnati who is interested in a career in marketing research. I am highly motivated, eager to learn, and I enjoy working with all types of people. I am excited by the prospect of working for a firm like Acme Marketing Research Associates, where I can apply my leadership and problem-solving skills in a professional setting.

As a mathematics major, I have developed the analytical proficiency that is necessary for working through complex problems. My courses in statistics have especially prepared me for data analysis, and my more theoretical courses have taught me how to construct an effective argument. My leadership training and experiences have given me the ability to work effectively in groups and have taught me the benefits of both individual and group problem solving. My work on the Strategic Planning Committee has given me an introduction to market analysis by teaching me skills associated with strategic planning. Finally, from my theatrical experience, I have gained the poise to make presentations in front of small and large groups alike. I believe these experiences and others have shaped who I am and have helped me to develop many of the skills necessary to be successful. I am interested in learning more and continuing to grow.

I look forward to having the opportunity for an interview with you. I have enclosed my résumé with my school address and phone number. Thank you for your consideration. I hope to hear from you soon.

Sincerely,
Elisa C. Vardin

Figure A.3
Sample cover letter

Prepare a professional résumé

The **résumé** is a brief summary of your skills and accomplishments and is your "silent sales representative" (Stewart & Cash, 2000, p. 274). Although there is no universal format for a résumé, there is some agreement on what should be included:

1. **Contact information:** Your name, addresses (current and permanent), telephone numbers, and e-mail address. This may sound easy, but consider your contact information from the potential employers' perspective. If you go by a nickname, think twice before using it for your contact information. Think also about your e-mail address. If your e-mail address is something personal like redwingsfan@ yahoo.com or hottee@aol.com, create a separate account with a more professional-sounding name to use on your résumé. Finally, since recruiters typically telephone to set up an interview, think about your voice-mail message. If you have a novelty phone message such as a recording of Ozzy Osbourne's voice asking the caller to "leave a $%*# message," replace it with a more professional-sounding salutation.

2. **Career objective:** A one-sentence objective describing your job search goal.

3. **Employment history:** A list of your paid work experiences, beginning with the most recent. List the name and address of the organization, your employment dates, your title, key duties, and noteworthy accomplishments. Try not to leave gaps in your work history because doing so can raise a red flag to a potential employer. Rather, if you left a paid job while you worked as a stay-at-home parent, say so in a brief line.

4. **Education:** List the names and addresses of the schools you have attended (including specialized military schools), the degrees or certificates you have earned (or expect to earn), and the dates of attendance and graduation. Also list academic honors received with degrees or certificates.

5. **Relevant professional affiliations:** List the names of the organizations, dates of membership, and offices you held in them.

6. **Military background (if applicable):** List branch and dates of service, last rank held, significant commendations, and discharge status.

7. **Special skills:** List language fluencies, technical expertise, computer expertise, multimedia competencies, and any other skills related to your job goal.

8. **Community service:** List significant involvement in community service organizations, clubs, and other volunteer efforts.

9. **References:** List or have available the names, addresses, e-mail addresses, and phone numbers of at least three people who will speak well of your ability, your work product, and your character.

Prepare your résumé so that it is easy to read, highlights your accomplishments, and is short. Good résumés are generally one (and not more than two) pages long.

Figure A.4 displays a sample résumé for a recent college graduate.

Web Resource A.5

Skill Learning Activity A.5
Web Resource A.6
Web Resource A.7

Electronic Cover Letters and Résumés

Employers like electronic résumés because they can sift through large numbers, looking only for particular qualifications or characteristics. Candidates like electronic résumés because they can send essentially the same materials online, saving time and money. In fact, many large employers now expect to receive your résumé electronically. As a result, most job search experts now recommend that you have your résumé available in four formats: a print version, a scannable version, a plain text format version, and an e-mail version. These are not separate résumés; rather, they contain

résumé
a written summary of your skills and accomplishments

Elisa C. Vardin

2326 Tower Avenue
Cincinnati, Ohio 45220
Phone: (513) 861-2497
E-mail: ElisVardin@UC.edu

PROFESSIONAL OBJECTIVE

To use my intellectual abilities, quantitative capabilities, communication skills, and proven leadership to further the mission of a high-integrity marketing research organization.

EDUCATIONAL BACKGROUND

University of Cincinnati, Cincinnati, OH, B.A. in Mathematics, June 2009. GPA 3.36. Dean's List.

National Theater Institute at the Eugene O'Neill Theater Center, Waterford, CT. Fall 2008. Acting, Voice, Movement, Directing, and Playwriting.

WORK AND OTHER BUSINESS-RELATED EXPERIENCE

Reynolds & Dewitt, Cincinnati, OH. Summer 2008. Intern at brokerage/ investment management firm. Provided administrative support. Created new databases, performance comparisons, and fact sheets in Excel and Word files.

Mummers Theatre Guild, University of Cincinnati, Spring 2008–Spring 2009. Treasurer. Responsible for all financial/accounting functions for this undergraduate theater community.

Breakthough, Cincinnati, Cincinnati Country Day School, Cincinnati, OH. Summer 2007. Teacher in program for at-risk junior high students. Taught seventh-grade mathematics, sixth- and seventh-grade speech communication, sign language; academic advisor; club leader. Organized five-hour diversity workshop and three-hour tension-reduction workshop for staff.

Strategic Planning Committee, Summit Country Day School, Cincinnati, OH. Fall 2003–2004. One of two student members. Worked with the board of directors developing the first Strategic Plan for a 1,000-student independent school (pre-K through 12).

AYF International Leadership Conference, Miniwanca Conference Center, Shelby, MI. Summer 2002–2003. Participant in international student conference sponsored by American Youth Foundation.

PERSONAL

Musical theater: lifetime involvement, including leads and choreography for several shows. A cappella singing group, 2006–2009; director 2007–2008. Swing Club 2007–2009, president and teacher of student dance club. Junior high youth group leader, 2006. Math tutor, 2005. Aerobics instructor, 2008–2009. University of Cincinnati Choral Society, 2005–2009. American Sign Language instructor, Winter 2007, 2008.

TECHNICAL SKILLS AND TRAINING: SAS, PASW, Excel, Access, Word. Univariate and multivariate statistics (2 courses), regression analysis (2 courses).

REFERENCES: Available on request.

Figure A.4
Sample résumé

Web Resource A.8
Web Resource A.9

How do you
present yourself
successfully in a
job interview?

the same information but are prepared so that they can be easily received by a prospective employer. Specific information on how to develop each version is available on the Web.

Preparing to Be Interviewed

Once you submit your résumé/cover letter package, you need to prepare for the interview you hope to get. In this section, we offer four suggestions to prepare for a job interview: research the organization, prepare a self-summary, practice answering difficult questions, and prepare your questions.

1. **Do your homework.** If you haven't yet done extensive research on the position and the organization, do so before you go to the interview. Be sure you know the organization's products and services, areas of operation, ownership, and financial health. Nothing puts off interviewers more than applicants who arrive at an interview knowing little about the organization. You can easily begin your research by looking at the organization's home page online. Be sure to look beyond the "Work for Us" or "Frequently Asked Questions" links. Find more specific information such as pages that target potential investors, report company stock performance, and describe the organization's mission (Slayter, 2006). Likewise, pictures can suggest the type of organizational culture you can expect—formal or informal dress, collaborative or individual work spaces, diversity, and so on. Researching these details will help you decide whether the organization is right for you, as well as help you form questions to ask during the interview.

2. **Prepare a self-summary.** You should not have to hesitate when an interviewer asks you why you are interested in the job. You should also be prepared to describe your previous accomplishments. Form these statements as personal stories with specific examples that people will remember (Beshara, 2006). Robin Ryan (2000), one of the nation's foremost career authorities, advises job seekers to prepare a 60-second general statement they can share with a potential employer. She advises job seekers to identify which aspects of their training and experience would be most valued by a potential employer. She suggests making a five-point agenda that can (a) summarize your most relevant experience and (b) "build a solid picture emphasizing how you *can* do the job" (p. 10). Once you have your points identified, practice communicating them fluently in 60 seconds or less.

3. **Prepare a list of questions about the organization and the job.** The employment interview should be a two-way street, where you size up the company as they are sizing you up. So you will probably have a number of specific questions to ask the interviewer. For example, "Can you describe a typical workday for the person in this position?" or "What is the biggest challenge in this job?" Make a list of your questions and take it with you to the interview. It can be difficult to come up with good questions on the spur of the moment, so you should prepare several questions in advance. One question we do not advise asking during the interview, however, is "How much money will I make?" Save salary, benefits, and vacation-time negotiations until after you have been offered the job.

4. **Rehearse the interview.** Several days before the interview, spend time outlining the job requirements and how your knowledge, skills, and experiences meet those requirements. Practice answering questions commonly asked in interviews, such as those listed in Figure A.5.

- In what ways does your transcript reflect your ability?
- Can you give an example of how you work under pressure?
- What are your major strengths? Weaknesses?
- Can you give an example of when you were a leader and what happened?
- Tell me a time when you tried something at work that failed. How did you respond to the failure?
- Tell me about a time you had a serious conflict with a co-worker. How did you deal with the conflict?
- What have you done that shows your creativity?
- What kind of position are you looking for?

Figure A.5
Frequently asked interview questions

Guidelines for Job Interviewees

The actual interview is your opportunity to sell yourself to the organization. Although interviews can be stressful, your preparation should give you the confidence you need to relax and communicate effectively. Believe it or not, the job interview is somewhat stressful for the interviewer as well. Most companies do not interview potential employees every day. Moreover, the majority of interviewers have little or no formal training in the interview process. Your goal is to make the interview a comfortable conversation for both of you.

Use these guidelines to help you have a successful interview.

1. **Dress appropriately.** You want to make a good first impression, so it is important to be well groomed and neatly dressed. Although "casual" or "business casual" is common in many workplaces, some organizations still expect employees to be more formally dressed. If you don't know the dress code for the organization, call the human resources department and ask.
2. **Arrive on time.** The interview is the organization's first exposure to your work behavior, so you don't want to be late. Find out how long it will take you to travel by making a dry run at least a day before. Plan to arrive 10 or 15 minutes before your appointment.
3. **Bring supplies.** Bring extra copies of your résumé, cover letter, and references, as well as the list of questions you plan to ask. You will also want to have paper and a pen so that you can make notes.
4. **Use active listening.** When we are anxious, we sometimes have trouble listening well. Work on attending, understanding, and remembering what is asked. Remember that the interviewer will be aware of your nonverbal behavior, so be sure to make and keep eye contact as you listen.
5. **Think before answering.** If you have prepared for the interview, make sure that as you answer the interviewer's questions, you also tell your story. Take a moment to consider how your answers portray your skills and experiences.
6. **Be enthusiastic.** If you come across as bored or disinterested, the interviewer is likely to conclude that you would be an unmotivated employee.
7. **Ask questions.** As the interview is winding down, be sure to ask the questions you prepared that have not already been answered. You may also want to ask how well the interviewer believes your qualifications match the position, and what your strengths are.

Web Resource A.10

In the interview at the opening of this appendix, Terrence didn't really probe Bobby's answers. If Terrence had probed, his evaluation of Bobby's competence might have been different. Even though Terrence did not do his part in probing, if Bobby had been an effective and prepared interviewee, he could have expanded on his answers anyway:

TERRENCE: So, Bobby, you want to work here at Qwik In and Out?

BOBBY: Yes. I'm a marketing major at CSCTU and this job would provide great experience for me.

TERRENCE: Well, you understand that you will be working alone at night, right?

BOBBY: Yes, and that will work well with my class schedule. I used to close at my job at the Burger Barn so I'm used to working at night.

TERRENCE: It says on your application that you went to Highlands High School. Is that right?

BOBBY: Yes, I graduated with honors two years ago.

TERRENCE: And now you're a student at CSCTU?

BOBBY: Yes. I'm in my second year, but credit-wise I'm a junior.

TERRENCE: Will school interfere with your work schedule?

BOBBY: Not at all. My program at CSCTU doesn't offer night classes, so this is perfect in that regard.

TERRENCE: Is there anything else I should know?

BOBBY: Yes. I really want this job and if you decide to hire me, you will find that I am a hard worker, responsible, and enjoy serving people.

TERRENCE: Well, I've got several other people to talk to, and I'll let you know by Monday what I decide.

BOBBY: Okay. Thanks for taking the time to interview me, and I look forward to talking with you again on Monday.

Conversation and Analysis

Skill Learning Activity A.6

Use your Premium Website for *Communicate!* to access the **Skill Learning Activity A.6**, which is a video clip of Elliott Miller's job interview at Community Savings and Loan. As you watch the video, notice how well both Karen Bourne and Elliott Miller follow the guidelines for effective interviews. You can record your observations and respond to analysis questions by clicking on "Critique" in the menu bar at the top of the screen. When you've answered all the questions, click "Done" to compare your answers to those provided by the authors.

Elliott Miller is a second-semester senior who has double-majored in business and communication. Today he is interviewing with Community Savings and Loan, which is recruiting managerial trainees. Elliott has dressed carefully. He has on his good charcoal suit, a light blue shirt, a conservative necktie, and wingtips. At 10 a.m. sharp, he knocks on the office door of Karen Bourne, the person with whom he has an interview. She is in her mid-thirties and dressed in a conservative navy blue suit. She opens the door and offers her hand to Elliott.

Conversation

BOURNE: Mr. Miller, I see you're right on time. That's a good start. (*They shake hands.*)

MILLER: Thank you for inviting me to interview today.

BOURNE: Sit down. (*He sits in the chair in front of her desk; she sits behind the desk.*) So you're about to finish college are you? I remember that time in my own life—exciting and scary!

MILLER: It's definitely both for me. I'm particularly excited about the job here at Community Savings and Loan.

BOURNE (*smiles*): Then there's a mutual interest. We had a lot of applications, but we're interviewing only eight of them. What I'd like to do is get a sense of your interests and tell you about our managerial trainee program here, so that we can see if the fit between us is as good as it looks on paper. Sound good to you?

MILLER: Great.

BOURNE: Let me start by telling you about a rather common problem we've had with our past managerial trainees. Many of them run into a problem—something they have trouble learning or doing right. That's normal enough—we expect that. But a lot of trainees seem to get derailed when that happens. Instead of finding another way to approach the problem, they get discouraged and give up. So I'm very interested in hearing what you've done when you've encountered problems or roadblocks in your life.

MILLER: Well, I can remember one time when I hit a real roadblock. I was taking an advanced chemistry course, and I just couldn't seem to understand the material. I failed the first exam, even though I'd studied hard.

BOURNE: Good example of a problem. What did you do?

MILLER: I started going to all the tutorial sessions that grad assistants offer. That helped a little, but I still wasn't getting the material the way I should. So I organized a study team and offered to pay for pizzas so that students who were on top of the class would have a reason to come.

BOURNE (*nodding with admiration*): That shows a lot of initiative and creativity. Did the study team work?

MILLER (*smiling*): It sure did. I wound up getting a B in the course, and so did several other members of the study team who had been in the same boat I was in early in the semester.

BOURNE: So you don't mind asking for help if you need it?

MILLER: I'd rather do that than flounder, but I'm usually pretty able to operate independently.

BOURNE: So you prefer working on your own to working with others?

MILLER: That depends on the situation or project. If I have all that I need to do something on my own, I'm comfortable working solo. But there are other cases in which I don't have everything I need to do something well—maybe I don't have experience in some aspect of the job or I don't have a particular skill or I don't understand some perspectives on the issues. In cases like that, I think teams are more effective than individuals.

BOURNE: Good. Banking management requires the ability to be self-initiating and also the ability to work with others. Let me ask another question. As I was looking over your transcript and résumé, I noticed that you changed your major several times. Does that indicate you have difficulty making a commitment and sticking with it?

MILLER: I guess you could think that, but it really shows that I was willing to explore a lot of alternatives before making a firm commitment.

BOURNE: But don't you think that you wasted a lot of time and courses getting to that commitment?

MILLER: I don't think so. I learned something in all of the courses I took. For instance, when I was a philosophy major, I learned about logical thinking and careful reasoning. That's going to be useful to me in management. When I was majoring in English, I learned how to write well and how to read others' writing critically. That's going to serve me well in management too.

BOURNE: So what led you to your final decision to double-major in business and communication? That's kind of an unusual combination.

MILLER: It seems a very natural one to me. I wanted to learn about business because I want to be a manager in an organization. I need to know how organizations work, and I need to understand different management philosophies and styles. At the same time, managers work with people, and that means I have to have strong communication skills.

Following Up After the Interview

Once the interview is over, you can set yourself apart from the other applicants by following these important steps:

Web Resource A.11

1. Write a thank-you note. It is appropriate to write a short note thanking the interviewer for the experience and again expressing your interest in the job.
2. Self-assess your performance. Take time to critique your performance. How well did you do? What can you do better next time?
3. Contact the interviewer for feedback. If you don't get the job, you might call the interviewer and ask for feedback. Be sure to be polite and to indicate that you are only calling to get some help on your interviewing skills. Actively listen to the feedback, using questions and paraphrases to clarify what is being said. Be sure to thank the interviewer for helping you.

Skill Learning Activity A.7

To practice what you've learned about job interviews in this appendix, use your Premium Website for *Communicate!* to complete **Skill Learning Activity A.7: Mock Interview.** In this activity, you will work with a partner to prepare and participate in two interviews, one in which you will use your partner's job advertisement, résumé, and cover letter to prepare and interview your partner for a job, and the other in which your partner will use the material you supply to interview you for a job.

Strategies for Interviews with the Media

Today we live in a media-saturated environment where any individual may be approached by a newsperson and asked to participate in an on-air interview. For example, we have a friend who became the object of media interest when the city council in his town refused to grant him a zoning variance so he could complete building a new home on his property. In the course of three days, his story became front-page news in his town, and reports about his situation made the local radio and TV news shows. You might be asked for an interview at public meetings, at the mall, or within the context of your work or community service. For example, you may be asked to share your knowledge of your organization's programs, events, or activities. Because media interviews are likely to be edited in some way before they are aired and because they reach a wide audience, there are specific strategies you should use to prepare for and participate in them.

How do you
participate in a
media interview?

Before the Interview

The members of the media work under very tight deadlines, so it is crucial that you respond immediately to media requests for an interview. When people are insensitive to media deadlines, they can end up looking like they have purposefully evaded the interview and have something to hide. When you speak with the media representative, clarify what the focus of the interview will be and how the information will be presented. At times, the entire interview will be presented; however, it is more likely that the information from the interview will be edited or paraphrased and not all of your comments will be reported.

As you prepare for the interview, identify three or four **talking points**, that is, the central ideas you want to present as you answer the questions during a media interview. For example, before our friend was interviewed by the local TV news anchor, he knew that he wanted to emphasize that he was a victim of others' mistakes: (1) he had hired a licensed architect to draw the plans; (2) the city inspectors had repeatedly approved earlier stages of the building process; (3) the city planning commission had voted unanimously to grant him the variance; and (4) he would be out half the cost of the house if he were forced to tear it down and rebuild. Consider how you will tailor your information to the specific audience in terms they can understand. Consider how you will respond to tough or hostile questions.

During the Interview

Media interviews call for a combination of interviewing, nonverbal communication, and public speaking skills (Boyd, 1999). There are many strategies to be followed during a media interview:

1. Present appropriate nonverbal cues. Inexperienced interviewees can often look or sound tense or stiff. By standing up during a phone interview, your voice will sound more energetic and authoritative. With on-camera interviews, when checking your notes, move your eyes but not your head. Keep a small smile when listening. Look at the interviewer, not into the camera.
2. Make clear and concise statements. It is important to speak slowly, to articulate clearly, and to avoid technical terms or jargon. Remember that the audience is not familiar with your area of expertise.
3. Realize that you are always "on the record." Say nothing as an aside or confidentially to a reporter. Do not say anything that you would not want quoted. If you do not know an answer, do not speculate, but indicate that the question is outside of your area of expertise. Do not ramble during the interviewer's periods of silence. Do not allow yourself to be rushed into an answer.
4. Learn how to bridge. Media consultant Joanna Krotz (2006) defines a **bridge** as a transition you create so that you can move from the interviewer's subject to the message you want to communicate. To do this, you first answer the direct question and then use a phrase such as "What's important to remember, however . . .," "Let me put that in perspective . . .," or "It's also important to know . . ."

talking points
the three or four central ideas you will present as you answer the questions that are asked during a media interview.

bridge
a transition you create in a media interview so that you can move from the interviewer's subject to the message you want to communicate.

Skill Learning Activity A.8

With careful preparation, specific communication strategies during the interview, and practice, one can skillfully deliver a message in any media interview format.

Summary

Interviewing can be a productive way to obtain information from an expert for a paper, an article, or a speech. The key to effective interviewing begins with a highly structured protocol identifying a series of good questions. Your protocol should use a variety of question types. Primary questions stimulate response; follow-up questions ask for additional information. Open questions allow for flexible responses; closed questions require very brief answers. Neutral questions allow the respondent free choice; leading questions require the person to answer in a particular way. When you are interviewing for information, you will want to define the purpose, select the best person to interview, develop a protocol, and conduct the interview according to the protocol.

When you are interviewing a prospective applicant for a job, become familiar with the data contained in the interviewee's application form, résumé, letters of recommendation, and test scores, if available. Be careful how you present yourself, do not waste time, do not ask questions that violate fair employment practice legislation, and give the applicant an opportunity to ask questions. At the end of the interview, explain to the applicant what will happen next in the process.

If you are a job seeker, your first goal is to submit a résumé and cover letter that will get you an interview. Begin by taking the time to learn about the company and prepare your cover letter and résumé to highlight strengths you have that match the company's needs. Electronic cover letters and résumés have become popular and need special preparation. For the interview itself, you should dress appropriately, be prompt, be alert, look directly at the interviewer, give yourself time to think before answering difficult questions, ask intelligent questions about the company and the job, and show enthusiasm for the position.

If you are asked for an interview from the media, prepare by understanding the focus and format of the interview and considering the few main points you want to convey. During the media interview, you should present appropriate nonverbal cues, make clear and concise statements, realize everything you say is on the record, and learn to use bridges as transitions to your message.

A Question of Ethics

What Would You Do?

Ken shifted in his chair as Ms. Goldsmith, his interviewer, looked over his résumé.

"I have to tell you that you have considerably more experience than the average applicant we usually get coming straight out of college," Ms. Goldsmith said. "Let's see, you've managed a hardware store, been a bookkeeper for a chain of three restaurants, and were the number-one salesman for six straight months at a cell phone store."

"That's right," Ken said. "My family has always stressed the value of hard work, so I have worked a full-time job every summer since I entered junior high school, right through my last year of college. During the school year, I usually worked four to six hours a day after class."

"Very impressive," Ms. Goldsmith said. "And still you managed to get excellent grades and do a considerable amount of volunteer work in your spare time. What's your secret?"

"Secret?" said Ken nervously. "There's no secret—just a lot of hard work."

"Yes, I see that," said Ms. Goldsmith. "What I mean is that there are only 24 hours in a day and you obviously had a lot on your plate each day, especially for someone so young. How did you manage to do it?"

Ken thought for a moment before answering. "I only need five hours of sleep a day." He could feel Ms. Goldsmith's eyes scrutinizing his face. He hadn't exactly lied on his résumé—just exaggerated a little bit. He had, in fact, helped his father run the family hardware store for a number of years. He had helped his aunt, from time to time, keep track of her restaurant's receipts. He had also spent one summer selling cell phones for his cousin. Of course, his family always required him to do his schoolwork first before they let him

help at the store, so Ken often had little time to help at all, but there was no reason Ms. Goldsmith needed to know that.

"And you can provide references for these jobs?" Ms. Goldsmith asked.

"I have them with me right here," said Ken, pulling a typed page from his briefcase and handing it across the desk.

1. Are the exaggerated claims Ken made in his résumé ethical? Do the ethics of his actions change at all if he has references (family members) who will vouch for his claims?

2. Many people justify exaggerating or even lying on their résumés by saying that everybody does it and then rationalizing that, if they don't do it too, they will be handicapping their chances to get a good job. If the consequences of acting ethically diminish your economic prospects, are you justified in bending the rules? Explain your answer. If you think bending the rules is acceptable in such circumstances, how far can you bend them before you cross the line into unacceptable behavior?

Communicate! Active Online Learning

Now that you have read Appendix: Interviewing, use your Premium Website for *Communicate!* for quick access to the electronic resources that accompany this text. These resources include

- **Study tools** that will help you assess your learning and prepare for exams (*digital glossary, key term flash cards, review quizzes*).
- **Activities and assignments** that will help you hone your knowledge, analyze communication situations (*Skill Learning Activities*), and build your public speaking skills throughout the course (*Communication on Your Feet speech assignments, Action Step activities*). Many of these activities allow you to compare your answers to

those provided by the authors, and, if requested, submit your answers to your instructor.

- **Media resources** that will help you explore communication concepts online (*Web Resources*), develop your speech outlines (*Speech Builder Express 3.0*), watch and critique videos of communication situations and sample speeches (*Interactive Video Activities*), upload your speech videos for peer reviewing and critique other students' speeches (*Speech Studio online speech review tool*), and download chapter review so you can study when and where you'd like (*Audio Study Tools*).

This chapter's Key Terms, Skill Learning Activities, and Web Resources are also featured on the following pages.

Key Terms

bridge (201)
closed questions (187)
cover letter (192)
interview (186)

interview protocol (186)
job seeker (192)
leading questions (188)
neutral questions (188)
open questions (187)

primary questions (187)
résumé (194)
secondary questions (187)
talking points (201)

Skill Learning Activities

A.1: Open and Closed Questions (188)

Indicate which of the following questions are open and which are closed. If the question is open, write a closed question seeking similar information; if the question is closed, write an open question. Make sure your questions are neutral rather than leading.

1. What leads you to believe that Sheldon will be appointed?
2. How many steps are there in getting a book into print?
3. Will you try out for the Shakespeare play this year?
4. When are you getting married?
5. Have you participated in the Garden Project?

When you're done with this activity, compare your answers to the authors' at the Premium Website for *Communicate!* Look for them in the Skill Learning activities for Appendix: Interviewing.

A.2: Information Interviews (190)

Select a televised interview (for example, a news program, infomercial, or congressional hearing) for analysis. You may want to videotape it so that you can watch it several times. Count the number of open, closed, neutral, leading, and follow-up questions. After viewing the interview, analyze it. Was there a good balance of questions? Did the interviewer ask appropriate follow-up questions? What was the apparent goal of the interview? Was it reached? What grade would you give the interviewer? Why? What were the interviewer's strengths? Weaknesses? When you have finished analyzing the interview, write a paragraph discussing your analysis.

To help you complete this activity, you can use the tally sheet provided in your Premium Website for *Communicate!* Look for it in the Skill Learning activities for Appendix: Interviewing.

A.3: Interviewing an Interviewer (192)

Make an appointment to interview a human resource manager who is responsible for employment interviewing. Prepare an interview protocol that probes this manager about his or her interviewing practices. After the interview, compare this manager's practice to the text discussion. Submit your protocol, interview notes, and a short essay that describes what you have learned to your instructor.

A.4: Thinking Like an Interviewer (192)

Read the sample résumé shown in Figure A.4 or find another sample résumé more to your interest online by using your Premium Website for *Communicate!* to access **Web Resource A.10: Sample Résumés Online.** Analyze the résumé based on the position for which it was written and on the candidate's education, experience, and skills. Write 10 primary questions you would ask the job candidate if you were going to interview him or her for the position.

A.5: Résumé and Cover Letter (194)

Read the help wanted ads in your local newspaper or online until you locate a job you would enjoy. Write a résumé and cover letter applying for this position. To link you to an online résumé service to draft and print your résumé, access **Web Resource A.7: Résumé Builder.** When you have completed your résumé and cover letter, if requested, submit them to your instructor.

A.6: Elliott Miller's Interview (198)

After you've watched the video of Elliott Miller and Karen Bourne and have read the transcript of their conversation, answer the following questions.

1. Did Ms. Bourne provide a good opening for the interview?
2. How effectively do you think Mr. Miller handled the tough questions that Ms. Bourne asked?

3. Did Mr. Miller seem well prepared for the interview?
4. Identify leading questions asked by Ms. Bourne and evaluate how Mr. Miller responded to them.

When you're done with this activity, compare your answers to the authors' at the Premium Website for *Communicate!* Look for them in the Skill Learning activities for Appendix: Interviewing.

A.7: Mock Interview (200)

Work with a partner to prepare and participate in two interviews, one in which you will use your partner's ad, résumé, and cover letter to prepare and interview your partner for a job, and the other in which your partner will use the material you supply to interview you for a job. (Use an ad for a job that you'd consider applying for right now.)

1. You are the interviewer
   a. For what job did you interview your partner?
   b. List your interview questions for your partner.
2. You are the interviewee
   a. For what job did your partner interview you?
   b. List the answers you provided during your interview.

A.8: Critiquing a Media Interview (202)

Select a TV interview program like *The NewsHour with Jim Lehrer, Larry King Live,* or some other program whose focus is a lengthy interview with an expert, media personality, or political leader. Tape the interview so that you can replay it during your analysis. Make a list of the questions the interviewer asked and analyze them to determine which were the primary, secondary, and follow-up questions. What was the mix of open and closed questions? How did this mix affect the tone of the interview and the amount and kind of information offered by the interviewee? What percentage of the questions were neutral versus leading? Were the leading questions confrontational or cooperative? How did these questions affect the tone of the interview and the amount or kind of information offered by the interviewee? What do you think the purpose of this interview was? How effective was the interviewer in accomplishing this purpose? What one thing might the interviewer have done better?

Web Resources

A.1: E-mail Interviews (190)

Visit Writing-World.com to read useful tips for conducting electronic interviews with e-mail.

A.2: 150 Typical Job Interview Questions (191)

Prepare for a job interview by visiting QuintCareers.com, which provides a list of questions typically asked in interviews.

A.3: Discrimination Laws and Interviewing (191)

Salary.com provides helpful information about illegal interview questions, including a list of sample illegal questions and how you might deal with these types of questions during an interview.

A.4: Ten Cover Letter Don'ts (193)

This page at Monster.com features a list of several cover letter blunders to avoid.

A.5: What Is Your Objective? (194)

Visit this page at Money-Zine.com for help in formulating a career objective statement for your résumé.

A.6: Résumé Pet Peeves (194)

The ResumeDoctor.com Resource Center features this article about how to avoid the top twenty résumé pet peeves identified by 2,500 recruiters. (Click on the link "Recruiter Resume 'Pet Peeve' Survey Results and Articles.")

A.7: Sample Résumés Online (197)

This site provides several links to sample résumés. Look under the headings "Occupation" and "Problem Solved" for links to samples that pertain to specific job types and common résumé-writing challenges.

A.8: Résumé Builder (194)

Visit Buildaresume.com for help in drafting your résumé online. This free service allows you to prepare and edit your résumé and print it from any computer anytime.

A.9: Internet-Ready Résumés (196)

RileyGuide.com provides advice about how to prepare your résumé for e-mailing or posting on the Internet.

A.10: Virtual Interview (196)

Visit this page at Monster.com to sharpen your interviewing skills, answer sample questions, and receive help to improve your answers. (Click on the links under the heading "Virtual Interviews.")

A.11: Notable Notes (200)

Visit this page at About.com for links to sample thank-you notes to follow up on an interview.

Self Review

part 2

Interpersonal Communication

Interpersonal Communication from Chapters 6 through 8

What kind of an interpersonal communicator are you? This analysis looks at specific behaviors that are characteristic of effective interpersonal communicators. On the line provided for each statement, indicate the response that best captures your behavior: 1, almost always; 2, often; 3, occasionally; 4, rarely; 5, never.

_____ When I communicate with a person from another culture, I make an effort to keep an open mind and accept ambiguity in our interactions. (Ch. 6)

_____ When engaging in intercultural communication, I listen carefully to what the other person is saying and adjust my communication to that person and our situation. (Ch. 6)

_____ I make an effort to spend time with my friends, I share my feelings with them, and I provide them with comfort and support when they are feeling vulnerable. (Ch. 7)

_____ I maintain intimacy in my closest relationships by being dependable and responsive. (Ch. 7)

_____ I describe objectively to others my negative feelings about their behavior toward me without withholding or blowing up. (Ch. 8)

_____ I am quick to praise people for doing things well. (Ch. 8)

_____ I criticize people for their mistakes only when they ask for criticism. (Ch. 8)

_____ When I find myself in conflict with another person, I am able to discuss the issue openly without withdrawing or appearing competitive or aggressive. (Ch. 8)

Based on your responses, select the interpersonal communication behavior that you would most like to change. Write a communication improvement plan similar to the sample goal statement in Chapter 1 (page 000). If you would like verification of your self-review before you write a contract, have a friend or a co-worker complete this same analysis for you.

You can complete this Self-Review online and, if requested, e-mail it to your instructor. Go to your Premium Website for Communicate! to access Part II Self-Review.

Randy Faris/Flirt/CORBIS

Communicating in Groups

Questions you will be able to answer after reading this chapter:

- What makes a group different from a mere assembly of people?
- What are the characteristics of healthy groups?
- How do groups develop?
- What are some types of groups we might participate in?
- How can you evaluate group dynamics?

"Hi Mom, I'm just calling to tell you that I'm not going to make it home for dinner again tonight. Jennifer was supposed to close tonight and she just called in sick. So Bob asked me if I would close—I'm the only one in the store right now who knows how to do it."

"I can't believe it! Tonight is Sarah's last night at home before she deploys, and you know that Grandma and Grandpa are coming over for a big family dinner. What's wrong with you, Darla? Two nights ago you weren't home because you were playing softball; last night you begged off, claiming you had a group meeting for some class project; and now you're going to miss your sister's going-away dinner? I just don't understand you. Isn't your family important to you at all? I mean, where do we fall in your priorities? It seems to me that you have a lot of commitments to other people and that we are always last."

"But Mom, ..."

Kangah/iStockphoto

The Dark Side of Online Social Groups

Pop Comm!

Imogen D'Arcy was only 13 when she hanged herself in her bathroom because, despite being described as fit and well-liked, she felt fat and ugly (Stokes, 2008). Laura Dunnegan developed an eating disorder at 7. Sixteen years later she sees her disorder as a "lifestyle option" rather than as a disease that may kill her (Croucher, 2008). What do these girls have in common? Both regularly visited Websites where they received encouragement to pursue their distorted self-images.

In this chapter, we focus on healthy groups, but the Internet provides unprecedented opportunity for groups with unhealthy goals to flourish. Extreme examples include Websites that offer tips about how to commit suicide quickly and painlessly. Most consider these Websites to be dangerous and unethical, but some have argued that they can help people reach out and connect. "Ama Terasu," the 24-year-old creator of one such site, explains, "I think it has saved my life, because it has enabled me to open up about things online." (Harding 2004)

There is similar debate about online "pro-ana" (promoting anorexia nervosa) communities,

Like Darla in the opening scenario, you probably belong to many formal and informal groups. Each group has different purposes and different expectations of you. But one thing all groups have in common is that their effectiveness depends on members' communication. In fact, year after year, surveys conducted by the National Association of Colleges and Employers report "the ability to work well in groups" is one of the top ten skills sought in college graduates. Although students are often asked to do group projects, very few graduate from college with any formal training in how to participate effectively in groups.

In this chapter and the one that follows, we will help you understand how groups function and how you can communicate most effectively in them. We begin by explaining the characteristics of groups that differentiate them from other collections of people. Next, we describe the stages of development that groups follow over the course of their existence. Then we identify different types of groups and the communication challenges you might face in each one. We end this chapter by discussing how you can evaluate the effectiveness of groups and group members.

Characteristics of Healthy Groups

Take a moment to think about the groups of people you interact with consistently. Examples may range from student clubs to groups of friends you hang out with on weekends to family groups you interact with on special occasions to study groups to online chat rooms or interest groups on social networking sites. What makes each of these a group rather than a mere assembly of people? Scholars generally agree that a **group** is a collection of three or more people who interact and attempt to influence

> What makes a group different from a mere assembly of people?

sites where people with eating disorders can find support and share their experiences without judgment. These are the types of sites D'Arcy visited before she died and that Dunnegan frequently visits. Although initially it may seem these sites provide a positive environment, they often encourage people to develop and continue dangerous and pathological behaviors. For example, pro-ana sites often feature advice on how to starve effectively.

C. J. Pascoe (2008), a sociologist who studies teenagers and digital media at the University of California, Berkeley, thinks pro-ana Websites present a danger primarily because, before the Internet, anorexics had to check into a psychiatric hospital to find others like themselves. Now, with pro-ana Websites, they can find community without having to seek treatment. But creators of pro-ana groups argue they are fighting isolation and supporting others, and some pro-ana groups do legitimately focus on recovery (Peng, 2008).

In the *British Journal of Social Psychology*, David Giles (2006) suggests that pro-ana

Websites—and other sites that promote unhealthy behaviors such as unsafe sex, smoking, and self-harm—may have no offline equivalent, saying, "The Internet offers a perfect sanctuary for people with interests that are unacceptable to the general public. By serving as a counter-culture to official discourse around health and illness, the Web may serve to undermine the professionals so that more and more people find ways of opting out of conventional society (e.g., health care) if they can locate supportive communities online (p. 2)."

On the other hand, Pascoe (2008) believes that the subversion of mainstream society available online is not always a bad thing. An example is the vast online community of gay, lesbian, bisexual, and transgendered (GLBT) teenagers. These teens, who can have a difficult time finding friends or dates in their physical communities, can easily find other GLBT teenagers online. "It's a double-edged sword when it comes to subcultures," says Pascoe. "For better or for worse, kids who are marginalized can find community online (p. 2)."

each other in order to accomplish a common purpose. In a social group that purpose may be to have a good time, in a study group to get a good grade, in a work group to help an organization accomplish a task, and in a family to ensure that members survive and thrive. **Group communication**—all the verbal and nonverbal messages shared with or among members of the group—is what makes our participation in these different groups a positive or negative experience. **Healthy groups** are characterized by ethical goals, interdependence, cohesiveness, productive norms, accountability, and synergy.

healthy group
a group characterized by ethical goals, interdependence, cohesiveness, productive norms, accountability, and synergy.

Healthy Groups Have Ethical Goals

At times, the goals of a group may not be ethical either because the goal itself is unethical or because fulfilling the goal requires some or all group members to behave in ways that are not in their own best interest. For example, recent news reports have been filled with stories about investment firms built on Ponzi schemes (fraudulent investments) that have financially ruined clients who trusted them. Likewise, some children live in divorced families where the parents' goal seems to be to use the children as foils to harm each other. Criminal gangs are highly effective groups who may make lots of money but do so at the expense of society at large and who risk the lives of members to accomplish their illicit goals. In this chapter's Pop Comm! feature, "The Dark Side of Online Social Groups," you can read about online groups with unethical goals. By contrast, healthy groups have goals that benefit the members and the larger society. Fulfilling these goals may require sacrifice and hard work, but accomplishing them does not depend on any illegal or immoral behavior.

What are the characteristics of healthy groups?

group
a collection of three or more people who interact and attempt to influence each other in order to accomplish a common purpose

group communication
all the verbal and nonverbal messages shared with or among members of the group

Healthy Groups Are Interdependent

In **interdependent groups**, members rely on each other's skills and knowledge to accomplish the group goals. One concrete way to understand interdependence is to observe a musical group. Consider, for instance, a symphony orchestra. One reason the music we hear is so beautiful has to do with the fact that the violins, violas, cellos, and basses not only sound different but are each performing a different part made up of differing notes. If any of the musicians did not do their part well, we would hear it. Likewise, in any group, if one person doesn't choose to blend but instead tries to do all the "work," or if everyone in a group does the same piece of "work" while other pieces are left unattended, that group is not interdependent and is also not as effective as it could be.

Healthy Groups Are Cohesive

Cohesiveness is the force that brings group members closer together (Eisenberg, 2007). In a highly cohesive group, members genuinely like and respect each other and work cooperatively to reach the group's goals (Evans & Dion, 1991). Because cohesiveness is such an important characteristic of healthy groups, many newly formed groups will engage in **team-building activities** designed to build rapport and develop trust among members (Midura & Glover, 2005). Research suggests that five factors help foster cohesiveness in groups (Balgopal, Ephross, & Vassil, 1986; Widmer & Williams, 1991; Wilson, 2005). First, a group develops cohesiveness when members are attracted to its purpose. Daniel, for example, joined the local Lions Club because he was attracted to group's goal of community service. Second, groups are generally more cohesive when membership in them is voluntary. If Daniel had joined the Lions Club because he felt obligated to do so, cohesiveness would have suffered. Third, members feel free to express their honest opinions even when they disagree with others. Fourth, members support, encourage, and provide positive feedback to each other. Finally, members perceive the group to be achieving its goals and celebrate their accomplishments. When the Lions Club surpassed their previous fundraising record for the annual Journey for Sight 5K Community Run, they celebrated the accomplishment with a picnic in the park, which fostered cohesiveness.

Healthy Groups Develop and Abide by Productive Norms

Norms are expectations about the way group members are to behave while in the group. Healthy groups develop norms that help them achieve their goals (Shimanoff, 1992) and foster cohesiveness (Shaw, 1981). Norms can be developed through formal discussions or informal group processes (Johnson & Johnson, 2003, p. 27). Some groups choose to formulate explicit **ground rules**, prescribed behaviors designed to help the group meet its goals and conduct its conversations. These may include sticking to the agenda, refraining from interrupting others, making brief comments rather than lengthy monologues, expecting everyone to participate, focusing on issues rather than personalities, and sharing decision making. Did your family have formal rules about going out on school nights or curfews? These are also examples of explicit ground rules.

interdependent group
group in which members rely on each other's skills and knowledge to accomplish the group goals

cohesiveness
force that brings group members closer together.

team-building activities
activities designed to build rapport and develop trust among members.

norms
expectations for the way group members will behave while in the group.

ground rules
prescribed behaviors designed to help the group meet its goals and conduct its conversations.

Skill Learning Activity 9.1

Most clubs follow a set of norms to keep the meetings on track. What norms might this group follow and why?

Spencer Grant/PhotoEdit

In most groups, however, norms evolve informally. When we join a new group, we act in ways that were considered appropriate in the groups we participated in previously. When members of our new group respond positively to our actions, an informal norm is established. For example, suppose Daniel and two others show up late for a Lions Club meeting. If the latecomers are greeted with disapproving glares, then Daniel and the others will learn that this group has an on-time norm. A group may never actually discuss informal norms, but all veteran group members understand what they are, behave in line with them, and educate new members about them.

We sometimes find ourselves struggling to act appropriately in different groups we belong to because each seems to abide by different norms. This can be especially true for people who move from one country to another, as was the case for Dr. Mina Tsay, an assistant professor at Boston University who emigrated from Taiwan to the United States and maintains strong ties with groups in both cultures. Read her story in the Diverse Voices feature.

Web Resource 9.1

Managing Competing Group Norms

by Mina Tsay, Ph.D.

Diverse Voices

Assistant Professor of Communication
Boston University

Although I emigrated from Taiwan to the United States when I was only two years old, my memories are still surprisingly vivid. What I remember most is clinging to my mother as we faced our first blustery winter in Boston, Massachusetts. As a naturalized Chinese American growing up in Boston, I faced numerous challenges in managing competing group norms regarding "acceptable" or even "desirable" behavior. I can probably best illustrate these challenges by focusing on my experiences (a) speaking Chinese at home and English at school, (b) attending both American and Chinese schools while growing up, (c) traveling to Taiwan to visit my extended family, and (d) engaging in rich interactions with Chinese international students at college.

The first conflicting norm I remember struggling with was whether to speak English or Mandarin,

which is my native language and the most common Chinese dialect. I always spoke Mandarin at home but was expected to speak English at school. My parents made it very clear that they did not want me to forget how to speak Mandarin. This norm was so important to them that they enrolled my sister and me in a Chinese school in a suburb outside of Boston when I was in third grade.

I must admit I did not fully appreciate the workload at Chinese school during my early years. But, I developed several close friendships and gradually came to enjoy learning calligraphy, diabolo, literature, and dance. Being involved in these activities exposed me to Chinese art, culture, traditions, and rituals. Learning these customs was exceptionally rewarding, but being enrolled in both schools made it difficult for me to shift from the norms of one school setting to those of another, primarily in terms of linguistic expectations, standards of discipline, and social values. I often felt conflicted. In Chinese school, I became grounded in and celebrated my cultural roots.

(Continued)

Then, when I went to American school, I found myself compromising some of my Chinese cultural norms in order to be accepted by my peers.

At home and at Chinese school, I adhered to behavioral norms focused on discipline, a strong work ethic, and respect for elders. At American school, I had to adjust my norms in ways that seemed to conflict with those of my cultural heritage in order to fully engage in conversations and activities with my American friends there. I had to seek ways to assimilate and adhere to norms of their autonomous value system in order to "fit in."

Adjusting to competing norms at Chinese and American schools here in the United States was demanding, but I also faced this challenge when I traveled to Taiwan to visit relatives. In Taiwan, I would often sense a strong pull to adhere to norms in the other direction. Being around my extended family, it was comforting to know that they held similar politeness, spiritual, and collectivist norms. On the other hand, sometimes, my relatives would say that I was acting more American than Chinese. At times like these, I again felt the struggle of trying to adhere to competing norms.

Back in the United States as a college student at the University of Michigan and then at the Pennsylvania State University, I also recall feeling torn between competing norms when Chinese international students would make remarks that I had become "Westernized." Those comments made me feel apprehensive about whether I was losing aspects of my cultural identity. Such realizations encouraged me to seek ways to consciously integrate the norms of two worlds in order to maintain my unique sense of self. For example, I have negotiated standards and customs that help to both preserve my own Chinese norms and assimilate to American norms with regard to independence, discipline, religion, group identification, and life goals.

As a Chinese American, I continue to face the need to negotiate between competing norms, trying my best to integrate norms of both cultural worlds. When I meet new people and encounter new situations, I consciously try to adapt my behavioral norms in order to "fit in." Although these cultural negotiations are challenges, I choose to view them as opportunities to develop and cultivate a more refined sense of self. After all, I am a Chinese American, which means I honor and value both sets of norms, those grounded in my Chinese roots and those I have acquired as an American naturalized citizen.

Used with permission.

Healthy Groups Are Accountable

Accountability means all group members are held responsible for adhering to the group norms and working toward the group's goal. This means a group will sanction a member who violates a group norm. The severity of the sanction depends on the importance of the norm that was violated, the extent of the violation, and the status of the person who violated the norm. Violating a norm that is central to a group's performance or cohesiveness will generally receive a harsher sanction than violating a norm that is less central. Minor violations or violations by a newcomer generally receive more lenient sanctions. As a new Lions Club member, for example, Daniel's sanction was merely a stern look from the others. Group members who have achieved higher status in the group also tend to receive more lenient sanctions or escape sanctioning altogether.

Being accountable can also mean changing counterproductive norms. For example, suppose a few folks tell jokes, stories, and generally ignore attempts by others to begin more serious discussion about community service issues at the Lions Club meetings. If the group does not effectively sanction this behavior, then it could become a counterproductive group norm. As a result, work toward the group's goals could

accountability
group members being held responsible for adhering to the group norms and working toward the group's goal.

be delayed, set aside, or perhaps even forgotten. If counterproductive behavior continues for several meetings and becomes a norm, it will be very difficult (though not impossible) to change.

What can a group member do to try to change a norm? You can help your group change a counterproductive norm by (1) observing the norm and its outcome, (2) describing the results of the norm to the group, and (3) soliciting opinions of other members of the group (Renz & Greg, 2000, p. 52). For instance, Daniel observed that every Lions Club meeting began 15–20 minutes late and that this was making it necessary to schedule additional meetings. When members became frustrated at holding extra meetings, he could bring up his observations and the consequences and ask the group for their reaction.

Photo and Co/Riser/Getty Images

Healthy Groups Are Synergetic

The old saying "two heads are better than one" captures an important characteristic of healthy groups. **Synergy** is the multiplying force of a group of individuals working together that results in a combined effort greater than any of the parts (Henman, 2003). For instance, the sports record books are filled with "no-name teams" that have won major championships over opponents with more talented players. A healthy group can develop a collective intelligence and a dynamic energy that translate into an outcome that exceeds what even a highly talented individual could produce. When a group has ethical goals and is interdependent, cohesive, and held accountable to productive norms, the group is well on its way toward achieving synergy.

When underdog teams win championships, it is often because their combined efforts resulted in synergy. Have you ever been on an underdog team that went on to win a big game or championship? Do you think synergy played a role? Why or why not?

Stages of Group Development

Just as interpersonal relationships go through identifiable life cycles, so too do groups move through stages of development. Although numerous models have been proposed to describe the stages of group development, psychologist, Bruce Tuckman's (1965) model has been widely accepted because it identifies central issues facing a group at each stage. In this section, we describe each of these stages and the nature of communication during each one.

How do groups develop?

Forming

Forming is the initial stage of group development, and it is characterized by orientation, testing, and dependence. Members try to understand precisely what the goal is, what role they will play in reaching the goal, and what the other group members are like. As the goal becomes clearer, members assess how their skills, talents, and abilities might be used in accomplishing it. Members also begin to develop relationships and to test what behaviors will be acceptable in the group. Group interactions are likely to be polite and tentative as members become acquainted with each other and find their place in the group. Any real disagreements between people often remain unacknowledged during this stage because members want to be perceived as flexible and likable. During the forming stage, you should express positive attitudes; refrain from abrasive or disagreeable comments; make appropriately benign self-disclosures and wait to see

synergy
the multiplying force of a group working together that results in a combined effort greater than any of the parts.

forming
the initial stage of group development characterized by orientation, testing, and dependence.

Jetta Productions/Iconica/Getty Images

Why is storming an important stage of group development?

Web Resource 9.2

storming
the stage of group development characterized by conflict and power plays as members seek to have their ideas accepted and to find their place within the group's power structure.

groupthink
a deterioration of mental efficiency, reality testing, and moral judgment that results from in-group pressure to conform.

norming
the stage of group development during which the group solidifies its rules for behavior, resulting in greater trust and motivation to achieve the group goal.

performing
the stage of group development when the skills, knowledge, and abilities of all members are combined to overcome obstacles and meet goals successfully.

if they are reciprocated; and try to be friendly, open, and interested in others (Anderson, 1988).

Storming

As members figure out the goal and become comfortable with the other group members, they begin to express their honest opinions and vie for power and position. This signals the beginning of the second stage of group development. The **storming** stage is characterized by conflict and power plays as members seek to have their ideas accepted and to find their place within the group's power structure. Constructive disagreements help the group clarify its goal and the resolution of power plays clarifies the group structure and what is expected of each member. During this storming stage, the politeness exhibited during forming may be replaced by snide comments, sarcastic remarks, or pointedly aggressive exchanges between some members. While storming, members may take sides and form coalitions. Although storming occurs in all groups, some groups manage it better than others. When storming is severe, it can threaten the group's survival. However, if a group does not storm, it may experience **groupthink**, a deterioration of mental efficiency, reality testing, and moral judgment that results from in-group pressure to conform (Janis, 1982, p. 9). To avoid groupthink, we should encourage constructive disagreement, avoid name-calling and inflammatory language, and use the active listening skills with an emphasis on paraphrasing and honest questioning (Anderson, 1988).

Norming

Norming is the third stage of group development and is characterized by increased cohesion, collaboration, emerging trust among members, and motivation to achieve the group goal. Having expressed honest opinions, resolved major differences, and sorted out specific roles, members become loyal to each other and to the group goal. During this stage, members come to appreciate their differences, strengthen their relationships, and freely express their ideas and opinions. Members accept the norms established by the group and provide positive and constructive feedback to each other.

Performing

Performing is the fourth stage of group development and is characterized by harmony, productivity, problem-solving, and shared leadership. During this stage, the group capitalizes on the skills, knowledge, and abilities of all members to work toward achieving its goal. During this stage, conversations are focused on sharing task-related information and problem-solving. Groups cannot achieve their full potential in this stage unless they have successfully resolved storming conflicts and developed productive norms.

Adjourning

Adjourning is the stage of group development characterized by celebration of goal accomplishment and disengagement. Adjourning begins when the group recognizes that it has reached its goal. The group will engage in some type of formal or informal celebration during which they recognize their accomplishment and the role that each member played. They may rehash parts of their work and try to capture what they have learned about group process or their own behavior. Finally, group members will begin to disengage from their relationships with each other. The group may formally disband while some members continue to see each other in social settings, or the group may continue to exist with a new goal. The new goal will inevitably cause the members to revisit the earlier stages of group development, but the cohesion, trust, and norms developed earlier are likely to help the group move quickly and more smoothly through these stages.

With this basic understanding of the stages of group development, we now turn to describing types of groups.

Skill Learning Activity 9.2

Types of Groups

Most of us can identify many different groups to which we belong at any point in time; each one is focused on a common purpose, goal, or objective. You have probably noticed that what is expected of you varies from group to group. Scholars who study groups find it useful to categorize groups according to their purpose. This allows scholars to better understand how groups with similar purposes behave and what effects they have on their members. Let's look at the most common group types: families, social friendship groups, support groups, interest groups, service groups, and work groups.

> What are some types of groups we might participate in?

Families

A **family** is "a group of intimates who through their communication generates a sense of home and group identity, complete with strong ties of loyalty and emotion, and experiences a history and a future" (Galvin, Byland, & Brommel, 2007). Families can be nuclear (consisting of two parents who live together with their biological or adopted children), single parent (consisting of one adult living with his or her children), extended (consisting of a parent or parents and children living with grandparents, cousins, aunts and uncles, or other relatives), blended (consisting of committed or married adults living with the children of their previous marriages and relationships as well as the children of their union), or mixed (consisting of people of different races).

Not all families work the same way. Contemporary research on families suggests four different ways families function when facing an issue (Koerner & Fitzpatrick, 2002). In protective families, issues are not discussed and are decided solely by the family authority figure. In the movie *The Sound of Music*, prior to Maria's arrival, the Von Trapp family exemplified this family dynamic. In consensual families, all members engage in conversation about an issue but a family authority figure still makes the final decision. Many television sitcoms from the 1950s and 1960s such as *Father Knows Best*, *Leave It to Beaver*, and *The Brady Bunch* portray families with a benevolent and self-sacrificing father filling this role. In pluralistic families, all members engage in conversation about an issue and everyone participates in the decision-making. These families may have formal family meetings to decide important family issues. The popular 1980s television sitcom *Full House*, where three men raised the children together, operated in this way. Finally, in laissez-faire families, members may converse about an issue, but each member makes his or her own decision and is responsible for its consequences. The cartoon family portrayed on *The Simpsons* tends to function this way.

We initially learn how to act in groups based on the ways our family members interacted with each other while we were growing up. Of course, the conversational norms we learned may change as a result of the experiences we have in additional groups throughout our lives. Which family type did you grow up in? Do you think your conversational norms for participating in groups are consistent with what you experienced growing up? Why or why not?

adjourning
the stage of group development in which members assign meaning to what they have done and determine how to end or maintain interpersonal relations they have developed.

family
a group of intimates who through their communication generates a sense of home and group identity, complete with strong ties of loyalty and emotion, and experiences a history and a future

One of the major responsibilities of healthy families is to talk in ways that build one another's self-concept and self-esteem. So it is important that family members (1) praise each other: "Manuel you got a B on that spelling test, good for you!"; (2) offer statements of acceptance and support: "You know that I would rather you go to college, but your mom and I will support your decision to join the Navy"; and (3) verbally express love: "Nevah, you know I love you no matter what."

Social Friendship Groups

A **social friendship group** is composed of friends who have a genuine concern about each other's welfare and enjoy spending time together. Their interactions are characterized by "interpersonal ties and positive, amiable preexisting relationships among members" (Thompson, 2003, p. 239). Most of us belong to more than one social friendship group during our lives. You may have had a group of friends you were close to in high school, a group of buddies you were close to when you served in the military, or a group of friends you play golf or softball with regularly. Sometimes people who work together evolve into a social friendship group when they begin to get together for social activities outside of work. Social friendship groups may initially form around a shared interest like a book club or Bible study, but as members spend time together and find they enjoy one another's company, they may evolve into a social friendship group. Popular TV programs such as *Friends*, *Seinfeld*, and *Sex in the City* are examples of sitcom social friendship groups.

Because social friendship groups fill our needs to be accepted and to belong, communication in these groups should (1) encourage quieter members to participate in conversations: "Hey, Jules, you haven't had a chance to catch us up on how your Dad is doing"; (2) protect members from playful harassment: "Hey Jenna, back off, you've been aiming your put downs at Pam all evening"; (3) provide opportunities for friends to disclose problems and receive support; "Hey, Zach, I heard that your sister was diagnosed with Hodgkins lymphoma. How are you doing?"

Everett Collection

Can you identify ways that this social friendship group was similar to a family and ways in which it was different?

social friendship group
a group comprised of friends who have a genuine concern about each other's welfare and enjoy spending time together.

support group
a group comprised of people who come together to bolster each other by providing encouragement, honest feedback, and a safe environment for expressing deeply personal feelings about a problem common to the members.

Support Groups

Support groups are composed of people who come together to bolster each other by providing encouragement, honest feedback, and a safe environment for expressing deeply personal feelings about a problem common to the members. Support groups include well-known fellowships like Alcoholics Anonymous (AA) and Narcotics Anonymous, survivor or caregiver support groups formed by local chapters of a national organization like the Leukemia and Lymphoma Society or the Alzheimer's Association, grief groups at local synagogues and churches, and neighborhood stay-at-home-dads groups. Until recently, support groups met face to face, but today there are thousands of online support groups connecting people who have never met face to face.

Support groups must create an environment where members feel safe to disclose highly personal information. So members need to make sure that their messages follow the guidelines in Chapter 8 for comforting, which include clarifying supportive intentions, buffering face threats, using other-centered language, framing, and selectively offering advice.

Interest Groups

An **interest group** is composed of individuals who come together because they share a concern, hobby, or activity. These groups may be formal with defined goals and tasks (such as a 4-H club or community theater troupe) or they may be informal (like a neighborhood book or gardening club). They may be part of a larger organization like La Raza, the Urban League, or the Houston Area Apple Users Group. Some interest groups are externally focused on a common political or social issue and adopt an agenda to achieve change. MADD (Mothers Against Drunk Drivers) is an example. Other interest groups are internally focused on increasing skills or knowledge of their members. Toastmasters, for instance, is focused on helping its members improve their public speaking skills. Some interest groups meet online. Meetup.com is an Internet site that helps people find others who share their interests.

Because interest group members share some passion, all members ought to have an opportunity to communicate their expertise by (1) encouraging members to share success stories: "I'm really glad that Brian was able to get Ace Hardware to donate all the bathroom fixtures for our project. Brian, can you tell us what you said and did?" and (2) doing so in ways that all members highlight what they know without demeaning the knowledge or opinions of others: "I really liked hearing Brian's story and I'd like to hear about how other people approach getting donations."

Service Groups

Service groups are composed of individuals who come together to perform hands-on charitable works or to raise money to help organizations that perform such work. Service groups may be local affiliates of larger secular or religious service organizations like Break Away, Lions Club International, Red Cross, Salvation Army, B'nai B'rith, and Habitat for Humanity. Other service groups are local and function independently. Small soup kitchens, urban gardening groups, and community beautification groups perform charitable work that may include raising funds and interfacing with government agencies.

Because service groups are both voluntary and task-oriented, they need to be dedicated to the task as well as sensitive to the ego and emotional needs of members. So communication should (1) be clear about individual tasks, roles, and responsibilities: "Jim, as I remember it, today you agreed to work on patching the roof."; (2) encourage and praise member accomplishments: "I was really impressed with how sensitive you were when you turned her down for another bag of groceries"; and (3) be polite: "Mary, it would be great if you would please work with Yvonne on stuffing envelopes for that mailing. Thanks so much!"

Work Groups

A **work group** is a collection of three or more people formed to solve a problem or accomplish a specific task. Examples of work groups include class project groups (established to create a joint presentation, paper, or other learning project) and work teams (established as needed to perform specific activities in the workplace). Effective work groups have clearly defined goals, an appropriate number of members, and diversity in the skills and viewpoints of its members.

interest group
a group comprised of individuals who come together because they share a common concern, hobby, or activity.

service group
a group comprised of individuals who come together to perform hands-on charitable works, or to raise money to help organizations that perform such work.

work group
a collection of three or more people formed to solve a problem.

An effective **work group goal** is a clearly stated future state of affairs desired by enough members to motivate the group to work toward achieving it (Johnson & Johnson, 2003). Effective work group goals are specific. For example, the crew at a local fast food restaurant that began with the goal of "increasing profitability of the restaurant" made the goal more specific in this way: "During the next quarter, the second shift night crew will increase profitability by reducing food costs by 1 percent. They will do so by throwing away less food due to precooking." Effective work group goals are also consistent in that they serve a common purpose. That is, achieving one goal does not prevent the achievement of another. For the fast food crew, all members must believe that reducing the amount of precooked food on hand will not interfere with maintaining their current level of service. Effective work group goals are challenging. Achieving them will require hard work and team effort. Finally, effective work group goals are acceptable in that all members feel personally committed to achieving them. People tend to support things they help create. So group members who participate in setting the goals are likely to exert high effort to achieve them as well.

What is the best size for a work group? In general, research suggests that the best size is the smallest number of people capable of effectively achieving the goal (Sundstrom, DeMeuse, & Futrell, 1990). For many situations, this might mean as few as three to five people. As the size of the group increases, the time spent discussing and deciding also increases. When only Jeff, Bryan, and Sue are in a group, for instance, there are only four relationships to manage (Jeff–Sue; Bryan–Jeff; Bryan–Sue; Bryan–Sue–Jeff). Adding members also means more relationships to manage. Smaller groups can make decisions more quickly than larger ones. However, if the goals and issues are complex, a group with more members is more likely to have the breadth of information, knowledge, and skills needed to make high-quality decisions. As groups grow in size and complexity, however, the opportunities for each member to participate drop and because people tend to be more satisfied when they can actively participate, the most desirable size for most work group situations is five to seven members (Bonito, 2000).

More important than the number of people is the right combination of people in the work group. Effective work groups are likely to be composed of people who offer different but relevant knowledge and skills (Valacich, George, Nonamaker, & Vogel, 1994). A **heterogeneous group** is usually better than a **homogeneous group**. In homogeneous groups, members are likely to know the same things, come at the problem from the same perspective, and, consequently, be likely to overlook some important information or take shortcuts in the problem-solving process. In contrast, groups composed of heterogeneous members are more likely to have diverse information, perspectives, and values, and, consequently, discuss issues more thoroughly before reaching a decision. For example, a group composed of seven nurses who are all young white females would be considered a homogeneous group; a group composed of nurses, doctors, nutritionists, and physical therapists who differ in age, race, and

work group goal
a future state of affairs desired by enough members of the group to motivate the group to work toward its achievement.

heterogeneous group
group in which various demographics, levels of knowledge, attitudes, and interests are represented.

homogeneous group
group in which members have a great deal of similarity.

sex would be considered a heterogeneous group. The heterogeneous medical group would probably make a more comprehensive decision about a patient's care than the homogeneous group of nurses.

Work groups are usually more task oriented than other groups. So, much of the communication focuses on task-related issues and should (1) seek collaboration to resolve conflicts: "Felicia, I'm having a problem that I need your help with"; (2) update other members on the status of individual efforts: "I thought you all should know that I will be about two days late with that feasibility report as the woman who was providing me with the cost data is on vacation"; and (3) appropriately credit the contributions of other team members: "Today I am presenting the findings, but I think you should know that Len did the initial research and Mavis did the quantitative analysis that led to these conclusions."

Evaluating Group Dynamics

Group dynamics is the way a group interacts to achieve its goal. Effective groups periodically stop and evaluate how their interactions are affecting what they are accomplishing and how members perceive themselves and others. At times you may be asked to provide a formal evaluation of the group dynamics of a class project group or other work team. One way you might evaluate members is to describe how each member performed his or her specific tasks and how well his or her communication contributed to the cohesiveness, problem solving, and conflict resolution processes in the group. Figure 9.1 is one example you can use for evaluating class project group member participation. Alternatively, in a class project group, members could prepare a "reflective thinking process paper," which details in paragraph form what each member did well and could improve upon as well as a self-analysis of their own contributions and what they could do to improve.

Like the evaluations business managers make of employees, these evaluations serve to document the efforts of group members. They can be submitted to the instructor, just as they would be submitted to a supervisor. In business, these documents provide a basis for determining promotion, merit pay, and salary adjustments. In the classroom, they can provide a basis for determining one portion of each member's grade.

> How might you evaluate participation in groups?

group dynamics
the way a group interacts to achieve its goal.

Group Dynamics Evaluation Form

Meeting date: ——————————————————

Your name: ————————————————————

Directions

After each required group meeting, provide ethical critiques for both your group members and yourself. Rate each individual on his or her performance in the group. Justify the rating with specific examples. As you rate each member, consider the following:

- commitment to the group goal
- fulfills individual assignments
- manages interpersonal conflicts
- encourages group participation
- helps keep the discussion on track

Figure 9.1
Group dynamics evaluation form

Yourself ————————————————————————————————

Circle overall individual rating

0   1   2   3   4   5   6   7
(poor)   (met requirements)   (excellent)

Tasks accomplished:

Tasks assigned:

Ethical critique:

Group member ——————————————————————————————

Circle overall individual rating

0   1   2   3   4   5   6   7
(poor)   (met requirements)   (excellent)

Tasks accomplished:

Tasks assigned:

Ethical critique:

Group member ——————————————————————————————

Circle overall individual rating

0   1   2   3   4   5   6   7
(poor)   (met requirements)   (excellent)

Tasks accomplished:

Tasks assigned:

Ethical critique:

Group member ——————————————————————————————

Circle overall individual rating

0   1   2   3   4   5   6   7
(poor)   (met requirements)   (excellent)

Tasks accomplished:

Tasks assigned:

Ethical critique:

Group member ——————————————————————————————

Circle overall individual rating

0   1   2   3   4   5   6   7
(poor)   (met requirements)   (excellent)

Tasks accomplished:

Tasks assigned:

Ethical critique:

Figure 9.1
(continued)

A Question of Ethics

What Would You Do?

The community service and outreach committee of Students in Communication was meeting to determine what cause should benefit from their annual fund-raising talent contest.

"So," said Mark, "does anyone have any ideas about whose cause we should sponsor?"

"Well," replied Glenna, "I think we should give it to a group that's doing literacy work."

"Sounds good to me," replied Mark.

"My aunt works at the Boardman Center as the literacy coordinator, so why don't we just adopt them?" asked Glenna.

"Gee, I don't know much about the group," said Reed.

"Come on, you know, they help people learn how to read," replied Glenna sarcastically.

"Well, I was kind of hoping we'd take a look at sponsoring the local teen runaway center," offered Angelo.

"Listen, if your aunt works at the Boardman Center," commented Leticia, "let's go with it."

"Right," said Pablo, "that's good enough for me."

"Yeah," replied Heather, "let's do it and get out of here."

"I hear what you're saying, Heather," Mark responded, "I've got plenty of other stuff to do."

"No disrespect meant to Glenna, but wasn't the Boardman Center in the news because of questionable use of funds?" countered Angelo. "Do we really know enough about them?"

"OK," said Mark, "enough discussion. I've got to get to class. All in favor of the literacy program at the Boardman Center indicate by saying aye. I think we've got a majority. Sorry, Angelo—you can't win them all."

"I wish all meetings went this smoothly," Heather said to Glenna as they left the room. "I mean, that was really a good meeting."

1. What did the group really know about the Boardman Center? Is it good group discussion practice to rely on a passing comment of one member?
2. Regardless of whether the meeting went smoothly, is there any ethical problem with this process? Explain.

Summary

We participate in a variety of groups throughout our lives. A group is more than a mere assembly of people in that all members involved share a common goal, purpose, or objective. Although some groups form around purposes that have negative consequences, we focus on the characteristics of healthy groups—groups that are formed around a constructive purpose, goal, or objective. These characteristics are ethical goals, interdependence, cohesiveness, productive norms, accountability, and synergy.

Just as interpersonal relationships move through life cycles, so groups move through stages of development. These stages are forming, storming, norming, performing, and adjourning. Ultimately, moving through these stages successfully results in achieving group goals.

Because we participate in so many different groups, researchers have categorized group types based on purposes. For example, family groups share a mutual commitment to the group and its members and may operative protectively, consensually, pluralistically, or laissez-faire. Social friendship groups focus on purposes regarding a genuine concern for one another's welfare and pleasure in spending time together. Support groups come together to bolster each other by providing encouragement, honest feedback, and a safe environment for expressing deeply personal feelings about a problem common to the members. Interest groups form because the individuals share a common concern, hobby, or activity. Service groups perform hands-on charitable works and/or raise money to help organizations that perform such work. Work groups are collections of three or more people who must interact and influence each other to solve problems and accomplish a task. Examples of work groups are class project groups and work teams.

Sometimes you might be asked to evaluate how you and other members participate in a group. Doing so might help your instructor grade group dynamics or help your employer determine merit pay or bonuses.

Communicate! Active Online Learning

Now that you have read Chapter 9, use your Premium Website for *Communicate!* for quick access to the electronic resources that accompany this text. These resources include

- **Study tools** that will help you assess your learning and prepare for exams (*digital glossary, key term flash cards, review quizzes*).
- **Activities and assignments** that will help you hone your knowledge, analyze communication situations (*Skill Learning Activities*), and build your public speaking skills throughout the course (*Communication on Your Feet speech assignments, Action Step activities*). Many of these activities allow you to compare your answers to those provided by the authors,

and, if requested, submit your answers to your instructor.

- **Media resources** that will help you explore communication concepts online (*Web Resources*), develop your speech outlines (*Speech Builder Express 3.0*), watch and critique videos of communication situations and sample speeches (*Interactive Video Activities*), upload your speech videos for peer reviewing and critique other students' speeches (*Speech Studio online speech review tool*), and download chapter review so you can study when and where you'd like (*Audio Study Tools*).

This chapter's Key Terms, Skill Learning Activities, and Web Resources are also featured on the following pages.

Key Terms

accountability (212)
adjourning (215)
cohesiveness (210)
forming (213)
family (215)
ground rules (210)
group (208)
group communication (208)

group dynamics (219)
groupthink (214)
healthy group (209)
heterogeneous group (218)
homogeneous group (218)
interdependent group (210)
interest group (217)
norming (214)
norms (210)

performing (214)
service group (217)
social friendship group (216)
storming (214)
support group (216)
synergy (213)
team-building activities (210)
work group (217)
work group goal (218)

Skill Learning Activities

9.1: Cohesiveness in Homogeneous versus Heterogeneous Groups (210)

Identify two groups (for example, a sports team, study group, fraternal or community group, or work team) to which you belong; one should have a diverse membership and the other should have members who are similar (see page 218).

Analyze the demographic differences in each group. When you have completed this analysis, write a paragraph that discusses cohesiveness in each group. How cohesive is each group? Are both groups equally cohesive? Was it easier to establish cohesiveness in one of the groups? What real or potential pitfalls result from the level of cohesiveness in each group?

To help you complete this activity, you can use the demographic analysis provided in your Premium Website for *Communicate!* Look for it in the Skill Learning activities for Chapter 9.

9.2: Stages of Group Development (215)

Think of a group to which you have belonged for less than one term (if you have an assigned group in this course, use it). Now, write a paragraph that begins by identifying the stage of development the group is currently in and then describe how this group transitioned through each of the previous stages of group development. What event(s) do you recall as turning points, marking the group's movement from one stage to another? Has the group become stuck in a stage, or has it developed smoothly? What factors contributed to that? What can you do to help this group succeed in the stage it is in and to transition to the next stage?

Web Resources

9.1: Setting Group Norms (211)

This site at Brushy Fork Institute, a group dedicated to advancing leadership and community development in the Appalachians, features information on setting norms that contribute to group effectiveness.

9.2: Groupthink (214)

This site features an article whose purpose is to raise awareness about groupthink and to provide suggestions that can help task-oriented groups avoid this phenomenon.

⊙ Problem Solving in Groups

Questions you will be able to answer after reading this chapter:

- What are the steps in the systematic problem solving process?
- How does leadership function most effectively in problem solving groups?
- What are group member responsibilities when participating in meetings?
- How can groups communicate their solutions to others?

Members of the campus chapter of the Public Relations Student Society of America (PRSSA) chatted while Dolores, the chapter president, distributed the agenda. The recession had taken its toll on the chapter's membership, and the original budget was now unrealistic. They would have to cut corners somewhere to make ends meet. When all the members had received a copy of the agenda, Dolores began, "Well, we all know why we're here this evening. We've got to decide what to do to balance our budget. It's not going to be fun, but let's get started." After a few seconds of silence, Dolores asked, "Drew, what have you been thinking?"

"Well, I don't know," Drew replied, "I haven't really given it much thought." *(There were nods of agreement all around the table.)*

"Well," Jeremy said, "I'm not sure I even remember what our projected expenses are."

"But when I sent you the e-mail reminder, I attached a detailed spreadsheet and some questions to think about before this meeting," Dolores replied.

"Oh, is that what that was?" Bethany asked. "I read the part about the meeting, but I guess I didn't get a chance to look at the attachment."

Dolores responded, "We've got some tough decisions to make. Do we cut our donations to the food pantry? Do we cut the travel support we give to those planning to attend the annual convention? Do we stop printing our monthly newsletter and just offer the online version? Do we raise our monthly dues? Do we add another fundraising project?"

"Anything you think would be appropriate is OK with me," Dawn said.

"Well, I'm not comfortable making these decisions alone. Let's each of us plan to review the materials I sent and meet again tomorrow night with some ideas, okay?" Dolores suggested. *(There were nods of agreement around the table.)* "Meeting adjourned."

As the group dispersed, Dolores overheard Drew whisper to Dawn, "These meetings sure are a waste of time, aren't they?"

Perhaps you have been to a meeting like this one. If so, you were probably just as frustrated as the people in this vignette. When group meetings are ineffective, it is easy to point the finger at the leader. But as was the case with this group, the responsibility for the "waste of time" lies not with one person but with the group and the complex nature of problem solving in groups. Although working in groups can have its disadvantages, it is the preferred approach in business and industry today (O'Hair, O'Rourke, & O'Hair, 2001; Snyder, 2004; Teams, 2004). Leaders in business and industry realize that when groups work effectively to solve problems, they provide a deeper analysis of problems, generate a greater breadth of ideas and potential solutions, promote positive group morale, and lead to increased productivity. You can expect to work in groups to solve problems your organization faces during your professional life. These meetings may be in face-to-face or in virtual settings through e-mail, discussion boards, or video conferencing (Tullar & Kaiser, 2000). You will also encounter group problem solving in community groups, service groups, and even in your family.

In this chapter you will learn an effective process for group problem solving, the leadership skills needed to effectively manage group interactions during problem solving, the responsibilities that group members share, and ways that a group can effectively communicate the results of its deliberations to others.

The Problem Solving Process

When a group of people tackles a problem together, they may use an orderly series of steps or a less-structured spiral pattern in which they refine, accept, reject, modify, combine ideas, and circle back to previous discussion as they go along. To observers, groups that follow an orderly sequence of steps—finishing each before moving to the next one—appear to be more organized and are generally more efficient, completing their deliberations more quickly. Groups that follow a spiral sequence of activities may be less efficient, but they can also arrive at effective solutions. For example, when a group is presented with a problem, members will often immediately begin to offer solutions. But after a while most groups realize they can't decide on a solution until

> **What are the steps in the systematic problem solving process?**

they figure out the criteria for a good solution, or they may realize that each member has a different idea about what the problem is. A group needs to deal with these tasks before it can move to making a decision.

Whether the deliberations are linear or spiral, groups that arrive at high-quality decisions accomplish the six tasks that make up what is known as the Systematic Problem Solving Process. This process, first described by John Dewey in 1933 and since revised by others, is still the best approach to individual or group problem solving (Duch, Groh, & Allen, 2001; Edens, 2000; Levin, 2001). By understanding the steps in problem solving and guiding your group to use them systematically, you can help your group to be both effective and efficient.

Step One: Identify and Define the Problem

The first step is to identify the problem and define it in a way that all group members understand and agree with. Even when a group is commissioned by an outside agency that provides a description of the problem, the group still needs to understand precisely what is at issue and needs to be resolved. Many times what appears to be a problem is only a symptom of a problem, and if the group focuses on solutions that eliminate only a symptom, the underlying problem will remain. For example in the opening vignette, the group's budget crisis was described as stemming from a recession-related membership drop. How does the group know that the inability to fund the budget is the problem and not just a symptom of the problem? What if their membership drop has some other cause? If that is the case, then cutting the budget may be a temporary fix but will not solve the problem. One way to see if you have uncovered the root cause or real problem is to ask, "If we solve this problem, are we confident that the consequences of the problem will not reoccur?" If we cut the budget, are we confident that we won't have to cut it further? If not, then we probably need to look further for the root problem. We will need to look more closely at causes for the drop in membership and other ways besides dues for funding the budget. The real problem may be how to fund the budget.

Once your group agrees about the nature of the root problem you will want to draft a **problem definition**, which is a formal written statement describing the problem. An effective problem definition is stated as a question of fact, value, or policy; it contains only one central idea; and it uses specific, precise, and concrete language. **Questions of fact** ask the group to determine what is true or to what extent something is true. "What percentage of our projected expenses can be covered with our existing revenue?" is a question of fact. **Questions of value** ask the group to determine or judge whether something is right, moral, good, or just. Questions of value often contain words such as *good, reliable, effective,* or *worthy*—for instance, "What is the most effective way to recruit new members?" **Questions of policy** concern what course of action should be taken or what rules should be adopted to solve a problem—for example, "Should we sponsor an annual fund-raising event with the local Public Relations Society of America (PRSA) chapter in order to help fund our budget?" After some discussion, the student chapter decided that the problem they needed to solve was a policy question that could be best stated: "How can we increase our revenues in order to meet our budget in the current economic conditions?"

Step Two: Analyze the Problem

Analysis of a problem entails finding out as much as possible about the problem. Most groups begin this process with each member sharing information he or she already knows about the problem through previous experiences. Some groups don't move

Skill Learning Activity 10.1
Web Resource 10.1

problem definition
a formal written statement describing a problem.

question of fact
a question asked to determine what is true or to what extent something is true.

question of value
a question asked to determine or judge whether something is right, moral, good, or just.

question of policy
a question asked to determine what course of action should be taken or what rules should be adopted to solve a problem.

- What are the symptoms of this problem?
- What are the causes of this problem?
- Can this problem be subdivided into several smaller problems that each may have individual solutions?
- What have others who have faced this problem done?
- How successful have they been with the solutions they attempted?
- How is our situation similar and different from theirs?
- Does this problem consist of several smaller problems? If so, what are their symptoms, causes, previously tried solutions, and so forth?
- What would be the consequences of doing nothing?
- What would be the consequences of trying something and having it fail?

Figure 10.1
Questions to guide problem analysis

beyond this level of analysis, which maybe OK if the group consists of individuals who are expert in the important areas related to the problem. But when this is not the case, the group needs to search for additional information. Members may be assigned to collect and examine information about the problem that is published in materials available at the library and on the Internet. Other members may interview experts, and still others may conduct surveys to gather information from particular target groups. The information gathered by group members should help the group to answer key questions about the nature of the problem such as those listed in Figure 10.1.

The PRSSA chapter, for example, might interview the dean of Student Affairs to understand how in the past other campus groups increased their revenues and to learn of any campus policies that govern fund-raising by student groups. Some group members might network with other student groups on campus and PRSSA chapters at other schools. Finally, the group could survey former members to understand why they dropped out of the group and what might entice them to rejoin, as well as survey eligible students who are not members to find out what would entice them to join.

During the information gathering and analysis step, it is important to consciously encourage members to share information they have found that is new or contradicts the sentiments or preferences expressed in the group. It is difficult for most of us to give up our pet theories or preferred worldviews. A group that is willing to consider new and unexpected information will more deeply analyze the problem and, therefore, will likely come to a more effective solution.

Step Three: Determine Criteria for Judging Solutions

Criteria are standards or measures used for judging the merits of proposed solutions. They provide a blueprint for how the group will evaluate the virtues of each alternative solution. Research suggests that when groups develop criteria before they think about specific solutions, they are more likely to come to a decision that all members can accept (Young, Wood, Phillips, & Pedersen, 2007). Without clear criteria, group members may argue for their preferred solution without regard to whether it will adequately address the problem and whether it is feasible. Figure 10.2 provides a list of questions that can help a group think about the types of criteria that a solution might need to meet.

Once you've agreed on the list of solution criteria, the group needs to prioritize the list. Although rank ordering the list from most to least important may be unwieldy and counterproductive, it is probably useful to agree which criteria are major (must meet) and which are minor (would like to see).

criteria
standards or measures used for judging the merits of proposed solutions.

- What are the quantitative and qualitative measures of success that a solution must be able to demonstrate?
- Are there resource constraints that a good solution must meet (costs, time, manpower)?
- Is solution simplicity a factor?
- What risks are unacceptable?
- Is ease of implementation a consideration?
- Is it important that no constituency be unfairly harmed or advantaged by a solution?

Figure 10.2
Questions to guide discussion of solution criteria

Based on their research and discussion, the PRSSA chapter agreed on three major criteria and one minor criterion. A good plan would comply with the university's policy on fund-raising by student groups. It would need to cost less than $500 to implement. It would need to raise at least $4,000. It would not require more than 20 hours of work from each member.

Step Four: Identify Alternative Solutions

Ending up with a good solution depends on having a wide variety of possible solutions to choose from. So one of the most important activities of problem solving is coming up with solution ideas. Many groups fail at generating solution ideas because they criticize the first ideas expressed; this discourages members from taking the risk to put their ideas out for the group to consider. One way to encourage everyone's ideas is to use the technique of brainstorming. **Brainstorming** is an uncritical, non-evaluative process of generating possible solutions by being creative, suspending judgment, and combining or adapting ideas. When brainstorming, the group agrees to a freewheeling session when members offer ideas without censoring themselves. During this time other members may build on ideas that have been presented, combine two or more ideas, or even offer off-the-wall thoughts. What members may not do is criticize, poke fun at, or in any other way evaluate the ideas. While the group is brainstorming, one member should be recording the ideas, preferably in a manner that allows all members to see them (on a white board, smart board, or overhead projector, for instance).

When individuals are freed from the fear of criticism, a group may quickly generate 20 or more solution ideas. When members trust each other to abide by the rules, brainstorming is fun and productive.

The PRSSA chapter brainstormed and came up with these ideas:

Web Resource 10.2

- Place an ad on the Communication Department's Website to recruit members.
- Place an ad on the college Website to recruit members.
- Ask faculty to allow PRSSA members to do 2-minute "testimonials" in classes as a way of recruiting members.
- Text-message all the people we know about upcoming PRSSA events.
- Run a monthly raffle at the PRSA meetings. The winning ticket would get 4 hours of work from a PRSSA member.
- Find PRSA chapter members whose businesses would sponsor student scholarships to the national convention.
- Set up a consulting program to provide public relations help to other student groups for a fee.
- Set up a consulting program to provide public relations help to small businesses for a fee.

brainstorming
an uncritical, non-evaluative process of generating possible solutions by being creative, suspending judgment, and combining or adapting ideas.

- Do a virtual newsletter instead of a printed one.
- Double membership dues.
- Co-sponsor a golf outing with the local PRSA chapter.
- Raffle off a spring break getaway for six to St. Thomas.

Step Five: Evaluate Solutions and Decide

With a list of potential solutions in hand, the group must then sort through them to find the one or ones that will best solve the problem. To do this, the group needs to compare each of the alternatives to the decision criteria they established earlier. If a lot of solutions were generated during brainstorming, the group will probably want to quickly review the list and eliminate those that obviously do not meet the criteria. Then it can concentrate on evaluating the remaining solutions, talking about how well each meets specific criteria and comparing the positive features of each. This discussion may result in only one solution that meets all the criteria, but often there will be more than one viable solution.

Decision making is the process of choosing among alternatives. Sometimes your group may not be responsible for choosing among the remaining alternatives. Instead you will present the results of your work to others who will make the actual decision. At other times your group will make the decision. Five methods are commonly used to reach a group decision. Methods that require greater agreement among members are more time consuming.

1. **The expert opinion method.** Once the group has eliminated those alternatives that do not meet the criteria, the group asks the member who has the most expertise to make the final choice. Obviously, this method is quick and useful if one member is much more knowledgeable about the issues or has a greater stake in the implementation of the decision. The PRSSA chapter, for instance, might ask its president to make the final choice.
2. **The average group opinion method.** In this approach, each group member ranks each of the alternatives that meet all the criteria. Their rankings are then averaged, and the alternative receiving the highest average becomes the choice. This method is useful for routine decisions or when a decision needs to be made quickly. It can also be used as an intermediate straw poll so the group can eliminate low-scoring alternatives before moving to a different process for making the final decision.
3. **The majority rule method.** In this method, the group votes on each alternative, and the one that receives a majority of votes (50 percent + 1) is selected. Although this method is considered democratic, it can create problems. If the majority voting for an alternative is slight, then nearly as many members oppose the choice as support it. If these minority members strongly object to the choice, they may sabotage implementation of the solution either actively or passively.
4. **The unanimous decision method.** In this method, the group must continue deliberation until every member of the group believes that the same solution is the best. As you would expect, it is very difficult to arrive at a truly unanimous decision, and to do so takes a lot of time. When a group reaches unanimity, however, each member is likely to be committed to selling the decision to others and helping to implement it.
5. **The consensus method.** This method is an alternative to the unanimous decision method. In consensus, the group continues deliberation until all members of the group find an acceptable solution, one they can support and are committed to helping implement. Some group members may believe there is a better solution than the one chosen, but all feel they can live with the chosen solution. Arriving at consensus, though easier than reaching unanimity, is still difficult. Although the majority rule method is widely used, the consensus method is a wise investment if the group needs everyone's support to implement the decision successfully.

decision making
the process of choosing among alternatives.

Sometimes a group will choose only one solution. But frequently a group will decide on a multi-pronged approach that combines two or three of the acceptable solutions. The PRSSA chapter, for instance, reached consensus on a plan to place ads on both the college and department Websites and to launch a text-message campaign 24 hours before their next meeting. They also decided to approach PRSA chapter members and ask them to sponsor student members to the national convention. Finally, they decided to explore the feasibility of setting up a consulting program.

Step Six: Implement the Agreed-Upon Solution

Finally, the group may be responsible for implementing the agreed-upon solution or, if the group is presenting the solution to others for implementation, making recommendations for how the solution should be implemented. The group has already considered implementation in terms of selecting a solution, but now must fill in the details. What tasks are required by the solution(s)? Who will carry out these tasks? What is a reasonable time frame for implementation generally and for each of the tasks specifically?

Skill Learning Activity 10.2

> How does leadership function most effectively in problem solving groups?

Skill Learning Activity 10.3

informal or emergent leaders
members who gain power because they are liked and respected by the group

shared leadership functions
the sets of roles that group members perform to facilitate the work of the group and help maintain harmonious relationships between members.

task roles
sets of behaviors that help a group acquire, process, or apply information that contributes directly to completing a task or goal.

Shared Leadership

When we think of leadership, we typically think of a person who is in charge. It was once thought that leaders were "born"—that some people inherited personality and other traits that made them naturally suited to be leaders. Later, the emphasis moved to the notion that leaders were "made" and that if we could identify the specific behaviors of leadership, then any person could learn them and become an effective leader. Then, we recognized who became a leader and the behaviors that made a leader effective varied depending on the task, the situation, and the followers. The most recent thinking is that leadership is a set of functions that can be performed by one, more than one, or all group members at various times. In other words, leadership is most often a shared activity in which different members perform various functions based on their unique strengths and expertise (Fairhurst, 2001). A group, then, may have a formal leader, but in actuality, throughout the life of the group, a series of **informal leaders** (also called emergent leaders) will arise to help the group meet the challenges the group faces. People who assume the role of a leader behave and communicate in specific ways that fulfill important leadership functions.

Shared leadership functions are the sets of roles that you or other members perform to facilitate the work of the group and help maintain harmonious relationships between members. A **role** is a specific pattern of behavior that group members perform based on their skills and their perception about the needs of the group at that time. When leadership roles are effectively performed, the group will function smoothly and members will enjoy each other and working on the task. There are three sets of leadership roles that must be performed by members if a group is to be successful: task roles, maintenance roles, and procedural roles.

Task Roles

Task roles help the group acquire, process, or apply information that contributes directly to completing a task or goal.

- Information or opinion givers provide content for the discussion. People who perform this role are well informed on the content of the task and share what they know with the group. Your ability to assume this role depends on your command of high-quality information that the group needs in order to complete its task. "Well, the articles I read seem to agree that..." and "Based on how my sorority raised money for the Ronald McDonald House, we could..." are statements typical of information and opinion givers.

- Information or opinion seekers probe others for their ideas and opinions during group meetings. Typical comments by those performing this role include "Before going further, what information do we have about how raising fees is likely to affect member-ship?" or "How do other members of the group feel about this idea?"

- Information or opinion analyzers help the group to scrutinize the content and the reasoning of discus-sions. They may question what is being said and help members understand the hidden assumptions in their statements. Information or opinion analyzers make statements such as "Enrique, you're generalizing from only one instance. Can you give us some others?"

Maintenance Roles

Maintenance roles are the sets of behaviors that help the group to develop and maintain cohesion, commitment, and positive working relationships. We engage in maintenance leadership any time we manage participation, foster collabora-tion to resolve conflict, or integrate fun into the group experience. Managing participation means giving everyone an opportunity to share ideas and information with the group and ensuring that no group member or members dominate the discussion. Fostering col-laboration to resolve conflict means acting as an unbiased mediator when disagreements between members become heated so that the conflict is resolved as a win-win.

Integrating fun into the group experience means intervening in the group's pro-cess in order to reduce tension by encouraging the group to relax, laugh, and enjoy each other's company. We know that humor has a positive impact on group communi-cation. Noted psychotherapist and business consultant S. M. Sultanoff (1993) explains that "humor facilitates communication, builds relationships, reduces stress, provides perspective, and promotes attending and energizes" (para 2). Fortune 500 companies such as General Electric, AT&T, Kodak, Lockheed, and IBM all emphasize the value of workplace humor in their training programs.

Members who undertake maintenance leadership roles will be supporters, inter-preters, harmonizers, mediators, or interpreters.

- Supporters encourage others in the group. When another member contributes to the group, supporters show appreciation through their nonverbal or verbal behavior. Nonverbally, supporters may smile, nod, or vigorously shake their heads. Verbally, they demonstrate support through statements like "Good point, Ming," "I really like that idea, Nikki," or "It's obvious you've really done your homework, Janelle."

- Interpreters are familiar with the differences in the social, cultural, and gender orien-tations of group members and use this knowledge to help group members understand each other. Interpreters are especially important in groups whose members are cultur-ally diverse (Jensen & Chilberg, 1991). For example, an interpreter might say, "Paul, Lin Chou is Chinese, so when she says that she will think about your plan she might mean that she does not support your ideas, but she doesn't want to embarrass you in front of the others." Or an interpreter might say, "Jim, most of us are from the South and consider it impolite to begin business before we socialize and catch up with one

Some members provide information to the group, others help maintain harmonious relations among group members, and still others help the group stay on track. When you are part of a problem solving group, which roles do you usually assume?

maintenance roles
sets of behaviors that help a group develop and maintain cohesion, commitment, and positive working relationships.

A good logistics coordinator leads by providing for the physical needs of the group and its members. Can you think of a group experience you have had in which no one provided this type of leadership?

another." When groups do not have a member to serve in the interpreter leadership role and members come from different cultures, effective group process can suffer. This was the case for Lily Herakova when she came to the United States from Bulgaria to study. You can read Lily's story in the Diverse Voices feature in this chapter.

- Harmonizers intervene in the group's discussion when conflict is threatening to harm group cohesiveness or the relationship between specific group members. Harmonizers are likely to make statements such as "Tom, Jack, hold it a second. I know you're on opposite sides of this, but let's see where you might have some agreement" or "Cool it, everybody, we're coming up with some good stuff; let's not lose our momentum by getting into name-calling."

- Mediators are neutral and impartial arbiters who guide the discussion so that members who have conflicting ideas find a mutually acceptable resolution. Mediators do this by maintaining their own neutrality, keeping the discussion focused on issues and not personalities, helping to identify areas of common ground, and working to find a mutually satisfying solution to the disagreement using paraphrasing and perception checking.

- Tension relievers recognize when group members are stressed or tired and then intervene to relieve the stress or reenergize the group usually through humor. People who are effective in this leadership role might tell a joke, kid around, or tell a lighthearted story so that the group is refreshed when it returns to the task. In some situations, a single well-placed one-liner will get a laugh, break the tension or monotony, and jolt the group out of its lethargy. Although the tension reliever momentarily distracts the group from its task, this action helps the group remain cohesive.

Procedural Roles

Procedural leadership roles are sets of behaviors that directly support the group process. This includes providing logistical support for the group, managing the group's interaction, and keeping records of the group's accomplishments and decisions.

- Logistics coordinators arrange for appropriate spaces for group meetings, procure the supplies and equipment that will be needed by the group, and manage other details so that the group's physical needs are met. The logistics coordinator's leadership role is usually carried out behind the scenes, but the successful performance of this role is crucial to a group's ability to be efficient and effective. Making arrangements so that the group has appropriate space, furniture, and equipment and providing for the physical needs of members during the meeting allows the group to efficiently work on its tasks

- Expediters keep track of what the group is trying to accomplish and help move the group through the agenda. When the group has strayed, expediters will make statements like "I'm enjoying this, but I can't quite see what it has to do with resolving the issue" or "Let's see, aren't we still trying to find out whether these are the only criteria that we should be considering?"

- Gatekeepers manage the flow of conversation so that all members have an equal opportunity to participate. If one or two members begin to dominate the conversation, the gatekeeper acknowledges this and invites other group members to participate. Gatekeepers also notice nonverbal signals that indicate that a member

procedural leadership roles

sets of behaviors that directly support a group process.

The Effects of Cultural Diversity When Problem Solving in Groups

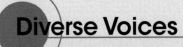

by Lily Herakova

Ph.D. student, University of Massachusetts, Amherst

I'll never forget the day—it must have been early October—the rural Minnesota town where I had arrived from Bulgaria to pursue my dreams of attaining a diverse and challenging education was still holding on to the warm traces of summer. In history class that day, the professor assigned us to work in what he called "problem solving groups." We were to review each other's papers and offer suggestions for improvement. He said, "Use this not only as an editing exercise, but as a problem solving activity. I want you to rely on your group partners' responses to move toward solutions of problems you might be having in your papers." Because I was not sure I understood the professor, I asked for clarification. One of my classmates explained that we were to identify problem areas in the papers and make suggestions for improvement to the author. Then, through further discussion with group members, the author was to make sense of the comments and use the ones he or she agreed with to improve the manuscript. I realize today that the professor's definition of a problem solving group was pretty loosely defined. We would not be working together as a group to arrive at a solution to one problem. However, we did have to work in groups to solve problems. So, to be most effective, it would be important to engage in shared leadership.

The bright sunshine outside the classroom window carried me away and, in my mind, I was back in my parents' bedroom in Bulgaria. That was where our family computer was and where, consequently, I did a lot of my paper writing and editing. (Nostalgia has a strange way of creeping in to the most mundane activities.) Although I hadn't ever been asked to do so in a class with my

peers before, I thought to myself: "I know how to do this. I've done it plenty of times. In fact, it's kind of cool that professors here in the United States allow us time in class to 'problem-solve' and learn from each other." Confident in my understanding, I began reading my classmates' papers. I was going to help "solve problems" and help my group mates improve their papers.

I was fairly confident because back home in Bulgaria my friends and I often reviewed each others' papers and offered suggestions for improvement. Although I had never heard of the concept of "problem solving in groups," it seemed to me I actually had experience in doing so. You see, in Bulgaria computers and printers were scarce and it cost a lot of money to hire someone to type and print your term paper. So my parents agreed to let my friends use our computer to type and print their papers. Because classes in Bulgaria were usually large lectures where we rarely knew our professors, our insecurities about expectations abounded. Our collaborative paper writing was our way of checking perceptions in terms of identifying and defining the goals (e.g., problem) of the assignment, getting information from each other (e.g., analyzing the problem), and developing papers that met the assignment guidelines (e.g., solution). So, we did actually solve problems in groups. It was just something my friends and I did informally as opposed to as an in-class activity.

My friends and I would assemble in my parents' sunny bedroom to "problem solve" about the goal of the assignment and help each other prepare papers that met the goal. One of us dictated the draft of her paper while another typed using only her two pointer-fingers. The other group members listened and offered on-the-spot suggestions for revising the essay in ways that more clearly met the goal (at least what we believed it to be) of the assignment. In our informal problem solving

(*Continued*)

sessions, my Bulgarian classmates and I would offer conflicting opinions, argue, and laugh about our "mistakes." We straightforwardly pointed out when we thought something in the text was wrong, and quietly swallowed our pride as the others made candid comments and offered constructive criticism. For example, members might say, "This sentence doesn't make any sense," "It's grammatically weird," "It's completely missing a verb," or "How is this even relevant?" Responses to this feedback ranged from anger—"I give up! No one seems to get me!"—to much quieter resignation—"Fine I'll just do it your way…." Most of the time, though, reactions fell somewhere in between. We often dove into long conversations about what someone actually wanted to say and why it wasn't coming through that way on paper.

Though sometimes painful to hear, more often than not, these group sessions helped me. Comments the others made sometimes hurt my pride but often deepened the analysis of my paper and always clarified my thoughts and my writing. As often happens, what seems so obvious to the writer might not be so obvious to the reader, and what the writer might overlook becomes a glaring oversight to the reader. At least that was my experience…my friends helped me define the problems in my papers and our conversations suggested possible solutions. Ultimately, we all benefitted because we produced papers that usually met and often exceeded the expectations of the instructor.

So, in history class that day in rural Minnesota, I felt I had the proper experience to participate effectively in what he called "problem solving" groups! I proceeded confidently to read the papers. When I read one of the papers and it was mostly composed of incomplete sentences, I said to the author, "This will make so much more sense if you would write in complete sentences. It's kind of hard to get what you mean when you're missing verbs." In retrospect, I only remember what I said because of the reaction that followed. She immediately raised her hand to call the instructor over to our group and said, "I don't know why you let her respond to our papers. She's not even a native English speaker, and she's telling me I don't know how to write! I want someone else to read my paper." I believed I was acting appropriately in my role as an information analyzer, which was what our instructor expected us to do. My group member, however, was unwilling to listen (regardless of whether I may have been correct) because English was not my first language. I would argue that she responded in a self-centered way that hurt the functioning of the group toward our overall goal.

To this day, I don't know for certain if her reaction was due to cultural differences (perhaps ethnocentrism), an inability to accept feedback (especially accepting constructive criticism), or some other issue. Throughout the years, however, this experience has stayed with me as an unresolved confusion—why did my nationality matter in terms of functioning as an analyzer in the group? Did it somehow automatically disqualify me from having a good command of the English language or a good understanding of history? I could have taken her response personally and been hurt by it, but, interestingly, this was not my reaction. Instead, throughout my education as an undergraduate student, a master's student, and now a Ph.D. student in the United States, I keep this question in the forefront of my mind when asked to work in a group to solve problems: How can we problem solve together without creating new problems out of our good-natured attempts to "help," especially when cultural diversity might play a role?

Skill Learning Activity 10.4
Web Resource 10.3

wishes to speak. The gatekeeper is the one who sees that Juanita is on the edge of her chair, eager to comment, and says, "We haven't heard from Juanita, and she seems to have something she wants to say."

- Recorders take careful notes of what the group has decided and the evidence upon which the decisions are based. Recorders usually distribute edited copies of their notes to group members prior to the next meeting. Sometimes these notes are published as minutes, which become a public record of the group's activities.

Making Meetings Effective

The disastrous meeting experience recorded in the chapter opener stemmed from poor meeting management skills by both the meeting facilitator and by those who attended the meeting. In a recent survey, business consultant Dike Drummond (2004) discovered that over 50 percent of managers spend at least six hours per week in meetings and these same managers feel 50 percent of their meeting time is wasted! To ensure that your meetings are not a waste of your time or that of others, let's look at guidelines for meeting leaders and meeting participants.

> What are group member responsibilities when participating in meetings?

Guidelines for Meeting Leaders

Most of us will be responsible for convening a group meeting at some point in our lives. Whether you are leading the meeting for a class project, a task force at work, or substituting for your manager at the monthly department meeting, knowing how to effectively plan for, facilitate, and follow up after meetings are useful skills.

Before the meeting

1. Prepare and distribute an agenda. An **agenda** is an organized outline of the information and decision items that will be covered during a meeting. It is a road map that lets the members know the purpose of the meeting and what they are expected to accomplish as a result of attending. Agenda items should move the group toward its goals and should not include items that could be accomplished without the presence (albeit in a face-to-face or virtual environment) of all of the meeting attendees.

   You can identify the items for your agenda by
   - reviewing your notes and the formal minutes of the previous meeting;
   - identifying what the group decided would be its work between meetings; and
   - identifying what decisions it expected to make in the next session.

   Then you can structure the agenda into information items and decision items, having members report on their assignments and then, based on what has been learned or accomplished, moving to make relevant decisions.

   It is critical to distribute the agenda at least 24 hours before the meeting so that members have time to prepare. You can e-mail the agenda, post it to the group's Web page, or hand-deliver it. None of us likes to come to a meeting and be embarrassed because we have forgotten to complete an assignment, and most of us don't like to be called on to make decisions that we have not had time to think about. Being unprepared is one of the main reasons that time is wasted in meetings. As the meeting leader, you are responsible for providing the information that members need in order to come prepared. Figure 10.3 shows an agenda for a group that is meeting to decide which one of three courses to offer over the Internet next semester.

2. Decide who should attend the meeting. In most cases, all members of a group will attend meetings. Occasionally, one or more members of the group may not need to attend a particular meeting but may only need to be informed of the outcomes later.

3. Manage meeting logistics. You may choose to enact this role or to ask another group member to do this. But even if you delegate these tasks, it remains your responsibility to make sure that the meeting arrangements are appropriate. If the group is meeting face to face you will want a room that is appropriate to the size and work of the group, and you will want to make sure that all of the equipment that the group needs is on hand and operational. The room should be set up so that it encourages group interaction. This usually means that members can sit around a table or in a circle with plenty of desk/table space for writing. If the entire group or some group

agenda
an organized outline of the information and decision items that will be covered during a meeting.

March 1, 2009

To: Campus computer discussion group

From: Janelle Smith

Re: Agenda for discussion group meeting

Meeting Date: March 8, 2009

Place: Student Union, Conference Room A

Time: 3:00 p.m. to 4:30 p.m.

Meeting objectives
- We will familiarize ourselves with each of three courses that have been proposed for Internet-based delivery next semester.
- We will evaluate each course against the criteria we developed last month.
- We will use a consensus decision process to determine which of the three courses to offer.

Agenda for Group discussion
- Review and discussion of Philosophy 141 (Report by Justin)
- Review and discussion of Art History 336 (Report by Marique)
- Review and discussion of Communication 235 (Report by Kathryn)

Consensus building discussion and decision
- Which proposals fit the criteria?
- Are there non-criteria-related factors to consider?
- Which proposal is more acceptable to all members?

Discussion of next steps and task assignments

Set date of next meeting

Figure 10.3
Agenda for Internet course committee

members are attending the meeting from remote locations you will need to make sure that the technology needed to conference them in has been provided. Because groups become less effective in long meetings, a meeting should last no longer than ninety minutes. If a meeting must be planned for a longer period of time, use segments of no longer than ninety minutes with scheduled breaks to avoid fatigue.

4. **Speak with each participant prior to the meeting.** As the leader, it is important for you to understand members' positions and personal goals. Time spent discussing issues in advance allows you to anticipate conflicts that might emerge and plan how to manage them so that the group makes effective decisions and maintains cohesiveness.

During the meeting

1. **Review and modify the agenda.** Begin the meeting by reviewing the agenda and modifying it based on members' suggestions. Because things can change between distribution of the agenda and the meeting, reviewing the agenda ensures that the group will be working on items that are still relevant. Reviewing the agenda also gives members a chance to give input into what is to be discussed.

2. **Monitor member interaction.** If other group members are assuming the task-related, maintenance, and procedural functions, you need do nothing. But when there is a need for a particular role and no one is assuming it, you should do so. For example,

if you notice that some people are talking more than their fair share and no one is trying to draw out quieter members, you should assume the gatekeeper role and invite reluctant members to comment on the discussion. Similarly, if a discussion becomes too heated, you may need to take on the role of harmonizer so relationships are not unduly strained.

3. Monitor the time. It is easy for a group to get bogged down in a discussion. Although another group member may serve as expediter, it is your responsibility as meeting leader to make sure that the group stays on schedule.

4. Praise in public and reprimand in private. Meetings provide an excellent opportunity to praise individuals or the entire group for jobs well done. Being recognized among one's peers often boosts self-esteem, group morale, and synergy. Conversely, criticizing individuals or the entire group during a meeting has the opposite effect. The humiliation of public criticism can deflate self-esteem, group morale, and motivation.

5. Check periodically to see if the group is ready to make a decision. You should listen carefully for agreement among members and move the group into its formal decision-making process when the discussion is no longer adding insight.

6. Implement the group's decision rules. You are responsible for executing the decision-making rule the group has agreed to use. If the group is deciding by consensus, for example, you must make sure all members feel they can support the chosen alternative. If the group is deciding by majority rule, you call for the vote and tally the results.

7. Summarize decisions and assignments. You should summarize what has happened and what is left to accomplish, as well as reiterate task assignments made during the meeting, and review what is left to accomplish or decide.

8. Set the next meeting. You should clarify with members when, and if, future meetings are necessary. The overall purposes of the next meeting will dictate what you'll put in the next agenda.

© 2002 Ted Goff

© 2002 Ted Goff www.tedgoff.com

"At 10:01, Mr. Holtz fell asleep. At 10:17, Ms. Sommer fell asleep. At 10:31, everyone else fell asleep. Those are the minutes of our last meeting."

Following up

1. Review the meeting outcomes and process. A good leader learns how to be more effective by reflecting on how well the meeting went. Did the meeting accomplish its goals? Was group cohesion improved or damaged in the process? What will you do differently next time to improve the experience?

2. Prepare and distribute a meeting summary. Although in some groups, a member serves as the recorder and distributes minutes, many groups rely on their leader. Having a written record of what was agreed to and accomplished as well as assignments that members agreed to complete prior to the next meeting and the decision items the group agreed to consider next time gives members an opportunity to review the group's progress and to correct any mistakes in the record. If the group has a recorder, you should review the minutes and compare them to your notes before they are distributed. Summaries are most useful when they are distributed within two or three days of the meeting when everyone's memories are still fresh.

3. Repair damaged relationships. If the debate during the meeting was heated, some members may have damaged their relationships or left the meeting angry or hurt. You should help repair relationships by seeking out these participants and talking with them. Through empathic listening, you can soothe hurt feelings and spark a recommitment to the group.

4. Conduct informal progress reports. When participants have been assigned specific task responsibilities, you should periodically check in to see if they have encountered any problems in completing those tasks and how you might help them.

Guidelines for Meeting Participants

Just as there are guidelines for effective conveners/formal leaders to follow before, during, and after meetings, there are also guidelines to help meeting participants.

Before the meeting

As the chapter opener illustrated, too often people think of group meetings as a "happening" that requires attendance but no preparation. Countless times we have observed people arriving at a meeting unprepared even though they are carrying packets of material they received in advance. To be worthwhile, meetings should not be treated as impromptu events but as carefully planned interactions that pool information from well-prepared individuals. Here are some important steps for members to take prior to attending a meeting.

1. **Study the agenda.** Consider the purpose of the meeting and determine what you need to do to be prepared. If you had an assignment, make sure that you will be ready to report on it.
2. **Study the minutes.** If this is one in a series of meetings, read the minutes and your own notes from the previous meeting. What happened at the previous meeting should provide the basis for preparing for the next one.
3. **Do your homework.** Read the material distributed prior to the meeting and do your own research to become better informed about items on the agenda. If no material is provided, then identify the issues and learn what you need to know to be a productive group member. Bring any materials you find that may help the group accomplish the agenda. If some members will not be able to attend, solicit their ideas about the agenda.
4. **List questions.** Make a list of questions related to agenda items that you would like to have answered during the meeting.
5. **Plan to play a leadership role.** Consider which leadership functions and roles you are best at. Decide what you will do to play those roles to the best of your ability.

Some people wait until the last minute to prepare for meetings. Do you find it annoying to attend meetings where people come unprepared to participate?

Tony Freeman/PhotoEdit

During the meeting

Go into the meeting planning to be a full participant. If there are five people in the group, all five should be participating.

1. **Listen attentively.** Concentrate on what others are saying so that you can use your material to complement, supplement, or counter what is presented.
2. **Stay focused.** It is easy to get off track during meetings. Keep your comments focused on the specific agenda item under discussion. If others get off the subject, do what you can to get the discussion back on track.
3. **Ask questions.** Honest questions, whose answers you do not already know, help stimulate discussion and build ideas.

4. **Take notes.** Even if someone else is responsible for providing the official minutes, you'll need notes that help you follow the discussion's line of development. Also, these notes will help you remember what has been said and any responsibilities you have agreed to take on after the meeting.

5. **Play devil's advocate.** When you think an idea has not been fully discussed or tested, be willing to voice disagreement or encourage further discussion.

6. **Monitor your contributions.** Especially when people are well prepared, they have a tendency to dominate discussion. Make sure that you are neither dominating the discussion nor abdicating your responsibility to share insights and opinions.

Web Resource 10.4

Following these guidelines for participating responsibly in meetings will make them a more pleasant and productive experience. Although most meetings used to be conducted face to face, today more meetings are occurring via teleconference, video conference, and online social networks. Engaging responsibly in virtual meetings has some unique challenges, particularly in staying focused and listening attentively.

Following up

When meetings end, too often people leave and forget about what took place until the next meeting. But what happens in one meeting provides a basis for what happens in the next. You must do your part to prepare to move forward at the next meeting.

1. **Review and summarize your notes.** Try to do this shortly after the meeting while ideas are still fresh in your mind. Make notes of what needs to be discussed next time.

2. **Evaluate your effectiveness.** How effective were you in helping the group move toward achieving its goals? Where were you strong? Where were you weak? What should you do next time to improve and how? For example, if you didn't speak up as much as you would have liked to, perhaps you'll decide to write down questions or topics when they come to you and use them as notes to encourage you to speak up next time.

3. **Review decisions.** Make notes about what your role was in making decisions. Did you do all that you could have done? If not, what will you do differently next time, why, and how?

4. **Communicate progress.** Inform others who need to know about information conveyed and decisions made in the meeting.

5. **Complete your tasks.** Make sure you complete all assignments you received in the meeting.

6. **Review minutes.** Compare the official meeting minutes to your own notes, and report any significant discrepancies to the member who prepared the minutes.

Skill Learning Activity 10.5

Conversation and Analysis

Use your Premium Website for *Communicate!* to access **Skill Learning Activity 10.6,** which is a video clip of the Student Government Financial Committee meeting. As you watch the conversation, observe the group's dynamics. Is its goal clear? Is its membership sufficiently diverse? What stage of group development does the committee appear to be in? Are the members using the problem solving method? What roles are being played by each member? Do they appear to be prepared for the meeting? You can respond to these analysis questions by clicking on "Critique" in the menu bar at the

Problem Solving in Cyberspace: *Dungeons & Dragons* and *World of Warcraft*

Pop Comm!

AP Photo/Eckehard Schulz

For some, the role-playing games *Dungeons & Dragons* and *World of Warcraft* might conjure up the stereotypical image of a teenage boy typing away at his computer, alone. But role-playing games are actually social interactions that encourage successful group problem solving, incorporating the six steps we discuss

in this chapter: identifying and defining the problem, analyzing the problem, developing criteria for evaluation solutions, brainstorming possible solutions, selecting one, and implementing it.

Dungeons & Dragons, the first modern role-playing game of its kind (Williams, Hendricks, & Winkler, 2006), is typically played among a group of friends at a table, without a computer. A Dungeon Master narrates and creates rules for a fantasy story, and people at the table act as the story's characters. Together, the players work to defeat monsters, find treasure, gain experience, and face other challenges. One of the creators of *Dungeons & Dragons*, Gary Gygax, said in a 2006 telephone interview, "The essence of a role-playing game is that it is a group, cooperative experience. There is no winning or losing" (Schiesel, 2008). *Newsweek*'s Patrick Enright remembers his own *Dungeons & Dragons* experiences as a boy (Ebeling, 2008):

Skill Learning Activity 10.6

Jason Harris/Thomson Higher Education/ Wadsworth Publishing Group

top of the screen. When you've answered all the questions, click "Done" to compare your answers to those provided by the authors.

As members of the Student Government Financial Committee, Davinia, Joyce, Thomas, and Pat make decisions on how much funding, if any, to give to various student groups that request support from the funds collected from student fees. They are meeting for the first time in a campus cafeteria.

Conversation

THOMAS: Well, we've got 23 applications for funding and a total of $19,000 that we can distribute.

DAVINIA: Maybe we should start by listing how much each of the 23 groups wants.

JOYCE: It might be better to start by determining the criteria that we will use to decide if groups get any funding from student fees.

DAVINIA: Yeah, right. We should set up our criteria before we look at applications.

If you suddenly wanted to attack your traveling companions with a broadsword or a Finger of Death spell, there was nothing stopping you. The amazing thing is how rarely that happened. Unless the neighborhood bully joined in (and almost never did those tanned, skinned-kneed fellas venture into our dank lairs), we all helped each other and together defeated whatever dragon or monster we were battling. Yes, I'll say it: *Dungeons & Dragons* taught me everything I need to know about teamwork.

Dungeons & Dragon inspired *World of Warcraft*, a popular MMORPG (massively multiplayer online role-playing game). *World of Warcraft* differs from *Dungeons & Dragons* in that it is played online, and the game, instead of a human Dungeon Master, regulates the story and the rules. To significantly advance in the game, players must still work with others to defeat monsters, find treasure, and gain experience, but they communicate with one another using text or voice chat programs (Newman, 2007).

In a *Business Week Online* article, researcher John Seely Brown and business consultant John Hagel (2009) argue that many aspects of *World of Warcraft* encourage group problem solving and can even be applied as innovative workplace strategies. These aspects include

- Creating opportunities for teams to self-organize around challenging performance targets.
- Providing opportunities to develop tacit knowledge without neglecting the exchange of broader knowledge.
- Encouraging frequent and rigorous performance feedback.

But beyond the application to real-life situations, many fans of role-playing find that the complexities of group problem solving make things more interesting and more exciting. In *The Escapist*, an online magazine about video games, Ray Huling (2008) writes of *Dungeons & Dragons*, "Players can mitigate the chaos inherent in a game's dice by agreeing to ignore rolls, but they can also intensify chaos by pissing off (or on!) huge barbarians. The group decides whether encouraging mischief-makers adds to the game." He adds, "Group dynamics produce unforeseen complications, which often maximize fun."

THOMAS: Sounds good to me. Pat, what do you think?

PAT: I'm on board. Let's set up criteria first and then review the applications against those.

JOYCE: OK, we might start by looking at the criteria used last year by the Financial Committee. Does anyone have a copy of those?

THOMAS: I do. *(He passes out copies to the other three people.)* They had three criteria: service to a significant number of students, compliance with the college's nondiscrimination policies, and educational benefit.

DAVINIA: What counts as "educational benefit"? Did last year's committee specify that?

JOYCE: Good question. Thomas, you were on the committee last year. Do you remember what they counted as educational benefit?

THOMAS: The main thing I remember is that it was distinguished from artistic benefit—like a concert or art exhibit or something like that.

PAT: But can't art be educational?

Jason Harris/Thomson Higher Education/ Wadsworth Publishing Group

DAVINIA: Yeah, I think so. Thomas, Joyce, do you?

THOMAS: I guess, but it's like art's primary purpose isn't to educate.

JOYCE: I agree. It's kind of hard to put into words, but I think educational benefit has more to do with information and the mind, and art has more to do with the soul. Does that sound too hokey? *(Laughter.)*

PAT: OK, so we want to say that we don't distribute funds to any hokey groups, right? *(More laughter.)*

DAVINIA: It's not like we're against art or anything. It's just that the funding we can distribute is for educational benefit, right? *(Everyone nods.)*

JOYCE: OK, let's move on to another criterion. What is the significant number of students?

THOMAS: Last year we said that the proposals for using money had to be of potential interest to at least 20 percent of students to get funding. How does that sound to you?

PAT: Sounds OK as long as we remember that something can be of potential interest to students who aren't members of specific groups. Like, for instance, I might want to attend a program on Native American customs even though I'm not a Native American. See what I mean?

DAVINIA: Good point—we don't want to define student interest as student identity or anything like that. *(Nods of agreement.)*

THOMAS: OK, so are we agreed that 20 percent is about right with the understanding that the 20 percent can include students who aren't in a group applying for funding? *(Nods.)* OK, then, do we need to discuss the criterion of compliance with the college's policies on nondiscrimination?

Communicating Group Solutions

Once a group has completed its deliberations, it is usually expected to communicate what it has decided to someone or some other body. **Deliverables** are tangible or intangible products of your work that must be provided to someone else. Although some deliverables are objects, typically the deliverables from problem solving groups are communications of the information gathered, analyses, decisions, and recommendations of the group. These kinds of intangible deliverables can be communicated in written formats, oral formats, or visual and audiovisual formats.

> How can groups communicate their solutions to others?

Written Formats

deliverables
tangible or intangible products of work that must be provided to someone else.

written brief
a very short document that describes a problem, background, process, decision, and rationale so that a reader can quickly understand and evaluate a group's product.

1. Written brief. A **written brief** is a very short document that describes the problem, background, process, decision, and rationale so that the reader can quickly understand and evaluate the group's product. Most briefs are one or two pages long. When preparing a brief, begin by describing your group's task. What problem were you attempting to solve and why? Then briefly provide the background information the reader will need to evaluate whether the group has adequately studied the problem. Present solution steps and timelines for implementation as bullet points so that the reader can quickly understand what is being proposed. Close with a sentence or very short paragraph that describes how the recommendation will solve the problem, as well as any potential side effects.

2. Comprehensive report. A **comprehensive report** is a written document that provides a detailed review of the problem solving process used to arrive at the recommendation. A comprehensive report is usually organized into sections that parallel the problem solving process.

   Because comprehensive reports can be very long, they usually include an executive summary. An **executive summary** is a one-page synopsis of the report. This summary contains enough information to acquaint readers with the highlights of the full document without reading it. Usually, it contains a statement of the problem, some background information, a description of any alternatives, and the major conclusions.

Oral Formats

1. Oral brief. An **oral brief** is essentially a summary of a written brief delivered to an audience by a group member. Typically, an oral brief can be delivered in less than 10 minutes.
2. Oral report. An **oral report** is similar to a comprehensive report. It provides a more detailed review of a group's problem solving process. Oral reports can range from 30 to 60 minutes.
3. Symposium. A **symposium** is a set of prepared oral reports delivered sequentially by group members before a gathering of people who are interested in the work of the group. A symposium may be organized so that each person's speech focuses on one step of the problem solving process, or it may be organized so that each speaker covers all of the steps in the problem solving process as they relate to one of several issues or recommendations that the group worked on or made. In a symposium format, the speakers usually sit together at the front of the room. One member acts as moderator, offering the introductory and concluding remarks and providing transitions between speakers. When introduced by the moderator, each speaker may stand and walk to a central spot, usually a lectern. Speakers who are going to use PowerPoint visuals should coordinate their slides so that there can be seamless transitions between speakers. Symposiums often conclude with a question-and-answer session facilitated by the moderator, who directs one or more of the members to answer based on their expertise. Questions can be directed to individuals or to the group as a whole.
4. Panel discussion. A **panel discussion** is a structured problem solving discussion held by a group in front of an audience. One member serves as moderator, introducing the topic and providing structure by asking a series of planned questions that panelists answer. Their answers and the interaction among them provide the supporting evidence. A well-planned panel discussion seems spontaneous and interactive but requires careful planning and rehearsal to ensure that all relevant information is presented and that all speakers are afforded equal speaking time. After the formal discussion, the audience is often encouraged to question the participants. Perhaps you've seen or heard a panel of experts discuss a topic on a radio or television talk show like *Sports Center* or *The View*.

Virtual Reports

1. Remote access reports. A **remote access report (RAR)** is a computer-mediated audiovisual presentation of the group's process and outcome that others can receive through e-mail, Web posting, and so forth. Prepared by one or more members of the group, the RAR is prepared in PowerPoint or other computer software and provides a visual overview of the group's process, decisions, and

---

comprehensive report
a written document that provides a detailed review of the problem solving process used to arrive at a recommendation.

executive summary
a one-page synopsis of a comprehensive report.

oral brief
a summary of a written brief delivered to an audience by a group member.

oral report
a detailed review of a group's problem solving process delivered to an audience by one or more group members.

symposium
a set of prepared oral reports delivered sequentially by group members before a gathering of people who are interested in the work of the group.

panel discussion
a structured problem solving discussion held by a group in front of an audience.

panel discussion
a structured problem solving discussion held by a group in front of an audience.

remote access report (RAR)
a computer-mediated audiovisual presentation of a group's process and outcome that others can receive electronically.

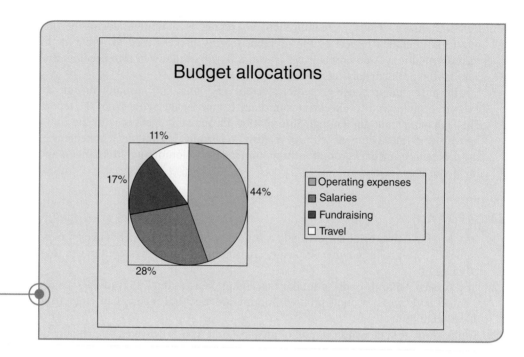

Figure 10.4

Example of a slide in a remote access report

recommendations. Effective RARs consist of no more than 15 to 20 slides. Slides are titled and content is presented in outline or bullet-point phrases or key words (rather than complete sentences or paragraphs), as well through visual representations of important information. For example, a budget task force might have a slide with a pie chart depicting the portions of the proposed budget that are allocated to operating expenses, salaries, fundraising, and travel (see Figure 10.4). RARs may be self-running so that the slides automatically forward after a certain number of seconds, but it is better to let the viewer choose the pace and control when the next slide appears. RARs can be silent or narrated. When narrated, a voice-over accompanies each slide, providing additional or explanatory information.

2. Streaming videos. A **streaming video** is a pre-recording that is sent in compressed form over the Internet. You are probably familiar with streaming video from popular Websites such as YouTube. Streaming videos are a great way to distribute oral briefs, but they also can be used to distribute recordings of oral reports, symposiums, or panel presentations. Streaming videos are useful when it is inconvenient for some or all the people who need to know the results of the group's work to meet at one time or in one place.

Speech Assignment: Communicate on Your Feet

Panel Discussion

The Assignment

Form a small group with 3–5 classmates. As a group, decide on a social issue or problem you would like to study in depth. Then select one group member to serve as moderator and the others as expert panelists. Each member should do research to find out all they can about the issue, why it is a problem, how it affects people and to what degree, as well as

streaming video
a pre-recording that is sent in compressed form over the Internet.

potential ideas for solving it. The moderator's role is to come up with 4–6 good questions to ask the panelists. The panelists should prepare notes about the research they discovered.

On the day determined by the instructor, you will engage in a 15- to 20-minute panel discussion in front of your classmates. The moderator will guide the discussion by asking questions of the panelists, as well as asking for questions from the class.

Suggested Format

1. Moderator thanks audience for coming and introduces the panelists and the topic.
2. Moderator asks panelists a series of questions, letting a different panelist respond first each time.
3. Moderator asks follow-up questions when appropriate.
4. Moderator asks for questions from the audience.
5. Moderator thanks the panelists and the audience members for participating.

A Question of Ethics

What Would You Do?

"You know, Sue, we're going to be in deep trouble if the group doesn't support McGowan's resolution about dues reform."

"Well, we'll just have to see to it that all the arguments in favor of that resolution are heard, but in the end it's the group's decision."

"That's very democratic of you, Sue, but you know that if it doesn't pass, you're likely to be out on your tail."

"That may be, Heather, but I don't see what I can do about it."

"You don't want to see. First, right now the group respects you. If you would just apply a little pressure on a couple of the members, you'd get what you want."

"What do you mean?"

"Look, this is a good cause. You've got something on just about every member of the group.

Take a couple of members aside and let them know that this is payoff time. I think you'll see that some key folks will see it your way."

1. Should Sue follow Heather's advice? Why or why not?
2. Is it appropriate to use personal influence to affect the outcome of group decisions? If you answered yes, at what point does the use of personal influence cross the line from ethical to unethical behavior? If you answered no, explain why personal influence shouldn't be one of the many factors groups consider when making decisions?

Summary

In this chapter, you learned about an effective process for problem solving developed by John Dewey over 75 years ago. That six-step process consists of identifying and defining the problem, analyzing the problem, developing criteria for evaluating solutions, brainstorming possible solutions, selecting a solution, and implementing it.

You also learned about the leadership skills needed to effectively manage group interactions during problem solving. These shared leadership skills focus on task, maintenance, and procedural roles.

Then, we explained your responsibilities as group convener and as group participant before, during, and after meetings. Finally, we talked about the different formats you might choose from to share your solutions with others. These formats can be written, oral, or visual/audiovisual. By following the guidelines we offer in this chapter, you will find your participation in problem solving groups to be both pleasant and productive.

Communicate! Online

Now that you have read Chapter 10, use your Premium Website for *Communicate!* for quick access to the electronic resources that accompany this text. These resources include

- **Study tools** that will help you assess your learning and prepare for exams (*digital glossary, key term flash cards, review quizzes*).
- **Activities and assignments** that will help you hone your knowledge, analyze communication situations (*Skill Learning Activities)*, and build your public speaking skills throughout the course (*Communication on Your Feet speech assignments, Action Step activities*). Many of these activities allow you to compare your answers to those provided by the authors, and, if requested, submit your answers to your instructor.

- **Media resources** that will help you explore communication concepts online (*Web Resources*), develop your speech outlines (*Speech Builder Express 3.0*), watch and critique videos of communication situations and sample speeches (*Interactive Video Activities*), upload your speech videos for peer reviewing and critique other students' speeches (*Speech Studio online speech review tool*), and download chapter review so you can study when and where you'd like (*Audio Study Tools*).

This chapter's Key Terms, Skill Learning Activities, and Web Resources are also featured on the following pages, and you can find this chapter's Communicate on Your Feet assignment in the body of the chapter.

Key Terms

agenda (235)
brainstorming (228)
comprehensive report (243)
criteria (227)
decision making (229)
executive summary (243)
informal or emergent leader (230)

maintenance roles (231)
oral brief (243)
oral report (243)
panel discussion (243)
problem definition (226)
procedural roles (232)
question of fact (226)
question of policy (226)

question of value (226)
remote access report
   (RAR) (243)
shared leadership functions (230)
streaming video (244)
symposium (243)
task roles (230)
written brief (242)

Skill Learning Activities

10.1: Stating Problems (226)

Indicate whether each of the following is a question of fact, a question of value, or a question of policy. When you're done with this activity, compare your answers to the authors' at the Premium Website for *Communicate!* Look for them in the Skill Learning activities for Chapter 10.

1. What should we do to increase the quality of finished parts?
2. Do police stop African American drivers more frequently than other drivers?
3. Should television news organizations use exit polls to call elections?
4. Is John guilty of involuntary manslaughter?
5. Is seniority the best method of handling employee layoffs?
6. What is the best vacation plan for our family?

10.2: How Does Your Group Solve Problems? (230)

Analyze a situation in which a group to which you belong attempted to solve a problem. Write a paragraph in which you answer the following questions. Did the group use all six of the problem solving steps listed in this chapter? If not, which steps did the group overlook? Were there any steps the group should have placed more emphasis on? Was the group successful in its efforts to solve the problem? Explain why you think this was or was not the case.

10.3: Emerging Informal Leadership in CBS's *Survivor* Series (230)

Watch a recent episode of one of the popular CBS *Survivor* series. Select one tribe and identify the dominant roles that each member of the group seems to play in that episode. Who is vying for informal leadership? How are they trying to gain or maintain their leadership? What do you think will happen to each leader candidate?

To help you complete this activity, use the link to the Website for each *Survivor* series provided in your Premium Website for *Communicate!* (Look for it in the Skill Learning Activities for Chapter 10.) Click on the "Video" link in the menu at the top of the home page to access video to each season's episodes. Click on the "Recaps" link for the group you chose and see how well your predictions held up. Write a short essay describing what you have learned.

10.4: Identifying Roles (234)

Match the typical comment to the role it is most characteristic of. When you're done with this activity, compare your answers to the authors' at the Premium Website for *Communicate!* Look for them in the Skill Learning Activities for Chapter 10.

Roles
a. aggressor
b. analyzer
c. expediter
d. gatekeeper
e. harmonizer
f. information or opinion giver
g. information or opinion seeker
h. interpreter
i. supporter
j. tension reliever

Comments

1. Did anyone discover if we have to recommend only one company?
2. I don't have time to help with that.
3. I think Rick has an excellent idea.
4. Stupid idea, Katie. Why don't you stop and think before you open your mouth?
5. Kwitabe doesn't necessarily agree with you, but he would consider it rude to openly disagree with someone who is older.
6. Josiah, in your plan weren't you assuming that we'd only need two days rest for rehearsal?
7. Lisa, I understand your point. What do you think about it, Paul?
8. Okay, so we've all agreed that we should begin keeping time logs. Now shouldn't we be thinking about what information needs to be on them?
9. Wow, it's getting tense in here. If we don't chill out soon, we're likely to spontaneously combust. And, hello, that'll be a problem because we're the only engine company in this area of town, right?
10. Barb, I don't think that your position is really that different from Saul's. Let me see if I can explain how they relate.

11. I've visited that home before, and I found that both the mom and dad are trying very hard to help their son.

10.5: Member Meeting Responsibilities (239)

Recall the last time you attended a small group problem solving meeting. On a scale of 1 to 5 (1 = not at all, 2 = poorly, 3 = somewhat, 4 = well done, 5 = to the best of my ability), rate yourself on how well you carried out each of the preparation, participation, and follow-up guidelines. Analyze your responses and determine how effectively you participated in that meeting. What do you need to work on to become a more valuable member of a problem solving group? Why? Write a paragraph in which you describe what you have learned.

To help you complete this activity, you can use the check sheet provided in your Premium Website for *Communicate!* Look for it in the Skill Learning Activities for Chapter 10.

10.6: Group Communication (240)

After you've watched the video of Thomas, Davinia, Joyce, and Pat and have read the transcript of their conversation, answer the following questions.

1. Is the group's goal clear?
2. Do they have sufficient diversity in their membership?
3. What stage of group development do they seem to be in?
4. Are they using the problem solving method?
5. What roles are being played by each member?
6. Do they appear to be prepared for the meeting?

When you're done with this activity, compare your answers to the authors' at the Premium Website for *Communicate!* Look for them in the Skill Learning Activities for Chapter 10.

Web Resources

10.1: What's Your Problem? (226)

This page at the Website for the Sheridan Institute of Technology and Advanced Learning suggests that later stages of problem solving move more quickly if the group has thoroughly studied, discussed, and agreed on the problem.

10.2: Rules for Brainstorming (228)

This site at the Center for Leadership and Community Engagement, George Mason University, features a list of rules to guide the brainstorming process.

10.3: Identifying Your Team Player Style (234)

Determine whether you are a contributor, collaborator, communicator, or challenger using this survey at the Professional Teambuilding Website.

10.4: Taking Notes (239)

For useful tips on how to take minutes in meetings, visit this page at the MeetingWizard.org Website.

Self Review

Group Communication

Group Communication from Chapters 9 and 10

How effective are you at working in problem solving groups? The following state-ments can help you evaluate your effectiveness in group settings. Use this scale to assess the frequency with which you perform each behavior: 1 = always; 2 = often; 3 = sometimes; 4 = rarely; 5 = never.

_____   I enjoy working with others to accomplish goals. (Ch. 9)

_____   I adapt my behavior to the norms of the group. (Ch. 9)

_____   I am comfortable with conflict. (Ch. 9)

_____   I actively listen and keep an open mind during problem solving discussions. (Ch. 10)

_____   I avoid performing self-centered roles in the group. (Ch. 10)

_____   I am equally adept at performing task and maintenance roles in the group. (Ch. 10)

_____   I come to group meetings prepared. (Ch. 10)

_____   During group meetings, my active participation makes positive contributions to goal accomplishment and maintaining good relationships. (Ch. 10)

_____   After meetings, I complete tasks I have been assigned and review meeting notes and minutes. (Ch. 10)

To verify this self-analysis, have a friend or fellow group member complete this review for you. Based on what you have learned, select the group communication behavior you would most like to improve. Write a communication improvement plan similar to the sample goal statement in Chapter 1 (page 18).

You can complete this Self-Review online and, if requested, e-mail it to your instructor. Use your Premium Website for Communicate! _to access Part 3 Self-Review under the chapter resources for Chapter 10, then click on "Part 3 Self-Review."_

Will Hart/PhotoEdit

Developing and Researching a Speech Topic

Questions you will be able to answer after reading this chapter:

- How can you choose a good topic for your speech?
- What can you do to make sure that your speech topic and goal are appropriate?
- How can you adapt your speech goal to your audience?
- What are the three types of information sources for speeches?
- How can you evaluate sources to ensure that the information they provide is unbiased and true?
- Why is it important for you to make a record of the information you find?
- How do you orally cite sources during your speech?

Donna is a marine biologist. She knows that her audience wants to hear her talk about marine biology, but she doesn't know what aspect of the topic she should focus on.

Romeo has been invited to speak to a student assembly at the inner-city middle school he attended. He has a lot he could say to these students who are so much like him. He really wants them to understand what they need to do now to have a chance to go to college. However, he's not sure how to organize his thoughts.

Dan is taking a required public speaking class. His first speech is scheduled for two weeks from tomorrow. As of today, he doesn't have the foggiest idea what he is going to talk about and he's scared to death.

Do any of these situations seem familiar? Do you identify with Dan? You may be taking this course as part of a graduation requirement and the thought of giving a speech can be overwhelming. However, developing public speaking skills is important. Why? Because when you are able to express your ideas to an audience, you are empowered. In a public forum, an effective speaker can stimulate and influence the thinking of others in ways that can improve their lives and the lives of those around them. In the workplace, effective public speaking skills are essential to advancement. Whether presenting oral reports and proposals, responding to questions, or training other workers, management-level and professional employees spend much of their work lives in activities that include or draw on public speaking skills.

Luckily, public speaking skills are not inborn; they are learned. In the chapters that follow, we will explain how you can improve your public speaking through careful preparation. In Chapters 11 through 14, you will learn a simple speech planning process that consists of the five Action Steps listed in Figure 11.1. Then in the final two chapters, we present more detailed information on organizing and developing informative and persuasive speeches, which are the two most common types.

Action Step 1
Determine a Specific Speech Goal that is Adapted to the Audience and Occasion.

Action Step 2
Gather and Evaluate Information to Develop the Content of Your Speech.

Action Step 3
Organize Your Material to Meet the Needs of Your Particular Audience.

Action Step 4
Adapt the Verbal and Visual Material to the Needs of Your Specific Audience.

Action Step 5
Practice Presenting Your Speech

Figure 11.1
Speech plan action steps

This chapter is devoted to explaining how to complete the first two action steps.

Action Step 1: Determine a Specific Speech Goal That Is Adapted to the Audience and Occasion

Speech planning begins by identifying a goal for your speech. To prepare a specific goal, you will need a list of topics that are appropriate to your specific audience and to the occasion. From these you will be able to select one and to write a goal statement for your speech.

Identify Topics

Good speech topics are developed from subjects that interest you and that you already know something about. What do you know a lot about? What has interested you enough so that you have gained some expertise? These subjects are a good source for speech topics. What is the difference between subject and topic? A **subject** is a broad area of knowledge; for example, you may have expertise in the subject of movies, cognitive psychology, computer technology, hip-hop culture, Asian art, or the politics of the Middle East. A **topic** is narrower and is a subset or specific aspect of a subject. If your subject is movies, you might feel qualified to speak on a variety of topics such as how the Academy Awards nomination process works; the relationships between movie producers, directors, and distributors; or how technology is changing movie production. Similarly, if your subject area is computer technology, you might be able to speak on cloud technology or Web 2.0.

Let's look at how you can identify subject areas that interest you and then, from those subject areas, identify and select specific topics you might use for the speeches you will present.

List Subjects

You can identify potential subjects for your speeches by listing subjects that (1) are important to you—that you find interesting and exciting—and (2) you know something about. Subjects may be related to careers that interest you, your major area of study, special skills or competencies that you have or admire, your hobbies, your leisure and volunteer activities, as well as your social, economic, or political interests. So if sales and marketing are your majors and your intended career, playing WoW online and snowboarding are your favorite activities, and you are a literacy volunteer who is concerned about the falling rate of high school graduation, then these are subject areas from which you can identify topics for your speeches.

At this point, it is tempting to think, "The audience is going to be bored if I talk about what interests me." In reality, all subject areas can interest an audience. Have you ever been drawn into a subject because the person you were talking to was so excited by the subject and good at explaining it? If you speak on a topic that you know something about and that really interests you, you will find it easy to be appear knowledgeable and to communicate your enthusiasm to others. Figure 11.2 is the list of subjects that Holly, a beginning speech student, identified for the speeches she was to give this term in her speech class. She identified subjects under three broad

subject
a broad area of knowledge.

topic
some specific aspect of a subject.

Major and career interests	Hobbies and activities	Issues and concerns
teaching	social networking	endangered birds
Web site design	rowing	child pornography on the Internet and child abuse
information systems	Big Brotherss Big Sisters organization	personal privacy and the Internet
technology trainer	birding	water pollution
computer-aided design	photography	parenting education

Figure 11.2
Holly's subject list

headings: (1) major subject and career interests, (2) hobbies and activities, and (3) issues or concerns.

Brainstorm and Concept Map for Topic Ideas

Because a topic is only one aspect of a subject, you can identify many topics within a subject. Two methods for identifying topics are brainstorming and concept mapping.

Brainstorming is an uncritical, nonevaluative process of generating associated ideas. When you brainstorm, you list as many ideas as you can without evaluating them. Holly, for example, decided she wanted to give a speech on the subject of social networking. By brainstorming, she was able to a list topics that included: the history of social networking, future trends in social networking, comparisons between popular social networking sites; the downside of social networking, and the social impacts of online social networks.

A second tool you can use to identify specific topics from a general subject area is concept mapping. **Concept mapping** is a visual means of exploring connections between a subject and related ideas (Callison, 2001). To generate connections, you might ask yourself questions about your subject, focusing on who, what, where, when, and how. Holly used concept mapping to identify topics related to endangered birds. In Figure 11.3 you can see what Holly's concept map looked like.

You can create a list of potential topics by completing Action Step 1.a: Brainstorm and Concept Map for Topics.

When you brainstorm, you will come up with many topics from one subject. Try it!

Web Resource 11.1

brainstorming
an uncritical, nonevaluative process of generating associated ideas.

concept mapping
A visual means of exploring connections between a subject and related ideas.

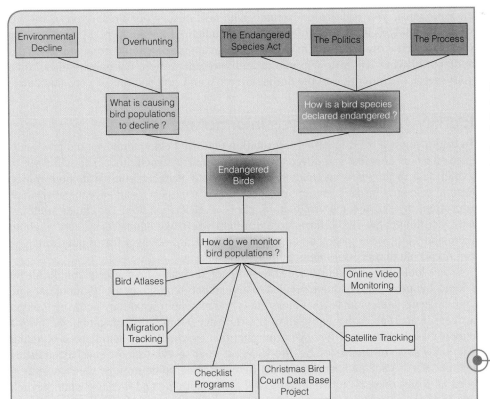

Figure 11.3
Concept map for endangered birds

Action Step 1.a

Brainstorm and Concept Map for Topics

1. Develop a subject list.
   a. Divide a sheet of paper into three columns. Label column 1 "major or vocational interest," label column 2 "hobby or activity," and label column 3 "concern or issue."
   b. Working on one column at a time, identify subjects of interest to you. Try to identify at least 3 subjects in each column.
   c. Place a check mark next to subject in each column you would most enjoy speaking about.
   d. Keep these lists for future use in choosing a topic for an assigned speech.
2. For each subject you have checked, brainstorm a list of topics that relate to it.
3. Then, for each subject you have checked, develop a concept map to identify smaller topic areas and related ideas that might be developed into future speeches.

Analyze the Audience

How can you analyze your audience and setting so that your speech topic and goal are appropriate?

Because speeches are presented to a particular audience, before you can finally decide on your topic, you need to understand who will be in your prospective audience. **Audience analysis** is the study of the intended audience for your speech. Understanding your prospective audience will help you select an appropriate topic from your list. Your audience analysis will also help you in **audience adaptation**, the process of tailoring your speech's information to the needs, interests, and expectations of your audience.

Identify Audience Analysis Information Needs

To begin, you will want to gather information that will help you understand how audience members are alike and different from you and from each other. You will want to gather data to help you understand basic audience characteristics or **demographics**. Helpful demographic information includes things such as each audience member's age, education, gender, income, occupation, race, ethnicity, religion, geographic uniqueness, and language. This information will help you make educated inferences about them and adapt your speech accordingly. Figure 11.4 presents a list of questions you can use to obtain necessary demographic information.

Let's look at an example to see how audience analysis data can help you decide on a topic. Suppose that you have decided to give a speech on blogging. If you're not sure your audience understands what blogging is you may infer what they know by looking at their demographics. Is almost all of the audience young, well-educated, and from a middle class background? If so, you can infer that they will have heard about blogging and know some of the basics. So you will gear your speech to more specialized information. But if your audience is from different demographic groups, then you might need to survey them about what they know about blogging and then use what they tell you to pick an appropriate topic within the general subject of blogging. For example,

audience analysis
the study of the intended audience for your speech.

audience adaptation
the process of tailoring your information to the needs, interests, and expectations of your speech audience.

demographics
data to help you understand basic audience characteristics

imagine that one of the topics that interests you is the dangers or "dark side" of blogging. If your audience is made up primarily of 18–22 year-old college students, you can assume they know what blogging is and so this topic would probably be a good one for this audience. If you discover that one or two audience members are older than that, you can avoid marginalizing them by briefly defining blogging in your opening remarks so that they aren't completely lost. But if you discover that most of your audience members are older and have never read or written a blog, then this topic may not be appropriate for this audience or you may need to spend more time acquainting the audience with blogging before moving to a discussion of the dangers of blogging.

You will also want to collect subject-related audience data, including: how knowledgeable audience members are in your subject area, their initial level of interest in the subject, their attitude toward the subject, and their attitude toward you as a speaker. Once you determine what your audience already knows about your subject, you can eliminate familiar topics that might bore them and choose a topic that will present them with new information and new insights. When you understand the initial level of interest that audience members have regarding your subject, you can choose a topic that builds on that interest, or you will need to adapt your material so that it captures their interest. Understanding your audience's attitude toward your subject is especially important when you want to influence their beliefs or move them to action. Because there is a limit to how persuasive any one speech can be, knowing your audience members' attitudes toward your subject will enable you to choose a topic that affects your audience's position without alienating them.

Gather Audience Data

There are four main methods you can use to gather the information you need for an audience analysis:

1. **Conduct a survey.** Although it is not always feasible, the most direct and most accurate way to collect audience data is to survey the audience. A **survey** is a questionnaire designed to gather information from people. Some surveys are done as interviews; others are written forms that are completed by audience members. Survey questions or items can be: two-sided items (respondents choose between two answers), multiple response items (respondents choose between several items),

survey
a questionnaire designed to gather information from people.

Age: Average age and age range?
Educational level: Percentage with high school, college, or postgraduate education?
Gender: Percentages of men and women?
Occupation: Single (or dominant) occupation or industry or diverse occupations and industries?
Socioeconomic background: Percentage lower, medium, upper income?
Ethnicity: Dominant culture of group if any? Other co-cultures represented?
Religion: Religions represented? Is one preponderant?
Community: Single neighborhood, city, state, country? Or mixed?
Language: Common spoken language? Other first languages shared by a significant minority?
Knowledge of the subject: What do they know? How varied is their knowledge?
Attitude toward subject: What do they feel or think about the subject?

Figure 11.4
Demographic and subject-specific audience analysis questions

scaled items (respondents choose between levels of intensity in a response), or open-ended items (respondents reply in any way they see fit). Figure 11.5 gives examples of each type of question.

2. **Informally observe.** If the members of the audience are people whom we know, such as classmates or coworkers, we can learn a lot about them by just watching. For instance, after a couple of classes, we can determine the approximate average age of the class members, the ratio of men to women, and the general cultural makeup. As we listen to classmates talk, we learn about their knowledge of, and interest in, certain issues.

3. **Question a representative.** When we are invited to make a speech, we can ask the contact person for audience information. You should specifically ask for data that are somewhat important for you as you choose a topic or work to adapt your

---

Two-sided question
Are you _____ a man _____ a woman?

Question with multiple responses
Which is the highest educational level you have completed? _____ less than high school _____ high school _____ attended college _____ associate's degree _____ bachelor's degree _____ master's degree _____ doctorate degree _____ postdoctorate

Scaled items
How much do you know about Islam? _____ not much _____ a little _____ some _____ quite a lot _____ detailed knowledge

Open-ended item
What do you think about labor unions?

Figure 11.5
Sample survey questions

Action Step 1.b

Analyze Your Audience

1. Decide on the audience characteristics (demographics and subject-specific information that you need in order to choose a topic and adapt to your audience).
2. Choose a method for gathering audience information.
3. Collect the data.

 To help you complete this step, you can use the worksheet provided in your Premium Website for *Communicate!* Look for it in the Action Steps for Chapter 11. Save your completed worksheet so you can use the information to guide you as you choose your topic. You will also refer to it as you complete other steps of the speech planning process.

material. For the blogging speech, for example, you would want to know if the audience members have a basic understanding of what it is.

4. **Make educated guesses.** If you can't get information in any other way, you can make informed guesses based on indirect data such as the general profile of people in a certain community or the kinds of people likely to attend the event or occasion.

Analyze the Setting

The location and occasion make up the speech **setting.** Answers to several questions about the setting should also guide your topic selection and other parts of your speech planning.

1. **What are the special expectations for the speech?** Every speaking occasion is surrounded by expectations. At an Episcopalian Sunday service, for example, the congregation expects the minister's sermon to have a religious theme. Likewise, at a national sales meeting, the field representatives expect to hear about new products. For your classroom speeches, a major expectation is that your speech will meet the criteria set for the assignment.

2. **What is the appropriate length for the speech?** The time limit for classroom speeches is usually quite short, so you will want to choose a topic that is narrow enough to be accomplished in the brief time allowed. For example, "Two Major Causes of Environmental Degradation" could be presented as a 10-minute speech, but "A History of Human Impact on the Environment" could not. Speakers who speak for more or less time than they have been scheduled can seriously interfere with the program of an event and lose the respect of both their hosts and their audience.

3. **How large will the audience be?** Although audience size may not directly affect the topic you select, it will affect how you adapt your material and how you present the speech. For example, if the audience is small (up to about 50), you can talk without a microphone and move about if you choose to do so. For larger audiences, you might have a microphone that may limit your range of movement.

4. **Where will the speech be given?** Rooms vary in size, shape, lighting, and seating arrangements. Some are a single level, some have stages or platforms, and some have tiered seating. The space affects the speech. For example, in a long narrow room, you may have to speak loudly to be heard in the back row. The brightness of the room and the availability of shades may affect what kinds of visual aids you can use. So you will want to know and consider the layout of the room as you plan your speech. At times, you might request that the room be changed or rearranged so that the space is better suited to your needs.

5. **What equipment is necessary to give the speech?** Would you like to use a microphone, lectern, flip chart, overhead projector and screen, or a hookup for your laptop computer during your speech? If so, you need to check with your host to make sure that the equipment can be made available to you. In some cases, the unavailability of equipment may limit your topic choice. Regardless of what arrangements have been made, however, experienced speakers expect that something may go wrong and are always prepared with alternative plans. For example, although computer slide shows can be very effective, there are often technological glitches that interfere with their use, so many speakers prepare overheads or handouts and bring them along as backup.

Bob Daemmrich/PhotoEdit

How does the setting and the occasion dictate what a speaker will talk about at a graduation ceremony?

setting
the occasion and location for your speech.

Skill Learning Activity 11.1

Action Step 1.c

Understand the Speech Setting

Hold a conversation with the person who arranged for you to speak and get answers to the following questions:

1. What are the special expectations for the speech? _____
2. What is the appropriate length for the speech? _____
3. How large will the audience be? _____
4. Where will the speech be given? _____
5. What equipment is necessary to give the speech? _____

Write a short paragraph mentioning which aspects of the setting are most important for you to consider in speech preparation and why.

Select a Topic

Armed with your topic lists and the information you have collected on your audience and setting, you are ready to select an appropriate topic. Are there some topics on your list that are too simple or too difficult for this audience? Eliminate them. Are some topics likely to bore the audience and you can't think of any way to pique their interest. Eliminate them. How does the audience's demographic profile mesh with each topic? Are some ill suited to this demographic profile? Eliminate them. At the end of this process, you should have several topics that would be appropriate for your audience.

Action Step 1.d

Select a Topic

Use your responses to Action Steps 1.a, 1.b, and 1.c to complete this step.

1. Write each of the topics that you checked in Action Step 1 on the lines below:

   _____   _____   _____
   _____   _____   _____
   _____   _____   _____

2. Using the information you compiled in Action Step 1.b, the audience analysis, compare each topic to your audience profile. Draw a line through topics that seem less appropriate for your audience.
3. Using the information you compiled in Action Step 1.c, your analysis of the setting, compare the remaining topics to the requirements of the setting. Eliminate topics that seem less suited to the setting.
4. From the topics that remain, choose the one that you would find most enjoyable to present. Circle that topic.

 To complete this activity, you can use the worksheet provided in your Premium Website for *Communicate!* Look for it in the Action Steps for Chapter 11.

Now consider the setting. Are some of the remaining topics inappropriate for the expectations of the audience or too broad for the time allocated, or do they require equipment that is unavailable in this setting? If so, eliminate them.

From the topics that still remain after considering the audience and the setting, you should choose the one that you would find most enjoyable to share with the audience as your speech topic.

Write a Speech Goal

Once you have chosen your topic, you are ready to identify the general goal of your speech and to write a specific goal statement tailored to the audience and setting.

Identify Your General Goal

The **general goal** is the overall intent of the speech. Most speeches generally intend to entertain, inform, or persuade, even though each type can include elements of the other types. Consider the following examples: Conan O'Brien's opening monologue on *The Tonight Show* is intended to entertain, even though it may include material that is persuasive. President Obama's campaign speeches were intended to persuade, even though they may also have been informative. In this book, we focus the general goals of informing and persuading. These are the kinds of speeches you will most likely present in academic, professional, and community settings.

> How can you adapt your speech goal to your audience?

Phrase a Specific Goal Statement

The **specific goal**, or specific purpose of your speech, is a single statement that identifies the exact response you want from the audience after they have listened to your speech. A specific goal statement for an informative speech usually specifies whether you want the audience to learn about, understand, or appreciate the topic. "I would like the audience to understand the four major criteria used for evaluating a diamond" is a goal statement for an informative speech. A specific goal statement for a persuasive speech specifies whether you want the audience to accept the belief that you are presenting: "I want my audience to believe that the militarization of space is wrong," or to act a certain way: "I want my audience to donate money to the United Way." Figure 11.6 gives further examples of informative and persuasive speech goals.

general speech goal
the overall intent of your speech.

specific speech goal
a single statement of the exact response the speaker wants from the audience.

Informative Goals
Increasing understanding: I want my audience to understand the three basic forms of a mystery story.
Increasing knowledge: I want my audience to learn how to light a fire without a match.
Increasing appreciation: I want my audience to appreciate the intricacies of spider-web designs.

Persuasive Goals
Reinforce belief: I want my audience to maintain its belief in drug-free sports.
Change belief: I want my audience to believe that SUVs are environmentally destructive.
Motivation to act: I want my audience to join Amnesty International.

Figure 11.6
Informative and persuasive speech goals

To create a well-worded specific goal statement, follow these guidelines:

1. **Write a first draft of your speech goal, using a complete sentence that specifies the response you want from the audience.** Julia, who has been concerned with and is knowledgeable about the subject of illiteracy, drafts the following statement of her general speech goal: "I want my audience to be informed about the effects of illiteracy." Julia's draft is a complete sentence, and it specifies the response she wants from the audience: to be informed about the effects of illiteracy. Her phrasing tells us that she is planning to give an informative speech.

2. **Revise the draft statement until it focuses clearly on the desired audience reaction.** The draft "I want my audience to understand illiteracy" is a good start, but it is extremely broad. Just what is it about illiteracy that Julia wants the audience to understand? She narrows the statement: "I want my audience to understand three effects of illiteracy." This version is more specific than her first draft, but it still does not clearly capture her intention, so she revises it further: "I would like the audience to understand three effects of illiteracy in the workplace." Now the goal is limited by Julia's focus not only on the specific number of effects but also on a specific situation. If Julia wanted to persuade her audience, her specific goal might be "I want my audience to believe that illiteracy in the workplace is a major problem."

3. **Make sure the goal statement contains only one central idea.** Suppose Julia had written the following specific goal statement: "I want the audience to understand the nature of illiteracy and innumeracy." This would need to be revised because it includes two distinct ideas: illiteracy and innumeracy. Although these problems may be related, because both make it difficult for people to function in society, the causes of illiteracy and innumeracy are different. It would be difficult to adequately address both within one speech. So Julia would need to realize this statement includes two topic ideas and to choose between them. If your goal statement includes the word *and*, you may have more than one idea and will need to narrow your focus.

Skill Learning Activity 11.2

Action Step 1.e

Write a Specific Goal

Type of speech_____

1. Write a draft of your specific speech goal, using a complete sentence that specifies the type of response you want from the audience: *to learn about, to understand,* or *to appreciate* the topic.
2. Review the specific goal statement. If it contains more than one idea, select one and redraft your specific goal statement.
3. Test the infinitive phrase. Does the infinitive phrase express the specific audience reaction desired? If not, revise the infinitive phrase.

Write your final wording of the specific goal:

_____

_____

 You can complete this activity online with Speech Builder Express, a speech organization and development program that will help you complete some of the action steps in this book to develop your speech. Access Speech Builder Express at your Premium Website for *Communicate!*

Crafting a Specific Speech Goal That Meets Audience Needs

Communication Skill

Skill	Use	Procedure	Example
The process of identifying a speech purpose that draws on the speaker's knowledge and interests and is adapted to a specific audience and setting.	To identify a speaking goal that matches speaker interest and expertise, audience needs and interests, and setting.	1. Identify topics within subject areas in which you have interest and expertise. 2. Analyze your audience's demographic characteristics, interests, and attitudes toward your subject. 3. Understand the occasion and the location for the speech. 4. Select a topic that will meet the interests and needs of your audience and setting. 5. Write a specific speech goal that clearly states the exact response you want from your audience.	Ken first writes, "I want my audience to know what to look for in buying a dog." As he revises, he writes, "I want my audience to understand four important considerations in buying the perfect dog." Once Ken has a goal with a single focus and a clearly specified, desired audience reaction, he tests his first version by writing two differently worded versions.

Action Step 2: Gather and Evaluate Information to Develop the Content of Your Speech

To select and then use the most effective information to support your speech, you must be able to locate and evaluate appropriate sources of information, identify and select the information most relevant to your speech, draw information from multiple cultural perspectives, and then record the information in a way that will help you prepare for and present your speech.

Locate and Evaluate Information Sources

How can you quickly find the best information related to your specific speech goal? It depends. Speakers usually start by assessing their own knowledge, experience, and personal observations. Then they move to secondary resources, which includes information about the topic that has been discovered by other people and is available in public sources. They might do an electronic search for relevant books, articles, general references, and Web sites. Occasionally, when other resources do not have the information needed, they may conduct their own study by doing a survey, interviewing experts, or performing an experiment.

Personal Knowledge, Experience, and Observation

If you have chosen to speak on a topic you know something about, you are likely to have material that you can use as examples and personal experiences in your speech. For instance, musicians have special knowledge about music and instruments, entrepreneurs know about starting up businesses, and marine biologists about marine reserves. So Erin, a skilled rock climber, can draw from her own knowledge and experience for her speech "Rappelling Down a Mountain."

For many topics, the knowledge you've gained from experience can be supplemented with careful observation. If, for instance, you were planning to talk about how a small claims court works or how churches help the homeless find shelter and job training, you could learn more by attending small claims sessions or visiting a church's outreach center. By focusing on specific behaviors and taking notes on your observations, you could make a record of specifics to use in your speech.

Sharing your personal knowledge, experience, and observations can also bolster your credibility if you inform your audience about your credentials—your experiences or education that qualifies you to speak with authority on a specific subject. For Erin, establishing her credentials means briefly mentioning her training and expertise as a rock climber before she launches into her observations about unqualified climbers.

> What are three types of information sources for speeches?

Web Resource 11.2
Web Resource 11.3
Web Resource 11.4
Web Resource 11.5

Secondary Research

Secondary research is the process of locating information about your topic that has been discovered by other people. Libraries house various sources of secondary research. Most libraries store information about their holdings in electronic databases. Users retrieve the information at computer terminals in the library or over the Internet. If you don't know how to access your school's library resources online, you can call the help desk at your library. If you have difficulty using library search tools, your library probably offers a short seminar or you can ask a research librarian for help. Secondary resources include the following types of materials:

Books

If your topic has been around for at least six months, there are likely to be books written about it. To find them, you can do a keyword search of an online database. Although books are excellent sources of in-depth material about a topic, books are not a good resource if your topic is very new or if you're looking for the latest information on a topic.

Articles

Articles, which may contain more current or highly specialized information on your topic than a book would, are published in **periodicals**—magazines and journals that appear at regular intervals. The information in periodical articles is often more current than that in books because many periodicals are published weekly, biweekly, or monthly. However, articles don't provide as much in-depth information as you'd find in a book. Articles are often a good source of information for highly specialized topics. Today, most libraries subscribe to electronic databases that index periodical articles. Check with your librarian to learn what electronic indexes your college or university subscribes to.

secondary research
the process of locating information about your topic that has been discovered by other people.

periodicals
magazines and journals that appear at fixed intervals.

Newspapers

Newspaper articles are excellent sources of facts about and interpretations of both contemporary and historical issues. Keep in mind, however, that most authors of newspaper articles are journalists who are not experts on the topics they write about. So, it is best not to rely solely on newspaper articles for your speech. Today most newspapers are available online, which makes them very accessible. Two electronic newspaper indexes that are most useful if they are available to you are the *National Newspaper Index*, which indexes five major newspapers: the *New York Times*, the *Wall Street Journal*, the *Christian Science Monitor*, the *Washington Post*, the *Los Angeles Times*, and *Newsbank*, which provides not only the indexes but also the text of articles from more than 450 U.S. and Canadian newspapers.

Encyclopedias

An encyclopedia can be a good starting point for your research. Encyclopedias give an excellent overview of many subjects and can acquaint you with the basic terminology and ideas associated with a topic. But because encyclopedias provide only overviews, they should never be the sole research base for your speech. Wikipedia, the online collaborative encyclopedia has become a popular research tool, but it is also a controversial source of information. To understand the controversy about this and similar online resources, read the Pop Comm! feature "To Wikipedia or Not to Wikipedia? Good Question."

Statistical sources

Statistical sources present numerical information on a wide variety of subjects. When you need facts about demography, continents, heads of state, weather, or similar subjects, access one of the many single-volume sources that report such data. Two of the most popular sources in this category are *The Statistical Abstract of the United States* (available online), which provides numerical information on various aspects of American life, and *The World Almanac and Book of Facts*.

Web Resource 11.6

Biographical references

When you need an account of a person's life, you can turn to one of the many biographical references that are available. In addition to full-length biographies and encyclopedia entries, consult such reference books as *Who's Who in America* and *International Who's Who*. Your library may also carry other biographical references such as *Contemporary Black Biography, Dictionary of Hispanic Biography, Native American Women, Who's Who of American Women, Who's Who Among Asian Americans*, and many more.

Government documents

If your topic is related to public policy, government documents may provide useful information. For Internet links to several frequently used U.S. federal government documents, consult Web Resource 11.6: Government Publications Online through your Premium Website for *Communicate!*. Similar documents for other countries, states, and cities may be found by using a search engine.

Internet-based resources

In addition to printed resources (many of which you can access online), you may find resources for your speech that are only available on the Internet. For example, you can access electronic databases, bulletin boards, and scholarly and professional electronic discussion groups, as well as Web sites and Web pages authored by individuals and groups.

F. Pedrick/The Image Works

Have you ever taken a class at your library on online research? If not, consider doing so. You can save yourself lots of time and locate great sources of useful information.

Pop Comm!

To Wikipedia or Not to Wikipedia?: That's a Good Question

Of Wikipedia, *The Office*'s Michael Scott opined, "Wikipedia is the best thing ever. Anyone in the world can write anything they want about any subject, so you know you are getting the best possible information." Funny, right? Not for John Seigenthaler, a well-respected journalist who was a friend and aide to President John F. Kennedy and Attorney General Robert F. Kennedy in the 1960s. Seigenthaler was a victim of a hoax article posted to Wikipedia that falsely claimed he had been suspected in the assassinations of John and Robert Kennedy. The hoax upset Seigenthaler not only because the article defamed his character, but also because Wikipedia editors didn't discover and correct it for over four months (Seigenthaler, 2005). Shortly after Seigenthaler published an article in *USA Today* about the incident, Wikipedia announced that it had barred unregistered users from creating new articles, and later the site enacted a policy that prevented the public from creating new articles about living people without editorial review (Helm, 2005; Cohen, 2009). These moves signaled a change from Wikipedia's initial desire to provide a free online encyclopedia that the public could create collaboratively.

Wikipedia is one of the top ten Web sites used worldwide, offering 2,665,263 articles covering

Primary Research

Primary research is the process of conducting your own study to acquire information for your speech. It is much more labor intensive and time consuming than secondary research, and in the professional world, it is much more costly. If, after making an exhaustive search of secondary sources, you cannot locate the information you need, you might consider getting it through one of the following primary research methods:

Surveys

You can gather information directly from a group of people through the use of a questionnaire. If you decide to conduct your own survey, consult Web Resource 11.7 Conducting Surveys, which you can access through your Premium Website for *Communicate!* This resource will provide you with important tips for collecting good information.

Web Resource 11.7

primary research
the process of conducting your own study to acquire information for your speech.

Interviews

You can locate someone who is an acknowledged expert on your topic and ask for their opinions on your topic. The appendix after Chapter 8 provides information about conducting interviews.

over 2 million topics (Smith, 2008). Nonetheless, the Seigenthaler hoax and other incidents have spurred a "credibility" backlash against the site. For example, U.S courts have begun ruling that Wikipedia cannot be used as legal evidence—in April 2009, a New Jersey judge reversed an initial ruling that Wikipedia could be used to plug an evidentiary gap, saying that because "anyone can edit" the online encyclopedia, it is not a reliable source of information (Gallagher, 2009). In addition, many educators discourage their students from using Wikipedia as a research tool, and some schools have even banned access to it completely. The site prompts comments such as "Better to make such a site off-limits to students . . . if it will get them to rely on more authentic research sources for their writing" (Crovitz & Smoot, 2008). Even Wikipedia founder Jimmy Wales cautions against relying on the Web site as a primary source: "People shouldn't be citing encyclopedias in the first place. [Rather,] Wikipedia and other encyclopedias should be solid enough to give good, solid background information to inform your studies for a deeper level" (Helm, 2005).

But some educators argue that student use of Wikipedia can provide invaluable teaching moments. Jade Tippett of Ukiah High School suggests, "By showing students how Wikipedia entries are developed by dynamic consensus, as opposed to 'authoritative' sourcing, we can get to deeper levels of the 'what is truth' conversation" ("Wikipedia: Friend or Foe?" 2009). David Geary of the Harris County Department of Education says that although he hesitates to call Wikipedia "factual," he believes that information contributed to Wikipedia is often reflective of a popular cultural viewpoint ("Wikipedia: Friend or Foe?" 2009). And in *English Journal*, Darren Crovitz and W. Scott Smoot (2009) write, "Talking with [students] about how the site operates is essential in helping them move from passive acceptors of information to practicing analyzers and evaluators."

So, to Wikipedia or not to Wikipedia? A moderate approach advocates using Wikipedia as a starting point for research rather than a primary source. Here's a tip: Use the Notes section at the end of Wikipedia articles to find links to the published sources that support and inform each article. These sources include books; magazine, newspaper, and journal articles; original interviews; court decisions; and similar authoritative sources.

Experiments

You can design a study to test a hypothesis that you have. Then, based on your analysis, you can report the results in your speech.

Evaluate Sources

Information sources vary in the accuracy, reliability, and validity of the information they present. So before you use the information from a source in your speech, you will want to evaluate it. Four criteria you can use are authority, objectivity, currency, and relevance.

> How can you evaluate sources to ensure that the information they provide is unbiased and accurate?

1. **Authority.** The first test of a resource is the expertise of its author and/or the reputation of the publishing or sponsoring organization. When the author is named, you can check his or her credentials through biographical references or look on the Internet for a home page listing professional qualifications. Use your library's electronic periodical indexes or check the Library of Congress to see what else the author has published in the field.

   On the Internet, some information is anonymous or credited to someone whose background is not clear. In these cases, your ability to trust the information depends on evaluating the qualifications of the sponsoring organization.

On the Internet, URLs ending in ".gov" (governmental), ".edu" (educational), and ".org" are noncommercial sites with institutional publishers. The URL ".com" indicates that the sponsor is a for-profit organization and may be selling something. If you do not know whether you can trust the source, then do not use the information.

2. Objectivity. Although all authors have a viewpoint, you will want to be wary of information that is overly slanted. Documents that have been published by business, government, or public interest groups should be carefully scrutinized for obvious biases and good public-relations fronts. To evaluate the potential biases in books and articles, read the preface or identify the thesis statement. These often reveal the author's point of view. When evaluating a Web site with which you are unfamiliar, look for its purpose. Most home pages contain a purpose or mission statement (sometimes in a link called "About Us"). Armed with this information, you are in a better position to recognize the biases in the information.

3. Currency. In general, newer information is more accurate than older. So when evaluating your sources, be sure to consult the latest information you can find. One of the reasons for using Web-based sources is that they can provide more up-to-date information than printed sources (Munger, Anderson, Benjamin, Busiel, & Pardes-Holt, 2000). But just because a source is found online does not mean that the information is timely. To determine how current the information is, you will need to find out when the book was published, the article was written, the study was conducted, or the article was placed on the Web or revised. Web page dates are usually listed at the end of the article. If there are no dates listed, you have no way of judging how current the information is.

Action Step 2.a

Locate and Evaluate Information Sources

The goal of this activity is to help you compile a list of potential sources for your speech.

1. Identify gaps in your knowledge that you would like to fill.
2. Identify a person, an event, or a process that you could observe to broaden your personal knowledge base.
3. Brainstorm a list of keywords that are related to your speech goal.
4. Working with your library's catalog, periodical indexes (including InfoTrac College Edition), and general references discussed in this chapter, find and list specific resources that appear to provide information for your speech.
5. Using a search engine, identify organizationally sponsored and personal Web sites that may be sources of information for your speech.
6. Identify a person you could interview for additional information for your speech.
7. Skim the resources you have identified to decide which are likely to be most useful.
8. Evaluate each resource to determine how much faith you can place in the information.

4. **Relevance.** During your research, you will likely come across a great deal of interesting information. Whether that information is appropriate for your speech is another matter. Relevant information is directly related to your topic and supports your main points, making your speech easier to follow and understand. Irrelevant information will only confuse listeners, so you should avoid using it no matter how interesting it is.

Skill Learning Activity 11.3
Web Resource 11.8

Identify and Select Relevant Information

Types of information that you may find in your sources include factual statements, expert opinions, and elaborations.

Factual Statements

Factual statements are those that can be verified. *A recent study confirmed that preschoolers watch an average of 28 hours of television a week* and *The microprocessor, which was invented by Ted Hoff at Intel in 1971, made the creation of personal computers possible* are both statements of fact that can be verified. One way to verify whether a statement is accurate is to check it against other sources on the same subject. Never use any information that is not carefully documented unless you have corroborating sources. Factual statements may be statistics or examples.

1. **Statistics.** **Statistics** are numerical facts. *Only five of every ten local citizens voted in the last election* or *The national unemployment rate for May 2009 was 9.4 percent* can provide impressive support for a point, but if statistics are poorly used in a speech, they may be boring and, in some instances, downright deceiving. When you use statistics, follow these guidelines:
   - Use only statistics that you can verify to be reliable. Taking statistics from only the most reliable sources and double-checking any startling statistics with another source will guard against the use of faulty statistics.
   - Use only recent statistics so your audience will not be misled.
   - Use statistics comparatively. You can show growth, decline, gain, or loss by comparing two numbers.
   - Use statistics sparingly. A few pertinent numbers are far more effective than a battery of statistics.
   - No statistic is completely accurate, and statistics can be manipulated to prove things that a more honest rendering would belie. So before you use a statistic, be sure to evaluate the source and to cross check the method used to collect and interpret the data (Frances, 1994).

2. **Examples.** **Examples** are specific instances that illustrate or explain a general factual statement. One or two short examples like the following ones provide concrete detail that makes a general statement more meaningful to the audience: *One way a company increases its power is to buy out another company. Recently, Delta bought out Northwest and thereby became the world's largest airline company. Professional billiard players practice many long hours every day. Jennifer Lee practices up to 10 hours a day when she is not in a tournament.*

factual statements
statements that can be verified.

statistics
numerical facts.

examples
specific instances that illustrate or explain a general factual statement.

Expert Opinions

Expert opinions are interpretations and judgments made by an authority in a particular subject area. They can help explain what facts mean or put them in perspective. *Watching 28 hours of television a week is far too much for young children, but may be OK for adults* and *Having a firewire port on your computer is absolutely necessary* are opinions. Whether they are expert opinions depends on who made the statements. An **expert** is a person who has mastered a specific subject, usually through long-term study and who is recognized by other people in the field as being a knowledgeable and trustworthy authority.

Elaborations

Both factual information and expert opinions can be elaborated upon through anecdotes and narratives, comparisons and contrasts, or quotable explanations and opinions.

1. Anecdotes and narratives. **Anecdotes** are brief, often amusing stories; **narratives** are accounts, personal experiences, tales, or lengthier stories. Because holding audience interest is important and because audience attention is likely to be captured by a story, anecdotes and narratives are worth looking for or creating. The key to using them is to be sure the point of the story directly addresses the point you are making in your speech. Good stories and narratives may be humorous, sentimental, suspenseful, or dramatic.

2. Comparisons and contrasts. One of the best ways to give meaning to new ideas or facts is through comparison and contrast. **Comparisons** illuminate a point by showing similarities, whereas **contrasts** highlight differences. Although comparisons and contrasts may be literal, like comparing and contrasting the murder rates in different countries or during different eras, they may also be figurative.

   - *Figurative comparison*: "In short, living without health insurance is as much of a risk as having uncontrolled diabetes or driving without a safety belt" (Nelson, 2006, p. 24).
   - *Figurative contrast:* "If this morning you had bacon and eggs for breakfast, I think it illustrates the difference. The eggs represented 'participation' on the part of the chicken. The bacon represented 'total commitment' on the part of the pig!" (Durst, 1989, p. 325).

3. Quotations. At times, information you find will be so well stated that you want to quote it directly in your speech. Because the audience is interested in listening to your ideas and arguments, you should avoid using quotations that are too long or too numerous. But when you find that an author or expert has worded an idea especially well, quote it directly and then verbally acknowledge the person who said or wrote it. Using quotations or close paraphrases without acknowledging their source is **plagiarism**, the unethical act of representing another person's work as your own.

expert opinions
interpretations and judgments made by authorities in a particular subject area.

expert
a person who has mastered a specific subject, usually through long-term study.

anecdotes
brief, often amusing stories.

narratives
accounts, personal experiences, tales, or lengthier stories.

comparisons
illuminate a point by showing similarities.

contrasts
highlight differences.

plagiarism
the unethical act of representing a published author's work as your own.

Draw Information from Multiple Cultural Perspectives

How we perceive facts and what opinions we hold often are influenced by our cultural background. Therefore, it is important to draw information from a variety of cultural perspectives by seeking sources with different cultural orientations and by interviewing experts with diverse cultural backgrounds. For example, when Carrie was preparing for her speech on proficiency testing in grade schools, she purposefully searched for articles written by noted Hispanic, Asian American, African American, and European American authors. In addition, she interviewed two local school superintendents—one from an urban district and one from a suburban district. Because she consciously worked to develop diverse sources of information, Carrie felt confident that her speech would more accurately reflect all sides of the debate on proficiency testing.

Record Information

As you find facts, opinions, and elaborations that you want to use in your speech, you need to record the information accurately and keep a careful account of your sources so you can cite them appropriately during your speech.

> Why is it important to make a record of the information you find?

Prepare Research Cards

How should you keep track of the information you plan to use? Although it may seem easier to record all material from one source on a single sheet of paper (or to photocopy source material), sorting and arranging material is much easier when each item is recorded separately. Recording each piece of information on its own research card allows you to easily find, arrange, and rearrange individual pieces of information as you prepare your speech.

Make a research card for each factual statement, expert opinion, or elaboration you find. To prepare a research card, begin by writing a keyword or category heading that captures the main idea of this piece of information and identifies the subcategory to which the information belongs. Next, record the specific fact, opinion, or elaboration statement. Any part of the information item that is quoted directly from the source should be enclosed in quotation marks. Finally, record the bibliographic information you will need for your source list.

The exact bibliographic information you record depends on the type of source (such as book, article, or Web site) and the style guide (such as APA or MLA) you are using. Generally for a book, you will record the names of authors, title of the book, the place of publication and the publisher, the date of publication, and the page or pages from which the information is taken. For a periodical or newspaper, you will record the name of the author (if given), the title of the article, the name of the publication, its volume and issue numbers, the date, and the page number from which the information is taken. For online sources, include the URL for the Web site, the heading under which you found the information, the author, the date (if given), and the sponsoring organization or publisher. Be sure to record enough source information so you can relocate the material if you need to. Figure 11.7 provides a sample research card.

The number of sources you will need depends, in part, on the type of speech you are giving and your own expertise. For a narrative/personal experience, you obviously will be the main, if not the only, source. For informative reports and persuasive speeches, however, speakers ordinarily draw from multiple sources. For a five-minute speech on swine flu in which you plan to talk about causes, symptoms, and means of transmission, you might have two or more research cards under each heading. Moreover, the cards should come from a number of different sources. Selecting and using information from

Topic: Swine Flu

Heading: Swine Flu Myths

Influenza A (subtype H1N1) is a flu strain commonly found in pigs, but you cannot get this virus by eating pork.

"Influenza in Pigs: Questions and Answers: Key Facts about Swine Influenza (Swine Flu)." April 23, 2009. Centers for Disease Control and Prevention. http://www.cdc.gov/flu/swineflu/key_facts.htm

Figure 11.7

A sample research card

Action Step 2.b

Prepare Research Cards: Record Facts, Opinions, and Elaborations

The goal of this step is to review the source material you identified in Action Step 2.a and to record specific items of information that you might wish to use in your speech.

1. Carefully read all print and electronic sources (including Web site material) you have identified and evaluated as appropriate sources for your speech. Review your notes and any tapes from interviews and observations.

2. As you read an item (fact, opinion, example, illustration, statistic, anecdote, narrative, comparison/contrast, quotation, definition, or description) that you think might be useful in your speech, record it on a research card or on the appropriate electronic note card form available on the Premium Website for *Communicate!* If you are using an article from a periodical that you read online, use the periodical research card form.

 Go to your Premium Website for *Communicate!* to access this activity online. Look for it in the Action Steps for Chapter 11. There you can view samples of research cards prepared by another student, use online forms to prepare your own research cards, print them out to use as you prepare your speech, and, if requested, e-mail them to your instructor.

several sources helps you develop an original approach to your topic, insures a broader research base, makes it more likely that you will uncover the various opinions related to your topic, and reduces the likelihood that you will plagiarize the ideas of another.

Cite Sources in Speeches

Although it is important to credit the sources of your information in all of your communication, there are three reasons that it is crucial to cite the sources of your information within your speech. First, speeches, like essays and research papers, are public, so it is plagiarism to present information that you have learned from secondary sources as though it were your own. Second, doing so is also unethical behavior because it prevents the audience from accurately evaluating the source of the information. When a topic is

How do you orally cite sources during your speech?

controversial, knowing the source of the information can be critical to the audience's ability to trust it. Third, citing the source of your information adds to your credibility because it demonstrates to the audience that you have studied the topic. You should make a habit of using **oral footnotes,** which are references to the original sources, made at the points in the speech where information from those sources is presented. An oral footnote includes enough information for listeners to identify and evaluate the source for themselves. Figure 11.8 gives several examples of appropriate oral footnotes.

oral footnote
references to an original source, made at the point in the speech where information from that source is presented.

"Thomas Friedman, noted international editor for *The New York Times,* stated in his book *The World Is Flat* . . ."

"In an interview with *New Republic* magazine, Governor Arnold Schwarzenegger stated . . . "

"According to an article in last week's *Newsweek* magazine, the average college graduate . . ."

"In the latest Gallup poll cited in the February 10 issue of *The New York Times Online* . . . "

"But to get a complete picture, we have to look at the statistics. According to the 2010 *Statistical Abstracts,* the level of production for the European Economic Community fell from . . . "

"In June of 2009, during her keynote speech at the U.S.–India Business Council's 34th Anniversary Summit, Secretary of State Hillary Clinton stated . . . "

Figure 11.8
Appropriate oral footnotes

Action Step 2.c

Citing Sources

On the back of each research card, write a short phrase that you can use in your speech as an oral footnote.

Speech Assignment: **Communicate on Your Feet**

Citing Oral Footnotes

The Assignment

Do secondary research on a topic assigned to the class by your instructor. For that topic, create research cards and oral footnotes for the following kinds of sources:

- One newspaper article
- One journal or magazine article
- One book
- One Internet source

Be prepared when called on in class to present the information on your research card with an appropriate oral footnote. Be prepared to critique the oral footnotes your classmates present and to hear critiques of yours.

A Question of Ethics

What Would You Do?

When Mr. Allen gave the class its final public speaking assignment, Alessandra decided that she would deliver a speech on the limited educational opportunities for women in the developing world. This topic was close to her heart, as her mother had struggled for years to improve education for women in her native country of Eritrea before immigrating to the United States. Moreover, Alessandra had already done quite a bit of reading on the topic in the past.

As chance would have it, Alessandra came down with the flu the week before her speech was due and was flat on her back for four days before she finally recovered. Because she was so far behind in her studies, Alessandra didn't begin working on her speech until the afternoon before it was due. Still, by midnight, she had completed what she felt was a strong draft.

The next morning she cleaned up a few typos and errors in her outline and then practiced delivering it the next two hours. Just before leaving for school, she read the instructions one last time to double check that she had done everything correctly. Were her eyes playing tricks on her? The speech needed to be supported by no fewer than five published sources, yet she had cited only four. How could she have overlooked this detail? Alessandra thought frantically. She could ask for an extension, but she had too much other schoolwork to do in the coming days and needed to complete this project now. She could leave her speech as it was, but Mr. Allen was a stickler for little details and he'd certainly lower her grade over the missing source.

Alessandra had, of course, read other books on her topic in the past, even if she hadn't cited them in her speech. Although she couldn't remember the specific details of these books, she recalled their general message well enough. That was the solution! She would write a few quotations from one of the books based on her memory, drop them into her speech—she knew just the spot—and then update her references with credit information pulled from the Internet.

In less than a half an hour, Alessandra completed her emergency revisions to her speech and was on her way to class.

1. Although blatantly fabricating information from a source is clearly unethical, what about someone like Alessandra writing quotations based on her memory of earlier reading?
2. What ethical obligations does Alessandra have to her sources?

Summary

Five simple action steps can help you to prepare effective speeches: (1) determine a specific speech goal that is adapted to the audience and occasion; (2) gather and evaluate material to use in the speech; (3) organize and develop the material in a way that is suited to the audience and occasion; (4) choose visual and other presentational aids; and (5) practice delivering the speech.

To accomplish the first action step—determining a specific speech goal—begin identifying a topic by listing subjects you are interested in and know something about. Then for each subject, generate topic ideas by brainstorming or concept mapping. To select an appropriate topic, gather and analyze data about your audience members' information needs. The data should include demographic- and subject-related specifics. You can gather the data by conducting a survey, informally observing, questioning an audience representative, or by making educated guesses. When selecting a topic, you will also want to know about the speech setting and the occasion. Based on your audience and setting analyses, you can eliminate topics that would be inappropriate and then select your personal favorite from among the topics that remain. Once you have a topic, identify whether your general goal is to entertain, inform, or persuade. Finally, develop a specific goal—a single statement that identifies the exact response you want from your audience.

The second action step of the speech preparation process is to gather and evaluate material to use in your speech. The three general sources for information are (1) your personal knowledge, experiences, and observations; (2) secondary source research; and (3) primary source research. If you are an expert on your topic, you may already have most of the information you will need to use in your speech. But usually you will also need to do secondary research in resources like books, periodical articles, newspaper accounts, encyclopedia entries, statistical sources, biographical references, government documents, and Internet-based information on your topic. In rare instances, you may need to conduct primary research to get the information you need by surveying, interviewing, or conducting experiments. Before you use any information you find, you will want to evaluate it by testing its authority (expertise of the author and reputation of the publication), objectivity, currency (newness), and relevance (fit). The information you find will include factual statements (statistics and examples), expert opinions, and elaborations (anecdotes and narratives, comparisons and contrasts, and quotations). You will want to draw information from multiple cultural perspectives so that you accurately reflect what is known about your topic.

As you review your sources, you will want to record the information you find on research cards. Each card should contain only one factual statement, opinion, or elaboration so that you can easily access, sort, and arrange the pieces of information as you prepare your speech. On each research card, identify the information with a keyword or category so you can group similar items. You will also want to note the appropriate bibliographic information on each card so that you can relocate the source if you need to and prepare your source list. Finally, on the back of each research card, write a short oral footnote that you can use during your speech.

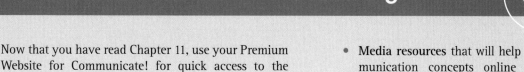

Communicate! Active Online Learning

Now that you have read Chapter 11, use your Premium Website for Communicate! for quick access to the electronic resources that accompany this text. These resources include

- **Study tools** that will help you assess your learning and prepare for exams (*digital glossary, key term flash cards, review quizzes*).
- **Activities and assignments** that will help you hone your knowledge, analyze communication situations (*Skill Learning Activities)*, and build your public speaking skills throughout the course (*Communicate on Your Feet speech assignments, Action Step activities*). Many of these activities allow you to compare your answers to those provided by the authors, and, if requested, submit your answers to your instructor.

- **Media resources** that will help you explore communication concepts online (*Web Resources*), develop your speech outlines (*Speech Builder Express 3.0*), watch and critique videos of communication situations and sample speeches (*Interactive Video Activities*), upload your speech videos for peer reviewing and critique other students' speeches (*Speech Studio online speech review tool*), and download chapter review so you can study when and where you'd like (*Audio Study Tools*).

This chapter's Key Terms, Skill Learning Activities, and Web Resources are also featured on the following pages, and you can find this chapter's Communicate on Your Feet assignment and Action Step activities in the body of the chapter.

Key Terms

anecdotes (268)
audience adaptation (254)
audience analysis (254)
brainstorming (253)
comparisons (268)
concept mapping (253)
contrasts (268)
demographics (254)

examples (267)
expert (268)
expert opinions (268)
factual statements (267)
general speech goal (259)
narratives (268)
oral footnotes (271)
periodicals (262)
plagiarism (268)

primary research (264)
secondary research (262)
setting (257)
specific speech goal (259)
statistics (267)
subject (252)
survey (255)
topic (252)

Skill Learning Activities

11.1: Audience and Setting (257)

Attend a public speech delivered outside your school. If your schedule makes going to a live speech difficult, you may watch a speech delivered on TV or cable (try C-SPAN). When watching the speech, give close consideration to the audience and the setting and evaluate how they might have influenced the speaker. Was the speech pitched directly at the immediate interests of the audience? If not, did the speaker attempt to draw connections between his or her topic and the audience's interests? Did the speaker use any particular words or gestures to connect better with the audience? What about the manner in which the speaker was dressed; how might this have played with the audience? Can you discern any influence the setting might have played on the speaker?

11.2: Recognizing a Specific Goal (260)

Find a speech online about a topic that interests you. (Try sites such as AmericanRhetoric.com or www.whitehouse.gov/briefing_room.) Then read that speech to identify the speaker's goal. Was the goal clearly stated in the introduction? Was it implied but nevertheless clear? Was it unclear? Note how this analysis can help you clarify your own speech goal. Write a paragraph explaining what you have learned.

11.3: Evaluating Online Sources (260)

The Internet can be a gold mine for a researcher, but the challenge can be knowing the fool's gold from the real thing. Pick a subject at random and search the Internet for information on it. Find five reliable and five unreliable online sources on the subject, explaining your rationale for your evaluation of each source.

Web Resources

11.1: Brainstorming (253)

For ideas about how to use brainstorming for developing speech topics, check out the handout "Brainstorming and Topic Development," prepared by the Auburn University English Center.

11.2: Statistics Online (262)

The *Statistical Abstract of the United States* contains a summary of social, political, and economic statistics on the United States.

11.3: Online Biographical References (262)

LibrarySpot.com provides numerous links to online biographical references.

11.4: Online Encyclopedias (262)

LibrarySpot.com also provides numerous links to online encyclopedias.

11.5: Quotations Online (262)

Bartleby.com features links to Web-based sources of quotations. Scroll down to the Quotations section.

11.6: Government Publications Online (263)

The Central Library at Vanderbilt University hosts an excellent site that features links to several frequently used U.S. government documents.

11.7: Conducting Surveys (264)

If you want to conduct your own survey, *Online* magazine at InfoToday.com features important tips for collecting information.

11.8: Analyzing Information Sources (267)

Visit this site, hosted by Cornell University, to read about criteria you can use to evaluate the credibility of your sources.

Organizing Your Speech

Questions you'll be able to answer after reading this chapter:

- How can you determine the main points of your speech?
- How can you construct a thesis statement for your speech?
- How can you prepare a well-written speech outline?
- How can you create effective transitions?
- How can you create an effective introduction to your speech?
- How can you create an effective conclusion for your speech?

"Troy, Mareka gave an awesome speech on recycling paper. I didn't realize the efforts that other universities are making to help the environment and I haven't heard so many powerful stories in a long time."

"Yeah, Brett, I agree; the stories were interesting. But, you know, I had a hard time following the talk. I couldn't really get a hold of what the main ideas were. Did you?"

"Well, she was talking about recycling and stuff, . . . but now that you mention it, I'm not sure what she really wanted us to think or do about it. I mean, it was really interesting, but kind of confusing too."

Troy and Brett's experience is not that unusual. We often hear speeches that are packed with interesting information and delivered in ways that hold our attention, but when we reflect on what was said, we find it difficult to recall the speaker's main ideas, or even the overall goal of the speech. Although every speech should have an introduction, a body, and a conclusion, not all speeches that have these components are well organized. So, we may listen to a speech and find that even though we have been entertained, the speaker's words have no lasting impact on us.

Well-constructed speeches have impact. When a speech is over, we must remember not only the opening joke or a random story, but we must also remember the main ideas that the speaker presented. In this chapter, we describe the third of the five speech-plan action steps. When you have completed this step, you can be confident that your speech not only will maintain your audience's interest but will help your audience understand and remember what you have said.

Action Step 3: Organize Your Material to Meet the Needs of Your Particular Audience

Organizing, the process of selecting and structuring ideas you will present in your speech, is guided by the audience analysis you conducted during the first step of the speech plan. Your audience will have certain expectations about what you will say and how you will organize it. When the audience's expectations are violated, they may get frustrated and "tune out" or even become hostile. The Pop Comm! feature "And the Winner Is…" discusses how the Academy Awards' audience reacted to the acceptance speeches by winners such as Michael Moore and Sally Field, who violated audience expectations.

As you're learning in this chapter, you continue your preparation by organizing the information you have gathered into an outline. To do so, begin by developing the body of your speech and then your introduction and conclusion.

Developing the Body of the Speech

Once you have analyzed the audience, developed a speech goal, and assembled information on your topic, you are ready to craft the body of your speech by (a) determining the main points; (b) writing a thesis statement; (c) outlining the body of the speech; (d) selecting and ordering the supporting material (examples, statistics, illustrations, quotations, and so on) that elaborates on or supports each of your main points; and (e) preparing sectional transitions.

Determining Main Points

The **main points** of a speech are the two to five central ideas you want to present, each stated as a complete sentence. You will want to limit the number of main points so that your audience members can keep track of your ideas and so that you can develop each idea with an appropriate amount of supporting material. Usually, the difference between a 5-minute speech and a 25-minute speech with the same speech goal is not the number of main ideas presented but the extent to which each main point is developed.

For some topics and goals, determining the main points is easy. Erin, who plays Division I volleyball for her college, didn't need to do much research for her speech on how to spike a volleyball. And because she will be speaking to a group of athletes, it was easy for her to group the actions into three steps: the proper approach, a powerful swing, and an effective follow-through.

How can you determine the main points of your speech?

---

organizing
the process of selecting and arranging the main ideas and supporting material to be presented in the speech in a manner that makes it easy for the audience to understand.

main points
complete sentence representations of the main ideas used in your thesis statement.

And the Winner Is . . .

AP Photo/Kevork Djansezian

The MTV Video Vanguard Awards, the People's Choice Awards, the Emmys, the Grammys, the Tonys, the Oscars—each year it seems as though there are more and more entertainment awards shows to keep us, well, entertained. Do you watch any of these shows? If so, why? To see what the celebrities are wearing? To view outstanding performances by your favorite artists? Or to hear what your favorite star says in an acceptance speech?

Acceptance speeches, long a staple of awards shows, can be a bane to the award show's producers and a way for celebrities to become even more famous—or infamous. Consider some of the more unconventional Oscar acceptance speeches. When James Cameron won the award for best director in 1998 for his movie *Titanic*, he first requested a moment of silence for the victims of the *Titanic* disaster, then proclaimed, "I am the king of the world!" In 2003 Michael Moore chastised the U.S. president in his speech, saying "Shame on you Mr. Bush, shame on you." In 1985 Sally Field famously, and very enthusiastically, proclaimed, "You like me, right now, you really like me!" And Greer Garson, who won the award for best actress in 1942, still holds the record for the longest Oscar speech—it lasted for seven minutes ("The ten most memorable," 2008).

Pop Comm!

To help Oscar nominees give effective and well-received speeches, award-winning actor Tom Hanks, a vice-president of the organization that presents the awards, has released a DVD of speech tips such as "Instead of hugging everyone within a 10-row radius, you might have to settle for a few fast high-fives as you sprint down the aisle." He also cautions against reading from a list or thanking a long list of people, and he recommends saying something witty, creative, and memorable ("Hanks for the Oscars," 2006).

Because Oscar speeches are often extensively covered in the media, many sources offer additional tips to nominees. Communication expert Bill Lampton suggests that people don't try to be funny if humor is not their strength and that they remember to keep the speech concise (Goodale, 2005). *The New York Times* advises Oscar nominees to avoid addressing political issues (Iorio, 1995). Media trainer T. J. Walker emphasizes the importance of being prepared, saying, "Preparedness is the only way to be truly spontaneous." As an example, he cites former President Clinton, who has a conversational style that always sounds extemporaneous. Walker explains, "He is still working from a scripted speech, but he knows it inside and out and that allows him to feel prepared and relaxed" (Goodale, 2005).

Feeling prepared and comfortable may encourage sincere emotional expression, which is what many Oscar viewers most appreciate. For Kirwan Rockefeller, pop culture professor at the University of California, Irvine, Halle Berry's 2002 acceptance speech for best actress was a great example of speaking from the heart. "Berry's speech was poignant and full of emotion," he said. "Everybody loves to see an Oscar winner cry and be humble and be really surprised" (Goodale, 2005).

But for other topics and goals, determining main points can be more difficult. For example Emming wants to speak on choosing a credit card. His specific goal statement is "I want the audience to understand the criteria for choosing a credit card." As he did his research, he uncovered numerous interesting facts related to the topic, but he has had trouble figuring out how to group them. When you find yourself in this situation, you will need to do further work to determine the main ideas you want to present.

How should you proceed? First, list the ideas you have found that relate to your specific goal. Like Emming, you may have a very long list. Second, eliminate ideas that your audience analysis suggests that your audience already understands. Third, see if some of the ideas can be grouped under a broader concept. Fourth, eliminate ideas for which you do not have strong support in the sources you consulted. Fifth, eliminate ideas that might be too complicated for this audience to comprehend in the time you have to explain them. Finally, from the ideas that remain, choose three to five that are the most important for your audience to understand if you are to accomplish your specific speech goal.

Let's look at how Emming used these steps to identify the main points for his speech on criteria for choosing a credit card. Emming had some thoughts about possible main ideas for the speech, but it wasn't until he completed most of his research, sorted through what he had collected, and thought about it, that he was able to choose his main points.

First, he listed ideas (in this case nine) that were discussed in the research materials he had found about choosing a credit card:

> what is a credit card
> interest rates
> credit ratings
> convenience
> discounts
> annual fee
> institutional reputation
> reward points
> rebates

Second, Emming eliminated the idea "what is a credit card" because he knew that his audience already understood this. This left him with eight ideas—still too many for his speech. Third, Emming noticed that several ideas seemed to be related. "Discounts," "reward points," and "rebates" are all types of incentives that card companies offer to entice people to choose their card. So Emming grouped these three ideas together under the single heading of "incentives." Fourth, Emming noticed that he had uncovered considerable information on interest rates, credit ratings, discounts, annual fees, rebates, and frequent flyer points, but he had very little information on convenience or institutional reputation, so he crossed out those two ideas.

Finally, Emming considered each of the six remaining ideas in light of the five-minute time limit for his speech. He decided to cross out credit ratings because, although people's credit ratings influence the types of cards and interest rates for which they might qualify, Emming believed that he could not adequately explain this idea in the short time available. In fact, he believed that explaining credit ratings to this audience might take a lot longer than five minutes and wasn't as basic as some of the other ideas he had listed. When he was finished with his analysis and synthesis, his list looked like this:

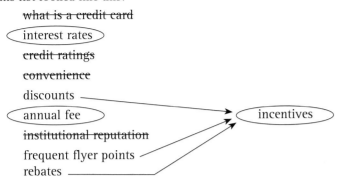

~~what is a credit card~~
interest rates
~~credit ratings~~
~~convenience~~
discounts
annual fee
~~institutional reputation~~
frequent flyer points
rebates
incentives

This process left Emming with three broad points he could develop in his speech: interest rates, annual fee, and incentives. When you want to talk about a topic that includes numerous types, categories, and so on, follow Emming's steps to reduce the number of your main points to between two and five.

> How can you construct a thesis statement for your speech?

Writing a Thesis Statement

A **thesis statement** is a one- or two-sentence summary of your speech that states your general and specific goals and previews the main points of your speech. Thus, your thesis statement provides a blueprint from which you will organize the body of your speech.

Now let's consider how you arrive at this thesis statement. Recall that Emming determined three main ideas that he wanted to talk about in his speech on choosing a

thesis statement
a one- or two-sentence summary of your speech that states your general and specific goals and previews the main points of your speech.

Action Step 3.a

Determining Main Points

The goal of this activity is to help you determine three to five main ideas or main points that you will present in your speech.

1. List all the ideas you have found that relate to the specific goal of your speech.
2. If there are more than five:
   a. Draw a line through each idea that you believe the audience already understands, that you have no supporting information for, or that just seems too complicated for the time allowed.
   b. Look for ideas that can be grouped under a larger heading.
3. From the ideas that remain, choose the two to five that you think will make the best main points for your audience.

 You can complete this activity online with Speech Builder Express, view a student sample of this activity, and, if requested, e-mail your completed activity to your instructor. Use your Premium Website for Communicate! to access the Action Step activities for Chapter 12.

Skill Learning Activity 12.1
Web Resource 12.1

credit card: interest rates, annual fee, and incentives. Based on his general and specific goals and the main points he had determined, Emming was able to write his thesis statement: "Three criteria you should use to find the most suitable credit card are level of real interest rate, annual fee, and advertised incentives."

Outlining the Body of the Speech

Once you have a thesis statement, you can begin to outline your speech. A **speech outline** is a sentence representation of the hierarchical and sequential relationships between the ideas presented in the speech. Your outline may have three hierarchical levels of information: main points (numbered with Roman numerals), subpoints that support a main point (ordered with capital letters), and sometimes sub-subpoints that support a subpoint (numbered with Arabic numbers). Figure 12.1 shows the general form of the speech outline system.

Writing your main points and subpoints in complete sentences will help you clarify the relationships between main points and subpoints. Once you have worded each main point and determined its relevant subpoints, you will choose a pattern of organization that fits your thesis. The order of your main points will depend on the pattern of organization that you choose.

> How can you prepare a well-written speech outline?

Wording main points

Recall that Emming determined that interest rates, annual fee, and incentives are the three major criteria for finding a suitable credit card and his thesis statement was "Three criteria that you should use to find the most suitable credit card are level of real interest rate, annual fee, and advertised incentives." So Emming's first draft of the main points of his speech might look like this:

   I. Examining the interest rate is one criterion that you can use to find a credit card that is suitable for where you are in life.

   II. Another criterion that you can use to make sure you find a credit card that is suitable for where you are in life is to examine the annual fee.

   III. Finding a credit card can also depend on weighing the advertised incentives, which is the third criterion that you will want to use to be sure that it is suitable for where you are in life.

speech outline
a sentence representation of the hierarchical and sequential relationships between the ideas presented in a speech.

Action Step 3.b ●

Writing a Thesis Statement

The goal of this activity is to use your specific goal statement and the main points you have identified to develop a well-worded thesis statement for your speech.

1. Write the specific goal you developed in Chapter 11 with Action Step 1.e.
2. List the main points you determined in Action Step 3.a.
3. Now write a complete sentence that includes both your specific goal and your main points.

You can complete this activity online with Speech Builder Express, view a student sample of this activity, and, if requested, e-mail your completed activity to your instructor. Use your Premium Website for Communicate! *to access the Action Step activities for Chapter 12.*

I. Main point one
   A. Subpoint A for main point one
      1. Sub-subpoint one for subpoint A of main point one
      2. Sub-subpoint two for subpoint A of main point one
   B. Subpoint B of main point one

II. Main point two
   A. Subpoint A for main point two
      1. Sub-subpoint one for subpoint A of main point two
      2. Sub-subpoint two for subpoint A of main point two
   B. Subpoint B of main point two
   C. Subpoint C of main point two
      1. Sub-subpoint one for subpoint C of main point two
      2. Sub-subpoint two for subpoint C of main point two
      3. Sub-subpoint three for subpoint C of main point two

III. Main point three
   A. Subpoint A for main point three
      1. Sub-subpoint one for subpoint A of main point three
      2. Sub-subpoint two for subpoint A of main point three
   B. Subpoint B of main point three
     ... and so on.

Figure 12.1
General form for a speech outline

Study these statements. Do they seem a bit vague? Sometimes, the first draft of a main point is well expressed and doesn't need additional work. More often, however, our first attempt doesn't quite capture what we want to say. So we need to rework the statements to make them clearer. Testing our main points with two questions can help us as we revise.

1. Is the relationship of each main point statement to the goal statement clearly specified? Based on this question, Emming revised his main points like this:
   I. A low interest rate is one criterion that you can use to select a credit card that is suitable for where you are in life.
   II. Another criterion that you can use to make sure you find a credit card that is suitable for where you are in life is to look for a card with no annual fee or a very low one.
   III. Finding a credit card can also depend on weighing the value of the advertised incentives against the increased annual cost or interest rate, which is the third criterion that you will want to use to be sure that it is suitable for where you are in life.

2. Are the main points parallel in structure? Main points are **parallel** to each other when their wording follows the same structural pattern, often using the same introductory words. Parallel structure helps the audience recognize main points by recalling a pattern in the wording. Based on this, Emming revised his main points to make them parallel:
   I. The first criterion for choosing a credit card is a relatively low interest rate.
   II. A second criterion for choosing a credit card is no annual fee or a low annual fee.
   III. A third criterion for choosing a credit card is the value of the advertised incentives compared to the increased annual cost or interest rate.

parallel
wording in more than one sentence that follows the same structural pattern, often using the same introductory words.

Selecting an organizational pattern for main points

A speech can be organized in many different ways. Your objective is to use a structure that will help the audience make the most sense of the material. You will want to choose an organizational pattern that makes your main points easy for your audience to understand. Although there are numerous organizational patterns, four fundamental patterns for beginning speakers are time (or sequential) order, narrative order, topic order, and logical reasons order.

1. **Time order,** sometimes called *sequential order* or *chronological order*, arranges main points by a chronological sequence or by steps in a process. When you are explaining how to do something, how to make something, how something works, or how something happened, you will want to use time order. Erin's audience will find it easiest to understand the process of spiking a volleyball if she uses time order for her main points (good approach, powerful swing, good follow-through). Imagine how difficult it would be for her audience if Erin began by talking about a powerful swing, then discussed a good-follow through, and ended by describing a good approach. Could her audience understand her point? Probably. But they would have to work much harder than if she ordered the topics sequentially. Let's look at another example of time order.

   Thesis statement: The four steps involved in developing a personal network are to analyze your current networking potential, to position yourself in places for opportunity, to advertise yourself, and to follow up on contacts.

      I. First, analyze your current networking potential.
      II. Second, position yourself in places for opportunity.
      III. Third, advertise yourself.
      IV. Fourth, follow up on contacts.

   Although the use of "first," "second," and so on, is not a requirement when using a time order, their inclusion helps audience members keep track of the sequence.

2. **Narrative order** dramatizes the thesis with a story or series of stories that includes characters, settings, and a plot. While a narrative may be presented in chronological order, it may also use a series of flash backs or flash forwards to increase the dramatic effect. The main points in a narrative may be the events in a single story that highlights the thesis, or the main points may be individual stories, each of which dramatizes the thesis. Narrative order is a particularly effective way of developing a thesis when you tell stories that are emotionally compelling. Lonna wanted her audience to understand how AIDS affects the lives of survivors, so she chose to develop this thesis by using a narrative order and tell her personal story.

   Thesis statement: Today, I want you to understand what it is like to live with AIDS. So I am going to share the story of my life before contracting AIDS, my life today with AIDS, and my future plans knowing that I have AIDS.

      I. My life before I contracted AIDS was pretty typical for a middle-class white girl.
      II. My life today is anything but typical as I balance my schoolwork and social life with weekly visits to the doctor and daily physical and drug therapy.
      III. My future life plans have changed dramatically because I have AIDS.

   Here's how Lonna could also use a narrative order that shares several stories:

   Thesis statement: Today, I want you to understand what it is like to live with AIDS. So I am going to share the stories of Robert, Emma, and me.

time, or sequential, order
organizing the main points by a chronological sequence, or by steps in a process.

narrative order
dramatizes the thesis using a story or series of stories that includes characters, settings, and a plot.

    I. Robert's story is about a 27-year-old store manager with AIDS.

   II. Emma's story is about a 3-year-old toddler with AIDS.

  III. My story is about a 20-year-old college student with AIDS.

3. **Topic order** arranges the main points of the speech by categories or divisions of a subject. This is a common way of ordering main points because nearly any subject may be subdivided or categorized in many different ways. The order of the topics may go from general to specific, least important to most important, or some other logical sequence. In the following example, the most important point is presented last and the second most important point is presented first, which is the order that the speaker believes is most suitable for the audience and speech goal.

    Thesis statement: To maintain good health, let's discuss three proven methods for ridding our bodies of harmful toxins: staying hydrated, reducing animal foods, and eating natural whole foods.

    I. One proven method for ridding our bodies of harmful toxins is reducing our intake of animal products.

   II. A second proven method for ridding our bodies of harmful toxins is eating more natural whole foods.

  III. A third proven method for ridding our bodies of harmful toxins is keeping well hydrated.

4. **Logical reasons order** is used when the main points are the rationale or proof that supports the thesis.

    Thesis statement: Donating to the United Way is appropriate because your one donation can be divided among many charities, you can stipulate which specific

topic order
organizing the main points of the speech by categories or divisions of a subject.

logical reasons order
emphasizes when the main points provide proof supporting the thesis statement.

Action Step 3.c

Organizing and Outlining the Main Points of Your Speech

The goal of this activity is to help you phrase and order your main points.

1. Write your thesis statement (Action Step 3.b).
2. Underline the two to five main points determined for your thesis statement.
3. For each underlined item, write one sentence that summarizes what you want your audience to know about that idea.
4. Review the main points as a group.
    a. Is the relationship of each main point statement to the goal statement clearly specified? If not, revise.
    b. Are the main points parallel in structure? If not, revise.
5. Choose an organizational pattern for your main points, and write them in this order. Place a "I." before the main point you will make first, a "II." before your second point, and so on.

You can complete this activity online using Speech Builder Express, view a student sample of this activity, and, if requested, e-mail your completed activity to your instructor. Use your Premium Website for Communicate! to access the Action Step activities for Chapter 11.

Skill Learning Activity 12.2

charities you wish to support, and a high percentage of your donation goes to charities.

I. When you donate to the United Way, your one donation can be divided among many charities.

II. When you donate to the United Way, you can stipulate which charities you wish to support.

III. When you donate to the United Way, you know that a high percentage of your donation will go directly to the charities you've selected.

Although these four organizational patterns are the most basic ones, in Chapters 15 and 16 you will be introduced to several other patterns that are appropriate for informative and persuasive speaking.

Selecting and Outlining Supporting Material

Although the main points provide the basic structure or skeleton of your speech, whether your audience understands, believes, or appreciates what you have to say usually depends on your supporting material—the information you use to develop the main points. You can identify supporting material by sorting your research cards into piles that correspond to each of your main points. The goal is to see what information you have to develop each point. When Emming sorted his research cards, he discovered that for his first point, interest rates, he had the following support:

Jim MacMillan/AP Photos

If you were giving a speech on the phenomenon of soldiers creating blogs about their combat experiences, what organizational pattern do you think would best suit your speech?

- Most "zero percent" cards carry an average of 8 percent after a specified 0 percent interest period.
- Some cards carry as much as 21 percent after the first year.
- Some cards offer a grace period.
- Department store interest rates are often higher than bank rates.
- *Variable rate* means that the interest rate can change from month to month.
- Even fixed rates on some cards can be raised to as much as 32 percent if you make a late payment.
- *Fixed rate* means the interest rate will stay the same.
- Many companies offer "zero percent" for up to 12 months.
- Some companies offer "zero percent" for a few months.

Once you have listed each of the supporting items, look for relationships between them that will allow you to group ideas under a broader heading and eliminate ideas that don't really belong. Then select the ideas that best support the main idea and develop them into complete sentences. When Emming did this, he came up with two statements for grouping the supporting information about his first main point. These two statements became his subpoints. He also had material that supported each subpoint. Here is Emming's expanded outline for his first main point:

    I. The first criterion for choosing a credit card is a low interest rate.

        A. Interest rates are the percentages that a company charges you to carry a balance on your card past the due date.

            1. Most credit cards carry an average of 8 percent after a specified 0 percent interest period.

            2. Some cards carry as much as 21 percent after the first year.

            3. Many companies quote low rates (0%–3%) for a specific period.

        B. Interest rates can be variable or fixed.

            1. A *variable rate* means that the percent charged can vary from month to month.

            2. A *fixed rate* means that the rate will stay the same.

            3. Even a card with a fixed rate can be raised to as much as 32 percent if you make a late payment.

The outline includes the supporting points of a speech, but it does not include all the development of them. For instance, Emming could use personal experiences, examples, illustrations, anecdotes, statistics, or quotations to elaborate on main points and subpoints. But these are not detailed on the outline. Emming will choose these developmental materials later as he considers how to verbally and visually adapt to his audience.

Skill Learning Activity 12.3

Action Step 3.d

Selecting and Outlining Supporting Material

The goal of this activity is to help you develop and outline your supporting material. Complete the following steps for each of your main points.

1. List the main point.
2. Using your research cards, list the key information related to that main point.
3. Analyze that information and cross out items that seem less relevant or don't fit.
4. Look for items that seems related and can be grouped under a broader heading.
5. Try to group information until you have between two and five supporting points for the main point.
6. Write those supporting subpoints in full sentences.
7. Write the supporting sub-subpoints in full sentences.
8. Repeat this process for all main points.
9. Write an outline using Roman numerals for main points, capital letters for supporting points, and Arabic numbers for material related to supporting points.

You can complete this activity online using Speech Builder Express and, if requested, e-mail your completed activity to your instructor. Use your Premium Website for Communicate! *to access the Action Step activities for Chapter 12.*

Preparing Section Transitions and Signposts

Once you have outlined your main points, subpoints, and potential supporting material, you will want to consider how you will move smoothly from one main point to another. **Transitions** are words, phrases, or sentences that show the relationship between or bridge two ideas. Transitions act like tour guides leading the audience from point to point through the speech. Good transitions are important in writing, but they are even more important in speaking. If listeners get lost or think they have missed something, they cannot check back as they can when reading. Transitions can come in the form of section transitions or signposts.

Section transitions are complete sentences that show the relationship between or bridge major parts of the speech. They summarize what has just been said and preview the next main idea. For example, suppose Noel has just finished the introduction of his speech on what it's like to be in a color guard and is now ready to launch into his main points. Before stating his first main point, he might say, "There are many benefits to participating in a color guard, one of which is the physical benefits you get from the workouts." When his listeners hear this transition, they are signaled to mentally prepare to listen to and remember the first main point. When he finishes his first main point, he will use another section transition to signal that he is finished speaking about the first main point and is moving on to the second main point: "Now that we understand some of the physical benefits, we can move on to some of the friendship benefits."

Section transitions are important for two reasons. First, they help the audience follow the organization of ideas in the speech. If every member of the audience were able to pay complete attention to every word, then perhaps section transitions would not be needed. But our attention rises and falls during a speech, so we often find ourselves wondering where we are. Section transitions give us a mental jolt and say, "Pay attention." Second, section transitions are important in helping us retain information. We may remember something that was said once in a speech, but our retention is likely to increase markedly if we hear something more than once.

In a speech, if we forecast main points, then state each main point, and use section transitions between each point, audiences are more likely to follow and remember the organization. To help remember and use section transitions, write them in complete sentences on your speech outline.

> **How can you create effective transitions?**

transitions
words, phrases, or sentences that show the relationship between or bridge ideas.

section transition
complete sentence that shows the relationship between or bridge major parts of the speech.

Action Step 3.e

Preparing Section Transitions

The goal of this exercise is to help you prepare section transitions. Section transitions appear as parenthetical statements before or after each main point. Using complete sentences:

1. Write a transition from your first main point to your second.
2. Write a transition from each remaining main point to the one after it.
3. Add these transitional statements to your outline.

 You can complete this activity online with Speech Builder Express, view a student sample of this activity, and, if requested, e-mail your completed activity to your instructor. Use your Premium Website for Communicate! to access the Action Step activities for Chapter 12.

Signposts are single words or phrases that connect pieces of supporting material to their main point or subpoint. Signposts are briefer than section transitions, and their only goal is to show relationships among or emphasize important supporting material. Sometimes signposts number ideas: *first*, *second*, *third*, and *fourth*. Sometimes they help the audience focus on a key idea: *foremost*, *most important*, or *above all*. Signposts can also be used to introduce an explanation: *to illustrate*, *for example*, *in other words*, *essentially*, or *to clarify*. Signposts can also signal that a lengthy anecdote, or even the speech itself, is coming to an end: *in short*, *finally*, *in conclusion*, or *to summarize*. Just as section transitions serve as the glue that holds your big-picture main points together, signposts connect your subpoints and supporting material within each main point.

Creating the Introduction

Once you have developed the body of the speech, you can decide how to begin your speech. The introduction of your speech establishes your relationship with your audience, so it is worth your time to develop two or three different introductions and then select the one that seems best for this particular audience. Although your introduction may be very short, it should gain the audience's attention and motivate them to listen to all that you have to say. An introduction is generally no more than 10 percent of the length of the entire speech, so for a five-minute speech (approximately 750 words), an introduction of about 30 seconds (approximately 60–85 words) is appropriate.

An effective introduction achieves three goals: it gains attention, it points out how your topic is relevant to the listener, and it reveals your thesis statement (specific speech goal and main points). In addition, effective introductions can help you begin to establish your credibility, set the tone for the speech, and create a bond of goodwill between you and the audience.

Gaining Attention

An audience's physical presence does not guarantee that people will actually listen to your speech. Your first goal, then, is to create an opening that will win your listeners' attention by arousing their curiosity and motivating them to continue listening. Although your introductions are limited only by your imagination, let's look at several techniques you can use to get your audience's attention and also to stimulate their interest in what you have to say: startling statements, questions, jokes, personal references, quotations, stories, and suspense.

Startling statements

A startling statement is a sentence or two that grabs your listeners' attention by shocking them in some way. Because they were shocked, audience members stop what they were doing or thinking about and focus on the speaker. Chris used a startling statement to get his listeners' attention for his speech about how automobile emissions contribute to global warming:

> **Look around. Each one of you is sitting next to a killer. That's right. You are sitting next to a cold-blooded killer. Before you think about jumping up and running out of this room, let me explain. Everyone who drives an automobile is a killer of the environment. Every time you turn the key to your ignition, you are helping to destroy our precious surroundings.**

Once Chris's startling statement grabbed the attention of his listeners, he went on to state his speech goal and preview his main points.

Michael Blann

Section transitions mentally prepare the audience to move to the next main idea.

How can you create an effective introduction to your speech?

signposts
short word or phrase transitions that connect pieces of supporting material to the main point or subpoint they address.

Rhetorical and direct questions

Questions encourage the audience think about something related to your topic Questions can be *rhetorical* or *direct*. A **rhetorical question** seeks a mental rather than a direct response. Notice how a student began her speech on counterfeiting with three short, rhetorical questions:

> What would you do with this $20 bill if I gave it to you? Take your friend to a movie? Treat yourself to a pizza and drinks? Well, if you did either of these things, you could get in big trouble—this bill is counterfeit!
>
> Today I want to explain the extent of counterfeiting in America and what our government is doing to curb it.

Unlike a rhetorical question, a **direct question** demands an overt response from the audience, usually by a show of hands. For example, here's how Stephanie introduced her speech on seatbelt safety:

> By a show of hands, how many of you drove or rode in an automobile to get here today? Of those of you who did, how many of you actually wore your seatbelt?

Direct questions get audience attention because they require a physical response. However, getting listeners to actually respond can sometimes pose a challenge.

Jokes

A **joke** is an anecdote or a piece of wordplay designed to be funny and make people laugh. To get audience attention, a joke needs to meet the "three-r test": it must be realistic, relevant, and repeatable (Humes, 1988). In other words, the joke can't be too far-fetched, unrelated to the speech purpose, or potentially offensive to some listeners. For example, one of your authors gave a speech recently about running effective meetings to a group of business professionals. She began with, "As many of you know, I'm a college professor, so I just couldn't resist giving you a quiz." She then handed out a 12-item personal-learning-styles inventory to the audience members. As she distributed it, she explained, "The nice thing about *this* quiz though is that you can't be wrong. You'll all get 100 percent." The audience laughed with relief. Be careful with humorous attention-getters—and consider how you will handle the situation if nobody laughs.

Personal references

A **personal reference** is a brief account of something that happened to you or a hypothetical situation that listeners can imagine themselves in. In addition to getting attention, a personal reference can engage listeners as active participants. A personal reference opening, like this one, may be suitable for a speech of any length:

> Say, were you panting when you got to the top of those four flights of stairs this morning? I'll bet there were a few of you who vowed you're never going

rhetorical question
a question seeking a mental rather than a vocal response.

direct question
a question that demands an overt response from the audience, usually by a show of hands.

joke
anecdote or a piece of wordplay designed to be funny and make people laugh.

personal reference
a brief account of something that happened to you or a hypothetical situation that listeners can imagine themselves in.

to take a class on the top floor of this building again. But did you ever stop to think that maybe the problem isn't that this class is on the top floor? It just might be that you are not getting enough exercise.

Quotations

A **quotation** is a comment made by and attributed to someone other than the speaker. A particularly vivid or thought-provoking quotation can make an excellent introduction to a speech of any length, especially if you can use your imagination to relate the quotation to your topic. For instance, notice how Sally Mason, provost at Purdue University, used a quotation to get the attention of her audience, the Lafayette, Indiana, YWCA:

> There is an ancient saying, "May you live in interesting times." It is actually an ancient curse. It might sound great to live in interesting times. But interesting times are times of change and even turmoil. They are times of struggle. They are exciting. But, at the same time, they are difficult. People of my generation have certainly lived through interesting times and they continue today. (Mason, 2007, p. 159)

Stories

A **story** is an account of something that has happened (actual) or could happen (hypothetical). Most people enjoy a well-told story, so a story can make a good attention getter. One drawback of stories is that they can be lengthy. So use a story only if it is short or if you can abbreviate it to make it appropriate for your speech length. Matt used a story to get audience attention for his speech about spanking as a form of discipline:

> One rainy afternoon, four-year-old Billy was playing "pretend" in the living room. He was Captain Jack Sparrow, staving off the bad guys with his amazing sword-fighting skills. Then it happened. Billy knocked his mother's very expensive china bowl off the table. Billy hung his head and began to cry. He knew what was coming, and sure enough it did. The low thud of his mother's hand on his bottom brought a sting to his behind and a small yelp from his mouth. Billy got a spanking.

Suspense

To create **suspense**, you word your attention-getter so that it generates uncertainty and excites the audience. When your audience wonders, "What is she leading up to?" you have created suspense. A suspenseful opening is especially valuable when your audience is not particularly interested in hearing about your topic. Consider the attention-getting value of this introduction:

> It costs the United States more than $116 billion per year. It has cost the loss of more jobs than a recession. It accounts for nearly 100,000 deaths a year. I'm not talking about cocaine abuse—the problem is alcoholism. Today I want to show you how we can avoid this inhumane killer by abstaining from it.

By putting the problem, alcoholism, at the end, the speaker encourages the audience to try to anticipate the answer. And because the audience may well be thinking "narcotics," the revelation that the answer is alcoholism is likely to make them interested in hearing what the speaker has to say.

Establishing Listener Relevance

Even if you successfully get the attention of your listeners, to *keep* their attention you will need to motivate them to listen to your speech. You can do this by creating a clear

quotation
a comment made by and attributed to someone other than the speaker.

story
an account of something that has happened (actual) or could happen (hypothetical).

suspense
wording your attention-getter so that it generates uncertainty and excites the audience.

listener relevance link, a statement of how and why your speech relates to or might affect your audience. Sometimes your attention-getting statement will serve this function, but if it doesn't, you will need to provide a personal connection between your topic and your audience. Notice how Tiffany created a listener relevance link for her speech about being a vegetarian by asking her audience to consider the topic in relation to their own lives:

> Although a diet rich in eggs and meat was once the norm in this country, more and more of us are choosing a vegetarian lifestyle to help lower blood pressure, reduce cholesterol, and even help prevent the onset of some diseases. So as I describe my experience, you may want to consider how *you* could alter your diet.

When creating a listener relevance link, answer these questions: Why should my listeners care about what I'm saying? In what way(s) might they benefit from hearing about it? How might my speech address my listeners' needs or desires for such things as health, wealth, well-being, self-esteem, or success?

Stating the Thesis

Because audiences want to know what the speech is going to be about, it's important to state your thesis, which will introduce them to the specific goal and main points of your speech. For his speech about romantic love, after Miguel gained the audience's attention, he introduced his thesis, "In the next five minutes, I'd like to explain to you that romantic love consists of three elements: passion, intimacy, and commitment."

Stating main points in the introduction is necessary unless you have some special reason for not revealing the details of the thesis. For instance, after getting the attention of his audience, Miguel might say, "In the next five minutes, I'd like to explain the three aspects of romantic love," a statement that specifies the number of main points, but leaves stating specifics for transition statements immediately preceding main points. Now let's consider three other goals you might have for your introduction.

Establishing Your Credibility

If someone hasn't formally introduced you before you speak, the audience members are going to wonder who you are and why they should pay attention to what you have to say. So another goal of the introduction may be to begin to build your credibility. For instance, it would be natural for an audience to question Miguel's qualifications for speaking on the topic of romantic love. So after his attention-getting statement he might say, "As a child development and family science major, last semester I took an interdisciplinary seminar on romantic love, and I am now doing an independent research project on commitment in relationships." Remember that your goal is to highlight why you are a credible speaker on this topic, but not to imply that you are *the* or even *a* final authority on the subject.

Setting a Tone

The introductory remarks may also reflect the emotional tone that is appropriate for the topic. A humorous opening will signal a lighthearted tone; a serious opening signals a more thoughtful or somber tone. For instance, a speaker who starts with a rib-tickling story is putting the audience in a lighthearted mood. If that speaker then says, "Now let's turn to the subject of abortion [or nuclear war, or global warming]," the audience will be confused by the introduction that signaled a far different type of subject.

listener relevance link
a statement of how and why your speech relates to or might affect your audience

Action Step 3.f

Writing Speech Introductions

The goal of this activity is to create choices for how you will begin your speech.

1. For the speech body you outlined earlier, write three different introductions—using a startling statement, rhetorical or direct question, joke, personal reference, quotation, story, or suspense—that you believe meet the goals of effective introductions and that you believe would set an appropriate tone for your speech goal and audience.
2. Of the three you drafted, which do you believe is the best? Why?
3. Next, plan how you will introduce your thesis statement.
4. Develop a very short statement that will establish your credibility.
5. Consider how you might establish goodwill during the introduction.
6. Write that introduction in outline form.

 You can complete this activity online with Speech Builder Express, view a student sample of this activity, and, if requested, e-mail your completed activity to your instructor. Use you Premium Website for Communicate! *to access the Action Step activities for Chapter 12.*

Creating a Bond of Goodwill

In your first few words, you may also establish how your audience will feel about you as a person. If you're enthusiastic, warm, and friendly and give a sense that what you're going to talk about is in the audience's best interest, it will make them feel more comfortable about spending time listening to you.

For longer speeches, you will have more time to accomplish all five goals in the introduction. But for shorter speeches, like those that you are likely to be giving in class, you will first focus on getting attention, establishing listener relevance, and stating the thesis; then you will use very brief comments to try to build your credibility, establish an appropriate tone, and develop goodwill.

Crafting the Conclusion

Shakespeare said, "All's well that ends well." A strong conclusion will summarize the main ideas and will leave the audience with a vivid impression of what they have learned. Even though the conclusion is a relatively short part of the speech—seldom more than 5 percent (35 to 40 words for a five-minute speech)—it is important that your conclusion be carefully planned. It should achieve two major goals: summarize your speech goal and main points and provide a clincher that leaves a vivid impression of your message in the minds of your audience or compels them to action.

As with your speech introduction, you should prepare two or three conclusions and then choose the one you believe will be the most effective with your audience.

> How can you create an effective conclusion for your speech?

Summary

An effective speech conclusion will include a restatement of your speech goal and summary of the main points. An appropriate summary for an informative speech on how to improve your grades might be "So I hope you now understand [informative goal] that three techniques to help you improve your grades are to attend classes regularly, to develop a positive attitude toward the course, and to study systematically [main points]." A short ending for a persuasive speech on why you should lift weights might be "So remember that three major reasons why you should consider lifting weights [persuasive goal] are to improve your appearance, to improve your health, and to accomplish both with a minimum of effort [main points]."

Jeff Greenberg/PhotoEdit

When you end your speech with an emotional conclusion, you really drive your point home. Can you recall conclusions from speeches you have heard? Were they emotional?

clincher
a one- or two-sentence statement that provides a sense of closure by driving home the importance of your speech in a memorable way.

appeal
describes the behavior you want your listeners to follow after they have heard your arguments.

Clincher

Although summaries help you achieve the first goal of an effective conclusion, you'll need to develop additional material to achieve the second goal: leaving the audience with a vivid impression or appealing to action. You can achieve this goal with a **clincher**—a one- or two-sentence statement that provides a sense of closure by driving home the importance of your speech in a memorable way. Very often, effective clinchers also achieve closure by referring back to the introductory comments in some way. You can provide closure and create vivid impressions using any of the attention-getters described earlier in this chapter. For example, in Tiffany's conclusion to her speech about being a vegetarian, she mentioned the personal reference she made in her introduction about a vegetarian Thanksgiving dinner:

> So now you know why I made the choice to become a vegetarian and how this choice affects my life today. As a vegetarian, I've discovered a world of food I never knew existed. Believe me, I am salivating just thinking about the meal I have planned for this Thanksgiving: fennel and blood orange salad; followed by baked polenta layered with tomato, Fontina, and Gorgonzola cheeses; an acorn squash tart, marinated tofu; and with what else but pumpkin pie for dessert!

Sounds good doesn't it? Clinchers with vivid imagery are effective because they leave listeners with a picture imprinted in their minds.

The appeal to action is a common clincher for a persuasive speech. The **appeal** describes the behavior that you want your listeners to follow after they have heard your arguments. Notice how David M. Walker, former comptroller general of the United States, concluded his speech on fiscal responsibility with a strong appeal to action:

> The truth is that all sectors of society have a dog in this fiscal fight and transformation effort. If government stays on its current course, we'll all end up paying a big price, especially our kids and grandkids.

Action Step 3.g

Creating Speech Conclusions

The goal of this activity is to help you create choices for how you will conclude your speech.

1. For the speech body you outlined earlier, write three different conclusions that review important points you want the audience to remember and leave the audience with vivid imagery or an emotional appeal.
2. Which do you believe is the best? Why?
3. Write that conclusion in outline form.

You can complete this activity online with Speech Builder Express, view a student sample of this activity, and, if requested, e-mail your completed activity to your instructor. Use you Premium Website for Communicate! *to access the Action Step activities for Chapter 12.*

Speech Assignment: **Communicate on Your Feet**

The Assignment

1. Identify a favorite toy, game, food, or hobby you had as a child.
2. Come up with a thesis statement and three main points you could talk about for that toy, game, food, or hobby.
3. Prepare an introduction, section transitions, and conclusion for a "speech" about that toy, game, food, or hobby. But do not prepare any supporting material.
4. At your instructor's request, come to the front of the room and deliver the introduction, section transitions, and conclusion for a speech on that topic.
5. Be prepared to hear critiques from your classmates and to offer suggestions on theirs as well.

Over its 200-plus years of existence, the United States has faced many great challenges. We've always risen to those challenges, and I'm confident we'll eventually do so this time as well. After all, it's always a mistake to underestimate American resolve when we set our minds to accomplish something.

But we need to act, and act soon. Baby boomers like myself are on course to become the first generation of Americans who leave things in worse shape than when we found them. Fortunately, such a legacy isn't carved in stone. Turning things around won't be easy, and it's not going to happen overnight. But we all need to be part of the solution. By applying our collective energy, expertise, and experience to looming problems; by making some difficult decisions; and by accepting some degree of shared sacrifice, we can ensure a brighter future for this great nation, for our children and grandchildren, and for those who will follow them. (Walker, 2006, p. 762).

Skill Learning Activity 12.4

Listing Sources

Regardless of the type or length of speech, you'll want to prepare a list of the sources you are going to use in the speech. Although you may be required to prepare this list for the speeches you give in this course and other courses you take, in real settings, this list will enable you to direct audience members to the specific source of the information you have used, and will allow you to quickly find the information at a later date. The two standard methods of organizing source lists are (1) alphabetically by author's last name or (2) by content category, with items listed alphabetically by author within each category. For speeches with a short list, the first method is efficient. But for long speeches with a lengthy source list, it is helpful to group sources by content categories.

There are many formal bibliographic style formats you can use in citing sources (for example, MLA, APA, Chicago, CBE). The "correct" form differs by professional or academic discipline. Check to see if your instructor has a preference about which style you use for this class.

Regardless of the particular style, however, the specific information you need to record differs somewhat, depending on whether the source is a book, a periodical, a newspaper, or an Internet source or Web site. The elements that are essential to all are author, title of publication, date of publication, and page numbers. Figure 12.2

	MLA style	APA style
Book	Miller, Roberta B. *The Five Paths to Persuasion: The Art of Selling Your Message.* New York: Warner Business Books, 2004. Print.	Miller, R. B. (2004). *The five paths to persuasion: The art of selling your message.* New York: Warner Business Books.
Edited book	Janzen, Rod. "Five Paradigms of Ethnic Relations." *Intercultural Communication 10th ed.* Eds. Larry Samovar and Richard Porter. Belmont, CA: Wadsworth, 2003. 36–42. Print.	Janzen, R. (2003). Five paradigms of ethnic relations. *Intercultural communication* (10th ed.) (L. Samovar & R. Porter, Eds.). Belmont, CA: Wadsworth, 36–42.
Academic journal	Barge, J. Kevin. "Reflexivity and Managerial Practice." *Communication Monographs* 71 (Mar. 2004): 70–96. Print.	Barge, J. K. (2004, March). Reflexivity and managerial practice. *Communication Monographs, 71,* 70–96.
Magazine	Krauthammer, Charles. "What Makes the Bush Haters So Mad?" *Time* 22 Sept. 2003: 84. Print.	Krauthammer, C. (2003, September 22). What makes the Bush haters so mad? *Time,* 84.
Newspaper	Cohen, Richard. "Wall Street Scandal: Whatever the Market Will Bear." *The Cincinnati Enquirer* 17 Sept. 2003: C6. Print.	Cohen, R. (2003, September 17). Wall Street scandal: Whatever the market will bear. *The Cincinnati Enquirer,* p. C6.
Electronic article based on print source	Friedman, Thomas L. "Connect the Dots." *The New York Times.* 25 Sept. 2003. Web. 20 Aug. 2004. <http://www.nytimes.com/2003/09/25/opinion/25FRIED.html>.	Friedman, T. L. (2003, September 25). Connect the dots. *The New York Times.* Retrieved from http://www.nytimes.com/2003/09/25/opinion/25FRIED.html

Figure 12.2

Examples of the MLA and APA citation forms for speech sources

Electronic article from Internet-only publication	Osterweil, Neil, and Michelle Smith. "Does Stress Cause Breast Cancer?" *Web M.D. Health.* WebMD Inc. 24 Sept. 2003. Web. 20 Aug. 2004. <http://my.webmd.com/contents/article/74/89170.htm?z3734_00000_1000_ts_01>.	Osterweil, N., & Smith, M. (2003, September 24). Does stress cause breast cancer? *Web M.D. Health.* Retrieved from http://my.webmd.com/contents/article/74/89170.htm?z3734_00000_1000_ts_01
Electronic article retrieved from database	Grabe, Mark. "Voluntary Use of Online Lecture Notes: Correlates of Note Use and Note Use as an Alternative to Class Attendance." *Computers and Education* 44 (2005): 409–21. *ScienceDirect.* Web. 28 May 2006. <http://www.sciencedirect.com/>.	Grabe, M. (2005). Voluntary use of online lecture notes: Correlates of note use and note use as an alternative to class attendance. *Computers and Education* 44, 409–421. Retrieved from ScienceDirect.
Movie	*Pirates of the Caribbean: Dead Man's Chest.* Dir. Gore Verbinksi. Perf. Johnny Depp, Orlando Bloom, Keira Knightly. 2006. Walt Disney Pictures, 2007. DVD.	Verbinksi, G. (Director). (2006). *Pirates of the Caribbean: Dead man's chest* [Motion picture]. Burbank, CA: Walt Disney Pictures.
Television program	Gordon, Keith, dir. "Truth Be Told." By Drew Z. Greenberg and Tim Schlattmann. *Dexter.* Showtime. 10 Dec. 2006. Television.	Greenberg, D. Z., & Schlattmann, T. (Writers), & Gordon, K. (Director). (2006, December 10). Truth be told [Television series episode]. In *Dexter.* Manos, J., Jr. (Executive producer), New York, NY: Showtime.
Music recording	Nirvana. "Smells Like Teen Spirit." *Nevermind.* Geffen, 1991. CD.	Nirvana. (1991). Smells like teen spirit. On *Nevermind* [CD]. Santa Monica, CA: Geffen.
Personal interview	Mueller, Bruno (diamond cutter at Fegel's Jewelry). Personal interview. 19 March 2004.	APA style dictates that personal interviews are not included in a reference list. Rather, cite this type of source orally in your speech, mentioning the name of the person you interviewed and the date of the interview.

Figure 12.2
(continued)

gives examples of Modern Language Association (MLA) and American Psychological Association (APA) citations for the most commonly used sources.

Action Step 3.h helps you compile a list of sources used in your speech. Figure 12.3 gives an example of this activity completed by a student in this course.

Compiling a List of Sources

Dixon, Dougal. *The Practical Geologist.* (New York: Simon & Schuster, 1992.)

Farver, John, professor of Geology. Personal interview. June 23, 2006.

Klein, Cornelius. *Manual of Mineralogy,* 2nd ed. (New York: Wiley, 1993.)

Montgomery, Carla W. *Fundamentals of Geology,* 3rd ed. (Dubuque, IA: Wm. C. Brown, 1997.)

Figure 12.3
Student response to Action Step 3.h

Action Step 3.h

Compiling a List of Sources

The goal of this activity is to help you record the list of sources you used in the speech.

1. Review your research cards, separating those with information you have used in your speech from those you have not.
2. List the sources of information used in the speech by copying the bibliographic information recorded on the research cards.
3. For short lists, organize your list alphabetically by the last name of the first author. Be sure to follow the form shown in Figure 12.2. If you did not record some of the bibliographic information on your research card, you will need to revisit the library, database, or other source to find it.

 You can complete the activity online with Speech Builder Express, view a student sample of this activity, and, if requested, e-mail your completed activity to your instructor. Use your Premium Website for Communicate! to access the Action Step activities for Chapter 12.

Reviewing the Outline

Now that you have created all of the parts of the outline, it is time to put them together in complete outline form and edit them to make sure the outline is well organized and well worded. Use this checklist to complete the final review of the outline before you move into adaptation and rehearsal.

1. **Have I used a standard set of symbols to indicate structure?** Main points are indicated by Roman numerals, major subdivisions by capital letters, minor subheadings by Arabic numerals, and further subdivisions by lowercase letters.
2. **Have I written main points and major subdivisions as complete sentences?** Complete sentences help you to see (1) whether each main point actually develops your speech goal and (2) whether the wording makes your intended point. Unless the key ideas are written out in full, it will be difficult to follow the next guidelines.

Organizing the Speech

Communication Skill

Skill
The process of identifying main points, constructing a thesis statement, outlining the body of the speech, developing section transitions, creating an introduction, crafting a conclusion, and cataloguing a list of sources.

Use
To create a hierarchy and sequence of ideas that help a particular audience to easily understand the speaker's ideas and the goal of the speech.

Procedure
1. Identify your main ideas.
2. Write a thesis statement.
3. Outline the body of the speech by carefully wording main points, selecting an organizational pattern, selecting and organizing support, and preparing section transitions.
4. Create introductions and select the best one.
5. Create conclusions and select the best one.
6. List sources.

Example
The **three aspects** of romantic love are passion, intimacy, and commitment.
I. Passion is the first aspect of romantic love to develop.
II. Intimacy is the second.
III. Commitment is the third.
Example for "passion":
A. Passion is a compelling feeling of love.
B. (Focus on function.)
C. (Discuss maintenance.)
Transition from I to II: Although passion is essential to a relationship, passion without intimacy is just sex.
Possible introduction: What does it mean to say "I'm in love"? And how can you know whether what you are experiencing is not just a crush?
Possible conclusion: Developing romantic love involves passion, intimacy, and commitment.
Sample entry: Sternberg, Robert J., and Michael L. Barnes, eds. *The Psychology of Love.* New Haven, CT: Yale University Press, 1988.

3. Do main points and major subdivisions each contain a single idea? This guideline ensures that the development of each part of the speech will be relevant to the point. Thus, rather than

I. The park is beautiful and easy to get to.

divide the sentence so that both parts are separate:

I. The park is beautiful.
II. The park is easy to get to.

The two-point example sorts out distinct ideas so that the speaker can line up supporting material with confidence that the audience will see and understand its relationship to the main points.

4. Does each major subdivision relate to or support its major point? This principle, called subordination, insures that you don't wander off point and confuse your audience. For example:

I. Proper equipment is necessary for successful play.
   A. Good gym shoes are needed for maneuverability.
   B. Padded gloves will help protect your hands.
   C. A lively ball provides sufficient bounce.
   D. And a good attitude doesn't hurt.

Notice that the main point deals with equipment. A, B, and C (shoes, gloves, and ball) all relate to the main point. But D, attitude, is not equipment and should appear under some other main point, if at all.

5. Are potential subdivision elaborations indicated? Recall that it is the subdivision elaborations that help to build the speech. Because you don't know how long it might take you to discuss these elaborations, it is a good idea to include more than you are likely to use. During rehearsals, you may discuss each a different way.

6. Does the outline include no more than one-third the total number of words anticipated in the speech? An outline is only a skeleton of the speech—not a complete manuscript with letters and numbers attached. The outline should be short enough to allow you to experiment with different methods of development during practice periods and to adapt to audience reaction during the speech itself. An easy way to judge whether your outline is about the right length is to estimate the number of words that you are likely to be able to speak during the actual speech and compare this to the number of words in the outline (counting only the words in the outline minus speech goal, thesis statement, headings, and list of sources). Because approximate figures are all you need, to compute the approximate maximum words for your outline, start by assuming a speaking rate of 160 words per minute. (Last term, the speaking rate for the majority of speakers in my class was 140 to 180 words per minute.) Thus, using the average of 160 words per minute, a three- to five-minute speech would contain roughly 480 to 800 words, and the outline should be 160 to 300 words. An 8- to 10-minute speech, roughly 1,280 to 1,600 words, should have an outline of approximately 426 to 533 words.

Now that we have considered the various parts of an outline, let us put them together for a final look. The outline in Figure 12.4 illustrates the principles in practice. The commentary to the right of the outline relates each part of the outline to the guidelines we have discussed.

OUTLINE

General goal: I want to inform my audience.

Specific goal: I would like the audience to understand the major criteria for finding a suitable credit card.

Thesis statement: Three criteria that will enable audience members to find the credit card that is most suitable for them are level of real interest rate, annual fee, and advertised incentives.

Introduction

I. How many of you have been hounded by credit card vendors outside the Student Union?

II. They make a credit card sound like the answer to all of your dreams, don't they?

III. Today I want to share with you three criteria you need to consider carefully before deciding on a particular credit card: interest rate, annual fee, and advertised incentives.

Body

I. The first criterion for choosing a credit card is to select a card with a lower interest rate.

 A. Interest rates are the percentages that a company charges you to carry a balance on your card past the due date.
   1. Most credit cards carry an average of 8 percent.
   2. Some cards carry as much as 32 percent.
   3. Many companies offer 0 interest rates for up to 12 months.
   4. Student credit cards typically have higher interest rates.
   5. Some student credit cards carry APRs below 14%.
 B. Interest rates can be variable or fixed.
   1. Variable rates mean that the rate can change from month to month.
   2. Fixed rates mean that the rate will stay the same.
   3. Even cards with fixed rates can be raised to as much as 32% if you make a late payment.

ANALYSIS

Write your general and specific goals at the top of the page. Refer to the goal to test whether everything in the outline is relevant.

The thesis statement states the elements that are suggested in the specific goal. In the speech, the thesis serves as a forecast of the main points.

The heading *Introduction* sets the section apart as a separate unit. The introduction attempts to (1) get attention and (2) lead into the body of the speech as well as establish credibility, set a tone, and gain goodwill.

The heading Body sets this section apart as a separate unit. In this example, main point I begins a topical pattern of main points. It is stated as a complete sentence.

The two main subdivisions designated by A and B indicate the equal weight of these points. The second-level subdivisions—designated by 1, 2, and 3 for major subpoint A, and 1 and 2 for major subpoint B— give the necessary information for understanding the subpoints.

The number of major and second-level subpoints is at the discretion of the speaker. After the first two levels of subordination, words and phrases may be used in place of complete sentences for elaboration.

Figure 12.4
Sample complete outline
(continued on next page)

(*Transition:* Now that we have considered interest rates, let's look at the next criterion.)

II. A second criterion for choosing a suitable credit card is to select a card with no annual fee.
   A. The annual fee is the cost the company charges you for extending you credit.
   B. The charges vary widely.
      1. Most cards have no annual fee.
      2. Some companies still charge fees.

(*Transition:* After you have considered interest and fees, you can weigh the incentives that the company promises you.)

III. A third criterion for choosing a credit card is to weigh the incentives.
   A. Incentives are extras that you get for using a particular card.
      1. Some companies promise rebates.
      2. Some companies promise frequent flyer miles.
      3. Some companies promise discounts on "a wide variety of items."
      4. Some companies promise "cash back" on your purchases.
   B. Incentives don't outweigh other criteria.

Conclusion

I. So, if you exercise care in examining interest rates, annual fees, and incentives, you can choose the credit card that's right for you.
II. Then your credit card may truly be the answer to your dreams.

Sources

Bankrate Monitor. Web. <http://www.Bankrate.com>.

Barrett, Lois. "Good Credit 101." *Black Enterprise* Oct. 2006. Web. <http://www.blackenterprise.com/ArchiveOpen.asp?Source=ArchiveTab/2006/10/1006-16.htm>.

"Congratulations, Grads—You're Bankrupt: Marketing Blitz Buries Kids in Plastic Debt." *Business Week.* 2001 May 21: , 48. Print.

This transition reminds listeners of the first main point and forecasts the second. Main point II, continuing the topical pattern, is a complete sentence that parallels the wording of main point I. Notice that each main point considers only one major idea.

This transition summarizes the first two criteria and forecasts the third.

Main point III, continuing the topical pattern, is a complete sentence paralleling the wording of main points I and II. Throughout the outline, notice that main points and subpoints are factual statements. The speaker adds examples, experiences, and other developmental material during practice sessions.

The heading *Conclusion* sets this section apart as a separate unit. The content of the conclusion is intended to summarize the main ideas and leave the speech on a high note. The conclusion also provides closure by referring back to the idea mentioned in the introduction, a credit card is the answer to your dreams.

A list of sources should always be a part of the speech outline. The sources should show where the factual material of the speech came from. The list of sources is not a total of all sources available—only those that were used, directly or indirectly. Each of the sources is shown in proper form.

Figure 12.4
(continued)

Hennefriend, Bill. *Office Pro* 64 Oct. 2004:
17–20. Print.

Lankford, Kimberly. "The 31% Credit-card Trap,"
Kiplinger's January 2007: 96–98. Print.

"Protect Your Credit Card." *Kiplinger's* (Dec.
2004): 88. Print.

Ramachandran, Nisha. "Harvesting Rewards."
U.S. News and World Report 31 July 2005.
Web. <http://www.usnews.com/
biztech/articles/050808/8rewards.htm>.

Figure 12.4
(continued)

A Question of Ethics

As Marna and Gloria were eating lunch together, Marna happened to ask Gloria, "How are you doing in Woodward's speech class?"

"Not bad," Gloria replied. "I'm working on this speech about product development. I think it will be really informative, but I'm having a little trouble with the opening. I just can't seem to get a good idea for getting started."

"Why not start with a story—that always worked for me in class."

"Thanks, Marna; I'll think on it."

The next day when Marna ran into Gloria again, she asked, "How's that introduction going?"

"Great. I've prepared a great story about Mary Kay—you know, the cosmetics woman? I'm going to tell about how she was terrible in school and no one thought she'd amount to anything. But she loved dabbling with cosmetics so much that she decided to start her own business—and the rest is history."

What Would You Do?

"That's a great story. I really like that part about being terrible in school. Was she really that bad?"

"I really don't know—the material I read didn't really focus on that part of her life. But I thought that angle would get people listening right away. And after all, I did it that way because you suggested starting with a story."

"Yes, but . . . "

"Listen, she did start the business. So what if the story isn't quite right? It makes the point I want to make—if people are creative and have a strong work ethic, they can make it big."

1. What are the ethical issues here?
2. Is anyone really hurt by Gloria's opening the speech with this story?
3. What are the speaker's ethical responsibilities?

Summary

Organizing is the process of selecting and structuring ideas you will present in your speech; it is guided by your audience analysis. Once you have analyzed your audience, created a speech goal, and assembled a body of information on your topic, you are ready to identify the main ideas you wish to present in your speech and to craft them into a well-phrased thesis statement.

Once you have identified a thesis, you will prepare the body of the speech. The body of the speech is hierarchically ordered through the use of main points and subpoints. Once identified, main points and their related subpoints are written in complete sentences, which should be checked to make sure that they are clear, parallel in structure, meaningful, and limited in number to five or less. The sequential relationship between main point ideas and among subpoint ideas depends on the organizational pattern that is chosen. The four most basic organizational patterns are time, narrative, topic, and logical reasons order. You will want to choose an organizational pattern that best helps your audience understand and remember your main points. Main point sentences are written in outline form using the organizational pattern selected.

Subpoints support a main point with definitions, examples, statistics, personal experiences, stories, quotations, and so on. These subpoints also appear in the outline below the main point to which they belong. An organizational pattern will also be chosen for each set of subpoints.

Once the outline of the body is complete, transitions between the introduction and the body, between main points within the body, and between the body and the conclusion need to be devised so that the audience can easily follow the speech and identify each main point. Similarly, signposts should be placed appropriately to connect subpoints and supporting material together.

The organization process is completed by creating (1) an introduction that gets audience attention, introduces the thesis, establishes listener relevance and speaker credibility, sets the tone for the speech, and creates goodwill; (2) a conclusion that summarizes the main points and creates a vivid impression; and (3) a list of sources compiled from the bibliographic information recorded on research cards.

The complete draft outline should be reviewed as revised to make sure that you have used a standard set of symbols, used complete sentences for main points and major subdivisions, limited each point to a single idea, related minor points to major points, and made sure the outline length is no more than one-third the number of words of the final speech.

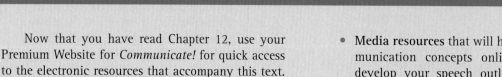

Communicate! Active Online Learning

Now that you have read Chapter 12, use your Premium Website for *Communicate!* for quick access to the electronic resources that accompany this text. These resources include

- **Study tools** that will help you assess your learning and prepare for exams (*digital glossary, key term flash cards, review quizzes*).
- **Activities and assignments** that will help you hone your knowledge, analyze communication situations (*Skill Learning Activities*), and build your public speaking skills throughout the course (*Communication on Your Feet speech assignments, Action Step activities*). Many of these activities allow you to compare your answers to those provided by the authors, and, if requested, submit your answers to your instructor.

- **Media resources** that will help you explore communication concepts online (*Web Resources*), develop your speech outlines (*Speech Builder Express 3.0*), watch and critique videos of communication situations and sample speeches (*Interactive Video Activities*), upload your speech videos for peer reviewing and critique other students' speeches (*Speech Studio online speech review tool*), and download chapter review so you can study when and where you'd like (*Audio Study Tools*).

This chapter's Key Terms, Skill Learning Activities, and Web Resources are also featured on the following pages, and you can find this chapter's Communicate on Your Feet assignment and Action Step activities in the body of the chapter.

Key Terms

appeal (292)
clincher (292)
direct question (288)
joke (288)
listener relevance link (290)
logical reasons order (283)
narrative order (282)

main points (276)
organizing (276)
parallel (281)
personal reference (288)
rhetorical question (288)
section transition (286)
signpost (287)

speech outline (280)
story (289)
suspense (289)
thesis statement (279)
time order (282)
topic order (283)
transitions (286)

Skill Learning Activities

12.1: Identifying Thesis Statements (280)

Access the American Rhetoric Online Speech Bank. Select five speeches and listen to the audio recordings or read the printed transcript of each speech. As you listen to or read the speeches, identify and write down the thesis statements in each. Not all speeches necessarily have explicit thesis statements, but all speeches have an implied thesis or purpose. If you feel any one of the speeches you have selected does not contain an explicit thesis, identify its implied thesis or purpose.

12.2: Identifying Main Points (284)

Choose one of the speeches you listened to or read in Skill Learning Activity 12.1. Listen to or read it again, but this time identify and write down the main points in each. What type of organizational pattern is the speaker using in the speech?

12.3: Identifying Supporting Materials (285)

Using the speech you chose in Skill Learning Activity 12.1, list the various types of support the speaker uses to develop each main point. Does the speaker acknowledge the sources of this information? Are there types of support that you thought should have been used that are missing from this speech?

Does the speaker seem to rely on one type of support to the exclusion of others? Why do you suppose that the speaker chose the types of support that were used?

12.4: Identifying Transition Statements, Introductions, and Conclusions (293)

Using the same speech you chose for Skill Learning Activity 12.1:

1. Identify the transition statements the speaker used to move from one main point to another.
2. Identify the type of introduction the speaker used. Do you think it was effective? If so, why? If not, why not?
3. Identify the type of conclusion the speaker used. Why do you think the speaker chose to end the speech in this way? Was the conclusion effective? If so, why? If not, why not?

Web Resources

12.1: Writing Different Types of Thesis Statements (280)

Visit this site at Purdue University for guidance in writing analytical, expository, and persuasive thesis statements.

Biggie Productions/Riser/Getty Images

⊙ Adapting Verbally and Visually

Questions you'll be able to answer after reading this chapter:

- What can you do to demonstrate the relevance of your speech to your audience?
- How can you establish common ground in your speech?
- What can you do to bolster your credibility as a speaker?
- How can you help your audience comprehend and retain your message?
- What can you do to adapt to the cultural differences between you and your audience?
- What are the different types of presentational aids?
- What criteria can you use to select presentational aids?
- What guidelines should you follow to construct and integrate presentational aids?

Nathan had asked his friend George to listen to one of his speech rehearsals. He finished the final sentences of the speech, "So, now you know what a Meckel's diverticulum is, who is most susceptible, and what it's symptoms are. And now I'd like to end as I began with the rules of 2s. But I'd like to add one more. Please don't blow off acute abdominal pain as only a stomach ache because doing so could lead "2" death." Then, he asked George, "So, what do you think?"

"You're giving the speech to your classmates, right?"

"Yeah."

"And they're mostly mass media majors?"

"Uh-huh."

"Well, it was a good speech, but it was awfully technical and I didn't hear anything that showed that you had media majors in mind. Why would they want to know about this?"

Nathan may have chosen his topic and main points with his audience in mind, but as he prepared, he forgot that an effective speech is one that is adapted to the specific audience. Recall from Chapter 11 that **audience adaptation** is the process of customizing your speech to your specific audience. Audience adaptation depends on audience analysis. You used the results of your audience analysis in Action Step 1.b to identify your topic, decide on a specific purpose, and select main points. Now you are going to learn how to use your audience analysis as you develop that speech. In this chapter, we will look at Action Step 4: Adapt the Verbal and Visual Material to the Needs of Your Specific Audience. You will use your knowledge of your audience as you consider what specific verbal material you will present and how you will represent that material visually with presentational aids.

Action Step 4: Adapt the Verbal and Visual Material to the Needs of Your Specific Audience

The skill of adapting involves both verbally and visually adapting by preparing presentational aids that facilitate audience understanding.

Adapting to Your Audience Verbally

As you select supporting material and make language choices for your speech, you will want to consider how they (1) demonstrate relevance, (2) establish common ground, (3) enhance your credibility and the credibility of the material you are presenting, (4) help the audience comprehend and remember the information, and (5) reflect the cultural diversity in your audience.

Relevance

Your first challenge will be to adapt your speech so the audience sees its **relevance** to them. Listeners pay attention to and are interested in ideas that have a personal impact (when they can answer the question, What does this have to do with me?); they are bored when they don't see how the speech relates to them. You can help the audience perceive your speech as relevant by including supporting material that is timely, proximate, and has a personal impact.

Establish timeliness

Listeners are more likely to be interested in information they perceive as **timely**—they want to know how they can use the information *now*. For example, in a speech about the hazards of talking on cell phones while driving, J. J. quickly established the topic's relevance in his introduction:

> Most of us in this room, as many as 90 percent in fact, are a danger to society. Why? Because we talk or text on our cell phones while driving. Although driving while phoning (DWP) seems harmless, a recent study conducted by the Nationwide Mutual Insurance Company reports that DWP is the most common cause of accidents today—even more common than driving under the influence (DUI)! Did you know that when you talk on the phone when you're driving— even if you do so on a hands-free set—you're four times more likely to get into a serious crash than if you're not doing so? That's why several states have actually banned the practice. So this issue is far from harmless and is one each of us should take seriously.

What can you do to help your audience see the relevance of your speech to them?

audience adaptation
the process of customizing your speech material to your specific audience.

relevance
adapting the information in the speech so that audience members view it as important to them.

timely
showing how information is useful now or in the near future.

Establish proximity

Your listeners are more likely to be interested in information that has **proximity**, a relationship to their personal "space." Psychologically, we pay more attention to information that is related to our "territory"—to us, our family, our neighborhood, or our city, state, or country. You have probably heard speakers say something like this: "Let me bring this closer to home by showing you…" and then make their point by using a local example. As you review the supporting material you collect for your speech, look for statistics and examples that have proximity for your audience. For example, J. J. used the latest DWP accident statistics in his state and used a story reported in the local paper of a young mother who was killed while DWPing.

Demonstrate personal impact

When you present information that can have a serious physical, economic, or psychological impact on audience members, they are more likely to be interested in what you have to say. For example, notice how your classmates' attention picks up when your instructor says that what is said next "will definitely be on the test." Your instructor understands that this "economic" impact (not paying attention can "cost") is enough to refocus most students' attention on what is being said.

As you prepare your speech, incorporate ideas that create personal impact for your audience. In a speech about toxic waste, you might show a serious physical impact by providing statistics on the effects of toxic waste on the health of people in your state. You may be able to demonstrate serious economic impact by citing the cost to the taxpayers of a recent toxic waste cleanup in your city. Or you might be able to illustrate a serious psychological impact by finding and recounting the stresses faced by one family (that is demographically similar to the audience) with a long-term toxic waste problem in their neighborhood. To drive home the impact of DWP, toward the end of his speech, J.J. introduced John, his high school friend, who had come to class with J.J. and who is now paralyzed and wheelchair-bound because his girlfriend crashed into another car while she was dialing her cell phone.

How can you establish relevance in a speech about driving while phoning?

Michael Ventura/Alamy

Common Ground

Each person in the audience is unique, with differing knowledge, attitudes, philosophies, experiences, and ways of perceiving the world. They may or may not know others in the audience. So it is easy for them to assume that they have nothing in common with you or with other audience members. Yet when you speak, you will be giving one message to that diverse group. **Common ground** is the background, knowledge, attitudes, experiences, and philosophies that are shared by audience members and the speaker. Effective speakers use their audience analysis to identify areas of similarity; then they use the adaptation techniques of personal pronouns, rhetorical questions, and common experiences to create common ground.

> How can you establish common ground in your speech?

Use personal pronouns

The simplest way to establish common ground between yourself and the members of your audience is to use **personal pronouns**: *we*, *us*, and *our*. For example, in a speech given to an audience whose members are known to be sympathetic to legislation limiting violence in children's programming on TV, notice the different effects of using an unspecific noun and a personal pronoun:

> I know that most *people* are worried about the effects that violence on TV is having on young children.
> I know that most of *us* worry about the effects that violence on TV is having on young children.

proximity
a relationship to personal space.

common ground
the background, knowledge, attitudes, experiences, and philosophies that are shared by audience members and the speaker.

personal pronouns
we, us, and our: pronouns that refer directly to members of the audience.

By using *us* instead of *most people*, the speaker includes the audience members, and this gives them a stake in listening to what is to follow.

Ask rhetorical questions

A **rhetorical question** is one whose answer is obvious to audience members and to which they are not really expected to reply. Rhetorical questions create common ground by alluding to information that is shared by audience members and the speaker. They are often used in speech introductions but can also be effective as transitions and in other parts of the speech. For instance, notice how this transition, phrased as a rhetorical question, creates common ground:

Mark Peterson/CORBIS

In what ways do you think the speaker in this situation could create common ground with the audience?

> **When you have watched a particularly violent TV program, have you ever asked yourself, "Did they really need to be this graphic to make the point"?**

Rhetorical questions are meant to have only one answer that highlights similarities between audience members and leads them to be more interested in the content that follows.

Draw from common experiences

You can also develop common ground by sharing personal experiences, examples, and illustrations that embody what you and the audience have in common. For instance, in a speech about the effects of television violence, you might allude to a common viewing experience:

> Remember how sometimes at a key moment when you're watching a really frightening scene in a movie, you may quickly shut your eyes? I vividly remember slamming my eyes shut over and over again during the scariest scenes in *Texas Chainsaw Massacre, The Blair Witch Project,* and *Halloween.*

To create material that draws on common experiences, you must first analyze how you and your audience members are similar in the exposure you have had to the topic or in other areas that you can then relate to your topic.

Skill Learning Activity 13.1

Speaker Credibility

Credibility is the confidence that an audience places in the truthfulness of what a speaker says. Some people are widely known as experts in a particular area and have proven to be trustworthy and likeable. When these people give a speech, they don't have to adapt their remarks to establish their credibility. However, most of us—even if we are given a formal introduction to acquaint the audience with our credentials and character—will still need to adapt our remarks to build audience confidence in the truthfulness of what we are saying. Three adaptation techniques can affect how

rhetorical questions
questions whose answers are obvious to the audience and to which they are not expected to reply.

credibility
the level of confidence that an audience places in the truthfulness of what a speaker says.

credible we are perceived to be: demonstrating knowledge and expertise, establishing trustworthiness, and displaying personableness.

Demonstrate knowledge and expertise

When listeners perceive that you are a knowledgeable expert, they will perceive you as credible. Their assessment of your **knowledge and expertise** depends on how well you convince them that you are qualified to speak on this topic. You can demonstrate your knowledge and expertise through direct and indirect means.

You directly establish expertise when you disclose your experiences with your topic including formal education, special study, demonstrated skill, and your track record. Audience members will also assess your expertise through indirect means, such as how prepared you seem and how much firsthand involvement you demonstrate through personal examples and illustrations. Audiences have an almost instinctive sense of when a speaker is winging it, and most audiences distrust a speaker who does not appear to have command of the material. Speakers who are overly dependent on their notes or who hem and haw, fumbling to find ways to express their ideas, undermine the confidence of the audience. When your ideas are easy to follow and are clearly expressed, audience members perceive you to be more credible.

Similarly, when your ideas are developed through specific statistics, high-quality examples, illustrations, and personal experiences, audience members are likely to view you as credible. Recall how impressed you are with instructors who always seem to have two or three perfect examples and illustrations and who are able to recall statistics without looking at their notes. Compare them to instructors who seem tied to the textbook and don't appear to know much about the subject beyond their prepared lecture. In which instance do you perceive the instructor to be more knowledgeable?

Establish trustworthiness

Your **trustworthiness** is the extent to which the audience members believe that what you say is accurate, true, and in their best interests. The more your audience sees you as trustworthy, the more credible you will be. People assess others' trustworthiness by judging their character and their motives. So you can establish yourself as trustworthy by following ethical standards and by honestly explaining what is motivating you to speak.

As you plan your speech, you need to consider how to demonstrate your character: that you are honest, industrious, dependable, and a morally strong person. For example, when you credit the source of your information as you speak, you confirm that the information is true—that you are not making it up—and you signal your honesty by not taking credit for someone else's ideas. Similarly, if you present the arguments evenly on both sides of an issue, instead of just the side you favor, audience members will see you as fair-minded.

How trustworthy you appear to be will also depend on how the audience views your motives. If people believe that what you are saying is self-serving rather than in their interests, they will be suspicious and view you as less trustworthy. Early in your speech, then, it is important to show how audience members will benefit from what you are saying. For example, in his speech on toxic waste, Brandon might describe how one community's ignorance of the dangers of toxic waste disposal allowed a toxic waste dump to be located in their community, with subsequent serious health issues. He can then share his motive by saying something like: "My hope is that this speech will give you the information you need to thoughtfully participate in decisions like these that may face your community."

What can you do to bolster your credibility as a speaker on your topic?

knowledge and expertise
how well you convince your audience that you are qualified to speak on the topic.

trustworthiness
the extent to which audience members believe that what you say is accurate, true, and in their best interests.

ALEXIS C. GLENN/UPI/Landov

Do you think Steven Colbert is trustworthy? Why or why not?

Display personableness

We have more confidence in people we like. **Personableness** is the extent to which you project an agreeable or pleasing personality. The more your listeners like you, the more likely they are to believe what you tell them. We quickly decide how much we like a new person based on our first impressions. As a speaker trying to build credibility with an audience, you should look for ways to adapt your personal style to one that will help the audience like you and perceive you as credible.

Besides dressing in a way that is appropriate for the audience and occasion, you can increase the chances that the audience will like you by smiling at individual audience members before beginning your remarks and by looking at individuals as you speak, acknowledging them with a quick nod. You can also demonstrate personableness by using appropriate humor.

Information Comprehension and Retention

Although your audience analysis helped you select a topic that was appropriate for your audience's current knowledge level, you will need to adapt the information you present so that audience members can easily understand it and remember it when you are through. Five guidelines that can aid you are (1) appealing to diverse learning styles, (2) orienting the audience with internal reviews, (3) choosing clear language, (4) using vivid language and examples, and (5) comparing unfamiliar ideas with those the audience recognizes.

What can you do to help your audience comprehend and retain your message?

Appeal to diverse learning styles

A **learning style** is a person's preferred way of receiving information. Because people differ in how they prefer to learn, you should present your ideas in ways that make it easy for all audience members to understand and remember what you are saying. Kolb's (1984) cycle of learning cycle of learning conceptualizes learning style preferences along four dimensions: feeling, watching, thinking, and doing. Because your audience is likely to have people with a diversity of learning styles, you will want to adapt your ideas so that they can be understood and remembered by people who prefer different styles. Kolb argues that even though individuals might prefer learning in one these four ways, we all learn best when we engage with material in all four ways. So it makes sense to adapt your speech in ways that address all four dimensions. Figure 13.1 illustrates the cycle.

personableness
the extent to which you project an agreeable or pleasing personality.

learning style
a person's preferred way of receiving information.

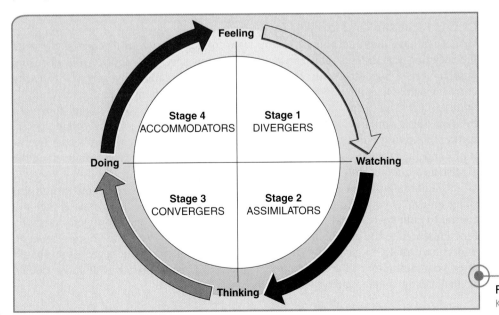

Figure 13.1
Kolb's cycle of learning

To address the feeling (concrete experience) dimension, you can offer personal stories or examples that appeal to the senses and emotions. J. J. did this when he shared the story about the young mother and when he introduced his wheelchair-bound friend. To address the watching (reflective observation) dimension, you should include visual materials to reinforce important points. You might also integrate rhetorical questions that encourage your listeners to reflect on some of the ideas you present. J. J. did so, for example, when he asked his audience whether they knew serious automobile accidents are more commonly related to driving while phoning than driving under the influence. To address the thinking (abstract conceptualization) dimension, you should support your ideas with detailed definitions, explanations, facts, and statistics. To address the doing (active experimentation) dimension, you can identify ways that the audience can become personally involved in doing something related to your ideas. J. J. talked about turning off cell phones before starting the car or pulling over to the side of the road to answer or make a call.

Orient the audience with internal reviews

Listeners who are confused or have forgotten previous information from your speech lose interest in what is being said. If your speech is more than a couple of minutes long, you can use internal reviews to remind and orient your audience. Suppose your goal is to inform your audience about the three phases of clinical trials that a cancer drug must pass in order to win FDA approval. After explaining the goals of the first phase, the types of patients recruited, the type of information that must be provided to the FDA, and the FDA's review process, you are ready to move on to an explanation of the next phase. But your audience may still be trying to process the information you have presented on the first phase. You can use an internal review to summarize the first phase and to preview phase two: "So the goal of the first phase is to see whether a drug that has been found to be safe in animals is safe in a small number of humans who have the cancer. Phase I trials are not designed to determine whether the drug works or not. It is in the next phase, Phase II, that we begin to answer that question.

Choose specific and familiar language

Words can have many meanings, so you want to make sure your listeners understand the meaning you intend. You can do so by using specific language and choosing familiar terms. Specific words clear up the confusion caused by general words by narrowing the focus in some way. For example, saying "a banged-up Honda Civic" is more specific than "a car." Narrowing the meaning encourages your listeners to picture the same thing you are. Similarly, you can narrow a term such as "blue-collar worker" further by saying "construction worker" and even further by saying "bulldozer operator." Choosing specific language is one way to make sure your listeners understand the precise meaning you intend.

Using familiar terms is just as important as using specific words. Avoid **jargon** and **slang** unless (1) you define them clearly the first time you use them and (2) they are central to your speech goal. For instance, in a speech on the major problems faced by functionally illiterate people in the workplace, it will be important to your audience to understand what you mean by "functionally illiterate." Early in the speech, you should offer your definition: "By 'functionally illiterate,' I mean people who have trouble accomplishing simple reading and writing tasks."

jargon
the unique technical terminology of a trade or profession.

slang
informal, nonstandard vocabulary and definitions assigned to words by a social group or subculture.

© 1999 Ted Goff

©1999 Ted Goff www.tedgoff.com

"To access soup, interface opener tool and rotate can to reformat container configuration."

Use vivid language and examples

Because listeners cannot reread what you have said, you must speak in ways that help them remember your message. You can do so by using **sensory language** that appeals to the senses of seeing, hearing, tasting, smelling, and feeling. Here is how Marla appealed to the senses when describing the downhill skiing experience:

> As you climb the hill, you squint because the bright winter sunshine glistening on the snow is almost blinding *[sight]*. Just before you take off, you gently slip your goggles over your eyes. The bitter cold of them stings your nose *[touch and feel]*. You start the descent, and as you gradually pick up speed, the taste of air and ice and snow in your mouth invigorates you *[taste]*. An odd silence fills the air, and you hear only the swish of your skis against the snow *[sound]* until, at last, you arrive at the bottom of the hill. As you enter the warming house, you feel your fingers thaw in the warm air *[feel]*, and the familiar aroma of the wood stove *[smell]* comforts you as you pour yourself a cup of hot chocolate.

Sensory language and examples help audience members understand and remember abstract, complex, and novel material. A vivid example can help us understand a complicated concept. So as you prepare your speech, you will want to adapt by choosing

sensory language
language that appeals to the senses.

Ken Redding/Surf/Corbis

You can help listeners remember by appealing to the senses.

How can you adapt to cultural differences between you and members of your audience?

real or hypothetical examples and illustrations to help your audience understand the new information you present.

Compare unknown ideas with familiar ones

An easy way to adapt your material to your audience is to compare your new ideas with ones the audience already understands. For example, if you wanted an audience of 18- to 24-year-olds to feel the excitement that was generated when telegrams were first introduced, you might compare it to the public response when cell phones became widely available. In the speech on functional illiteracy, if you want your audience of literates to sense what functionally illiterate people experience, you might compare it to the experience of living in a country where one is not fluent in the language.

Adapting to Cultural Differences

When you address an audience composed of people from ethnic and language groups different from your own, you should make three adaptations: being understandable when you are speaking in your second language, showing respect by choosing bias-free language, and creating common ground by choosing culturally appropriate supporting material.

Work to be understood when speaking in your second language

When the first language spoken by audience members is different from yours, they may not be able to understand what you are saying because you may speak with an accent, mispronounce words, choose inappropriate words, and misuse idioms. Speaking in a second language can make you anxious and self-conscious. But most audience members are more tolerant of mistakes made by a second-language speaker than they are of those made by a native speaker. Likewise, they will work hard to understand a second-language speaker.

Nevertheless, when you are speaking in a second language, you have an additional responsibility to make your speech as understandable as possible. You can help your audience by speaking more slowly and articulating as clearly as you can. By slowing your speaking rate, you give yourself additional time to pronounce difficult sounds and choose words whose meanings you know. You also give your audience members additional time to adjust their ears so that they can more easily process what you are saying. You can also use visual aids to reinforce key terms and concepts as you move through you speech. Doing so assures listeners that they've heard you correctly.

One of the best ways to improve when you are giving a speech in a second language is to practice the speech in front of friends and associates who are native speakers. Ask them to take note of words and phrases that you mispronounce or misuse. Then they can work with you to correct the pronunciation or to choose other words that better express your idea. Also, keep in mind that the more you practice speaking the language, the more comfortable you will become with the language and with your ability to relate to the audience members.

Choose nonoffensive language

Some words, phrases and references may be offensive to some cultural groups. When you use these in a speech, you are being disrespectful of the feelings of your audience. Respectful language choices are those that will not offend any of your listeners.

Disrespectful language includes expressions that some people perceive as sexist, racist, demeaning, insulting, or offensive. Any words, examples, or stories that belittle a person or a group of people based on their race, sex, religion, age, class, education, or occupation are disrespectful.

Profane or vulgar language can also offend some audience members and should be avoided in a public address. Although casual swearing—profanity injected into regular conversation—occurs more today than in the past, research has shown that people who pepper their formal speeches with it are often perceived as abrasive, as well as lacking in character and emotional control (DuFrene & Lehman, 2002; O'Connor, 2000).

Respectful language is also gender neutral and avoids stereotypes. *Firefighter* rather than *fireman*, *server* rather than *waitress*, and *flight attendant* rather than *stewardess* are examples of bias-free language choices.

You will also want to avoid offensive examples and stories. Dirty jokes and racist, sexist, or other -ist examples show your disregard for the feelings of some of your audience members and are likely to turn off not only those who you are demeaning but also other members of the audience. You might recall when comedian Chris Rock hosted the 2003 MTV music awards and introduced Eminem as someone who "saves a lot of money on Mother's Day" and P. Diddy as "being sued by more people than the Catholic church" (MTV Music Awards, 2003). Although some audience may have thought these remarks were funny, others surely did not. And although remarks such as these may be accepted from Chris Rock the comedian, your audience is unlikely

Action Step 4.a

Adapting to Your Audience Verbally

The goal of this activity is to help you plan how you will verbally adapt your material to the specific audience.

Write your thesis statement: _____

Review the audience analysis that you completed in Action Steps 1.b and 1.c. As you review the speech outline that you completed in Action Steps 3.a–3.h, plan the supporting material you will use to verbally adapt to your audience by answering the following questions:

1. How can I adapt this material so that it is relevant to this audience by showing its timeliness, proximity, and personal impact?

2. How can I establish common ground by using personal pronouns, asking rhetorical questions, and drawing from common experiences?

3. How can I establish my credibility by demonstrating my knowledge and expertise, my trustworthiness, and my personableness?

4. How can I make this material easier for the audience to comprehend by addressing diverse learning styles, orienting them with internal reviews, speaking clearly, using sensory language and examples, and comparing unknowns with what your audience knows?

5. How can I adapt to the cultural differences between my audience and me?

 You can complete this activity online, view another student's sample of this activity, and, if requested, e-mail your completed activity to your instructor. Use your Premium Website for Communicate! *to access the Action Step activities for Chapter 13.*

to find your use of this type of humor appropriate or effective. As a general rule of thumb: When in doubt, leave it out.

Choose culturally appropriate supporting material

Much of your success in adapting to the audience hinges on establishing common ground and drawing on common experiences. When you are speaking to audiences who are vastly different from you, you should learn as much as you can about their culture so that you can develop the material in a way that is meaningful to them. This may mean conducting additional library research to find statistics and examples that are meaningful to the audience. Or it may require you to elaborate on ideas that would be self-explanatory in your own culture. For example, suppose that Maria, a Mexican American exchange student, was giving a personal narrative speech on her quinceañera party when she turned 15 for her speech class at Yeshiva University in Israel. Because students in Israel have no experience with the Mexican coming-of-age tradition of quinceañera parties, they would have had trouble understanding the significance of this event if Maria had not used her knowledge of the Bar Mitzvah and Bat Mitzvah coming-of-age ritual celebrations in Jewish culture and related it to them.

In the Diverse Voices feature, Ann Neville Miller provides insights into public speaking practices in Kenya and how Kenyans must adapt their speeches to appeal to their audiences' shared experiences and knowledge.

Public Speaking Patterns in Kenya

by Ann Neville Miller

Diverse Voices

One of the major differences in adapting to different groups is understanding their expectations and their reactions to your words. In this excerpt, Ann Neville Miller describes the different purposes of public speaking in Kenya and how those purposes influence how Kenyan speakers adapt their words to the expectations of their audiences.

Much public speaking in the United States is informative or persuasive in purpose; ceremonial occasions for public speaking are less common. This is due, in part, to the stress that mainstream U.S. culture places on informality. The average Kenyan, in contrast, will give far more ceremonial speeches in life than any other kind of speech. These may be speeches of greeting, introduction, tribute, and thanks, among others. Life events, both major and minor, are marked

by ceremonies, and ceremonies occasion multiple public speeches.

This means that, unlike the majority of people in the United States, who report that they fear speaking in public, possibly even more than they fear death (Richmond & McCroskey, 1995), for most Kenyans, public speaking is an unavoidable responsibility. For example, when a Kenyan attends a church service or other event away from home, he or she will often be asked to stand up and give an impromptu word of greeting to the assembly. In more remote areas, where literacy rates are low and there is little access to electronic media, this word of greeting also can serve an informative purpose because the one who has traveled often brings news of the outside world. The *harambee*, a kind of community fund-raising event peculiar to Kenya, is characterized by the presence of both a guest of honor and various dignitaries of a stature appropriate to the specific occasion, all of whom are likely at some point to address the gathering. Weddings and funerals overflow with ceremonial speeches; virtually any relative, friend, or business associate of the newly married or deceased may give advice or pay tribute. Older members of the bride's family, for example, may remind her how important it is to feed her husband well, or warn the groom that in their family men are expected never to abuse their wives, but to settle marital disputes with patience. Even the woman selected to cut the cake expects to give a brief word of exhortation before performing her duty. The free dispensing of advice, a hallmark of Kenyan wedding celebrations, would be out of place at most receptions in the United States, where the focus of speeches is normally more on remembrances and well-wishing.

In fact, when it comes to marriage, speech making begins long before the actual wedding day, at bridal negotiations where up to 40 or 50 people from the two families attempt to settle on a bride price. At these negotiations especially, but also in other ceremonial speeches, "deep" language replete with proverbs and metaphors is expected. The family of the man may explain that their son has seen a beautiful flower, or a lovely she-goat, or some other item in the compound of the family of the young lady and that they would like to obtain it for their son. In a negotiation of this type that I recently attended, the speaker for the bride's relatives explained that the family would require 20 goats as a major portion of the bride price. Because both parties were urban dwellers and would have no space to keep that many animals, the groom's family conferred with each other and determined that the bride's family really wanted cash. They settled on what they considered to be a reasonable price per goat, multiplied it by 20, and presented the total amount through a designated spokesperson to the representative of the bride. The original speaker from the bride's family looked at the money and observed dryly that goats in the groom's area were considerably thinner than those the bride's family were accustomed to! This type of indirect communication, the subtlety of which affords immense satisfaction and sometimes amusement to both speaker and listener, is a form of the high-context communication described by [Edward T.] Hall. A full appreciation of the speech requires extensive knowledge of shared experiences and traditions.

Excerpted from Ann Neville Miller, "Public Speaking Patterns in Kenya." In Larry A. Samovar, Richard E. Porter, & Edwin R. McDaniel, eds., Intercultural Communication: A Reader (11th ed., pp. 238–245). Belmont, CA: Wadsworth, 2006.

Adapting to Audiences Visually

Because of the influence of mass media, today's audiences are visually oriented. As a result, your audience is likely to expect you to use **presentational aids** to provide a visual component to your speech. A **presentational aid** is any visual, audio, or audiovisual material used in a speech for the purpose of helping the audience understand some point the speaker is making. The most common form of presentational aid is a **visual aid**—a form of supporting material that allows the audience to see as well as hear information.

There are several benefits to using presentational aids. First, they enable you to adapt to an audience's level of knowledge by clarifying and dramatizing your verbal message. Second, they help audiences retain the information because people are better able to remember what they both see and hear rather than what they only hear (Tversky, 1997). Third, presentational aids help listeners whose learning styles are based on visual cues (Kolb, 1984). Fourth, presentational aids are persuasive. In fact, some research suggests that speakers who use presentational aids are almost two times more likely to convince listeners than those who do not have presentational aids (Hanke, 1998). Finally, using presentational aids helps you feel more confident.

presentational aid
any visual, audio, or audiovisual material used in a speech for the purpose of helping the audience understand some point the speaker is making.

visual aid
a form of supporting material that allows the audience to see as well as to hear information.

Speakers report that when they use presentational aids, they tend to be less anxious and have more confidence (Ayres, 1991).

The important role of presentational aids in speech giving has lead to a new form of entertainment. In Ignite speech contests (many of which take place in bars), speakers compete by giving informative speeches with a slide show. You can read more about "Ignite Nights" in the Pop Comm! feature "Ignite: The Power(Point) of eXtreme Audience Adaptation."

> What are the different types of presentational aids?

Types of Presentational Aids

Presentational aids range from those that are ready-made and simple to use to those that require practice to use effectively and must be custom produced for the specific speech. In this section, we describe the types of presentational aids that you can consider using as you prepare your speech.

Actual objects

Actual objects are inanimate or animate physical samples of the idea you are communicating. Inanimate objects make good visual aids if they are (1) large enough

---

Ignite: The Power(Point) of eXtreme Audience Adaptation

Pop Comm!

Ignite Baltimore/Mike Subelsk

Ignite asks speakers, "If you had five minutes on stage, what would you say? What if you only got 20 slides and they rotated automatically after 15 seconds?" ("What Is Ignite?"). Ignite challenges speakers to engage in what could be called extreme audience adaptation, sharing information in a timely and relevant manner so that it is easily comprehended by its techie audience. The entire focus of Ignite presentations is on what the target demographic wants to see: short and fast communication.

Ignite is a style of presentation that began in Seattle in 2006, created by Brady Forrest of O'Reilly Radar, a blog sponsored by the computer-book publisher O'Reilly Media, and Bre Pettis of *Make Magazine,* which is devoted to DIY technology projects. Started as a way to provide fun, informal conferences for people working in the technology industry, the events have spread to cities all over the United States and beyond, including Sydney, Australia, and Buenos Aires, Argentina (Guzman, 2009). Ignite events are free of charge, only relying on sponsors to provide food and drink.

Speeches at Ignite events range from "Fighting Dirty in Scrabble" to "Causal Inference Is Hard," or "How I Learned to Stop Worrying and Love Counterfactuals" to "How I Learned to Appreciate Dance: Being Married to a Ballerina" to "Geek Generation" ("Ignite Seattle 7," 2009). The emphasis on extreme brevity as a way to share ideas is reflected in Ignite Seattle's tagline: "Enlighten us, but make it quick" (*Ignite Seattle,* n.d.). Aside from their strict limits on presentation

to be seen by all audience members, (2) small enough to carry to the site of the speech, (3) simple enough to understand visually, and (4) safe. A volleyball or a Muslim prayer rug would be appropriate in size for most classroom audiences. A smart phone might be OK if the goal was simply to show what a smart phone looks like, but it might be too small if you want to demonstrate how to use the phone's specialized functions.

Some animate objects also make effective visual aids. On occasion, *you* can be an effective visual aid. For instance, you can use descriptive gestures to show the height of a tennis net; you can use posture and movement to show the motions involved in a golf swing; or you can use your attire to illustrate the traditional attire of a particular country. Sometimes it can be appropriate to use another person as a visual aid, such as when Jenny used a friend to demonstrate the Heimlich maneuver. Animals can also be effective visual aids. For example, Josh used his AKC Obedience Champion dog to demonstrate the basics of dog training. But keep in mind that some animals placed in unfamiliar settings can become difficult to control and can distract from your message.

structure, Ignite events are low on rules—most cities' Ignite Web sites say in their basic guidelines, "We want Ignite to be about promoting and sharing burning ideas. If those ideas happen to take the form of . . . any other self-serving commercial interest, then so be it. We're fine with it, really. But whatever you present had better be interesting" ("Basic Guidelines," n.d.).

Luciana Lopez (2008) of *The Oregonian* calls Ignite events "attention deficit theater," and these events are indeed tailored to a generation increasingly comfortable with pared-down forms of communication, such as text messaging and Twitter. Event organizer Jason Prothero says, "[Ignite is] a deliberate attempt to avoid what sucks about presentations. They're boring" (Neznanski, 2008). An online review of Ignite Seattle recommends that "all presentations should be five minutes long," explaining: "Anyone who knows PowerPoint presentations knows that a 'five-minute presentation,' after including setup time, switching between applications, waiting for your web browser demo to respond, etc., lasts a half hour but feels like an eternity. Ignite's presentation style is a slap in the face to convention" (Weill, 2006). Another online reviewer wrote, "The messages were succinct and powerful because the speakers knew they didn't have time for the clutter that normally pops up in conferences" (Raybould, 2007).

Part of Ignite's success has been its ability to adapt to the interests of its various audiences. For example, co-creator Brady Forrest attempts to balance the gender of the speakers and to keep topics only moderately techie so that more audience members can relate (Guzman, 2009). Ignite Bend in Oregon has applied Ignite's presentation style to community organization, and IgniteChange in Boston focuses on social justice (Guzman, 2009).

In addition, Ignite's message has spread so rapidly because of its incorporation of online social networking tools. Ignite Web sites feature real-time Twitter feeds, Flickr photos and streaming videos, and links to individual blog posts that review Ignite events. Of Ignite's intense Internet focus, Luciana Lopez (2008) says, "This crowd was so wired, organizers went online to update folks waiting to get inside the [theater]."

Extreme audience adaptation? Perhaps for now—sounds like pretty soon *everybody* will be doing it. If you'd like to see for yourself what Ignite is all about, visit the Ignite Seattle Web site at www.igniteseattle.com.

Models

When an object is too large or too small, too complex to understand visually, or potentially unsafe or uncontrollable, a model of the object can be an effective visual aid. A **model** is a three-dimensional scaled-down or scaled-up version of an actual object, and it may also be scaled-down to aid understanding. In a speech on the physics of bridge construction, a scale model of a suspension bridge would be an effective visual aid. Likewise, in a speech on genetic engineering, a scaled-up model of the DNA double helix might help the audience understand what happens during these microscopic procedures.

Photographs

If an exact reproduction of material is needed, enlarged still photographs are excellent visual aids. In a speech on smart weapons, enlarged before-and-after photos of target sites would be effective in helping the audience understand the pinpoint accuracy of these weapons.

Simple drawings and diagrams

Simple drawings and diagrams are easy to prepare. If you can use a compass, a straight-edge, and a ruler, you can draw well enough to prepare a simple diagram. Or with a little practice, you can use a basic computer drawing program to prepare one. For instance, if you are making the point that water-skiers must hold their arms straight, their back straight, and their knees bent slightly, a stick figure (see Figure 13.2) will illustrate the point. Stick figures may not be as aesthetically pleasing as professional drawings or photographs, but they can still be effective. In fact, elaborate, detailed drawings may not be worth the time and effort, and actual photographs may be so detailed that they obscure the point you wish to make. Likewise, a simple **diagram**, a type of drawing that shows how the whole relates to its parts, can be more effective than a photograph because you can choose how much detail to include. Andria's diagram of the human body and its pressure points, for example, worked well to clarify her message visually (see Figure 13.3).

Maps

Like drawings and diagrams, maps are relatively easy to prepare. Simple maps allow you to orient audiences to landmarks (mountains, rivers, and lakes), states, cities, land routes, weather systems, and so on. Commercial maps are available, but simple maps can be customized so that audience members are not confused by visual information that is irrelevant to your purpose. Figure 13.4 shows a map that focuses on weather systems.

model
a three-dimensional scaled-down or scaled-up version of an actual object.

diagram
a type of drawing that shows how the whole relates to its parts.

Figure 13.2
Sample drawing

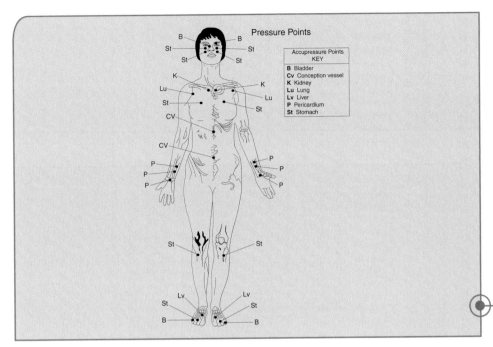

Figure 13.3
Sample diagram

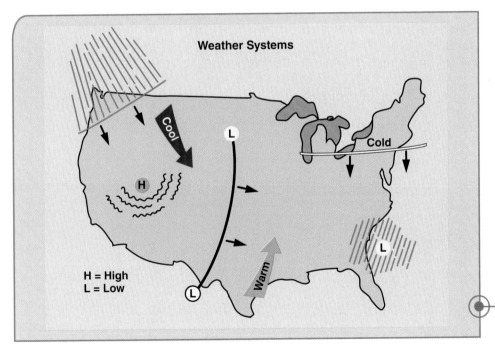

Figure 13.4
Sample map

Charts

A **chart** is a graphic representation that distills a lot of information and presents it in an easily interpreted visual format. Word charts, flow charts, and organizational charts are the most common. A **word chart** is used to preview, review, or highlight important ideas covered in a speech. In a speech on Islam, a speaker might make a word chart that lists the five pillars of Islam, as shown in Figure 13.5. A **flow chart** uses symbols and connecting lines to diagram the progressions through a complicated process. Tim

charts
graphic representations that present information in easily interpreted formats

word charts
used to preview, review, or highlight important ideas covered in a speech.

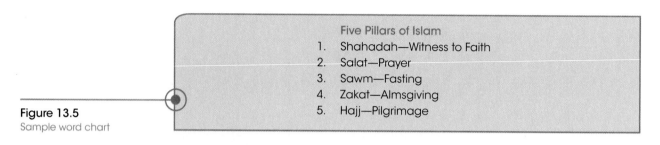

Figure 13.5
Sample word chart

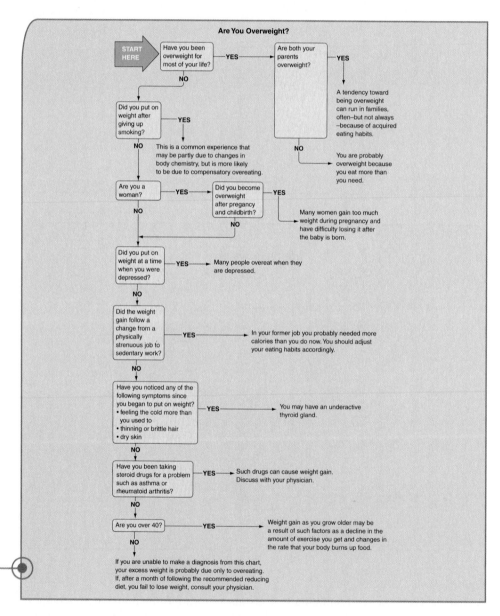

Figure 13.6
Sample flowchart

flow charts
use symbols and connecting lines to diagram the progressions through a complicated process.

used a flow chart to help listeners move through the sequence of steps to determine whether they might be overweight (Figure 13.6) Organizational charts are a common type of flow chart that shows the chain of command in an organization. The chart in Figure 13.7 illustrates the organization of a student union board.

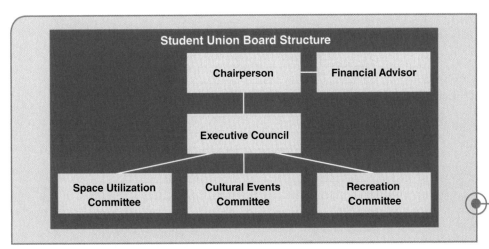

Figure 13.7
Sample organizational chart

Graphs

A **graph** is a diagram that presents numerical information. Bar graphs, line graphs, and pie graphs are the most common forms of graphs.

A **bar graph** is a diagram that uses vertical or horizontal bars to show relationships between two or more variables at the same time or at various times on one or more dimensions. For instance, Jacqueline used a bar graph to compare the amounts of caffeine found in one serving each of brewed coffee, instant coffee, tea, cocoa, and cola (see Figure 13.8).

A **line graph** is a diagram that indicates the changes in one or more variables over time. In a speech on the population of the United States, for example, the line graph in Figure 13.9 helps by showing the population increase, in millions, from 1810 to 2000.

graph
a chart that compares information.

bar graphs
charts that present information using a series of vertical or horizontal bars.

line graphs
charts that indicate changes in one or more variables over time.

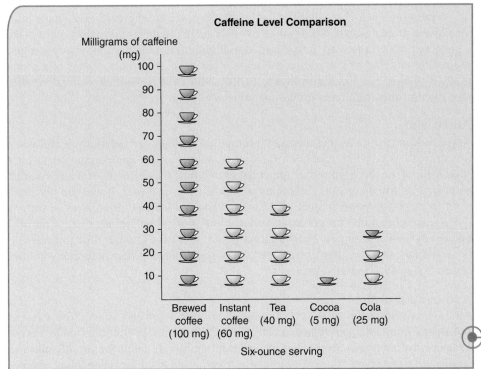

Figure 13.8
Sample bar graph

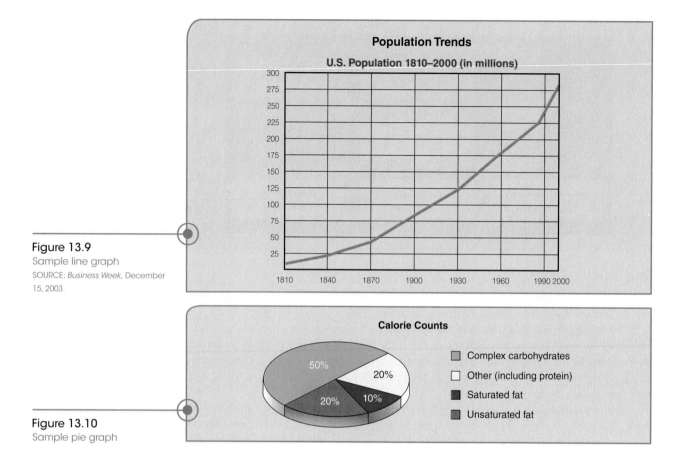

Figure 13.9

Sample line graph

SOURCE: *Business Week*, December 15, 2003.

Figure 13.10

Sample pie graph

A **pie graph** is a chart that shows the relationships among parts of a single unit. Ideally, pie graphs should have two to five "slices," or wedges—more than eight make a pie graph difficult to read during a speech. If your graph includes too many wedges, use a different kind of graph or consolidate several less important wedges into a category of "Other," as Jim did in Figure 13.10 to show the percentage of total calories that should come from the various components of food.

Audio aids

Audio aids enhance a verbal message through sound. They are especially useful when it is difficult, if not impossible, to describe a sound in words. For example, in David's speech about the three types of trumpet mutes and how they alter the trumpet's sound, he played his trumpet so that listeners could hear what he meant. If you can't or don't want to make your own sounds, you can use recorded excerpts from sources such as famous speeches, radio programs, interviews, and musical recordings or environmental sounds. Before using an audio aid, make sure you have enough time to present it (it should take no more than about 5 percent of your speaking time) and that you have access to a quality sound system.

Audiovisual aids

Audiovisual aids enhance a verbal message through sight and sound. You can use short clips from films and videos to demonstrate concepts or processes or to expose audiences to important people. For example, in his speech about the use of robots in automobile production, Chad, who worked as a technician at the local Ford plant, showed

pie graphs
charts that help audiences visualize the relationships among parts of a single unit.

audio aids
a presentation aid that enhances a verbal message through sound.

audiovisual aids
a presentation aid that enhances a verbal message through sight and sound.

a 20-second video clip of a car being painted in a robotic paint booth. As with audio aids, your audiovisual aid should take no more than 5 percent of your speaking time.

Criteria for Choosing Presentational Aids

Now that you understand the various types of presentational aids, you have to decide what content you want to highlight in a presentational aid and the best way to do so. Some simple guidelines can help you make good choices.

What criteria can you use to select presentational aids?

1. Create aids for important information that the audience needs to understand and remember.
2. Create aids for ideas that are complex or difficult to explain verbally but would be easy for members to understand visually.
3. Create aids that are appropriate for the size of the audience.
4. Limit the number of aids so that they do not distract from you as speaker.
5. Use media aids only when equipment is readily available and you know how to operate it.
6. Consider preparation time and expense when choosing aids.

Web Resource 13.1

Designing Effective Presentational Aids

However simple your presentational aids, you still need to produce them carefully. You may need to find or create charts, graphs, diagrams, maps, or drawings. You may need to search for and prepare photographs. You may look for audio or audiovisual snippets and then convert them to a format that you can use at your speech site.

Action Step 4.b

Adapting to Your Audience Visually

The goal of this activity is to help you decide which visual aids you will use in your speech.

1. Identify the key ideas in your speech that you could emphasize with a presentational aid to increase audience interest, understanding, or retention.
2. For each idea you have identified, list the type of presentational aid you think would be most appropriate to develop and use.
3. For each idea you plan to enhance with an aid, decide on the method or aid you will use to present it.
4. Write a brief paragraph describing why you chose the types of presentational aids and methods that you did. Be sure to consider how your choices will affect your preparation time and the audience's perception of your credibility.

You can use Speech Builder Express to complete this activity, or you can complete it online, download a Visual Aids Planning Chart to keep track of your decisions, view a student sample of this activity, and, if requested, e-mail your work to your instructor. Use your Premium Website for Communicate! to access the Action Step activities for Chapter 14.

As you approach your design task, you must first determine whether you will design your aids by hand or use computer presentation software. Regardless of which you choose, there are several guidelines that you will want to follow.

1. **Limit the reading required of the audience.** The audience should not spend a long time reading your presentational aid; you want them listening to you. So limit the total number of lines on an aid to six or fewer, and write points as short phrases rather than complete sentences.

2. **Customize presentational aids from other sources.** We often get ideas for our aids from other sources, and the tendency is to include everything that was in the original. But if the original source includes information that is irrelevant to your purpose or audience, you should customize your aid to include only the information you want to present. For example, Jia Li was preparing a speech on alcohol abuse by young adults. During her research she found a graph of the 2005 statistics called "Current, Binge, and Heavy Alcohol Use among Persons Aged 12 or Older by Age." This graph presented information pertaining to drinkers from ages 12 to 65+, which was much more information than Jia Li needed. So she simplified it for her presentation and used only the information for young adults ages 16 to 29.

3. **Use a photo, print, or type size that can be seen easily by your entire audience.** Check your photo, charts, and lettering for size by moving as far away from the presentational aid as the farthest person in your audience will be sitting. If you can see the image, read the lettering, and see the details from that distance, your aid is large enough; if not, create another sample and check it again.

4. **Use a print style that is easy to read.** Avoid fancy print styles; your goal is presentation aids that are easy to read. In addition, some people think that printing in all capital letters creates emphasis, but the combination of uppercase and lowercase letters is easier to read than uppercase only—even when the ideas are written in short phrases.

5. **Make sure information is laid out in a way that is visually pleasing.** Visually pleasing material is artistically arranged while not losing its communicative function. So visuals that will appeal to the audience are neatly prepared, not crowded, have space separating ideas, use color strategically, and use typefaces and indenting to visually display the relationships between the ideas.

6. **Use pictures or other visual symbols to add interest.** A presentational aid should consist of more than just words (Booher, 2003). Even on a word chart, visual symbols can increase retention by appealing to diverse learning styles (Kolb, 1984; Long, 1997). If you are working with computer graphics, consider adding clip art. Most computer graphics packages have a wide variety of clip art that you can import to your document. You can also buy relatively inexpensive software packages that contain thousands of clip art images. A relevant piece of clip art can make the image look both more professional and more dramatic. Be careful, though; clip art can be overdone. Don't let your message be overpowered by unnecessary pictures or animations.

7. **Use color strategically.** Although black and white can work well for your visual aids, you should consider using color. Color when used strategically can emphasize points. Here are some suggestions for incorporating color in your graphics:

   - Choose a single background color to use on all of your presentation aids. Then choose a different color of type for each main point and use it on all visuals related to that main point.

- Use the same color to show similarities and opposite colors (on a color wheel) to depict differences between ideas.
- Use bright colors, such as red, to highlight important information. Be sure to avoid using red and green together, however, since audience members who are color-blind may not be able to distinguish them.
- Make sure that the color of the type can be easily seen on the background.
- Use no more than two or three colors on any presentation aid that is not a photograph.

Pretend you are your audience. Sit as far away as they will be sitting, and evaluate the colors. Assess your color choices for their readability and appeal from the perspective of your audience.

8. Use presentation software to prepare professional looking presentational aids. **Presentation software** is a computer program that enables you to electronically prepare and store your visual aids using a computer. Microsoft's *PowerPoint*, Adobe's *Captivate*, and Apple's *Keynote 3* are popular presentation software programs. The visuals you create on a computer can become overhead transparencies or handouts, or they can be displayed directly on a screen or TV monitor as a computerized slide show. Aids developed with presentation software give a very polished look to your speech and allow you to develop and deliver complex multimedia presentations that are expected in many professional settings.

Computerized slide shows have quickly become the presentational aid of choice today. Unfortunately, too often these shows do not adhere to the most important function of effective presentational aids: to enhance and complement the verbal message and not to replace it. The speaker should not be relegated to the role of projectionist. On the other hand, well-designed and well-presented computerized slide shows greatly enhance audience interest, understanding, and memory as well as the audience's perceptions of the speaker's credibility.

When you are unfamiliar with the software, using it to prepare your presentational aids will be time-consuming. But if you start simply, over time you will become more adept at creating professional-quality aids. Like hand-prepared presentational aids, those you prepare with presentation software need to be created with your specific audience in mind.

Let's see if we can put all of these principles to work. Figure 13.11 contains a lot of important information, but notice how unpleasant it is to the eye. As you can see, this visual aid ignores all principles. However, with some thoughtful simplification, this speaker could produce the visual aid shown in Figure 13.12, which sharpens the focus by emphasizing the key words (*reduce, reuse, recycle*), highlighting the major details, and adding clip art for a professional touch.

presentation software
a computer program that enables you to electronically prepare and store your visual aids using a computer.

Skill Learning Activity 13.2

I WANT YOU TO REMEMBER THE THREE R'S OF RECYCLING

Reduce the amount of waste people produce, like overpacking or using material that won't recycle.

Reuse by relying on cloth towels rather than paper towels, earthenware dishes rather than paper or plastic plates, and glass bottles rather than aluminum cans.

Recycle by collecting recyclable products, sorting them correctly, and getting them to the appropriate recycling agency.

Figure 13.11
A cluttered and cumbersome visual aid

The Three R's of Recycling

Reduce waste

Reuse

    cloth towels
    dishes
    glass bottles

Recycle

    collect
    sort
    deliver

Figure 13.12
A simple but effective visual aid

Methods for Displaying Presentational Aids

Once you have decided on the specific presentational aids for your speech, you will need to choose the method to display them. Methods for displaying aids vary in the type of preparation they require, the amount of specialized training needed to use them effectively, and the professionalism they convey. Some methods, such as writing on a chalkboard, require little preparation. Other methods, such as computerized slide show presentations, can require extensive preparation. Similarly, it's easy to use an object or a flip chart, but you will need training to properly set up and run a computerized slide show presentation. Finally, the quality of your visual presentation will affect your perceived credibility. A well-run computerized slide show is impressive, but technical difficulties can make you look unprepared. Hand-drawn charts and graphs that are hastily or sloppily developed mark you as an amateur, whereas professional-looking visual aids enhance your credibility. Speakers can choose from the following methods for displaying presentational aids.

Posters

The easiest method for displaying simple drawings, charts, maps, photos, and graphs is by mounting them on stiff cardboard or foamcore. Then the visual can be placed on an easel or in a chalk tray when it is referred to during the speech. Because posters tend to be fairly small, use them only with smaller audiences (30 people or less).

Whiteboards or Chalkboards

Because a whiteboard or chalkboard is a staple in every college classroom, many novice (and ill-prepared) speakers rely on this method for displaying their visual aids. Unfortunately, the whiteboard or chalkboard is easy to misuse and to over-use. Moreover, they are not suitable for depicting complex material. Writing on a whiteboard or chalkboard is appropriate only for very short items of information that can be written in a few seconds. Nevertheless, being able to use a whiteboard or chalkboard effectively should be a part of any speaker's repertoire.

Whiteboards or chalkboards should be written on prior to speaking or during a break in speaking. Otherwise, the visual is likely to be either illegible or partly obscured by your body as you write. Or you may end up talking to the board instead of to the audience. Should you need to draw or write on the board while you are talking, you should practice doing it. If you are right-handed, stand to the right of what you are drawing. Try to face at least part of the audience while you work. Although it may seem awkward at first, your effort will allow you to maintain contact with your audience and will allow the audience to see what you are doing while you are doing it.

"Chalk talks" are easy to prepare, but they are the most likely to result in damage to speaker credibility. It is the rare individual who can develop well-crafted visual aids on a whiteboard or chalkboard. More often, they signal a lack of preparation.

Flip Charts

A **flip chart,** a large pad of paper mounted on an easel, can be an effective method for presenting visual aids. Flip charts (and easels) are available in many sizes. For a presentation to four or five people, a small tabletop version works well; for a larger audience, a larger-size pad (30″ × 40″) is needed.

Flip charts are prepared before the speech, using colorful markers to record the information. At times, a speaker may record some of the information before the speech begins and then add information while speaking.

When you are preparing a flip chart, leave several pages between each visual on the pad. If you discover a mistake or decide to revise, you can tear out that sheet without disturbing the order of other visuals you may have prepared. After you have finished all the visuals, tear out all but one sheet between each of them. This blank sheet serves as both a transition page and a cover sheet. Because you want your audience to focus on your words and not on visual material that is no longer being discussed, you can flip to the empty page until you are ready to talk about the next visual. Also, the empty page between visuals ensures that heavy lines or colors from the next one will not show through.

For flip charts to be effective, information that is handwritten or drawn must be neat and appropriately sized. Flipchart visuals that are not neatly done detract from speaker credibility. Flipcharts can be comfortably used with smaller audiences (less than one hundred people) but are not appropriate for larger settings. It is especially important when creating flip charts to make sure that the information is written large enough to be easily seen by all audience members.

Handouts

At times it may be useful for each member of the audience to have a personal copy of the visual aid. For these situations, you can prepare a handout (material printed on sheets of paper). On the plus side, you can prepare handouts quickly, and all the people in the audience can have their own professional-quality copy to refer to and take with them from the speech. On the minus side, distributing handouts is distracting and has the potential for losing audience members' attention when you want them to be looking at you.

Before you decide to use handouts, carefully consider why they would be better than some other method. Handouts are effective for information you want listeners to refer to after the speech, such as a set of steps to follow later, useful telephone numbers and addresses, or mathematical formulas.

flip chart
a large pad of paper mounted on an easel; it can be an effective method for presenting visual aids.

If you decide on handouts, distribute them at the end of the speech. If you want to refer to information on the handout during the speech, create another visual aid that you can reveal when discussing it during your speech. Tim used a handout for his flow chart about determining whether you are overweight. He wanted listeners to take it home with them to refer to later. But for his speech, he also created a flow chart on a poster.

Document Cameras

Another simple way to project drawings, charts, photos, and graphs is using a document camera, such as an Elmo. An Elmo is a document camera that allows you project images without transferring them to an acetate film. Be sure to transfer drawings, charts, photos, and graphs from their source onto a sheet of 8 1/2″ x 11″ piece of paper so that you can display them smoothly and professionally.

CD/VCR/DVD Players and LCD Projectors

To show TV, film, and video clips for a classroom speech, a VCR or DVD player and a television monitor should be sufficient. For larger audiences, however, you will need to use multiple monitors or, ideally, an LCD multimedia projector. An LCD projector connects to a VCR/DVD player or computer and projects images from them onto a screen, which makes the images easy to see by all members of a large audience. An LCD projector is also ideal for displaying computerized slideshows such as those you create using PowerPoint.

Computer-Mediated Slide Show

You can present computerized slide shows using an LCD projector or a large monitor connected to an onsite computer that has presentation software compatible with the one you used in making your aids. Because you can't always anticipate problems with onsite projection equipment, come with back-up aids such as transparencies or handouts. When you present your slide show during your speech, ensure that the audience members focus their attention on you when you're not talking about one of your slides. To redirect their attention from your slide show to you, insert blank screens between your slides or press the B key on your computer to display a blank screen.

Web Resource 13.2

Speech Assignment: **Communicate on Your Feet**

Battle of the Visual Aids

The Assignment

Form groups of four or five people. Your instructor will provide you with three sample visual aids that might be used in a speech. Based on the criteria and guidelines you learned in this chapter, evaluate each visual aid and select the best one. At your instructor's request, one member of each team should go to the front of the room and give a 2- to 3-minute speech that makes a case for why the visual aid you selected is the best of the three. After all groups have made their presentations, vote as a class on the best one and discuss why.

A Question of Ethics

What Would You Do?

Kendra, I heard you telling Jim about the speech you're giving tomorrow. You think it's a winner, huh?"

"You got that right, Omar. I'm going to have Bardston eating out of the palm of my hand."

"You sound confident."

"This time I have reason to be. See, Professor Bardston's been talking about the importance of audience adaptation. These last two weeks that's all we've heard—adaptation, adaptation."

"What does she mean?"

"Talking about something in a way that really relates to people personally."

"OK—so how are you going to do that?"

"Well, you see, I'm giving this speech on abortion. Now here's the kick. Bardston let it slip that she's a supporter of Right to Life. So what I'm going to do is give this informative speech on the Right to Life movement. But I'm going to discuss

the major beliefs of the movement in a way that'll get her to think that I'm a supporter. I'm going to mention aspects of the movement that I know she'll like."

"But I've heard you talk about how you're pro-choice."

"I am—all the way. But by keeping the information positive, she'll think I'm a supporter. It isn't as if I'm going to be telling any lies or anything."

1. In a speech, is it ethical to adapt in a way that resonates with your audience but isn't in keeping with what you really believe?
2. Could Kendra have achieved her goal using a different method? How?

Summary

Audience adaptation is the process of customizing your speech to your specific audience. You need to consider both how to adapt verbally with your supporting material and language choices and visually (and audiovisually) by using presentational aids to help the audience understand and remember what you are saying.

First, you adapt to the audience verbally by (1) demonstrating relevance through showing how the information you are presenting is timely, proximate, and has personal impact on the audience; (2) establishing common ground by using personal pronouns, asking rhetorical questions, and drawing from common experiences; (3) demonstrating credibility through showing your knowledge and expertise and establishing your trustworthiness; (4) ensuring that your material is easily comprehended by the audience; and (5) adapting to language and cultural differences between you and your audience.

As you plan the aids you will use with your speech, consider the time and cost of preparation, the impact on audience understanding and memory, and the effect on speaker credibility. To design effective aids: (1) use printing or type size that can be seen easily by your entire audience; (2) use a typeface that is easy to read and pleasing to the eye; (3) use upper- and lowercase type; (4) limit the lines of type to six or less; (5) include only items of information that you will emphasize in your speech; (6) make sure information is laid out in a way that is aesthetically pleasing; (7) add clip art where appropriate; and (8) use color to reinforce your meaning.

You adapt to audiences by developing and using appropriate presentational aids. The most common types of aids are objects, models, photographs, slides, simple drawings and diagrams, maps, charts, and graphs. There are various methods speakers can use to display presentational aids, including posters, whiteboards or chalkboards, flip charts, handouts, document cameras, CD/VCR/DVD players and LCD projectors, and computer-mediated slide shows. You might also use audio or audiovisual materials.

Communicate! Active Online Learning

Now that you have read Chapter 13, use your Premium Website for *Communicate!* for quick access to the electronic resources that accompany this text. These resources include

- **Study tools** that will help you assess your learning and prepare for exams (*digital glossary, key term flash cards, review quizzes*).
- **Activities and assignments** that will help you hone your knowledge, analyze communication situations (*Skill Learning Activities*), and build your public speaking skills throughout the course (*Communication on Your Feet speech assignments, Action Step activities*). Many of these activities allow you to compare your answers to those provided by the authors, and, if requested, submit your answers to your instructor.

- **Media resources** that will help you explore communication concepts online (*Web Resources*), develop your speech outlines (*Speech Builder Express 3.0*), watch and critique videos of communication situations and sample speeches (*Interactive Video Activities*), upload your speech videos for peer reviewing and critique other students' speeches (*Speech Studio online speech review tool*), and download chapter review so you can study when and where you'd like (*Audio Study Tools*).

This chapter's Key Terms, Skill Learning Activities, and Web Resources are also featured on the following pages, and you can find this chapter's Communicate on Your Feet assignment and Action Step activities in the body of the chapter.

Key Terms

audience adaptation (305)
bar graphs (321)
charts (319)
common ground (306)
credibility (307)
diagram (318)
flip chart (327)
flow charts (318)
graph (321)
jargon (310)

knowledge and expertise (308)
line graphs (321)
model (318)
personal pronouns (306)
personableness (309)
personalize (000)
pie graph (322)
presentation software (325)
proximity (306)

relevance (305)
rhetorical questions (307)
sensory language (311)
slang (310)
timely (305)
trustworthiness (308)
visual aid (315)
word charts (319)

Skill Learning Activities

13.1: Creating Common Ground (307)

Search online for the article "A Question of Real American Black Men," by Bailey B. Baker Jr., *Vital Speeches,* April 15, 2002. (Two good search resources are InfoTrac College Edition and AccessMyLibrary.com.

You can find a link to the first on your Premium Website, and the second is free on the Web with registration.) Analyze how this speaker uses personal pronouns, rhetorical questions, common experiences, and personalized information to create common ground. Write a short essay describing the conclusions of your analysis.

13.2: Evaluating Visual Aids (325)

Analyze speeches or other public presentations such as lectures, articles, essays, newscasts, and infomercials that you can find on campus, in print, online, or via television. Evaluate the use of at least one item from each of the following visuals aids: (1) objects, (2) models, (3) photographs, (4) slides, (5) film/video clip, (6) drawings, (7) maps, (8) charts, and (9) graphs. How effectively does the speaker or author use each item to illustrate or support his or her speech or presentation? Are there ways the speaker might have used the visual aid more effectively? Would a different type of visual aid have conveyed the presentation's message more clearly?

Web Resources

13.1: Visual Aids (323)

This site at the U.S. Department of Labor features a thorough discussion of the methods and guidelines for using visual aids in presentations.

13.2: PowerPoint Tips & Tutorials (328)

This site at Bates College provides a concise but informative list of tips for creating and displaying PowerPoint slides effectively. Be sure to click on the link "PowerPoint: Web Image Capturing and Basic Slide Show" for links to PowerPoint tutorials and an excellent discussion about copyright issues related to Web text and images.

14

Mel Yates/Cultura (RF)/Jupiter Images

Overcoming Speech Apprehension by Practicing Delivery

Questions you will be able to answer after reading this chapter:

- What are the symptoms and causes of public speaking apprehension?
- What techniques can you use to manage public speaking apprehension?
- What can you do to use your voice effectively?
- What can you do to use your body effectively?
- What are the three most common delivery methods?
- What can you do to conduct effective rehearsal sessions?
- How can you use presentational aids effectively during your speech?
- What criteria can you use to evaluate the effectiveness of a speech?

When Gwen finished speaking, virtually everyone in the audience reacted by applauding, smiling, and saying to people around them, "That was a great speech."

Miguel turned to his friend Justin and said, "I can see why people are excited; the information was good and easy to follow. I thought it was excellent."

Justin replied, "Miguel, I've heard many speeches that had excellent information and were well organized, but what made this speech so much better was her presentation. She talked with us, developed ideas fully, and most of all, used her voice and body language in ways that helped her get her point across—and she didn't appear to be nervous at all!"

As Justin and his classmates have recognized, the difference between a good speech and a great speech is often how well it is delivered. Although delivery can't compensate for a poorly researched, poorly organized, or poorly developed speech, it can take a well-researched, well-organized, and well-developed speech and make it a powerful vehicle for accomplishing your speech goal. Although some people seem to be naturally fluent and comfortable speaking to a group, most of us are a bit frightened about the prospect and not really comfortable with our abilities to effectively present our ideas.

Action Step 5: Practice Presenting Your Speech

In this chapter, we're going to explain the fifth Action Step: Practice Presenting Your Speech. We begin by discussing stage fright, or public speaking apprehension, which most of us face. Then we discuss the characteristics of an effective delivery style and how to use your voice and body effectively when giving a speech. Next, we describe the three most common methods for delivering a speech and introduce a speech practice process designed to make your rehearsal sessions productive. Finally, we offer some criteria you can use to evaluate your speeches and, as an example, we apply the criteria to a sample student speech.

Public Speaking Apprehension

Most people feel some fear about speaking in public. So if you're a bit unnerved, you are in good company. In fact, as many as 76 percent of experienced public speakers feel fearful before presenting a speech (Hahner, Sokolof, & Salisch, 2001). Did you know, for example, that Academy Award–winning actress Meryl Streep, singer Barbra Streisand, and evangelist Billy Graham all experience fear of public speaking? In spite of their fear, they are all effective public speakers because they employ the strategies for managing nervousness that you will read about in this chapter. **Public speaking apprehension**, a type of communication anxiety (or nervousness), is the level of fear you experience when anticipating or actually speaking to an audience. Today, you can benefit from the results of a significant amount of research about public speaking apprehension and methods for managing it.

> What are the symptoms and causes of public speaking apprehension?

Symptoms and Causes

The symptoms of pubic speaking apprehension vary from individual to individual and range from mild to debilitating. Symptoms can be physical, emotional, or cognitive. Physical symptoms may be stomach upset (or butterflies), flushed skin, sweating, shaking, light-headedness, rapid or pounding heartbeats, and verbal disfluencies such as stuttering and vocalized pauses ("like," "you know," "ah," "um," and so on). Emotional symptoms include feeling anxious, worried, or upset. Cognitive symptoms include negative self-talk, which is also the most common cause of speech apprehension (Richmond & McCroskey, 2000).

In addition to negative self-talk, previous experience, modeling, and negative reinforcement have also been found to be leading causes of public speaking apprehension. Previous experience has to do with being socialized to fear public speaking as a result of modeling and negative reinforcement (Richmond & McCroskey, 2000). Modeling has to do with observing how your friends and family members react to speaking in public. If they tend to be quiet and reserved and avoid public speaking, your fears may

public speaking apprehension
a type of communication anxiety (or nervousness), is the level of fear you experience when anticipating or actually speaking to an audience.

stem from modeling. Negative reinforcement concerns how others have responded to your public speaking endeavors. If you experienced negative reactions, you might be more apprehensive about speaking in public than if you had been praised for your efforts (Motley, 1997).

Our level of public speaking apprehension is not static. Rather, it varies over the course of giving a speech. Research has identified three phases of speaking anxiety: anticipation, confrontation, and adaptation (Behnke & Carlile, 1971). The anticipation phase is the anxiety you experience before giving the speech, both while preparing it and waiting to speak. The confrontation phase is the surge of anxiety you feel as you begin delivering your speech; this usually falls once you get into your speech. The adaptation phase is the period during which your anxiety level gradually decreases; it typically begins about one minute into the presentation and tends to level off after about five minutes.

So researchers have found that the level of apprehension varies over the course of giving a speech and that there are various symptoms and causes of apprehension. But the apprehension we feel does not have to affect how well we present our speeches.

> What techniques can you use to manage public speaking apprehension?

Managing Your Apprehension

Would we be better off if we could be totally free from nervousness? Based on years of study, Gerald Phillips (1977) concluded that "learning proceeds best when the organism is in a state of tension" (p. 37). In fact, it helps to be a little nervous to do your best. Not only that, if you are lackadaisical, you probably won't do a good job (Motley, 1997).

Because at least some tension is constructive, the goal is not to eliminate nervousness but to learn how to manage it. There are five techniques you can use to manage public speaking apprehension: communication orientation, visualization, systematic desensitization, cognitive restructuring, and public speaking skills training.

Communication orientation

performance orientation
seeing public speaking as a situation in which a speaker must impress an audience with knowledge and delivery, and seeing audience members as hypercritical judges.

communication orientation
seeing a speech situation as an opportunity to talk with a number of people about a topic that is important to the speaker and to them.

visualization
a method to reduce apprehension by developing a mental picture of yourself giving a masterful speech.

systematic desensitization
a method to reduce apprehension by gradually visualizing increasingly more frightening speaking events.

Communication orientation motivation (COM) techniques help you adopt a communication rather than a performance orientation toward speeches (Motley, 1997). When you have a **performance orientation**, you see public speaking as a situation in which you must *impress* the audience with your knowledge and delivery, and you view audience members as hypercritical judges who will notice and judge even minor mistakes. On the other hand, when you have a **communication orientation**, you view your speech as an opportunity to talk with a number of people about a topic that is important to you and to them. You focus on your audience and getting the message across so that they understand your thoughts. You are not concerned about impressing the audience or worried about them judging you.

Visualization

Visualization helps you develop a mental picture of yourself giving a masterful speech. You have probably heard reports of how athletes use visualization to improve sports performance, and you may have used it before athletic competitions yourself. If you visualize yourself going through your entire speech preparation and speech making process successfully, research has found that you are likely to be more successful when you actually deliver the speech (Ayres & Hopf, 1990). By visualizing themselves speaking effectively, people seem to lower their general apprehension and report fewer negative thoughts when they actually speak (Ayres, Hopf, & Ayres, 1994). So, you will want to use visualization activities as part of your speech preparation.

An interesting study of the use of visualization in sports performances looked at players trying to improve their foul-shooting percentages (Scott 1997). In the study the players were divided into three groups. One group never practiced, another group practiced, and a third group visualized practicing. As we would expect, those who practiced improved far more than those who didn't. What seems amazing is that those who only visualized practicing improved almost as much as those who practiced. Imagine what can happen when you visualize yourself giving a great speech *and* you practice as well!

Web Resource 14.1

To listen to an audio exercise that guides you through a visualization experience, access **Web Resource 14.1: Visualizing Your Success.**

Systematic desensitization

Systematic desensitization can help you reduce apprehension by gradually visualizing and engaging in increasingly more frightening speaking events. The process starts with consciously tensing and then relaxing muscle groups in order to learn how to recognize the difference between the two states. Then, while in a relaxed state, you first imagine yourself and then engage in successively more stressful situations—for example, researching a speech topic in the library, practicing the speech out loud to a roommate, and finally, giving a speech. The ultimate goal of systematic desensitization is to transfer the calm feelings we attain while visualizing to the actual speaking event. Calmness on command—it works.

Cognitive restructuring

Cognitive restructuring is designed to help you systematically rebuild your thoughts about public speaking by replacing anxiety-arousing negative self-talk with anxiety-reducing positive self-talk. The process consists of four steps.

AP Photo/Mark J. Terrill

1. To change your negative thoughts, you must first identify them. Write down all the fears that come to mind when you know you must give a speech.
2. Consider whether or not these fears are rational. (Most are irrational because public speaking is not life threatening.)
3. Develop positive coping statements to replace each negative self-talk statement.
4. Incorporate your positive coping statements into your life so they become second nature. You can do this by writing your statements down and reading them aloud to yourself each day, as well as before you give a speech. The more you repeat your coping statements, the more natural they will become (see Figure 14.1).

Public speaking skills training

Public speaking skills training is the systematic teaching of the skills associated with preparing and delivering an effective public speech, with the intention of reducing public speaking apprehension. Skills training is based on the assumption that some of our anxiety about speaking in public is due to not knowing how to be successful—we lack the knowledge and behaviors to be effective. Therefore, if we learn the processes and behaviors associated with effective speech making, then we will be less anxious (Kelly, Phillips, & Keaten, 1995). Public speaking skills include those associated with the processes of goal analysis, audience and situation analysis, organization, delivery, and self-evaluation.

Do you use positive self-talk to pump yourself up before you have an important event? Do the same before you speak. If you believe you can, you will.

cognitive restructuring
a method to systematically rebuild thoughts about public speaking by replacing anxiety-arousing negative self-talk with anxiety-reducing positive self-talk.

public speaking skills training
the systematic teaching of the skills associated with preparing and delivering an effective public speech, with the intention of improving speaking competence and thereby reducing public speaking apprehension.

Beth decided to try cognitive restructuring to reduce her anxiety about giving speeches in front of her classmates. Here are the positive statements she developed to counter her negative self-talk:

Negative self-talk
1. I'm afraid I'll stumble over my words and look foolish.
2. I'm afraid everyone will be able to tell that I am nervous.
3. I'm afraid my voice will crack.
4. I'm afraid I'll sound boring.

Positive coping statements
1. Even if I stumble, I will have succeeded as long as I get my message across.
2. They probably won't be able to tell I'm nervous, but as long as I focus on getting my message across, that's what matters.
3. Even if my voice cracks, as long as I keep going and focus on getting my message across, I'll succeed at what matters most.
4. I won't sound bored if I focus on how important this message is to me and to my audience. I don't have to do somersaults to keep their attention, because my topic is relevant to them.

Figure 14.1
Negative self-talk versus positive coping statements

Skill Learning Activity 14.1

All five of these methods for reducing public speaking apprehension have successfully helped people manage their anxiety (Dwyer, 2000). For most people, using several of them yields the best results.

Characteristics of an Effective Delivery Style

Think about the best speaker you have ever heard. What made this person stand out in your mind? In all likelihood, how the speaker delivered the speech had a lot to do with it. **Delivery** is how a message is communicated orally and visually through the use of voice and body to be conversational and animated.

Use a Conversational Style

You have probably heard ineffective speakers whose delivery was overly dramatic, too formal, or affected. And you've probably heard ineffective speakers who just read their speeches or sounded mechanical. In contrast, effective delivery has a **conversational style**—your audience feels you are talking *with* them, not *at* them. The hallmark of a conversational style is spontaneity. **Spontaneity** is the ability to sound natural as you speak—as though you are really thinking about the ideas and about getting them across to your audience. Your speech doesn't sound rehearsed, memorized, or read no matter how many times you've practiced it.

How can you make your thoroughly prepared and practiced speech sound spontaneous? One effectively strategy is to learn the *ideas* of the speech instead of trying to memorize its words. You develop spontaneity in public speaking by getting to know the ideas in your speech as well as you know the route you take to school or to work. When you know the ideas this well, you can focus on talking with your audience about your ideas in an organized, professional, and natural way.

Be Animated

Have you ever been bored by a professor reading a well-structured lecture while looking at the lecture notes rather than the students and making few gestures other than

delivery
how a message is communicated orally and visually through the use of voice and body to be conversational and animated.

conversational style
an informal style of presenting a speech so that your audience feels you are talking with them, not at them.

spontaneity
a naturalness that seems unrehearsed or memorized.

turning the pages? Even a well-written speech given by an expert can bore an audience unless its delivery is **animated**, that is, lively and dynamic.

How can you be animated? The secret is to focus on conveying the passion you feel about your topic to your audience through your voice and body. In everyday life, all of us differ in how animated we are when we speak. When we are excited to share something with someone, however, almost all of us become more animated in our delivery. It is this level of liveliness that you want to duplicate when you deliver your speech.

For most of us, appearing conversational and animated requires considerable practice. So, in the next two sections, we'll focus on how you can use your voice and your body to deliver your speech effectively.

Effective Use of Your Voice

Your voice is the vehicle that communicates the ideas in your speech to your audience. The sound of your voice affects your success in getting those ideas across. How your voice sounds depends on its pitch, volume, rate, and quality.

Pitch is the highness or lowness of the sounds produced in your larynx by the vibration of your vocal cords. Just as the pitch of a guitar string is changed by making it tighter or looser, so the pitch of your voice is changed by tightening and loosening the vocal cords. Natural pitch varies from person to person, but adult men generally have lower voices than women and children.

Volume is how loudly or softly you speak. You control your volume by how forcefully you expel air through your vocal cords. When you push a lot of air through your vocal cords, you speak loudly. When you push less air through, your volume drops.

Rate is how fast you talk. In your speeches, you will want to vary your rate. Present new or difficult ideas more slowly. Speak more quickly when covering material that you expect to be more easily understood.

Quality is the tone or timbre of your voice and what distinguishes it from others—it's how you sound to others. Voices that are nasal, breathy, harsh, or hoarse can be unpleasant to listen to and may distract from the message. The vocal quality that is most easily understood is clear and pleasant to the ear.

By effectively using your pitch, volume, rate, and quality, you can achieve the animated, conversational quality that will help your audience listen to your speech.

As you practice and deliver your speech, take note of *how* you sound. Strive to use your voice so that what you say is both intelligible and vocally expressive.

Speak Intelligibly

To be **intelligible** means to be understandable. All of us have experienced situations in which we couldn't understand what was being said because the speaker was talking too softly or too quickly or had a voice that was compromised in some way. If you are not intelligible, your listeners are bound to struggle with your verbal message. By practicing using appropriate pitch, volume, rate, and vocal quality, you can improve the likelihood that you will be intelligible to your audience.

What can you do to use your voice effectively?

animated
lively and dynamic

pitch
the highness or lowness of the sounds produced by the vibration of your vocal cords.

volume
the degree of loudness of the tone you make as you expel air through your vocal cords.

rate
the speed at which you talk.

quality
the tone, timbre, or sound of your voice.

intelligible
understandable

© 2004 by Sidney Harris

"LADIES AND GENTLEMEN... IS *THAT* MY VOICE?... I NEVER HEARD IT AMPLIFIED BEFORE. IT SOUNDS SO WEIRD. HELLO. HELLO. I CAN'T BELIEVE IT'S ME. WHAT A STRANGE SENSATION. ONE, TWO, THREE... HELLO. WOW..."

Most of us speak at a pitch that is appropriate for us and intelligible to listeners. However, some people naturally have voices that are higher or lower in register or become accustomed to talking in tones that are either above or below their natural pitch. Speaking at an appropriate pitch is particularly important if your audience includes people who have hearing loss because they may find it difficult to hear a pitch that is too high or too low.

In normal conversation, pitch fluctuates frequently, and perhaps even a bit more when giving a speech. For example, in English a sentence that is meant to be a question is vocalized with rising pitch. If pitch doesn't rise at the end of a question, listeners may interpret the sentence as a statement instead.

The volume of your voice should be loud enough to be heard easily by the audience members in the back of the room but not so loud as to cause discomfort to listeners seated in the front. You can vary your volume to emphasize important information. For example, you may speak louder when as you introduce each of your main points.

The rate at which you speak should be appropriate to the information you are presenting. If you peak too slowly, your listeners' minds may wander from you and your message. If you speak too quickly, especially when sharing complex ideas and arguments, your listeners may not have enough time to process the information completely. Because nervousness may cause you to speak more quickly than normal, monitor your rate and adjust if you are speaking more quickly than normal.

In addition to vocal characteristics, your articulation and accent can affect intelligibility. **Articulation** is using the tongue, palate, teeth, jaws, and lips to shape vocalized sounds that combine to produce a word. Many of us suffer from minor articulation and **pronunciation** problems such as adding an extra sound ("athalete" for *athlete*), leaving out a sound ("libary" for *library*), transposing sounds ("revalent" for *relevant*), and distorting sounds ("truf " for *truth*). **Accent** is the inflection, tone, and speech habits typical of native speakers of a language. When you misarticulate or speak with a heavy accent during a conversation, your listeners can ask you to repeat yourself until they understand you. But in a speech setting, audience members are unlikely to interrupt to ask you to repeat what you have just said. If your accent is strong or very different from that of most of your audience, practice pronouncing key words so that you are easily understood; speak slowly to allow your audience members more time to process your message; and consider reinforcing important points with visual aids.

Use Vocal Expressiveness

Vocal expressiveness is produced by the variety you create in your voice through changing pitch, volume, and rate, stressing certain words, and using pauses. These contrasts clarify the emotional meaning of your message and help animate your delivery. Generally, speeding up your rate, raising your pitch, and increasing your volume reinforce emotions such as joy, enthusiasm, excitement, anticipation, and a sense of urgency or fear. Slowing down your rate, lowering your pitch, or decreasing your volume can communicate resolution, peacefulness, remorse, disgust, or sadness.

A total lack of vocal expressiveness produces a **monotone**—a voice in which the pitch, volume, and rate remain constant, with no word, idea, or sentence differing significantly in sound from any other. Although few people speak in a true monotone, many severely limit themselves by using only two or three pitch levels and relatively unchanging volume and rate. An actual or near monotone not only lulls an audience to sleep but, more important, diminishes the chances of audience understanding. For instance, if the sentence "Congress should pass laws limiting the sale of pornography" is presented in a monotone, listeners will be uncertain whether the speaker is

Skill Learning Activity 14.2

articulation
using the tongue, palate, teeth, jaw movement, and lips to shape vocalized sounds that combine to produce a word.

pronunciation
the form and accent of various syllables of a word.

accent
the articulation, inflection, tone, and speech habits typical of the native speakers of a language.

vocal expressiveness
the contrasts in pitch, volume, rate, and quality that affect the meaning an audience gets from the sentences you speak.

monotone
a voice in which the pitch, volume, and rate remain constant, with no word, idea, or sentence differing significantly from any other.

concerned with *who* should be take action, what Congress should *do*, or *what* the laws should be.

Pauses, moments of silence strategically used to enhance meaning, can mark important ideas. If you use one or more sentences in your speech to express an important idea, pause before each sentence to signal that something important is coming or pause afterward to allow the idea to sink in. Pausing one or more times within a sentence can also add impact. Nick included several short pauses within and a long pause after his sentence "Our government has no compassion (*pause*), no empathy (*pause*), and no regard for human feeling" (*longer pause*).

Effective use of voice—that is, voice that is both intelligible and vocally expressive—is particularly challenging when delivering speeches in a second language. Read Raj Gaur's story "Mommy, Why Does Raj Talk Funny?" in the Diverse Voices feature to learn how he deals with these challenges.

pauses
moments of silence strategically used to enhance meaning.

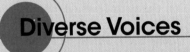

"Mommy, Why Does Raj Talk Funny?"

by Raj Gaur

Graduate student, University of Kentucky

I grew up in India. In my home we spoke Hindi, but from the time I began school at 5 years old, I was also taught English. So, by the time I was 14 years old I was fluent in English—at least what I thought of at the time as English. Ten years ago, I came to the United States and have since learned that the English I speak is somewhat different from the English that is spoken here in the United States. These differences sometimes make it difficult for me to be understood by some Americans. You see, the English I learned as a child is a nativization of English that might more accurately be called "Indian English." What is nativization?

Nativization is the unconscious process of adapting a foreign language so it conforms to the linguistic style and rhetorical patterns of the native language spoken in a particular culture. Since the primary purpose of language is to create shared meaning, it is not surprising that over time the new language gets modified in ways that make it easier for members of the new cultural group to communicate about experiences that may be unique to their cultural experiences. You are familiar with the ways American English differs between regions and among groups within the United States, as well as differences between British English and American English. If there are differences among native English speakers, imagine what happens when a cultural group like Indians whose native language is Hindi adopts English as a second language! As you would probably expect, they adapt English by using some of the grammar, syntax, and pronunciation rules that characterize their first language, as well as by adopting some of the rhetorical and idiomatic expressions that they use in their mother tongue. It's not that Indians consciously decide to make these changes. Rather, the changes simply occur as the new language, in this case English, is used in everyday conversations with other Indians.

Today, more people speak English as a second language than speak it as a native language. So it is not surprising that we can talk about British English, American English, West Indies

(Continued)

English, Asian English, Indian English, and so forth. While the same basic English grammar and vocabulary are taught worldwide, the English spoken by many of us who use it as a second language is not exactly the "educated" English we were taught in school. So the Indian English that was commonly spoken in my neighborhood when I was growing up was modified to use some of the grammar, syntax, and pronunciation rules of our primary language, Hindi.

In India, most of the people I knew spoke English just like I did and I had no problem understanding them or being understood by them. So imagine my consternation when after arriving in the United States some of my American colleagues, professors, and students had trouble understanding me when I spoke. What made this particularly interesting was that I didn't seem to have as much trouble understanding others or being understood when I wrote in English. Rather, it was when I spoke that I got quizzical looks and requests to repeat myself.

What I now understand is that there are major differences between the way certain words are pronounced by those speaking American English and those speaking Indian English. Some of these differences are due to the rules each type of English uses for accenting the syllables within a word. All words are made up of what linguists call *phonemes*. These are basic sound units like "pit," "bit," "can," "plor," etc. When two or more phonemes are combined, they form words with one or more syllables. So the word that is spelled "m-a-r-b-l-e" has two syllables made up of two phonemes, "mar" and "bel." In American English, which phonemes are accented depends on each phoneme's position within a word—the syllable in which it occurs, not the phoneme itself. So a phoneme like "pho" may be accented in some words but not in others. For example, in the word *photo* the "pho" is accented and the "to" is not, while in the word *photography* the "pho" is not accented. In American English, as a general rule, words with more than one syllable alternate between accented and unaccented syllables. So if the first syllable is accented the second is not and vice versa. But in Hindi, whether a particular syllable is accented or not depends on the phoneme itself. Some phonemes always receive

an accent and others do not regardless of their position in a word. So in Indian English, the phoneme "pho" is pronounced the same whether the speaker is using the word *photo* or *photography*. If you speak American English, you are used to hearing "pho·tog´·ra·phy´" but when I pronounce it in Indian English, I say "pho´·to·graph´·y." If you're an American English speaker and you hear me say this, you may not understand me or may think, "Oh he just mispronounced that word." But to me, your pronunciation sounds just as strange because in India, that is how we pronounce the word.

Now consider how the American English rules for accenting every other syllable and the Indian English rules that require phonemes to carry the same stress accent regardless of their syllable placement result in spoken language patterns that are radically different from each other in their cadence. Cadence includes both rhythm and intonation. American English sounds more rhythmic because of the every-other-syllable accent pattern, while Indian English sounds more arrhythmic. Since accented syllables are generally given emphasis by increasing the volume of the voice, Indian English and American English also differ in intonation patterns. So when I give a lecture or talk with an American, the manner in which I accent phonemes will make my English sound very different than what my American listeners are used to hearing. As a result, they sometimes have trouble understanding what I am saying.

There are also syntactic differences between Indian and American English. You will recall that syntax is the rules of a particular language for how words are supposed to be put together to form complete ideas. The syntactic issue that I have struggled most with is the use of articles (*a, an, the,* etc.). In Hindi, we may or may not use articles and this practice also guides our Indian English. So an Indian English student may say, "I go to university in city of Mumbai," rather than "I go to *the* university in *the* city of Mumbai. Another syntactic difference that is common to speakers of Indian English is to form questions without using an auxiliary verb (do, should, can, must, etc.). In Hindi, auxiliary verbs are not required when forming an interrogatory sentence. So in Indian English I may ask, "I know you?" rather than "*Do*

I know you?" or "I finish it?" rather than "*Should* (or *Can* or *Must*) I finish it?"

Nativization of English can also be perceived at the idiomatic level when I attempt to express Indian sensibilities and Indian realities to my American friends. To clarify, as a speaker of Indian English, I sometimes exploit the syntactic structures of the language by directly translating Hindi idioms to English. For example, I might say "wheatish complexion" in Indian English to mean "not dark-skinned, tending toward light." Or I might use the phrase "out of station'" to mean "out of town," which has its origins denoting army officers posted to far-off places during the British rule. Indians also commonly substitute "hotel" for "restaurant," "this side" and "that side" for "here" and "there," "cent per cent" for "100 percent," and "reduce weight" for "lose weight."

Rhetorical devices—for instance, metaphors, similes, allusions, and hyperbole—make speeches more interesting. Metaphors and symbols that are unique to Indian experience—Indian mythology, flora and fauna, social customs, localized attitudes and behaviors—provide a basis for some unique stylistic devices in Indian English. So, in a routinely used expression "Himalayan blunder" for "grave mistake," the size of Himalaya is used as a metaphor to convey the gravity of mistake. The use of *Gandhi* (who is often referred to as *Mahatma* meaning the "Great Soul") as an allusion to "the great soul" is also very common in Indian English. The use of (the river) "Ganges" and "cow" as metaphors for *pure* is also very commonplace and unique to Indian English.

Any one of these English adaptations might not pose problems, but taken together they make the brand of English that I speak very different from that of my American friends. Indian English has evolved over a long period of time and English is now integrated into much of Indian culture. English is taught in schools, business is conducted in English, and English is used in government dealings. Nonetheless, the English of Delhi is not the English of London, or Berlin, or New York, or Lexington, Kentucky. And I find it ironic that after living in the United States for nearly ten years now and struggling to be understood by Americans, my friends in India now complain about my English too. They say it's too American!

Used with permission

References

Don't care for Nano or No-No: Mamta. (2009, March 23). Hindustan Times. *Retrieved March 23, 2009, from http://www. hindustantimes.com.*

Kachru, Braj B. (1992) The Other Tongue: English Across Cultures. *Urbana, Illinois: University of Illinois Press.*

Kachru, Braj B. (1986). The Alchemy of English: the Spread, Functions, and Models Of Non-native Englishes. *Oxford: Pergamon Press.*

Guj riots a national shame, not IPL going abroad: PC. (2009, March 23). The Financial Express. *Retrieved March 23, 2009, from http://www.expressindia.com.*

Patrolling intensified in sea, on shores in Tamil Nadu. (2009, March 23). Press Trust of India. *Retrieved March 23, 2009, from http://www.ptinews.com.*

Wiltshire, C. & Moon, R. (2003). Phonetic stress in Indian English vs. American English. World Englishes, 22(3), 291–303.

Zardari is 5th biggest loser in world: Foreign policy magazine. (2009, March 23). NDTV. *Retrieved March 23, 2009, from http://www.ndtv.com.*

Effective Use of Your Body

Because your audience can see as well as hear you, how you use your body contributes to the impression of conversational and animated delivery. The body language elements that affect delivery are facial expressions, gestures, movement, eye contact, posture, poise, and appearance.

What can you do to use your body effectively?

Facial Expressions

Facial expressions are the eye and mouth movements that convey your personableness and can help you animate your speech. When you talk with friends, your facial expressions are naturally animated. Your audiences expect your expressions to be similarly

facial expression
eye and mouth movements.

animated when you give a speech. Speakers who do not vary their facial expressions during their speech but instead wear a deadpan expression, a perpetual grin, or a permanent scowl tend to be perceived as boring, insincere, or stern. Audiences respond positively to natural facial expressions that appear to spontaneously reflect what you're saying and how you feel about it.

Gestures

Gestures—the movements of your hands, arms, and fingers—can help intelligibility. You can use gestures to describe or emphasize what you are saying, refer to presentational aids, or clarify structure. For example, as Aaron began to speak about the advantages of wireless DSL, he said, "on one hand" and lifted his right hand face up. When he got to the disadvantages, he lifted his left hand face up as he said, "on the other hand."

Some people who are nervous when giving a speech, clasp their hands behind their backs, bury them in their pockets, or grip the lectern. Unable to pry their hands free gracefully, they wiggle their elbows weirdly or appear stiff.

As with facial expressions, effective gestures must appear spontaneous and natural even though they are carefully planned and practiced. When you practice and then deliver your speech, leave your hands free so that they will be available to gesture as you normally do.

Movement

Movement is changing the position or location of your entire body. During your speech, it is important to engage only in **motivated movement**, movement with a specific purpose such as emphasizing an important idea, referencing a presentational aid, or clarifying macrostructure. To emphasize a particular point, you might move closer to the audience. To create a feeling of intimacy before telling a personal story, you might walk out from behind a lectern and sit down on a chair placed at the edge of the stage. Each time you begin a new main point, you might take a few steps to one side of the stage or the other. To use motivated movement effectively, you need to practice when and how you will move.

Avoid such unmotivated movement as bobbing, weaving, shifting from foot to foot, or pacing from one side of the room to the other because unplanned movements distract the audience from your message. Because many unplanned movements result from nervousness, you can minimize them by paying mindful attention to your body as you speak. At the beginning of your speech, stand up straight on both feet. If you find yourself fidgeting, readjust and position you body with your weight equally distributed on both feet.

gestures
movements of hands, arms, and fingers that illustrate and emphasize what is being said.

movement
changing the position or location of the entire body.

motivated movement
movement with a specific purpose.

Using appropriate facial expressions, gestures, and motivated movement enhances your intelligibility and expressiveness.

PictureNet/Flame/Corbis

Eye Contact

Eye contact is looking directly at the people to whom you are speaking. In speechmaking, it involves looking at people in all parts of an audience throughout the speech. As long as you are looking at someone (those in front of you, in the left rear of the room, in the right center of the room, and so on) and not at your notes or the ceiling, floor, or window, everyone in the audience will perceive you as having good eye contact with them. Generally, you should look at your audience at least 90 percent of the time, glancing at your notes only when you need a quick reference point. Maintaining eye contact is important for several reasons.

1. **Maintaining eye contact helps audiences concentrate on the speech.** If you do not look at audience members while you talk, audience members are unlikely to maintain eye contact with you. This break in mutual eye contact often decreases concentration on the message.

2. **Maintaining eye contact increases the audience's confidence in you, the speaker.** Just as you are likely to be skeptical of people who do not look you in the eye as they converse, so too audiences will be skeptical of speakers who do not look at them. In the United States, eye contact is perceived as a sign of sincerity. Speakers who fail to maintain eye contact with audiences are perceived almost always as ill at ease and often as insincere or dishonest (Burgoon, Coker, & Coker, 1986).

3. **Maintaining eye contact helps you gain insight into the audience's reaction to the speech.** Because communication is two-way, audience members are communicating with you at the same time you are speaking to them. In public speaking, the audience members typically "speak" through body language. Audience members who are bored might yawn, look out the window, slouch in their chairs, and even sleep. If audience members are confused, they will look puzzled; if they agree with what you say or understand it, they might nod their heads. By monitoring your audience's behavior, you can adjust by becoming more animated, offering additional examples, or moving more quickly through a point.

When speaking to large audiences of 100 or more people, you must create a sense of looking listeners in the eye even though you actually cannot. This process is called **audience contact.** You can create audience contact by mentally dividing your audience into small groups. Then, at random, talk for four to six seconds with each group as you move through your speech.

Posture

Posture is the manner in which you hold your body. In speeches, an upright stance and squared shoulders communicate a sense of confidence. As you practice, be aware of your posture and adjust it so that you do not slouch and keep your weight equally distributed on both feet.

Poise

Poise is a graceful and controlled use of the body that gives the impression that the speaker is self-assured, calm, and dignified. Mannerisms that convey nervousness, such as swaying from side to side, drumming fingers on the lectern, taking off or putting on glasses, jiggling pocket change, smacking the tongue, licking the lips, or scratching the nose, hand, or arm should be noted during practice sessions and avoided.

eye contact
looking directly at the people to whom we are speaking.

audience contact
when speaking to large audiences, creating a sense of looking listeners in the eye even though you actually cannot.

posture
the position or bearing of the body.

poise
graceful and controlled use of the body.

Appearance

Some speakers think that what they wear doesn't or shouldn't affect the success of their speech. But your **appearance**—the way you look to others—is important. Studies show that a neatly groomed and professional appearance sends important messages about a speaker's commitment to the topic and occasion, as well as about the speaker's credibility (Bates, 1992; Lawrence & Watson, 1991). Your appearance should complement your message, not detract from it. Three guidelines can help you decide how to dress for your speech.

1. Consider your audience and the occasion of your speech. Dress a bit more formally than you expect members of your audience to dress. If you dress too formally, your audience is likely to perceive you to be untrustworthy and insincere (Phillips & Smith, 1992), and if you dress too casually, your audience may view you as uncommitted to your topic or disrespectful of them or the occasion (Morris, Gorham, Cohen, & Huffman, 1996).

2. Consider your topic and purpose. In general, the more serious your topic, the more formally you should dress. For example, if your topic is AIDS and you are trying to convince your audience to be tested for HIV, you will want to look like someone who is an authority by dressing the part. In contrast, if your topic is skateboarding and you are trying to convince your audience that they would enjoy visiting the new skateboard park on campus, you might dress more casually.

appearance
the way we look to others.

Political Comedy and the Credibility of Our Leaders

Pop Comm!

Dana Edelson/NBCU Photo Bank Via AP Images

What was your impression of vice-presidential candidate Sarah Palin when she said, "I can see Russia from my house" in response to a question about her foreign policy credentials? Did her statement help convince you that—wait, hold on a minute. Did Palin really say that? No! Comedian Tina Fey said it when she imitated Palin on *Saturday Night Live* in 2008. What Palin actually said was "[Y]ou

can actually see Russia from land here in Alaska, from an island in Alaska" (Associated Press, 2008). But within 48 hours after Fey's impression was posted to the Web, 5 million people had watched it (Hinckley, 2008), and over a year later, what many people remember about Palin is Fey's unflattering impression of her.

Does biting political comedy like the kind featured on *Saturday Night Live, The Daily Show*, and *The Colbert Report* undermine the credibility of our political leaders? If so, is that okay? Mocking political figures for entertainment has been going on since at least the time of the ancient Greek playwrights, and most likely for centuries before. What's new today is that, increasingly, this type of entertainment is spilling into the serious commentary we receive about political figures. Today, many people include the "fake news" provided by entertainment programs in their overall consumption of news (Associated Press Strategic Planning, 2008, pp. 5, 45; "*The*

3. Avoid extremes. Your attire shouldn't detract from your speech. Avoid gaudy jewelry, over- or undersized clothing, and sexually suggestive attire. Remember you want your audience to focus on your message, so your appearance should be neutral, not distracting.

All speakers need to practice in order to become effective at using their voice and body in a speech. Even though there are best practices for using your voice and body effectively in a public speaking situation, each of us tends to develop our own unique style. Sometimes a speaker's vocal style or mannerisms become a "signature" and, if the speaker is a celebrity (such as a politician, singer, actor or actress), comedians may impersonate him or her for a laugh. Unfortunately, doing so can undermine the person's credibility. For more about this practice and its consequences, read the Pop Comm! feature in this chapter, "Political Comedy and the Credibility of Our Leaders."

Skill Learning Activity 14.3
Web Resource 14.2

Delivery Methods

Speeches vary in the amount of content preparation and practice you do ahead of time. Both of these factors influences how a speech is delivered. The three most common delivery methods are impromptu, scripted, and extemporaneous.

What are the three most common delivery methods?

Daily Show," 2008). Not only that, blogs and mainstream news sources such as *The Huffington Post, The New York Times,* and MSNBC comment on and air the really popular comedy bits, such as snippets of *The Daily Show* interviews, Amy Poehler's *SNL* imitation of Hillary Clinton, and Will Ferrell's impressions of George W. Bush. As a result, in addition to getting unbiased news about political figures from mainstream sources, many people also see mocking portrayals.

How does the ridiculing of political figures affect our opinions? Citing a study by Jody Baumgartner and Jonathan S. Morris of East Carolina University where participants watched episodes of *The Daily Show, The Washington Post's* Richard Morin (2006) wrote, "The results showed that the participants rated both [2004 presidential] candidates more negatively after watching Stewart's program. Participants also expressed less trust in the electoral system and more cynical views of the news media." But on the blog *MyDD,* Matt Stoller interpreted the same study differently: "This is a woefully misleading representation of the study ... [T]he authors of the study concluded that we don't know what the effect of *The Daily Show* is on voting patterns. They mused that it could be positive, or it could be negative" (Clark, 2006). Jessica Clark (2006) of the newsmagazine *In These Times* argues that the fact that politically humorous TV shows decrease our trust is not necessarily a bad thing—skepticism is a sane response to the problems in the media and in politics, and it encourages explorations of authenticity.

Furthermore, political leaders can use satirical TV shows to enhance their credibility. For example, candidates John McCain and Barack Obama both appeared on *Saturday Night Live* during the 2008 presidential race. John McCain was able to poke fun at Obama's prime-time infomercial with a sketch of his own, selling plates on the QVC network that commemorated town hall meetings between him and Obama—which were blank, because the meetings never happened (Bentley, 2008). McCain's appearance increased his likeability. Even Obama remarked, "John McCain was funny yesterday ... [T]hat's part of what our politics should be about, being able to laugh at each other, but also laugh at ourselves" (Gay, 2008).

Impromptu Speeches

At times, you may be called on to speak on the spot. An **impromptu speech** is one that is delivered with only seconds or minutes of advance notice for preparation and is usually presented without referring to notes of any kind. You may have already been called on in this class to give an impromptu speech, so you know the pressure this delivery method creates.

You can improve your impromptu performances by practicing mock impromptu speeches. For example, if you are taking a class in which the professor calls on students at random to answer questions, you can prepare by anticipating the questions that might be asked on the readings for the day and practice giving your answers. Over time, you will become more adept at organizing your answers and thinking on your feet.

Scripted Speeches

At the other extreme, you might carefully prepare a complete written manuscript of each word you will speak in your presentation. Then you will either memorize or read the text to the audience from a printed document or teleprompter. A **scripted speech** is one that is prepared by creating a complete written manuscript and delivered by rote memory or reading a written copy.

Obviously, effective scripted speeches take a great deal of time to prepare because both an outline and a word-for-word transcript must be prepared and perhaps memorized. When you memorize a scripted speech, you face the increased anxiety of forgetting your lines. When you read a scripted speech, you must become adept at looking at the script with your peripheral vision so that you don't appear to be reading and you sound conversational and animated.

Because of the time and skill required to effectively prepare and deliver a scripted speech, scripted speeches are usually reserved for important occasions that have important consequences. Political speeches, keynote addresses at conventions, commencement addresses, and CEO remarks at annual stockholder meetings are examples of occasions when a scripted speech might be worth the effort.

Extemporaneous Speeches

Most speeches, whether in the workplace, in the community, or in class, are delivered extemporaneously. An **extemporaneous speech** is researched and planned ahead of time, but the exact wording is not scripted and will vary from presentation to presentation. When speaking extemporaneously, you may refer to simple notes you have prepared to remind you of the ideas you want to present and the order in which you want to present them.

Extemporaneous speeches are the easiest to give effectively. Unlike impromptu speeches, when speaking extemporaneously, you are able to prepare your thoughts ahead of time, have notes to prompt you, and practice what you might actually say. Unlike scripted speeches, extemporaneous speeches do not require as lengthy a preparation process to be effective. In the next section, we describe how to rehearse successfully for an extemporaneous speech.

Rehearsal

Rehearsing is practicing the presentation of your speech aloud. Is it really necessary to practice a speech out loud? A speech that is not practiced out loud is likely to be far less effective than it would have been had you given yourself sufficient time to revise, evaluate, and mull over all aspects of the speech (Menzel & Carrell, 1994). Figure 14.2 provides a useful timetable for preparing a classroom speech.

impromptu speech
a speech that is delivered with only seconds or minutes of advance notice for preparation and is usually presented without referring to notes.

scripted speech
a speech that is prepared by creating a complete written manuscript and delivered by rote memory or by reading a written copy.

extemporaneous speech
a speech that is researched and planned ahead of time, although the exact wording is not scripted and will vary from presentation to presentation.

rehearsing
practicing the presentation of your speech aloud.

7 days before	Select topic; begin research
6 days before	Continue research
5 days before	Outline body of speech
4 days before	Work on introduction and conclusion
3 days before	Finish outline; find additional material if needed; have all visual aids completed
2 days before	First rehearsal session
1 day before	Second rehearsal session
Due date	Give speech

Figure 14.2
Timetable for preparing a speech

In this section, we describe how to rehearse effectively by preparing speaking notes, handling presentational aids, and recording, analyzing, and refining delivery.

Preparing Speaking Notes

Prior to your first rehearsal session, prepare a draft of your speaking notes. **Speaking notes** are a word or phrase outline of your speech designed to help trigger your memory. The best notes contain the fewest words possible written in lettering large enough to be seen instantly at a distance.

To develop your notes, begin by reducing your speech outline to an abbreviated outline of key phrases and words. Then, if you have details in the speech which you must cite accurately—such as a specific example, a quotation, or a set of statistics—add these in the appropriate spots. Next, indicate exactly where you plan to share presentational aids. Finally, incorporate delivery cues indicating where you want to make use of your voice and body to enhance intelligibility or expressiveness. For example, indicate where you want to pause, gesture, or make a motivated movement. Capitalize, underline, or highlight words you want to stress. Use slash marks (//) to remind yourself to pause (see Figure 14.3).

For a three- to five-minute speech, you will need no more than three 3 × 5-inch note cards to record your speaking notes. For longer speeches, you might need one card for the introduction, one for each main point, and one for the conclusion. If your speech contains a particularly important and long quotation or a complicated set of statistics, you can record this information in detail on a separate card.

During practice sessions, use the notes as you will when you actually give the speech. If you will use a lectern, set the notes on the speaker's stand or, alternatively, hold them in one hand and refer to them only when needed. How important is it to construct good note cards? Speakers often find that the act of making a note card is so effective in helping cement ideas in the mind that during practice, or later during the speech itself, they rarely use the notes at all.

Handling Presentational Aids

Many speakers think that once they have prepared good presentational aids, they will have no trouble using them in the speech. However, many speeches with good aids have become a shambles because the aids were not well handled. You can avoid problems by following these guidelines:

1. **Carefully plan when to use presentational aids.** Indicate on your outline (and mark on your speaking notes) exactly when you will reveal and conceal each aid. Practice introducing and using your aids until you can use them comfortably and smoothly.

What can you do to conduct effective rehearsal sessions?

What are some key guidelines to follow when using presentational aids during your speech?

speaking notes
word or phrase outlines of your speech.

Note Card 1

Intro

(PAUSE and LOOK LISTENERS IN THE EYE)

How many hounded by vendors?

credit card — answer — dreams

Three criteria: 1 IR, // 2 Fee, // 3 Incentives //

Note Card 2

Body

(walk right)

1st C: Examine interest rates

IRs are % that a company charges to carry balance

- Average of 8%
- As much as 32%!! (*Kiplinger's* Jan. 2007)
- Start as low as 0 up to 12 months
  — Student cards higher (*Business Week* May 21, 2001)
  — Some below 14%

IRs variable or fixed

- Variable—change month to month
- Fixed—stay same
  — Even fixed rates can be raised after late payment

(walk left to VISUAL AID)

(Considered IRs: look at next criterion)

Note Card 3

2nd C: Examine the annual fee

AF charges vary

(SHOW VISUAL AID)

- Most, no annual fee
- Some companies do have fee (AMEX)

(COVER VISUAL AID)

(walk left)

(After considered interest and fees, weigh benefits)

3rd C: Weigh incentives

- Rebates (*US News* July 31, 2005)
- Freq flyer miles
- Discounts
  — Cash back on purchases

Incentives not outweigh other factors

Conclusion

(walk back to center)

So, 3 criteria: IRs, annual fees, inducements

Then your credit card may truly be—answer—dreams.

Figure 14.3

Note cards

2. Consider audience needs carefully. As you practice, eliminate any presentational aid that does not contribute directly to the audience's attention to, understanding of, or retention of the key ideas in the speech.

3. Share a presentational aid only when talking about it. Because presentational aids will draw audience attention, practice sharing them only when you are talking about them, and then removing them when they are no longer the focus of attention.

   A single visual or audiovisual aid may contain several bits of information. To keep audience attention where you want it, you can prepare the aid so that you only expose the portion you are currently discussing. This is particularly true when using computerized slideshows. Practice using the "B" key for black screen when you aren't directly referencing the aid, as well as the slideshow animation feature to make concepts appear only when you are ready to talk about them.

4. Display visual and audio aids so that everyone in the audience can see and hear them. It's frustrating not to be able to see or hear an aid. Try to practice in the space where you will give your speech so you will know how to adjust the equipment to make visual images easily seen and sounds clearly heard from all points in the room. If you cannot practice in the space ahead of time, be sure to arrive early enough on the day of the presentation to practice quickly with the equipment you will use.

5. Talk to your audience, not to the presentational aid. Although you will want to acknowledge the presentational aid by looking at it occasionally, it is important to keep your eye contact focused on your audience. As you practice, resist the urge to stare at your presentational aid.

6. Resist the temptation to pass objects through the audience. People look at, read, handle, and think about whatever they hold in their hands. While they are so occupied, they are not likely to be listening to you. It is better to project the images in front of the audience and save handouts for distribution after the speech.

Recording, Analyzing, and Refining Speech Delivery

As with any other activity, effective speech delivery requires practice, and the more you practice, the better your speech will be. During practice sessions, you have three major goals. First, you will practice wording your ideas so they are clear, inclusive, and vivid. Second, you will practice your speech by working with your voice and body so that your ideas are delivered conversationally and expressively. Third, you will practice using presentational aids. As part of each practice, you will want to analyze how well it went and set goals for the next practice session.

Let's look at how you can proceed through several practice rounds.

First practice

Your initial rehearsal should include the following steps:

1. Record (audio and video) your practice session. If you do not own a recorder, try to borrow one. You may also want to have a friend sit in on your practice.

2. Read through your complete sentence outline once or twice to refresh memory. Then put the outline out of sight and practice the speech using only the note cards you have prepared.

3. Make the practice as similar to the speech situation as possible, including using the presentational aids you've prepared. Stand up and face your imaginary audience. Pretend that the chairs, lamps, books, and other objects in your practice room are people.
4. Write down the time that you begin.
5. Begin speaking. Regardless of what happens, keep going until you have presented your entire speech. If you goof, make a repair as you would have to do if you were actually delivering the speech to an audience.
6. Write down the time you finish. Compute the length of the speech for this first rehearsal.

Analysis

Listen to and watch the recording and look at your complete outline. How did it go? Did you leave out any key ideas? Did you talk too long on any one point and not long enough on another? Did you clarify each of your points? Did you adapt to your anticipated audience? (If you had a friend or relative watch and listen to your practice, have him or her help with your analysis.) Were your note cards effective? How well did you do with your presentational aids? Make any necessary changes before your second rehearsal.

Second practice

Repeat the six steps outlined for the first rehearsal. By practicing a second time right after your analysis, you are more likely to make the kind of adjustments that begin to improve the speech.

Additional practices

After you have completed one full rehearsal session, consisting of two practices and the analysis in between them, put the speech away until that night or the next day. Although you should rehearse the speech at least one more time, you will not benefit if you cram all the practices into one long rehearsal time. You may find that a final practice right before you go to bed will be very helpful; while you are sleeping, your subconscious will continue to work on the speech. As a result, you are likely to find significant improvement in your mastery of the speech when you practice again the next day.

How many times you practice depends on many variables, including your experience, your familiarity with the subject, and the length of your speech.

Criteria for Evaluating Speeches

In addition to learning to prepare and present speeches, you are learning to evaluate (critically analyze) the speeches you hear. From an educational standpoint, critical analysis of speeches provides the speaker with an analysis of where the speech went right and where it went wrong, and it also gives you, the critic, insight into the methods that you can incorporate or avoid in your own speeches. In this section, we look at some general criteria for evaluating public speeches.

What criteria can you use to evaluate speeches?

The critical assumption is that if a speech has good content that is adapted to the audience, is clearly organized, and is delivered well, it is likely to achieve its goal. Thus, you can evaluate any speech by answering questions that relate to the basics of content, structure, and delivery. Figure 14.4 is a speech critique checklist. You can use this checklist to analyze your first speech during your rehearsal period and to critique sample student speeches at the end of this chapter as well as speeches delivered by your classmates.

Action Step 5

Rehearsing Your Speech

The goal of this activity is to rehearse your speech, analyze it, and rehearse it again. One complete rehearsal includes a practice, an analysis, and a second practice.

1. Find a place where you can be alone to practice your speech. Follow the six points of the first practice as listed on p. 349–350.
2. Listen to and watch the recording. Review your outline as you watch and listen and then answer the following questions.
   Are you satisfied with how well
   The introduction got attention and led into the speech? _____
   Main points were clearly stated? _____ And well developed? _____
   Material adapted to the audience? _____
   Section transitions were used? _____
   The conclusion summarized the main points? _____ Left the speech on a high note? _____
   Presentational aids were used? _____
   Ideas were expressed vividly? _____ And clearly? _____
   Sounded conversational throughout? _____
   Sounded animated? _____ Sounded intelligible? _____
   Used natural gestures and movement ? _____ Used effective eye contact? _____ Facial expression? _____ Posture? _____ Appearance? _____
   List the three most important changes you will make in your next practice session:
   One: _____
   Two: _____
   Three: _____
3. Go through the six steps outlined for the first practice again.

Then assess: Did you achieve the goals you set for the second practice?
_____

Reevaluate the speech using the checklist and continue to practice until you are satisfied with all parts of your presentation.

You can complete this activity online, print out copies of the Rehearsal Analysis Sheet, see a student sample of a practice round, and, if requested, e-mail your work to your instructor. Use your Premium Website for Communicate! *to access the Action Step activities for Chapter 14.*

Thinking Critically About Speeches

Check all items that were accomplished effectively.

Content

_____ 1. Was the goal of the speech clear?
_____ 2. Did the speaker establish common ground and adapt the content to the audience's interests, knowledge, and attitudes?
_____ 3. Did the speaker use a variety of kinds of developmental material?
_____ 4. Did the speaker use and verbally cite credible information?
_____ 5. Were presentational aids appropriate and well used?

Structure

_____ 6. Did the introduction gain attention, establish relevance and goodwill, and lead into the speech?
_____ 7. Were the main points clear, parallel, and in meaningful complete sentences?
_____ 8. Did section transitions lead smoothly from one point to another?
_____ 9. Was the language clear, inclusive, and vivid?
_____ 10. Did the conclusion tie the speech together by summarizing the goal and main points and providing closure?

Delivery

_____ 11. Did the speaker appear and sound spontaneous and conversational?
_____ 12. Did the speaker appear and sound animated?
_____ 13. Did the speaker sound intelligible?
_____ 14. Did the speaker sound vocally expressive?
_____ 15. Did the speaker sound fluent?
_____ 16. Did the speaker look at the audience?
_____ 17. Did the speaker have good posture and poise?
_____ 18. Were the speaker's gestures and movement appropriate?
_____ 19. Did the speaker have good facial expressions?
_____ 20. Was the speaker's appearance appropriate?

Based on these criteria, evaluate the speech as (check one):
_____ excellent _____ good _____ satisfactory _____ fair _____ poor

Figure 14.4
Speech critique checklist

Speech Assignment: **Communicate on Your Feet**

Presenting Your First Speech

The Assignment

1. Follow the Action Steps to prepare an informative or persuasive speech. The time and other parameters for this assignment will be announced by your instructor.

2. Criteria for evaluation include all the essentials of topic and purpose, content, organization, and presentation, but special emphasis will be placed on clarity of goal, clarity and appropriateness of main points, and delivery (items that are grouped under the boldface headings in the Speech Critique Checklist in Figure 14.4). As you

practice your speech, you can use the checklist to ensure that you are meeting the basic criteria in your speech. In addition, you may want to refer to the sample student outline and speech that follow this assignment box.

3. Prior to presenting your speech, prepare a complete sentence outline and a written plan for adapting your speech to the audience. If you have used Speech Builder Express to complete the action step activities online, you will be able to print out a copy of your completed outline. Your adaptation plan should describe how you plan to verbally and visually adapt your material to the audience.

If you completed the Action Step activities in Chapter 13, you can use them for the basis of your written adaptation plan.

Sample Informative Speech

Understanding Hurricanes
Adapted from a speech by Megan Soileau from the University of Kentucky*

This section presents a sample informative speech adaptation plan, outline, and transcript by a student in an introductory speaking course.

1. Review the outline and adaptation plan developed by Megan Soileau in preparing her speech on hurricanes.
2. Then read the transcript of her speech.
3. Use the Speech Critique Checklist from Figure 14.4 to help you evaluate this speech.
4. Use your Premium Website for *Communicate!* to watch a video clip of student Chet Harding presenting Megan's speech in class.
5. Write a paragraph of feedback to Megan, describing the strengths of her presentation and what you think she might do next time to be more effective.

You can use your Premium Website for *Communicate!* to complete this activity online, print a copy of the Informative Speech Evaluation Checklist, compare your feedback to that of the authors, and, if requested, e-mail your work to your instructor. Access the Interactive Video Activities for Chapter 14.

Adaptation Plan

1. **Key aspects of audience.** Because audience members have probably seen television coverage on hurricanes but don't really know much about them, I will need to provide basic information.
2. **Establishing and maintaining common ground.** My main way of establishing common ground will be by using inclusive personal pronouns (*we, us, our*).
3. **Building and maintaining interest.** I will build interest by pointing out how hurricanes even affect the weather in Kentucky and by using examples.
4. **Audience knowledge and sophistication.** Because most of the class has probably not been in a hurricane, I will provide as much explanatory information as I can.

*Used with permission of Megan Soileau.

5. **Building credibility.** I will build credibility through solid research and oral citation of sources. Early on, I'll mention where I live on the Gulf Coast and the fact that I have lived through several hurricanes
6. **Audience attitudes.** I expect my audience to be curious about hurricanes, especially since Hurricane Katrina received so much media attention. So I will give them information to help them become more knowledgeable about them.
7. **Adapt to audiences from different cultures and language communities.** Because hurricanes occur on coasts all over the world, I don't need to adapt to different cultures or language communities. However, I will consider how to make the topic relevant to people who do not live on a coast.
8. **Use presentational aids to enhance audience understanding and memory.** I will use several PowerPoint slides to highlight the effects of hurricanes.

Speech Outline: Understanding Hurricanes

General purpose: To inform

Speech goal: In this speech, I am going to familiarize the audience with the overall effects of hurricanes: how they work, ways they affect our whole country, and the toll they have on the people who live in their direct paths.

Introduction
I. Think about a time you've been absolutely terrified (whether it was by a person, event, or situation) and all you wanted to do was go home and be with your family and friends. Now imagine the feeling you might have if you were that afraid, but you had no idea if your home would even be there when you arrived.
II. This is the reality for many people living on the coastlines of the United States. Hurricanes affect the lives of those living in their direct paths, but they can also cause spin-off weather that affects the entire country.
III. I have lived about 45 minutes from the Gulf Coast of Texas my entire life and have seen and experienced the destruction caused by hurricanes firsthand, especially in the past three years. *(Slide 1: Picture of hurricane that hit my hometown last year)*
IV. Today I'd like to speak with you about the way hurricanes work, the ways they affect our entire country, and most importantly, the toll they have on the people who live in their direct paths.

Body
I. To begin, let's discuss how hurricanes form and the varying degrees of intensity of them so we can be better informed when we watch news broadcasts and read newspaper reports about them.
   A. Several basic conditions must be present for a hurricane to form.
      1. According to award-winning Discovery Communications Website HowStuffWorks.com, hurricanes form "when an area of warm low pressure air rises and cool, high pressure seizes the opportunity to move in underneath it." This causes a center to develop. This center may eventually turn into what is considered a hurricane.
      2. The warm and moist air from the ocean rises up into these pressure zones and begins to form storms. As this happens, the storm continues to draw up more warm moist air, and a heat transfer occurs because of the cool air being heated, causing the air to rise again.

3. "The exchange of heat creates a pattern of wind that circulates around a center" (the eye of the storm) "like water going down a drain."
4. The "rising air reinforces the air that is already" being pulled up from the surface of the ocean, "so the circulation and speeds of the wind increase."

B. Classifications of these types of storms help determine their intensity so we can prepare properly for them.
1. Winds that are less than 38 miles per hour are considered tropical depressions.
2. Tropical storms are winds ranging from 39 to 73 miles per hour.
3. And lastly hurricanes are storms with wind speeds of 74 miles per hour and higher.
4. When storms become classified as hurricanes, they become part of another classification system that is displayed by the Saffir-Simpson Hurricane Scale.
    a. Hurricanes are labeled as Categories 1–5 based on their wind-intensity level or speed. *(Slide 2: Hurricane scale chart)*
    b. Hurricane Ike was labeled differently at different places. *(Slide 3: Map showing the different places Ike was labeled in the different categories)*

Transition: Knowing how and where hurricanes occur help us determine how our daily lives, even here in Kentucky, may be affected when one hits.

II. A hurricane can affect more than just those living in its direct path, and these effects can actually be seen across the country in terms of the environment and the economy.
A. Hurricanes affect wildlife in negative ways.
1. According to the *Beaumont Enterprise* on October 7, 2008; Christine Rappleye reported that the storm surge (a wall of water) of Hurricane Ike brought in up to 14 feet of water across some parts of Southeast Texas.
2. Dolphins were swept inland with the surge and then, when the waters flowed back out to sea, dolphins were left stranded in the marsh.
3. Some were rescued, but not all. This dolphin was rescued from a ditch. *(Slide 4: Dolphin being rescued)*

B. Hurricanes also affect the economy as prices climb close to all-time highs when hurricanes hit.
1. According to economist Beth Ann Bovino, quoted in the September 29, 2005 issue of *The Washington Post*, gas prices skyrocket when a hurricane like Katrina, Rita, or Ike hits.
    a. Paul Davidson said, in a September 12, 2008 article in *USA Today*, that in anticipation of Hurricane Ike, 12 refineries in Texas were shut down. "This is 17% of the U.S. refining capacity" he said.
    b. That's why even residents here in Lexington saw a dramatic spike in gas prices immediately following Ike's landfall.
2. Energy costs to heat and cool our homes also rise.
    a. When we consumers have to pay more to heat and cool our homes, we also have less to spend eating out at restaurants.
    b. And we have less to spend on nonessentials at the mall.
    c. So, economically we all feel the ripple effect when hurricanes hit.

Transition: So, yes, we all feel the effects of hurricanes, but we should not overlook the dramatic ways in which people who live in the direct path of a hurricane are affected.

III. When a hurricane hits, many of these people become homeless, at least for a while, and suffer emotionally and financially as they evacuate to places all over the country, including Kentucky!

    A. People who go through hurricanes suffer extreme emotional effects.

        1. Evacuation is stressful because people have to pack up what they can and have no way of knowing if their home will still be standing or inhabitable when they return. *(Slides 5 and 6: Before and after pictures from Hurricane Ike)*

        2. Even returning home is emotionally taxing because returning home means rebuilding homes, neighborhoods, and even memories.

        3. Though we try to get back to a "normal" life, it can never really be the same as it once was. Instead, it's what Silicon Valley venture capitalist and investor Roger McNamee calls the "new normal" in his book: *The New Normal: Great Opportunities in a Time of Great Risk.*

    B. Because they have to rebuild their homes and lives, people also go through financial difficulties.

        1. People battle with insurance companies about whether a home has wind or water damage as they seek financial assistance. (Insurance companies will often claim that it is the one—wind or water—the homeowner is uninsured for.)

        2. Price gouging is another financial challenge hurricane victims face.

            a. When families and businesses begin the process of rebuilding, people come from outside areas to help with labor and materials and will charge exorbitant fees.

            b. An example of this is when my father needed people to help remove two trees from our home in September 2005 after Hurricane Rita.

Conclusion

I. Hurricanes affect victims who live in their direct path and the country as a whole.

II. To understand these effects, we talked about how hurricanes work, how they affect our country and daily lives, and the impacts they have on the lives of people who live through them.

III. Maybe knowing some of these facts will help each of us appreciate our homes and our families just a little bit more. *(Handout: Hurricane tracking charts)*

References

Associated Press. (2008, October 8). Windstorm costs insurers $550M. *Newark Advocate*, p. x.

Bovino, B. A. (2005, September 29). Hurricanes impact national economy. *The Washington Post*, Retrieved from http://washingtonpost.com/wp-dym/content/discussion/2005/09/28/D12005092801431.html

Davidson, P. (2008, September 12). Ike blows gasoline prices higher." *USA Today*, p. x.

Marshall, B., Freudenrich, C., & Lamb, R. How hurricanes work. Retrieved from http://www.howstuffworks.com/hurricanes.htm

McNamee, R. (2004). *The new normal: Great opportunities in a time of great risk.* New York: Penguin.

Rappleye, C. (2008, October 7). Hurricane strands marine mammals, damages facility for the stranded. *Beaumont Enterprise*.

Speech and Analysis

Speech	Analysis

Speech

Think about a time you've been absolutely terrified whether it was by a person, event, or situation and all you wanted to do was go home and be with your family and friends.

Now imagine the feeling you might have if you were that afraid, but you had no idea if your home would even be there when you arrived. This is the reality for many people living on the coastlines of the United States. Hurricanes affect the lives of those living in their direct paths, but they can also affect the entire country.

I have lived about forty-five minutes from the Gulf Coast of Texas my entire life and have seen and experienced the destruction caused by hurricanes first hand, especially in the past three years. *(Slide 1: Picture of hurricane that hit my hometown last year.)* This is a picture of my hometown when a hurricane hit it last year.

Today I'd like to speak with you about the way hurricanes work, the ways they affect our whole country and, most importantly, the toll they have on the people who live in their direct paths.

To begin, let's discuss how hurricanes form and the varying degrees of intensity of them so we can be better informed when we watch news broadcasts and read newspaper reports about them.

Several basic conditions must be present for a Hurricane to form. According to award-winning Discovery Communications Website HowStuffWorks.com, hurricanes form "when an area of warm low pressure air rises and cool, high pressure seizes the opportunity to move in underneath it." This causes a center to develop. This center may eventually turn into what is considered a hurricane. The warm and moist air from the ocean rises up into these pressure zones and begins to form storms. As this happens the storm continues to draw up more warm moist air and a heat transfer occurs because of the cool air being heated, causing the air to rise again. "The exchange of heat creates a pattern of wind that circulates around a center" (the eye of the storm) "like water going down a drain." The "rising air reinforces the air that is already" being pulled up from the surface of the ocean, "so the circulation and speeds of the wind increase."

Classifications of these types of storms help determine their intensity so we can prepare properly

Analysis

Megan opens by using an analogy to help get her audience emotionally involved in her speech, then quickly introduces her topic.

Notice how Megan establishes her credibility by sharing that grew up near the Gulf Coast of Texas and has been a hurricane victim herself. The first slide adds emotional appeal to her point.

Megan concludes her introduction by previewing her main points clearly.

Megan does a nice job of incorporating a listener relevance link into her first main point statement.

Here Megan offers an oral footnote to add credibility. Noting that the Website is an award-winning one helps her here.

for them. Winds that are less than 38 miles per hour are considered tropical depressions. Tropical storms have winds that range from 39 to 73 miles per hour. And lastly hurricanes are storms with wind speeds of 74 miles per hour and higher.

When storms become classified as a hurricane, they become part of another classification system that is displayed by the Saffir-Simpson Hurricane Scale. Hurricanes are labeled as categories 1–5 based on their wind intensity level or speed. *(Slide 2: Hurricane scale chart)* Hurricane Ike was labeled differently at different places. *(Slide 3: Map showing the different places Ike was labeled in the different categories.)*

Showing the hurricane scale chart and the map depicting Hurricane Ike at different categories visually reinforces what Megan describes in her verbal message.

Knowing how and where hurricanes occur helps us determine how our daily lives, even here in Kentucky, may be affected when one hits.

Megan does a nice job tying together the two main points, which makes for a fluent section transition.

A hurricane can affect more than just those living in its direct path, and these effects can actually be seen across the country in terms of the environment and the economy.

Hurricanes affect wildlife in negative ways. According to the *Beaumont Enterprise* on October 7, 2008, Christine Rappleye reported that the storm surge, which is basically a wall of water, that Hurricane Ike brought in across some parts of Southeast Texas was about 14 feet in some places. Dolphins were swept inland with the surge and then, when the waters flowed back out to sea, dolphins were left stranded in the marsh. Some were rescued, but not all. This dolphin was rescued from a ditch. *(Slide 4: Dolphin being rescued)*

Here Megan not only describes the 14-foot wall of water Hurricane Ike transported into Texas but also reinforces it with the picture on her PowerPoint slide.

Hurricanes also affect the economy. Prices climb close to all time highs when hurricanes hit. According to economist Beth Ann Bovino, quoted in the September 29, 2005 issue of *The Washington Post*, gas prices skyrocket when a hurricane like Katrina, Rita, or Ike hit. Paul Davidson said in a September 12, 2008 article in *USA Today* that in anticipation of Hurricane Ike, 12 refineries in Texas were shut down. "This is 17% of the U.S. refining capacity," he said. That's why even residents here in Lexington saw a dramatic spike in gas prices immediately following Ike's landfall.

By indicating that Beth Ann Bovino is an economist makes this oral footnote stand out as very credible.

Here Megan reminds her audience that even in Lexington, Kentucky, hurricanes have an impact, which is felt in higher gas prices and energy costs.

Energy costs to heat and cool our homes also rise. When consumers have to pay more to heat and cool our homes, we also have less to spend eating out at restaurants. And we have less to spend on nonessentials at the mall. So, economically we all feel the ripple effect when hurricanes hit.

Here Megan could have developed her main point with an example or a concrete story.

So, yes, we all feel the effects of hurricanes, but we should not overlook the dramatic ways in which people who live in the direct path of a hurricane are affected.

When a hurricane hits, many of these people become homeless, at least for a while, and suffer emotionally and financially as they evacuate to places all over the country, including Kentucky!

People who go through hurricanes suffer extreme emotional effects. Evacuation is stressful because people have to pack up what they can and have no way of knowing if their home will still be standing or inhabitable when they return, *(Slides 5 and 6: Before and after pictures from Hurricane Ike)*

Even returning home is emotionally taxing because returning home means rebuilding homes, neighborhoods, and even memories. Though we try to get back to a "normal" life, it can never really be the same as it once was. Instead, it's what Silicon Valley venture capitalist and investor Roger McNamee calls the "new normal" in his book *The New Normal: Great Opportunities in a Time of Great Risk.*

Because they have to rebuild their homes and lives, people also go through financial difficulties. People battle with insurance companies about whether a home has wind or water damage as they seek financial assistance. (Insurance companies will often claim that it is the one—wind or water—the homeowner is uninsured for.)

Price gouging is another financial challenge hurricane victims face. When families and businesses begin the process of rebuilding, people come from outside areas to help with labor and materials and will charge exorbitant fees. An example of this is when my father needed people to help remove two trees from our home in September 2005 after Hurricane Rita.

To close, I'd like to remind you that hurricanes affect victims who live in their direct path and the country as a whole. To understand some of these effects, we talked about how hurricanes work, how they affect our country and daily lives, and the impacts they have on the lives of people who live through them. Maybe knowing some of these facts will help each of us appreciate our homes and our families just a little bit more. *(Handout: Hurricane tracking charts)*

Again, Megan offers a clear and fluent section transition.

Again, Megan makes her emotional appeal stronger by showing before and after pictures.

Megan could have developed this point a bit more, perhaps by giving a specific example.

Megan does a nice job concluding her speech by summarizing her main points and tieing back to her introduction.

Notice how Megan waits until the end of her speech to distribute her handout. That way, she kept the focus on her message during the speech

All in all, this is a well-presented, informative speech with sufficient documentation.

A Question of Ethics

What Would You Do?

Nalini sighed loudly as the club members of Toastmasters International took their seats. It was her first time meeting with the public speaking group, and she didn't want to be there, but her mom had insisted that she join the club in the hopes that it would help Nalini transfer from her community college to the state university. It wasn't that the idea of public speaking scared Nalini. She had already spent time in front of an audience as the lead singer of the defunct emo band Deathstar. To Nalini's mind, public speaking was just another type of performance, like singing or acting, albeit a stuffy form better suited to middle-aged men and women than people her age, a sentiment that explained why she wanted to be elsewhere at the moment.

After the club leader called the meeting to order, he asked each of the new members to stand, introduce themselves, and give a brief speech describing their background, aspirations, and reasons for joining the club. "Spare me," Nalini muttered loud enough for those next to her to hear. The club leader then called on a young woman to Nalini's left, who rose and began to speak about her dream of becoming a lawyer and doing public advocacy work for the poor. After the young

woman sat down, the club members applauded politely. Nalini whistled and clapped loudly and kept on clapping after the others had stopped.

The club leader, somewhat taken aback, called on Nalini next. She rose from her seat and introduced herself as the secret love child of a former president and a famous actress. Nalini then strung together a series of other fantastic lies about her past and her ambitions. She concluded her speech by saying that she had joined the club in the hopes that she could learn how to hypnotize audiences into obeying her commands. After Nalini sat, a few of the club members applauded quietly, while others cast glances at each other and the club leader.

1. Is mocking behavior in a formal public speaking setting, either by an audience member or a speaker, an ethical matter? Explain your answer.
2. What ethical obligations does an audience member have to a speaker? What about a speaker to his or her audience?

Summary

Although speeches may be presented impromptu, by manuscript, or by memory, the material you have been reading is designed to help you present your speeches extemporaneously—that is, carefully prepared and practiced, but with the exact wording determined at the time of utterance.

Even though almost all of us experience public speaking apprehension, only 15 percent or less experience high levels of fear. The signs of speaking apprehension, or stage fright, vary from individual to individual. The causes of apprehension are still being studied—in fact, some speaking apprehension may be inborn. You can learn to manage apprehension by practicing visualization, systematic desensitization, and cognitive restructuring techniques, and by preparing carefully and rehearsing your speech.

The major elements of speech delivery are embedded within your use of voice (pitch, volume, rate, quality, articulation, and pronunciation) and use of body (facial expression, gestures, movement, eye contact, posture, poise, and appearance).

Three of the most common types of speech delivery are impromptu speaking (talking on the spot), scripted speeches (completely written manuscripts), and extemporaneous speaking (speeches that are researched and planned but not scripted).

Effective delivery requires rehearsal. Experienced speakers schedule and conduct rehearsal sessions. Once their outline is complete, effective speakers usually rehearse at least twice, often using speech notes on cards that include key phrases and words.

In many cases, speakers may use presentational aids to help audiences understand and remember the material. To be effective, presentational aids need to be carefully planned, shared only when being talked about, and displayed so that all can see and hear them.

In addition to preparing and presenting, you should also evaluate speeches, focusing on content, structure, and delivery.

Communicate! Active Online Learning

Now that you have read Chapter 14, use your Premium Website for *Communicate!* for quick access to the electronic resources that accompany this text. These resources include

- **Study tools** that will help you assess your learning and prepare for exams (*digital glossary, key term flash cards, review quizzes*).
- **Activities and assignments** that will help you hone your knowledge, analyze communication situations (*Skill Learning Activities*), and build your public speaking skills throughout the course (*Communication on Your Feet speech assignments, Action Step activities*). Many of these activities allow you to compare your answers to those provided by the authors, and, if requested, submit your answers to your instructor.

- **Media resources** that will help you explore communication concepts online (*Web Resources*), develop your speech outlines (*Speech Builder Express 3.0*), watch and critique videos of communication situations and sample speeches (*Interactive Video Activities*), upload your speech videos for peer reviewing and critique other students' speeches (*Speech Studio online speech review tool*), and download chapter review so you can study when and where you'd like (*Audio Study Tools*).

This chapter's Key Terms, Skill Learning Activities, and Web Resources are also featured on the following pages, and you can find this chapter's Communicate on Your Feet assignment, Action Step activity, and speech analysis activity in the body of the chapter.

Key Terms

accent (338)
animated (337)
appearance (344)
articulation (338)
audience contact (343)
cognitive restructuring (335)
communication orientation (334)
conversational style (336)
delivery (336)
extemporaneous speech (346)
eye contact (343)
facial expression (341)

gestures (342)
impromptu speech (346)
intelligible (337)
monotone (338)
motivated movement (342)
movement (342)
pauses (339)
performance orientation (334)
pitch (337)
poise (343)
posture (343)
pronunciation (338)
public speaking apprehension (333)

public speaking skills training (334)
rate (337)
rehearsing (346)
quality (337)
scripted speech (346)
speaking notes (347)
spontaneity (336)
systematic desensitization (335)
visualization (334)
vocal expressiveness (338)
volume (337)

Skill Learning Activities

14.1: Controlling Nervousness (336)

Interview one or two people who give frequent speeches (such as a minister, a politician, a lawyer, a businessperson, or a teacher). Ask what is likely to make them more or less nervous about giving the speech. Find out how they cope with their nervousness. Write a short paragraph summarizing what you have learned from the interviews. Then identify the behaviors used by those people that you believe might work for you.

14.2: Articulation Practice (338)

The goal of this activity is to practice articulating difficult word combinations. To find a list of sentences that are difficult to articulate, go to jimpowell.com, click on "Directing Tips," and then on "Articulation Exercises." Practice saying each of these sentences until you can do so without error.

14.3: Evaluating Speaker Vocal and Body Action Behaviors (345)

Attend a public speech event on campus or in your community. Watch and evaluate the speaker's use of vocal characteristics (voice and articulation), body action (facial expressions, gestures, movement, poise, and posture), animation, spontaneity, and eye contact. Which vocal or body action behaviors stood out and why? How did the speaker's use of voice, body actions, animation, spontaneity, and eye contact contribute to or detract from the speaker's message? What three things could the speaker have done to improve the delivery of the speech?

Web Resources

14.1: Visualizing Your Success (335)

Try out this visualization exercise. It features a recorded and printed script that can help you manage your anxiety as your prepare to deliver your speech.

14.2: Body Motions and Audience Attention (345)

To explore how body motions affect audience attention during a speech, go to the Presentation-Pointers site and read the article "Capture an Audience's Attention: Points on Posture, Eye Contact, and More" by Marjorie Brody. Presentation-Pointers.com is a site that features many articles about how to give effective speeches.

Carl & Ann Purcell/Encyclopedia/CORBIS

Informative Speaking

Questions you will be able to answer after reading this chapter:

- What are the characteristics of informative speaking?
- What are the major methods of informing?
- What are the two most common informative speech frameworks?
- What are the major elements of process speeches?
- What are the major types of expository speeches?

The campus had been fortunate to hear a number of excellent speakers at this year's *Future of Energy* series and tonight would be no different. Interested students, faculty, and invited guests had taken their seats, and listened as the speaker was introduced by the director of the university's Center for the Study of the Environment. Now, Susan Cischke, Vice President of Sustainability, Environment and Safety Engineering for Ford Motor Company, walked to the microphone to begin her speech entitled "Sustainability, Environment, and Safety Engineering."

This is but one of many scenes played out every day when experts deliver speeches to help others understand complex information. In this chapter, we focus specifically on the characteristics unique to good informative speaking and the methods you can use to develop an effective informative speech.

An **informative speech** is one whose goal is to explain or describe facts, truths, and principles in a way that stimulates interest, facilitates understanding, and increases the likelihood of remembering. In short, informative speeches are designed to educate audiences. Informative speeches answer questions about a topic, such as who, when, what, where, why, how to, and how does. For example, your informative speech might describe who popular singer-songwriter Lady Gaga is, define what Scientology is, compare and contrast the similarities and differences between Twitter and Facebook as social networking sites, narrate the story of Al Franken's campaign for U.S. Senate, or demonstrate how to create and post a video on a Web site like YouTube. Informative speaking is different from other speech forms (such as speaking to persuade, to entertain, or to celebrate) in that your goal is simply to achieve mutual understanding about an object, person, place, process, event, idea, concept or issue.

In this chapter, we describe five distinguishing characteristics of informative speeches and five methods of informing. Then, we discuss two common types of informative speeches (process and expository speeches) and provide an example of an informative speech.

> **What are the characteristics of informative speaking?**

informative speech
a speech that has a goal to explain or describe facts, truths, and principles in a way that increases understanding.

intellectually stimulating
information that is new to audience members.

Rangers, guides, and interpreters work to become experts so they can tailor their presentations to the needs of specific audiences. If you were listening to this ranger, what would you want to know?

Characteristics of Effective Informative Speaking

Effective informative speeches are intellectually stimulating, relevant, creative, memorable, and address diverse learning styles.

Intellectually Stimulating

Your audience will perceive information to be **intellectually stimulating** when it is new to them and when it is explained in a way that piques their curiosity and excites their interest. By *new* information, we mean information that most of your audience is unfamiliar with or new insights into a topic with which they are already familiar.

If your audience is unfamiliar with your topic, you should consider how you might tap the members' natural curiosity. Imagine that you are an anthropology major who is interested in prehistoric humans, not an interest shared by most members of your audience. You know that in 1991, a 5,300-year-old man, Ötzi, as he has become known, was found surprisingly well preserved in an ice field in the mountains between Austria and Italy. Even though the discovery was big news at the time, it is unlikely that most of your audience knows much about it. You can draw on their natural curiosity, however, as you present "Unraveling the Mystery of the Iceman," in which you describe scientists' efforts to understand who Ötzi was and what happened to him ("Ötzi, the Ice Man," n.d.).

© David R. Frazier/PhotoEdit

If your audience members are familiar with your topic, you will need to identify information that will be new to them. Begin by asking yourself, What about my topic do listeners probably not know? Then consider depth and breadth as you answer the question. *Depth* has to do with going into more detail than people's general knowledge of the topic. If you've ever watched programs on the *Food Channel*, that's what they do. Most people know basic recipes, but these programs show new ways to cook the same foods. *Breadth* has to do with how your topic relates to associated topics. Trace did this when he informed his audience about type 1 diabetes. He discussed not only the physical and emotional effects of diabetes on the person who has it, but also the emotional and relational effects on family and friends. As you can see, when your topic is one that audience members are familiar with, you will need to explore a new angle on it if you are going to stimulate them intellectually.

Relevant

A general rule to remember when preparing your informative speeches is this: Don't assume your listeners will recognize how the information you share is relevant to them. Incorporate **listener relevance links**, statements that clarify how a particular point may be important to a listener, throughout the speech. As you prepare each main point, ask yourself, How would knowing this information make my listeners happier, healthier, wealthier, and so forth? Or you can compare unfamiliar aspects of your topic to something your listeners are likely to be familiar with. Trace did this when he compared the relational effects of living with diabetes to living with other chronic diseases such as heart disease and diverticulitis.

Creative

Your audience will perceive your information to be **creative** when it yields different or original ideas and insights. You may never have considered yourself to be creative, but that may be because you have never worked to develop innovative ideas. Contrary to what you may think, creativity is not a gift that some have and some don't; rather, it is the result of hard work. Creativity comes from good research, time, and productive thinking.

Creative informative speeches begin with good research. The more you learn about the topic, the more you will have to think about and the more you will be able to develop it creatively. Speakers who present information creatively have given themselves lots of supporting material to work with.

For the creative process to work, you have to give yourself time. Rarely do creative ideas come just before a deadline. Instead, they are likely to come when we least expect them, when we're driving our car, preparing for bed, or daydreaming. The creative process depends on having time to mull over ideas. If you complete a draft of your outline several days before you speak, you'll have time to consider how to present your ideas creatively.

For the creative process to work, you have to think productively. Productive thinking occurs when we contemplate something from a variety of perspectives. Then, with numerous ideas to choose from, we can select the ones that are best suited to our particular audience. In the article "A Theory about Genius," Michael Michalko describes eight tactics that can be used to become better at productive thinking. You can access this article at the Premium Website for *Communicate!* Look for **Web Resource 15.1.**

Let's look at how productive thinking can help to identify different approaches to a topic. Suppose you want to give a speech on climatic variation in the United States,

Web Resource 15.1

listener relevance links
statements that clarify how a particular point may be important to a listener.

creative
using information in a way that yields different or original ideas and insights.

and in your research, you ran across the data shown in Figure 15.1. By looking at the data from different perspectives, you can identify several possible ways to develop your speech. For instance, you might notice that the yearly high temperatures vary less than the yearly low temperatures. Most people wouldn't understand why this is so and would be curious about this. Or you might notice that it hardly ever rains on the West Coast in the summer. In fact, Seattle, a city that most of us consider to be rainy, receives less than an inch of rain in July, which is three inches less than any eastern city and five inches less than Miami. Again, an explanation of this anomaly would probably interest most audience members. Looking at these data in yet another way reveals that although most of us might think of July as a month that is relatively dry, cities in the Midwest and on the East Coast get more rainfall than we might expect in July.

Productive thought can also help us to create alternative ways to make the same point. Again, using the information in Figure 15.1, we can quickly create two ways to support the point "Yearly high temperatures in U.S. cities vary far less than yearly low temperatures."

Skill Learning Activity 15.1

> **Alternative A:** Of the 13 cities in this table, 10 cities, or 77 percent, had yearly highs of 95 degrees or more. Four cities, or 30 percent, had yearly lows above freezing; and only three cities, or 23 percent, had low temperatures of more than 15 degrees below zero.
>
> **Alternative B:** Cincinnati, Miami, Minneapolis, New York, and St. Louis, cities at different latitudes, all had yearly high temperatures of 95 to 98 degrees. In contrast, the lowest temperature for Miami was 50 degrees, whereas the lowest temperatures for Cincinnati, Minneapolis, New York, and St. Louis were -7, -27, -2, and -9 degrees, respectively.

Memorable

If your speech is really informative, your audience will hear a lot of new information but will need your help in remembering the most important. Emphasizing your specific

City	Yearly Temperature (in degrees Fahrenheit)		Precipitation (in inches)	
	High	Low	July	Annual
Chicago	95	−21	3.7	35
Cincinnati	98	−7	3.3	39
Denver	104	−3	1.9	15
Los Angeles	104	40	trace	15
Miami	96	50	5.7	56
Minneapolis	95	−27	3.5	28
New Orleans	95	26	6.1	62
New York	98	−2	4.4	42
Phoenix	117	35	0.8	7
Portland, ME	94	−18	3.1	44
St. Louis	97	−9	3.9	37
San Francisco	94	35	trace	19
Seattle	94	23	0.9	38

Figure 15.1

Temperature and precipitation highs and lows in selected U.S. cities

Technique	Use	Example
Presentational aids	To provide audience members with a visual or auditory memory of important or difficult material	A diagram of the process of making ethanol
Repetition	To give the audience a second or third chance to retain important information by repeating or paraphrasing it	"The first dimension of romantic love is passion; that is, it can't really be romantic love if there is no sexual attraction."
Transitions	To help the audience understand the relationship between the ideas being presented, including primary and supporting information	"So the three characteristics of romantic love are passion, intimacy, and commitment. Now let's look at each of the five ways you can keep love alive. The first is through small talk."
Humor and other emotional anecdotes	To create an emotional memory link to important ideas	"True love is like a pair of socks, you have to have two, and they've got to match. So you and your partner need to be mutually committed and compatible."
Mnemonics and acronyms	To provide an easy memory prompt for a series or a list	"You can remember the four criteria for evaluating a diamond as the four Cs: carat, clarity, cut, and color." "As you can see, useful goals are SMART: S for specific, M for measurable, A for action-oriented, R for reasonable, and T for time-bound. That's SMART."

Figure 15.2
Techniques for making informative speech material memorable

goal and making sure your main points are stated in parallel language are good starting points. Figure 15.2 summarizes ways to use presentational aids, repetition, transitions, humor, and mnemonics and acronyms to help your audience remember information you believe to be most important.

Skill Learning Activity 15.2
Web Resource 15.2

Address Diverse Learning Styles

Because the members of your audience learn differently, you will be most successful at informing all your audience when you present your information in ways that appeal to all styles of learning. You can appeal to people who prefer to learn through the feeling dimension by providing concrete, vivid images, examples, stories, and testimonials. Address the watching dimension by using visual aids. Address the thinking dimension by including definitions, explanations, and statistics. Address the doing dimension by encouraging your listeners to do something during the speech or afterward. Rounding the learning cycle in this way ensures that you address the diverse learning style preferences of your audience and make the speech understandable, meaningful, and memorable for all.

Methods of Informing

We can inform through description, definition, comparison and contrast, narration, and demonstration. Let's look more closely at each of these patterns.

What are the major methods of informing?

Description

Description is the informative method used to create an accurate, vivid, verbal picture of an object, geographic feature, setting, event, person, or image. This method usually answers an overarching who, what, or where question. If the thing to be described is simple and familiar (like a light bulb or a river), the description may not need to be detailed. But if the thing to be described is complex and unfamiliar (like a sextant or holograph), the description will need to be more exhaustive. Descriptions are, of course, easier if you have a presentational aid, but verbal descriptions that are clear and vivid can create mental pictures that are also informative. To describe something effectively, you can explain its size, shape, weight, color, composition, age, condition, and spatial organization. Although your description may focus on only a few of these, each characteristic is helpful to consider as you create your description.

description
the informative method used to create an accurate, vivid, verbal picture of an object, geographic feature, setting, person, event, or image.

You can describe size subjectively, such as large or small, and objectively by noting specific numerical measures. For example, you can describe New York City subjectively as the largest in the United States or more objectively as home to more than 8 million people with more than 26,000 people per square mile.

You can describe shape by reference to common geometric forms like round, triangular, oblong, spherical, conical, cylindrical, or rectangular, or by reference to common objects such as a book or a milk carton. For example, the Lower Peninsula of Michigan is often described as a left-hand mitten. Shape is made more vivid by using adjectives, such as *smooth*, *jagged*, and so on.

How might you describe a NASCAR automobile?

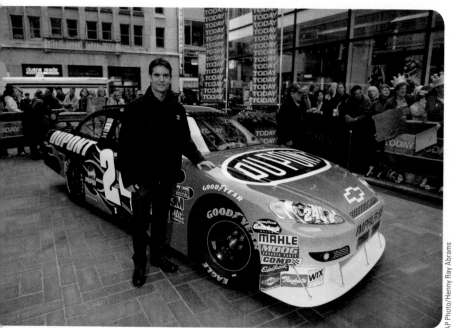

AP Photo/Henny Ray Abrams

You can describe weight subjectively, such as heavy or light, and objectively by pounds and ounces or kilograms and grams. As with size, you can clarify weight with comparisons. For example, you can describe a Humvee (Hummer) as weighing about 7,600 pounds or about as much as three Honda Civics.

You can describe color by coupling a basic color (such as black, white, red, or yellow) with a common object. For instance, instead of describing something as puce or ocher, you might describe the object as "eggplant purple" or "clay pot orange."

You can describe the composition of something by indicating what it is made of, such as by saying the building was made of brick, concrete, wood, or siding. In some cases, you might be clearer by describing what it looks like rather than what it is. For example, you might say something looks metallic, even if it is made of plastic rather than metal.

You can describe something by its age and by its condition. For example, describing a city as old and well kept gives different mental pictures than does describing a city as old and war torn.

Finally, you can describe by spatial organization going from top to bottom, left to right, outer to inner, and so on. A description of the Sistine Chapel, for example, might go from the floor to the ceiling, and a description of a NASCAR automobile might go from the body to the engine to the interior.

Definition

definition
a method of informing that explains the meaning of something.

synonym
a word that has the same or similar meaning.

antonym
a word that is a direct opposite.

comparison and contrast
a method of informing that explains something by focusing on how it is similar and different from other things.

Definition is a method of informing that explains the meaning of something. There are four ways to define something.

First, you can define a word or idea by classifying it and differentiating it from similar ideas. For example, in a speech on vegetarianism, you might use information from the Vegan Society's Web site (http://www.vegansociety.com) to develop a definition of a vegan: "A vegan is a vegetarian who is seeking a lifestyle free from animal products for the benefit of people, animals, and the environment. Vegans eat a plant-based diet free from all animal products including milk, eggs, and honey. Vegans also don't wear leather, wool, or silk and avoid other animal-based products."

Second, you can define a word by explaining its derivation or history. For instance, the word *vegan* is made from the beginning and end of the word *vegetarian* and was coined in the United Kingdom in 1944, when the Vegan Society was founded. Offering this etymology will help your audience to remember the meaning of *vegan*.

Third, you can define a word by explaining its use or function. For example, in vegan recipes, you can use tofu or tempeh to replace meat and soy milk to replace cow's milk.

The fourth, and perhaps the quickest way you can define something, is by using a familiar synonym or antonym. A **synonym** is a word that has the same or a similar meaning; an **antonym** is a word that has the opposite meaning. So you could define a *vegan* by comparing it to the word *vegetarian*, which is a synonym, or to the word *carnivore*, which is an antonym.

How might a presentational aid help enhance your informative speech on vegans?

Comparison and Contrast

Comparison and contrast is a method of informing that focuses on how something is similar to and different from other things. For example, in a speech on vegans, you might tell your audience how vegans are similar and different from other types of vegetarians. You can point out that like vegetarians, vegans don't eat meat. In contrast, semi-vegetarians

Joshua Wold/veganfoodpyramid.com

eat fish or poultry. Like lacto-vegetarians, vegans don't eat eggs, but unlike this group and lacto-ovo-vegetarians, vegans don't use dairy products. So of all vegetarians, vegans have the most restrictive diet. Because comparisons and contrasts can be figurative or literal, you can use metaphors and analogies as well as making direct comparisons.

Narration

Narration is a method of informing that recounts an autobiographical or biographical event, a myth, a story, or some other account. Narrations usually have four parts. First, the narration orients the listener by describing when and where the event took place and by introducing the important people or characters. Second, the narration explains the sequence of events that led to a complication or problem, including details that enhance the development. Third, the narration discusses how the complication or problem affected the key people in the narrative. Finally, the narration recounts how the complication or problem was solved. The characteristics of a good narration include a strong story line; use of descriptive language and detail that enhance the plot, people, setting, and events; effective use of dialogue; pacing that builds suspense; and a strong voice (Baerwald, n.d.).

Narrations can be presented in a first-, second-, or third-person voice. When you use first person, you report what you have personally experienced or observed, using the pronouns *I*, *me*, and *my* as you recount the events. "Let me tell you about the first time I tried to water-ski" might be the opening for a narrative story told in first person. When you use second person, you place your audience at the scene by using the pronouns *you* and *your*. You might say, for example, "Imagine that you have just gotten off the plane in Hong Kong. You look at the signs, but can't read a thing. Which way is the terminal?" When you use third person, you describe to your audience what has happened, is happening, or will happen to other people by using pronouns like *he*, *her*, and *they*. "When the students arrived in Venice for their study-abroad experience, the first thing they saw was…"

narration
a method of informing that explains something by recounting events or stories.

demonstration
a method of informing that explains something by showing how it is done, by displaying the stages of a process, or by depicting how something works.

The TV program *How I Met Your Mother* is an example of informing using the first-person narrative method. How does this technique capture and maintain audience interest?

Demonstration

Demonstration is a method of informing that shows how something is done, displays the stages of a process, or depicts how something works. Demonstrations range from very simple with a few easy-to-follow steps (such as how to iron a shirt) to very complex (such as explaining how a nuclear reactor works). Regardless of whether the topic is simple or complex, effective demonstrations require expertise, developing a hierarchy of steps, and using visual language and aids.

In a demonstration, experience with what you are demonstrating is critical. Expertise gives you the necessary background to supplement bare-bones instructions with personal, lived experience. Why are TV cooking shows so popular? Because

Sonja Flemming/CBS/Getty Images

the chef doesn't just read the recipe and do what it says. Rather, while performing each step, the chef shares tips that aren't mentioned in any cookbook. It is the chef's experience that allows him or her to say that one egg will work as well as two, or how to tell if the cake is really done.

In a demonstration, you organize the steps from first to last so that your audience will be able to remember the sequence of actions accurately. Suppose that you want to demonstrate the steps in using a touch-screen voting machine. If you present 14 separate points, your audience is unlikely to remember them. However, if you group them under the following four headings, chances are much higher that your audience will be able to remember most of the items: I. Get ready to vote; II. Vote; III. Review your choices; and IV. Cast your ballot.

Chris Gordon/WireImage/Getty Images

A carefully prepared and well-organized demonstration can help listeners retain information.

Although you could explain a process with only words, most demonstrations show the audience the process or parts of the process. That's in part why TV shows like *What Not to Wear* and *Flip This House* are so popular. If what you are explaining is relatively simple, you can demonstrate the entire process from start to finish. However, if the process is lengthy or complex, you may choose to pre-prepare the material for some of the steps. Although you will show all stages in the process, you will not have to take the time for every single step as the audience watches. For example, many of the ingredients used by TV chefs are already cut up and measured into little bowls.

Effective demonstrations require practice. Remember that under the pressure of speaking to an audience, even the simplest task can become difficult. (Did you ever try to thread a needle with 25 people watching you?) As you practice, you will want to consider the size of your audience and the configuration of the room. Be sure that all of the audience will be able see what you are doing. You may find that your demonstration takes longer than the time limit you have been given. In these cases, you might want to pre-prepare the material for a step or two.

Common Informative Speech Frameworks

Two of the most common frameworks for structuring or organizing informative speech ideas are process frameworks and expository frameworks.

Skill Learning Activity 15.3

> What are the two most common informative speech frameworks?

Process Speech Frameworks

The goal of a **process speech** is to demonstrate how something is done or made, or how it works. Effective process speeches require you to carefully delineate the steps in the process and the order in which they occur. Then you group the steps and develop concrete explanations for each step and substep. Process speeches rely heavily on the demonstration method of informing.

process speech
a speech that demonstrates how something is done or made, or how it works.

What are the major elements of process speeches?

For example, Allie is a floral designer and has been asked by her former art teacher to speak on the basics of floral arrangement to a high school art class. The teacher has allotted five minutes for her presentation. In preparing for the speech, Allie recognized that in five minutes she could not complete arranging one floral display of any size, let alone help students understand how to create various effects. So she opted to demonstrate only parts of the process and bring arrangements in various stages of completion as additional presentational aids. For example, the first step in floral arranging is to choose the right vase and frog (flower holder). So she brought in vases and frogs of various sizes and shapes to display as she explained how to choose a vase and frog based on the types of flowers used and the desired visual effect. The second step is to prepare the basic triangle of blooms, so she began to demonstrate how to place the flowers she had brought to form a triangle. Rather than hurrying and trying to arrange everything perfectly in the few seconds she had, she brought out several partially finished arrangements that she had stored behind a draped table. These showed carefully completed triangles that used other types of flowers. The third step is placing additional flowers and greenery to complete an arrangement and achieve various artistic effects. Again, Allie demonstrated how to place several blooms, and then, as she described them, she brought out several completed arrangements that illustrated various artistic effects. Even though Allie did not physically perform all of each step, her visual presentation was an excellent demonstration of floral arranging.

Although some process speeches require you to demonstrate, others are not suited to demonstrations. For these, you can use visual aids to help the audience see the steps in the process. In a speech on making iron, it wouldn't be possible to demonstrate the process in a classroom; however, a speaker would be able to greatly enhance the verbal description by showing pictures or drawings of each stage.

In process speeches, the steps are the main points, and the speech is organized in time order, so the earlier steps are discussed before later ones.

To see a sample process speech, "Flag Etiquette" by Cindy Gardner, use your Premium Website for *Communicate!* to access the Interactive Video Activities for Chapter 15. In addition to watching this speech, you can also read Cindy's adaptation plan, outline, and manuscript and analyze them using the process speech evaluation form provided.

Web Resources 15.3

Expository Speech Frameworks

The goal of an **expository speech** is to provide carefully researched, in-depth knowledge about a complex topic. For example, "understanding the health care debate," "the origins and classification of nursery rhymes," "the sociobiological theory of child abuse," and "viewing gangsta rap as poetry" are all topics on which you could give an interesting expository speech. Lengthy expository speeches are known as lectures.

What are the major types of expository speeches?

expository speech
an informative presentation that provides carefully researched, in-depth knowledge about a complex topic.

oral footnotes
oral references to the original source of particular information at the point of presenting it during a speech.

All expository speeches require that the speaker use an extensive research base for preparing the presentation, choose an organizational pattern that helps the audience understand the material being discussed, and use a variety of the informative methods to sustain the audience's attention and comprehension of the material presented.

Even college professors who are experts in their fields draw from a variety of source material when they prepare their lectures. You will want to acquire your information from reputable sources. Then as you are speaking, you will want to cite the sources for the information you present. You do so in the form of **oral footnotes**—oral references to the original source of particular information at the point of presenting it during a speech. In this way, you can establish the trustworthiness of the information you present and also strengthen your own credibility.

Speech Assignment: **Communicate on Your Feet**

A Process Speech

1. Follow the speech plan Action Steps to prepare a process speech. Your instructor will announce the time limit and other parameters for this assignment.

2. Criteria for evaluation include the general criteria of topic and purpose, content, organization, and presentation, but special emphasis will be placed on how intellectually stimulating the topic is made for the audience, how creatively ideas are presented, and how clearly the important information is emphasized.

3. Prior to presenting your speech, prepare a complete sentence outline and source list (bibliography) as well as a written plan for adapting your speech to the audience. If you have used Speech Builder Express to complete the action step activities online, you will be able to print out a copy of your completed outline and source list. Your adaptation plan should describe how you plan to verbally and visually adapt your material to the audience and how you will address the following issues:

   - Establish common ground
   - Build and maintain audience interest
   - Adjust to the audience's knowledge and sophistication
   - Build speaker credibility
   - Adapt to the audience's attitudes toward your speech goal
   - Adapt to audiences from different cultures and language communities (if relevant for you in this speech)
   - Use presentational aids to enhance audience understanding and memory

Expository speakers also must choose an organizational pattern that is best suited to the material they will present. Different types of expository speeches are suited to different organizational patterns, so it is up to the speaker to arrange the main points of the speech so they flow in a manner that aids audience understanding and memory.

Finally, a hallmark of effective expository speaking is that it uses various methods of informing for developing material. Within one speech, a speaker may use descriptions, definitions, comparisons and contrasts, narration, and short demonstrations to develop the main points.

Expository speeches include speeches that explain a political, economic, social, religious, or ethical issue; those that explain events or forces of history; those that explain a theory, principle, or law; and those that explain a creative work.

Exposition of political, economic, social, religious, or ethical issues

An expository speech can help the audience understand the background or context of a political, economic, social, religious, or ethical issue. In such a speech, you would explain the forces that gave rise to the issue and are continuing to affect it. You may also present the various positions that are held about the issue and the reasoning behind these positions. Finally, you may discuss various ways that have been presented for resolving the issue.

Coloring the News: Is the Information Provided by the Media Biased?

Pop Comm!

Kevin Lamaque/Reuters/Landov

MANDEL NGAN/AFP/Getty Images

When you watch a newscast or read an online news article, do you expect the information you receive to be objective and reported without any kind of bias? Or do you assume that all news is biased in some way? Or do you assume bias only from certain sources, such as FOX News or MSNBC, which have both been accused of, respectively, a conservative and a liberal bias.

What makes us think that the news we receive is biased or unbiased? One of the factors is presentation. One journalist who personifies a professional, unbiased delivery—even almost thirty years after his final broadcast as a news anchor—is Walter Cronkite. Cronkite anchored and reported for the *CBS Evening News* from 1962 to 1981 and was so admired and respected that he was named "the most trusted man in America" in a 1972 poll. He delivered the news in a calm, straightforward manner no

matter what he was reporting, betraying emotion only rarely, such as when he announced the death of President John F. Kennedy. He also took pains to ensure that he would be clearly understood by listeners, training himself to speak 124 words per minute, which is 40 words per minute slower than the average American speaks (Hinckley, 2009). And he always made it very clear when he was veering from the reporting the news to expressing an opinion. A tireless advocate of objective journalism, he once said, "[The journalist's] job is only to hold up the mirror—to tell and show the public what has happened." (Leopold, 2009).

Contrast this image of responsible, reliable reporting with the information we receive from many cable TV news programs today. In an effort to fulfill cable TV's demand for 24-hour-a-day programming, even respected news organizations

---

The general goal of your speech is to inform, not to persuade. So you will want to present all sides of controversial issues, without advocating which side is better. You will also want to make sure that the sources you are drawing from are respected experts and are objective in what they report. Finally, you will want to present complex issues in a straightforward manner that helps your audience understand them, while not oversimplifying knotty issues. Figure 15.3 provides examples of topic ideas for an expository speech about a political, economic, social, religious, or ethical issue.

For example, while researching a speech on drilling for oil and natural gas in Arctic National Wildlife Refuge (ANWR), you need to be careful to consult articles and experts on all sides of this controversial issue and fairly represent and incorporate their

such as CNN must present not only the "hard news" but also news analysis, sensational graphics, and chitchat among program hosts. As a result, the news many people watch blurs the lines between opinion, entertainment, and the straightforward presentation of facts. In addition, some cable news anchors and show hosts have become the subject of controversy for their on-air rants, partisan attacks, and melodramatic grandstanding, including Bill O'Reilly, Keith Olbermann, and Geraldo Rivera—all of whom are reporters who were trained in the principles of fair reporting.

Another factor that makes us suspect the information in news reports is biased is how events are covered. News coverage during presidential campaigns tends to generate a lot of interest and analysis. During the 2008 presidential race, some charged the media was showing bias in support of Democratic candidate Barack Obama. *The Washington Post's* Deborah Howell (2008) reported that during the first week of June 2008, Obama dominated political stories by 142 to Republican candidate John McCain's 96, a 3-to-1 advantage. Although she acknowledged that numbers weren't everything and that Obama generated a lot of coverage because he was the first African American nominee and initially less well-known than McCain, she argued that readers deserved comparable coverage of both candidates.

Nonetheless, there is little consensus in the debate over media bias. People disagree not only about the issue of bias itself, but also about how to determine if there is bias, or if such a determination is even possible. For example, expert statistical analysis of media bias, such as *A Measure of Media Bias* by Tim Groseclose and Jeffrey Milyo, has been disputed by other experts who believed there were faults in this study's research methods (Liberman, 2005). And *Scientific American's* Vivian B. Martin (2008) writes, "Most media scholars do not think the issue of bias can be settled by a formula."

Whatever your thoughts about media bias, you'll be a better-informed consumer if you learn how to evaluate news source bias critically. Fairness and Accuracy in Reporting (FAIR) provides a helpful list of factors that can contribute to bias in news reporting ("What's Wrong with the News?" n.d.):

- Corporate ownership
- Advertiser influence
- Official agendas
- Telecommunications policy
- The public relations industry
- Pressure groups
- The narrow range of debate
- Censorship
- Sensationalism

FAIR also recommends asking the following critical questions when evaluating news information ("How to Detect Bias," n.d.):

- Who are the sources?
- Is there a lack of diversity?
- From whose point of view is the news reported?
- Are there double standards?
- What are the unchallenged assumptions?
- Is the language loaded?
- Is there a lack of context?
- Do the headlines and stories match?
- Are stories on important issues featured prominently?

gay marriage	stem cell research	health care
affirmative action	school vouchers	hate speech
school uniforms	media bias	home schooling
immigration	downloading music	eating disorders

Figure 15.3
Topic ideas for expository speeches about political, economic, social, religious, or ethical issues

views in your outline. You will want to discuss all important aspects of this complex issue, including the ecological, economic, political (national, state, and local), and technological aspects. If time is limited, you might discuss just one or two of these aspects, but you should at least inform the audience of the other considerations that affect the issue.

We often think of broadcast news programs as unbiased. However, as you read the Pop Comm! feature "Coloring the News: Is the Information Provided by the Media Biased?" consider how that is not necessarily true.

Exposition of historical events and forces

A second important type of expository speech is one that explains historical events or forces. It has been said that those who don't understand history may be destined to repeat it. So an expositional speech about historical events and forces can be fascinating for its own sake, but it can also be relevant for what is happening today. As an expository speaker, you have an obligation during your research to seek out stories and narratives that can enliven your speech. And you will want to consult sources that analyze the events you describe so that you can discuss their impact at the time they occurred and the meaning they have today. Although many of us know the historical fact that the United States developed the atomic bomb during World War II, an expository speech on the Manhattan Project that dramatizes the international race to produce the bomb and tells the stories of the main players would add to our understanding of the inner workings of secret, government-funded research projects and might also place modern arms races and the fear of nuclear proliferation in historical context. Figure 15.4 proposes examples of topic ideas for an expository speech about historical events and forces.

Exposition of a theory, principle, or law

The way we live is affected by natural and human laws and principles and is explained by various theories. Yet there are many theories, principles, and laws that we do not completely understand or we don't understand how they affect us. Ann expository speech can inform us by explaining these important phenomena. The main challenge for an expository speaker is to find material that explains the theory, law, or principle in language that is understandable to the audience. You will want to search for or create examples and illustrations that demystify complicated concepts and terminology. Effective examples and comparing unfamiliar ideas with those that the audience already knows are techniques that can help you with this kind of speech. In a speech on the psychological principles of operant conditioning, a speaker could help the audience understand the difference between continuous reinforcement and intermittent reinforcement with the following explanation:

> When a behavior is reinforced continuously, each time the person performs the behavior, a reward is given, but when the behavior is reinforced intermittently, the reward is not always given when the behavior is displayed. Behavior that is learned by continuous reinforcement disappears quickly when the reward no longer is provided, but behavior that is learned by intermittent reinforcement continues for long periods of time, even when not reinforced.

Figure 15.4

Topic ideas for expository speeches about historical events and forces

slavery	the papacy	Irish immigration to the U.S.
women's suffrage	the colonization of Africa	the Vietnam War
the Olympics	building the Great Pyramids	the Ming Dynasty
the Crusades	the Industrial Revolution	the Balfour Declaration

Every day you can see the effects of how a behavior was conditioned. For example, take the behavior of putting a coin in a machine. If the machine is a vending machine, you expect to be rewarded every time you "play." And if the machine doesn't dispense the item, you might wonder if the machine is out of order and "play" just one more coin or you might bang on the machine. In any case, you are unlikely to put in more than one more coin. But suppose the machine is a slot machine or a machine that dispenses instant winner lottery tickets. How many coins will you "play" before you stop and conclude that the machine isn't going to give you what you want? Why the difference? Because you were conditioned to a vending machine on a continuous schedule, but a slot machine or automatic lottery ticket dispenser "rewards" you on an intermittent schedule.

Figure 15.5 provides some examples of topic ideas for an expository speech about a theory, principle, or scientific law.

Exposition of creative work

Courses in art, theatre, music, literature, and film appreciation give students tools by which to recognize the style, historical period, and quality of a particular piece or group of pieces. Yet most of us know very little about how to understand a creative work, so presentations designed to explain creative works like poems, novels, songs, or even famous speeches can be very instructive for audience members.

When developing a speech that explains a creative work, you will want to find information on the work and the artist who created the it. You will also want to find sources that educate you about the period in which this work was created and inform you about the criteria that critics use to evaluate works of this type. For example, if you wanted to give an expository speech on Fredrick Douglass's Fourth of July Oration given in Rochester, New York in 1852, you might need to orient your audience by first reminding them of who Douglass was. Then you would want to explain the traditional expectations for Fourth of July speakers in the mid-1800s. After this, you might want to summarize the speech and perhaps share a few memorable quotes. Finally, you would want to discuss how speech critics view the speech and why the speech is considered a great speech.

Figure 15.6 presents examples of topics for expository speeches about creative works. Figure 15.7 is a checklist that you can use to analyze any informative speech you rehearse or to critique the speeches of others.

natural selection	diminishing returns	psychoanalytic theory
gravity	Boyle's law	Maslow's hierarchy of needs
global warming	number theory	intelligent design
feminist theory	color theory	social cognitive theory

Figure 15.5
Topic ideas for expository speeches about theories, principles, or laws

hip-hop music	the films of Alfred Hitchcock	inaugural addresses
Impressionist painting	the love sonnets of Shakespeare	the *Harry Potter* series
salsa dancing	Kabuki theater	iconography
women in cinema	children's book illustration	fad dances

Figure 15.6
Topic ideas for expository speeches about creative works

You can use this form to critique informative speeches you hear in class. As you listen, outline the speech and identify which informative speech framework the speaker is using. Then answer the questions that follow.

Informative Speech Critique

Process Speech
Expository Speech:
_____ Exposition of political, economic, social, religious, or ethical issue
_____ Exposition of historical events or forces
_____ Exposition of a theory, principle, or law
_____ Exposition of creative work

General Criteria
_____ 1. Was the specific goal clear?
_____ 2. Were the main points developed with breadth and depth of appropriate supporting material?
_____ 3. Was the introduction effective in creating interest and introducing the main points?
_____ 4. Was the speech organized and easy to follow?
_____ 5. Was the language clear, inclusive, vivid, and appropriate?
_____ 6. Was the conclusion effective in summarizing the main points and providing closure?
_____ 7. Was the vocal delivery intelligible, conversational, and expressive?
_____ 8. Did the body actions appear poised, natural, spontaneous, and appropriate?

Specific Criteria for Process Speeches
_____ 1. Was the introduction clear in previewing the process to be explained?
_____ 2. Was the speech easy to follow and organized in a time order?
_____ 3. Were presentational aids used effectively to clarify the process?
_____ 4. Did the process use a demonstration method effectively?

Specific Criteria for Expository Speeches
_____ 1. Was the specific goal of the speech to provide well-researched information on a complex topic?
_____ 2. Did the speaker effectively use a variety of methods to convey the information?
_____ 3. Did the speaker emphasize the main ideas and important supporting material?
_____ 4. Did the speaker present in-depth, high-quality, appropriately cited information?

Figure 15.7
Informative speech
evaluation checklist

Speech Assignment: Communicate on Your Feet

An Expository Speech

1. Follow the speech plan Action Steps to prepare a five- to eight-minute informative speech in which you present carefully researched, in-depth information about a complex topic. Your instructor will announce other parameters for this assignment.

2. Criteria for evaluation include all the general criteria of topic and purpose, content, organization, and presentation, but special emphasis will be placed on how intellectually stimulating the topic is made for the audience, how creatively ideas are presented, and how clearly the important information is emphasized. Use the informative speech evaluation checklist in Figure 15.7 to critique yourself as you practice your speech.

3. Prior to presenting your speech, prepare a complete-sentence outline, a reference list (bibliography), and a written plan for adapting your speech to the audience. If you have used Speech Builder Express to complete the action step activities online, you will be able to print out a copy of your completed outline and source list. Your adaptation plan should describe how you plan to verbally and visually adapt your material to the audience and how you will address the following issues:

- Establish common ground
- Build and maintain audience interest
- Adjust to the audience's knowledge and sophistication
- Build speaker credibility
- Adapt to the audience's attitudes toward your speech goal
- Adapt to audiences from different cultures and language communities (if relevant for you in this speech)
- Use presentational aids to enhance audience understanding and memory

Sample Informative Speech

Making Ethanol
by Louisa Greene*

This section presents a sample expository speech adaptation plan, outline, and transcript given by a student in an introductory speaking course.

1. Review the outline and adaptation plan developed by Louisa Greene in preparing her speech on ethanol.
2. Then read the transcript of her speech.
3. Use the Informative Speech Evaluation Checklist from Figure 15.7 to help you evaluate this speech.
4. Use your Premium Website for *Communicate!* to watch a video clip of Louisa presenting her speech in class.
5. Write a paragraph of feedback to Louisa, describing the strengths of her presentation and what you think she might do next time to be more effective.

You can use your Premium Website for *Communicate!* to complete this activity online, print a copy of the Informative Speech Evaluation Checklist, compare your feedback to that of the authors, and, if requested, e-mail your work to your instructor. Access the Interactive Video Activities for Chapter 15.

*Used with permission of Louisa Greene.

Adaptation Plan

1. **Speaking directly to the audience:** I will begin my speech by asking the audience a question. Throughout the speech I will refer to the audience's previous knowledge and experience.
2. **Building credibility:** Early in the speech I will tell the audience about how I got interested in ethanol when I built a still as a science fair project in high school. I will also tell them that I am now a chemical engineering major and am hoping to make a career in the alternative fuel industry.
3. **Getting and maintaining interest:** Because my audience is initially unlikely to be interested in how to produce ethanol, I will have to work hard to interest them and to keep their interest throughout the speech. I will try to gain their interest in the introduction by relating the production of ethanol, the fuel, to the production of "white lightning," the illegal alcohol, which might be of more interest to the average college student. Throughout the speech, I will use common analogies and metaphors to explain the complex chemical processes. Finally, I will use a well-designed PowerPoint presentation to capture attention.
4. **Facilitating understanding:** Throughout the speech I will use analogies and metaphors and simple language to help the audience understand complex technical and chemical processes. I will use transitions and signposts to differentiate the steps in the process. The PowerPoint slides will provide a visual reinforcement for each step.
5. **Increasing retention:** Early in the speech I will give a brief overview of the four-step process used to make ethanol. Then as I speak about each step, I will use color-coded PowerPoint slides with headers to reinforce the step being discussed. Finally, I will review the steps twice during my conclusion.

Speech Outline

General goal: To inform

Specific goal: I want my audience to understand the process for making ethanol from corn.

Introduction

I. Did you know that cars were originally designed to run on ethanol?
   A. Henry Ford was an ethanol enthusiast.
   B. In World War II about 75% of German and American military vehicles were powered by ethanol.
   C. In 1978 Robert Warren built a still to produce what he called "liquid sunshine," which you may know as ethanol.
II. Both moonshine and ethanol are easily produced using the same method since both are pure or almost pure alcohol.
III. Today, I'm going to explain to you the commercial process that turns corn into alcohol.
IV. The four steps in the commercial process of making ethanol are first, preparing the corn by making a mash; second, fermenting the mash by adding yeast to make beer; third, distilling the ethanol from the beer; and fourth, processing the remaining whole stillage to produce co-products such as animal feed. *(Slide 1. Shows the four step flow process)*

Body

I. The first step in the commercial process of making ethanol, preparing the mash, has two parts: milling the corn and breaking the starch down into simple sugars. *(Slide 2. Title: Preparation. Shows corn flowing from a silo into a hammer mill and then into a holding tank where yeast is added)*
   A. The corn is emptied into a bin and passes into a hammer mill where it is ground into coarse flour.
   B. After milling the corn flour, a starch, must be broken down so that it becomes simple sugars by mixing in water and enzymes to form a thick liquid called slurry.
      1. First the water and corn flour are dosed with the enzyme alpha-amylase and heated.
      2. Then the starchy slurry is heated to help the enzyme do its work.
      3. Later gluco-amylase, is added to finish the process of turning the starch to simple sugar.

Transition: Once the starch has been turned to sugar, the mash is ready for fermentation.

II. The second step of the commercial process for making ethanol is fermenting the mash by adding yeast. *(Slide 3. Title: Fermentation. Shows yeast added to the mash in a fermenter and carbon dioxide being released to form "beer")*
   A. The mash remains in the fermenters for about 50 hours.
   B. As the mash ferments, the sugar is turned into alcohol and carbon dioxide.

Transition: This fermented mash must next be distilled.

III. The third step of the commercial process for making ethanol is distilling the fermented mash, now called "beer" by passing it through a series of columns where the alcohol is removed from the mash. *(Slide 4. Title: Distillation of Ethanol. Animated slide showing beer flowing into distillation tank, heat being applied to the beer, ethanol vapors being released and captured in a condenser)*
   A. Distillation is the process of boiling a liquid and then condensing the resulting vapor in order to separate out one component of the liquid.
   B. In most ethanol production, distillation occurs through the use of cooling columns.
   C. Once the ethanol has reached the desired purity or proof, it is denatured to be made undrinkable.

Transition: Once the mash has been distilled, it is ready to be converted into co-products.

IV. The fourth step in commercial production is converting the remaining whole stillage into co-products. *(Slide 5. Title: Co-product. Shows a tank with remaining whole solids flowing into a condenser with output flowing into a bin of animal feed)*

Conclusion

I. As you can see, producing ethanol is a simple four-step process: preparing the corn into a slurry or mash, fermenting the slurry into "beer," distilling the "beer" to release the ethanol, and processing the remaining water and corn solids into co-products. *(Slide 6: Same as Slide 1)*
II. With today's skyrocketing gas prices, you can see why this simple process of making liquid sunshine has resulted in an increase of ethanol plants for cars that can use E-85 fuel.

Work Cited

DENCO. (n.d.). Tour the plant. Retrieved from http://www.dencollc.com/DENCO%20 WebSite_files/Tour.htm.

Northwest Iowa Community College Business and Industry Center. (2004, May 7). Module 2: Science and technology. *Ethanol*. Retrieved from http://www.nwicc. com/pages/continuing/business/ethanol/Module2.htm.

Renewable Fuels Association. (n.d.). The industry—Statistics. Retrieved from http:// www.ethanolrfa.org/industry/statistics/.Tham, M. T. (1997). *Distillation" An introduction*. Retrieved from http://lorien.ncl.ac.uk/ming/distil/distil0.htm.

Warren, Robert. "Make your own fuel." http://running_on_alcohol.tripod.com/index. html. Last updated 8/18/2006. Accessed 2:30 p.m. CDT 7/3/2007.

Speech and Analysis

Speech

Did you know that the first Model Ts were designed to run on ethanol and that Henry Ford said that ethanol was the fuel of the future? Or that in World War II about 75 percent of the German and American military vehicles were powered by ethanol since oil for gasoline was difficult to obtain? In 1978, during the first Arab oil embargo, when gas soared from 62 cents a gallon to $1.64, Californian Robert Warren and others built stills to produce what he called, no, not "white lightning" but "liquid sunshine," which we call ethanol.

I became interested in ethanol in high school when I built a miniature ethanol still as a science fair project. I'm now a chemical engineering major and hope to make a career in the alternative fuel industry. So, today, I'm going to explain to you the simple process that takes corn and turns it into liquid sunshine. Specifically I want you to understand the process that is used to make ethanol from corn.

The four steps in the commercial process of making ethanol are first, preparing the corn by making a mash; second, fermenting the mash by adding yeast to make "beer"; third, distilling the ethanol from the "beer"; and fourth, processing the remaining whole stillage to produce co-products like animal feed. *(Slide 1)*

The first step in the commercial process of making ethanol, preparing the mash, has two parts: milling the corn and breaking the starch down into simple sugars. *(Slide 2)*

The corn, which has been tested for quality and stored in a silo, is emptied into a bin and passes into a hammer mill where it is ground into coarse flour.

Analysis

Louisa begins this speech with a series of rhetorical questions designed to pique the audience's interest in her topic. Because at the time she prepared the speech, gasoline prices were once again soaring, these questions coupled with the example of Robert Warren's solution to a similar problem provide a provocative introduction to the general topic of ethanol.

At this point Louisa personalizes the topic with a self-disclosure that also establishes her credibility. Although the introduction does a good job of gaining attention and interest, it doesn't explain why the audience should care about how ethanol is produced. So this transition to the thesis statement seems abrupt.

This is a clear statement of her thesis. The PowerPoint slide is a simple but effective tool to visually reinforce the verbal description.

Throughout the speech Louisa does a good job of using signposts to help her audience follow each step of the process. Notice how Louisa has nested two steps, milling and breaking starch into sugar under the more general heading of "preparation." This grouping keeps the main points to a manageable number and will help her audience to remember the steps and substeps. Her second slide is simple but effective since it reinforces the two substeps.

One thing Louisa could do better throughout the speech is to offer listener relevance links. Because the audience might not be interested in the topic,

This is done to expose more of the corn's starchy material so that these starches can be more easily broken down into sugar.

In your saliva, you have enzymes that begin to break the bread and other starches you eat into sugar. In your stomach, you have other enzymes that finish this job of turning starch to simple sugar so your body can use the energy in the food you eat. In the commercial production of ethanol, a similar transformation takes place.

To break the milled corn flour starch into sugar, the milled flour is mixed with water and alpha-amylase, the same enzyme that you have in your saliva, and is heated. The alpha-amylase acts as Pac-Men and takes bites out of the long sugar chains which are bound together in the starch. What results are broken bits of starch that need further processing to become glucose. So later, gluco-amylase, which is like the enzyme in your stomach, is added, and these new Pac-Men bite the starchy bits into simple glucose sugar molecules. Now this mixture of sugar, water, and residual corn solids, called slurry or mash, is ready to be fermented.

The second step in the commercial production of ethanol is to ferment the mash by adding yeast in an environment that has no oxygen and allowing the mixture to "rest" while the yeast "works." *(Slide 3)* This is accomplished by piping the slurry into an oxygen free tank called a fermenter, adding the yeast, and allowing the mixture to sit for about 50 hours. Without oxygen, the yeast feeds on the sugar and gives off ethanol and carbon dioxide as waste products. Eventually, deprived of oxygen, the yeast dies.

This is similar to what happens when we add yeast to bread dough. But in bread dough, the carbon dioxide is trapped in the dough and causes it to rise, and the alcohol is burned off when the bread is baked.

In ethanol production, the carbon dioxide is not trapped in the watery slurry. Since it is as a gas, it bubbles out of mixture and is captured and released into the outside air. The ethanol however, remains in the mixture that is now called "beer" with the water and the nonfermentable corn solids. At the end of fermentation process, it is the ethanol in the mixture that retains much of the energy of the original sugar. At this point we are now ready to separate or distill the ethanol from the other parts of the beer.

The third step in the commercial production of ethanol is distillation, which is the process of purifying a liquid by heating it and then condensing its vapor. So for example, if you boiled your tap water and condensed the steam that was produced, you would have

she should remind them of its relevance whenever possible.

Louisa helps the audience understand the unfamiliar starch-to-sugar conversion by comparing it to the familiar process of digestion.

The Pac-Man analogy also helps the audience to visualize what is occurring during the starch to sugar conversion.

The last sentence in this paragraph is an excellent transition between the two main points.

Even though she used an effective transition statement, Louisa continues to help the audience stay with her by using the signpost "second step." Her third slide, a visual of the "fermentation equation," nicely simplifies the complex chemistry that underlies fermentation.

By comparing fermentation in corn mash to bread making, Louisa is able again to make the strange familiar, and she contrasts what happens to the alcohol and the carbon dioxide in ethanol production and bread.

She uses another effective transition statement to signal to her audience that she will be moving to the third step.

Again she uses a signpost to reinforce to the audience that what follows is a description of the third step.

purified water with no minerals or other impurities. But distilling ethanol is a bit more complicated since both the ethanol and the water in the beer are liquids and can be vaporized into steam by adding heat.

Luckily, different liquids boil at different temperatures, and since ethanol boils at 173° F while water boils at 212°F, we can use this boiling point difference to separate the two. So to simplify what is really a more complex process, *(Slide 4)* in the commercial distillation of ethanol, a column or series of columns are used to boil off the ethanol and the water and then to separate these vapors so that the ethanol vapors are captured and condensed back into pure liquid ethanol. The liquid ethanol is then tested to make sure that it meets the specifications for purity and proof. At this point, ethanol is drinkable alcohol and would be subject to a $20 per gallon federal excise tax. To avoid this it is "denatured"—made undrinkable by adding gasoline to it. After this, the ethanol is ready to be transported from the plant.

The fourth step in the commercial production process is converting the whole stillage into co-products. *(Slide 5)* One of the greatest things about producing ethanol is that the water and nonfermentable corn solids which are left after the ethanol is distilled aren't just thrown out as waste. Instead, the remaining water and nonfermentable corn solids can also be processed to make co-products that are primarily used as animal feed.

So as you have seen, the process of making ethanol is really quite simple. *(Slide 6)* One, prepare the corn by milling and breaking its starch into sugar. Two, ferment the mash using yeast. Three, distill off the ethanol from the beer, and four, process the co-products.

In 1980, when Robert Warren was operating his still, only 175 million gallons of ethanol were being commercially produced in the United States. Twenty-five years later, according to the Renewable Fuels Association, 4.85 billion gallons were produced. That's a whopping 2,674% increase! And it is a trend that is continuing. Automobile manufacturers and service stations are gearing up to satisfy the increased demand for E-85, a fuel that is 85% ethanol. And you may already own a car that is a flexible fuel vehicle. So keep an eye out at your local service station for that green-handled pump. And when you see it, think of the four easy steps, preparation, fermentation, distillation, and processing co-products that were used to produce it.

I'd be happy to answer any questions you may have.

Her fourth slide is much more elaborate than the others. The animation in the slide helps the audience to visualize how distillation works. It would have been more effective, however, had she been able to control the motion so that each stage was animated as she talked about it instead of having quickly moving animation and then a static image.

The last sentence serves as an internal conclusion to the fourth step.

A signpost marks the beginning of her brief discussion of the fourth main point. The slide is so simple that it really isn't needed to aid audience understanding, but it is a visual reinforcement of this step, and the audience has been conditioned to expect one slide per point.

Louisa begins the conclusion with a summary of her main points. The sixth slide, a repetition of the first slide, visually closes the loop and reinforces the four steps.

The conclusion then makes a circular reference back to Robert Warren, who was introduced at the beginning of the speech. Then Louisa uses the statistics on ethanol production to drive home the point that ethanol is once again an important fuel source and that in the near future ethanol may be a fuel used by members of the audience.

Notice how cleverly Louisa uses the final statement to once again reinforce the four steps of the ethanol production process. By leaving the sixth slide on the screen until the end of her speech, she is able to point to it as she provides this quick recap.

Louisa could have offered a better ending clincher by tying her final sentence back to her introductory comments about Henry Ford. For example, she might have said, "Almost a century later, it seems that what Henry Ford said will be coming true. Look for a green-handled pump coming soon to a gas station near you."

A Question of Ethics

After class, as Gina and Paul were discussing what they intended to talk about in their process speeches. Paul said, "I think I'm going to talk about how to make a synthetic diamond."

Gina was impressed. "That sounds interesting. I didn't know you had expertise with that."

"I don't. But the way I see it, Professor Henderson will really be impressed with my speech because my topic will be so novel."

"Well, yeah," Gina replied, "but didn't he stress that for this speech we should choose a topic that was important to us and that we knew a lot about?"

What Would You Do?

"Sure," Paul said sarcastically, "he's going to be impressed if I talk about how to maintain a blog? Forget it. Just watch—everyone's going to think I make diamonds in my basement, and I'm going to get a good grade."

1. Is Paul's plan unethical? Why?
2. What should Gina say to challenge Paul's last statement?

Summary

An informative speech is one that has a goal to explain or describe facts, truths, and principles in a way that stimulates interest, facilitates understanding, and increases likelihood that audiences will remember. In short, informative speeches are designed to educate an audience.

Effective informative speeches are intellectually stimulating, relevant, creative, memorable, and address diverse learning styles. Informative speeches will be perceived as intellectually stimulating when the information is new and when it is explained in a way that excites interest. Informative speeches are creative when they produce new or original ideas or insights. Informative speeches stimulate memory when they round the four-stage cycle of learning.

We can inform by describing something, defining it, comparing and contrasting it with other things, narrating a story about it, or demonstrating it.

Two common frameworks for informative speeches are process speeches, in which the steps of something are shown, and expository speeches, which are well-researched explanations of complex ideas. Expository speeches can explain political, economic, social, religious, or ethical issues; events or forces of history; a theory, principle, or law; or a creative work.

Communicate! Active Online Learning

Now that you have read Chapter 15, use your Premium Website for *Communicate!* for quick access to the electronic resources that accompany this text. These resources include

- **Study tools** that will help you assess your learning and prepare for exams (*digital glossary, key term flash cards, review quizzes*).

- **Activities and assignments** that will help you hone your knowledge, analyze communication situations (*Skill Learning Activities*), and build your public speaking skills throughout the course (*Communication on Your Feet speech assignments, Action Step activities*). Many of these activities allow you to compare your answers to those provided by the authors, and, if requested, submit your answers to your instructor.

- **Media resources** that will help you explore communication concepts online (*Web Resources*), develop your speech outlines (*Speech Builder Express 3.0*), watch and critique videos of communication situations and sample speeches (*Interactive Video Activities*), upload your speech videos for peer reviewing and critique other students' speeches

(*Speech Studio online speech review tool*), and download chapter review so you can study when and where you'd like (*Audio Study Tools*).

This chapter's Key Terms, Skill Learning Activities, and Web Resources are also featured on the following pages, and you can find this chapter's Communicate on Your Feet assignment and speech activity in the body of the chapter.

Key Terms

antonym (369)
comparison and contrast (369)
creative (365)
definition (369)
demonstration (370)

description (368)
expository speech (372)
informative speech (364)
intellectually stimulating (364)
listener relevance links (365)
narration (370)

process speech (371)
synonym (369)

Skill Learning Activities

15.1: Creating through Productive Thinking (366)

Use the data in the table below to practice productive thinking. Create a list of all of the speech ideas suggested by these data.

Annual dropout rates of U.S. high school students, 1999

Characteristics	Dropout rate (%)
Average total	4.7
Sex	
Male	4.3
Female	5.1
Race and Hispanic origin	
White	4.4
White non-Hispanic	3.8
Black	6.0
Asian and Pacific Islander	4.5
Hispanic (of any race)	7.1
Family income	
Less than $20,000	9.0
$20,000–$39,000	3.8
$40,000 and over	2.3
Grade level	
10th grade	2.7
11th grade	3.7
12th grade	8.5

Source: U.S. Census Bureau, Current Population Survey, October 1999.

15.2: Techniques to Emphasize Important Information (367)

Access Web Resource 15.2 and read "Characteristics of Change Agents," a speech by Billy O. Wireman. Analyze the techniques the speaker used to emphasize important points. How could the speaker have improved his emphasis? Can you identify specific places and techniques where this aspect of the speech could have been improved? Write an essay in which you analyze this aspect of the speech and make specific recommendations for improving it.

To help you complete this activity, you can use the data sheet provided in your Premium Website for *Communicate!* Look for it in the Skill Learning activities for Chapter 15.

15.3: Evaluating Demonstrations (371)

Watch an informative speech involving a demonstration, and evaluate how effectively the speaker performed the demonstration. (Do-it-yourself and home improvement TV programs, like those on the cable DIY, Style, and HGTV channels, often feature demonstrations.) Did the speaker perform a complete or modified demonstration? Did the speaker use only the tools, equipment, or other items needed to perform the demonstrated task, or did he or she also use other items, such as visual aids? How effective was the demonstration overall? Were there any areas of the demonstration the speaker could have improved?

Web Resources

15.1: A Theory about Genius (365)

To read about techniques that can help stimulate "productive" rather than "reproductive" thought, go to creativity expert Michael Michalko's Website and find the article "A Theory about Genius" in the Library of Articles.

15.2: Change Agents (367)

To analyze a speech for its use of emphasis, use AccessMyLibrary.com (free with registration) to find the article "Characteristics of Change Agents" by Billy O. Wireman.

⊙ Persuasive Speaking

Questions you will be able to answer after reading this chapter:

- How do people listen to and evaluate persuasive messages?
- What are the different types of persuasive speaking goals or propositions?
- How does the target audience's initial attitude toward your topic affect your proposition?
- How do you develop strong arguments to support your proposition?
- What are some common fallacies to avoid when developing your arguments?
- How can you increase audience involvement through emotional appeals?
- How can you demonstrate goodwill in your speech?
- How might you motivate your audience to act?
- What are some common organizational patterns for persuasive speeches?

As the canvassing volunteers walked out of the auditorium, Dan remarked, "Wow, after an hour and a half of dull speeches, I was about to go to sleep, but two minutes into Kate Tucker's speech, I was wide awake."

"Me too," Lydia replied. "I mean, with each point she made I could see more people listening closely, nodding, and agreeing with what she had to say."

"Not only were her reasons easy for me to understand," agreed Stan, "but she had the facts to support each point. How could you not believe what she had to say and want to do what you can to help the cause?"

"Yes, and she was so passionate about what we need to do. That really got me pumped up to get out there and do my part," noted Trace. "If only everyone who spoke tonight had been that good."

Although it is easy to get excited about a powerful speech, real-life attempts to persuade others require speakers to be knowledgeable about forming arguments and adapting them to the needs of the audience. A **persuasive speech** is one whose goal is to influence the attitudes, values, beliefs, or behavior of audience members. It is the most demanding speech challenge because it not only requires the skills you've studied so far but also an understanding of how to convince audience members to alter their attitudes, beliefs, values, or behavior.

In this chapter, you will learn how to prepare an effective persuasive speech. We begin by presenting a theoretical model that explains how people process persuasive messages. Then, we use this model to describe how you can meet the challenge of developing an effective persuasive speech. To do this, you will build arguments that are convincing to your audience, use emotion to increase your audience's involvement, develop your credibility by demonstrating goodwill, use incentives to motivate your audience, and choose an effective persuasive organizational pattern.

How We Process Persuasive Messages: The Elaboration Likelihood Model (ELM)

Do you remember listening carefully and thoughtfully to an idea someone was trying to convince you about? Do you remember consciously thinking over what had been said and making a deliberate decision? Do you remember other times when you only half-listened and made up your mind quickly based on your gut feeling about the truthfulness of what had been said? What determines how closely we listen to and how carefully we evaluate the hundreds of persuasive messages we hear each day? Richard Petty and John Cacioppo (1996) developed a model that explains how likely people are to spend time elaborating on information (such as the arguments in a speech), using their critical thinking skills, rather than processing the information in a simpler, less critical manner. Called the Elaboration Likelihood Model (ELM), this theory can be used by speakers to develop persuasive speeches that will be influential with audience members, regardless of how they process information.

The model suggests that people process information in one of two ways. One way is intense and time consuming. People using what is called the "central route" listen carefully, think about what is said, and may even mentally elaborate on the message. The second way, called the "peripheral route," is a shortcut that relies on simple cues such as a quick evaluation of the speaker's credibility, or a gut check on what the listener feels about the message.

According to the ELM, what determines if we use the central or peripheral route is how important we perceive the issue to be for us. When we feel involved with an issue, we are willing to expend the energy necessary for processing on the central route. When the issue is less important to us, we take the peripheral route. So, how closely audience members will follow the speaker's argument depends on how involved they feel with the topic. For example, a person with a chronic illness that is expensive to treat is more likely to pay attention to and evaluate proposals to change health care benefits. Listeners who are healthy will probably quickly agree with suggestions from someone they perceive to be credible or go along with a proposal that seems compassionate.

The ELM also suggests that when listeners form attitudes as a result of central processing (critical thinking), they are less likely to change their minds than when their attitudes are based on peripheral cues. You can probably remember times when you were swayed at the moment by a powerful speaker but on later reflection regretted your decision and changed your mind. Likewise, you probably have some strongly

> How do people listen to and evaluate persuasive messages?

persuasive speech
a speech that has a goal to influence the attitudes, values, beliefs, or behavior of audience members.

Scott Olson/Getty Images

held beliefs that are based on information you have heard and spent time thinking about.

When you prepare a persuasive speech, you will draw on this theory by developing your topic in a way that will increase the likelihood that your audience members feel personally involved with the topic. You will want to develop sound reasons so that audience members who use the central, critical thinking approach to your speech will find your arguments convincing. For members who are less involved, you will want to appeal to their emotions and include information that enables them to see you as credible.

What type of audience would this be for a speaker whose goal was to convince them that U.S. armed forces should pull out of Iraq and Afghanistan? What led you to your conclusion?

What are the different types of persuasive speaking goals or propositions?

Writing Persuasive Speech Goals as Propositions

A persuasive speech's specific goal is stated as a proposition. A **proposition** is a declarative sentence that clearly indicates the speaker's position on the topic. For example, "I want to convince my audience that pirating copyrighted media (illegally downloading music and movies) is wrong." The goal of a persuasive speech is to get the audience to agree with what the speaker is advocating. The goal may focus on what the audience's attitude or belief should be, what they should value, or how they should act. The three major types of persuasive goals are stated as propositions of fact, value, or policy.

Types of Persuasive Goals

A **proposition of fact** is a statement designed to convince your audience that something did or did not exist or occur in the past, is or is not true in the present, or will or will not occur in the future. A proposition of fact takes a position on something not known for certain but that can be argued for as true or plausible. Although propositions of fact may or may not be true—both positions are arguable—they are stated as true. For example, you could argue a proposition of fact that "Smoking marijuana leads to the use of more dangerous drugs" or "Smoking marijuana is less dangerous than drinking alcohol." Other examples are "There is [or is not] a God"; "Thanks to the messaging opportunities of the Internet, the postal service will eventually cease to exist"; and "Global warming is destroying the earth" are propositions of fact.

A **proposition of value** is a statement designed to convince your audience that something is good, bad, desirable, undesirable, fair, unfair, moral, immoral, sound, unsound, beneficial, harmful, important, or unimportant (Hill & Leeman, 1997). You can attempt to persuade your audience that something has more value than something else, or you can attempt to persuade them that something meets valued standards. "A low-fat diet is actually better than a fat-free diet" is an example of the former, and "Multilingual education is beneficial to children" is an example of the latter.

proposition
a declarative sentence that clearly indicates the speaker's position on the topic.

proposition of fact
a speech goal designed to convince the audience that something is or is not true.

proposition of value
a speech goal designed to convince the audience that something is good, fair, moral, sound, etc., or its opposite.

A **proposition of policy** is a statement designed to convince your audience that a specific course of action should be taken. **Propositions of policy** will implore listeners using phrases such as *do it/don't do it*, *should/shouldn't*, and *must/must not*. "All college students should be required to take an oral communication skills course in order to graduate" and "We must vote for the tax levy to build a downtown entertainment center" are propositions of policy. Figure 16.1 provides several examples of how propositions of fact, value, and policy can be developed from the same topic idea.

Tailoring Your Proposition to Your Audience

As you consider your topic and the proposition you will argue, you'll want to understand the opinions your audience members currently have about your topic.

Audience members' opinions about your speech topic can range from highly favorable to highly opposed and can be visualized as lying on a continuum like the one in Figure 16.2. Even though an audience will include individuals with opinions at nearly every point along the continuum, generally their opinions will tend to cluster in one area of the continuum. For instance, most of the audience members represented in Figure 16.2 were "mildly opposed," even though a few people were more hostile and a few had favorable opinions. This cluster point would be your **target audience**, the group of people you most want to persuade.

The initial attitude of your target audience toward your topic can be classified as "in favor" (already supportive), "neutral" (uninformed, impartial, or apathetic), or "opposed" (against a particular belief or holding an opposite point of view). You develop your proposition based on where your target audience stands initially. Generally, when your target audience is opposed, seek incremental change. When your target audience is neutral, seek agreement. And when your target audience is in favor , seek action. So for the target audience represented on the continuum in Figure 16.2, you would

> How does the target audience's initial attitude toward your topic affect your proposition?

proposition of policy
a speech goal designed to convince the audience that a specific course of action should be taken.

target audience
the group of people a speaker most wants to persuade

Propositions of fact	Propositions of value	Propositions of policy
Mahatma Gandhi was the father of passive resistance.	Mahatma Gandhi was a moral leader.	Mahatma Gandhi should be given a special award for his views on passive resistance.
Pharmaceutical advertising to consumers increases prescription drug prices.	Advertising of new prescription drugs on TV is better than marketing new drugs directly to doctors.	Pharmaceutical companies should be prohibited from advertising prescription drugs on TV.
Using paper ballots is a reliable method for voting in U.S. elections.	Paper ballots are better than electronic voting machines.	Using paper ballots should be required for U.S. elections.

Figure 16.1
Examples of persuasive speech propositions

Highly opposed	Opposed	Mildly opposed	Neither in favor nor opposed	Mildly in favor	In favor	Highly in favor
2	2	11	1	2	2	0

Figure 16.2
Sample opinion continuum

develop a proposition seeking incremental change in attitude, belief, or value. Let's look a bit closer at each of these types of audiences and how you should focus your speech.

Opposed

If your target audience is very much opposed to your goal, it is unrealistic to believe that you will be able to change their attitude from opposed to in favor in only one short speech. Instead, when dealing with a hostile (strongly opposed) target audience, seek incremental change, that is, attempting them to move only a small degree in your direction. For example, if you determine that your audience is likely to be opposed to the proposition "I want to convince my audience that gay marriage should be legalized," you might rephrase your proposition to "I want to convince my audience that committed gay couples should be able to have the same legal protection that is afforded to committed heterosexual couples through state-recognized civil unions." Then brainstorm potential objections, questions, and criticisms that might arise, and shape your speech around them.

Neutral

If your target audience is neutral, you can be straightforward with the reasons in support of your proposition. But you should consider whether they are uninformed, impartial, or apathetic about your topic. If they are **uninformed**, that is, they do not know enough about a topic to have formed an opinion, you will need to provide the basic arguments and information. For example, if your target audience is uninformed about gay marriage, you might need to begin by highlighting the legal benefits of marriage. Make sure that each of your reasons is well supported with good information. If your target audience is **impartial**, that is, they know the basics about your topic but have no opinion, you will want to provide more elaborate or secondary arguments and more robust evidence. Perhaps your audience knows the legal benefits of marriage but needs to understand how gay partners who do not have these benefits are disadvantaged. When target audience members have no opinion because they are **apathetic**, you will need to find ways to personalize the topic for them so that they see how it relates to them or their needs. In other words, you need to provide answers to a question such as, "I'm not gay, so why should I care?" You can do this by including listener relevance links for each main point in your speech.

In favor

If your target audience is only mildly in favor of your proposal, your task is to reinforce and strengthen their beliefs. Audience members who favor your topic will benefit from an elaboration of the reasons for holding these beliefs. They may become further committed to the belief by hearing additional or new reasons and more recent evidence that supports it.

© Robert Brenner/PhotoEdit

Is it more challenging to try to change the attitude of a hostile audience, or to persuade people who are neutral to give money to a cause?

uninformed
not knowing enough about a topic to have formed an opinion.

impartial
knowing the basics about a topic but still having no opinion about it.

apathetic
having no opinion because one is uninterested, unconcerned, or indifferent to a topic.

If your target audience strongly agrees with your position, then you can consider a proposition that builds on that belief and moves the audience to act on it. So, for example, if the topic is gay marriage, and your audience poll shows that most audience members strongly favor the idea, then your goal may be "I want my audience members to walk in Saturday's march in support of gay marriage" or "I want my audience members to e-mail their state representatives and urge them to support legislation allowing our state to extend the right to marry to gay couples."

Skill Learning Activity 16.1
Web Resource 16.1

Developing Arguments (Logos) That Support Your Proposition

Persuasive speeches develop an **argument** that is the collective reasons and evidence used to support the proposition. Aristotle, the ancient Greek philosopher who is credited with first articulating how people attempt to persuade, used the term **logos** to denote the logical reasoning used to develop an argument. So, the main points of your persuasive speeches are reasons that argue for your proposition. You will choose your reasons and the evidence that supports them from the information you have acquired during your research.

> How do you develop strong arguments to support your proposition?

Finding Reasons to Use as Main Points

Reasons are main point statements that summarize several related pieces of evidence and show *why* the listener should believe or do something. For example, suppose your speech proposition is "I want the audience to believe home ownership is good for a society." Based on your research, you develop six potential reasons:

I. Home ownership builds strong communities.
II. Home ownership reduces crime.
III. Home ownership increases individual wealth.
IV. Home ownership increases individual self-esteem.
V. Home ownership improves the value of a neighborhood.
VI. Home ownership is growing in the suburbs.

Once you have identified reasons, you can weigh and evaluate each and choose the three or four that have the highest quality. You can judge the quality of each reason by asking the following questions:

1. **Is the reason directly related to proving the proposition?** Sometimes, we find information that can be summarized into a reason, but that reason doesn't directly argue the proposition. For instance, you may have uncovered a lot of research that supports the notion that "home ownership is growing in the suburbs." Unfortunately, it isn't clear how the growth of home ownership in the suburbs benefits society as a whole. When choosing reasons, eliminate those that are only tangentially related to your proposition.

2. **Do I have strong evidence to support a reason?** Some reasons sound impressive but cannot be supported with solid evidence. For example, the second reason, "Home ownership reduces crime," sounds like a good one, but if the only proof you have is an opinion expressed by one person whose expertise is questionable, or if, in your research, you discover that although crime is lower in areas with high home ownership, there is little evidence to suggest a cause-and-effect relationship, you should eliminate this reason from consideration.

3. **Will this reason be persuasive for this audience?** Suppose that you have a lot of factual evidence to support the reason "Home ownership encourages self-esteem."

argument
the collective reasons and evidence used to support a proposition.

logos
the logical reasoning a speaker uses to develop an argument.

reasons
main point statements that summarize several related pieces of evidence and show why you should believe or do something.

This reason might be very persuasive to an audience of social workers, psychologists, and teachers, but it would probably be less important to an audience of financial planners, bankers, and economists. Once you have identified reasons that are related to the proposition and have strong evidence to support them, choose to use as main points of your speech the three or four that you believe will be most persuasive for your particular audience.

Selecting Evidence to Support Reasons

Although a reason may seem self-explanatory, audience members will need information that backs it up before they will believe it. As you researched, you may have discovered more evidence to support a reason than you will have time to use. So, you will have to select the pieces of evidence you will present.

Verifiable factual statements are a strong type of evidence to support reasons. Suppose, for example, that you were attempting to convince people that Alzheimer's research should be better funded, and you want to use the reason "Alzheimer's disease is an increasing health problem in the United States." A factual statement that supports this reason would be "According to a 2003 article in the *Archives of Neurology*, the number of Americans with Alzheimer's has more than doubled since 1980 and is expected to continue to grow, affecting between 11.3 and 16 million Americans by the year 2050."

Statements from people who are experts on a subject can also be used as evidence to support a reason. For example, the statement "According to the Surgeon General, 'By 2050, Alzheimer's disease may afflict 14 million people a year'" is an expert opinion.

Let's look at an example of how fact and expert opinion evidence can be used in combination to support a proposition.

> *Proposition:* I want the audience to believe that playing violent video games leads children to become aggressive and violent in real life.
> *Reason:* Playing violent video games increases aggressive emotions in children.
> *Support:* Studies measuring the emotional responses of adolescents to playing violent video games when compared with emotional responses of children playing nonviolent games have shown that violent games increase aggressive emotions. [*fact*] Adolescents themselves often seem to recognize this. In their study published in a 1998 issue of *Psychological Reports*, Griffiths and Hunt observed that when asked to name the "bad things" about computer games, many students reported that they make people more moody and aggressive. [*opinion*] And the same study also found that students who were more "addicted" to video games were significantly more likely to be in a bad mood before, during, and after play than were non-addicted students. [*fact*]

Regardless of whether the evidence is based on expert opinions or facts, you will want to use the best evidence you have found to support your point. You can use the answers to the following questions to help you select evidence that is likely to persuade your audience:

1. **Does the evidence come from a well-respected source?** This question involves both the people who offered the opinions or compiled the facts and the book, journal, or Internet source in which they were reported. Just as some people's opinions are more reliable than others, some printed and Internet sources are more reliable than others. Be especially careful of undocumented information. Eliminate evidence that comes from a questionable, unreliable, or biased source.

2. **Is the evidence recent and, if not, is it still valid?** Things change, so information that was accurate for a particular time may not be valid today. As you look at your evidence, consider when the evidence was gathered. Something that was true five years ago may not be true today. A trend that was forecast a year ago may have been revised since then. A statistic that was reported last week may be based on data that were collected three years ago. So whether it is a fact or an opinion, you want to choose evidence that is valid today.

   For example, the evidence "The total cost of caring for individuals with Alzheimer's is at least $100 billion according to the Alzheimer's Association and the National Institute on Aging," was cited in a 2003 NIH publication. But it is based on information from a study using 1991 data that were updated to 1994 data before being published. As a result, we can expect that today, annual costs would be higher. If you choose to use this evidence, you should disclose the age of the data used in the study and indicate that today, the costs would be higher.

3. **Does the evidence really support the reason?** Just as reasons need to be relevant to the proposition, evidence needs to be relevant to the reason. Some of the evidence you have found may be only indirectly related to the reason and should be eliminated in favor of evidence that provides more central support.

4. **Will this evidence be persuasive for this audience?** Finally, just as when you select your reasons, you will want to choose evidence that your particular audience is likely to find persuasive. So, if you have your choice of two quotations from experts, you will want to use the one from the person your audience is likely to find more credible.

Types and Tests of Arguments

An argument is the logical relationship between the proposition and the reasons or between the reasons and the evidence. If your audience is not convinced that your supporting evidence provides a convincing argument for your reason, they will not agree with it. And if your audience doesn't buy the argument from your reasons, they will not support your proposition.

You can develop several kinds of arguments:

1. **Arguing from example.** You **argue from example** when the reasons you offer are examples of the proposition or when the evidence you offer are examples of the reasons. For instance, if you say, "Anyone who studies can get As" and offer as evidence "Tom, Jane, and Josh studied and they all got As," you would be making an argument from example. An argument from example asserts that what is true in some instances is true in all instances. When arguing from example, you can make sure that your argument is valid by answering the following questions:

   - Were enough instances (or examples) cited so that listeners understand that they are not isolated or handpicked examples?
   - Were the instances typical and representative?
   - Are the negative instances really atypical?

   If the answer to any of these questions is no, then consider making your argument in a different way.

2. **Arguing from analogy.** You **argue from analogy** when you support your reason with a single comparable example that is so significantly similar to the subject that it offers strong proof. For example, if you support your proposition "Children who play violent video games for two or more hours per day act more aggressively" by saying, "Children who watch violent television programs for two or

arguing from example
support a claim by providing one or more individual examples.

arguing from analogy
support a claim with a single comparable example that is significantly similar to the subject of the claim.

more hours per day act more aggressively than children who don't," you would be arguing from analogy. An argument from analogy asserts that what is true or will work in one set of circumstances is true or will work in a comparable set of circumstances. When arguing from analogy, make sure your argument is valid by answering these questions:

- Are the subjects really comparable (for example, are video games really similar to television programs in all important ways)? If they are not, then your argument is not valid.
- Are any of the ways that the subjects are dissimilar important to the conclusion? If so, the reasoning is not sound.

3. **Arguing from causation.** You **argue from causation** when you cite evidence that one or more events always or almost always bring about, lead to, create, or prevent a predictable event or set of effects. If you support your proposition "Fewer Americans will be buying new homes in the next year" by saying, "Unemployment is higher than it has been in decades" and "Banks are applying tougher standards for loan approvals," you would be arguing from causation. Your argument can be boiled down to "The lack of sufficient funds causes a reduction in the number of homes being bought." The general form of a causal argument is if A, which is known to bring about B, has happened, then we can expect B to occur. To make sure your causal arguments are sound, you should answer the following questions:

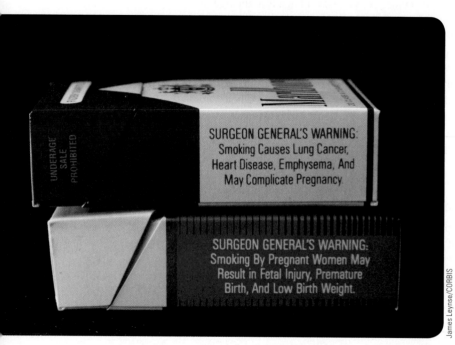

SURGEON GENERAL'S WARNING: Smoking Causes Lung Cancer, Heart Disease, Emphysema, And May Complicate Pregnancy.

SURGEON GENERAL'S WARNING: Smoking By Pregnant Women May Result in Fetal Injury, Premature Birth, And Low Birth Weight.

James Leynse/CORBIS

When the government makes manufacturers place warning labels on products, it is trying to influence consumers by reasoning from causation. Do such labels work to persuade you? Why or why not?

arguing from causation
support a claim by citing evidence that shows one or more events always or almost always bring about, lead to, create, or prevent another event or effect.

arguing from sign
support a claim by citing information that signals the claim.

- Are the events alone enough to cause the stated effect?
- Do other events accompanying the events cited actually cause the effect?
- Is the relationship between causal events and effect consistent?

If the answer to one of these questions is "No," the reasoning is not sound.

4. **Arguing from sign.** You **argue from sign** when you offer events as outward signals of the truth of your proposition or reason. For example, you might support your point that the recession is worsening by noting that the local soup kitchens have experienced an increase in the number of people they are serving. Your argument would be "Longer lines at soup kitchens are a sign of the worsening recession." To test this kind of argument, you should ask the following questions:

- Does the sign cited always or usually signal the conclusion drawn?
- Are a sufficient number of signs present?
- Are contradictory signs also in evidence?

If your answer to the first two of these questions is no or yes to the third question, then your reasoning is not sound.

Avoiding Fallacies in Your Reasons and Argument

As you develop your reasons and the argument that you will make, you should be sure to avoid fallacies or errors in your reasoning. Five common fallacies are the following:

1. **Hasty generalization.** A **hasty generalization** presents a generalization that is either not supported with evidence or is supported with only one weak example. Because the supporting material that is cited should be representative of all the supporting material that could be cited, enough supporting material must be presented to satisfy the audience that the instances are not isolated or handpicked. Because you can find an example or statistic to support almost anything, avoiding hasty generalizations requires you to be confident that the instances you cite as support are typical and representative of your claim. For example, someone who argued "All Akitas are vicious dogs" based on the sole piece of evidence "My neighbor's Akita bit my best friend's sister" would be guilty of a hasty generalization. It is hasty to generalize about the temperament of a whole breed of dogs based on a single action of one dog.

2. **False cause.** A **false cause** fallacy occurs when the alleged cause fails to be related to or to produce the effect. The Latin term for this fallacy is *post hoc, ergo propter hoc,* meaning "after this, therefore because of this." Just because one thing happened after another does not mean that the first necessarily caused the second. Don't be like people who blame monetary setbacks or illness on black cats or broken mirrors, and be careful that you don't present a coincidental event as causal unless you can prove the causal relationship. To claim that school violence is caused by listening to Marilyn Manson's shock rock music is an example of a false cause fallacy. When one event follows another, there may be no connection at all, or the first event might be just one of many causes that contribute to the second.

3. **Ad hominem.** An **ad hominem** fallacy supports a claim by attacking or praising the character of someone or something. *Ad hominem* literally means "to the man" [sic]. For example, if Jamal's support for his claim that his audience members should buy an iPhone is that Steve Jobs, co-founder and CEO of Apple Inc., is a genius, he would be making an ad hominem argument. Jobs's intelligence isn't really a reason to buy a particular cell phone. Television commercials that feature celebrities using the product are often guilty of committing ad hominem fallacies.

4. **Either-or.** An **either-or** fallacy supports a claim by suggesting there are only two alternatives when, in fact, others exist. This kind of fallacy oversimplifies a complex issue. For example, when Robert argued, "We'll either have to raise taxes or close the library," he committed an either-or fallacy. He reduced a complex issue to one oversimplified solution when there were many other possible solutions for keeping the library open.

5. **Straw person.** A **straw person** fallacy occurs when a speaker weakens the opposing position by misrepresenting it in some way and then attacking that misrepresented (straw person) position. For example, in her speech advocating a seven-day waiting period to purchase handguns, Colleen favored regulation, not prohibition, of gun ownership. Bob argued in opposition claiming, "It is our constitutional right to bear arms." However, Colleen did not advocate abolishing the right to bear arms. Bob distorted Colleen's position, making it easier for him to refute.

Have you ever watched an infomercial and been convinced to purchase the product? If so, did the product live up to your expectations? Probably not. Infomercials attempt to develop arguments that convince consumers to buy their products. Although these arguments may seem compelling, a student of persuasion will quickly identify common reasoning fallacies. You can read more about the history

What are some common fallacies to avoid when developing your arguments?

Skill Learning Activity 16.2

hasty generalization
a fallacy that presents a generalization that is either not supported with evidence or is supported with only one weak example.

false cause
a fallacy that occurs when the alleged cause fails to be related to, or to produce, the effect.

ad hominem
a fallacy that occurs when one attacks the person making the argument, rather than the argument itself.

either-or
a fallacy that occurs when a speaker supports a claim by suggesting there are only two alternatives when, in fact, others exist.

straw person
a fallacy that occurs when a speaker weakens the opposing position by misrepresenting it in some way and then attacks that weaker (straw person) position.

of infomercials, how they've changed over time, and what we can expect of them in the future in the Pop Comm! feature "You Too Can Have Six-Pack Abs in Only Three Weeks."

Increasing Audience Involvement Through Emotional Appeal (Pathos)

> How can you increase audience involvement through emotional appeals?

As you will recall, the ELM suggests that people are more likely to listen to and think about information when they feel personally involved in the topic. We are more likely to be involved in a topic when we have an emotional stake in it. If you can give your audience members an emotional stake in what you are saying, they are more likely to listen to and think about your arguments. Aristotle labeled these appeals to emotion **pathos**. You can increase your audience members' involvement by evoking negative or positive emotions in your speeches (Nabi, 2002, p. 292).

Negative emotions are disquieting, so when people experience them, they look for ways to eliminate the discomfort. You might tap any number of negative emotions in your speech. The five most common are fear, guilt, shame, anger, and sadness. Notice

pathos
appeals to emotion.

You Too Can Have Six-Pack Abs in Only Three Weeks!

  **Pop Comm!**

AP Photo/Chris O'Meara

Body by Jake, Body Dome, Bun & Thigh Max, and Smart Abs all promise you can trim and tone your way to a better body in just minutes a day. Besides promising to be the most effective exercise equipment ever, what do all these products have in common? They're the subject of infomercials. Infomercials are television and online programs designed to look like 30- or 60-minute talk shows, but they're actually extended commercials that focus on a product's

extraordinary features and offer testimonials of its effectiveness.

Infomercials are a relatively new phenomenon in advertising—until 1984 the Federal Communications Commission banned program-length commercials, and the ban is still in effect for products that are marketed to children (Head, Spann, & McGregor, 2001). Although infomercials are viewed with skepticism and derision by some, others view them as "an example of capitalism at its best" ("Billy Mays," 2009). Whatever you think of infomercials, you can't deny that they are everywhere. Even Barack Obama took advantage of the infomercial format when he campaigned for president. Providing direct communication at low production costs, his 30-minute commercial played on seven networks and was watched by 33.55 million viewers (Carter, 2008). Democratic strategist Joe Lockhart thought Obama's strategy was wise: "The benefit is you get to make your closing argument in a dramatic way without

in the following statement how fear personalizes the statistics on heart disease and piques your interest in listening to what the speaker has to say:

> One out of every three Americans age 18 and older has high blood pressure. It is the primary cause of stroke, heart disease, heart failure, kidney disease, and blindness. It triples a person's chance of developing heart disease, and boosts the chance of stroke seven times and the chance of congestive heart failure six times. Look at the person on your right; look at the person on your left. If they don't get it, chances are you will. Today, I'd like to convince you that you are at risk of developing high blood pressure.

Positive emotional involvement can also lead audience members to more carefully consider your proposition and arguments. When you evoke positive emotions, audience members will look for ways to sustain or further enhance the feeling. Five of the most common positive emotions you can evoke are happiness/joy, pride, relief, hope, and compassion. For example, notice how the speaker used the emotion of pride to pique interest in a speech designed to get the audience to sign up for an alternative spring break experience with Habitat for Humanity:

> Imagine you are an Olympian who has won your event and now stands on the podium with a medal around your neck as they play your national anthem.

the filter of the media. It gives you more context and texture than a 30-second or 60-second ad" (Cummings, 2008).

Infomercials have even become sources of entertainment. In 2008 and 2009, the Snuggie—"A blanket with sleeves!"—and a similar product, the Slanket, were frequently referenced in popular culture, from YouTube parodies ("The Cult of Snuggie") to *30 Rock* storylines (with Liz Lemon asserting, "It's not product placement; I just like it!"). And when "infomercial king" Billy Mays passed away unexpectedly in June 2009, many were inspired to affectionately celebrate his influence. A "Billy Mays Gangsta Remix" grew to quick popularity on YouTube (mastamokei, 2008), and a Facebook page "RIP Billy Mays (We Will Miss Your Infomercials)" (n.d.) was created, gaining 175,000 fans, many of them posting about their favorite Billy Mays product. An Internet application was even created in his honor: "Billy Mays Caps Lock: Turn your Caps Lock key into a Billy Mays key!" (Haller, 2009).

Despite the fun we like to have with infomercials, they have come under criticism in recent years. Many Americans put at least part of the blame for the economic recession on advertising, claiming that it often causes people to buy things they don't need and can't afford (Crain, 2009). But consumer suspicion of the ability of infomercials in particular to deceive is nothing new. For example, in 2002 Guthy-Renker, the largest producer of television infomercials, became the subject of a class-action lawsuit, which claimed Guthy-Renker made exaggerated claims of profitability and promoted an Internet "shopping mall" that was simply a scam ("Timothy D. Naegele & Associates," 2002).

Because advertisements are inherently persuasive, it's important to view them with a critical eye, although certainly not all ads and infomercials make false claims. But with infomercials, it can be especially easy to overlook misleading claims because infomercials typically have a compelling spokesperson like Billy Mays or a popular celebrity like Jessica Simpson (Mannes, 2009). Charm and personality can distract consumers from what's really being said in a persuasive message. If you suspect you see questionable claims in an infomercial, be careful before you buy. A good rule of thumb is to first contact the Better Business Bureau (www.bbb.org) and see if there have been any complaints lodged about the company advertising the product. If there have, buyer beware!

Web Resource 16.2

Imagine opening your mail and finding out that you have gotten into the top ranked graduate program in the country. Now imagine that you are standing on the front porch of a brand new home that you have helped to build and are being hugged by the mother of four children who, thanks to your selfless work, will no longer have to share a one-bedroom fifth-floor walk-up. Imagine the pride? How long has it been since you felt so good? Well, folks, that's just what you'll experience and much more when you sign up to work with the Habitat for Humanity house being constructed in your community.

Some of the techniques you might use to appeal to emotions in your speeches include vivid stories and testimonials, startling statistics, emotion-packed listener relevance links, striking presentational aids, provocative language, and animated vocal delivery and body language.

Cueing Your Audience Through Credibility (Ethos): Demonstrating Goodwill

You cannot expect that everyone in your audience will choose the central processing route when listening to your speech. Some will still pay minimal attention to your arguments and instead will use simple cues and process your message using the peripheral route. The most important cue for those who process information along the peripheral route is the credibility of the speaker. Aristotle used the term **ethos** to characterize such appeals to credibility. One crucial characteristic for motivating uninvolved audience members to believe what you are saying is your goodwill. **Goodwill** is the audience members' perception that the speaker (1) understands, (2) empathizes with, and (3) is responsive to them. In other words, goodwill is the audience members' belief that your intentions toward them are for their good. Audience members who perceive the speaker as exhibiting goodwill toward them are more willing to believe what the speaker is saying.

You can demonstrate that you understand your audience by personalizing your information. Information you gleaned from your audience analysis can help you. For example, Meg, a union rep trying to convince the membership to accept a new contract change to health care benefits, might build goodwill by personalizing one aspect of the proposal:

> I know that about 40 percent of you have little use for eye care, which is part of the new package. But for the 60 percent of you who wear glasses or have dependents who wear glasses, this plan will not only pay for your annual eye exam, but it will also pay 30 percent of the cost of new glasses or 25 percent of the new cost of contact lenses. This will mean about $250 in your pocket each year, and with less overtime predicted for this year, that's a real benefit.

Speakers also demonstrate goodwill by empathizing with their audience. Empathizing requires you to go beyond understanding and to identify emotionally with audience members' views. This doesn't mean, however, that you accept their views as your own. It means only that you acknowledge their views as valid. Even when your speech is designed to change audience members' views, the sensitivity you show to their feelings will demonstrate goodwill. For example, the union rep might demonstrate empathy by saying this:

> I can imagine what it will be like for some of you who, under this new plan, will go to the drugstore and find that there is now a high co-pay required for a drug you take that is no longer on the formulary. But I also guarantee that

How can you demonstrate goodwill in your speech?

ethos
appeals to credibility.

goodwill
the audience perception that the speaker understands, empathizes with, and is responsive to them.

the plan formulary will have drugs that your doctor can prescribe that will be direct substitutes, or you will be able to appeal the co-pay.

Finally, to demonstrate goodwill, you will want to show your responsiveness to the audience. Being responsive is showing you care about the audience by acknowledging their feedback, especially subtle negative cues. The union rep can demonstrate responsiveness by referencing feedback that the membership had provided earlier:

> Before we started negotiations, we surveyed you, asking what changes you wanted to see in the health care program. Seventy-five percent of you said that your number-one concern was keeping the office visit co-pay at $10, and in this contract we were able to do that.

Or, if she notices that some members of the audience are looking disgusted and shaking their heads, she might respond:

> I can see that some of you are disappointed with the increase in premiums. So am I. I wish we could have done better on this issue. But the fact is, health care costs have risen 15 percent nationwide this year, and our usage has exceeded this average.

By establishing your goodwill, you enhance your credibility with the audience, which is especially important for audience members who are not personally involved with your topic.

In addition to demonstrating goodwill, several other techniques of good speaking can increase the audience's perception of your credibility. These include doing the following things you have learned about in previous chapters: (1) explain your qualifications, (2) establish common ground, (3) use and cite orally evidence from respected sources, (4) be vocally expressive, (5) dress appropriately, and (6) convey confidence with your posture, poise, and eye contact.

Motivating Your Audience to Act Through Incentives

When your speech proposition is aimed at influencing your audience members' attitudes or beliefs, you will use emotional appeals to encourage them to become involved with your topic. But when you want to influence your audience to act on what you have said, you will need to provide motivation by showing how what you are asking them to do will meet their needs. **Motivation,** "forces acting on or within an organism to initiate and direct behavior" (Petri, 1996, p. 3), is often a result of incentives that meet needs.

An **incentive** is a reward promised if a particular action is taken or goal is reached (Petri, 1996). Incentives can be physical (food, shelter, money, sex), psychological (self-esteem, peace of mind), or social (acceptance, popularity, status) rewards. Incentives are valuable only to the extent that they can satisfy a need felt by the audience members, and the value of the incentive for taking the action must not be outweighed by costs associated with the action.

How might you motivate your audience to act?

motivation
forces acting on or within an organism to initiate and direct behavior.

incentive
a reward promised if a particular action is taken or goal is reached.

Using Incentives to Satisfy Unmet Needs

Incentives are more likely to motivate people when they satisfy an important unmet need. Various ways for categorizing needs have been developed. One of the most widely recognized is Maslow's hierarchy of needs. Abraham Maslow divided people's needs into five categories, illustrated in Figure 16.3: (1) physiological needs, including food, drink, and life-sustaining temperature; (2) safety and security needs, including long-term survival and stability; (3) belongingness and love needs, including the need to identify with friends, loved ones, and family; (4) esteem needs—ego gratification including material goods, recognition, and power or influence; (5) cognitive needs; (6) aesthetic needs; and (7) self-actualization needs, including the need to develop one's self to realize one's full potential and engage in creative acts (Maslow, 1954). Maslow believed that these needs were hierarchical; that is, that "lower order" needs had to be met before we would be motivated by "higher order" needs. In theory, then, a person cannot be motivated to meet an esteem need of gaining recognition until basic physiological, safety, and belongingness and love needs have been met.

The hierarchical nature of needs is still debated because there is evidence that at times, some people will sacrifice lower order needs to satisfy higher order ones. Nevertheless, as a speaker, when you can tie the incentives that accompany your proposal with unmet audience needs, you increase the likelihood that the audience will take the action you are proposing. Let's see how this could work in the volunteering for literacy speech with a college student audience. Suppose that, during the speech, you point out that people who volunteer 30 hours or more a year receive a recognition certificate and are invited to attend a private dinner with the stars of the hot band that will be headlining the big spring campus concert. After announcing this you add,

> I know that although most of you care about literacy, you're thinking about what else you could do with that hour. But the really cool part of spending your time as a literacy volunteer is that you will feel good about yourself because you have improved someone's life, and you also will be able to list this service and recognition on your résumé. As a bonus, you'll get to brag to your friends about having dinner with several celebrities.

In the first part of this short statement, you have enumerated three incentives that are tied to volunteering: a physical incentive (a recognition certificate), a psychological incentive of enhanced self-concept (I feel good about myself because I have helped someone else), and a social incentive (having dinner with an elite group and meeting celebrities). In the second part you have also tied each incentive to a need that it can

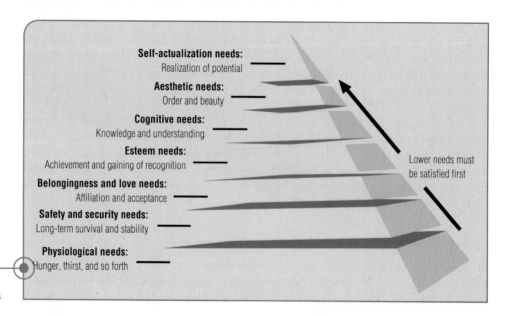

Figure 16.3
Maslow's hierarchy of needs

satisfy. With enhanced résumés, people are more likely to get jobs that provide money for food and shelter. If by helping someone else, we feel better about ourselves, then we have met a self-actualization need. And by attending the private dinner, we might satisfy both esteem needs and belongingness needs.

Creating Incentives That Outweigh Costs

As you prepare your speech, you must be concerned with presenting the incentives that meet the needs of your audience, and you also need to understand the potential costs for audience members who act in line with your proposal. For example, in the literacy speech, one obvious cost is the hour of free time each week that might subtract from time audience members spend with their friends or family. This could create a potential deficit in their belongingness need. To address this concern, you could point out, "Now, I know you might be concerned about the time this will take away from your friends or family, but relax. Your friends and family are likely to understand and admire you [*esteem need substitute for belongingness*]. Also, at the literacy center, you're going to have time before the tutoring starts to meet other volunteers [*belongingness*], and they are some really cool people [*esteem*]. I know a couple who just got engaged, and they met through their volunteering [*big-time belongingness*]."

If, through your audience analysis, you discover that you cannot relate your proposition to meeting basic audience needs, or if the analysis reveals that the costs associated with your proposition would outweigh the incentives, then you probably need to reconsider what you are asking the audience to do. For example, if you discover that most of your audience members are overcommitted, then it is probably unrealistic to think you will be able to convince them to volunteer an hour a week. You may need to modify your proposition and persuade them to donate a book or money to buy a book for the literacy library.

Finally, if your incentives are going to motivate your audience members, they must be convinced that there is a high likelihood that if they act as you suggest, they will receive the incentives. It is important, therefore, that you discuss only incentives that are closely tied to the action you are requesting and are received by almost all people who act in the recommended way. Although there is an annual award for the literacy volunteer who has donated the most time that year, mentioning this in your speech is unlikely to motivate the audience because only one person receives it and the cost is very high.

When you want to move audience members to action, you need to understand their needs and explain the incentives they can receive by taking the action you suggest. You also need to make sure that the incentives you mention fulfill unmet needs in the audience.

Skill Learning Activity 16.3

Organizational Patterns for Persuasive Speeches

Having developed a proposition, selected evidence to support your reasons, identified ways to increase audience involvement through emotional appeals, determined how you will enhance your credibility by developing goodwill, and identified the incentives you will use to motivate your audience, you are ready to choose a pattern to organize your speech. The most common patterns for organizing persuasive speeches include statement of reasons, comparative advantages, criteria satisfaction, refutative, problem-solution, problem-cause-solution, and motivated sequence. In this section, we describe and illustrate these persuasive organizational patterns. So that you can contrast the

What are some common organizational patterns for persuasive speeches?

patterns and better understand their use, we will illustrate each pattern by examining the same topic with slightly different propositions that use the same or similar reasons.

Statement of Reasons

The **statement of reasons** pattern attempts to prove propositions of fact by presenting the best-supported reasons in a meaningful order. For a speech with three reasons or more, place the strongest reason last because this is the reason you believe the audience will find most persuasive. Place the second strongest reason first because you want to start with a significant point. Place the other reasons in between.

Proposition: I want my audience to believe that passing the proposed school tax levy is necessary.

I. The income will enable the schools to restore vital programs. [*second strongest*]
II. The income will enable the schools to give teachers the raises they need to keep up with the cost of living.
III. The income will allow the community to maintain local control and will save the district from state intervention. [*strongest*]

Comparative Advantages

The **comparative advantages pattern** attempts to prove that something has more value than something else. A comparative advantages approach to a school tax proposition would look like this:

Proposition: I want my audience to believe that passing the school tax levy is better than not passing it. [*compares the value of change to the status quo*]

I. Income from a tax levy will enable schools to reintroduce important programs that had to be cut. [*advantage 1*]
II. Income from a tax levy will enable schools to avoid a tentative strike by teachers who are underpaid. [*advantage 2*]
III. Income from a tax levy will enable us to retain local control of our schools, which will be lost to the state if additional local funding is not provided. [*advantage 3*]

Criteria Satisfaction

The **criteria satisfaction pattern** seeks audience agreement on criteria that should be considered when evaluating a particular idea and then shows how the proposition that the speaker is advocating satisfies the criteria. A criteria satisfaction pattern is especially useful when your audience is opposed to your proposition, because it approaches the proposition indirectly by first focusing on the criteria that the audience may agree with before introducing the specific solution. A criteria satisfaction organization for the school levy would look like this:

Proposition: I want my audience to believe that passing a school levy is a good way to fund our schools.

I. We can all agree that a good school funding method must meet three criteria:
   A. A good funding method results in the reestablishment of programs that have been dropped due to budget constraints.
   B. A good funding method results in fair pay for teachers.
   C. A good funding method generates enough income to maintain local control, avoiding state intervention.

statement of reasons pattern
a straightforward organization in which you present the best-supported reasons you can find.

comparative advantages pattern
an organization that allows you to place all the emphasis on the superiority of the proposed course of action.

criteria satisfaction pattern
an organization that first seeks audience agreement on criteria that should be considered when they evaluate a particular proposition and then shows how the proposition satisfies those criteria.

II. Passage of a local school tax levy is a good way to fund our schools.
    A. A local levy will allow us to re-fund important programs.
    B. A local levy will allow us to give teachers a raise.
    C. A local levy will generate enough income to maintain local control and avoid state intervention.

Refutative

The **refutative pattern** helps you organize your main points so that you persuade by both challenging opposing arguments and bolstering your own. This pattern is particularly useful when the target audience opposes your position. Begin by acknowledging the merit of opposing arguments and then provide evidence of their flaws. Once listeners understand the flaws, they will be more receptive to the arguments you present to support your proposition. A refutative pattern for the school tax proposition might look like this:

Proposition: I want my audience to agree that a school levy is the best way to fund our schools.

II. Opponents of the tax levy argue that the tax increase will fall only on property owners.
    A. Landlords will recoup property taxes in the form of higher rents.
    B. Thus, all people will be affected.
III. Opponents of the tax levy argue that there are fewer students in the school district, so schools should be able to function on the same amount of revenue.
    A. Although there are fewer pupils, costs continue to rise.
        1. Salary costs are increasing.
        2. Energy costs are increasing.
        3. Maintenance costs are increasing.
        4. Costs from unfunded federal and state government mandates are rising.
    B. Although there are fewer pupils, there are many aging school buildings that need replacing or retrofitting.
IV. Opponents of the tax levy argue that parents should be responsible for the excessive cost of educating their children.
    A. A free public education is a hallmark of our democracy and ensures the future of our country.
    B. Parents today are already paying more than previous generations.
        1. Activity fees
        2. Lab fees
        3. Book fees
        4. Transportation fees
    C. Of school-age children today in this district, 42 percent live in families that are below the poverty line and have limited resources.

refutative pattern
an organization that challenging opposing arguments while bolstering your own.

Problem-Solution

The **problem-solution pattern** attempts to argue that a particular problem can be solved by implementing the recommended solution. This organization works well when the audience is neutral or agrees only that there is a problem but has no opinion about a particular solution. In a problem-solution speech, the claim ("There is a problem that can be solved by X") is supported by three reasons that take the general form: (1) There

problem-solution pattern
an organization that argues that a particular problem can be solved by implementing a recommended solution.

is a problem that requires action. (2) Proposal X will solve the problem. (3) Proposal X is the best solution to the problem, because it will lead to positive consequences and minimize or avoid negative ones. A problem-solution organization for the school tax proposition might look like this:

> *Proposition:* The current fiscal crisis in the school district can be solved through a local tax levy.
>
> I. The current funding is insufficient and has resulted in program cuts, labor problems resulting from stagnant wages, and a threatened state take-over of local schools. [*statement of problem*]
> II. The proposed local tax levy is large enough to solve these problems. [*solution*]
> III. The proposed local tax levy is the best means of solving the funding crisis.

Problem-Cause-Solution

The **problem-cause-solution pattern** is similar to the problem-solution pattern, but it has a main point about the causes of the problem and the solution is designed to alleviate those causes. This pattern is particularly useful for addressing seemingly intractable problems that have been dealt with unsuccessfully in the past as a result of treating symptoms rather than underlying causes. A problem-cause-solution organization for the school tax proposition might look like this:

> *Proposition:* The current fiscal crisis in the school district can be solved through a local tax levy.
>
> I. The current funding is insufficient and has resulted in program cuts, labor problems, and a threatened state takeover of local schools. [*statement of problem*]
> II. These problems exist due to dwindling government support and increasing costs for operating expenses. [*causes*]
> III. The proposed local tax levy will solve these problems by supplementing government support and enhancing operating budgets. [*solution*]

Motivated Sequence

The **motivated sequence pattern** combines a problem-solution pattern with explicit appeals designed to motivate the audience to act. The motivational sequence pattern is a unified five-point sequence that replaces the normal introduction-body-conclusion model with (1) an attention step, (2) a need step that fully explains the nature of the problem, (3) a satisfaction step that explains how the proposal solves the problem in a satisfactory manner, (4) a visualization step that provides a personal application of the proposal, and (5) an action appeal step that emphasizes the direction that audience action should take. A motivational pattern for the school tax levy proposition would look like this:

> *Proposition:* I want my audience to vote in favor of the school tax levy on the November ballot.
>
> I. Comparisons of worldwide test scores in math and science have refocused our attention on education. [*attention*]
> II. The shortage of money is resulting in cost-cutting measures that compromise our ability to teach basic academic subjects well. [*need, statement of problem*]
> III. The proposed increase is large enough to solve those problems in ways that allow for increased emphasis on academic need areas. [*satisfaction, how the proposal solves the problem*]

problem-cause-solution pattern
an organization that demonstrates that there is a problem caused by specific things that can be alleviated with the proposed solution that addresses the causes.

motivated sequence pattern
an organization that combines the problem solution pattern with explicit appeals designed to motivate the audience to act.

IV. Think of the contribution you will be making to the education of your children and also to efforts to return our educational system to the world-class level it once held. [*visualization of personal application*]

V. Here are "Vote Yes" buttons that you can wear to show you are willing to support this much-needed tax levy. [*action appeal showing specific direction*]

Yann Arthus-Bertrand/Terra/Corbis

Because motivational patterns are variations of problem-solution patterns, the underlying assumption is similar: When the current means are not solving the problem, a new solution that does solve the problem should be adopted. Figure 16.4 is a checklist that you can use to analyze any persuasive speech you rehearse or to critique the speeches of others.

How would you apply each of the organizational patterns described in this chapter to a speech about rebuilding the wetlands of Louisiana to help reduce the effects of a large hurricane on New Orleans?

You can use this form to critique a persuasive speech to convince that you hear in class. As you listen to the speaker, outline the speech, paying close attention to the reasoning process the speaker uses. Also note the claims and support used in the arguments and identify the types of warrants being used. Then answer the questions that follow.

General Criteria

_____ 1. Was the proposition clear? Could you tell the speaker's position on the issue?

_____ 2. Was the introduction effective in creating interest and involving the audience in the speech?

_____ 3. Was the speech organized using an appropriate persuasive pattern?

_____ 4. Was the language clear, vivid, inclusive, and appropriate?

_____ 5. Was the conclusion effective in summarizing what had been said and mobilizing the audience to act?

_____ 6. Was the speech delivered conversationally and expressively?

_____ 7. Did the speaker establish credibility by demonstrating:

_____ expertise?

_____ personableness?

_____ trustworthiness?

Primary Criteria

_____ 1. Was the specific goal phrased as a proposition (were you clear about the speaker's position on the issue)?

_____ 2. Did the proposition appear to be adapted to the initial attitude of the target audience?

_____ 3. Were emotional appeals used to involve the audience with the topic?

Skill Learning Activity 16.4
Web Resource 16.3

Figure 16.4

Persuasive speech evaluation checklist

4. Were the reasons used in the speech
   _____ directly related to the proposition?
   _____ supported by strong evidence?
   _____ persuasive for the particular audience?
5. Was the evidence [*support*] used to back the reasons [*claims*]
   _____ from well-respected sources?
   _____ recent and/or still valid?
   _____ persuasive for this audience?
   _____ typical of all evidence that might have been used?
   _____ sufficient [*enough evidence cited*]?
6. Could you identify the types of arguments that were used?
   _____ Did the speaker argue from example?   _____ If so, was it valid?
   _____ Did the speaker argue from analogy?   _____ If so, was it valid?
   _____ Did the speaker argue from causation?   _____ If so, was it valid?
   _____ Did the speaker argue from sign?   _____ If so, was it valid?
7. Could you identify any fallacies of reasoning in the speech?
   _____ hasty generalizations
   _____ arguing from false cause
   _____ ad hominem attacks
   _____ straw person
   _____ either-or
_____ 8. Did the speaker demonstrate goodwill?
9. If the speech called for the audience to take action,
   _____ did the speaker describe incentives and relate them to audience needs?
   _____ did the speaker acknowledge any costs associated with the action?
10. Did the speaker use an appropriate persuasive organizational pattern?
    _____ statement of reasons
    _____ comparative advantages
    _____ criteria satisfaction
    _____ refutative
    _____ problem-solution
    _____ problem-cause-solution
    _____ motivated sequence

Overall evaluation of the speech (check one):
_____ excellent _____ good _____ average _____ fair _____ poor

Figure 16.4
(Continued)

Use the information from this checklist to support your evaluation.

Speech Assignment: **Communicate on Your Feet**

A Persuasive Speech

1. Follow the speech plan Action Steps to prepare a speech in which you change audience belief. Your instructor will announce the time limit and other parameters for this assignment.
2. Criteria for evaluation include all the general criteria of topic and purpose, content, organization, and presentation, but special

emphasis will be placed on the primary persuasive criteria of how well the speech's specific goal was adapted to the audience's initial attitude toward the topic, the soundness of the reasons, the evidence cited in support of them, and the credibility of the arguments.

3. Use the persuasive speech evaluation checklist in Figure 16.4 to critique yourself as you practice your speech.

4. Prior to presenting your speech, prepare a complete sentence outline and source list (bibliography). If you have used Speech Builder Express to complete the Action Step activities online, you will be able to print out a copy of your completed outline and source list. Also prepare a written plan for adapting your speech to the audience. Your adaptation plan should address the following issues:

- How does your goal adapt to whether your prevailing audience attitude is in favor, no opinion, or opposed?
- What reasons will you use, and how will the organizational pattern you select fit your topic and audience?
- How will you establish your credibility with this audience?
- How will you motivate your audience?
- How you will organize your reasons?

Sample Persuasive Speech

Sexual Assault Policy a Must
by Maria Lucia R. Anton

This section presents the outline and transcript of a sample persuasive speech developed and presented by college student Maria Lucia R. Anton at the 1994 Interstate Oratorical Association competition. It is now published in an anthology of the winning speeches by college students that year. An adaptation plan was not required, so the one provided here has been created as an example for you to use as you develop your own persuasive speech.

1. Review the outline and adaptation plan for Maria's speech to petition her school's administration to create and implement a sexual assault prevention policy.
2. Then read the transcript of Maria's speech.
3. Use the persuasive speech evaluation checklist from Figure 16.4 to help you evaluate this speech.
4. Write a paragraph of feedback to Maria describing the strengths of her speech and what you think she might do next time to be more effective.

You can use your Premium Website for *Communicate!* to complete this activity online, print a copy of the persuasive speech evaluation checklist, compare your feedback to that of the authors, and, if requested, e-mail your work to your instructor. Access the speech activities for Chapter 16.

Adaptation Plan

1. **Audience analysis:** My audience is composed of traditional-age college students with varying majors and classes. Most are European Americans from working- or middle-class backgrounds.
2. **Background knowledge:** My perception is that my audience knows about sexual assault on college campus, but not about the nuances of it.
3. **Creating and maintaining interest:** I will involve my audience by appealing to several emotions including guilt, sadness, relief, hope, and most of all, compassion. I will use representative examples as short stories.
4. **Organization:** I have organized my speech using the motivated sequence.
5. **Building credibility:** I will build credibility initially by pausing and looking listeners in the eye before beginning. Throughout the speech I will cite strong sources. I will dress professionally and sound emotionally convinced about the topic. I will provide credibility at the end by pausing and looking listeners in the eye for a moment after appealing to them with my call to action.
6. **Motivation:** The incentive that I will offer is that the audience members can act to create a sexual assault policy on their campuses. Doing so will appeal to hope and safety.

Outline

General purpose: To persuade

Speech goal: I want my audience to petition the administration on their campus to formulate and implement a sexual assault prevention policy.

Attention

I. "If you want to take her blouse off, you have to ask. If you want to touch her breast, you have to ask. If you want to move your hand down to her genitals, you have to ask. If you want to put your finger inside her, you have to ask." [*quotation from Antioch College's sexual offense policy*]
   A. The policy consists of three major points:
      1. If you have an STD, you must disclose it to a potential partner.
      2. It is not acceptable to knowingly take advantage of someone who is under the influence of alcohol or drugs.
      3. Obtaining consent is an ongoing process in any sexual interaction.
   B. The policy is designed to create a safe campus environment.

Need

II. Sexual assault on college campuses is a problem across the nation.
   A. Carlton College in Northfield, Minnesota, was sued for $800,000 in damages by four university women. [Time *magazine article*]
   B. Although college administration know of enrolled rapists, they need not say or do anything.
   C. One in every four college women have been assault victims. [Ms. Magazine *survey*]

D. Between 30 and 40 percent of male students reported they might force someone to have sex if they knew they would escape punishment. [Ms. Magazine *survey*]

E. The effects of sexual assault on victims is disturbing.

Transition: Many campuses are open invitations for sexual assault. The absence of a policy is a grand invitation.

Satisfaction

III. We need to push for sexual assault policies on our campuses.
   A. Antioch policy example.
   B. Fundamental points for any sexual assault policy.
      1. Input from students, faculty, staff, and administration is crucial when developing the policy.
      2. The policy must be publicized in many venues including the student handbook, newspaper, and radio station.
      3. Educational programs must be developed to educate the campus community about the sexual assault policy.
      4. Campuses should outline a step-by-step procedure for reporting and addressing sexual assault perpetrators.

Transition: It is pertinent that universities provide support to victims through such policies and procedures if college campuses are to be a safe environment for all students.

Visualization

IV. All students should feel safe leaving the classroom at night.
   A. The wheels of justice turn too slowly when sending victims to the local police.
   B. Without a policy, there are no specific penalties to prosecute offenders.
   C. With a policy, would-be offenders will think twice.
   D. With a policy, there is at least a chance that justice will be served.

Action

V. We students must voice our concerns.
   A. We must form petitions to demand that our universities create sexual assault policies.
   B. We must not stop until we've succeeded and our campuses have sexual assault policies.

Speech and Analysis

Speech

"If you want to take her blouse off, you have to ask. If you want to touch her breast, you have to ask. If you want to move your hand down to her genitals, you have to ask. If you want to put your finger inside her, you have to ask."

What I've just quoted is part of the freshman orientation at Antioch College in Ohio. In the sexual

Analysis

Attention
This opening attracts our attention by personalizing the Antioch sexual offense prevention policy. Notice how the emotional impact of the policy changes as the acts described become more intimate.

offense policy of this college, emphasis is given to three major points: (1) If you have a sexually transmitted disease, you must disclose it to a potential partner; (2) to knowingly take advantage of someone who is under the influence of alcohol, drugs, and/or prescribed medication is not acceptable behavior in the Antioch community; (3) obtaining consent is an ongoing process in any sexual interaction. The request for consent must be specific to each act.

The policy is designed to create a "safe" campus environment, according to Antioch President Alan Guskin. For those who engage in sex, the goal is 100 percent consensual sex. It isn't enough to ask someone if they would like to have sex; you have to get verbal consent every step of the way.

This policy has been highly publicized and you may have heard it before. The policy addresses sexual offenses such as rape, which involves penetration, and sexual assault, which does not. In both instances, the respondent coerced or forced the primary witness to engage in nonconsensual sexual conduct with the respondent or another.

Sexual assault has become a reality in many campuses across the nation. Carleton College in Northfield, Minnesota, was sued for $800,000 in damages by four university women. The women charged that Carleton was negligent in protecting them against a known rapist. From the June 1991 issue of *Time* magazine:

> Amy had been on campus for just five weeks when she joined some friends to watch a video in the room of a senior. One by one the other students went away, leaving her alone with a student whose name she didn't even know. "It ended up with his hands around my throat," she recalls. In a lawsuit she has filed against the college, she charges that he locked the door and raped her again and again for the next four hours. "I didn't want him to kill me, I just kept trying not to cry." Only afterwards did he tell her, almost defiantly, his name. It was on top of the "castration list" posted on women's bathroom walls around campus to warn other students about college rapists. Amy's attacker was found guilty of sexual assault but was only suspended.

Julie started dating a fellow cast member in a Carleton play. They had never slept together, she charges in a civil suit, until he came to her dorm room one night, uninvited, and raped her. She struggled to hold her life and education together, but finally could

Maria Lucia draws on language specific to the Antioch policy, referring to the "respondent" and the "primary witness." This language could be confusing to the audience. It would have been clearer to use the terms "aggressor" and "victim."

She could have helped the audience to better understand the purpose of the speech if she had previewed what was to come. As it is, the transition to the next step in the motivated sequence is very abrupt, which makes it difficult to follow.

Need

Maria Lucia's first subpoint in support of the need for campus sexual offense prevention policies is an excellent case example with first-person narratives that dramatize the problem and pack a powerful emotional punch.

manage no longer and left school. Only later did Julie learn that her assailant was the same man who had attacked Amy.

Ladies and gentlemen, the court held that the college knew this man was a rapist. The administration may have been able to prevent this from happening if they had expelled the attacker, but they didn't. My campus has no reports of sexual assault. Is the administration waiting for someone to be assaulted before it formulates a sexual assault policy? This mistake has been made elsewhere; we don't have to prove it again.

Perhaps some statistics will help you understand the magnitude of the problem. According to *New Statesman and Society,* June 21, 1991, issue:

- A 1985 survey of sampled campuses by *Ms. Magazine* and the National Institute of Mental Health found that one in every four college women were victims of sexual assault, 74 percent knew their attackers. Even worse, between 30 and 40 percent of male students indicated they might force a women to have sex if they knew they would escape punishment.
- In just one year, from 1988 to 1989, reports of student rape at the University of California increased from two to eighty.

These numbers are indeed disturbing. But more disturbing are the effects of sexual assault: a victim feeling the shock of why something this terrible was allowed to happen; having intense fears that behind every dark corner could be an attacker ready to grab her, push her to the ground, and sexually assault her; many waking moments of anxiety and impaired concentration as she remembers the attack; countless nights of reliving the traumatic incident in her sleep; mood swings and depression as she tries to deal internally with the physical hurt and the emotional turmoil that this attack has caused.

Many campuses are open invitations for sexual assault. The absence of a policy is a grand invitation. I have never been sexually assaulted so why do I care so much about a policy? You know why—because I could be assaulted. I won't sit and wait to be among one out of every four women on my campus to be assaulted. The first step to keep myself out of the statistics is to push for a sexual assault policy on my campus. One way to do this is through a petition to the university.

Although the Antioch policy sounds a little far-fetched and has been the target of criticism in comedy routines such as those on *Saturday Night*

Here, the startling fact that administration knew the man was a rapist serves to heighten emotional appeal.

As the second subpoint supporting the need for these policies on campus the speaker cites several startling statistics. Although the percentage of college women who were victims of an attack is surprising, and the fact that about three quarters of them knew their attacker is shocking, it is the third statistic that stuns.

These statistics from a sample of campuses across the nation demonstrate the breadth of the problem. The increase of rapes at the University of California, however, needs more explanation.

The third subpoint describes the effects of sexual assault. Maria Lucia uses vivid language to paint a picture of the aftermath of an attack on the life of the victim. She could have heightened the emotional impact by personalizing the information using personal pronouns as she described the effects.

Live, and although students feel that formalizing such a policy is unnatural, many campuses are taking heed and revisiting their own policies. Campuses like mine don't have a sexual assault policy to revisit. Does yours?

By far the most controversial policy today is the one established at Antioch College. I'm not saying that we need one as specific as theirs, but every university has a responsibility to provide a safe environment for its students. Universities have an obligation to provide a sexual assault policy.

The following points are fundamental to the safety of the students and need to be addressed by universities:

1. Every campus should have a sexual assault policy that is developed with input from students, faculty, staff, and administration. The policy then needs to be publicized in the student handbook. The school newspaper should print and the campus radio broadcast the policy periodically to heighten awareness.
2. Campuses must institute programs to educate students and other campus personnel. Examples of these policies can include discussing the sexual assault policy during mandatory student orientation and conducting special workshops for faculty and other staff.
3. Campuses should outline a step-by-step written procedure to guarantee that sexual assault victims are assisted by the university. It is pertinent that they are not without support at this very critical time.

My vision is a campus where there is no place for any sexual assault. I want to leave the classroom at night knowing that my trip from the building to the car will not be one of fear for my personal safety.

You may be saying to yourself that there are laws to handle crimes like these. In the *Chronicle of Higher Education,* May 15, 1991 issue, Jane McDonnell, a senior lecturer in women's studies at Carleton, says colleges cannot turn their back on women. "We'd be abandoning victims if we merely sent them to the police," she says. "the wheels of justice tend to grind slowly and rape has one of the lowest conviction rates of any crime."

Satisfaction

The ideal satisfaction step shows in a point-by-point fashion how the proposed solution, in this case a sexual assault prevention policy, would satisfy the needs presented earlier. We would expect the speaker to tell us how such a policy would (1) prevent scenarios like the one at Carleton College, (2) change the statistics on date rape, (3) change male students' perceptions about the likelihood of punishment, and (4) offer support for the victims.

Maria Lucia handles this step very well although the organization of this section could be tighter. Specifically she should have laid out four points, not three, as fundamental to an effective policy. Point 4 would have addressed disciplinary procedures and penalties specific to sexual assault. She implies these are important but never makes the case.

Visualization

This section might have been more compelling had it been placed after the discussion of disciplinary procedures and victim support. The visualization also could have been developed a bit more. It would have been more effective had it been less "speaker specific" and instead invited the audience to visualize.

Here she points to negative visualization, that is, what we can expect if action to create sexual assault policies is not taken.

Without a policy, most institutions lack specific penalties for sexual assault and choose to prosecute offenders under the general student-conduct code. At Carleton College, for example, Amy's attacker was allowed back on campus after his suspension, and consequently he raped again.

Although the policy may not stop the actual assault, would-be offenders will think twice before committing sexual assault if they know they will be punished. In addition, it guarantees justice for victims of sexual assault. We need to make it loud and clear that sexual assault will not be tolerated.

Yes, universities have a big task in the struggle to prevent sexual assault.

You and I can actively assist in this task and can make a giant contribution to move it forward. On my campus, students have not only voiced their concerns, but we have also started a petition demanding that the university formulate a sexual assault policy.

The bottom line is that we need to prevent sexual assault on campus. The key to prevention is a sexual assault policy. If your university does not have a policy, then you need to petition your administration to have one. I know I won't stop my advocacy until I see a policy on my campus.

This transition to the action step doesn't really follow from the previous discussion.

Action
Here Maria Lucia offers a specific action to be taken by the audience, that is, to petition for a sexual assault prevention policy on their campuses. The way she phrases it, however, is not as compelling as it could be. She could have been more effective by making her call to action more direct.

She also fails to quickly review her main points and she doesn't provide much direction to the audience about how to go about petitioning.

The speech ends abruptly with an indirect emotional appeal to the audience's sense of guilt. She didn't really have a clincher. The speech seems to just end. Perhaps a tie back to the opening quotation and an appeal to compassion or hope would have served her purpose more effectively.

Summary

Persuasive speeches are designed to influence the beliefs and/or behavior of audience members. They present logical reasons but must also present those reasons in a way that motivates the audience to listen and think about what the speaker is saying. The elaboration likelihood model (ELM) suggests that when people hear an argument, they can process it one of two ways. Either they can listen carefully, think about the information, and elaborate its implications for themselves; or they can make decisions about what they are hearing based on simple cues about the speaker's credibility. According to the model, people who feel personally involved with a proposition are more likely to process it carefully.

So in preparing a persuasive speech, the speaker must choose a proposition (goal) that takes into account the target audience's initial attitude. A target audience may be opposed to the proposition, neutral (because they are uninformed, impartial, or apathetic), or in favor.

The speaker must choose good reasons and sound evidence. Reasons are main point statements that support the proposition. Evidence is information (facts, opinions, and so on) selected to support reasons. Then the speaker needs to identify and test the forms of argument that will be used in supporting the proposition and in supporting each reason. Four of the most common types of arguments are arguing from example, from analogy, from causation, and from sign. Speakers also need to check arguments so that they avoid five of the common fallacies that occur in reasoning: hasty generalizations, false cause, ad hominem, straw person, and either-or.

Speakers can use emotional appeals to increase audience members' involvement with the proposition. Both appeals to negative and positive emotions can be effective.

When speakers want their audience to act, they should also consider the incentives the audience has for acting in accord with the speakers' propositions and how these incentives meet the needs of the audience. Audience needs include physiological, safety, belongingness, esteem, and self-actualization. Speakers should also consider whether the costs that audience members may experience would outweigh the incentives attached to the proposition.

The reasons that support a proposition can be organized following one of several patterns, which include the statement of reasons pattern, the comparative advantages pattern, the criteria satisfaction pattern, the refutative pattern, the problem-solution pattern, the problem-cause-solution pattern, and the motivational sequence pattern.

Communicate! Active Online Learning

Now that you have read Chapter 16, use your Premium Website for *Communicate!* for quick access to the electronic resources that accompany this text. These resources include

- **Study tools** that will help you assess your learning and prepare for exams (*digital glossary, key term flash cards, review quizzes*).
- **Activities and assignments** that will help you hone your knowledge, analyze communication situations (*Skill Learning Activities*), and build your public speaking skills throughout the course (*Communication on Your Feet speech assignments, Action Step activities*). Many of these activities allow you to compare your answers to those provided by the authors, and, if requested, submit your answers to your instructor.

- **Media resources** that will help you explore communication concepts online (*Web Resources*), develop your speech outlines (*Speech Builder Express 3.0*), watch and critique videos of communication situations and sample speeches (*Interactive Video Activities*), upload your speech videos for peer reviewing and critique other students' speeches (*Speech Studio online speech review tool*), and download chapter review so you can study when and where you'd like (*Audio Study Tools*).

This chapter's Key Terms, Skill Learning Activities, and Web Resources are also featured on the following pages, and you can find this chapter's Communicate on Your Feet assignment and speech activity in the body of the chapter.

Key Terms

ad hominem (397)
apathetic (392)
arguing from analogy (395)
arguing from example (395)
arguing from sign (396)

arguing from causation (396)
argument (393)
comparative advantages pattern (404)
criteria satisfaction pattern (404)
either-or (397)

ethos (400)
false cause (397)
goodwill (400)
hasty generalization (397)
impartial (392)
incentive (401)

logos (393)
motivated sequence pattern (406)
motivation (401)
pathos (398)
persuasive speech (389)
problem-cause-solution pattern (406)

problem-solution pattern (405)
proposition (390)
proposition of fact (390)
proposition of policy (391)
proposition of value (390)
reasons (393)

refutative pattern (405)
statement of reasons pattern (404)
straw person (397)
target audience (391)
uninformed (392)

Skill Learning Activities

16.1: A Specific Goal Statement in a Persuasive Speech (393)

The goal of this activity is to find and analyze a specific goal statement.

1. Use your Premium Website for *Communicate!* to access **Web Resource 16.1: Maintaining the Faith** and read "Terrorism and Islam: Maintaining Our Faith," a speech by Mahathir Bin Mohamad, Prime Minister of Malaysia, given at the OIC Conference of Ministers of Endowments and Islamic Affairs, May 7, 2002. Identify the specific goal statement.
2. Given the composition of the audience, what do you think their initial attitude was toward the speaker's position?
3. Write a paragraph in which you analyze the speaker's goal statement. What type of specific speech goal is this? Does this goal seem appropriate for this audience? Explain your reasoning.

16.2: Giving Good Reasons and Evidence (397)

The goal of this activity is to analyze reasons and evidence.

1. Use your Premium Website for *Communicate!* to access **Web Resource 16.1: Maintaining the Faith** and read the speech "Terrorism and Islam: Maintaining Our Faith" by Mahathir Bin Mohamad. Identify each of the main points or reasons the speaker offers in support of his thesis.
2. Are his reasons good? Are they supported? Relevant? Adapted to the audience?
3. Analyze his supporting evidence. Assess the quality, currency, and relevance to his reasons.
4. Identify two kinds of reasoning links that he uses, and then test them using the appropriate questions. Are the links you tested logical? Explain.

5. Are there any fallacies that you can detect in his argument? Explain.

16.3: Motivating Audiences (403)

The goal of this activity is to analyze motivational tactics.

1. Use your Premium Website for *Communicate!* to access **Web Resource 16.1: Maintaining the Faith** and read the speech "Terrorism and Islam: Maintaining Our Faith" by Mahathir Bin Mohamad. Analyze the incentives that Mahathir presents.
2. What emotions do you think he hopes to arouse? What information does he present to stimulate emotions? Does he seem to phrase the ideas in a way that elicits those emotions? Explain.

16.4: Persuasive Organizational Methods (407)

The goal of this activity is to analyze organizational patterns.

1. Use your Premium Website for *Communicate!* to access **Web Resource 16.1: Maintaining the Faith** and read the speech "Terrorism and Islam: Maintaining Our Faith" by Mahathir Bin Mohamad. Analyze the organizational methods Mahathir uses.
2. How well does his pattern fit the attitudes you believe his audience holds toward his position? Are there other patterns that might have served him better?

Web Resources

16.1: Maintaining the Faith (393)

To read and analyze a speech about Islam in the modern world, go to AccessMyLibrary.com (free with registration) to find the article "Terrorism and Islam: Maintaining Our Faith," given by Mahathir Bin

Mohamad, Prime Minister of Malaysia, at a conference of ministers from Muslim countries in May 2002.

16.2: Evoking Negative and Positive Emotions (400)

Read more about how to appeal to various negative and positive emotions in an online section

called "Increasing Audience Involvement through Emotional Appeals."

16.3: Motivated Sequence Speech (407)

Read a transcript of a speech that uses the motivated sequence pattern. This speech includes an analysis by the authors of *Communicate!*

Self Review

part

4

Foundations of Communication

Public Speaking from Chapters 11 to 16

What kind of a public speaker are you? The following analysis looks at specifics that are basic to a public-speaking profile. Use this scale to assess the frequency with which you perform each behavior: 1 = always; 2 = often; 3 = sometimes; 4 = rarely; 5 = never.

_____ When I am asked to speak, I am able to select a topic and determine a speech goal with confidence. (Ch. 11)

_____ When I speak, I use material from a variety of sources. (Ch. 11)

_____ In my preparation, I construct clear main points and organize them to follow some consistent pattern. (Ch. 12)

_____ In my preparation, I am careful to be sure that I have developed ideas to meet audience needs. (Ch. 13)

_____ When I speak, I sense that my audience perceives my language as clear and vivid. (Ch. 13)

_____ I look directly at members of my audience when I speak. (Ch. 14)

_____ When I speak, my bodily actions help supplement or reinforce my ideas; I feel and look involved. (Ch. 14)

_____ I have confidence in my ability to speak in public. (Ch. 14)

_____ When I give informative speeches, I am careful to use techniques designed to get audience attention, create audience understanding, and increase audience retention. (Ch. 15)

_____ When I give persuasive speeches, I am careful to use techniques designed to build my credibility, prove my reasons, and motivate my audience. (Ch. 16)

To verify this self-analysis, have a friend or fellow group member complete this review for you. Based on what you have learned, select the public-speaking behavior you would most like to improve. Write a communication improvement plan similar to the sample goal statement in Chapter 1 (page 18).

You can complete this Self-Review online and, if requested, e-mail it to your instructor. Use your Premium Website for Communicate! *to access* **Part IV Self-Review** *under the chapter resources for Chapter 16.*

Abrams, J. (2007, Sept. 25). House panel debates hip-hop lyrics. *USA Today.com*. Retrieved from http://www.usatoday.com/news/washington/2007-09-25-3649050705_x.htm

African neck stretching. (2008–2009). Retrieved from African Tribes.Org Web site: http://www.african-tribes.org/african-neck-stretching.html

Ahladas, J. (1989, April 1). Global warming. *Vital Speeches of the Day* (381–384).

Ali, S. (2007, October 7). Close enough to touch was too far apart. *New York Times*. Retrieved from http://www.nytimes.com/2007/10/07/fashion/07love.html

Alsever, J. (2007, March 11). In the computer dating game, room for a coach. *New York Times*. Retrieved from http://www.nytimes.com/2007/03/11/business/yourmoney/11dating.html

Altman I. (1993). Dialectics, physical environments, and personal relationships. *Communication Monographs*, 60, 26–34.

American Museum of Natural History. (1999). Exhibition highlights. *Body Art: Marks of Identity*. Retrieved from http://www.amnh.org/exhibitions/bodyart/exhibition_highlights.html

Andersen, P. A., Hecht, M. L., Hoobler, G. D., & Smallwood, M. (2003). Nonverbal communication across cultures. In W. B. Gudykunst (Ed.), *Cross-cultural and intercultural communication*. Thousand Oaks, CA: Sage.

Anderson, J. (1988). Communication competency in the small group. In R. Cathcart & L. Samovar (Eds.), *Small group communication: A reader*. Dubuque, IA: Brown.

Anzaldúa, G. (1999). *Borderlands/La frontera: The new Mestiza*. San Francisco, CA: Aunt Lute Books.

Aron, A., Aron, E. N., Tudor, M., & Nelson, G. (2004). Close relationships as including other in the self. In H. T. Reis & C. E. Rusbult (Eds.), *Close relationships* (pp. 365–379). New York: Psychology Press.

Aronson, E. (1999). *The social animal*. New York: Worth.

Asch, S. E. (1946). Forming impressions of personality. *Journal of Abnormal and Social Psychology*, 9, 272–279.

Associated Press. (2008, December 17). "I can see Russia from my house!" *Brisbane Times*. Retrieved from http://www.brisbanetimes.com.au/articles/2008/12/16/1229189584297.html

Associated Press. (2009, July 21). Charges against Harvard scholar dropped. *MSNBC.com*. Retrieved from http://www.msnbc.msn.com/id/32010985/

Associated Press Strategic Planning. (2008, June). *A New Model for News Studying the Deep Structure of Young-Adult News Consumption* pp 5, 45; retrieved from http://www.ap.org/newmodel.pdf

Australian Museum. (2009). Shaping. *Body Art*. Retrieved from http://amonline.net.au/bodyart/shaping/

Ayres, J. (1991, June–December). Using visual aids to reduce speech anxiety. *Communication Research Reports*, 73–79.

Ayres, J., & Hopf, T. S. (1990, January). The long-term effect of visualization in the classroom: A brief research report. *Communication Education*, 39, 75–78.

Ayres, J., Hopf, T. S., & Ayres, D. M. (1994, July). An examination of whether imaging ability enhances the effectiveness of an intervention designed to reduce speech anxiety. *Communication Education*, 43, 252–258.

Baerwald, D. (n.d.). Narrative. Retrieved from Northshore School District Web site: http://ccweb.norshore.wednet.edu/writingcorner/narrative.html.

Balgopal, P. R., Ephross, P. H., & Vassil, T. V. (1986). Self-help groups and professional helpers. *Small Group Research, 17*, 123–137.

Baron, R. A., Byrne, D., & Branscombe, N. R. (2006). *Social psychology* (11th ed.). Boston: Allyn & Bacon.

Basic guidelines at Ignite Columbus. (n.d.). Retrieved from http://ignitecbus.com/?page_id=2

Bates, B. (1992). *Communication and the sexes*. Prospect Heights, IL: Waveland Press.

Baxter, L. (1982). Strategies for ending relationships: Two studies. *Western Journal of Speech Communication, 46*, 223–241.

Baxter, L. A., & Montgomery, B. M. (1996). *Relating: Dialogues and dialectics*. New York: Guilford.

Baxter, L. A., & West, I. (2003). Couple perceptions of their similarities and differences: A dialectical perspective. *Journal of Social and Personal Relationships, 20*, 491–514.

Becker, A. (2004). Television, disordered eating, and young women in Fiji: Negotiating body image and identity during rapid social change. *Culture, Medicine and Psychiatry, 28*(4), 533–559.

Beebe, S., & Masterson, J. (2006). *Communicating in groups: Principles and practices* (8th ed.). Boston: Pearson.

Behnke, R. R., & Carlile, L. W. (1971). Heart rate as an index of speech anxiety. *Speech Monographs, 38,* 66.

Bentley, J. (2008, November 2). McCain "fine gold" and a special guest on *Saturday Night Live. CBS News.com.* Retrieved from http://www.cbsnews.com/blogs/2008/11/02/politics/fromtheroad/entry4563297.shtml

Berger, C. (1987). Communicating under uncertainty. In M. Roloff and G. Miller (Eds.), *Interpersonal Processes: New Directions in Communication Research* (pp. 39–62). Newbury Park, CA: Sage.

Beshara, T. (2006). *The job search solution: The ultimate system for finding a great job now!* New York: AMACOM Books.

Billy Mays, the infomercial king; Death of a great American salesman; Want to know the secret of America's innovation edge? Call now! (2009, July 1). *Global Agenda.* Retrieved from InfoTrac College Edition.

Birdwhistell, R. (1970). *Kinesics and context.* Philadelphia: University of Pennsylvania Press.

Bommelje, R., Houston, J. M., & Smither, R. (2003). Personality characteristics of effective listeners: A five-factor perspective. *International Journal of Listening, 17,* 32–46.

Bonito, J. (2000). The effect of contributing substantively on perceptions of participation. *Small Group Research, 31,* 528–553.

Bonvillain, N. (2003). *Language, culture and communication: The meaning of messages* (4th ed.). Upper Saddle River, NJ: Prentice-Hall.

Booher, D. D. (2003). *Speak with confidence: Powerful presentations that inform, inspire, and persuade* [Adobe Digital Editions version]. New York: McGraw-Hill. doi: 10.1036/0071420789

Boon, S. D. (1994). Dispelling doubt and uncertainty: Trust in romantic relationships. In S. Duck (Ed.), *Dynamics of relationships* (pp. 86–111). Thousand Oaks, CA: Sage.

Boyd, A. (1999). *How to handle media interviews.* London: Mercury.

Buber, M. (1970). *I and thou* (W. Kaufman, Trans.). New York: Scribner.

Burgoon, J. K., & Bacue, A. E. (2003). Nonverbal communication skills. In J. O. Greene & B. R. Burleson (Eds.), *Handbook of communication and social interaction skills* (pp. 179–220). Mahwah, NJ: Erlbaum.

Burgoon, J. K., Blair, J. P., & Strom, R. E. (2008). Cognitive biases and nonverbal cue availability in detecting deception. *Human Communication Research, 34,* 572–599.

Burgoon, J. K., Coker, D. A., & Coker, R. A. (1986). Communicative effects of gaze behavior: A test of two contrasting explanations. *Human Communication Research, 12,* 495–524.

Burgoon, J. K., & Hoobler, G. D. (2002). Nonverbal signals. In M. L. Knapp & J. A. Daly (Eds.), *Handbook of interpersonal communication* (3rd ed., pp. 240–299). Thousand Oaks, CA: Sage.

Burke, K. (1968). *Language as symbolic action.* Berkeley: University of California Press.

Burleson, B. R. (2003). Emotional support skills. In J. O. Green & B. R. Burleson (Eds.), *Handbook of communication and social interaction skills* (pp. 551–594). Mahwah, NJ: Erlbaum.

Burleson, B. R., & Goldsmith, D. J. (1998). How the comforting process works: Alleviating emotional distress through conversationally induced reappraisals. In P. A. Andersen & L. K. Guerrero (Eds.), *Handbook of communication and emotion: Research, theory, applications, and contexts* (pp. 248–280). San Diego, CA: Academic Press.

Callison, D. (2001). Concept mapping. *School Library Media Activities Monthly, 17*(10): 30–32.

Carr, D. (2007, April 7). Network condemns remarks by Imus. *New York Times.* Retrieved from http://www.nytimes.com/2007/04/07/arts/television/07imus.htm

Carter, B. (2008, October 31). Infomercial for Obama is big success in ratings. *New York Times, 158*(54480), A19. Retrieved from InfoTrac College Edition.

Cegala, D. J., & Sillars, A. L. (1989). Further examination of nonverbal manifestations of interaction involvement. *Communication Reports, 2,* 45.

Chuang, R. (2004). An examination of Taoist and Buddhist perspectives on interpersonal conflict, emotions and adversities. In F. E. Jandt (Ed.), *Intercultural communication: A global reader* (pp. 38–50). Thousand Oaks, CA: Sage.

Clark, J. (2006, August 4). In politics, comedy is central. *In These Times.* Retrieved from http://www.inthesetimes.com/article/2745

Cleveland, H. (2009). The limits to cultural diversity. In L. A. Samovar, R. E. Porter, & E. R. McDaniel (Eds.), *Intercultural communication: A reader* (11th ed.; pp. 405–408). Belmont, CA: Thomson Wadsworth

Cohen N. (2009, August 24). Wikipedia to limit changes to articles on people. *New York Times.* Retrieved from http://www.nytimes.com/2009/08/25/technology/internet/25wikipedia.html?_r=1

Colapinto, J. (2006, August 11). Mad dog. *Rolling Stone.* Retrieved from http://www.rollingstone.com/politics/story/6417561/mad_dog

College learning for the new global century. (2007). *A Report from the National Leadership Council for Liberal Education and*

America's Promise. Washington D.C.: Association of American Colleges and Universities.

Crain, R. (2009, May 4). Deceitful financial infomercial tars entire advertising industry. *Advertising Age, 80*(16), 17. Retrieved from InfoTrac College Edition.

Croucher, M. (2008, February 29.) I just want to be thin. If it takes dying to get there—so be it. *The Epoch Times*. Retrieved from http://en.epochtimes.com/news/8-2-29/66794.html

Crovitz, D., & Smoot, W. S. (2009, January). Wikipedia: Friend, not foe. *English Journal, 98*(3), 91–97. Retrieved from http://www.nytimes.com/learning/teachers/archival/EnglishJournalArticle2.pdf

Cummings, J. (2008, October 29). Obama infomercial: Smart or overkill? *Politico*. Retrieved from http://www.politico.com/news/stories/1008/15056_Page2.html

Cupach, W. R., & Metts, S. (1986). Accounts of relational disclosure: A comparison of marital and non-marital relationships. *Communication Monographs, 53*, 319–321.

C. Vivian Stringer took the Imus firestorm in stride. (2008, March 1). *New York Daily News*. Retrieved from http://www.nydailynews.com/entertainment/arts/2008/03/02/2008-03-02_c_vivian_stringer_took_the_imus_firestor.html

Dahl, S. (2004). *Intercultural research: The current state of knowledge* (Middlesex University Discussion Paper no. 26). Available from SSRN: http://SSRN.com/abstract=658202

The Daily Show: Journalism, satire, or just laughs? (2008, May 8). *PewResearch.org* (Pew Research Center, Project for Excellence in Journalism). Retrieved from http://pewresearch.org/pubs/829/the-daily-show-journalism-satire-or-just-laughs

Demo, D. H. (1987). Family relations and the self-esteem of adolescents and their parents. *Journal of Marriage and the Family, 49*, 705–715.

Dindia, K. (2000a). Relational maintenance. In C. Hendrick & S. S. Hendrick (Eds.), *Close relationships: A sourcebook* (pp. 287–300). Thousand Oaks, CA: Sage.

Dindia, K. (2000b). Sex differences in self-disclosure, reciprocity of self-disclosure, and self-disclosure and liking: Three metaanalyses reviewed. In S. Petronio (Ed.), *Balancing the secrets of private disclosures* (pp. 21–36). Mahwah, NJ: Erlbaum.

Dindia, K., Fitzpatrick, M. A., & Kenny, D. A. (1997). Self-disclosure in spouse and stranger interaction: A social relations analysis. *Human Communication Research, 23*, 388–412.

Dindia, K., & Timmerman, L. (2003). Accomplishing romantic relationships. In J. O. Greene & B. R. Burleson (Eds.), *Handbook of communication and social interaction* (pp. 685–722). Mahwah, NJ: Erlbaum.

Donoghue, P. J., & Siegel, M. E. (2005). *Are you really listening?: Keys to successful communication*. Notre Dame, IN: Sorin Books.

Downey, G., Freitas, A. L., Michaelis, B., & Khouri, H. (2004). The self-fulfilling prophecy in close relationships: Rejection sensitivity and rejection by romantic partners. In H. T. Reis & C. E. Rusbult (Eds.), *Close relationships* (pp. 153–174). New York: Psychology Press.

Drummond, D. (2004). *Miracle meetings* [e-book]. Retrieved from http://www.superteams.com.

Duch, B. J., Groh, S. E., & Allen, D. E. (eds). (2001). *The power of problem-based learning*. Sterling, VA: Stylus.

Duck, S. (1987). How to lose friends without influencing people. In M. E. Roloff & G. R. Miller (Eds.), *Interpersonal processes: New directions in communication research*. Beverly Hills, CA: Sage.

Duck, S. (1999). *Relating to others*. Philadelphia: Open University Press.

Duck, S. (2007). *Human Relationships* (4th ed.). Thousand Oaks, Calif.: Sage.

DuFrene, D. D., & Lehman, C. M. (2002). Persuasive appeal for clean language. *Business Communication Quarterly, 65* (March), 48–56.

Dunkel, P., & Pialorsi, F. (2005). *Advanced listening comprehension: Developing aural and notetaking skills*. Boston: Thomson Heinle.

Durst, G. M. (1989, March 1). The manager as a developer. *Vital Speeches of the Day* (pp. 309–314).

Dwyer, K. K. (2000, January). The multidimensional model: Teaching students to self-manage high communication apprehension by self-selecting treatments. *Communication Education, 49*, 79.

Ebeling, R. (2008, March 6). So long, Dungeon Master. *Newsweek*. Retrieved from http://www.newsweek.com/id/119782

Edens, K. M. (2000). Preparing problem solvers for the 21st century through problem-based learning. *College Teaching, 48*, 55–60.

Eisenberg, J. (2007). Group cohesiveness. In R. F. Baumeister & K. D. Vohs (Eds.), *Encyclopaedia of Social Psychology* (pp. 386–388). Thousand Oaks, CA: Sage.

Estes, W. K. (1989). Learning theory. In A. Lesgold & R. Glaser (Eds.), *Foundations for a psychology of education* (pp. 1–49). Hillsdale, NJ: Erlbaum.

Evans, C., & Dion, K. (1991). Group cohesion and performance: A meta-analysis. *Small Group Research, 22*, 175–186.

Fairhurst, G. T. (2001). Dualism in leadership. In F. M. Jablin & L. M. Putnam (Eds.), *The new handbook of organizational communication* (pp. 379–439). Thousand Oaks, CA: Sage.

Farhi, P. (2009, February 19). Political pundits, overpopulating the news networks. *Washington Post*. Retrieved from http://www.washingtonpost.com/wp-dyn/content/article/2008/02/18/AR2008021802267.html

Forgas, J. P. (1991). Affect and person perception. In J. P. Forgas (Ed.), *Emotion and social judgments* (pp. 387–406). New York: Pergamon Press.

Forgas, J. P. (2000). Feelings and thinking: Summary and integration. In J. P. Forgas (Ed.), *Feeling and thinking: The role of affect in social cognition* (pp. 387–406). New York: Cambridge University Press.

Frances, P. (1994). Lies, damned lies . . . *American Demographics, 16*, p. 2.

Gallagher, M. P. (2009, April 27). Wikipedia held too malleable to be reliable as evidence. *New Jersey Law Journal.* n.p. Retrieved from Infotrac.

Galvin, K. M., Byland, C. L., & Brommel, B. J. (2007*). Family communication: Cohesion and change* (7th ed.). Boston: Allyn & Bacon.

Gangestad, S. W., & Snyder, M. (2000). Self-monitoring: Appraisal and reappraisal. *Psychological Bulletin, 126*, 530–555.

Gay, V. (2008, November 3). McCain's poignant appearance on *Saturday Night Live. Newsday.* Retrieved from InfoTrac.

Gibson, J. J. (1966). *The senses considered as perceptual systems.* Boston: Houghton Mifflin.

Gilbert, D., & Kahl, J. A. (1982). *The American class structure: A new synthesis.* Homewood, IL: Dorsey.

Giles, D. (2006). Constructing identities in cyberspace: The case of eating disorders. *British Journal of Social Psychology 45*(3): 463–477. Retrieved from http://www.brown.uk.com/eatingdisorders/giles2.pdf

Goodale, G. (2005, February 25). How to pen an Oscar speech. *The Christian Science Monitor.* Retrieved from InfoTrac College Edition.

Goodwin, S. (Executive Producer). (2009, July 23). Black and blue: Police and minorities [Radio broadcast transcript]. In *Talk of the Nation.* Retrieved from National Public Radio Web site: http://www.npr.org/templates/story/story.php?storyId=106928434

Graber, S. (2000). *The everything get-a-job book: From resume writing to interviewing to finding tons of job openings.* Avon, MA: Adams Media.

Guzman, M. (2009, April 16). A Seattle geek fest spreads its wings. *Seattle Pi.* Retrieved from http://www.seattlepi.com/business/405192_IGNITE16.html

Haffner, D. (2008, September 2). Bristol Palin, Mary Cheney and the limits of family privacy. *Huffington Post.* Retrieved from http://www.huffingtonpost.com/rev-debra-haffner/bristol-palin-mary-cheney_b_123164.html

Hahner, J. C., Sokoloff, M. A., & Salisch, S. L. (2001). *Speaking clearly: Improving voice and diction* (6th ed.). New York: McGraw-Hill.

Hall, B. J. (2002). *Among cultures: The challenge of communication.* Belmont, CA: Wadsworth.

Hall, E. T. (1959). *The silent language.* Greenwich, CT: Fawcett.

Hall, E. T. (1968). Proxemics. *Current Anthropology, 9,* 83–108.

Hall, E. T. (1969). *The hidden dimension.* Garden City, NY: Doubleday.

Haller, J. T. (2009, July 6). Billy Mays Caps Lock. Retrieved August 21, 2009, from http://johnhaller.com/jh/useful_stuff/billy_mays_caps_lock.

Hanke, J. (1998). The psychology of presentation visuals. *Presentations, 12*(5), 42–47.

Hanks for the Oscars speech advice, Tom! (2006, March 4). *Mail Online.* Retrieved from http://www.dailymail.co.uk/tvshowbiz/article-378755/Hanks-Oscars-speech-advice-Tom.html

Hansen, R. S., & Hansen, K. What do employers really want? Top skills and values employers seek from job-seekers. Retrieved from Quintessential Careers Web site: http;//www.quintcareers.com/job_skills_values.html

Harding, Andrew (2004, December 4). Japan's internet 'suicide clubs'. *BBC News.* Retrieved http://news.bbc.co.uk/2/hi/programmes/newsnight/4071805.stm

Hattie, J. (1992). *Self-concept.* Hillsdale, NJ: Erlbaum.

Hau, L. (2008, April 28). Timber! Newspaper circulation falls again. *Forbes.com.* Retrieved from http://www.forbes.com/2008/04/28/newspapers-circulation-advertising-biz-media-cx_lh_0428newspapers.html

Haubegger, C. (2000). I'm not fat, I'm Latina. In M. Adams, W. J. Blumenfeld, R. Castañeda, H. W. Hackman, M. L. Peters, & X. Zúñiga (Eds.), *Readings for diversity and social justice: An anthology on racism, anti-Semitism, sexism, heterosexism, ableism, and classism* (pp. 242–243). New York: Routledge.

Haviland, W. A. (1993). *Cultural anthropology.* Fort Worth, TX: Harcourt, Brace, Jovanovich.

Head, S. W., Spann, T., & McGregor, M. A. (2001). *Broadcasting in America: A survey of electronic media* (9th ed.). Boston: Houghton Mifflin.

Heider, F. (1958). *The psychology of interpersonal relations.* New York: Wiley.

Helm, B. (2005, December 14). Wikipedia: "A work in progress." *Business Week.* Retrieved from http://www.businessweek.com/technology/content/dec2005/tc20051214_441708.htm?chan=db

Hendrick, S.S. (1981). Self-disclosure and marital satisfaction. *Journal of Personality and Social Psychology.* 40, 1150–1159.

Henman, L. D. (2003). Groups as systems: A functional perspective. In R. Y. Hirokawa, R. S. Cathcart, L. A. Samovar, & L. D. Henman

(Eds.), *Small group communication theory and practice: An anthology* (8th ed., pp. 3–7). Los Angeles: Roxbury.

Henry Louis Gates, Jr., police report. (2009, July 23). *The Smoking Gun*. Retrieved from http://www.thesmokinggun.com/archive/years/2009/0723092gates2.html

Hill, B., & Leeman, R. W. (1997). *The art and practice of argumentation and debate*. Mountain View, CA: Mayfield.

Hinckley, D. (2008, October 7). *Saturday Night Live* is buzzworthy again, thanks to Tina Fey as Sarah Palin. *New York Daily News*. Retrieved from http://www.nydailynews.com/entertainment/tv/2008/10/07/2008-10-07_saturday_night_live_is_buzzworthy_again_.html

Hinckley, D. (2009, July 18). Walter Cronkite remains gold standard for journalists. *NYDailyNews.com*. Retrieved from http://www.nydailynews.com/entertainment/tv/2009/07/18/2009-07-18_he_remains_the_gold_standard_among_all.html

Hip-Hop Summit Action Network. (n.d.). Mission statement. Retrieved from http://www.hsan.org/content/main.aspx?pageid=7

Hip-Hop Summit Action Network. (2007, April 13) Differentiating between Don Imus and hip hop: A statement from Russell Simmons, Chairman, and Dr. Benjamin Chavis, President, of the Hip-Hop Summit Action Network. Retrieved from http://hsan.org/Content/Main.aspx?PageId=242

Hip-Hop Summit Action Network. (2007, April 23). Recommendation to the recording and broadcast industries: A statement by Russell Simmons and Dr. Benjamin Chavis on behalf of the Hip-Hop Summit Action Network. Retrieved from http://hsan.org/Content/Main.aspx?PageId=246

Hirokawa, R., Cathcart, R., Samovar, L., & Henman, L. (Eds.). (2003). *Small group communication theory and practice* (8th ed.). Los Angeles: Roxbury.

Hofstede, G. (1980). *Culture's consequences*. Beverly Hills, CA: Sage.

Hofstede, G. (Ed.). (1998). *Masculinity and femininity: The taboo dimension of national cultures*. Thousand Oaks, CA: Sage.

Hofstede, G. (2000). The cultural relativity of the quality of life concept. In G. R. Weaver (Ed.), *Cultural communication and conflict: Readings in intercultural relations*. Boston: Allyn & Bacon.

Honeycutt, J. M. (1993). Memory structures for the rise and fall of personal relationships. In S. Duck(Ed.), *Individuals in relationships* (pp. 60–86).Newbury Park, CA: Sage.

Holtgraves, T. (2002). *Language as social action: Social psychology and language use*. Mahwah, NJ: Erlbaum.

Hotz, R. L. (April 15, 1995). Official racial definitions have shifted sharply and often. *Los Angeles Times*, p. A14.

How to detect bias in news media. (n.d.) Retrieved from FAIR (Fairness and Accuracy in Reporting) Web site: http://www.fair.org/index.php?page=121

How to dress in women's professional attire. (2008). *eHow: How to do just about everything*. Retrieved from http://www.ehow.com/how_2064031_dress-womens-professional-attire.html.

Howell, D. (2008, August 17). Obama's edge in the coverage race. *Washington Post*. Retrieved from http://www.washingtonpost.com/wp-dyn/content/article/2008/08/15/AR2008081503100.html?sub=AR

Huling, R. (2008, May 27). "Dungeons & Dragons" owns the future. *The Escapist*. Retrieved from http://www.escapistmagazine.com/articles/view/issues/issue_151/4931-Dungeons-Dragons-Owns-the-Future.2

Humes, J. C. (1988). *Standing ovation: How to be an effective speaker and communicator*. New York: Harper and Row.

Ignite Seattle. (n.d.). Retrieved from http://www.igniteseattle.com/

Ignite Seattle 7 is happening on 8/3. (2009). *Ignite*. Retrieved from http://ignite.oreilly.com/2009/07/ignite-seattle-7-is-happening-on-83.html

Iorio, P. (1995, March 26). How not to blow the Oscar speech. *The New York Times*. Retrieved from InfoTrac College Edition.

Itzkoff, D. (2009, February 20). Police investigate photo in Chris Brown case. *New York Times*. Retrieved from http://www.nytimes.com/2009/02/21/arts/music/21arts-POLICEINVEST_BRF.html

Jackson, R. L., II (Ed.). (2004). *African American communication and identities*. Thousand Oaks, CA: Sage.

Jacobs, B. (2005, June). *Adolescents and self-cutting (self-harm): Information for parents* (Bringing Science to Your Life, Guide I-104). Retrieved from Cooperative Extension Service, College of Agriculture and Home Economics, New Mexico State University Web site: http://aces.nmsu.edu/pubs/_i/I-104.pdf

Jandt, F. E. (2001). *Intercultural communication: An introduction* (3rd ed.). Thousand Oaks, CA: Sage.

Janis, I. L. (1982). *Groupthink: Psychological studies of policy decisions and fiascoes*. Boston: Houghton Mifflin.

Janusik, L. A., & Wolvin, A. D. (2006). *24 hours in a day: A listening update to the time studies*. Paper presented at the meeting of the International Listening Association, Salem, OR.

Jensen, A. D., & Chilberg, J. C. (1991). *Small group communication: Theory and application*. Belmont, CA: Wadsworth.

Johnson, D., & Johnson, F. (2003). *Joining together: Group theory and group skills* (8th ed.). Boston: Allyn & Bacon.

Johnson, P. (2006, September 24). Cable rantings boost ratings. *USA Today*. Retrieved from http://www.usatoday.com/life/columnist/mediamix/2006-09-24-media-mix_x.htm

Jones, M. (2002*). Social psychology of prejudice*. Upper Saddle River, NJ: Prentice-Hall.

Jonsson, P. (2009, July 31). Was there a better way to conduct the Gates-Crowley debate? *Christian Science Monitor.* Retrieved from http://features.csmonitor.com/politics/2009/07/31/was-there-a-better-way-to-conduct-gates-crowley-debate/

Kaplan, R. M. (2002). *How to say it in your job search: Choice words, phrases, sentences and paragraphs for résumés, cover letters and interviews.* Paramus, NJ: Prentice-Hall.

Kapoun, J. (2000, January 25). Teaching undergrads Web evaluation: A guide for library instruction. *College and Research Library News, 59*(7). Retrieved from http://www.ala.org/ala/mgrps/divs/acrl/publications/crlnews/1998/jul/teachingundergrads.cfm

Kellerman, K. (1992). Communication: Inherently strategic and primarily automatic. *Communication Monographs, 59,* 288–300.

Kelly, L., Phillips, G. M., & Keaten, J. A. (1995). *Teaching people to speak well: Training and remediation of communication reticence.* Cresskill, NJ: Hampton.

King, A. E., Austin-Oden, D., & Lohr, J. M. (2009). Browsing for love in all the wrong places: Does research show that Internet matchmaking is more successful than traditional dating? *Skeptic* v15 i1 48(8). Retrieved from Infotrac.

Kleinman, S. (2007). *Displacing Place: Mobile Communication in the Twenty-First Century.* New York: Peter Lang.

Klyukanov, I. E. (2005). *Principles of intercultural communication.* New York: Pearson.

Knapp, M., & Daly, J. (2002). *Handbook of interpersonal communication.* Thousand Oaks, CA: Sage.

Knapp, M. L., & Hall, J. A. (2006). *Nonverbal communication in human interaction* (5th ed.). Belmont, CA: Thomson Wadsworth.

Knapp, M. L., & Vangelisti, A. L. (2000). *Interpersonal communication and human relationships* (4th ed.). Boston: Allyn & Bacon.

Koerner, A. F., & Fitzpatrick, M. A. (2002). Understanding family communication patterns and family functioning: The roles of conversation orientation and conformity orientation. In W. B. Gudykunst (Ed.), *Communication yearbook 26* (pp. 36–68). Mahwah, NJ: Erlbaum.

Kolb, D. (1984). *Experiential learning: Experience as the source of learning and development.* Englewood Cliffs, NJ: Prentice Hall.

Koncz, A. (2008). *Job outlook 2009.* Bethlehem, PA: National Association of Colleges and Employers.

Krotz, J. (2006). *6 tips for taking control in media interviews.* Retrieved from Microsoft Small Business Center Web site: http://www.microsoft.com/smallbusiness/resources/management/leadership-training/6-tips-for-taking-control-in-media-interviews.aspx#tipsfortakingcontrolinmediainterviews

Lawrence, S. G., & Watson, M. (1991). Getting others to help: The effectiveness of professional uniforms in charitable fund raising. *Journal of Applied Communication Research, 19,* 170–185.

Leary, M. R. (2002). When selves collide: The nature of the self and the dynamics of interpersonal relationships. In A. Tesser, D. A. Stapel, & J. V. Wood (Eds.), *Self and motivation: Emerging psychological perspectives* (pp. 119–145). Washington, D.C.: American Psychological Association.

Leopold, T. (2009, July 18). Former CBS anchor '"Uncle Walter" Cronkite dead at 92. *CNN.com.* Retrieved from http://www.cnn.com/2009/US/07/17/walter.cronkite.dead/index.html

Levin, B. B. (Ed.). (2001). *Energizing teacher education and professional development with problem-based learning.* Alexandria, MN: Association for Supervision and Curriculum Development.

Liberman, M. (2005, December 23). Multiplying ideologies considered harmful. Retrieved from http://itre.cis.upenn.edu/~myl/languagelog/archives/002724.html

Lim, L. (Reporter). (2007, March 19). Painful memories for China's footbinding survivors [Radio broadcast story]. In *Morning Edition.* Retrieved from National Public Radio Web site: http://www.npr.org/templates/story/story.php?storyId=8966942

Listening factoid. (2003). International Listening Association. Retrieved from http://www.listen.org/pages/factoids.html

Littlejohn, S. W., & Foss, K. A. (2008). *Theories of human communication* (9th ed.). Belmont, CA: Thomson Wadsworth.

Long, K. (1997, August 12). *Visual aids and learning.* Retrieved from University of Portsmouth, Audio Video Homepage: http://www.mech.port.ac.uk/av/AVALearn.htm

Lopez, L. (2008, February 5). Attention Deficit theater. *OregonLive.com.* Retrieved from http://www.oregonlive.com/entertainment/index.ssf/2008/02/attention_deficit_theater.html

Luckmann, J. (1999). *Transcultural communication in nursing.* New York: Delmar.

Luft, J. (1970). *Group processes: An introduction to group dynamics.* Palo Alto, CA: Mayfield.

Lulofs, R. S., & Cahn, D. D. (2000). *Conflict: From theory to action* (2nd ed.). Boston: Allyn & Bacon.

Maguire, J. (2007, February 22). Cicero's rules of rhetoric and our own shout-fest. *Maguire Online.* Retrieved from http://www.maguireonline.com/2007/02/ciceros_rules_of_rhetoric_and.php

Mannes, T. (2009, May 22). Infomercials standing by! *San Diego Union-Tribune.* Retrieved from InfoTrac College Edition.

Margulis, Stephen T. (1977). Concepts of privacy: Current status and next steps. *Journal of Social Issues 33*(3), 5–21.

Martin, J. N., & Nakayama, T. K. (2000). *Intercultural communication in contexts* (2nd ed.). Mountain View, CA: Mayfield.

Martin, M. M., Anderson, C. M., & Horvath, C. L. (1996). Feelings about verbal aggression: Justifications for sending and hurt from receiving verbally aggressive messages. *Communication Research Reports, 13*(1), 19–26.

Martin, V. B. (2008, September 26). Media bias: Going beyond fair and balanced. *Scientific American.* Retrieved from http://www.scientificamerican.com/article.cfm?id=media-bias-presidential-election

Maslow, A. H. (1954). *Motivation and personality.* New York: Harper & Row.

Mason, S. (2007, April). Equality will someday come. *Vital Speeches of the Day* (pp. 159–163).

mastamokei. (2008, April 30). Billy Mays gangsta remix [Video file]. Retrieved from www.youtube.com/watch?v=_tyct9l-fD8

Maul, K. (2009, February 25). Rihanna aftermath rouses ethics debate. *PR Week.* Retrieved from http://www.prweekus.com/Rihanna-aftermath-rouses-ethics-debate/article/127824

McCarthy, E. (2008, September 24). Matchmakers, matchmakers, making a mint. *Washington Post.* Retrieved from http://www.washingtonpost.com/wp-dyn/content/article/2008/09/23/AR2008092303669.html

McCarthy, M. (2005). New theme for Reebok. *USAToday.com.* Retrieved from http://usatoday.com/money/advertising/2005-02-09-reebok-usat_x.htm

McCartney, A. (2009, February 20). Rihanna won't discuss Chris Brown, but thanks fans [Television story]. Retrieved from *ABC News* Web site: http://abcnews.go.com/Entertainment/wireStory?id=6918527

McCroskey, J. C. (1977). Oral communication apprehension: A review of recent theory and research. *Human Communication Research, 4,* 78–96.

Mehrabian, A. (1972). *Nonverbal communication.* Chicago: Aldine.

Menzel, K. E., & Carrell, L. J. (1994). The relationship between preparation and performance in public speaking. *Communication Education, 43,* 17–26.

Merton, R. K. (1968). *Social theory and social structure.* New York: Free Press.

Michener, H. A., & DeLamater, J. D. (1999). *Social psychology* (4th ed.). Orlando, FL: Harcourt Brace.

Midura, D. W., & Glover, D. R. (2005). *Essentials of teambuilding.* Champaign, IL: Human Kinetics.

Morin, R. (2006, June 23). Jon Stewart, enemy of democracy? *Washington Post.* Retrieved from http://www.washingtonpost.com/wp-dyn/content/article/2006/06/22/AR2006062201474.html

Morris, T. L., Gorham, J., Cohen, S. H., & Huffman, D. (1996). Fashion in the classroom: Effects of attire on student perceptions of instructors in college classes. *Communication Education, 45,* 135–148.

Moser, K. (2006, May 25). New memorials: t-shirts, websites, autodecals. *Christian Science Monitor.* Retrieved from http://www.csmonitor.com/2006/0525/p15s01-lihc.html

Motley, M. (1997). COM therapy. In J. A. Daly, J. C. McCroskey, J. Ayres, T. Hopf, & D. M. Ayres (Eds.), *Avoiding communication: Shyness, reticence, and communication apprehension* (2nd ed., pp. 379–400). Cresskill, NJ: Hampton Press.

Mruk, C. (1999). *Self-esteem: Research, theory, and practice* (2nd ed.). New York: Springer.

MTV Video Music Awards (2003). Retrieved from http://www.imdb.com/title/tt0375940/

Munger, D., Anderson, D., Benjamin, B., Busiel, C., & Pardes-Holt, B. (2000). *Researching online* (3rd ed.). New York: Longman.

Mutz, D., Reeves, B., & Wise, K. (2003, May 27). *Exposure to mediated political conflict: Effects of civility of interaction on arousal and memory.* Paper presented at the annual meeting of the International Communication Association, San Diego, CA. Retrieved from http://www.allacademic.com/meta/p111574_index.html

Nabi, R. L. (2002). Discrete emotions and persuasion. In J. P. Dillard and M. Pfau (Eds.), *The persuasion handbook: Developments in theory and practice* (pp. 291–299). Thousand Oaks, CA: Sage.

Nelson J C. (2006). *Leadership.* Utah School Boards Association 83rd Annual Conference, Salt LakeCity, Utah. Retrieved from http://www.ama-assn.org/ama/pub/category/15860.html

Neville Miller, A. (2006). Public speaking patterns in Kenya. In L. A. Samovar, R. E. Porter, & E. R. McDaniel (Eds.), *Intercultural communication: A reader* (11th ed., pp. 238–245). Belmont, CA: Wadsworth.

Neuliep, J. W. (2006). *Intercultural communication: A contextual approach* (3rd ed.). Thousand Oaks, CA: Sage.

Newman, H. (2007). "World of Warcraft" players: Let's slay together. *Detroit Free Press.* Retrieved from InfoTrac.

Newman, M. (2007, April 10). Rutgers women to meet with Imus over remark. *New York Times.* Retrieved from http://www.nytimes.com/2007/04/10/business/media/10cnd-imus.html?hp

Neznanski, M. (2008, November 14). Sharing ideas quickly. *Gazette Times.* Retrieved from http://www.gazettetimes.com/articles/2008/11/14/news/community/3loc01_tech.txt

O'Connor, J. V. (2000). FAQs #1. Retrieved from Cuss Control Academy Web site: http://www.cusscontrol.com/faqs.html

Ogden, C. K., & Richards, I. A. (1923). *The meaning of meaning.* London: Kegan, Paul, Trench, Trubner.

O'Hair, D., O'Rourke, J., & O'Hair, M. (2001). *Business communication: A framework for success.* Cincinnati, OH: South-Western.

Olaniran, B. (2002–2003). Computer-mediated communication: A test of the impact of social cues on the choice of medium for resolving misunderstandings. *Journal of Educational Technology Systems, 31*(2), 205–222.

Omdahl, B. L. (1995). *Cognitive appraisal, emotion, and empathy.* Mahwah, NJ: Erlbaum.

Onkvisit, S., & Shaw, J. (1987). Self-concept and image congruence: Some research and managerial implications. *Journal of Consumer Marketing, 4*(1), 13–23

Otzi, the ice man. (n.d.). *Dig: The archaeology magazine for kids.* Retrieved from http://www.digonsite.com/drdig/mummy/22.html.

Parks, M. R. (2006). *Personal relationships and personal networks.* Mahwah, NJ: Erlbaum.

Pascoe, C. J. (2008, January 22). Interview in Growing up online [Television series episode]. In D. Fanning. (Executive producer) *Frontline.* Boston, MA: WGBH. Retrieved from http://www.pbs.org/wgbh/pages/frontline/kidsonline/interviews/pascoe.html

Patterson, B. R., Bettini, L., & Nussbaum, J. F. (1993). The meaning of friendship across the life-span: Two studies. *Communication Quarterly, 41,* 145.

Pearson, J. C., West, R. L., & Turner, L. H. (1995). *Gender & communication* (3rd ed.). Dubuque, IA: Brown & Benchmark.

Peng, T. (2008, November 23). Out of the shadows. *Newsweek.* Retrieved from http://www.newsweek.com/id/170528

Petri, H. L. (1996). *Motivation: Theory, research, and applications* (4th ed.). Belmont, CA: Wadsworth.

Petronio, S. (2002). *Boundaries of privacy: Dialectics of disclosure.* Albany: State University of New York Press.

Pew Research Center. (2007). *A portrait of "Generation Next": How young people view their lives, futures, and politics* (Survey Report) . Retrieved from http://people-press.org/report/300/a-portrait-of-generation-next

Phillips, G. (1977). Rhetoritherapy versus the medical model: Dealing with reticence. *Communication Education, 26,* 34–43.

Phillips, P. A., & Smith, L. R. (1992). *The effects of teacher dress on student perceptions* (Report No. SP 033-944). Retrieved from ERIC Document Services. (ED347151)

Plumb, T. (2006, August 31). Websites offer mourning for youths online. *Boston Globe.* Retrieved from http://www.boston.com/news/local/massachusetts/articles/2006/08/31/websites_offer_mourning_for_youths_online

Plumb, T. (2009). About Legacy.com, Inc. http://legacy.com/NS/About/

Rabby, M., & Walther, J. B. (2003). Computer mediated communication effects in relationship formation and maintenance. In D. J. Canary & M. Dainton (Eds.), *Maintaining relationships through communication* (pp. 141–162). Mahwah, NJ: Erlbaum.

Raybould, B. (2007, August 11). Gnomedex: Ignite Seattle. *Bold Words.* Retrieved from http://boldwords.wordpress.com/2007/08/11/gnomedex-ignite-seattle/

Rayner, S. G. (2001). Aspects of the self as learner: Perception, concept, and esteem. In R. J. Riding & S. G. Rayner (Eds.), *Self-perception: International perspectives on individual differences* (Vol. 2). Westport, CN: Ablex.

Reaves, J. (2001, July 31). Anorexia goes high tech. *Time.* Retrieved from http://www.time.com/time/health/article/0,8599,169660,00.html

Reebok marketing. (n.d.). Retrieved from http://corporate.reebok.com/en/about_reebok/faq_section/marketing/default.asp

Reebok's positioning. (n.d.). *About Reebok.* Retrieved from http://corporate.reebok.com/en/about_reebok/default.asp

Reebok Your Move campaign [Video file]. (n.d.). Retrieved from http://www.youtube.com/watch?v=IK_5TwmvuWo

Renz, M. A., & Greg, J. B. (2000). *Effective small group communication in theory and practice.* Boston: Allyn & Bacon.

Richmond, V. P., & McCroskey, J. C. (1995). *Communication: Apprehension, avoidance, and effectiveness* (4th ed.). Scottsdale, AZ: Gorsuch Scarisbrick.

Richmond, V. P., & McCroskey, J. C. (1997). *Communication apprehension, avoidance, and effectiveness* (5th ed.). Scottsdale, AZ: Gorsuch Scarisbrick.

Richmond, V. P., & McCroskey, J. C. (2000). *Communication: Apprehension, avoidance, and effectiveness* (5th ed.). Scottsdale, AZ: Gorsuch Scarisbrick.

RIP Billy Mays (We will miss your infomercials). (n.d.). Retrieved from http://www.facebook.com/pages/RIP-Billy-Mays-We-Will-Miss-Your-Infomercials/97433051622

Roloff, M.E., & Ifert, D.E. (2000). Conflict management through avoidance: Withholding complaints, suppressing arguments, and declaring topics taboo. In S. Petronio (Ed.), *Balancing the Secrets of Private Disclosures* (pp. 151–163). Mahwah, N.J.: LEA.

Rusbult, C. E., Olsen, N., Davis, J. L., & Hannon, P. A. (2004). Commitment and relationship maintenance mechanisms. In H. T. Reis & C. E. Rusbult (Eds.), *Key readings on close relationships* (pp. 287–304). Washington, D.C.: Taylor & Francis.

Ryan, R. (2000). *60 seconds & you're hired.* New York: Penguin Books.

Salopek, J. J. (1999). Is anyone listening? Training and Development, 531(9), 58–60.

Samovar, L. A., & Porter, R. E. (2001). *Communication between cultures* (4th ed.). Belmont, CA: Wadsworth.

Samovar, L. A., Porter, R. E., & McDaniel, E. R. (2007). *Communication between cultures* (6th ed.). Belmont, CA: Thomson Wadsworth.

Samovar, L. A., Porter, R. E., & McDaniel, E. R. (Eds.) (2006). *Intercultural communication: A reader* (11th ed.).Belmont, CA: Thomson Learning/Wadsworth.

Samovar, L. A., Porter, R. E., & McDaniel, E. R. (Eds.). (2009). *Intercultural communication: A reader* (12th ed.) . Belmont, CA: Cengage.

Samter, W. (2003). Friendship interaction skills across the lifespan. In J. O. Greene & B. R. Burleson (Eds.), *Handbook of communication and social interaction skills* (pp. 637–684). Mahwah, NJ: Erlbaum.

Schiesel, S. (2008, March 5). Gary Gygax, Game pioneer, dies at 69. *New York Times*. Retrieved from http://www.nytimes.com/2008/03/05/arts/05gygax.html

Schurman, A. (n.d.). A brief and rich body piercing history. *Life 123*. Retrieved from http://www.life123.com/beauty/style/piercings/body-piercing-history.shtml

Scott, P. (1997, January–February). Mind of a champion. *Natural Health, 27*, 99.

Seely Brown, J., & Hagel, J. (2009). How "World of Warcraft" promotes innovation. *Business Week Online*. Retrieved from Infotrac.

Seelye, K. Q. (2008, September 1). Palin's teen daughter is pregnant; new G.O.P. tumult. *New York Times*. Retrieved from http://www.nytimes.com/2008/09/02/us/politics/02PALINDAY.html

Seigenthaler J. (2005, November 29). A false Wikipedia "biography." *USA Today*. Retrieved from http://www.usatoday.com/news/opinion/editorials/2005-11-29-wikipedia-edit_x.htm

Shaw, M. E. (1981). *Group dynamics: The psychology of small group behavior* (3rd ed.). New York: McGraw-Hill.

Shedletsky, L. J., & Aiken, J. E. (2004). *Human communication on the Internet*. Boston: Pearson.

Shihab Nye, N. (2000). Long overdue. In *Post Gibran: An anthology of new Arab American writing*. Syracuse, NY: Syracuse University Press.

Shimanoff, M. (1992). Group interaction and communication rules. In R. Cathcart & L. Samovar (Eds.), *Small group communication: A reader*. Dubuque, IA: William C. Brown.

Slayter, M. E. (2006, January 14). Rehearse, rehearse, repeat: Have a rock-solid plan when preparing for an interview. *The Forum*, p. E3.

Smith, S. (2008). The case for using, but not citing, Wikipedia. *Prosecutor, Journal of the National District Attorneys Association, 42*(4), 31. Retrieved from Infotrac.

Snell, W.E., Belk, S.S., & Hawkins, R.C. II (1986). The masculine and feminine self-disclosure scale:The politics of masculine and feminine self presentation. *Sex Roles*, 15, 249.267.

Snyder, B. (2004). Differing views cultivate better decisions. *Stanford Business*. Retreived online at:http://www.gsb.stanford.edu/NEWS/bmag/sbsm0405/feature_workteams_gruenfeld.shtml

Solomon, M., Bamossy, G., & Askegaard, S. (2002). *Consumer behaviour: A European perspective* (2nd ed.) . Upper Saddle River, NJ: Prentice Hall Financial Times.

Spitzberg, B. H. (2000). A model of intercultural communication competence. In L. A. Samovar & R. E. Porter (Eds.), *Intercultural communication: A reader* (9th ed., pp. 375–387). Belmont, CA: Wadsworth.

Stephens, M. (1999). The new TV: Stop making sense. In R. E. Hiebert (Ed.), *Impact of mass media: Current issues* (4th ed.; pp. 16–22). White Plains, NY: Longman.

Stereotype. (2005). *The American Heritage New Dictionary of Cultural Literacy* (3rd ed.). Boston: Houghton Mifflin. Retrieved from Dictionary.com Web site: http://dictionary.reference.com/browse/stereotype

Stewart, C. J., & Cash, W. B. (2000). *Interviewing: Principles and practices* (9th ed.). Dubuque, IA: William C. Brown.

Stewart, L. P., Cooper, P. J., Stewart, A. D., & Friedley, S. A. (1998). *Communication and gender* (3rd ed.). Boston: Allyn & Bacon.

Stiff, J. B., Dillard, J. P., Somera, L., Kim, H., & Sleight, C. (1988). Empathy, communication and prosocial behavior. *Communication Monographs, 55*, 198–213.

Stokes, P. (2008, November 26). Perfectionist school girl hanged herself while worried about appearance. *Telegraph.co.uk*. Retrieved from http://www.telegraph.co.uk/news/uknews/3525738/Perfectionist-schoolgirl-hanged-herself-while-worried-about-appearance.html

Sultanoff, S. (1993). Tickling our funny bone: Humor matters in health. *International Journal of Humor Research, 6*, 89–104.

Sundstrom, E., DeMeuse, K. P., & Futrell, D. (1990, February). Work teams: Applications and effectiveness. *American Psychologist*, 120–133.

Tate, R. (2009, February 20). Battered Rihanna picture a media ethics lightning rod. *The Gawker*. Retrieved from http://gawker.com/5157078/battered-rihanna-picture-a-media-ethics-lightning-rod

Taylor, D. A., & Altman, I. (1987). Communication in interpersonal relationships: Social penetration theory. In M. E. Roloff & G. R. Miller (Eds.), *Interpersonal processes: New directions in communication research* (pp. 257–277). Beverly Hills, CA: Sage.

Taylor, J., & Hardy D. (2004). *Monster careers: How to land the job of your life.* New York: Penguin Books.

Teams that succeed (2004). *Harvard Business Review.* Boston: Harvard Business School Press.

The ten most memorable Oscar acceptances. (2008, February 22). *Times Online.* Retrieved from http://entertainment.timesonline.co.uk/tol/arts_and_entertainment/film/oscars/article3418375.ece?token=null&offset=0&page=1

Tengler, C. D., & Jablin, F. M. (1983). Effects of question type, orientation, and sequencing in the employment screening interview. *Communication Monographs, 50,* 261.

Terkel, S. N., & Duval, R. S. (Eds.). (1999). *Encyclopedia of ethics.* New York: Facts on File.

Thompson, L. L. (2003). *The social psychology of organizational behavior: Key readings.* New York: Taylor and Francis.

Thorndike, E. L. (1920). A constant error on psychological rating. *Journal of Applied Psychology, 4,* 25–29.

Thurlow, C., Lengel, L., & Tomic, A. (2004). *Computer mediated communication: Social interaction and the Internet.* Thousand Oaks, CA: Sage.

Timothy D. Naegele & Associates announces class action lawsuit against Guthy-Renker. (2002, June 26). *All Business.* Retrieved from http://www.allbusiness.com/crime-law/criminal-offenses-cybercrime/5968871-1.html

Ting-Toomey, S. (1999). *Communicating across cultures.* New York: Guilford Press.

Ting-Toomey, S. (2004). The matrix of face: An updated face-negotiation theory. In W. Gudykunst (Ed.), *Theorizing about Intercultural Communication* (pp. 71–92). Thousand Oaks, CA: Sage.

Ting-Toomey, S., Yee-Jung, K., Shapiro, R., Garcia, W., Wright, T., & Oetzel, J. G. (2000). Cultural/ethnic identity salience and conflict styles. *International Journal of Intercultural Relations, 23,* 47–81.

TMZ responds to LAPD internal investigation on battered Rihanna photo [Television story]. (2009, February 22). In *On the Record.* Retrieved from FOX News Network Web site: http://www.foxnews.com/story/0,2933,498157,00.html

Tuckman, B. W. (1965). Developmental sequence in small groups. *Psychological Bulletin, 6393,* 384–399.

Tullar, W., & Kaiser, P. (2000). The effect of process training on process and outcomes in virtual groups. *Journal of Business Communication, 37,* 408–427.

Tversky, B. (1997). Memory for pictures, maps, environments, and graphs. In D. G. Payne & F. G. Conrad (Eds.), *Intersections in basic and applied memory research* (pp. 257–277). Mahwah, NJ: Erlbaum.

U.S. Census Bureau. (2007). Hispanic Americans by the numbers. Retrieved from http://www.infoplease.com/spot/hhmcensus1.html

U.S. text message statistics. (2009, February 19). *Text message blog.* Retrieved from http://www.textmessageblog.mobi/2009/02/19/text-message-statistics-usa/

Valacich, J. S., George, J. F., Nonamaker, J. F., Jr., & Vogel, D. R. (1994). Idea generation in computer based groups: A new ending to an old story. *Small Group Research, 25,* 83–104.

Walker, D. M. (December 2006). America at a crossroads. *Vital Speeches of the Day* (pp. 752–762).

Walther, J. B. (1996). Computer-mediated communication: Impersonal, interpersonal and hyperpersonal interaction. *Western Journal of Communication, 57,* 381–398.

Walther, J. B., & Parks, M. R. (2002). Cues filtered out, cues filtered in: Computer-mediated communication and relationships. In M. C. Knapp & J. A. Daly (Eds.), *Handbook of interpersonal communication* (3rd ed.; pp. 529–563). Thousand Oaks, CA: Sage.

Ward, C. C., & Tracy, T. J. G. (2004). Relation of shyness with aspects of online relationship involvement. *Journal of Social and Personal Relationships, 21,* 611–623.

Watzlawick, P., Bavelas, J. B., & Jackson, D. D. (1967). *Pragmatics of human communication.* New York: Norton.

Weaver, J. B., III, & Kirtley, M. B. (1995). Listening styles and empathy. *Southern Communication Journal, 60,* 131–140.

Weill, J. (2006, December 18). All presentations should be five minutes long. *Jason Weill Web Productions.* Retrieved from http://weill.org/2006/12/08/all-presentations-should-be-five-minutes-long/

Weiten, W. (1998). *Psychology: Themes and variations* (4th ed.). Pacific Grove, CA: Brooks/Cole.

What is Ignite? (n.d.). *Ignite.* Retrieved from http://ignite.oreilly.com

What's wrong with the news? (n.d.). Retrieved from FAIR (Fairness and Accuracy in the News)Web site: http://www.fair.org/index.php?page=101

Whitestone McCallum, H. (n.d.). Frequently asked questions. *Heather.* Retrieved from http://www.heatherwhitestone.com/site/content/faqs.shtml

Widmer, W. N., & Williams, J. M. (1991). Predicting cohesion in a coacting sport. *Small Group Research, 22,* 548–570.

Wikipedia: Friend or foe? (2009). *Learning & Leading with Technology, 36*(8), 6. Retrieved from Infotrac.

Williams, J. (2009, July 31). Over beers, a taste of what's to come. *Boston Globe.* Retrieved from http://www.boston.com/news/nation/washington/articles/2009/07/31/over_beers_a_taste_of_whats_to_come/

Williams, J. P., Hendricks, S. Q., & Winkler, W. K. (Eds.). (2006). *Gaming as culture: Essays on reality, identity and experience in fantasy games*. Jefferson, NC: McFarland.

Wilson, C. (2002). The history of corsets. *eSSORTMENT: Information and advice you want to know*. Retrieved form http://www .essortment.com/all/historyofcors_rmue.htm

Wilson, G. L. (2005). *Groups in context: Leadership and participation in small groups* (7th ed.). New York: McGraw Hill.

Wolvin, A., & Coakley, C. G. (1996*). Listening* (5th ed.). Dubuque, IA: Brown & Benchmark.

Wood, J.T. *Relational Communication: Continuity & Change in Personal Relationships, 2nd Ed*. Belmont, CA: Wadsworth. 2000.

Wood, J. T. (2007). *Gendered lives: Communication, gender, and culture* (7th ed.). Belmont, CA: Wadsworth.

Wood, J. T., & Inman, C. (1993). In a different mode: Recognizing male modes of closeness. *Journal of Applied Communication Research, 21*, 279–295.

World Almanac and Book of Facts. Mahwah, NJ: World Almanac Books, 2001.

Wright, J. W. (2002). *New York Times Almanac*. New York: New York Times.

Young, K. S., Wood, J. T., Phillips, G. M., & Pedersen, D. J. (2007). *Group discussion: A practical guide to participation and leadership* (4th ed.). Long Grove, IL: Waveland Press.

Young, M. (2003). Integrating communication skills into the marketing curriculum: A case study. *Journal of Marketing Education, 25*, 57–70.

Zempke, R., Raines, C., & Filipczak (2000). *Generations at work*. New York: AMACOM Books.

Index

Italicized page numbers indicate materials in figures.

A

Accents, 338
Accommodation, 144, 177
Accountability, 212–213
Acquaintances, 134–135
Ad hominem fallacies, 397
Adaptation phase, 334
Adaptors, 69
Adjourning, 214–215
Age, communication and, 116
Agendas, 235, *236*
Aggressive behavior, 173–175
Ali, Saba, 146–147
Altruism, 128
Ambiguity, 127–128
American Psychological Association (APA), 294–295, *295*
Analogy, arguing from, 395–396
Analysis, critical. *See* Critical analysis
Anecdotes, 268
Animation, in delivery, 336–337
Anorexia, 240–241
Anticipation phase, 334
Antonyms, 369
Anxiety
    in communicating, 16, 35
    intercultural communication and, 112, 121, 123
    listening and, 197
    managing, 334–336
    in public speaking. *See* Public speaking apprehension
    scripted speeches and, 346
    symptoms/causes, 333–334
Anzaldúa, Gloria, 55–56
APA citation style, 294–295, *295*
Apathetic audiences, 392
Appeals to action, 292
Appearance
    gender differences in, 79
    nonverbal communication and, 76
    self-perceptions and, 30–31
    in speech presentation, 344–345
Appreciative listening, 91
Apprehension. *See* Anxiety; Communication apprehension; Public speaking apprehension
Arguments (persuasive). *See also* Persuasive speaking
    audience adaptation and, 391–393
    definition of, 395
    emotional appeal and, 398–400

fallacies in, 397–398
    main points, 393–394
    persuasive goals and, 390–391
    supporting evidence, 394–395
    types of, 395–396
Articles, 262–263
Articulation, 338
Artifacts, 74–75, 117
Assertiveness, 173–176, *175*
Assumptions, 123–124
Asynchronous technologies, 4
Attending, 92–93
Attention, 7, 24, 48
Attention, gaining, in speeches, 286–289, 305–306, 326–328, 349
Attitudes
    of audiences, 391–393
    common ground and, 306
    intercultural communication and, 127–128
    topic selection and, 256
Attributions, 40
Audience, 401–402
Audience adaptation, 304–331
    attitudes and, 391–393
    audience analysis and, 254–257
    common ground and, 306–307, 314
    for comprehension/retention, 309–312
    credibility and, 307–309
    cultural diversity and, 312–315
    definition of, 305
    intellectual stimulation and, 364–365
    interest and, 305–306
    memory aids and, 366–367
    presentational aids for, types of, 315–323
    presentational aids for, using, 323–328
    propositions and, 391–393
    relevance and, 305–306
    sample plans, 353–354, 380, 410
    setting and, 257
    topic selection and, 258–259
Audience analysis, 254–257. *See also* Audience adaptation
Audience contact, 343
Audience-based communication apprehension, 16
Audiovisual materials, 322–323
Autonomy, 150
Average group opinion method, 229
Avoidance, uncertainty, 121

B

Bar graphs, 321, *321*
Barriers, 123–127
Behavior, 168–170, 376–377. *See also* Nonverbal
    communication
Bias, media, 374–375
Bias-free language choice, 62, 313
Bibliographic style formats, 294
Biographies, 263
Blogs, 67
Body art, 80–81
Body language. *See* Kinesics
Body movement, 71
Body orientation, 70–71
Body type, 76
Books, 262
Boundaries, 172
Brainstorming, 228–229, 252, 253–254
Breadth, 365
Bridges, 201
Briefs, 242, 243
Buffering, 159

C

CA. *See* Communication apprehension
Cameras, document, 328
Causation, arguing from, 396
Causes, false, 397
CD players, 328
Chalkboards, 326–327
Channels, 6–7
Charts, 319–321, *319*
Chronemics (use of time), 75–78
Chronological order, 282
Citing sources, 270–272, 294–296, *295, 296,* 372
Cleveland, Harland, 13–14
Clichés, 56
Clinchers, 292–293
Clip art, 324
Closed questions, 187–188
Closedness, 150, 161
Clothing, nonverbal communication and, 76
CMC. *See* Computer-mediated communication
Co-cultures, 114–116
Codes, communication, 126
Cognitive restructuring, 335
Cohesiveness, 210, 231
Collaboration, 178–179, 231
Collectivist cultures, 30, 117–120,
    161, 174
Color, in presentational aids, 234–325
COM. *See* Communication orientation motivation
Comforting, 158–161. *See also* Listening
Common ground, 306–307, 314

Communication, 1–22
    anxiety and, 16, 135
    codes, 126
    competence in, 15–16, 127–130
    cultural influences on, 12
    definition of, 3
    elements of, 3–8
    ethics and, 14–15
    in groups. *See* Group communication
    learning and, 15
    nonverbal. *See* Nonverbal communication
    paraphrasing, 96
    principles, 10–15
    process model, 8
    in relationships. *See* Interpersonal communication
    settings. *See* Contexts
    skills, improving, 18, *19*
    verbal. *See* Verbal communication
Communication apprehension (CA), 16, 35. *See also* Public
    speaking apprehension
Communication competence, 15–16, 127–130
Communication orientation motivation (COM), 334
Communication Skills
    assertiveness, 175
    feelings, describing, 169
    paraphrasing, 96
    perception checking, 42
    specific language, using, 57
    speech goals, 261
    speech organization, 297
Comparative advantages pattern, 404
Comparisons, 268, 312, 369–370
Competence, communication, 15–16, 127–130
Comprehending, 91–97, 159, 309–312, 372
Comprehensive listening, 91
Comprehensive reports, 243
Compromising, 177–178
Computer-mediated communication (CMC), 59, 67, 136
Computer-mediated presentational aids, 243–244, 328
Concept mapping, 252, 253–254, *253*
Conclusions, speech, 291–293
Concrete words, 53
Confidentiality, 161. *See also* Privacy
Conflict management, 176–180, 231
Confrontation phase, 334
Connection, 150
Connotation, 50
Consensus method, 229
Constructed messages, 11
Constructive criticism, 102, *103,* 170–171
Content paraphrases, 94
Context-based communication apprehension, 16
Contexts
    analyzing, 257–258
    cultural differences in, 5, 51–52
    definition of, 4

disclosure and, 162
    expository speeches and, 373
    perception and, 40–41
    types of, 4–6, 8–10
Continuity of communication, 11
Continuous reinforcement, 376–377
Continuum, opinion, *391*
Contrasts, 268, 369–370
Control, 11–12
Controversial topics, 373–376
Conversation and Analysis
    employment interview, 198–200
    group problem solving, 239–242
    interpersonal communication, 179–180
    interpersonal relationships, 152–154
    interviewing, 198–200
    listening and responding, 104–106
Conversational style, 336
Coping statements, 335, *336*
Costs, incentives and, 403
Cover letters, 192–196, *193*
Creative works, expository speeches on, 377
Creativity, in expository speeches, 365–366
Credibility
    appearance and, 344–345
    communication competence and, 16
    definition of, 16
    evoking in speeches, 400
    goodwill and, 400–401
    humor and, 344–345
    of speakers, 307–308, 401
    in speeches, 290, 372
    trustworthiness and, 16, 266–267, 308, 372
Criteria, solution, 227
Criteria satisfaction pattern, 404
Critical analysis, 100, 351, *352*, 357–359, 382–384, 411–415
Critical listening, 92, 99–101
Critiquing others, 102, *103*, 170–171
Cronkite, Walter, 374
Cultural context, 5, 51–52, 68, 70, 315
Cultural diversity, 269, 312–314
Cultural immersion, 128
Culture shock, 112–113
Cultures
    barriers to communication between, 123–127
    behavior and, 174–175
    co-cultures and, 114–116
    comforting and, 160–161
    communication and, 112–117
    communication competence and, 127–130
    cultural identity of, 116–117
    definition of, 12, 112
    emotional responses and, 97
    eye contact and, 70
    gestures and, 69
    language and, 51–52

learning about, 128–129
    nonverbal communication and, 68
    norms and values of, 117–123, 127, 145
    physical space and, 75
    privacy and, 161
    self-perceptions and, 30–31, 32–33
    time orientation and, 75–76
    touch and, 71
    vocal volume and, 72. *See also* Vocalics
Culture-specific skills, 129–130
Curiosity, intellectual, 287, 364

D
Dating information, 54
Decision making, 229–230, 237
Decoding, 3
Definitions, 369
Deliverables, 242
Delivery, 336. *See also* Speech presentation
Demographics, 254
Demonstrations, 370–372
Denotation, 50
Depth, 365
Descriptions, 368–369
Desensitization, 335
Deteriorating relationships, 148–149
Developing relationships, 144–145
Diagrams, 318, *319*
Dialectics, 149–150
Dimensions, 310
Dimensions (learning cycle), 367–368
Direct questions, 288
Disagreement, 102
Disclosure
    definition of, 161
    of feelings, 167–168
    guidelines for, 161–162, 164
    intimacy and, 164
    maintaining privacy and, 171–172
    personal feedback and, 168–171
    of personal information, 165–166
    reciprocity and, 164–165
    in relationship life cycles, 141–143
Discrimination, 39
Discriminative listening, 91
Dissolving relationships, 148–149
Distortion, 31–34
Distractions, 7–8, 92–93
Diverse Voices
    concept of time, 77–78
    cultural perceptions, 32–33
    diversity, 13–14
    group norms, 211–212
    hearing impairment, 89–90
    individualism and collectivism, 119–120

Diverse Voices (*continued*)
  interpersonal relationships, 146–147
  languages of Gloría Anzaldúa, 55–56
  problem solving, cultural diversity and,
    233–234
  public speaking patterns, 314–315
  second language, speaking, 339–441
  self-disclosure, prejudice and, 162–163
Document cameras, 328
Doing dimension, 310, 368
Dominant cultures, 113–115
Drawings, 318, *318*
Drummond, Dike, 235
DVD players, 328

E

Ectomorphs, 76
Educated guesses, 257
Ego gratification, 402
Egocentricity, 128
Either-or fallacies, 397
Elaboration Likelihood Model (ELM), 389–390, 398
Elaborations, 268
Electronic resources, 263
ELM. *See* Elaboration Likelihood Model
Email, 67
Emblems, 69
Emoticons, 67, 70
Emotional support, 158–161. *See also* Listening
Emotions, 97, 101–102, 398–400
Empathy, 91, 95, 97, 130, 400–401
Emphasis, 57
Employment applications, 192–196
Employment interviews
  conducting (interviewer), 191–192
  following up (applicant), 200
  interview guidelines (applicant), 197–198
  preparing for (applicant), 196–197
Encoding, 3
Encyclopedias, 263
Endomorphs, 76
Esteem needs, 402
Ethics
  definition of, 14
  groups and, 208
  implications on communication, 14–15
  Internet and, 36
  in speeches, 271–272, 301, 329, 360, 385
Ethics issues
  audience adaptation, 329
  communication perspectives, 19–20
  expository speech topics, 385
  group decision making, 221, 245
  intercultural communication, 130
  interpersonal communication, 106, 180–181

  linguistic sensitivity, 63
  nonverbal communication, 83–84
  online ethics, 152
  resumes, exaggerating in, 202–203
  social perceptions, 43
  source citations in speeches, 272
  speaker/audience obligations, 360
  truthfulness in speeches, 301
Ethnicity, 114
Ethnocentrism, 124
Ethos, 400
Etymology, 369
Evaluating. *See* Critical analysis
Evidence, to support reasons, 394–395
Example, arguing from, 395
Executive summaries, 243
Expectations, 25, *25*, 164–165
Expediting (meetings), 232, 237
Experiences, perception and, 26
Experiments, 265
Expert opinion method, 229
Expert opinions, 268
Expertise, speaker credibility and, 308
Expository speeches, 372–378
Extemporaneous speeches, 346
Eye contact, 68–70, 343, 349

F

Facebook, 67
Facial expressions, 70, 341–342
Fact, proposition of, 390
Factual statements, 99–100
Fairness, 14
Fallacies (arguments), 397–398
False causes, 397
Families, 215–216
Fear
  about speaking with others, 16, 35
  as persuasive technique, 398–399
  of public speaking. *See* Public speaking apprehension
Feedback, 7–8, 141–143, 168–171
Feeling dimension, 310, 367
Feelings, 167–168, 171–172, 367–368
Feelings paraphrases, 94
Figurative comparisons/contrasts, 268
Filtering, 34
First impressions, 38. *See also* Social perceptions
Flattery, 170
Flexibility, 130
Flip charts, 327
Flow charts, 318, 319–320, *320*
Forcing, 177
Form (organization), 4
Forming, 213–214
Friends, 136–139

G

Gatekeepers, 232–234, 236–237
Gaur, Raj, 339–441
Gaze (eye contact), 68–70, 343, 349
Gender bias, in language, 62, 313
Gender differences
    in clothing style, 79
    co-cultures and, 114–115
    in comforting, 160–161
    in cultural norms/values,
        122–123
    in eye contact, 70
    in gestures, 69
    in intimacy, 138–139
    in language styles, 52
    in physical contact, 71, 145
    privacy and, 162
    in self-perceptions, 30–31
    in voices, 72, 337
General speech goal, 259
Generalizations, 54, 397
Generic language, 59
Gestures, 69–70, 342
Goals
    with acquaintances, 134–135
    communication improvement, 18, 19
    in constructive criticism, 171
    in expository speeches, 374
    in groups, 118, 218
    interviewing, 186, 192, 197
    language clarification, 54, 56
    listening, 91–92, 100
    persuasive, 259, 390–391
    in relationships, 143–144
    in responding, 101–102,
        159–160
    of resumés, 192, 194
    of speeches. See Speech goals
Goodwill, 291, 400–401
Government documents, 263
Graphs, 321–322
Grieving, 5–6
Grooming, 76, 79
Ground rules, 210
Group communication, 207–223
    of decisions, 242–244
    definition of, 208
    furniture placement and, 75
    group development and, 213–215
    group dynamics and, 219
    healthy groups and, 208–213
    humor in, 231, 232
    problem solving and. See Problem solving
    in small groups, definition of, 9
    types of groups and, 215–219
Group dynamics, 219–220

Groups
    accountability in, 212–213
    cohesiveness in, 210
    collectivist cultures and, 30, 118, 119–120
    communicating in. See Group communication
    conflict management in, 231
    cultural influences on, 112, 113
    decision methods in, 229
    definition of, 208
    development stages of, 213–215
    dynamics of, 219
    ethics and, 14, 208
    goals of, 118
    healthy, 208–213
    interdependence in, 210
    language communities, 48
    leadership in, 230–234
    perceptions of, 38–39
    problem solving in. See Problem solving
    separateness in, 13
    small, 9
    status in, 74
    trust and, 210, 214, 216
    types of, 215–219
    working in, 18, 118
Groupthink, 214

H

Halo effect, 38
Handouts, 327–328
Haptics (touch), 71
Harmonizers, 232
Hasty generalizations, 397
Haubegger, Christy, 32–33
Hearing impairment, 89–90
Herakova, Lily, 233–234
Heterogeneous groups, 218–219
Hierarchy of needs, 401–402
High power-distance cultures, 121–122
High uncertainty-avoidance
        cultures, 121
High-context cultures, 51, 315
Historical context, 4
Historical topics, 376
Hofstede, Geert, 117, 122
Home pages, 266
Homogeneous groups, 218–219
Honesty. See also Truthfulness
    assertiveness and, 138
    definition of, 14
    groups and, 210, 214, 216
    halo effect and, 38
    managing conflict and, 176
    trust and. See Trust
    trustworthiness and. See Trustworthiness

Humor
    credibility and, 344–345
    in group communication, 231, 232
    as memory aid, 367
    as speech opener, 288
    as tension reliever, 232

I

"I"-centered messages, 172
Ideal self-concept, 27
Ignite (presentation style), 316–317
Illustrators, 69
Immediacy, 11
Immersion, cultural, 128
Impartial audiences, 392
Impersonal communication, 134
Implementing solutions, 230
Implicit personality theories, 38
Impromptu speeches, 346
Improvement plan, 18, *19*
Incentives, 401–403
Inclusive language, 59
Incongruence, 31–32
Incremental change, 392
Indexing generalizations, 54
Individualistic cultures, 30, 117–120, 161, 174
Inferences, 99–100
Infomercials, 397–398
Informal leaders, 230
Information givers/seekers/analyzers, 230–231
Information ownership, 165
Information sources, 262–272
Informational interviews, 189–190
Informative goals, *259*
Informative methods, 368–371, 373
Informative speaking, 363–387
    characteristics of, 364–368
    definition of, 364
    evaluation checklist, *378*
    methods of, 368–371
    sample speech, 353–359, 379–384
    speech frameworks of, 371–378
Initiation, in relationships, 136
Integrity, 14
Intellectual stimulation, 364–365
Intelligible speaking, 337–338
Intercultural communication, 111–132
    barriers to, 123–127
    basic skills, 129–130
    co-cultures and, 114–116
    competence in, 127–130
    cultural identity and, 116–117
    cultural norms and values and, 117–123
    definition of, 113
    dominant cultures and, 113–115

Interdependence, group, 210
Interest groups, 217
Interests, 24–25
Interference (noise), 7–8
Intermittent reinforcement, 376–377
Internal noise, 7
Internal reviews, 310
Internet-based resources, 263
Interpersonal communication, 157–184
    comforting, 158–161
    definition of, 9
    disclosure guidelines for, 165–171
    expectations and, 164–165
    intimacy and, 164
    negotiating in, 172–176
    privacy issues in, 161–165, 171–172
Interpersonal relationships, 133–156
    communication skills for. *See* Interpersonal
        communication
    conflict in, 176–180
    dialectics in, 149–151
    life cycles of, 141–143
    stages of, 143–149
    trust in, 137–138, 148
    types of, 134–140
Interpreters, 231
Interpreting, 26
Interrupting, 93
Interviewees, 189–190
Interviews, 185–205, 264
    barriers to, 123–127
    definition of, 186
    with media, 200–202
    protocols for, 186, *187*
    questions for, 187–188, *197*
    structuring, 186–189, *187*, *189*
Intimacy, 137–140, 164
Intimate distance, 73
Intonation, 72. *See also* Vocalics
Intrapersonal communication, 9
Introductions, speech, 287–291

J

Jargon, 58, 310
Job interviews. *See* Employment interviews
Job seeker, 192
Johari window, 141–143, *141*, *143*
Jokes. *See* Humor

K

Kinesics (use of body), 69–71, 341–345. *See also* Nonverbal
        communication
Knowledge, 16, 308
Kolb's cycle of learning, 309–310, *309*, 367–368

L

Language
 appropriate use of, 58–63
 audience adaptation and, 310–312
 clarity of, 52–54
 cultural influences on, 51–52
 definition of, 48
 electronic communication and, 59
 ethnicity and, 114
 gender influences on, 52
 linguistic sensitivity and, 58–63
 meaning and, 49–51
 memorable messages and, 56–58
 purposes of, 49
Language communities, 48, 50
LCD projectors, 328
Leadership, 31, 214, 230–238
Leading questions, 188
Learning cycle, 309–310, *309*,
  367–368
Learning styles, 309–310, 315,
  367–368
Lectures. *See* Expository speeches
Legal issues, in speeches, 376–377
Line graphs, 321, *322*
Linguistic sensitivity, 58–63
Listener relevance links, 289–290, 365
Listening, 87–109, *99*
 attending and, 92–93
 comforting and, 158–161
 common ground and, 306–307
 comprehension/retention and, 91–97, 309–312,
   366–368, 372
 cultural diversity and, 309–312
 definition of, 88
 evaluating and. *See* Critical analysis
 intercultural communication and, 129–130
 interference with, 7
 nonverbal communication and, 92–93
 processes, 92, *103–104*
 relevance and, 305–306
 relevance links and, 289–290
 remembering and, 97–98, 309–312, 315,
   366–368
 responding and, 101–102
 speaker credibility and, 307–309
 types of, 88, 90–92
Literal comparisons/contrasts, 268
Liu, Min, 119–120
Logical reasons order, 283–284
Logistics (meetings), 232, 235–236
Logos, 393
Love needs, 402
Low power-distance cultures, 122
Low uncertainty-avoidance cultures, 121
Low-context cultures, 51

M

Main points
 definition of, 276
 identifying, 276–279
 organizing, 282–284
 writing, 280–281
Maintaining relationships, 145, 148
Maintenance leadership roles,
  230–231
Majority rule method, 229
Maps, 318, *319*
Maslow's hierarchy of needs, 401–402, *402*
Meaning, 3, 49–51, 52–54
Media bias, 374–375
Media images, 34
Mediators, 232
Meetings, 235–239
Memory aids, 98, 366–367, *367*
Mesomorphs, 76
Messages
 comforting and, 158–161
 definition of, 3
 persuasive. *See* Persuasive speaking
 relational aspects of, 11–12
 types of, 11
Metaphors, 56
Miller, Ann Neville, 314–315
MLA citation style, 294–295, *295*
Mnemonic devices, 98, *367*
Modeling, 333–334
Models, scale, 318
Modern Language Association (MLA), 294–295, *295*
Monochronic time orientation, 75–76
Monotone, 338–339
Moral dilemmas, 14
Motivated sequence pattern, 406–407
Motivation
 communication competence and, 15
 definition of, 401
 disclosure and, 162
 through incentives, 401–403
Mourning, 5–6
Movement, 71, 342
Multimedia projectors, 328
Multitasking, 75–76

N

Narrative order, 282–283
Narratives, 268, 370
Needs, 24, 401–402
Negative reinforcement, 334
Negotiating, 172–176
Nervousness. *See* Anxiety
Neutral attitudes, 391, 392
Neutral questions, 188

Neutralization, 151
Newspapers, 263
Noise, 7–8
Nonverbal communication, 66–86
    body, use of. *See* Kinesics
    characteristics of, 68
    computer-mediated communication and, 67
    cultural differences in, 68–70, 71, 73, 75–78, 80–81
    definition of, 67
    gender differences in, 70, 71, 72, 79
    how we look and, 76, 79
    improving, 79–83
    interpreting messages, 82
    listening and, 93
    personal space and, 73–75
    sending messages, 79–82
    time use and, 75–76, 77–78
    vocal characteristics of, 71–73, 337–339
Norming, 214
Norms
    of cultures, 117–123, 127
    of groups, 210–211
Notes, speaking, 347, *348*
Note-taking, 98
Novelty, 150
Nye, Naomi Shihab, 162–163

O

Objects, 316–317
Observing
    cultural differences, 128
    as data source, 242–243
    first impressions and, 38
Oculesics (eye contact), 68–70, 343, 349
Offensive language, 60–63, 312–314
Okigbo, Charles, 77–78
Open questions, 187–188
Open-mindedness, 128
Openness, 150, 161
Operant conditioning, 376–377
Opinion continuum, *391*
Opinion givers/seekers/analyzers,
        230–231
Opposing attitudes, 391–392
Oral reports, 243
Organization (form), 4
Organizational charts, 320, *320*
Organizational patterns
    for expository speeches, 373
    for main points, 282–284
    for persuasive speeches, 403–407
Organizing, 276. *See also* Speech organization
Other-centered messages, 159, 160
Other-imposed prophecies, 33
Outlining speeches. *See* Speech organization

P

Panel discussions, 243
Paralanguage, 71. *See also* Vocalics
Paralinguistics. *See* Paralanguage
Parallel, 281
Paraphrasing, 94–96
Participants, 3
Passive behavior, 173–175
Passive observation, 128
Pathos, 398
Pattern, 25
Pauses, in speech, 73, 339. *See also* Vocalics
Perception
    checking, 41–43, 97
    of communication competence, 15
    definition of, 24
    false, 32
    observing others, 38
    of others, 38–42
    process, 24–26
    of self. *See* Self-perceptions
    stereotypes and, 38–39
Performance orientation, 334
Performing, 214
Periodicals, 262
Personableness, 309
Personal distance, 73
Personal experiences, 26
Personal impact, on audiences, 306
Personal references, 288–289
Personal space, 73–74
Personality theories, 38
Personas, 36–37
Perspective taking, 97
Persuasive goals, *259*, 390–391
Persuasive speaking, 388–418
    audience involvement, 398–400
    demonstrating goodwill, 400–401
    developing arguments, 393–398
    evaluation checklist, *407–408*
    goals, 390–393
    incentives and, 401–403
    organizational patterns, 403–407
    presentational aids and, 315
    processing persuasive messages, 389–390
    sample speech, 409–415
Persuasive speech propositions, *391*
Photographs, 318
Physical context, 4
Physical incentives, 402
Physical interference, 7
Physical space, 74
Physiological needs, 402
Pie graphs, 321–322, *322*
Pitch, vocal, 72, 337–338
Plagiarism, 268

Platonic relationships, 137
Poise, 343
Policy, proposition of, 391
Political satire, 344–345
Polychronic time orientation, 75–76
Pop Comm!
  acceptance speeches, 277
  audience adaptation, 316–317
  body art, 80–81
  credibility, humor and, 344–345
  infomercials, 398–399
  listening, uncivil discourse and, 94–95
  media bias, 374–375
  mourning, 5–6
  offensive language, 60–61
  online dating, 138–139
  online social groups, 240–241
  privacy, media and, 166–167
  problem solving, 209
  self-concept, 28–29
  stereotypes and prejudice, 124–125
  Wikipedia, 264–265
Positive reinforcement, 170
Posters, 326
Posture, 70–71, 343
Power distance, 121–122
Practicing speeches. *See* Speech presentation
Praise, 170
Precise words, 53
Predictability, 150
Predictions, 32–33
Prejudice, 39, 124–126
Presentational aids
  benefits of, 315–316
  computer-mediated aids, 243–244, 328
  creativity and, *366*
  criteria for choosing, 323
  designing, 323–326
  displaying methods, 326–328
  handling during speech, 347–349
  in process speeches, 372
  types of, 316–323
Presentations. *See* Speech presentation
Pride, 399–400
Primary questions, 187
Primary research, 264–265
Principles, 376–377
Privacy
  definition of, 161
  disclosure rules and, 161–162, 164
  gender differences and, 162
  information co-ownership and, 165
  intimacy and, 164
  maintaining, 171–172
  personal feedback and, 168–171
  personal information and, 165–166

  reciprocity and, 164–165
  self-disclosure and, 141–143
  sharing feelings and, 167–168
Privacy management, 161
Problem analysis, 226–227, *227*
Problem definition, 226
Problem solving, 224–248
  brainstorming, 228–229
  communicating solutions in, 242–244
  decision making, 229–230
  effective meetings for, 235–242
  problem analysis, 226–227
  problem definition, 226
  shared leadership in, 230–234
  solutions, 227–230
Problem-cause-solution pattern, 406
Problem-solution pattern, 405–406
Procedural leadership roles, 232
Process speeches, 371–372
Productive thinking, 365–366
Projectors, 328
Pronouns, personal, 306
Pronunciation, 338
Prophecies, 32–33
Propositions, 390–393
Protocols, interviewing, 186, *187*
Proxemics (use of space), 73–75
Proximity, 306
Psychological context, 5
Psychological incentives, 402
Psychological interference, 7
Public communication, 9
Public distance, 73
Public speaking
  action steps for, *252*
  apprehension and. *See* Public speaking apprehension
  audience and. *See* Audience analysis
  developing speech content. *See* Speech content
  organizing speeches. *See* Speech organization
  practicing/presenting. *See* Speech presentation
Public speaking apprehension, 316, 333–336.
    See also Speech presentation
Pundits, 94–95
Purposes, communication, 10

Q

Quotations, 268, 289

R

Race, 114
RAR. *See* Remote access reports
Rate, speaking, 72, 337–338
Reacting, 93. *See also* Feedback
Reactions, of others, 27

Reasons, 393–398, 404
Recorders, 234
Recording information, 269–270
Reframing, 151, 160
Refutative pattern, 405
Rehearsing speeches, 346–351. *See also* Speech presentation
Relational dialectics, 149–150
Relationship transformation, 149
Relationships, 134. *See also* Interpersonal relationships
Relevance, 305, 365
Religion, 115
Remembering, 97–98, 309–312, 315, 366–368
Remote access reports (RAR), 243–244
Repetition, as memory aid, 98
Reports, 243–244
Research cards, 269–270
Respect, 14
Responding, 101–102. *See also* Feedback
Responses, of others, 27
Responsibility, 15
Responsiveness, 136, 401
Restructuring, cognitive, 335
Résumés, 192–196, *195*
Retention, 97–98, 309–312, 315, 366–368
Rhetorical questions, 288, 307
Roles, 36–37, 230–234
Romantic relationships, 137

S

Safety needs, 402
Sapir-Whorf hypothesis, 48
Saving face, 135
Scripted messages, 11
Scripted speeches, 346
Secondary questions, 187
Secondary research, 262–263
Section transitions, 286
Selection, 24
Self Reviews
    Part I: Foundations of Communication, 110
    Part II: Interpersonal Communication, 206
    Part III: Group Communication, 249
    Part IV: Public Speaking, 418
Self-actualization needs, 402
Self-concept, 26–35
Self-created prophecies, 32–33
Self-disclosure, 136, 141–143, 161
Self-esteem, 26, 28–31, 34–35
Self-fulfilling prophecies, 32
Self-monitoring, 36
Self-perceptions, 26–37
    accuracy of, 31–34
    developing, 28–30
    effects on communication, 34–35
    forming, 26–27

gender/cultural influences on, 30–31
    and presentation to others, 36–37
Self-talk, 34–35, 333, 335, *336*
Semantic noise, 7–8
Sensory language, 311–312
Sequential order, 282
Service groups, 217
Settings. *See* Contexts
Sex differences. *See* Gender differences
Sexual orientation, 115
Shared leadership, 230–234
Sign, arguing from, 396
Signposts, 287
Similes, 56
Simplicity, 25
Situational communication apprehension, 16
Skill Building
    assertive messages, 176
    clarifying general statements, 57
    feelings, 169
    paraphrasing, 96
    perception checking, 43
    questions, 96
Skills, communication, 16
Slang, 59, 310
Slide, example of RAR, *244*
Slide shows, 328
Small group communication. *See* Group communication
Social class, 115–116
Social construction, 36–37
Social context, 4
Social distance, 73
Social ease, 16
Social environment, 37
Social friendship groups, 216
Social incentives, 402
Social perceptions, 38–42
Solution criteria, 227–228, *228*
Solution evaluation, 229
Sources, citing, 270–272, 294–296, *295*, *296*, 372
Space, use of, 73–75
Speaking anxiety. *See* Public speaking apprehension
Speaking notes, 347, *348*
Specific speech goal, 259
Specific words, 53
Speech, critiquing, *103*
Speech adaptation. *See* Audience adaptation
Speech Assignments
    citing oral footnotes, 271
    communicating emotions nonverbally, 83
    critical listening, 100–101
    cultural knowledge, 129
    expository speech, 378–379
    friendship, 140
    introducing a classmate, 17–18
    meaning clarification, 62

panel discussion, 244–245
personal narrative, 173
persuasive speech, 408–409
process speeches, 373
self-concept, 35
speech presentation, 352–353
thesis statements, 293
visual aids, 328
Speech communities, 48, 50
Speech content, 261–272
  citations in, 270–272
  cultural influences on, 269
  information sources/types, 261–268
  record keeping and, 269–270
Speech goals, 251–261
  audience and, 254–257
  setting and, 257–258
  topics and, 252–254, 258–259
  types of, 259
  writing, 259–261
Speech organization, 275–303
  audience analysis and, 276
  citing sources, 294–296
  conclusions, 291–293
  introductions, 287–291
  main points, identifying, 276–281
  organization patterns and, 280–284
  outlines, *281*, 296–298, *299–301*, 354–356, 380–382, 410–411
  section transitions, 286
  signposts, 287
  speech body, outlining, 280–284
  supporting materials, 284–285
  thesis statement, 279–280
Speech outlines, 280. *See also* Speech organization
Speech Planning Action Steps, *251*
  Step 1: determining speech goal. *See* Speech goals
  Step 2: developing speech content. *See* Speech content
  Step 3: organizing speech. *See* Speech organization
  Step 4: adapting speech to audience. *See* Audience adaptation
  Step 5: practicing speech delivery. *See* Speech presentation
Speech practicing. *See* Speech presentation
Speech presentation, 336–362
  apprehension and, 316, 333–336
  body language and, 341–345
  critique checklist, *352*
  critiquing, 351, 357–359, 382–384, 411–415
  delivery, 336–337, 345–346
  humor in, 288, 367
  rehearsing, 346–351
  skills training for, 335
  speech samples, 353–359, 379–384, 409–415
  voice and, 337–341

Speech rehearsing, 346–351. *See also* Speech presentation
Speech research, 261–272
  citing sources, 270–272
  cultural diversity and, 269
  experiments, 265
  expository speeches and, 372
  locating information sources, 261–265
  recording information, 269–270
  selecting relevant information, 267–268
  sources, evaluating, 265–267
  sources, types of, 262–265
Speech setting, 257–258, 259
Speech topics
  audience analysis and, 254–257
  brainstorming/concept mapping, 253–254
  content development of. *See* Speech content
  for expository speeches, *377*
  goals of. *See* Speech goals
  identifying, 252–254
  selecting, 258–259
  setting analysis, 257–258
Spontaneity, 336
Spontaneous expressions, 11
Statement of reasons pattern, 404
Statistical sources, 263
Stereotypes, 38, 124–126
Stimuli, 25–26
Stories, in speeches, 289
Storming (group development), 214
Straw person fallacies, 397
Streaming videos, 244
Subject lists, *252*
Subjects, 252. *See also* Topics
Summaries, 292
Support groups, 216–217
Supporters, 231
Supporting material, 284–285, 287, 314
Supportive attitudes, 391, 392–393
Supportive messages, 101
Surveys, 255–256, *255*, *256*, 264
Suspense, in speeches, 289
Symbols, 3
Sympathy, in responding, 97
Symposia, 243
Synchronous technologies, 4
Synergy, 213
Synonyms, 369
Syntactic context, 50
Systematic desensitization, 335

T

Talk show hosts, 94
Talking points, 201

Target audiences, 391
Task leadership roles, 230–231
Temporal selection, 151
Tension relievers, 232
Territory, marking of, 74
Texting, 59, 67
Theoretical topics, 376–377
Thesis statements, 279–280, 282–283, 290
Thinking dimension, 310, 368
Timbre, vocal, 72. *See also* Vocalics
Time, 75–78
Time order, 282
Timeliness, 305
Timetable, speech preparation, *347*
Tone setting, 290
Topic order, 283
Topical segmentation, 151
Topics, 252. *See also* speech topics
Touch, 71
Traitlike communication apprehension, 16
Transformation, relationship, 149
Transitions, 286
Trust. *See also* Trustworthiness
    disclosure and, 143, 166
    in groups, 210, 214
    in interpersonal relationships, 137–138, 148
    intimacy and, 139–140
Trustworthiness. *See also* Truthfulness
    appearance and, 344
    of sources, 266–267
    speaker credibility and, 16, 308, 372
Truthfulness. *See also* Honesty; Trust
    critical listening for, 92
    definition of, 14
    evaluating, 99
    responding with, 101
Tsay, Mina, 211–212

U

Unanimous decision method, 229
Uncertainty avoidance, 121
Uncertainty reduction, 37
Uncivil discourse, 95–96
Understanding, 91–97, 159, 309–312,
        366–368, 372
Uninformed audiences, 392

V

Value, proposition of, 390
Values, cultural, 117–123, 127
VCRs, 328
Vegans, 369
Verbal communication, 47–65
    appropriate language use, 58–63
    clarity of, 52–54
    cultural context and, 51–52
    gender differences in, 52
    meaning and, 49–51
    memorable messages and, 56–58
    purposes of, 48–49
Video cassette players, 328
Video reports, 244
Virtual reports, 243–244
Visual aids, *325, 326*
    computer-mediated aids, 243–244, 328
    criteria for choosing, 323
    definition of, 315
    designing, 323–326
    display methods for, 326–328
    in process speeches, 372
    types of, 316–323
Visualization, 334–335
Vividness, 56, 289, 291–292, 311–312
Vocal characteristics, 71–73, 337–339
Vocal expressiveness, 338–339
Vocal quality, 72, 337–338
Vocalics (use of voice), 71–73, 337–339
Vocalized pauses, 333
Voice characteristics, 71–73, 337–339
Volume, vocal, 72, 337–338

W

Watching dimension, 310, 367
Web research sources, 263
White lies, 172
Whiteboards, 326–327
Wikipedia, 264–265
Withdrawing (interpersonal conflict), 177
Word charts, 319, *320*
Words, 48, 53
Work groups, 217–219
Workplace humor, 231, 232
Written reports, 242–243